W9-BFD-250

ESSENTIALS OF THE THEORY OF FICTION

Essentials of the Theory of Fiction

EDITED BY MICHAEL J. HOFFMAN

AND PATRICK D. MURPHY

Duke University Press   *Durham and London*   *1988*

Fourth printing, 1995
© 1988 Duke University Press
All rights reserved.
Printed in the United States of America
on acid-free paper ∞
Library of Congress Cataloging-in-Publication Data
appear on the last printed page of this book.

CONTENTS

Acknowledgments   ix

Preface   xi

Introduction   1

1   Henry James, *The Art of Fiction*   14

2   Virginia Woolf, *Mr. Bennett and Mrs. Brown*   24

3   E. M. Forster, *Flat and Round Characters*   40

4   M. M. Bakhtin, *Epic and Novel*   48

5   Edmund Wilson, *The Historical Interpretation of Literature*   70

6   Joseph Frank, *Spatial Form in Modern Literature*   85

7   Mark Schorer, *Technique as Discovery*   101

8   Lionel Trilling, *Manners, Morals, and the Novel*   115

9   R. S. Crane, *The Concept of Plot*   131

10   Roland Barthes, *Writing and the Novel*   143

11   Norman Friedman, *What Makes a Short Story Short?*   152

12   Wayne Booth, *Distance and Point-of-View: An Essay in Classification*   170

13   Ralph Freedman, *The Lyrical Novel: Retrospect and Prognosis*   190

14   Georg Lukács, *Marxist Aesthetics and Literary Realism*   203

15   Frank Kermode, *Literary Fiction and Reality*   218

16   J. Arthur Honeywell, *Plot in the Modern Novel*   238

17 Mitchell A. Leaska, *The Concept of Point of View* 251

18 William H. Gass, *The Concept of Character in Fiction* 267

19 Gérard Genette, *Time and Narrative in* A la recherche du temps perdu 277

20 William Freedman, *The Literary Motif: A Definition and Evaluation* 299

21 Gerald Prince, *Introduction to the Study of the Narratee* 313

22 George Levine, *Realism Reconsidered* 336

23 Mary Doyle Springer, *Approach to the Novella through Its Forms* 349

24 Seymour Chatman, *Discourse: Nonnarrated Stories* 366

25 Elaine Showalter, *Towards a Feminist Poetics* 380

26 Tzvetan Todorov, *Reading as Construction* 403

27 John Barth, *The Literature of Replenishment* 419

28 Ivo Vidan, *Time Sequence in Spatial Fiction* 434

29 Suzanne C. Ferguson, *Defining the Short Story: Impressionism and Form* 457

30 Rachel Blau DuPlessis, *Breaking the Sentence; Breaking the Sequence* 472

Index 493

TOPICAL CONTENTS

GENRE

Henry James, *The Art of Fiction* 14
M. M. Bakhtin, *Epic and Novel* 48
Ralph Freedman, *The Lyrical Novel: Retrospect and Prognosis* 190
John Barth, *The Literature of Replenishment* 419

NOVELLA AND SHORT STORY

Norman Friedman, *What Makes a Short Story Short?* 152
Mary Doyle Springer, *Approach to the Novella through Its Forms* 349
Suzanne C. Ferguson, *Defining the Short Story: Impressionism and Form* 457

NOVEL AND SOCIETY

Edmund Wilson, *The Historical Interpretation of Literature* 70
Lionel Trilling, *Manners, Morals, and the Novel* 115
Roland Barthes, *Writing and the Novel* 143
Elaine Showalter, *Towards a Feminist Poetics* 380

REALISM

George Lukács, *Marxist Aesthetics and Literary Realism* 203
Frank Kermode, *Literary Fiction and Reality* 218
George Levine, *Realism Reconsidered* 336

STRUCTURE

Joseph Frank, *Spatial Form in Modern Literature*   85

Mark Schorer, *Technique as Discovery*   101

William Freedman, *The Literary Motif: A Definition and Evaluation*   299

Rachel Blau DuPlessis, *Breaking the Sentence; Breaking the Sequence*   472

CHARACTER

Virginia Woolf, *Mr. Bennett and Mrs. Brown*   24

E. M. Forster, *Flat and Round Characters*   40

William H. Gass, *The Concept of Character in Fiction*   267

PLOT

R. S. Crane, *The Concept of Plot*   131

J. Arthur Honeywell, *Plot in the Modern Novel*   238

POINT OF VIEW

Wayne Booth, *Distance and Point-of-View: An Essay in Classification*   170

Mitchell A. Leaska, *The Concept of Point of View*   251

NARRATIVE

Gerald Prince, *Introduction to the Study of the Narratee*   313

Seymour Chatman, *Discourse: Nonnarrated Stories*   366

Tzvetan Todorov, *Reading as Construction*   403

TIME

Gérard Genette, *Time and Narrative in* A la recherche du temps perdu   277

Ivo Vidan, *Time Sequence in Spatial Fiction*   434

ACKNOWLEDGMENTS

Like all books this one was a collaborative effort, not simply because there were two editors but because others were heavily involved in advising and helping us. We should like to acknowledge the prompt, efficient, and cheerful help of Diana Dulaney and Carolyn Jentzen, who typed and prepared the manuscript. Bonnie Iwasaki-Murphy deserves thanks for her continued support and active interest in this project from inception to completion.

The University of California at Davis Academic Senate Committee on Research helped with a series of grants-in-aid. We are also very grateful for the enthusiastic support and intelligent, thoughtful editing of Reynolds Smith at the Duke University Press. We found especially helpful the many shrewd comments of that press's anonymous consultant readers. The book is much improved because of their suggestions, and because of the shrewd copy-editing of Mindy Conner.

PREFACE

When we first began to pursue the idea of editing this book, we naturally did some research into our potential competition. We discovered that no collection of essays on the theory of fiction had been published for more than ten years, and that all the older editions are now out of print. The many collections of essays on literary theory are of a more general nature, usually including *some* essays on fiction; but none exist that would serve the needs of a serious student of fiction who is interested in a coverage of that field or who wants a text for his or her own students to use in a course on the novel or other prose forms.

It seemed clear, then, that there is a serious need for such a text, because of the great proliferation of courses on prose fiction at colleges and universities across the United States and because the theory of fiction is one of the burgeoning subdivisions in the thriving study of literary theory. What is needed is a single text that contains within its covers the best essays written on the major topics in the theory of fiction so that the varied study of that field can be presented at its best.

We conceive of our audience as consisting of educated general readers as well as scholars who might wish to have major texts available in a single volume. Also included in our audience are those students who can use the book as an introduction to the field and those already knowledgeable who want an opportunity to experience fiction theory more broadly. Our criteria of selection were: (1) those texts traditionally considered "classics," (2) those that represent the various concerns of the most important scholars and thinkers, (3) those that are the best in their quality of thought and exposition, and (4) those that are the most readable and well written. The reader of this book should know that we have deliberately excluded essays that we found needlessly obscure or poorly written, no matter how much they might have represented the most "advanced" thinking in the field.

Within these strictures we have proceeded with both historical and topical foci. We present the essays in chronological order of their publication. This will enable any reader who wishes to read the book through from beginning to end to gain a good overview of the developing critical discussion of fiction throughout the current century. We have also attempted to represent the topics that have defined that discussion. To aid readers, students, and teachers in following that part of the discussion, we have also developed a topical table of contents, to be found immediately after the more conventional one, with the full understanding that many of the essays cannot be neatly categorized and might well be listed in more than one category. We nonetheless hope that our classifications will prove useful and enlightening.

Some readers may wish to start the book at the beginning and continue until the end; others may wish to dip in here and there, reading those essays that they may find interesting at the moment. Instructors may wish to use the essays to introduce fictional topics in conjunction with the reading of specific stories, novellas, or novels. One of us has already used the book in typescript as exactly that kind of supplemental text, and his students found both fictional and theoretical texts to be enhanced by such a juxtaposition. The book will also work well, we believe, when used in a more advanced course that stresses primarily the historical development of the theory of fiction.

In the Introduction we attempt to introduce readers to the theory of fiction, state something briefly about the history of the field, and describe the categories and terms under which the discussion has taken place. Unlike the introductions to many anthologies, ours says comparatively little about each of the essays we have chosen and their authors, reserving that kind of discussion for the headnotes that precede each of the essays. We think that such a placement of information will prove most useful to our readers. In the headnotes we try to state something about the central concern of each essay and relate it to others in the book. In this way we attempt to show how in a discipline like literary theory such essays are always in a kind of dialogue—occasionally explicit, perhaps most often implicit—with one another.

Finally, we wish to state that each of us was involved fully with the selection of texts and the drafting of prose. Producing this book was, we strongly believe, a collaboration in the best sense of that overused word.

INTRODUCTION

Who was the first storyteller? A lonely hunter consoling his fellows on a cold northern evening far from home? A mother calming a frightened child with tales of gods and demigods? A lover telling his intended of fantastic exploits, designed to foster his courtship? The reader can multiply the number of possibilities, but we shall never know the answer, for the impulse to tell stories is as old as the development of speech, older than the invention of writing. It has deep, psychological springs we do not fully comprehend, but the need to make up characters, and to place them in worlds that are parallel to our own or are perhaps wildly at variance with it, is part of the history of all peoples, cultures, and countries; there is no known human group that has not told tales.

Oral cultures are great sources for students of the theory of fiction. Researchers have established that in those that still exist, the storyteller (or bard) is highly revered for the ability to relate from memory a number of verse narratives of enormous length, told within the regularities of meter and conventional figures of language that aid the memory, containing the stories of characters known to listeners who share in a common folklore and myth. These stories, about familiar characters in recognizable situations, do not engage their audience in the mysteries of an unresolved plot, for the listeners know the story already, have heard it told before, and are often as familiar with its events as they are with events in their own lives. Then why do they listen? Beyond the story itself, the audience concerns itself with the voice and manner of the teller of the tale; the texture and density of the story's material; the fit of the characters with the audience's expectations about how human beings, gods, demigods, and mythic heroes behave in a world something like their own. For such people—just as for ourselves—fictions have an extraordinary explanatory power; they make clear why, for instance, there are seasons, why there is an underworld for the spirits of dead ancestors, why there is one royal line of descent and not another.

We begin this collection of essays on the theory of fiction with a discussion of so-called "primitive" origins because we believe that the impulse to tell tales and listen to them is akin to the impulse in "literate" cultures to write stories and read them, and as Claude Lévi-Strauss has shown us in *The Savage Mind* (*La Pensée Sauvage*) the science of primitive peoples is as sophisticated in its own purposes as the science in literate cultures; so too are the fictions. Tribal members in oral cultures may or may not have detailed discussions of the nature and forms of their fictions, but clearly they do make judgments as to the adequacy of the telling of stories, and the act of judgment is, after all, an act of criticism. Questions of judgment and interpretation, in fact, inform human discourse everywhere.

While we do not claim that the theory of fiction occupies much of the attention of tribal scholars, we do claim that the interpretation of works of literature, and in particular of fictional creation, is part of the written record of all literate cultures. It has constituted an extremely large and important part of literature since the times of the ancient Hebrews and Greeks, with its beginnings in Midrashic texts and in the writings of Plato and the sophists and, ultimately, in the most important literary critical text of Western antiquity, the *Poetics* of Aristotle.

The study of literature and literary theory—by which we mean the use of rhetorical, linguistic, and structural analysis as a means of interpreting texts—has, therefore, a long tradition in Western intellectual history, one employed quite heavily during certain periods and certainly appearing during the current century as a principal form of literate intellectual activity. In its forms of analysis, literary theory has been defined to a great extent by the kinds of texts to which it has been applied. In the *Poetics* Aristotle was concerned primarily with discussing the epic poem and the two dominant forms of drama, comedy and tragedy. For the most part, these were the most important forms, along with lyric poetry, written by the ancient

Greek authors that Aristotle studied. The fictions about which Aristotle could have written were, therefore, composed in verse or dialogue, not in prose, and the forms were not the prose fictional forms that dominate our time: the novel, the novellas, and the short story.

Historians of literature have argued at length about which prose fictions might qualify as the first novels. There were certainly prominent examples of lengthy prose fictions in the ancient world, with *The Golden Ass* of Apuleius and Petronius's *Satyricon* coming prominently to mind. But while these are extended narratives in prose, they do not, for most critics, fulfill the criteria for defining a novel formally in terms of the development of plot and character. Both tales are products of the early Christian centuries and were followed by more than a millennium in which the long fictional forms consisted mainly of verse epics and romances whose subject matter was the relatively conventional material of shared folklore and myth. Indeed, with some exceptions such as the Icelandic sagas and Boccaccio's *Decameron*, extended prose fictions did not begin to flourish in England and on the European continent until the sixteenth century, in the writings of Nashe and Lyly in England, Rabelais in France, and Cervantes in Spain. Some critics have called Cervantes' *Don Quixote*, published during the early years of the seventeenth century, the first European novel, and while the adventures of the man of La Mancha have been extraordinarily influential on later forms of prose fiction— Lionel Trilling finds its theme of illusion and reality to be the essence of the novel—*Don Quixote* did not found a tradition in which those writers who came after him self-consciously thought of themselves as writing "novels." Rather, Cervantes' book summed up and parodied the tradition of Medieval and Renaissance romance, with all its chivalric and courtly conventions. The self-conscious establishment of a tradition of novel writing did not come about with any lasting force until more than a century later, in an increasingly mercantile and industrial Europe where the middle classes were rapidly rising. The rising literacy that always accompanies trade and technology created an expanded reading public hungry for stories of people like themselves, in prose like that of the newspapers, journals, and scientific treatises that had come to dominate the new technology of print. For the middle classes poetry was identified with the aristocracy, except for such didactic verse as they sang in church.

England in the first half of the eighteenth century was a country dominated increasingly by trade and a mercantile middle class fortified by great prosperity, who used their profits to purchase for themselves the perquisites hitherto reserved for the landed aristocracy. The earliest British novels dramatized the rise of this new class. In addition, the development of a literate population, helped by the technology of print, made it possible for the first time for writers to earn a living through the sale of their printed works rather than through receiving patronage from a wealthy person of noble birth.

This new technology created a veritable writing industry in London, producing not only great masses of publications for science and various trades, but also the first newspapers, biographies, "confessions" of famous criminals, travel books, and ostensibly "true" accounts of how successful individuals found ways to thrive in the developing bourgeois culture. The works of Daniel Defoe are representative of this tendency; the ones we still read today were written as serious parodies of the forms developed in the popular press: *Robinson Crusoe* (1719), *A Journal of the Plague Year* (1722), and *Moll Flanders* (1722). All are written in a "nonliterary" prose of great lucidity and apparent functional utility. *Moll Flanders* and *Crusoe* are often called the great precursors of the British novel and taught in courses on that genre. The other great precursor of this period, Jonathan Swift's *Gulliver's Travels* (1728), uses the form of the travel tale to parody the society of England by placing it in various guises in exotic fictional settings.

While the works of Defoe and Swift are surely wonderful exercises of the fictional imagination, they were not written by authors working self-consciously in a new literary form. Not until two decades after the appearance of Lemuel Gulliver's *Travels into Several Remote Regions of the World* did the works of two writers, Samuel Richardson and Henry Fielding, announce the development of a new form. Richardson's epistolary novels, *Pamela* (1741) and *Clarissa* (1747–48), caught the imagination of England and much of Europe because of their sympathetic and extended treatment of character and their fashionable excesses of feeling. Fielding's work as a novelist began with a parody of Richardson's *Pamela* in a travesty called *Shamela* (1741). Having found his gift for comedy, Fielding then produced two of the best early novels in British literature: *Joseph An-*

drews (1742) and *Tom Jones* (1749), in each of which, but especially in the latter, he wrote justifications of his use of the new form. Calling his books comic epics in prose and rationalizing his procedures through reference to the works of classic Greek and Roman authors, Fielding more than anyone else wrote the first essays on the theory of fiction in British literature.

Although the tradition of the novel was established quite quickly and has ultimately come to dominate the common conception of "literature" for the reading public, no corresponding tradition of writings on the theory of fiction arose to follow Fielding's lead in that area. Works on literary theory continued to concentrate, as they had since Aristotle, on poetry and drama, and the main practitioners in the eighteenth century were primarily poets, such as John Dryden and Alexander Pope. The one major exception to that rule, Samuel Johnson—that extraordinary man of letters who worked in many forms including the novel—included little on the theory of fiction in his theoretical writings.

Well into the nineteenth century the novel remained for critics the stepchild among literary forms, popular with the mass reading public but not considered serious in the way of the lyric or the long poem. Major British critics continued to be poets, such as Samuel Taylor Coleridge and Matthew Arnold, but again neither had much to say about the novel. In France and Russia, however, critics including Sainte-Beuve and Belinsky, and the novelists Balzac and Stendhal did begin to write seriously about fiction. Nonetheless, the first writer to develop an extensive and lasting body of writing in English on the theory of fiction was the novelist Henry James, who—in a lengthy series of essays written over more than four decades and in the prefaces he wrote to the New York Edition (1907–1909) of his collected works—practically invented the field, along with many of the terms and concepts still most frequently used by people who write about fiction. Indeed, for instance, the Jamesian belief in the importance of the single point of view, and his belief that authors should not "intrude" by "telling" but should dramatize action became an almost tyrannical force in critical theory and novelistic practice during the first half of the twentieth century—as Wayne Booth demonstrates in *The Rhetoric of Fiction* (1961).

It may well be, however, that the most important example set by

James's writings on fictional theory, as well as by his own work as an artist, is to show that the writing of fiction is not simply a form of entertainment, but a serious art form, to be ranked with the lyric, the epic, and the drama and to be taken just as seriously by its practitioners. James's monastic commitment to writing, along with his belief that the exercise of craft is a form of moral commitment—a belief he learned from Flaubert and Turgenev—was so powerful that the theory of fiction has been dominated ever since by an emphasis on craft with less thought in general given to subject matter. It seems only fitting, then, to begin our collection of essays with James's "The Art of Fiction" (1884), an essay that reads like a manifesto for the position summarized above.

The nineteenth century has come to seem the great age of narrative, particularly in the realistic novel. Even though the theory of fiction in England had to await the advent of James, by the time of his death in 1917 fiction had come to be seen as the central act of literary creation—the area of real artistic commitment. In his early essays, for instance, Ezra Pound claimed that it was again time for poets to take their craft as seriously as the novelists take theirs. While for a time poet-critics such as Pound and T. S. Eliot continued to dominate literary theory—both of them strongly influenced by the *example* of James as an artist—from the 1920s on, major contributions were made to the theory of fiction by both scholars and practitioners.

As a result, a study of recent contributions made to the theory of fiction indicates that field to be a microcosm of both the concerns of literary theory and the general study of literature—particularly because the entire field of literature has become more and more a part of the academic enterprise. As, for instance, the study of poetry moved away from a concern with the poet's biography and the poem's subject matter, so did the study of fiction focus more on the ways the novel or story is constructed rather than on how facts of the author's life relate to details in the fiction.

While readers of this collection may wish to seek analogies between the concerns expressed in these essays and those expressed throughout the century in the study of poetry, drama, language, and rhetoric, the editors wish to focus the remainder of this introduction on the central concerns of the theory of fiction and on how they evolved throughout this century.

Genre

A number of the following essays treat an issue that has occupied many writers on fiction: that of defining the nature of each of the fictional genres. The first issue lies in deciding which works fall under the purview of the theory of fiction as distinct from theories of poetry and drama. Most writers draw the line between works written in prose and those written in verse—which is certainly the case with most of the essays in this collection. Still, some critics have claimed that Homer's *Iliad* and Chaucer's *Troilus and Criseyde* are, for instance, almost "perfect" novels, even though they are both long poems in the epic/romance traditions. Major theorists like Georg Lukács and Mikhail Bakhtin see the lines of fictional tradition as running from the epic to the novel; their major task is then to show how the two forms differ. For Bakhtin the fact that one form is written in verse, the other in prose, seems almost incidental. For other critics this distinction is crucial. Does the final distinction here become a cultural one, for example between historical cultures that use one form of discourse rather than another? Is there a difference in the way the world appears through the lenses of prose and verse?

Making distinctions among the prose fictional forms of the novel, novella, and short story have also occupied critics throughout the century. Are these distinctions simply ones of length between forms of up to 15,000 words, up to 50,000 words or more than 50,000 words? Do these arbitrary word lengths impose formal constraints on authors, so that novels, novellas, and short stories differ in their basic characters? The stort story is in fact an older form, attracting critical attention at least as early as the 1840s, in Edgar Allan Poe's classical essay on his countryman Nathaniel Hawthorne's *Twice-Told Tales*, but the novella did not emerge as a self-consciously viable form until the latter part of the nineteenth century. What does the actual word limit of the various forms mean to a writer when composing a work of fiction? What advantages does each form give writers that they cannot take advantage of in the others?

Narrative Voice and Point of View

Since the time of Henry James the related matters of narrative voice and point of view have formed a major part of the discussion of fiction. It is important to remember that both concepts are metaphoric, that the figure of point of view has to do with how the action is seen or experienced and that the figurative narrative voice is really silent and requires us to suppose from the words on the page how that voice might sound if someone were actually speaking them. Although figurative concepts, these notions have long had a powerful explanatory power for critics and readers, enabling us to understand that all narrative is written from a certain perspective and that one major fictional device is making the reader share in the experience from that perspective.

Henry James codified the concept of point of view by insisting that the narrative voice be purified of the kind of authorial commentary that he claimed interfered with the narrative flow. Moral judgments were to become implicit rather than explicit, and a single narrative perspective was to be carried through the story—either that of a character in the tale or that of a narrator whose voice was to become the flexible instrument that sustained a distance between the author and the fictional matter. Authors were not to demean their tasks by pretending that novels were merely "made up" and that they could cavalierly intervene any time they had a comment to make. The author was to become invisible, to be—in James Joyce's famous formulation in *A Portrait of the Artist as a Young Man*— "like the God of the creation, who remains within or behind or beyond or above his handiwork, invisible, refined out of existence, indifferent, paring his fingernails."

Such extraordinary narrative purity has remained an ideal throughout much of the current century, motivating the work of such writers as Joyce, Ernest Hemingway, William Faulkner, and Virginia Woolf. So strongly did this concept take hold of critics that it was not seriously challenged until Wayne Booth's *The Rhetoric of Fiction* (1961), which pointed out that not only had some of the greatest novels never strived for such purity but that in no work of fiction did the author *ever* disappear; that judgments were always present in the narrative tone and in all the various kinds of irony available to the narrator and the "implied author." Booth's influence has not only opened up earlier novels for our greater appreciation, it has also made more accessible to us a whole host of "postmodern" novels that make no attempt to hide the fact that they were written—that, in fact, make a fetish of their artificiality.

Plot

Discussions of plot have become much more sophisticated in recent criticism. Instead of simply seeing plot as a succession of events taking place in a narrative, critics have now begun to make important distinctions. They understand that major differences exist among the story embedded in the narrative, the actual narrative sequence (which is frequently *not* in the story's chronological order), and the various tensions between the two orders that authors have always self-consciously exploited.

In addition, there are many different types of plots, ranging from idyllic love stories to stories of war, murder, and mayhem to stories of ritual and religion to stories that are primarily intellectual discussions of ideas. And to advance the many different kinds of plots novelists employ many devices, including "flashes" forward and backward, involutions of temporal sequence, and telling the story more than once from the points of view of different characters. A good demonstration of the developing critical concept of plot lies in the sequence of essays in this book, which range from R. S. Crane's classic essay on *Tom Jones* to the extraordinary number of narrative sequential strategies enumerated and described by Gérard Genette in his discussion of Marcel Proust's multivolume novel, *Remembrance of Things Past (A la Recherche du Temps Perdu)*.

Character

What exactly is a character? Is it simply that entity which, for the most part, retains the same name from the beginning to the end of the work of fiction? Are fictional characters obliged to obey the same rules of human behavior as living people of flesh and blood?

If so, why, for instance, are we convinced by the characters in such novels as George Orwell's *Animal Farm*, in which animals speak and act like human beings?

What constitutes a good character? To borrow terminology from E. M. Forster's *Aspects of the Novel*, can we claim that "rounded" characters are more vivid and memorable than "flat" ones? Forster himself makes no such claim, but some of his followers have misread him as suggesting that he did. Can we really say that Leo Tolstoy's Anna Karenina (a rounded character) is more memorable than Herman Melville's Captain Ahab (a flat one)—to take two tragic characters as examples? Hardly. But the question does point out that fictional characters are defined not so much by what they are as by how they are used. The functions to which characters are put determine whether we shall see only one side of them or experience their many-sidedness. Captain Ahab's obsession is what defines him and controls the monomaniacal nature of the quest for Moby-Dick. To see him much outside of this defining obsession would soften him too much and would allow the momentum of the quest to flag. Anna Karenina's role, on the other hand, demands that we see her much more completely within a set of social situations and in many moods, for her fate is tied up with the mores of a large society and she does not assume the dominant role in it that Captain Ahab does in his. But with all their differences, both characters rank among the most memorable in the history of fiction.

The problem is made to seem even more complex when we consider comic characters, who are more often flat (Don Quixote) than round (Leopold Bloom), and characters in more recent fiction who are frequently both serious and comic, round and flat (e.g., the nameless narrator in Ralph Ellison's *Invisible Man*).

And what then do we think of the arguments made by the practitioners of the French *nouveau roman*, such as Alain Robbe-Grillet and Nathalie Sarraute, who recently claimed that the notion of character was passé, and that a new conception of the novel would have to be developed in which character no longer played a role as we know it. In such a new novel the writer could only record phenomena. What then is character: a speaking voice, a thinking mind, a feeling of spirit? The essays in *Essentials* trace the development of this continuing argument.

Fiction and Reality

The relationship of fictional worlds to those inhabited by readers has long been a subject for discussion in the theory of fiction. Are novels primarily representations of "reality," or are they all "made up"? How obliged are novelists to make what happens in their texts compare with what might have happened had the same events occurred in the "real world"? Is verisimilitude, for instance, an obligation for a writer?

Lionel Trilling claims in "Manners, Morals, and the Novel," that realism is the basic drive behind all fictional creation, that the life of individuals in society has been the stuff out of which novels have always been made. Other writers, such as George Levine, have identified realism more closely with certain periods of history (the nineteenth century) than with others (the twentieth century). Even, however, in modernist novels as different as Joyce's *Ulysses* and Faulkner's *Absalom, Absalom!,* one of the main thematic problems in each concerns the relatedness of fictional events to those of a specific moment in history, a single day in *Ulysses* or a more lengthy period, as in *Absalom, Absalom!*

But can we think of fictional reality in the same terms we use in thinking about history or about our own lives? Lives in fiction are surely more carefully determined than the lives that are lived by people who read books. Few lives have recurrent patterns, or perhaps even meaning, but they tend to repeat themselves almost obsessively and do not resolve themselves into the peculiar roundedness we feel when reading a satisfying plot. Novels do not have to end in death the way all lives and most biographies do. But we do not find characters to be well portrayed and developed unless something early in the novel has prepared us for what happens later. In this way novels are highly predictable and predetermined in ways unlike the randomness we all experience when living in a contingent world.

It seems, then, that we demand that novels and stories be plausible within the terms of their own fictional world and that such plausibility be measured not against whether that universe is truly a "represented" world but whether it is analogous to our own—that if some things happen then other things will follow, just as they might were we living in a universe constructed similar to the one in that "made-up" world. This, it seems to us, is as true of works of fiction written in the great "age of realism" of Dickens, Eliot, Stendhal, or Dostoevsky as it is of the more contrived but still essentially "realistic" novels of Joyce, Woolf, Faulkner, and Gabriel García Márquez, as well as works utilizing fantastic worlds, which often provide far more "realistic" or everyday details of their world than many avant-garde fictions.

Time and Space

Prose fiction is a temporal medium. It takes time for the reader of a novel to absorb its words, assimilate its concepts, and perceive its various elements. Characters are developed, and plots unfold in time. Like a symphony, a novel changes from one moment to the next, and the development of a given passage depends on other passages that have preceded it.

Novelists have often manipulated a story's temporal unfolding by telling a tale out of chronological order, and in that way exploiting the tension among story, narrative, and plot—a tension that we mentioned earlier. Even in fictions characterized primarily by straightforward, continuous chronology, the time of reading is almost always at variance with the time the plot takes to unfold; almost all novels cover a longer period of time than the number of hours even a slow reader might take to finish the book. (Even the occasional novel that tries to match reading and narrative time exactly goes therefore against the readers' expectations.) The exploitation of this tension becomes yet another device through which authors define the rhythms of their narratives. Some contemporary critics like Gérard Genette and Mieke Bal have developed elaborate typologies to describe the many ways in which the different temporal characteristics of a novel relate to one another.

Another concern of recent critics (e.g., Joseph Frank and Ivo Vidan) has been to describe the ways in which certain novels attempt to use "spatial" means to gain certain effects. As applied to fiction, space is even more metaphoric than the concept of time. Painting and sculpture are spatial forms, and because they exist in space (as does an unopened book), they can be experienced "all at once" in a single and instantaneous visual perception. A painting (as distinguished from one's understanding of it) does not unfold in time; it is all there at every moment, and its parts are not sequential but physically connected.

Many modernist novels have demanded that readers experience them all at once—an obviously impossible demand, given the temporal nature of the reading experience. But like a cubist painting, whose various elements are related simply by contiguity, novels like *Ulysses* or *The Sound and the Fury* can be understood only when they are perceived "all at once," for the various elements unfold not chronologically but in a fashion that seems at first to be almost random. It is often said that you cannot read such novels for the first time unless you have already read them. In other words, you must have their facts and their stories in your head (as you would when looking at a painting) before you can understand them as their narratives unfold. All students of fiction must therefore come to terms with the different conceptions of time conveyed in a nineteenth-century novel (like *Great Expectations* or *War and Peace*), with its emphasis on history and continuity, and the more fragmented modernist novel as it breaks with such seemingly old-fashioned concepts as causality and relatedness.

We hope this discussion of certain major topics in the theory of fiction will prove helpful to students, teachers, and scholars alike. Those topics and many others like them—metaphor, myth, setting, symbolism—are raised in much greater detail in the collection of texts that follow.

As prose fiction has developed from the early experiments of Cervantes' parodies, Richardson's epistolary works, and Hawthorne's sketches to the sophisticated experiments of modernism and postmodernism, literary criticism also has evolved. It has become more sophisticated as the result of efforts by critics to explain how fictions work their magic. The essays that follow, drawn from the past hundred years, and displaying that growth and change, are essential to any study of fiction in the latter part of the twentieth century.

1

The Art of Fiction

HENRY JAMES

■■■■■

Henry James has long been recognized as the major American author to bridge the transition from nineteenth-century realism to the impressionistic and modernistic fiction of the twentieth century. He is also the most important figure in effecting the transition of the criticism of fiction from the nineteenth-century journalistic review to the twentieth-century critical essay. James wrote "The Art of Fiction" as a reply to a lecture delivered by the Victorian novelist and historian Walter Besant at the Royal Institution in London in 1884. In these excerpts from that essay, James speaks not only as an author seeking the latitude necessary to develop his own method, but also as a literary critic determined to discourage prescriptive pronouncements about "the way in which fiction should be written." James the critic wishes to encourage descriptive criticism of actual novels, "what it [the novel] thinks of itself."

James echoes Besant in arguing for the novel as "one of the *fine* arts" on the basis of its formal qualities. This position stands in contradistinction to the popular contemporary argument that for a novel to qualify as *serious* literature it must engage a topic with a high moral purpose and resolution. James states unequivocally that "the only obligation to which in advance we may hold a novel . . . is that it be interesting." He draws a clear-cut distinction here that will recur throughout modern criticism and in the essays collected in this book: the appreciation and evaluation of literary works must be based on the primacy of formal or thematic qualities.

Henry James (1843–1916) is best known for many novels that have become classics of English language literature, including *The American* (1877), *Portrait of a Lady* (1881), *The Turn of the Screw* (1898), and *The Ambas-*

sadors (1903). He has also left us a legacy of well-known novellas and short stories, such as *Daisy Miller* (1879) and *The Beast in the Jungle* (1903). Much of his literary criticism is contained in the prefaces written for the New York edition of his works (1907–1917), which have been separately published in *The Art of the Novel* (1934), *The Future of the Novel* (1956), and other collections.

The only obligation to which in advance we may hold a novel, without incurring the accusation of being arbitrary, is that it be interesting. That general responsibility rests upon it, but it is the only one I can think of. The ways in which it is at liberty to accomplish this result (of interesting us) strike me as innumerable, and such as can only suffer from being marked out or fenced in by prescription. They are as various as the temperament of man, and they are successful in proportion as they reveal a particular mind, different from others. A novel is in its broadest definition a personal, a direct impression of life: that, to begin with, constitutes its value, which is greater or less according to the intensity of the impression. But there will be no intensity at all, and therefore no value, unless there is freedom to feel and say. The tracing of a line to be followed, of a tone to be taken, of a form to be filled out, is a limitation of that freedom and a suppression of the very thing that we are most curious about. The form, it seems to me, is to be appreciated after the fact: then the author's choice has been made, his standard has been indicated; then we can follow lines and directions and compare tones and resemblances. Then in a word we can enjoy one of the most charming of pleasures, we can estimate quality, we can apply the test of execution. The execution belongs to the author alone; it is what is most personal to him, and we measure him by that. The advantage, the luxury, as well as the torment and responsibility of the novelist, is that there is no limit to what he may attempt as an executant—no limit to his possible experiments, efforts, discoveries, successes. Here it is especially that he works, step by step, like his

"The Art of Fiction," by Henry James, is reprinted from *The Future of the Novel*, ed. Leon Edel, Vintage 1956, with permission of Leon Edel.

brother of the brush, of whom we may always say that he has painted his picture in a manner best known to himself. His manner is his secret, not necessarily a jealous one. He cannot disclose it as a general thing if he would; he would be at a loss to teach it to others. I say this with a due recollection of having insisted on the community of method of the artist who paints a picture and the artist who writes a novel. The painter *is* able to teach the rudiments of his practice, and it is possible, from the study of good work (granted the aptitude), both to learn how to paint and to learn how to write. Yet it remains true, without injury to the *rapprochement*, that the literary artist would be obliged to say to his pupil much more than the other, "Ah, well, you must do it as you can!" It is a question of degree, a matter of delicacy. If there are exact sciences, there are also exact arts, and the grammar of painting is so much more definite that it makes the difference.

I ought to add, however, that if Mr. Besant says at the beginning of his essay that the "laws of fiction may be laid down and taught with as much precision and exactness as the laws of harmony, perspective, and proportion," he mitigates what might appear to be an extravagance by applying his remark to "general" laws, and by expressing most of these rules in a manner with which it would certainly be unaccommodating to disagree. That the novelist must write from his experience, that his "characters must be real and such as might be met with in actual life"; that "a young lady brought up in a quiet country village should avoid descriptions of garrison life," and "a writer whose friends and personal experiences belong to the lower middle-class should carefully avoid introducing his characters into society"; that one should enter one's notes in a common-place book; that one's figures should be clear in outline; that making them clear by some trick of speech or of carriage is a bad method, and "describing them at length" is a worse one; that English Fiction should have a "conscious moral purpose"; that "it is almost impossible to estimate too highly the value of careful workmanship—that is, of style"; that "the most important point of all is the story," that "the story is everything": these are principles with most of which it is surely impossible not to sympathize. That remark about the lower middle-class writer and his knowing his place is perhaps rather chilling; but for the rest I should find it difficult to dissent from any one of these recommendations. At the same time, I should find it difficult positively to assent to them, with the exception, perhaps, of the injunction as to entering one's notes in a common-place book. They scarcely seem to me to have the quality that Mr. Besant attributes to the rules of the novelist—the "precision and exactness" of "the laws of harmony, perspective, and proportion." They are suggestive, they are even inspiring, but they are not exact, though they are doubtless as much so as the case admits of: which is a proof of that liberty of interpretation for which I just contended. For the value of these different injunctions—so beautiful and so vague—is wholly in the meaning one attaches to them. The characters, the situation, which strike one as real will be those that touch and interest one most, but the measure of reality is very difficult to fix.

. . . . Experience is never limited, and it is never complete; it is an immense sensibility, a kind of huge spider-web of the finest silken threads suspended in the chamber of consciousness, and catching every air-borne particle in its tissue. It is the very atmosphere of the mind; and when the mind is imaginative—much more when it happens to be that of a man of genius—it takes to itself the faintest hints of life, it converts the very pulses of the air into revelations. The young lady living in a village has only to be a damsel upon whom nothing is lost to make it quite unfair (as it seems to me) to declare to her that she shall have nothing to say about the military. Greater miracles have been seen than that, imagination assisting, she should speak the truth about some of these gentlemen. I remember an English novelist, a woman of genius,[1] telling me that she was much commended for the impression she had managed to give in one of her tales of the nature and way of life of the French Protestant youth. She had been asked where she learned so much about this recondite being, she had been congratulated on her peculiar opportunities. These opportunities consisted in her having once, in Paris, as she ascended a staircase, passed an open door where, in the household of a *pasteur*, some of the young Protestants were seated at table round a finished meal. The glimpse made a picture; it lasted only a moment, but that moment was experience. She had got her direct personal impression, and she turned out her type. She knew what youth was, and what Protestantism; she also had the advantage of having seen what it was to be French, so that she converted these ideas into a concrete image and produced a reality. Above all, however, she was blessed with the faculty which when you give it an inch takes an ell, and which for the artist is a much greater source of strength than any accident of residence or of place in the social scale. The power to guess the unseen from the seen, to trace the implication of things, to judge the whole piece by the pattern, the condition of feeling life in general so completely that you are well on your way to knowing any particular corner of it—this cluster of gifts may almost be said to constitute experience, and they occur in country and in town, and in the most differing stages of education. If experience consists of impressions, it may be said that impressions *are* experience, just as (have we not seen it?) they are the very air we breathe. Therefore, if I should certainly say to a novice, "Write from experience and experience only," I should feel that this was rather a tantalizing monition if I were not careful immediately to add, "Try to be one of the people on whom nothing is lost!"

I am far from intending by this to minimize the importance of exactness—of truth of detail. One can speak best from one's own taste, and I may therefore venture to say that the air of reality (solidity of specification) seems to me to be the supreme virtue of a novel—the merit on which all its other merits (including that conscious moral purpose of which Mr. Besant speaks) helplessly and submissively depend. If it be not there they are all as nothing, and if these be there, they owe their effect to the success with which the author has produced the illusion of life. The cultivation of this success, the study of this exquisite process, form, to my taste, the beginning and the end of the art of the novelist. . . . That his characters "must be clear in outline," as Mr. Besant says—he feels that down to his boots; but how he shall make them so is a secret between his good angel and himself. It would be absurdly simple if he could be taught that a great deal of "description" would make them so, or that on the contrary the absence of description and the cultivation of dialogue, or the absence of dialogue and the multiplication of "incident," would rescue him from his difficulties. Nothing, for instance, is more possible than that he be of a turn of mind for which this odd, literal opposition of description and dialogue, incident and description, has little meaning and light. People often talk of these things as if they had a kind of internecine distinctness, instead of melting into each other at every breath, and being intimately associated parts of one general effort of expression. I cannot imagine composition existing in a series of blocks, nor conceive, in any novel worth discussing at all, of a passage of description that is not in its intention narrative, a passage of dialogue that is not in its intention descriptive, a touch of truth of any sort that does not partake of the nature of incident, or an incident that derives its interest from any other source than the general and only source of the success of a work of art—that of being illustrative. A novel is a living thing, all one and continuous, like any other organism, and in proportion as it lives will it be found, I think, that in each of the parts there is something of each of the other parts. The critic who over the close texture of a finished work shall pretend to trace a geography of items will mark some frontiers as artificial, I fear, as any that have been known to history. There is an old-fashioned distinction between the novel of character and the novel of incident which must have cost many a smile to the intending fabulist who was keen about his work. It appears to me as little to the point as the equally celebrated distinction between the novel as the equally celebrated distinction between the novel and the romance—to answer as little to any reality. There are bad novels and good novels, as there are bad pictures and good pictures; but that is the only distinction in which I see any meaning, and I can as little imagine speaking of a novel of character as I can imagine speaking of a picture of character. When one says picture one says of character, when one says novel one says of incident, and the terms may be transposed at will. What is character but the determination of incident? What is incident but the illustration of character? What is either a picture or a novel that is *not* of character? What else do we seek in it and find in it? It is an incident for a woman to stand up with her hand resting on a table and look out at you in a certain way; or if it be not an incident I think it will be hard to say what it is. At the same time it is an expression of character. If you say you don't see it (character in *that—allons donc!*), this is exactly what the artist who has reasons of his own for thinking he *does* see it undertakes to show you. When a young man makes up his mind that he has not faith enough after all to enter the church as he intended, that is an incident, though you may not hurry to the end of the chapter to see whether perhaps he doesn't change once more. I do not say that these are extraordinary or startling incidents. I do not pretend to estimate the degree of interest proceeding from them, for this will depend upon the skill of the painter. It sounds almost puerile to say that some incidents are intrinsically much more important than others, and I need not take this precaution after having professed my sympathy for the major ones in remarking that the only classification of the novel that I can understand is into that which has life and that which has it not.

The novel and the romance, the novel of incident and that of character—these clumsy separations appear to me to have been made by critics and readers for their own convenience, and to help them out of some of their occasional queer predicaments, but to have little reality or interest for the producer, from whose point of view it is of course that we are attempting to consider the art of fiction. . . . If we pretend to respect the artist at all, we must allow him his freedom of choice, in the face, in particular cases, of innumerable presumptions that the choice will not fructify. Art derives a considerable part of its beneficial exercise from flying in the face of presumptions, and some of the most interesting experiments of which it is capable are hidden in the bosom of common things. Gustave Flaubert has written a story[2] about the devotion of a servant-girl to a parrot, and the production, highly finished as it is, cannot on the whole be called a success. We are perfectly free to find it flat, but I think it might have been interesting; and I, for my part, am extremely glad he should have written it; it is a contribution to our knowledge of what can be done—or what cannot. Ivan Turgenev has written a tale about a deaf and dumb serf and a lap-dog[3] and the thing is touching, loving, a little masterpiece. He struck the note of life where Gustave Flaubert missed it—he flew in the face of a presumption and achieved a victory.

So that it comes back very quickly, as I have said, to the liking: in spite of M. Zola, who reasons less powerfully than he represents, and who will not reconcile himself to this absoluteness of taste, thinking that there are certain things that people ought to like, and that they can be made to like. I am quite at a loss to imagine anything (at any rate in this manner of fiction) that people *ought* to like or dislike. Selection will be sure to take care of itself, for it has a constant motive behind it. That motive is simply experience. As people feel life, so they will feel the art that is most closely related to it. This closeness of relation is what we should never forget in talking of the effort of the novel. Many people speak of it as a factitious, artificial form, a product of ingenuity, the business of which is to alter and arrange the things that surround us, to translate them into conventional, traditional moulds. This, however, is a view of the matter which carries us but a very short way, condemns the art to an eternal repetition of a few familiar *clichés*, cuts short its development, and leads us straight up to a dead wall. Catching the very note and trick, the strange irregular rhythm of life, that is the attempt whose strenuous force keeps Fiction upon her feet. In proportion as in what she offers us we see life *without* rearrangement do we feel that we are touching the truth; in proportion as we see it *with* rearrangement do we feel that we are being put off with a substitute, a compromise and convention. It is not uncommon to hear an extraordinary assurance of remark in regard to this matter of rearranging, which is often spoken of as if it were the last word of art. Mr. Besant seems to me in danger of falling into the great error with his rather unguarded talk about "selection." Art is essentially selection, but it is a selection whose main care is to be typical, to be inclusive. . . .

Mr. Besant has some remarks on the question of "the story" which I shall not attempt to criticize, though they seem to me to contain a singular ambiguity, because I do not think I understand them. I cannot see what is meant by talking as if there were a part of a novel which is the story and part of it which for mystical reasons is not—unless indeed the distinction be made in a sense in which it is difficult to suppose that any one should attempt to convey anything. "The story," if it represents anything, represents the subject, the idea, the *donnée* of the novel; and there is surely no "school"— Mr. Besant speaks of a school—which urges that a novel should be all treatment and no subject. There must assuredly be something to treat; every school is intimately conscious of that. This sense of the story being the idea, the starting-point, of the novel, is the only one that I see in which it can be spoken of as something different from its organic whole; and since in proportion as the work is successful the idea permeates and penetrates it, informs and animates it, so that every word and every punctuation-point contribute directly to the expression, in that proportion do we lose our sense of the story being a blade which may be drawn more or less out of its sheath. The story and the novel, the idea and the form, are the needle and thread, and I never heard of a guild of tailors who recommended the use of the thread without the needle, or the needle without the thread. . . .

There is one point at which the moral sense and the artistic sense lie very near together; that is in the light of the very obvious truth that the deepest quality of a work of art will always be the quality of the mind of the producer. In proportion as that intelligence is fine will the novel, the picture, the statue partake of the substance of beauty and truth. To be constituted of such elements is, to my vision, to have purpose enough. No good novel will ever proceed from a superficial mind; that seems to me an axiom which, for the artist in fiction, will cover all needful moral ground: If the youthful aspirant take it to heart it will illuminate for him many of the mysteries of "purpose." There are many other useful things that might be said to him, but I have come to the end of my article, and can only touch them as I pass. The critic in the *Pall Mall Gazette*, whom I have already quoted, draws attention to the danger, in speaking of the art of fiction, of generalizing. The danger that he has in mind is rather, I imagine, that of particularizing, for there are some comprehensive remarks which, in addition to those embodied in Mr. Besant's suggestive lecture, might without fear of misleading him be addressed to the ingenuous student. I should remind him first of the magnificence of the form that is open to him, which offers to sight so few restrictions and such innumerable opportunities. The other arts, in comparison, appear confined and hampered; the various conditions under which they are exercised are so rigid and definite. But the only condition that I can think of attaching to the composition of the novel is, as I have already said, that it be sincere. This freedom is a splendid privilege, and the first lesson of the young novelist is to learn to be worthy of it.

Notes

1 Probably Anne Thackeray, Lady Ritchie, daughter of Thackeray, whose first novel *The Story of Elizabeth* corresponds to James's description.
2 *Un coeur simple.*
3 *Mumu.*

Mr. Bennett and Mrs. Brown

VIRGINIA WOOLF

▬▬▬

"On or about December, 1910, human character changed." So declares Virginia Woolf in "Mr. Bennett and Mrs. Brown," originally read before The Heretics Club of Cambridge, England, on May 18, 1924. This change, she goes on to claim, has produced a corresponding change in literature which requires the discarding of old prose writing habits and the adoption through experiment of new methods for shaping original forms and styles. Henry James declared that we may require of a novel only that it be "interesting," but Woolf argues that for the modern novel to fulfill that requirement it must break with the writing strategies of turn-of-the-century English novelists and forge new ones.

Such strategies must begin and end, according to Woolf, with a concern for character: "I believe that all novels . . . deal with character, and that it is to express character—not to preach doctrines, sing songs, or celebrate the glories of the British Empire, that the form of the novel, so clumsy, verbose, and undramatic, so rich, elastic, and alive, has been evolved." Like James, Woolf emphasizes the formal qualities of fiction over its thematic qualities. She declares the Edwardians, such as Arnold Bennett, John Galsworthy, and H. G. Wells, to be in the camp of social and historical novelists who are always concerned with issues outside the life of the novel they are writing; the Georgians, such as James Joyce, E. M. Forster, and, by implication, herself, she declares to be in the camp of innovative experimentalists who seek to capture through formal invention the change in human character that she believes has occurred. Woolf thus announces that what has become known as the modernist movement is the way forward for English literature: "Tolerate the spasmodic, the obscure, the fragmentary, the failure" because these experiments signal "the verge of one of the great ages of English literature." Time has borne out Woolf's claim, but we should ask ourselves whether her claim, that only through a central focus on character can the novel advance, is truly the source of this greatness.

Virginia Woolf (1882–1941) is best known as the author of such modernist novels as *Mrs. Dalloway* (1925), *To the Lighthouse* (1927), and *The Waves* (1931). She was also a prolific essayist and literary critic, a major feminist theorist (cf. *A Room of One's Own* [1929]), a diary writer, and letter writer, as well as a member of the famous Bloomsbury Group of British intellectuals. "Mr. Bennett and Mrs. Brown" appears in her collection *The Captain's Death Bed and Other Essays* (1950).

It seems to me possible, perhaps desirable, that I may be the only person in this room who has committed the folly of writing, trying to write, or failing to write, a novel. And when I asked myself, as your invitation to speak to you about modern fiction made me ask myself, what demon whispered in my ear and urged me to my doom, a little figure rose before me—the figure of a man, or of a woman, who said, "My name is Brown. Catch me if you can."

Most novelists have the same experience. Some Brown, Smith, or Jones comes before them and says in the most seductive and charming way in the world, "Come and catch me if you can." And so, led on by this will-o'-the-wisp, they flounder through volume after volume, spending the best years of their lives in the pursuit, and receiving for the most part very little cash in exchange. Few catch the phantom; most have to be content with a scrap of her dress or a wisp of her hair.

My belief that men and women write novels because they are lured on to create some character which has thus imposed itself upon them has the sanction of Mr. Arnold Bennett. In an article from which I will quote he says, "The foundation of good fiction is character-creating and nothing else. . . . Style counts; plot counts;

originality of outlook counts. But none of these counts anything like so much as the convincingness of the characters. If the characters are real the novel will have a chance; if they are not, oblivion will be its portion. . . ." And he goes on to draw the conclusion that we have no young novelists of first-rate importance at the present moment, because they are unable to create characters that are real, true, and convincing.

These are the questions that I want with greater boldness than discretion to discuss tonight. I want to make out what we mean when we talk about "character" in fiction; to say something about the question of reality which Mr. Bennett raises; and to suggest some reasons why the younger novelists fail to create characters, if, as Mr. Bennett asserts, it is true that fail they do. This will lead me, I am well aware, to make some very sweeping and some very vague assertions. For the question is an extremely difficult one. Think how little we know about character—think how little we know about art. But, to make a clearance before I begin, I will suggest that we range Edwardians and Georgians into two camps; Mr. Wells, Mr. Bennett, and Mr. Galsworthy I will call the Edwardians; Mr. Forster, Mr. Lawrence, Mr. Strachey, Mr. Joyce, and Mr. Eliot I will call the Georgians. And if I speak in the first person, with intolerable egotism, I will ask you to excuse me. I do not want to attribute to the world at large the opinions of one solitary, ill-informed, and misguided individual.

My first assertion is one that I think you will grant—that every one in this room is a judge of character. Indeed it would be impossible to live for a year without disaster unless one practised character-reading and had some skill in the art. Our marriages, our friendships depend on it; our business largely depends on it; every day questions arise which can only be solved by its help. And now I will hazard a second assertion, which is more disputable perhaps, to the effect that on or about December, 1910, human character changed.

I am not saying that one went out, as one might into a garden, and there saw that a rose had flowered, or that a hen had laid an egg. The change was not sudden and definite like that. But a change there was, nevertheless; and, since one must be arbitrary, let us date it about the year 1910. The first signs of it are recorded in the books of Samuel Butler, in *The Way of All Flesh* in particular; the plays of Bernard Shaw continue to record it. In life one can see the change, if I may use a homely illustration, in the character of one's cook. The Victorian cook lived like a leviathan in the lower depths, formidable, silent, obscure, inscrutable; the Georgian cook is a creature of sunshine and fresh air; in and out of the drawing-room, now to borrow the *Daily Herald*, now to ask advice about a hat. Do you ask for more solemn instances of the power of the human race to change? Read the *Agamemnon*, and see whether, in process of time, your sympathies are not almost entirely with Clytemnestra. Or consider the married life of the Carlyles and bewail the waste, the futility, for him and for her, of the horrible domestic tradition which made it seemly for a woman of genius to spend her time chasing beetles, scouring saucepans, instead of writing books. All human relations have shifted—those between masters and servants, husbands and wives, parents and children. And when human relations change there is at the same time a change in religion, conduct, politics, and literature. Let us agree to place one of these changes about the year 1910.

I have said that people have to acquire a good deal of skill in character-reading if they are to live a single year of life without disaster. But it is the art of the young. In middle age and in old age the art is practised mostly for its uses, and friendships and other adventures and experiments in the art of reading character are seldom made. But novelists differ from the rest of the world because they do not cease to be interested in character when they have learnt enough about it for practical purposes. They go a step further, they feel that there is something permanently interesting in character in itself. When all the practical business of life has been discharged, there is something about people which continues to seem to them of overwhelming importance, in spite of the fact that it has no bearing whatever upon their happiness, comfort, or income. The study of character becomes to them an absorbing pursuit; to impart character an obsession. And this I find it very difficult to explain: what novelists mean when they talk about character, what the impulse is that urges them so powerfully every now and then to embody their view in writing.

So, if you will allow me, instead of analysing and abstracting, I will tell you a simple story which, however pointless, has the merit of being true, of a journey from Richmond to Waterloo, in the hope that I may show you what I mean by character in itself; that you may realize the different aspects it can wear; and the hideous perils that beset you directly you try to describe it in words.

One night some weeks ago, then, I was late for the train and jumped into the first carriage I came to. As I sat down I had the strange and uncomfortable feeling that I was interrupting a conversation between two people who were already sitting there. Not that they were young or happy. Far from it. They were both elderly, the woman over sixty, the man well over forty. They were sitting opposite each other, and the man, who had been leaning over and talking emphatically to judge by his attitude and the flush on his face, sat back and became silent. I had disturbed him, and he was annoyed. The elderly lady, however, whom I will call Mrs. Brown, seemed rather relieved. She was one of those clean, threadbare old ladies whose extreme tidiness—everything buttoned, fastened, tied together, mended and brushed up—suggests more extreme poverty than rags and dirt. There was something pinched about her—a look of suffering, of apprehension, and, in addition, she was extremely small. Her feet, in their clean little boots, scarcely touched the floor. I felt that she had nobody to support her; that she had to make up her mind for herself; that, having been deserted, or left a widow, years ago, she had led an anxious, harried life, bringing up an only son, perhaps, who, as likely as not, was by this time beginning to go to the bad. All this shot through my mind as I sat down, being uncomfortable, like most people, at travelling with fellow passengers unless I have somehow or other accounted for them. Then I looked at the man. He was no relation of Mrs. Brown's I felt sure; he was of a bigger, burlier, less refined type. He was a man of business I imagined, very likely a respectable corn-chandler from the North, dressed in good blue serge with a pocket-knife and a silk handkerchief, and a stout leather bag. Obviously, however, he had an unpleasant business to settle with Mrs. Brown; a secret, perhaps sinister business, which they did not intend to discuss in my presence.

"Yes, the Crofts have had very bad luck with their servants," Mr. Smith (as I will call him) said in a considering way, going back to some earlier topic, with a view to keeping up appearances.

"Ah, poor people," said Mrs. Brown, a trifle condescendingly. "My grandmother had a maid who came when she was fifteen and stayed till she was eighty" (this was said with a kind of hurt and aggressive pride to impress us both perhaps).

"One doesn't come across that sort of thing nowadays," said Mr. Smith in conciliatory tones.

Then they were silent.

"It's odd they don't start a golf club there—I should have thought one of the young fellows would," said Mr. Smith, for the silence obviously made him uneasy.

Mrs. Brown hardly took the trouble to answer.

"What changes they're making in this part of the world," said Mr. Smith, looking out of the window, and looking furtively at me as he did so.

It was plain, from Mrs. Brown's silence, from the uneasy affability with which Mr. Smith spoke, that he had some power over her which he was exerting disagreeably. It might have been her son's downfall, or some painful episode in her past life, or her daughter's. Perhaps she was going to London to sign some document to make over some property. Obviously against her will she was in Mr. Smith's hands. I was beginning to feel a great deal of pity for her, when she said, suddenly and inconsequently:

"Can you tell me if an oak-tree dies when the leaves have been eaten for two years in succession by caterpillars?"

She spoke quite brightly, and rather precisely, in a cultivated, inquisitive voice.

Mr. Smith was startled, but relieved to have a safe topic of conversation given him. He told her a great deal very quickly about plagues of insects. He told her that he had a brother who kept a fruit farm in Kent. He told her what fruit farmers do every year in Kent, and so on, and so on. While he talked a very odd thing happened. Mrs. Brown took out her little white handkerchief and began to dab her eyes. She was crying. But she went on listening quite composedly to what he was saying, and he went on talking, a little louder, a little angrily, as if he had seen her cry often before; as if it were a painful habit. At last it got on his nerves. He stopped abruptly, looked out of the window, then leant towards her as he had been doing when I got in, and said in a bullying, menacing way, as if he would not stand any more nonsense:

"So about that matter we were discussing. It'll be all right? George will be there on Tuesday?"

"We shan't be late," said Mrs. Brown, gathering herself together with superb dignity.

Mr. Smith said nothing. He got up, buttoned his coat, reached his bag down, and jumped out of the train before it had stopped at Clapham Junction. He had got what he wanted, but he was ashamed of himself; he was glad to get out of the old lady's sight.

Mrs. Brown and I were left alone together. She sat in her corner opposite, very clean, very small, rather queer, and suffering intensely. The impression she made was overwhelming. It came pouring out like a draught, like a smell of burning. What was it composed of— that overwhelming and peculiar impression? Myriads of irrelevant and incongruous ideas crowd into one's head on such occasions; one sees the person, one sees Mrs. Brown, in the centre of all sorts of different scenes. I thought of her in a seaside house, among queer ornaments: sea-urchins, models of ships in glass cases. Her husband's medals were on the mantlepiece. She popped in and out of the room, perching on the edges of chairs, picking meals out of saucers, indulging in long, silent stares. The caterpillars and the oak-trees seemed to imply all that. And then, into this fantastic and secluded life, in broke Mr. Smith. I saw him blowing in, so to speak, on a windy day. He banged, he slammed. His dripping umbrella made a pool in the hall. They sat closeted together.

And then Mrs. Brown faced the dreadful revelation. She took her heroic decision. Early, before dawn, she packed her bag and carried it herself to the station. She would not let Smith touch it. She was wounded in her pride, unmoored from her anchorage; she came of gentlefolks who kept servants—but details could wait. The important thing was to realize her character, to steep oneself in her atmosphere. I had no time to explain why I felt it somewhat tragic, heroic, yet with a dash of the flighty and fantastic, before the train stopped, and I watched her disappear, carrying her bag, into the vast blazing station. She looked very small, very tenacious; at once very frail and very heroic. And I have never seen her again, and I shall never know what became of her.

The story ends without any point to it. But I have not told you this anecdote to illustrate either my own ingenuity or the pleasure of travelling from Richmond to Waterloo. What I want you to see in it is this. Here is a character imposing itself upon another person. Here is Mrs. Brown making someone begin almost automatically to write a novel about her. I believe that all novels begin with an old lady in the corner opposite. I believe that all novels, that is to say, deal with character, and that it is to express character—not to preach doctrines, sing songs, or celebrate the glories of the British Empire, that the form of the novel, so clumsy, verbose, and undramatic, so rich, elastic, and alive, has been evolved. To express character, I have said; but you will at once reflect that the very widest interpretation can be put upon those words. For example, old Mrs. Brown's character will strike you very differently according to the age and country in which you happen to be born. It would be easy enough to write three different versions of that incident in the train, an English, a French, and a Russian. The English writer would make the old lady into a "character"; he would bring out her oddities and mannerisms; her buttons and wrinkles; her ribbons and warts. Her personality would dominate the book. A French writer would rub out all that; he would sacrifice the individual Mrs. Brown to give a more general view of human nature; to make a more abstract, proportioned, and harmonious whole. The Russian would pierce through the flesh; would reveal the soul—the soul alone, wandering out into the Waterloo Road, asking of life some tremendous question which would sound on and on in our ears after the book was finished. And then besides age and country there is the writer's temperament to be considered. You see one thing in character, and I another. You say it means this, and I that. And when it comes to writing each makes a further selection on principles of his own. Thus Mrs. Brown can be treated in an infinite variety of ways, according to the age, country, and temperament of the writer.

But now I must recall what Mr. Arnold Bennett says. He says that it is only if the characters are real that the novel has any chance of surviving. Otherwise, die it must. But, I ask myself, what is reality? And who are the judges of reality? A character may be real to Mr. Bennett and quite unreal to me. For instance, in this article he says that Dr. Watson in *Sherlock Holmes* is real to him: to me Dr. Watson is a sack stuffed with straw, a dummy, a figure of fun. And so it is with character after character—in book after book. There is nothing that people differ about more than the reality of characters, especially in contemporary books. But if you take a larger view I think that Mr. Bennett is perfectly right. If, that is, you think of the novels which seem to you great novels—*War and Peace, Vanity Fair, Tristram Shandy, Madame Bovary, Pride and Prejudice, The Mayor of Casterbridge, Villette*—if you think of these books, you do at once think of some character who has seemed to you so real (I do not by that mean so lifelike) that it has the power to make you think not merely of it itself, but of all sorts of things through its eyes—of religion, of love, of war, of peace, of family life, of balls in country towns, of sunsets, moonrises, the immortality of the soul. There is hardly any subject of human experience that is left out of *War and Peace* it seems to me. And in all these novels all these great novelists have brought us to see whatever they wish us to see through some character. Otherwise, they would not be novelists; but poets, historians, or pamphleteers.

But now let us examine what Mr. Bennett went on to say—he said that there was no great novelist among the Georgian writers because they cannot create characters who are real, true, and convincing. And there I cannot agree. There are reasons, excuses, possibilities which I think put a different colour upon the case. It seems so to me at least, but I am well aware that this is a matter about which I am likely to be prejudiced, sanguine, and nearsighted. I will put my view before you in the hope that you will make it impartial, judicial, and broad-minded. Why, then, is it so hard for novelists at present to create characters which seem real, not only to Mr. Bennett, but to the world at large? Why, when October comes round, do the publishers always fail to supply us with a masterpiece?

Surely one reason is that the men and women who began writing novels in 1910 or thereabouts had this great difficulty to face—that there was no English novelist living from whom they could learn their business. Mr. Conrad is a Pole; which sets him apart, and makes him, however admirable, not very helpful. Mr. Hardy has written no novel since 1895. The most prominent and successful novelists in the year 1910 were, I suppose, Mr. Wells, Mr. Bennett, and Mr. Galsworthy. Now it seems to me that to go to these men and ask them to teach you how to write a novel—how to create characters that are real—is precisely like going to a boot maker and asking him to teach you how to make a watch. Do not let me give you the impression that I do not admire and enjoy their books. They seem to me of great value, and indeed of great necessity. There are seasons when it is more important to have boots than to have watches. To drop metaphor, I think that after the creative activity of the Victorian age it was quite necessary, not only for literature but for life, that someone should write the books that Mr. Wells, Mr. Bennett, and Mr. Galsworthy have written. Yet what odd books they are! Sometimes I wonder if we are right to call them books at all. For they leave one with so strange a feeling of incompleteness and dissatisfaction. In order to complete them it seems necessary to do something—to join a society, or, more desperately, to write a cheque. That done, the restlessness is laid, the book finished; it can be put upon the shelf, and need never be read again. But with the work of other novelists it is different. *Tristram Shandy* or *Pride and Prejudice* is complete in itself; it is self-contained; it leaves one with no desire to do anything, except indeed to read the book again, and to understand it better. The difference perhaps is that both Sterne and Jane Austen were interested in things in themselves; in character, in itself; in the book in itself. Therefore everything was inside the book, nothing outside. But the Edwardians were never interested in character in itself; or in the book in itself. They were interested in something outside. Their books, then, were incomplete as books, and required that the reader should finish them, actively and practically, for himself.

. . . . With all his powers of observation, which are marvellous, with all his sympathy and humanity, which are great, Mr. Bennett has never once looked at Mrs. Brown in her corner. There she sits in the corner of the carriage—that carriage which is travelling, not from Richmond to Waterloo, but from one age of English literature to the next, for Mrs. Brown is eternal, Mrs. Brown is human nature, Mrs. Brown changes only on the surface, it is the novelists who get in and out—there she sits and not one of the Edwardian writers has so much as looked at her. They have looked very powerfully, searchingly, and sympathetically out of the window; at factories, at Utopias, even at the decoration and upholstery of the carriage; but never at her, never at life, never at human nature. And so they have developed a technique of novel-writing which suits their purpose; they have made tools and established conventions which do their business. But those tools are not our tools, and that business is not our business. For us those conventions are ruin, those tools are death.

You may well complain of the vagueness of my language. What is a convention, a tool, you may ask, and what do you mean by saying that Mr. Bennett's and Mr. Wells's and Mr. Galsworthy's conventions are the wrong conventions for the Georgians? The question is difficult: I will attempt a short cut. A convention in writing is not much different from a convention in manners. Both in life and in literature it is necessary to have some means of bridging the gulf between the hostess and her unknown guest on the one hand, the writer and his unknown reader on the other. The hostess bethinks her of the weather, for generations of hostesses have established the fact that this is a subject of universal interest in which we all believe. She begins by saying that we are having a wretched May, and, having thus got into touch with her unknown guest, proceeds to matters of greater interest. So it is in literature. The writer must get into touch with his reader by putting before him something which he recognizes, which therefore stimulates his imagination, and makes him willing to co-operate in the far more difficult business of intimacy. And it is of the highest importance that this common meeting-place should be reached easily, almost instinctively, in the dark, with one's eyes shut. Here is Mr. Bennett making use of this common ground in the passage which I have quoted. The problem before him was to make us believe in the reality of Hilda Lessways. So he began, being an Edwardian, by describing accurately and minutely the sort of house Hilda lived in, and the sort of house she saw from the window. House property was the common ground from which the Edwardians found it easy to proceed to intimacy. Indirect as it seems to us, the convention worked admirably, and thousands of Hilda Lessways were launched upon the world by this means. For that age and generation, the convention was a good one.

But now, if you will allow me to pull my own anecdote to pieces, you will see how keenly I felt the lack of a convention, and how serious a matter it is when the tools of one generation are useless for the next. The incident had made a great impression on me. But how was I to transmit it to you? All I could do was to report as accurately as I could what was said, to describe in detail what was worn, to say, despairingly, that all sorts of scenes rushed into my mind, to proceed to tumble them out pell-mell, and to describe this vivid, this overmastering impression by likening it to a draught or a smell of burning. To tell you the truth, I was also strongly tempted to manufacture a three-volume novel about the old lady's son, and his adventures crossing the Atlantic, and her daughter, and how she kept a milliner's shop in Westminister, the past life of Smith himself, and his house at Sheffield, though such stories seem to me the most dreary, irrelevant, and humbugging affairs in the world.

But if I had done that I should have escaped the appalling effort of saying what I meant. And to have got at what I meant I should have had to go back and back and back; to experiment with one thing and another; to try this sentence and that, referring each word to my vision, matching it as exactly as possible, and knowing that somehow I had to find a common ground between us, a convention which would not seem to you too odd, unreal, and far-fetched to believe in. I admit that I shirked that arduous undertaking. I let my Mrs. Brown slip through my fingers. I have told you nothing whatever about her. But that is partly the great Edwardians' fault. I asked them—they are my elders and betters—How shall I begin to describe this woman's character? And they said: "Begin by saying that her father kept a shop in Harrogate. Ascertain the rent. Ascertain the wages of shop assistants in the year 1878. Discover what her mother died of. Describe cancer. Describe calico. Describe—" But I cried: "Stop! Stop!" And I regret to say that I threw that ugly, that clumsy, that incongruous tool out of the window, for I knew that if I began describing the cancer and the calico, my Mrs. Brown, that vision to which I cling though I know no way of imparting it to you, would have been dulled and tarnished and vanished for ever.

That is what I mean by saying that the Edwardian tools are the wrong ones for us to use. They have laid an enormous stress upon the fabric of things. They have given us a house in the hope that we may be able to deduce the human beings who live there. To give them their due, they have made that house much better worth living in. But if you hold that novels are in the first place about people, and only in the second about the houses they live in, that is the wrong way to set about it. Therefore, you see, the Georgian writer had to begin by throwing away the method that was in use at the moment. He was left alone there facing Mrs. Brown without any method of conveying her to the reader. But that is inaccurate. A writer is never alone. There is always the public with him—if not on the same seat, at least in the compartment next door. Now the public is a strange travelling companion. In England it is a very suggestible and docile creature, which, once you get it to attend, will believe implicitly what it is told for a certain number of years. If you say to the public with sufficient conviction: "All women have tails, and all men humps," it will actually learn to see women with tails and men with humps, and will think it very revolutionary and probably improper if you say: "Nonsense. Monkeys have tails and camels humps. But men and women have brains, and they have hearts; they think and they feel,"—that will seem to it a bad joke, and an improper one into the bargain.

In view of these facts—with these sounds in my ears and these fancies in my brain—I am not going to deny that Mr. Bennett has some reason when he complains that our Georgian writers are unable to make us believe that our characters are real. I am forced to agree that they do not pour out three immortal masterpieces with Victorian regularity every autumn. But, instead of being gloomy, I am sanguine. For this state of things is, I think, inevitable whenever from hoar old age or callow youth the convention ceases to be a means of communication between writer and reader, and becomes instead an obstacle and an impediment. At the present moment we are suffering, not from decay, but from having no code of manners which writers and readers accept as a prelude to the more exciting intercourse of friendship. The literary convention of the time is so artificial—you have to talk about the weather and nothing but the weather throughout the entire visit—that, naturally, the feeble are tempted to outrage, and the strong are led to destroy the very foundations and rules of literary society. Signs of this are everywhere apparent. Grammar is violated; syntax disintegrated; as a boy staying with an aunt for the week-end rolls in the geranium bed out of sheer desperation as the solemnities of the sabbath wear on. The more adult writers do not, of course, indulge in such wanton exhibitions of spleen. Their sincerity is desperate, and their courage tremendous; it is only that they do not know which to use, a fork or their fingers. Thus, if you read Mr. Joyce and Mr. Eliot you will be struck by the indecency of the one, and the obscurity of the other. Mr. Joyce's indecency in *Ulysses* seems to me the conscious and calculated indecency of a desperate man who feels that in order to breathe he must break the windows. At moments, when the window is broken, he is magnificent. But what a waste of energy! And, after all, how dull indecency is, when it is not the overflowing of a superabundant energy or savagery, but the determined and public-spirited act of a man who needs fresh air! Again, with the obscurity of Mr. Eliot. I think that Mr. Eliot has written some of the loveliest single lines in modern poetry. But how intolerant he is of the old usages and politenesses of society—respect for the weak, consideration for the dull! As I sun myself upon the intense and ravishing beauty of one of his lines, and reflect that I must make a dizzy and dangerous leap to the next, and so on from line to line, like an acrobat flying precariously from bar to bar, I cry out, I confess, for the old decorums, and envy the indolence of my ancestors who, instead of spinning madly through mid-air, dreamt quietly in the shade with a book. Again, in Mr. Strachey's books, *Eminent Victorians* and *Queen Victoria*, the effort and strain of writing against the grain and current of the times is visible too. It is much less visible, of course, for not only is he dealing with facts, which are stubborn things, but he has fabricated, chiefly from eighteenth-century material, a very discreet code of manners of his own, which allows him to sit at table with the highest in the land and to say a great many things under cover of that exquisite apparel which, had they gone naked, would have been chased by the men-servants from the room. Still, if you compare *Eminent Victorians* with some of Lord Macaulay's essays, though you will feel that Lord Macaulay is always wrong, and Mr. Strachey always right, you will also feel a body, a sweep, a richness in Lord Macaulay's essays which show that his age was behind him; all his strength went straight into his work; none was used for purposes of concealment or of conversion. But Mr. Strachey has had to open our eyes before he made us see; he has had to search out and sew together a very artful manner of speech; and the effort, beautifully though it is concealed, has robbed his work of some of the force that should have gone into it, and limited his scope.

For these reasons, then, we must reconcile ourselves to a season of failures and fragments. We must reflect that where so much strength is spent on finding a way of telling the truth, the truth itself is bound to reach us in rather an exhausted and chaotic condition. Ulysses, Queen Victoria, Mr. Prufrock—to give Mrs. Brown some of the names she has made famous lately—is a little pale and dishevelled by the time her rescuers reach her. And it is the sound of their axes that we hear—a vigorous and stimulating sound in my ears—unless of course you wish to sleep, when, in the bounty of his concern, Providence has provided a host of writers anxious and able to satisfy your needs.

Thus I have tried, at tedious length, I fear, to answer some of the questions which I began by asking. I have given an account of some of the difficulties which in my view beset the Georgian writer in all his forms. I have sought to excuse him. May I end by venturing to remind you of the duties and responsibilities that are yours as partners in this business of writing books, as companions in the railway carriage, as fellow travellers with Mrs. Brown? For she is just as visible to you who remain silent as to us who tell stories about her. In the course of your daily life this past week you have had far stranger and more interesting experiences than the one I have tried to describe. You have overheard scraps of talk that filled you with amazement. You have gone to bed at night bewildered by the complexity of your feelings. In one day thousands of ideas have coursed through your brains; thousands of emotions have met, collided, and disappeared in astonishing disorder. Nevertheless, you allow the writers to palm off upon you a version of all this, an image of Mrs. Brown, which has no likeness to that surprising apparition whatsoever. In your modesty you seem to consider that writers are different blood and bone from yourselves; that they know more of Mrs. Brown than you do. Never was there a more fatal mistake. It is this division between reader and writer, this humility on your part, these professional airs and graces on ours, that corrupt and emasculate the books which should be the healthy offspring of a close and equal alliance between us. Hence spring those sleek, smooth novels, those portentous and ridiculous biographies, that milk and watery criticism, those poems melodiously celebrating the innocence of roses and sheep which pass so plausibly for literature at the present time.

Your part is to insist that writers shall come down off their plinths and pedestals, and describe beautifully if possible, truthfully at any rate, our Mrs. Brown. You should insist that she is an old lady of unlimited capacity and infinite variety; capable of appearing in any place; wearing any dress; saying anything and doing heaven knows what. But the things she says and the things she does and her eyes and her nose and her speech and her silence have an overwhelming fascination, for she is, of course, the spirit we live by, life itself.

But do not expect just at present a complete and satisfactory presentment of her. Tolerate the spasmodic, the obscure, the fragmentary, the failure. Your help is invoked in a good cause. For I will make one final and surpassingly rash prediction—we are trembling on the verge of one of the great ages of English literature. But it can only be reached if we are determined never, never to desert Mrs. Brown.

3

Flat and Round Characters

E. M. FORSTER

—

In this brief excerpt from *Aspects of the Novel* (1927), E. M. Forster defines two basic types of characters, their qualities, functions, and importance for the development of a novel. "Flat" characters, he says, "are constructed round a single idea or quality." In addition, they undergo no change or development. If, in a sense, the flat character embodies an idea or quality, then the "round" character encompasses many ideas and qualities, undergoing change and development, as well as entertaining different ideas and characteristics. Forster uses Jane Austen to demonstrate his contention that "the test of a round character is whether it is capable of surprising in a convincing way." We may want to consider, given Forster's definitions, the relationship between the use of flat and round characters and the primacy of either formal or thematic concerns in creating particular works of fiction. If Virginia Woolf's claims have any validity, we may anticipate that modernist novels will demonstrate more attention to "round" character development, while novels that are oriented socially and thematically will rely largely on "flat" characters. Is this actually the case? Let us also consider why an author might choose either flat or round characters in a specific situation and how that choice might affect the advancement of a novel's plot or narrative structure.

E. M. Forster (1879–1970) was a major English prose stylist in the novel, the short story, and the literary essay. His most famous novels are *A Room With a View* (1908), *Howards End* (1910), and *A Passage to India* (1924). Many of his best essays are collected in *Arbinger Harvest* (1936).

We may divide characters into flat and round.

Flat characters were called "humorous" in the seventeenth century, and are sometimes called types, and sometimes caricatures. In their purest form, they are constructed round a single idea or quality: when there is more than one factor in them, we get the beginning of the curve towards the round. The really flat character can be expressed in one sentence such as "I never will desert Mr. Micawber." There is Mrs. Micawber—she says she won't desert Mr. Micawber, she doesn't, and there she is. Or: "I must conceal, even by subterfuges, the poverty of my master's house." There is Caleb Balderstone in *The Bride of Lammermoor*. He does not use the actual phrase, but it completely describes him; he has no existence outside it, no pleasures, none of the private lusts and aches that must complicate the most consistent of servitors. Whatever he does, wherever he goes, whatever lies he tells or plates he breaks, it is to conceal the poverty of his master's house. It is not his *idée fixe*, because there is nothing in him into which the idea can be fixed. He is the idea, and such life as he possesses radiates from its edges and from the scintillations it strikes when other elements in the novel impinge. Or take Proust. There are numerous flat characters in Proust, such as the Princess of Parma, or Legrandin. Each can be expressed in a single sentence, the Princess's sentence being, "I must be particularly careful to be kind." She does nothing except to be particularly careful, and those of the other characters who are more complex than herself easily see through the kindness, since it is only a by-product of the carefulness.

One great advantage of flat characters is that they are easily recognized whenever they come in—recognized by the reader's emotional eye, not by the visual eye, which merely notes the recurrence of a proper name. In Russian novels, where they so seldom occur, they would be a decided help. It is a convenience for an author when he can strike with his full force at once, and flat characters are very useful to him, since they never need reintroducing, never run away, have not to be watched for development, and provide their own atmosphere—little luminous disks of a pre-arranged size, pushed hither and thither like counters across the void or between the stars; most satisfactory.

A second advantage is that they are easily remembered by the reader afterwards. They remain in his mind as unalterable for the reason that they were not changed by circumstances; they moved through circumstances, which gives them in retrospect a comforting quality, and preserves them when the book that produced them may decay. The Countess in *Evan Harrington* furnishes a good little example here. Let us compare our memories of her with our memories of Becky Sharp. We do not remember what the Countess did or what she passed through. What is clear is her figure and the formula that surrounds it, namely, "Proud as we are of dear papa, we must conceal his memory." All her rich humour proceeds from this. She is a flat character. Becky is round. She, too, is on the make, but she cannot be summed up in a single phrase, and we remember her in connection with the great scenes through which she passed and as modified by those scenes—that is to say, we do not remember her so easily because she waxes and wanes and has facets like a human being. All of us, even the sophisticated, yearn for permanence, and to the unsophisticated permanence is the chief excuse for a work of art. We all want books to endure, to be refuges, and their inhabitants to be always the same, and flat characters tend to justify themselves on this account.

All the same, critics who have their eyes fixed severely upon daily life—as were our eyes last week—have very little patience with such renderings of human nature. Queen Victoria, they argue, cannot be summed up in a single sentence, so what excuse remains for Mrs. Micawber? One of our foremost writers, Mr. Norman Douglas, is a critic of this type, and the passage from him which I will quote puts the case against flat characters in a forcible fashion. The passage occurs in an open letter to D. H. Lawrence, with whom he is quarrelling: a doughty pair of combatants, the hardness of whose hitting makes the rest of us feel like a lot of ladies up in a pavilion. He complains that Lawrence, in a biography, has falsified the picture by employing "the novelist's touch," and he goes on to define what this is:

It consists, I should say, in a failure to realize the complexities of the ordinary human mind; it selects for literary purposes two or three facets of a man or woman, generally the most spectacular, and therefore useful ingredients of their character and disregards all the others. Whatever fails to fit in with these specially chosen traits is eliminated—must be eliminated, for otherwise the description would not hold water. Such and such are the data: everything incompatible with those data has to go by the board. It follows that the novelist's touch argues, often logically, from a wrong premise: it takes what it likes and leaves the rest. The facets may be correct as far as they go but there are too few of them: what the author says may be true and yet by no means the truth. That is the novelist's touch. It falsifies life.

Well, the novelist's touch as thus defined is, of course, bad in biography, for no human being is simple. But in a novel it has its place: a novel that is at all complex often requires flat people as well as round, and the outcome of their collisions parallels life more accurately than Mr. Douglas implies. The case of Dickens is significant. Dickens' people are nearly all flat (Pip and David Copperfield attempt roundness, but so diffidently that they seem more like bubbles than solids). Nearly every one can be summed up in a sentence, and yet there is this wonderful feeling of human depth. Probably the immense vitality of Dickens causes his characters to vibrate a little, so that they borrow his life and appear to lead one of their own. It is a conjuring trick; at any moment we may look at Mr. Pickwick edgeways and find him no thicker than a gramophone record. But we never get the sideway view. Mr. Pickwick is far too adroit and well-trained. He always has the air of weighing something, and when he is put into the cupboard of the young ladies' school he seems as heavy as Falstaff in the buck-basket at Windsor. Part of the genius of Dickens is that he does use types and caricatures, people whom we recognize the instant they re-enter, and yet achieves effects that are not mechanical and a vision of humanity that is not shallow. Those who dislike Dickens have an excellent case. He ought to be bad. He is actually one of our big writers, and his immense success with types suggests that there may be more in flatness than the severer critics admit.

Or take H. G. Wells. With the possible exceptions of Kipps and the aunt in *Tono Bungay*, all Wells' characters are as flat as a photograph. But the photographs are agitated with such vigour that we forget their complexities lie on the surface and would disappear if it were scratched or curled up. A Wells character cannot indeed be summed up in a single phrase; he is tethered much more to observation, he does not create types. Nevertheless his people seldom pulsate by their own strength. It is the deft and powerful hands of their maker that shake them and trick the reader into a sense of depth. Good but imperfect novelists, like Wells and Dickens, are very clever at transmitting force. The part of their novel that is alive galvanizes the part that is not, and causes the characters to jump about and speak in a convincing way. They are quite different from the perfect novelist who touches all his material directly, who seems to pass the creative finger down every sentence and into every word. Richardson, Defoe, Jane Austen, are perfect in this particular way; their work may not be great but their hands are always upon it; there is not the tiny interval between the touching of the button and the sound of the bell which occurs in novels where the characters are not under direct control.

For we must admit that flat people are not in themselves as big achievements as round ones, and also that they are best when they are comic. A serious or tragic flat character is apt to be a bore. Each time he enters crying "Revenge!" or "My heart bleeds for humanity!" or whatever his formula is, our hearts sink. One of the romances of a popular contemporary writer is constructed round a Sussex farmer who says, "I'll plough up that bit of gorse." There is the farmer, there is the gorse; he says he'll plough it up, he does plough it up, but it is not like saying "I'll never desert Mr. Micawber," because we are so bored by his consistency that we do not care whether he succeeds with the gorse or fails. If his formula were analysed and connected up with the rest of the human outfit, we should not be bored any longer, the formula would cease to be the man and become an obsession in the man; that is to say he would have turned from a flat farmer into a round one. It is only round people who are fit to perform tragically for any length of time and can move us to any feelings except humour and appropriateness.

So now let us desert these two-dimensional people, and by way of transition to the round, let us go to *Mansfield Park*, and look at Lady Bertram, sitting on her sofa with pug. Pug is flat, like most animals in fiction. He is once represented as straying into a rosebed in a cardboard kind of way, but that is all, and during most of the book his mistress seems to be cut out of the same simple material as her dog. Lady Bertram's formula is, "I am kindly, but must not be fatigued," and she functions out of it. But at the end there is a catastrophe. Her two daughters come to grief—to the worst grief known to Miss Austen's universe, far worse than the Napoleonic wars. Julia elopes; Maria, who is unhappily married, runs off with a lover. What is Lady Bertram's reaction? The sentence describing it is significant: "Lady Bertram did not think deeply, but, guided by Sir Thomas, she thought justly on all important points, and she saw therefore in all its enormity, what had happened, and neither endeavoured herself, nor required Fanny to advise her, to think little of guilt and infamy." These are strong words, and they used to worry me because I thought Jane Austen's moral sense was getting out of hand. She may, and of course does, deprecate guilt and infamy herself, and she duly causes all possible distress in the minds of Edmund and Fanny, but has she any right to agitate calm, consistent Lady Bertram? Is not it like giving pug three faces and setting him to guard the gates of Hell? Ought not her ladyship to remain on the sofa saying, "This is a dreadful and sadly exhausting business about Julia and Maria, but where is Fanny gone? I have dropped another stitch"?

I used to think this, through misunderstanding Jane Austen's method—exactly as Scott misunderstood it when he congratulated her for painting on a square of ivory. She is a miniaturist, but never two-dimensional. All her characters are round, or capable of rotundity. Even Miss Bates has a mind, even Elizabeth Eliot a heart, and Lady Bertram's moral fervour ceases to vex us when we realize this: the disk has suddenly extended and become a little globe. When the novel is closed, Lady Bertram goes back to the flat, it is true; the dominant impression she leaves can be summed up in a formula. But that is not how Jane Austen conceived her, and the freshness of her reappearances are due to this. Why do the characters in Jane Austen give us a slightly new pleasure each time they come in, as opposed to the merely repetitive pleasure that is caused by a character in

Dickens? Why do they combine so well in a conversation, and draw one another out without seeming to do so, and never perform? The answer to this question can be put in several ways: that, unlike Dickens, she was a real artist, that she never stooped to caricature, etc. But the best reply is that her characters though smaller than his are more highly organized. They function all round, and even if her plot made greater demands on them than it does, they would still be adequate. Suppose that Louisa Musgrove had broken her neck on the Cobb. The description of her death would have been feeble and ladylike—physical violence is quite beyond Miss Austen's powers—but the survivors would have reacted properly as soon as the corpse was carried away, they would have brought into view new sides of their character, and though *Persuasion* would have been spoiled as a book, we should know more than we do about Captain Wentworth and Anne. All the Jane Austen characters are ready for an extended life, for a life which the scheme of her books seldom requires them to lead, and that is why they lead their actual lives so satisfactorily. Let us return to Lady Bertram and the crucial sentence. See how subtly it modulates from her formula into an area where the formula does not work. "Lady Bertram did not think deeply." Exactly: as per formula. "But guided by Sir Thomas she thought justly on all important points." Sir Thomas' guidance, which is part of the formula, remains, but it pushes her ladyship towards an independent and undesired morality. "She saw therefore in all its enormity what had happened." This is the moral fortissimo—very strong but carefully introduced. And then follows a most artful decrescendo, by means of negatives. "She neither endeavoured herself, nor required Fanny to advise her, to think little of guilt or infamy." The formula is reappearing, because as a rule she does try to minimize trouble, and does require Fanny to advise her how to do this; indeed Fanny has done nothing else for the last ten years. The words, though they are negatived, remind us of this, her normal state is again in view, and she has in a single sentence been inflated into a round character and collapsed back into a flat one. How Jane Austen can write! In a few words she has extended Lady Bertram, and by so doing she has increased the probability of the elopements of Maria and Julia. I say probability because the elopements belong to the domain of violent physical action, and here, as already indicated, Jane Austen is feeble and ladylike. Except in her schoolgirl novels, she cannot stage a crash. Everything violent has to take place "off"—Louisa's accident and Marianne Dashwood's putrid throat are the nearest exceptions— and consequently all the comments on the elopement must be sincere and convincing, otherwise we should doubt whether it occurred. Lady Bertram helps us to believe that her daughters have run away, and they have to run away, or there would be no apotheosis for Fanny. It is a little point, and a little sentence, yet it shows us how delicately a great novelist can modulate into the round.

All through her works we find these characters, apparently so simple and flat, never needing reintroduction and yet never out of depth—Henry Tilney, Mr. Woodhouse, Charlotte Lucas. She may label her characters "Sense," "Pride," "Sensibility," "Prejudice," but they are not tethered to those qualities.

As for the round characters proper, they have already been defined by implication and no more need be said. All I need do is to give some examples of people in books who seem to me round so that the definition can be tested afterwards:

All the principal characters in *War and Peace,* all the Dostoevsky characters, and some of the Proust—for example, the old family servant, the Duchess of Guermantes, M. de Charlus, and Saint Loup; Madame Bovary—who, like Moll Flanders, has her book to herself, and can expand and secrete unchecked; some people in Thackeray— for instance, Becky and Beatrix; some in Fielding—Parson Adams, Tom Jones; and some in Charlotte Brontë, most particularly Lucy Snowe. (And many more—this is not a catalogue.) The test of a round character is whether it is capable of surprising in a convincing way. If it never surprises, it is flat. If it does not convince, it is a flat pretending to be round. It has the incalculability of life about it—life within the pages of a book. And by using it sometimes alone, more often in combination with the other kind, the novelist achieves his task of acclimatization and harmonizes the human race with the other aspects of his work.

4

Epic and Novel: Toward a Methodology
for the Study of the Novel

M . M . BAKHTIN

■

Mikhail Bakhtin began writing about literature in the 1920s, but only recently has his work been translated into English. These translations have produced widespread interest in what has become termed the "dialogic method." In this excerpt from "Epic and Novel," written in 1941, Bakhtin presents his conception of genre, in particular that of the novel, and he introduces some concepts which guide his method. For him a key difficulty and major point of interest in analyzing the novel lies in its being still a young genre that is developing and changing: "Of all the major genres only the novel is younger than writing and the book: it alone is organically receptive to new forms of mute perception, that is, to reading." Of major significance here is Bakhtin's argument that the novel is a *new* genre, qualitatively different from the epic in direct contrast to the claims of numerous other critics. Also important is Bakhtin's concept of the novel's ability to incorporate and satirize other genres as well as its own various styles: "This ability of the novel to criticize itself is a remarkable feature of this ever-developing genre."

In many ways, Bakhtin's excitement over the novel as a developing genre that "has become the leading hero in the dream of literary development" echoes Virginia Woolf's claims for modernist literature in the 1920s. For both writers the ability to experiment and innovate is an essential feature of literary leadership. One should also note that Bakhtin claims that the old poetics—that is, old literary theory—is inadequate to describe the modern novel. A new genre calls for new critical methods and viewpoints, ones that must begin as a descriptive poetics of the novels actually being written. Bakhtin sketches the characteristics of this genre by contrasting the novel with the epic, focusing on source material, the role of the narrator, the treatment of the hero, and the genre's relationship to the present.

Mikhail Bakhtin (1895–1975) has become famous for a collection of books and essays written over a nearly fifty-year period. The authorship of a few early works remains contested, primarily *The Formal Method* (1928; trans. 1978) and *Marxism and the Philosophy of Language* (1929; trans. 1973); he is definitely the author, however, of *The Dialogic Imagination* (1975; trans. 1981), *Problems of Dostoevsky's Poetics* (1929; trans. 1984), *Rabelais and His World* (1965; trans. 1968), and *Speech Genres and Other Late Essays* (1979; trans. 1986).

The study of the novel as a genre is distinguished by peculiar difficulties. This is due to the unique nature of the object itself: the novel is the sole genre that continues to develop, that is as yet uncompleted. The forces that define it as a genre are at work before our very eyes: the birth and development of the novel as a genre takes place in the full light of the historical day. The generic skeleton of the novel is still far from having hardened, and we cannot foresee all its plastic possibilities.

We know other genres, as genres, in their completed aspect, that is, as more or less fixed pre-existing forms into which one may then pour artistic experience. The primordial process of their formation lies outside historically documented observation. We encounter the epic as a genre that has not only long since completed its development, but one that is already antiquated. With certain reservations we can say the same for the other major genres, even for tragedy. The life they have in history, the life with which we are familiar, is the life they have lived as already completed genres, with a hardened and no longer flexible skeleton. Each of them has developed its own canon that operates in literature as an authentic historical force.

All these genres, or in any case their defining features, are considerably older than written language and the book, and to the present

"Epic and Novel" is reprinted from *The Dialogic Imagination: Four Essays by M. M. Bakhtin*, ed. Michael Holquist, trans. Caryl Emerson and Holquist. Reprinted with permission of the University of Texas Press, copyright 1981.

day they retain their ancient oral and auditory characteristics. Of all the major genres only the novel is younger than writing and the book: it alone is organically receptive to new forms of mute perception, that is, to reading. But of critical importance here is the fact that the novel has no canon of its own, as do other genres; only individual examples of the novel are historically active, not a generic canon as such. Studying other genres is analogous to studying dead languages; studying the novel, on the other hand, is like studying languages that are not only alive, but still young.

This explains the extraordinary difficulty inherent in formulating a theory of the novel. For such a theory has at its heart an object of study completely different from that which theory treats in other genres. The novel is not merely one genre among other genres. Among genres long since completed and in part already dead, the novel is the only developing genre. It is the only genre that was born and nourished in a new era of world history and therefore it is deeply akin to that era, whereas the other major genres entered that era as already fixed forms, as an inheritance, and only now are they adapting themselves—some better, some worse—to the new conditions of their existence. Compared with them, the novel appears to be a creature from an alien species. It gets on poorly with other genres. It fights for its own hegemony in literature; wherever it triumphs, the other older genres go into decline. Significantly, the best book on the history of the ancient novel—that by Erwin Rohde[1]—does not so much recount the history of the novel as it does illustrate the process of disintegration that affected all major genres in antiquity.

The mutual interaction of genres within a single unified literary period is a problem of great interest and importance. In certain eras— the Greek classical period, the Golden Age of Roman literature, the neoclassical period—all genres in "high" literature (that is, the literature of ruling social groups) harmoniously reinforce each other to a significant extent; the whole of literature, conceived as a totality of genres, becomes an organic unity of the highest order. But it is characteristic of the novel that it never enters into this whole, it does not participate in any harmony of the genres. In these eras the novel has an unofficial existence, outside "high" literature. Only already completed genres, with fully formed and well-defined generic contours, can enter into such a literature as a hierarchically organized, organic whole. They can mutually delimit and mutually complement each other, while yet preserving their own generic natures. Each is a unit, and all units are interrelated by virtue of certain features of deep structure that they all have in common.

The great organic poetics of the past—those of Aristotle, Horace, Boileau—are permeated with a deep sense of the wholeness of literature and of the harmonious interaction of all genres contained within this whole. It is as if they literally hear this harmony of the genres. In this is their strength—the inimitable, all-embracing fullness and exhaustiveness of such poetics. And they all, as a consequence, ignore the novel. Scholarly poetics of the nineteenth century lack this integrity: they are eclectic, descriptive; their aim is not a living and organic fullness but rather an abstract and encyclopedic comprehensiveness. They do not concern themselves with the actual possibility of specific genres coexisting within the living whole of literature in a given era; they are concerned rather with their coexistence in a maximally complete anthology. Of course these poetics can no longer ignore the novel—they simply add it (albeit in a place of honor) to already existing genres (and thus it enters the roster as merely one genre among many; in literature conceived as a living whole, on the other hand, it would have to be included in a completely different way).

We have already said that the novel gets on poorly with other genres. There can be no talk of a harmony deriving from mutual limitation and complementariness. The novel parodies other genres (precisely in their role as genres); it exposes the conventionality of their forms and their language; it squeezes out some genres and incorporates others into its own peculiar structure, reformulating and reaccentuating them. Historians of literature sometimes tend to see in this merely the struggle of literary tendencies and schools. Such struggles of course exist, but they are peripheral phenomena and historically insignificant. Behind them one must be sensitive to the deeper and deeper and more truly historical struggle of genres, the establishment and growth of a generic skeleton of literature.

Of particular interest are those eras when the novel becomes the dominant genre. All literature is then caught up in the process of "becoming," and in a special kind of "generic criticism." This occurred several times in the Hellenic period, again during the late Middle Ages and the Renaissance, but with special force and clarity beginning in the second half of the eighteenth century. In an era when the novel reigns supreme, almost all the remaining genres are to a greater or lesser extent "novelized": drama (for example Ibsen, Hauptmann, the whole of Naturalist drama), epic poetry (for example, *Childe Harold* and especially Byron's *Don Juan*), even lyric poetry (as an extreme example, Heine's lyrical verse). Those genres that stubbornly preserve their old canonic nature begin to appear stylized. In general any strict adherence to a genre begins to feel like a stylization, a stylization taken to the point of parody, despite the artistic intent of the author. In an environment where the novel is the dominant genre, the conventional languages of strictly canonical genres begin to sound in new ways, which are quite different from the ways they sounded in those eras when the novel was *not* included in "high" literature.

Parodic stylizations of canonized genres and styles occupy an essential place in the novel. In the era of the novel's creative ascendency—and even more so in the periods of preparation preceding this era—literature was flooded with parodies and travesties of all the high genres (parodies precisely of genres, and not of individual authors or schools)—parodies that are the precursors, "companions" to the novel, in their own way studies for it. But it is characteristic that the novel does not permit any of these various individual manifestations of itself to stabilize. Throughout its entire history there is a consistent parodying or travestying of dominant or fashionable novels that attempt to become models for the genre: parodies on the chivalric romance of adventure (*Dit d'aventures*, the first such parody, belongs to the thirteenth century), on the Baroque novel, the pastoral novel (Sorel's *Le Berger extravagant*),[2] the Sentimental novel (Fielding, and *The Second Grandison*[3] of Musäus) and so forth. This ability of the novel to criticize itself is a remarkable feature of this ever-developing genre.

What are the salient features of this novelization of other genres suggested by us above? They become more free and flexible, their language renews itself by incorporating extraliterary heteroglossia and the "novelistic" layers of literary language, they become dialogized, permeated with laughter, irony, humor, elements of self-parody and finally—this is the most important thing—the novel inserts into these other genres an indeterminacy, a certain semantic open-endedness, a living contact with unfinished, still-evolving contemporary reality (the open-ended present). As we will see below, all these phenomena are explained by the transposition of other genres into this new and peculiar zone for structuring artistic models (a zone of contact with the present in all its open-endedness), a zone that was first appropriated by the novel.

It is of course impossible to explain the phenomenon of novelization purely by reference to the direct and unmediated influence of the novel itself. Even where such influence can be precisely established and demonstrated, it is intimately interwoven with those direct changes in reality itself that also determine the novel and that condition its dominance in a given era. The novel is the only developing genre and therefore it reflects more deeply, more essentially, more sensitively and rapidly, reality itself in the process of its unfolding. Only that which is itself developing can comprehend development as a process. The novel has become the leading hero in the drama of literary development in our time precisely because it best of all reflects the tendencies of a new world still in the making; it is, after all, the only genre born of this new world and in total affinity with it. In many respects the novel has anticipated, and continues to anticipate, the future development of literature as a whole. In the process of becoming the dominant genre, the novel sparks the renovation of all other genres, it infects them with its spirit of process and inconclusiveness. It draws them ineluctably into its orbit precisely because this orbit coincides with the basic direction of the development of literature as a whole. In this lies the exceptional importance of the novel, as an object of study for the theory as well as the history of literature.

Unfortunately, historians of literature usually reduce this struggle between the novel and other already completed genres, all these aspects of novelization, to the actual real-life struggle among "schools" and "trends." A novelized poem, for example, they call a "romantic poem" (which of course it is) and believe that in so doing they have exhausted the subject. They do not see beneath the superficial hustle and bustle of literary process the major and crucial fates of literature and language, whose great heroes turn out to be first and foremost genres, and whose "trends" and "schools" are but second- or third-rank protagonists.

The utter inadequacy of literary theory is exposed when it is forced to deal with the novel. In the case of other genres literary theory works confidently and precisely, since there is a finished and already formed object, definite and clear. These genres preserve their rigidity and canonic quality in all classical eras of their development; variations from era to era, from trend to trend or school to school are peripheral and do not affect their ossified generic skeleton. Right up to the present day, in fact, theory dealing with these already completed genres can add almost nothing to Aristotle's formulations. Aristotle's poetics, although occasionally so deeply embedded as to be almost invisible, remains the stable foundation for the theory of genres. Everything works as long as there is no mention of the novel. But the existence of novelized genres already leads theory into a blind alley. Faced with the problem of the novel, genre theory must submit to a radical re-structuring.

Thanks to the meticulous work of scholars, a huge amount of historical material has accumulated and many questions concerning the evolution of various types of novels have been clarified—but the problem of the novel genre as a whole has not yet found anything like a satisfactory principled resolution. The novel continues to be seen as one genre among many; attempts are made to distinguish it as an already completed genre from other already completed genres, to discover its internal canon—one that would function as a well-defined system of rigid generic factors. In the vast majority of cases, work on the novel is reduced to mere cataloging, a description of all variants on the novel—albeit as comprehensive as possible. But the results of these descriptions never succeed in giving us as much as a hint of comprehensive formula for the novel as a genre. In addition, the experts have not managed to isolate a single definite, stable characteristic of the novel—without adding a reservation, which immediately disqualifies it altogether as a generic characteristic.

Some examples of such "characteristics with reservations" would be: the novel is a multi-layered genre (although there also exist magnificent single-layered novels); the novel is a precisely plotted and dynamic genre (although there also exist novels that push to its literary limits the art of pure description); the novel is a complicated genre (although novels are mass produced as pure and frivolous entertainment like no other genre); the novel is a love story (although the greatest examples of the European novel are utterly devoid of the love element); the novel is a prose genre (although there exist excellent novels in verse). One could of course mention a large number of additional "generic characteristics" for the novel similar to those given above, which are immediately annulled by some reservation innocently appended to them.

Of considerably more interest and consequence are those normative definitions of the novel offered by novelists themselves, who produce a specific novel and then declare *it* the only correct, necessary and authentic form of the novel. Such, for instance, is Rousseau's foreword to his *La Nouvelle Héloïse*, Wieland's to his *Agathon*,[4] Wezel's to his *Tobias Knouts*;[5] in such a category belong the numerous declarations and statements of principle by the Romantics on *Wilhelm Meister*, *Lucinde* and other texts. Such statements are not attempts to incorporate all the possible variants of the novel into a single eclectic definition, but are themselves part and parcel of the living evolution of the novel as a genre. Often they deeply and faithfully reflect the novel's struggle with other genres and with itself (with other dominant and fashionable variants of the novel) at a particular point in its development. They come closer to an understanding of the peculiar position of the novel in literature, a position that is not commensurate with that of other genres.

Especially significant in this connection is a series of statements that accompanied the emergence of a new novel-type in the eighteenth century. The series opens with Fielding's reflections on the novel and its hero in *Tom Jones*. It continues in Wieland's foreword to *Agathon*, and the most essential link in the series is Blankenburg's *Versuch über den Roman*.[6] By the end of this series we have, in fact, that theory of the novel later formulated by Hegel. In all these statements, each reflecting the novel in one of its critical stages (*Tom Jones*, *Agathon*, *Wilhelm Meister*), the following prerequisites for the novel are characteristic: (1) the novel should not be "poetic," as the word "poetic" is used in other genres of imaginative literature; (2) the hero of a novel should not be "heroic" in either the epic or the tragic sense of the word: he should combine in himself negative as well as positive features, low as well as lofty, ridiculous as well as serious; (3) the hero should not be portrayed as an already completed and unchanging person but as one who is evolving and developing, a person who learns from life; (4) the novel should become for the contemporary world what the epic was for the ancient world (an idea that Blankenburg expressed very precisely, and that was later repeated by Hegel).

All these positive prerequisites have their substantial and productive side—taken together, they constitute a criticism (from the novel's point of view) of other genres and of the relationship these genres bear to reality: their stilted heroizing, their narrow and unlifelike poeticalness, their monotony and abstractness, the pre-packaged and unchanging nature of their heroes. We have here, in fact, a rigorous critique of the literariness and poeticalness inherent in other genres and also in the predecessors of the contemporary novel (the heroic Baroque novel and the Sentimental novels of Richardson). These statements are reinforced significantly by the practice of these novelists themselves. Here the novel—its texts as well as the theory connected with it—emerges consciously and unambiguously as a genre that is both critical and self-critical, one fated to revise the fundamental concepts of literariness and poeticalness dominant at the time. On the one hand, the contrast of novel with epic (and the novel's opposition to the epic) is but one moment in the criticism of other literary genres (in particular, a criticism of epic heroization); but on the other hand, this contrast aims to elevate the significance of the novel, making of it the dominant genre in contemporary literature.

The positive prerequisites mentioned above constitute one of the high-points in the novel's coming to self-consciousness. They do not yet of course provide a theory of the novel. These statements are also not distinguished by any great philosophical depth. They do however illustrate the nature of the novel as a genre no less—if perhaps no more—than do other existing theories of the novel.

I will attempt below to approach the novel precisely as a genre-in-the-making, one in the vanguard of all modern literary development. I am not constructing here a functional definition of the novelistic canon in literary history, that is, a definition that would make of it a system of fixed generic characteristics. Rather, I am trying to grope my way toward the basic structural characteristics of this most fluid of genres, characteristics that might determine the direction of its peculiar capacity for change and of its influence and effect on the rest of literature.

I find three basic characteristics that fundamentally distinguish the novel in principle from other genres: (1) its stylistic three-dimensionality, which is linked with the multi-languaged consciousness realized in the novel; (2) the radical change it effects in the temporal coordinates of the literary image; (3) the new zone opened by the novel for structuring literary images, namely, the zone of maximal contact with the present (with contemporary reality) in all its open-endedness.

These three characteristics of the novel are all organically inter-related and have all been powerfully affected by a very specific rupture in the history of European civilization: its emergence from a socially isolated and culturally deaf semipatriarchal society, and its entrance into international and interlingual contacts and relationships. A multitude of different languages, cultures and times became available to Europe, and this became a decisive factor in its life and thought.

In another work[7] I have already investigated the first stylistic peculiarity of the novel, the one resulting from the active polyglossia of the new world, the new culture and its new creative literary consciousness. I will summarize here only the basic points.

Polyglossia had always existed (it is more ancient than pure, canonic monoglossia), but it had not been a factor in literary creation; an artistically conscious choice between languages did not serve as the creative center of the literary and language process. Classical Greeks had a feeling both for "languages" and for the epochs of language, for the various Greek literary dialects (tragedy is a polyglot genre), but creative consciousness was realized in closed, pure languages (although in actual fact they were mixed). Polyglossia was appropriated and canonized among all the genres.

The new cultural and creative consciousness lives in an actively polyglot world. The world becomes polyglot, once and for all and irreversibly. The period of national languages, coexisting but closed and deaf to each other, comes to an end. Languages throw light on each other: one language can, after all, see itself only in the light of another language. The naive and stubborn coexistence of "languages" within a given national language also comes to an end—that is, there is no more peaceful co-existence between territorial dialects, social and professional dialects and jargons, literary language, generic languages within literary language, epochs in language and so forth.

All this set into motion a process of active, mutual cause-and-effect and interillumination. Words and language began to have a different feel to them; objectively they ceased to be what they had once been. Under these conditions of external and internal interillumination, each given language—even if its linguistic composition (phonetics, vocabulary, morphology, etc.) were to remain absolutely unchanged—is, as it were, reborn, becoming qualitatively a different thing for the consciousness that creates in it.

In this actively polyglot world, completely new relationships are established between language and its object (that is, the real world)—and this is fraught with enormous consequences for all the already completed genres that had been formed during eras of closed and deaf monoglossia. In contrast to other major genres, the novel emerged and matured precisely when intense activization of external and internal polyglossia was at the peak of its activity; this is its native element. The novel could therefore assume leadership in the process of developing and renewing literature in its linguistic and stylistic dimension.

In the above-mentioned work I tried to elucidate the profound stylistic originality of the novel, which is determined by its connection with polyglossia.

Let us move on to the two other characteristics, both concerned with the thematic aspect of structure in the novel as a genre. These characteristics can be best brought out and clarified through a comparison of the novel with the epic.

The epic as a genre in its own right may, for our purposes, be characterized by three constitutive features: (1) a national epic past—in Goethe's and Schiller's terminology the "absolute past"—serves as the subject for the epic;[8] (2) national tradition (not personal experience and the free thought that grows out of it) serves as the source for the epic; (3) an absolute epic distance separates the epic world from contemporary reality, that is, from the time in which the singer (the author and his audience) lives.

Let us now touch upon several artistic features related to the above. The absence of internal conclusiveness and exhaustiveness creates a sharp increase in demands for an *external* and *formal* completedness and exhaustiveness, especially in regard to plot-line. The problems of a beginning, an end, and "fullness" of plot are posed anew. The epic is indifferent to formal beginnings and can remain incomplete (that is, where it concludes is almost arbitrary). The absolute past is closed and completed in the whole as well as in any of its parts. It is, therefore, possible to take any part and offer it as the whole. One cannot embrace, in a single epic, the entire world of the absolute past (although it is unified from a plot standpoint)—to do so would mean a retelling of the whole of national tradition, and it is sufficiently difficult to embrace even a significant portion of it. But this is no great loss, because the structure of the whole is repeated in each part, and each part is complete and circular like the whole. One may begin the story at almost any moment, and finish at almost any moment. The *Iliad* is a random excerpt from the Trojan cycle. Its ending (the burial of Hector) could not possibly be the ending from a novelistic point of view. But epic completedness suffers not the slightest as a result. The specific "impulse to end"—How does the war end? Who wins? What will happen to Achilles? and so forth—is absolutely excluded from the epic by both internal and external motifs (the plotline of the tradition was already known to everyone). This specific "impulse to continue" (what will happen next?) and the "impulse to end" (how will it end?) are characteristic only for the novel and are possible only in a zone where there is proximity and contact; in a zone of distanced images they are impossible.

In distanced images we have the whole event, and plot interest (that is, the condition of not knowing) is impossible. The novel, however, speculates in what is unknown. The novel devises various forms and methods for employing the surplus knowledge that the author has, that which the hero does not know or does not see. It is possible to utilize this authorial surplus in an external way, manipulating the narrative, or it can be used to complete the image of an individual (an externalization that is peculiarly novelistic). But there is another possibility in this surplus that creates further problems.

The distinctive features of the novelistic zone emerge in various ways in various novels. A novel need not raise any problematic questions at all. Take, for example, the adventuristic "boulevard" romance. There is no philosophy in it, no social or political problems, no psychology. Consequently none of these spheres provides any contact with the inconclusive events of our own contemporary reality. The absence of distance and of a zone of contact are utilized here in a different way:

in place of our tedious lives we are offered a surrogate, true, but it is the surrogate of a fascinating and brilliant life. We can experience these adventures, identify with these heroes; such novels almost become a substitute for our own lives. Nothing of the sort is possible in the epic and other distanced genres. And here we encounter the specific danger inherent in the novelistic zone of contact: we ourselves may actually enter the novel (whereas we could never enter an epic or other distanced genre). It follows that we might substitute for our own life an obsessive reading of novels, or dreams based on novelistic models (the hero of [Dostoevsky's] *White Nights*); Bovaryism becomes possible, the real-life appearance of fashionable heroes taken from novels—disillusioned, demonic and so forth. Other genres are capable of generating such phenomena only after having been novelized, that is, after having been transposed to the novelistic zone of contact (for example, the verse narratives of Byron).

Yet another phenomenon in the history of the novel—and one of extreme importance—is connected with this new temporal orientation and with this zone of contact: it is the novel's special relationship with extraliterary genres, with the genres of everyday life and with ideological genres. In its earliest stages, the novel and its preparatory genres had relied upon various extraliterary forms of personal and social reality, and especially those of rhetoric (there is a theory that actually traces the novel back to rhetoric). And in later stages of its development the novel makes wide and substantial use of letters, diaries, confessions, the forms and methods of rhetoric associated with recently established courts and so forth. Since it is constructed in a zone of contact with the incomplete events of a particular present, the novel often crosses the boundary of what we strictly call fictional literature—making use first of a moral confession, then of a philosophical tract, then of manifestos that are openly political, then degenerating into the raw spirituality of a confession, a "cry of the soul" that has not yet found its formal contours. These phenomena are precisely what characterize the novel as a developing genre. After all, the boundaries between fiction and nonfiction, between literature and nonliterature and so forth are not laid up in heaven. Every specific situation is historical. And the growth of literature is not merely development and change within the fixed boundaries of any given definition; the boundaries themselves are constantly changing. The shift of boundaries between various strata (including literature) in a culture is an extremely slow and complex process. Isolated border violations of any given specific definition (such as those mentioned above) are only symptomatic of this larger process, which occurs at a great depth. These symptoms of change appear considerably more often in the novel than they do elsewhere, as the novel is a developing genre; they are sharper and more significant because the novel is in the vanguard of change. The novel may thus serve as a document for gauging the lofty and still distant destinies of literature's future unfolding.

But the changes that take place in temporal orientation, and in the zone where images are constructed, appear nowhere more profoundly and inevitably than in the process of re-structuring the image of the individual in literature. Within the bounds of the present article, however, I can touch on this great and complex question only briefly and superficially.

The individual in the high distanced genres is an individual of the absolute past and of the distanced image. As such he is a fully finished and completed being. This has been accomplished on a lofty heroic level, but what is complete is also something hopelessly readymade; he is all there, from beginning to end he coincides with himself, he is absolutely equal to himself. He is, furthermore, completely externalized. There is not the slightest gap between his authentic essence and its external manifestation. All his potential, all his possibilities are realized utterly in his external social position, in the whole of his fate and even in his external appearance; outside of this predetermined fate and predetermined position there is nothing. He has already become everything that he could become, and he could become only that which he has already become. He is entirely externalized in the most elementary, almost literal sense: everything in him is exposed and loudly expressed: his internal world and all his external characteristics, his appearance and his actions all lie on a single plane. His view of himself coincides completely with others' views of him—the view of his society (his community), the epic singer and the audience also coincide.

In this context, mention should be made of the problem of self-praise that comes up in Plutarch and others. "I myself," in an environment that is distanced, exists not *in* itself or for *itself* but for the self's descendents, for the memory such a self anticipates in its descendents. I acknowledge myself, an image that is my own, but on this distanced plane of memory such a consciousness of self is alienated from "me." I see myself through the eyes of another. This coincidence of forms—the view I have of myself as self, and the view I have of myself as other—bears an integral, and therefore naive, character—there is no gap between the two. We have as yet no confession, no exposing of self. The one doing the depicting coincides with the one being depicted.[9]

He sees and knows in himself only the things that others see and know in him. Everything that another person—the author—is able to say about him he can say about himself, and vice versa. There is nothing to seek for in him, nothing to guess at, he can neither be exposed nor provoked; he is all of a piece, he has no shell, there is no nucleus within. Furthermore, the epic hero lacks any ideological initiative (heroes and author alike lack it). The epic world knows only a single and unified world view, obligatory and indubitably true for heroes as well as for authors and audiences. Neither world view nor language can, therefore, function as factors for limiting and determining human images, or their individualization. In the epic, characters are bounded, preformed, individualized by their various situations and destinies, but not by varying "truths." Not even the gods are separated from men by a special truth: they have the same language, they all share the same world view, the same fate, the same extravagant externalization.

These traits of the epic character, shared by and large with other highly distanced genres, are responsible for the exclusive beauty, wholeness, crystal clarity and artistic completedness of this image of man. But at the same time such traits account for his limitations and his obvious woodenness under conditions obtaining in a later period of human existence.

The destruction of epic distance and the transferral of the image of an individual from the distanced plane to the zone of contact with the inconclusive events of the present (and consequently of the future) result in a radical re-structuring of the image of the individual in the novel—and consequently in all literature. Folklore and popular-comic sources for the novel played a huge role in this process. Its first and essential step was the comic familiarization of the image of man. Laughter destroyed epic distance; it began to investigate man freely and familiarly, to turn him inside out, expose the disparity between his surface and his center, between his potential and his reality. A dynamic authenticity was introduced into the image of man, dynamics of inconsistency and tension between various factors of this image; man ceased to coincide with himself, and consequently men ceased to be exhausted entirely by the plots that contain them. Of these inconsistencies and tensions laughter plays up, first of all, the comic sides (but not only the comic sides); in the serio-comical genres of antiquity, images of a new order emerge—for example, the imposing, newly and more complexly integrated heroic image of Socrates.

Characteristic here is the artistic structuring of an image out of durable popular masks—masks that had great influence on the novelistic image of man during the most important stages of the novel's development (the serio-comical genres of antiquity, Rabelais, Cervantes). Outside his destiny, the epic and tragic hero is nothing; he is, therefore, a function of the plot fate assigns him; he cannot become the hero of another destiny or another plot. On the contrary, popular masks—Maccus, Pulcinello, Harlequin—are able to assume any destiny and can figure into any situation (they often do so within the limits of a single play), but they cannot exhaust their possibilities by those situations alone; they always retain, in any situation and in any destiny, a happy surplus of their own, their own rudimentary but inexhaustible human face. Therefore these masks can function and speak independent of the plot; but, moreover, it is precisely in these excursions outside the plot proper—in the Atellan *trices,*[10] in the *lazzi*[11] of Italian comedy—that they best of all reveal a face of their own. Neither an epic nor a tragic hero could ever step out in his own character during a pause in the plot or during an intermission: he has no face for it, no gesture, no language. In this is his strength and his limitation. The epic and tragic hero is the hero who, by his very nature, must perish. Popular masks, on the contrary, never perish: not a single plot in Atellan, Italian or Italianized French comedies provides for, or could ever provide for, the actual death of a Maccus, a Pulcinello or a Harlequin. However, one frequently witnesses their fictive comic deaths (with subsequent resurrections). These are heroes of free improvisation and not heroes of tradition, heroes of a life process that is imperishable and forever renewing itself, forever contemporary—these are not heroes of an absolute past.

These masks and their structure (the noncoincidence with themselves, and with any given situation—the surplus, the inexhaustibility of their self and the like), have had, we repeat, an enormous influence on the development of the novelistic image of man. This structure is preserved even in the novel, although in a more complex, deeply meaningful and serious (or serio-comical) form.

One of the basic internal themes of the novel is precisely the theme of the hero's inadequacy to his fate or his situation. The individual is either greater than his fate, or less than his condition as a man. He cannot become once and for all a clerk, a landowner, a merchant, a fiancé, a jealous lover, a father and so forth. If the hero of a novel actually becomes something of the sort—that is, if he completely coincides with his situation and his fate (as do generic, everyday heroes, the majority of secondary characters in a novel)—then the surplus inhering in the human condition is realized in the main protagonist. The way in which this surplus will actually be realized grows out of the author's orientation toward form and content, that is, the ways he sees and depicts individuals. It is precisely the zone of contact with an inconclusive present (and consequently with the future) that creates the necessity of this incongruity of a man with himself. There always remains in him unrealized potential and unrealized demands. The future exists, and this future ineluctably touches upon the individual, has its roots in him.

An individual cannot be completely incarnated into the flesh of existing sociohistorical categories. There is no mere form that would be able to incarnate once and forever all of his human possibilities and needs, no form in which he could exhaust himself down to the last word, like the tragic epic hero; no form that he could fill to the very brim, and yet at the same time not splash over the brim. There always remains an unrealized surplus of humanness; there always remains a need for the future, and a place for his future must be found. All existing clothes are always too tight, and thus comical, on a man. But this surplus of un-fleshed-out humanness may be realized not only in the hero, but also in the author's point of view (as, for example, in Gogol). Reality as we have it in the novel is only one of many possible realities; it is not inevitable, not arbitrary, it bears within itself other possibilities.

The epic wholeness of an individual disintegrates in a novel in other ways as well. A crucial tension develops between the external and the internal man, and as a result of the subjectivity of the individual becomes an object of experimentation and representation—and first of all on the humorous familiarizing plane. Coordination breaks down between the various aspects: man for himself alone and man in the eyes of others. This disintegration of the integrity that an individual had possessed in epic (and in tragedy) combines in the novel with the necessary preparatory steps toward a new, complex wholeness on a higher level of human development.

Finally, in a novel the individual acquires the ideological and linguistic initiative necessary to change the nature of his own image (there is a new and higher type of individualization of the image). In the antique stage of novelistic development there appeared remarkable examples of such hero-ideologues—the image of Socrates, the image of a laughing Epicurus in the so-called "Hypocratic" novel, the deeply novelized image of Diogenes in the thoroughly dialogized literature of the cynics and in Menippean satire (where it closely approximates the image of the popular mask) and, finally, the image of Menippius in Lucian. As a rule, the hero of a novel is always more or less an ideologue.

What all this suggests is a somewhat abstract and crude schematization for re-structuring the image of an individual in the novel.

We will summarize with some conclusions.

The present, in its all open-endedness, taken as a starting point and center for artistic and ideological orientation, is an enormous revolution in the creative consciousness of man. In the European world this reorientation and destruction of the old hierarchy of temporalities received its crucial generic expression on the boundary between classic antiquity and Hellenism, and in the new world during the late Middle Ages and Renaissance. The fundamental constituents of the novel as a genre were formed in these eras, although some of the separate elements making up the novel were present much earlier, and the novel's roots must ultimately be sought in folklore. In these eras all other major genres had already long since come to completion, they were already old and almost ossified genres. They were all permeated from top to bottom with a more ancient hierarchization of temporalities. The novel, from the very beginning, developed as a genre that had at its core a new way of conceptualizing time. The absolute past, tradition, hierachical distance played no role in the formation of the novel as a genre (such spatiotemporal categories did play a role, though insignificant, in certain periods of the novel's development, when it was slightly influenced by the epic—for example in the Baroque novel). The novel took shape precisely at the point when epic distance was disintegrating, when both the world and man were assuming a degree of comic familiarity, when the object of artistic representation was being degraded to the level of a contemporary reality that was inconclusive and fluid. From the very beginning the novel was structured not in the distanced image of the absolute past but in the zone of direct contact with inconclusive present-day reality. At its core lay personal experience and free creative imagination. Thus a new, sober artistic-prose novelistic image and a new critical scientific perception came into being simultaneously. From the very beginning, then, the novel was made of different clay than the other already completed genres; it is a different breed, and with it and in it is born the future of all literature. Once it came into being, it could never be merely one genre among others, and it could not erect rules for interrelating with others in peaceful and harmonious co-existence. In the presence of the novel, all other genres somehow have a different resonance. A lengthy battle for the novelization of the other genres began, a battle to drag them into a zone of contact with reality. The course of this battle has been complex and tortuous.

The novelization of literature does not imply attaching to already completed genres a generic canon that is alien to them, not theirs. The novel, after all, has no canon of its own. It is, by its very nature, not canonic. It is plasticity itself. It is a genre that is ever questing, ever examining itself and subjecting its established forms to review. Such, indeed, is the only possibility open to a genre that structures itself in a zone of direct contact with developing reality. Therefore, the novelization of other genres does not imply their subjection of an alien generic canon; on the contrary, novelization implies their liberation from all that serves as a brake on their unique development, from all that would change them along with the novel into some sort of stylization of forms that have outlived themselves.

I have developed my various positions in this essay in a somewhat abstract way. There have been few illustrations, and even these were taken only from an ancient period in the novel's development. My choice was determined by the fact that the significance of that period has been greatly underestimated. When people talk about the ancient period of the novel they have traditionally had in mind the "Greek novel" alone. The ancient period of the novel is enormously significant for a proper understanding of the genre. But in ancient times the novel could not really develop all its potential; this potential came to light only in the modern world. We indicated that in several works of antiquity, the inconclusive present begins to sense a greater proximity to the future than to the past. The absence of a temporal perspective in ancient society assured that this process of reorientation toward a real future could not complete itself; after all, there was no real concept of a future. Such a reorientation occurred for the first time during the Renaissance. In that era, the present (that is, a reality that was contemporaneous) for the first time began to sense itself not only as an incomplete continuation of the past, but as something like a new and heroic beginning. To reinterpret reality on the level of the contemporary present now meant not only to degrade, but to raise reality into a new and heroic sphere. It was in the Renaissance that the present first began to feel with great clarity and awareness an incomparably closer proximity and kinship to the future than to the past.

The process of the novel's development has not yet come to an end. It is currently entering a new phase. For our era is characterized by an extraordinary complexity and a deepening in our perception of the world; there is an unusual growth in demands on human discernment, on mature objectivity and the critical faculty. These are features that will shape the further development of the novel as well.

Notes

1 Erwin Rohde (1845–1898), *Der Griechesche Roman und seine Vorläufer* (1876, but many later editions, most recently published by F. Olds [Hildesheim, 1960]), one of the greatest monuments of nineteenth-century classical scholarship in Germany. It has never really been superseded. But see: Ben F.

Perry, *The Ancient Romances* (Berkeley, 1967) and Arthur Heiserman, *The Novel before the Novel* (Chicago, 1977). [Translator's note.]

2   Charles Sorel (1599–1674), an important figure in the reaction to the *preciosité* of such figures as Honoré d'Urfé (1567–1625), whose *L'Astrée* (1607–1627), a monstrous 5,500-page volume overflowing with highflown language, is parodied in *Le Berger extravagant* (1627). The latter book's major protagonist is a dyed-in-the-wool Parisian who reads too many pastoral novels; intoxicated by these, he attempts to live the rustic life as they describe it—with predictably comic results. [Translator's note.]

3   Johann Karl August Musäus (1735–1787), along with Tieck and Brentano, one of the great collectors of German folktales and author of several *Kunstmärchen* of his own (translated into English by Carlyle). Reference here is to his *Grandison der Zweite* (1760–1762, rewritten as *Der deutsche Grandison*, 1781–1782), a satire on Richardson. [Translator's note.]

4   Christoph Martin Wieland (1733–1813) is the author of *Geschichte des Agathon* (1767, first of many versions), an autobiographical novel in the guise of a Greek romance, considered by many to be the first in the long line of German *Bildungsromane*. [Translator's note.]

5   Reference here is to Johann Carl Wezel (1747–1819), *Lebensgeschichte Tobias Knouts, des Weisen, sonst der Stammler genannt* (1773), a novel that has not received the readership it deserves. A four-volume reprint was published by Metzler (Stuttgart, Afterword by Viktor Lange) in 1971. Also see, Elizabeth Holzberg-Pfenniger, *Der desorientierte Erzähler: Studien zu J. C. Wezels Lebensgeschichte des Tobias Knauts* (Bern, 1976). [Translator's note.]

6   Friedrich von Blankenburg (1744–1796), *Versuch über den Roman* (1774), an enormous work (over 500 pages) that attempts to define the novel in terms of a rudimentary psychology, a concern for *Tugend* in the heroes. A facsimile edition was published by Metzler (Stuttgart) in 1965. Little is known about Blankenburg, who is also the author of an unfinished novel with the imposing title *Beytrage zur Geschichte deutschen Reichs und deutschen Sitten*, the first part of which appeared a year after the *Versuch* in 1775. [Translator's note.]

7   Cf. the article "From the Prehistory of Novelistic Discourse" in *The Dialogic Imagination*.

8   Reference here is to "Über epische und dramatische Dichtung," cosigned by Schiller and Goethe, but probably written by the latter in 1797, although not published until 1827. The actual term used by Goethe for what Bakhtin is calling "absolute past" is *vollkommen vergangen*, which is opposed not to the novel, but to drama, which is defined as *vollkommen gegenwärtig*. The essay can be found in Goethe's *Sämtliche Werke* (Stuttgart and Berlin: Jubilaums-Ausgabe, 1902–1907), vol. 36, pp. 149–52. [Translator's note.]

9   Epic disintegrates when the search begins for a new point of view on one's own self (without any admixture of others' points of view). The expressive novelistic gesture arises as a departure from a norm, but the "error" of this

norm immediately reveals how important it is for subjectivity. First there is a departure from a norm, and then the problematicalness of the norm itself.

10 *Trices* are thought to have been interludes in the action of the Atellanae during which the masks often stepped out of character.

11 *Lazzi* were what we might now call "routines" or "numbers" that were not part of the ongoing action of the plot.

5

The Historical Interpretation
of Literature

EDMUND WILSON

■

Edmund Wilson's title reveals the basic critical orientation of his essay, one that is heavily influenced by historical and materialist philosophies, including Marxism. He begins by distinguishing "historical interpretation" from the kind of nonhistorical interpretation that T. S. Eliot practiced and that laid the foundation for what has come to be known as the "New Criticism." Wilson then distinguishes among forms of historical interpretation, ones that emphasize various dimensions of the historical context for literary production, such as the geographical, cultural, economic, and political. He focuses his negative remarks particularly on the form that emphasizes the immediate political element above, or to the exclusion of, other factors.

From these remarks, Wilson approaches the question of "how, in these matters of literary art, do we tell the good art from the bad." In part, in answering his own question, Wilson gravitates toward Mikhail Bakhtin's conception of the novel as a developing genre and Virginia Woolf's hope for the modernist movement. According to Wilson, "the experience of mankind on the earth is always changing as man develops and has to deal with new combinations of elements, and the writer who is to be anything more than an echo of his predecessors must always find expression for something which has never yet been expressed, must master a new set of phenomena which has never yet been mastered." While Woolf implies only a certain thematic orientation in her attention to character and Bakhtin suggests that the strength of the novel lies in its ability to engage the ideological dimensions of the present, Wilson explicitly states that the greatest literature *must* provide the reader with "deep satisfaction," making us feel that "we have been cured of some ache of disorder, relieved of some oppressive burden of uncomprehended events." For Wilson, then, there can be no art for art's sake, or formal experimentation sufficient unto itself to make a literary work great, but great literature inevitably engages important moral questions, a position we may want to consider in further detail in relation to other essays in this anthology, such as those of Lionel Trilling, Roland Barthes, and John Barth.

Edmund Wilson (1895–1972) served for many years as a contributor to such major periodicals as *Vanity Fair*, the *New Republic*, and the *New Yorker*, and as a leading reviewer of contemporary literature, theater, and art. His book *Axel's Castle* (1931) established him as a major critic of modern literature. *The Triple Thinkers*, from whose second edition (1948) this essay is taken, further enhanced that reputation. Many of his essays and reviews are collected in such volumes as *The Shores of Light* (1952).

I want to talk about the historical interpretation of literature—that is, about the interpretation of literature in its social, economic and political aspects.

To begin with, it will be worth while to say something about the kind of criticism which seems to be furthest removed from this. There is a kind of comparative criticism which tends to be non-historical. The essays of T. S. Eliot, which have had such an immense influence in our time, are, for example, fundamentally non-historical. Eliot sees, or tries to see, the whole of literature, so far as he is acquainted with it, spread out before him under the aspect of eternity. He then compares the work of different periods and countries, and tries to draw from it general conclusions about what literature ought to be. He understands, of course, that our point of view in connection with literature changes, and he has what seems to me a very sound conception of the whole body of writing of the past as something to which new works are continually being added, and which is not thereby merely increased in bulk but modified as a whole— so that Sophocles is no longer precisely what he was for Aristotle, or Shakespeare what he was for Ben Jonson or for Dryden or for Dr. Johnson, on account of all the later literature that has intervened between them and us. Yet at every point of this continual accretion, the whole field may be surveyed, as it were, spread out before the critic. The critic tries to see it as God might; he calls the books to a Day of Judgment. And, looking at things in this way, he may arrive at interesting and valuable conclusions which could hardly be reached by approaching them in any other way. Eliot was able to see, for example—what I believe had never been noticed before— that the French Symbolist poetry of the nineteenth century had certain fundamental resemblances to the English poetry of the age of Donne. Another kind of critic would draw certain historical conclusions from these purely esthetic findings, as the Russian D. S. Mirsky did; but Eliot does not draw them.

Another example of this kind of non-historical criticism, in a somewhat different way and on a somewhat different plane, is the work of the late George Saintsbury. Saintsbury was a connoisseur of wines; he wrote an entertaining book on the subject. And his attitude toward literature, too, was that of the connoisseur. He tastes the authors and tells you about the vintages; he distinguishes the qualities of the various wines. His palate was as fine as could be, and he possessed the great qualification that he knew how to take each book on its own terms without expecting it to be some other book and was thus in a position to appreciate a great variety of kinds of writing. He was a man of strong social prejudices and peculiarly intransigent political views, but, so far as it is humanly possible, he kept them out of his literary criticism. The result is one of the most agreeable and most comprehensive commentaries on literature that has ever been written in English. Most scholars who have read as much as Saintsbury do not have Saintsbury's discriminating taste. Here is a critic who has covered the whole ground like any academic historian, yet whose account of it is not merely a chronology but a record of fastidious enjoyment. Since enjoyment is the only thing he is looking for, he does not need to know the causes of things, and the historical background of literature does not interest him very much.

———

There is, however, another tradition of criticism which dates from the beginning of the eighteenth century. In the year 1725, the Neapolitan philosopher Vico published *La Scienza Nuova*, a revolutionary work on the philosophy of history, in which he asserted for the first time that the social world was certainly the work of man, and attempted what is, so far as I know, the first social interpretation of a work of literature. This is what Vico says about Homer:

> Homer composed the *Iliad* when Greece was young and consequently burning with sublime passions such as pride, anger and vengeance—passions which cannot allow dissimulation and which consort with generosity; so that she then admired Achilles, the hero of force. But, grown old, he composed the *Odyssey*, at a time when the passions of Greece were already somewhat cooled by reflection, which is the mother of prudence—so that she now admired Ulysses, the hero of wisdom. Thus also, in Homer's youth, the Greek people liked cruelty, vituperation, savagery, fierceness, ferocity; whereas, when Homer was old, they were already enjoying the luxuries of Alcinoüs, the delights of Calypso, the pleasures of Circe, the songs of the sirens and the pastimes of the suitors, who went no further in aggression and combat than laying siege to the chaste Penelope—all of which practices would appear incompatible with the spirit of the earlier time. The divine Plato is so struck by this difficulty that, in order to solve it, he tells us that Homer had foreseen in inspired vision these dissolute, sickly, and disgusting customs. But in this way he makes Homer out to have been but a foolish instructor for Greek civilization, since, however much he may condemn them, he is displaying for imitation these corrupt and decadent habits which were not to be adopted till long after the foundation of the nations of Greece, and accelerating the natural course which human events would take by spurring the Greeks on to corruption. Thus it is plain that the Homer of the *Iliad* must have preceded by many years the Homer who wrote the *Odys-*

sey; and it is plain that the former must belong to the northeastern part of Greece, since he celebrates the Trojan War, which took place in his part of the country, whereas the latter belongs to the southeastern part, since he celebrates Ulysses, who reigned there.

You see that Vico has here explained Homer in terms both of historical period and of geographical origin. The idea that human arts and institutions were to be studied and elucidated as the products of the geographical and climatic conditions in which the people who created them lived, and of the phase of their social development through which they were passing at the moment, made great progress during the eighteenth century. There are traces of it even in Dr. Johnson, that most orthodox and classical of critics—as, for example, when he accounts for certain characteristics of Shakespeare by the relative barbarity of the age in which he lived, pointing out, just as Vico had done, that "nations, like individuals, have their infancy." And by the eighties of the eighteenth century Herder, in his *Ideas on the Philosophy of History,* was writing of poetry that it was a kind of "Proteus among the people, which is always changing its form in response to the languages, manners, and habits, to the temperaments and climates, nay even to the accents of different nations." He said—what could still seem startling even so late as that—that "language was not a divine communication, but something men had produced themselves." In the lectures on the philosophy of history that Hegel delivered in Berlin in 1822–23, he discussed the national literatures as expressions of the societies which had produced them—societies which he conceived as great organisms continually transforming themselves under the influence of a succession of dominant ideas.

In the field of literary criticism, this historical point of view came to its first complete flower in the work of the French critic Taine, in the middle of the nineteenth century. The whole school of historian-critics to which Taine belonged—Michelet, Renan, Sainte-Beuve—had been occupied in interpreting books in terms of their historical origins. But Taine was the first of these to attempt to apply such principles systematically and on a large scale in a work devoted exclusively to literature. In the Introduction to his *History of English*

Literature, published in 1863, he made his famous pronouncement that works of literature were to be understood as the upshot of three interfusing factors: *the moment, the race, and the milieu.* Taine thought he was a scientist and a mechanist, who was examining works of literature from the same point of view as the chemist's in experimenting with chemical compounds. But the difference between the critic and the chemist is that the critic cannot first combine his elements and then watch to see what they will do: he can only examine phenomena which have already taken place. The procedure that Taine actually follows is to pretend to set the stage for the experiment by describing the moment, the race, and the milieu, and then to say: "Such a situation demands such and such a kind of writer." He now goes on to describe the kind of writer that the situation demands, and the reader finds himself at the end confronted with Shakespeare or Milton or Byron or whoever the great figure is—who turns out to prove the accuracy of Taine's prognosis by precisely living up to this description.

There was thus a certain element of imposture in Taine; but it was the rabbits he pulled out that saved him. If he had really been the mechanist that he thought he was, his work on literature would have had little value. The truth was that Taine loved literature for its own sake—he was at his best himself a brilliant artist—and he had very strong moral convictions which give his writing emotional power. His mind, to be sure, was an analytic one, and his analysis, though terribly oversimplified, does have an explanatory value. Yet his work was what we call creative. Whatever he may say about chemical experiments, it is evident when he writes of a great writer that the moment, the race, and the milieu have combined, like the three sounds of the chord in Browning's poem about Abt Vogler, to produce not a fourth sound but a star.

To Taine's set of elements was added, dating from the middle of the century, a new element, the economic, which was introduced into the discussion of historical phenomena mainly by Marx and Engels. The non-Marxist critics themselves were at the time already taking into account the influence of the social classes. In his chapters on the Norman conquest of England, Taine shows that the difference between the literatures produced respectively by the Normans and by the Saxons was partly the difference between a ruling class, on the one hand, and a vanquished and repressed class, on the other. And Michelet, in his volume on the Regency, which was finished the same year that the *History of English Literature* appeared, studies the *Manon Lescaut* of the Abbé Prévost as a document representing the point of view of the small gentry before the French Revolution. But Marx and Engels derived the social classes from the way that people made or got their livings—from what they called the *methods of production;* and they tended to regard these economic processes as fundamental to civilization.

The Dialectical Materialism of Marx and Engels was not really so materialistic as it sounds. There was in it a large element of the Hegelian idealism that Marx and Engels thought they had got rid of. At no time did these two famous materialists take so mechanistic a view of things as Taine began by professing; and their theory of the relation of works of literature to what they called the *economic base* was a good deal less simple than Taine's theory of the moment, the race and the milieu. They thought that art, politics, religion, philosophy, and literature belonged to what they called the *superstructure* of human activity; but they saw that the practitioners of these various professions tended also to constitute social groups, and that they were always pulling away from the kind of solidarity based on economic classes in order to establish a professional solidarity of their own. Furthermore, the activities of the superstructure could influence one another, and they could influence the economic base. It may be said of Marx and Engels in general that, contrary to the popular impression, they were tentative, confused and modest when it came down to philosophical first principles, where a materialist like Taine was cocksure. Marx once made an attempt to explain why the poems of Homer were so good when the society that produced them was from his point of view—that is, from the point of view of its industrial development—so primitive; and this gave him a good deal of trouble. If we compare his discussion of this problem with Vico's discussion of Homer, we see that the explanation of literature in terms of a philosophy of social history is becoming, instead of simpler and easier, more difficult and more complex.

Marx and Engels were deeply imbued, moreover, with the German admiration for literature, which they had learned from the age of

Goethe. It would never have occurred to either of them that *der Dichter* was not one of the noblest and most beneficent of human-kind. When Engels writes about Goethe, he presents him as a man equipped for "practical life," whose career was frustrated by the "misery" of the historical situation in Germany in his time, and re-proaches him for allowing himself to lapse into the "cautious, smug, and narrow" philistinism of the class from which he came; but En-gels regrets this, because it interfered with the development of the "mocking, defiant, world-despising genius," "der geniale Dichter," "der gewaltige Poet," of whom Engels would not even, he says, have asked that he should have been a political liberal if Goethe had not sacrificed to his bourgeois shrinkings his truer esthetic sense. And the great critics who were trained on Marx—Franz Mehring and Bernard Shaw—had all this reverence for the priesthood of literature. Shaw deplores the absence of political philosophy and what he re-gards as the middle-class snobbery in Shakespeare; but he celebrates Shakespeare's poetry and his dramatic imagination almost as enthusi-astically as Swinburne does, describing even those potboiling come-dies, *Twelfth Night* and *As You Like It*—the themes of which seem to him most trashy—as "the Crown Jewels of English dramatic po-etry." Such a critic may do more for a writer by showing him as a real man dealing with a real world at a definite moment of time than the impressionist critic of Swinburne's type who flourished in the same period of the late nineteenth century. The purely impressionist critic approaches the whole of literature as an exhibit of belletristic jewels, and he can only write a rhapsodic catalogue. But when Shaw turned his spotlight on Shakespeare as a figure in the Shavian drama of history, he invested him with a new interest as no other English critic had done.

The insistence that the man of letters should play a political role, the disparagement of works of art in comparison with political action, were thus originally no part of Marxism. They only became associated with it later. This happened by way of Russia, and it was due to special tendencies in that country that date from long before the Revolution or the promulgation of Marxism itself. In Russia there have been very good reasons why the political implications of literature should particularly occupy the critics. The art of Pushkin itself, with its marvelous power of implication, had certainly been partly created by the censorship of Nicholas I, and Pushkin set the tradition for most of the great Russian writers that followed him. Every play, every poem, every story, must be a parable of which the moral is *implied*. If it were stated, the censor would suppress the book as he tried to do with Pushkin's *Bronze Horseman*, where it was merely a question of the packed implications protruding a little too plainly. Right down through the writings of Chekhov and up almost to the Revolution, the imaginative literature of Russia presents the peculiar paradox of an art that is technically objective and yet charged with social messages. In Russia under the Tsar, it was inevitable that social criticism should lead to political conclusions, because the most urgent need from the point of view of any kind of improvement was to get rid of the tsarist regime. Even the neo-Christian moralist Tolstoy, who pretended to be non-political, was to exert a subversive influence, because his independent preaching was bound to embroil him with the Church, and the Church was an integral part of the tsardom. Tolstoy's pamphlet called *What Is Art?*, in which he throws overboard Shakespeare and a large part of modern literature, including his own novels, in the interest of his intransigent morality, is the example which is most familiar to us of the Russian criticism; but it was only the most sensational expression of a kind of approach which had been prevalent since Belinsky and Chernyshevsky in the early part of the century. The critics, who were usually journalists writing in exile or in a contraband press, were always tending to demand of the imaginative writers that they should dramatize bolder morals.

Even after the Revolution had destroyed the tsarist government, this state of things did not change. The old habits of censorship persisted in the new socialist society of the Soviets, which was necessarily made up of people who had been stamped by the die of the despotism. We meet here the peculiar phenomenon of a series of literary groups that attempt, one after the other, to obtain official recognition or to make themselves sufficiently powerful to establish themselves as arbiters of literature. Lenin and Trotsky and Lunacharsky had the sense to oppose these attempts: the comrade-dictators of Proletcult or Lev or Rapp would certainly have been just as bad as the Count Benckendorff who made Pushkin miserable, and when the Stalin bureaucracy, after the death of Gorky, got control of this department as of everything else, they instituted a system of repression that made Benckendorff and Nicholas I look like Lorenzo de' Medici. In the meantime, Trotsky, who was Commissar of War but himself a great political writer with an interest in belles-lettres, attempted, in 1924, apropos of one of these movements, to clarify the situation. He wrote a brilliant and valuable book called *Literature and Revolution*, in which he explained the aims of the government, analyzed the work of the Russian writers, and praised or rebuked the latter as they seemed to him in harmony or at odds with the former. Trotsky is intelligent, sympathetic; it is evident that he is really fond of literature and that he knows that a work of art does not fulfill its function in terms of the formulas of party propaganda. But Mayakovsky, the Soviet poet, whom Trotsky had praised with reservations, expressed himself in a famous joke when he was asked what he thought of Trotsky's book—a pun which implied that a Commissar turned critic was inevitably a Commissar still; and what a foreigner cannot accept in Trotsky is his assumption that it is the duty of the government to take a hand in the direction of literature.

This point of view, indigenous to Russia, has been imported to other countries through the permeation of Communist influence. The Communist press and its literary followers have reflected the control of the Kremlin in all the phases through which it has passed, down to the wholesale imprisonment of Soviet writers which has been taking place since 1935. But it has never been a part of the American system that our Republican or Democratic administration should lay down a political line for the guidance of the national literature. A recent gesture in this direction on the part of Archibald MacLeish, who seems a little carried away by his position as Librarian of Congress, was anything but cordially received by serious American writers. So long as the United States remains happily a non-totalitarian country, we can very well do without this aspect of the historical criticism of literature.

Another element of a different order has, however, since Marx's time been added to the historical study of the origins of works of literature. I mean the psychoanalysis of Freud. This appears as an extension of something which had already got well started before, which had figured even in Johnson's *Lives of the Poets*, and of which the great exponent had been Sainte-Beuve: the interpretation of works of literature in the light of the personalities behind them. But the Freudians made this interpretation more exact and more systematic. The great example of the psychoanalysis of an artist is Freud's own essay on Leonardo da Vinci; but this has little critical interest: it is an attempt to construct a case history. One of the best examples I know of the application of Freudian analysis to literature is in Van Wyck Brooks's book, *The Ordeal of Mark Twain*, in which Mr. Brooks uses an incident of Mark Twain's boyhood as a key to his whole career. Mr. Brooks has since repudiated the method he resorted to here, on the ground that no one but an analyst can ever know enough about a writer to make a valid psychoanalytic diagnosis. This is true, and it is true of the method that it has led to bad results where the critic has built a Freudian mechanism out of very slender evidence, and then given us what is really merely a romance exploiting the supposed working of this mechanism, in place of an actual study that sticks close to the facts and the documents of the writer's life and work. But I believe that Van Wyck Brooks really had hold of something important when he fixed upon that childhood incident of which Mark Twain gave so vivid an account to his biographer—that scene at the deathbed of his father when his mother had made him promise that he would not break her heart. If it was not one of those crucial happenings that are supposed to determine the complexes of Freud, it has certainly a typical significance in relation to Mark Twain's whole psychology. The stories that people tell about their childhood are likely to be profoundly symbolic even when they have been partly or wholly made up in the light of later experience. And the attitudes, the compulsions, the emotional "patterns" that recur in the work of a writer are of great interest to the historical critic.

These attitudes and patterns are embedded in the community and the historical moment, and they may indicate its ideals and its diseases as the cell shows the condition of the tissue. The recent scientific experimentation in the combining of Freudian with Marxist method, and of psychoanalysis with anthropology, has had its parallel development in criticism. And there is thus another element added to our equipment for analyzing literary works, and the problem grows still more complex.

The analyst, however, is of course not concerned with the comparative values of his patients any more than the surgeon is. He cannot tell you why the neurotic Dostoevsky produces work of immense value to his fellows while another man with the same neurotic pattern would become a public menace. Freud himself emphatically states in his study of Leonardo that his method can make no attempt to account for Leonardo's genius. The problems of comparative artistic value still remain after we have given attention to the Freudian psychological factor just as they do after we have given attention to the Marxist economic factor and to the racial and geographical factors. No matter how thoroughly and searchingly we may have scrutinized works of literature from the historical and biographical points of view, we must be ready to attempt to estimate, in some such way as Saintsbury and Eliot do, the relative degrees of success attained by the products of the various periods and the various personalities. We must be able to tell good from bad, the first-rate from the second-rate. We shall not otherwise write literary criticism at all, but merely social or political history as reflected in literary texts, or psychological case histories from past eras, or, to take the historical point of view in its simplest and most academic form, merely chronologies of books that have been published.

And now how, in these matters of literary art, do we tell the good art from the bad? Norman Kemp Smith, the Kantian philosopher, whose courses I was fortunate enough to take at Princeton twenty-five years ago, used to tell us that this recognition was based primarily on an emotional reaction. For purposes of practical criticism this is a safe assumption on which to proceed. It is possible to discriminate in a variety of ways the elements that in any given department go to make a successful work of literature. Different schools have at different times demanded different things of literature: *unity, symmetry, universality, originality, vision, inspiration, strangeness, suggestiveness, improving morality, socialist realism,* etc. But you could have any set of these qualities that any school of writing has called for and still not have a good play, a good novel, a good poem, a good history. If you identify the essence of good literature with any one of these elements or with any combination of them, you simply shift the emotional reaction to the recognition of the element or elements. Or if you add to your other demands the demand that the writer must have *talent*, you simply shift this recognition to the talent. Once people find some grounds of agreement in the coincidence of their emotional reactions to books, they may be able to discuss these elements profitably; but if they do not have this basic agreement, the discussion will make no sense.

But how, you may ask, can we identify this elite who know what they are talking about? Well, it can only be said of them that they are self-appointed and self-perpetuating, and that they will compel you to accept their authority. Impostors may try to put themselves over, but these quacks will not last. The implied position of the people who know about literature (as is also the case in every other art) is simply that they know what they know, and that they are determined to impose their opinions by main force of eloquence or assertion on the people who do not know. This is not a question, of course, of professional workers in literature—such as editors, professors, and critics, who very often have no real understanding of the products with which they deal—but of readers of all kinds in all walks of life. There are moments when a first-rate writer, unrecognized or out of fashion with the official chalkers-up for the market, may find his support in the demand for his work of an appreciative, cultivated public.

But what is the cause of this emotional reaction which is the critic's divining rod? This question has long been a subject of study by the branch of philosophy called esthetics, and it has recently been made a subject of scientific experimentation. Both these lines of inquiry are likely to be prejudiced in the eyes of the literary critic by the fact that the inquiries are sometimes conducted by persons who are obviously deficient in literary feeling or taste. Yet one should not deny the possibility that something of value might result from the speculations and explorations of men of acute minds who take as their primary data the esthetic emotions of other men.

Almost everybody interested in literature has tried to explain to himself the nature of these emotions that register our approval of artistic works: and I of course have my own explanation.

In my view, all our intellectual activity, in whatever field it takes place, is an attempt to give a meaning to our experience—that is, to make life more practicable; for by understanding things we make it easier to survive and get around among them. The mathematician Euclid, working in a convention of abstractions, shows us relations between the distances of our unwieldy and cluttered-up environment upon which we are able to count. A drama of Sophocles also indicates relations between the various human impulses, which appear so confused and dangerous, and it brings out a certain justice of Fate—that is to say, of the way in which the interaction of these impulses is seen in the long run to work out—upon which we can also depend. The kinship, from this point of view, of the purposes of science and art appears very clearly in the case of the Greeks, because not only do both Euclid and Sophocles satisfy us by making patterns, but they make much the same kind of patterns. Euclid's *Elements* takes simple theorems and by a series of logical operations builds them up to a climax in the square of the hypotenuse. A typical drama of Sophocles develops in a similar way.

Some writers (as well as some scientists) have a different kind of explicit message beyond the reassurance implicit in the mere feat of understanding life or of molding the harmony of artistic form. Not content with such an achievement as that of Sophocles—who has one of his choruses tell us that it is better not to be born, but who, by representing life as noble and based on law, makes its tragedy easier to bear—such writers attempt, like Plato, to think out and recommend a procedure for turning it into something better. But other departments of literature—lyric poetry such as Sappho's, for example—have *less* philosophical content than Sophocles. A lyric gives us nothing but a pattern imposed on the expression of a feeling; but this pattern of metrical quantities and of consonants and vowels that balance has the effect of reducing the feeling, however unruly or painful it may seem when we experience it in the course of our lives, to something orderly, symmetrical and pleasing; and it also relates this feeling to the more impressive scheme, works it into the larger texture, of the body of poetic art. The discord has been resolved, the anomaly subjected to discipline. And this control of his emotion by the poet has the effect at second hand of making it easier for the reader to manage his own emotions. (Why certain sounds and rhythms gratify us more than others, and how they are connected with the themes and ideas that they are chosen as appropriate for conveying, are questions that may be passed on to the scientist.)

And this brings us back again to the historical point of view. The experience of mankind on the earth is always changing as man develops and has to deal with new combinations of elements; and the writer who is to be anything more than an echo of his predecessors must always find expression for something which has never yet been expressed, must master a new set of phenomena which has never yet been mastered. With each such victory of the human intellect, whether in history, in philosophy or in poetry, we experience a deep satisfaction: we have been cured of some ache of disorder, relieved of some oppressive burden of uncomprehended events.

This relief that brings the sense of power, and, with the sense of power, joy, is the positive emotion which tells us that we have encountered a first-rate piece of literature. But stay! you may at this point warn: are not people often solaced and exhilarated by literature of the trashiest kind? They are: crude and limited people do certainly feel some such emotion in connection with work that is limited and crude. The man who is more highly organized and has a wider intellectual range will feel it in connection with work that is finer and more complex. The difference between the emotion of the more highly organized man and the emotion of the less highly organized one is a matter of mere gradation. You sometimes discover books—the novels of John Steinbeck, for example—that seem to mark precisely the borderline between work that is definitely superior and work that is definitely bad. When I was speaking a little while back of the genuine connoisseurs who establish the standards of taste, I meant, of course, the people who can distinguish Grade A and who prefer it to the other grades.

6

Spatial Form in Modern Literature

JOSEPH FRANK

━━━━

Joseph Frank broke new critical ground in his 1945 study of Djuna Barnes's *Nightwood*, analyzing a crucial technique of modernist literature, the substitution of spatial relationships for temporal progression as a formal metaphor of thematic development. Here we reprint the first half of Frank's essay, in which he presents his general conception of modern "spatial form." Starting with Gustave Flaubert and recognizing his efforts to duplicate the simultaneity of action possible in drama and later in film, Frank comments that "since language proceeds in time, it is impossible to approach this simultaneity of perception except by breaking up temporal sequence." According to Frank, "spatialization of form in the novel" provides an alternative to the chronological development normal to verbal structures, which can be read only in a linear fashion through time, unlike painting and the plastic arts, which can be visually apprehended instantaneously. Frank claims that while in poetry spatialization led to the "disappearance of coherent sequence . . . the novel, with its larger unit of meaning, can preserve coherent sequence within the unit of meaning and break up only the timeflow of narrative."

While Flaubert introduces this method, it does not become a dominant form, according to Frank, until James Joyce's *Ulysses* and Marcel Proust's *A la recherche du temps perdu* (one might want to compare Frank's treatment of this novel with Gérard Genette's later in this collection). Frank sees these two authors as embodying the more common approach to spatialization, one in which the authors "accept the naturalistic principle, presenting their characters in terms of those commonplace details, those descriptions of circumstance and environment, that we have come to regard as verisimilar."

Barnes, on the other hand, breaks with this tendency to present a literary equivalent of abstractionism. Although Frank does not allude to it, one might well compare Barnes's abstractionist spatialization with the experimental work of another expatriate American modernist, Gertrude Stein.

Frank's conception of spatial form has become a classical critical statement, one emended and developed by numerous other critics, such as Ivo Vidan, whose "Time Sequence in Spatial Fiction" appears later in this volume. But we should ask ourselves if spatialization is limited to being a formal principle of modernist fiction or if it can be integrated into a discussion of more traditional method of plot development?

In 1963 Professor Frank (b. 1918), who has spent most of his career at Princeton University, published *The Widening Gyre*, a full-length presentation of the critical conceptions contained in "Spatial Form in Modern Literature." In 1976 he published *F. M. Dostoevsky: Seeds of Revolt*, the first of a projected five-volume biography of that author. Subsequent volumes have appeared in 1983 and 1986.

For a study of esthetic form in the modern novel, Flaubert's famous county fair scene in *Madame Bovary* is a convenient point of departure. This scene has been justly praised for its mordant caricature of bourgeois pomposity, its portrayal—unusually sympathetic for Flaubert—of the bewildered old servant, and its burlesque of the pseudo-romantic rhetoric by which Rodolphe woos the sentimental Emma. At present, it is enough to notice the method by which Flaubert handles the scene—a method we might as well call cinematographic, since this analogy comes immediately to mind. As Flaubert sets the scene, there is action going on simultaneously at three levels, and the physical position of each level is a fair index to its spiritual significance. On the lowest plane, there is the surging, jostling mob in the street, mingling with the livestock brought to the exhibition; raised slightly above the street by a platform are the speech-making officials, bombastically reeling off platitudes to the attentive

"Spatial Form in Modern Literature," by Joseph Frank, is reprinted from *Sewanee Review* 53.2–3 (1945). Copyright 1945, 1983 University of the South. Reprinted with permission of the editor of the *Sewanee Review*.

multitudes; and on the highest level of all, from a window overlooking the spectacle, Rodolphe and Emma are watching the proceedings and carrying on their amorous conversation, in phrases as stilted as those regaling the crowds. Albert Thibaudet has compared this scene to the medieval mystery play, in which various related actions occur simultaneously on different stage levels; but this acute comparison refers to Flaubert's intention rather than to his method. "Everything should sound simultaneously," Flaubert later wrote, in commenting on this scene, "one should hear the bellowing of the cattle, the whisperings of the lovers and the rhetoric of the officials all at the same time."[1]

But since language proceeds in time, is it impossible to approach this simultaneity of perception except by breaking up temporal sequence. And this is exactly what Flaubert does: he dissolves sequence by cutting back and forth between the various levels of action in a slowly-rising crescendo until—at the climax of the scene—Rodolphe's Chateaubriandesque phrases are read at almost the same moment as the names of prize winners for raising the best pigs. Flaubert takes care to underline this satiric similarity by description, as well as by juxtaposition, as if he were afraid the reflexive relations of the two actions would not be grasped: "From magnetism, by slow degrees, Rodolphe had arrived at affinities, and while M. le Président was citing Cincinnatus at his plow, Diocletian planting his cabbages, and the emperors of China ushering in the new year with sowing-festivals, the young man was explaining to the young woman that these irresistible attractions sprang from some anterior existence."

This scene illustrates, on a small scale, what we mean by the spatialization of form in a novel. For the duration of the scene, at least, the time-flow of the narrative is halted: attention is fixed on the interplay of relationships within the limited time-area. These relationships are juxtaposed independently of the progress of the narrative; and the full significance of the scene is given only by the reflexive relations among the units of meaning. In Flaubert's scene, however, the unit of meaning is not, as in modern poetry, a word-group or a fragment of an anecdote, but the totality of each level of action taken as an integer: the unit is so large that the scene can be read with an illusion of complete understanding, yet with a total unawareness of the "dialectic of platitude" (Thibaudet) interweaving all levels, and finally linking them together with devastating irony. In other words, the struggle towards spatial form in Pound and Eliot resulted in the disappearance of coherent sequence after a few lines; but the novel, with its larger unit of meaning, can preserve coherent sequence within the unit of meaning and break up only the time-flow of narrative. (Because of this difference, readers of modern poetry are practically forced to read reflexively to get any literal sense, while readers of a novel like *Nightwood*, for example, are led to expect narrative sequence by the deceptive normality of language sequence within the unit of meaning). But this does not affect the parallel between esthetic form in modern poetry and the form of Flaubert's scene: both can be properly understood only when their units of meaning are apprehended reflexively, in an instant of time.

Flaubert's scene, although interesting in itself, is of minor importance to his novel as a whole, and is skillfully blended back into the main narrative structure after fulfilling its satiric function. But Flaubert's method was taken over by James Joyce, and applied on a gigantic scale in the composition of *Ulysses*. Joyce composed his novel of an infinite number of references and cross-references which relate to one another independently of the time-sequence of the narrative; and, before the book fits together into any meaningful pattern, these references must be connected by the reader and viewed as a whole. Ultimately, if we are to believe Stuart Gilbert, these systems of references form a complete picture of practically everything under the sun, from the stages of man's life and the organs of the human body to the colors of the spectrum; but these structures are far more important for Joyce, as Harry Levin has remarked, than they could ever possibly be for the reader. Students of Joyce, fascinated by his erudition, have usually applied themselves to exegesis. Unfortunately, such considerations have little to do with the perceptual form of Joyce's novel.

Joyce's most obvious intention in *Ulysses* is to give the reader a picture of Dublin seen as a whole—to re-recreate the sights and sounds, the people and places, of a typical Dublin day, much as Flaubert had re-created his provincial county fair. And, like Flaubert, Joyce wanted his depiction to have the same unified impact, the same sense of simultaneous activity occurring in different places. Joyce, as a matter of fact, frequently makes use of the same method as Flaubert—cutting back and forth between different actions occurring at the same time—and usually does so to obtain the same ironic effect. But Joyce had the problem of creating this impression of simultaneity for the life of a whole teeming city, and of maintaining it— or rather of strengthening it—through hundreds of pages that must be read as a sequence. To meet this problem, Joyce was forced to go far beyond what Flaubert had done; while Flaubert had maintained a clear-cut narrative line, except in the county-fair scene, Joyce breaks up his narrative and transforms the very structure of his novel into an instrument of his esthetic intention.

Joyce conceived *Ulysses* as a modern epic; and in the epic, as Stephen Dedalus tells us in *A Portrait of the Artist as a Young Man*, "the personality of the artist, at first sight a cry or a cadence and then a fluid and lambent narrative, finally refines itself out of existence, impersonalizes itself, so to speak . . . the artist, like the God of creation, remains within or beyond or above his handiwork, invisible, refined out of existence, indifferent, paring his fingernails." The epic is thus synonymous for Joyce with the complete self-effacement of the author; and, with his usual uncompromising rigor, Joyce carries this implication further than anyone had dared before. He assumes—what is obviously not true—that his readers are Dubliners, intimately acquainted with Dublin life and the personal history of his characters. This allows him to refrain from giving any direct information about his characters: such information would immediately have betrayed the presence of an omniscient author. What Joyce does, instead, is to present the elements of his narrative—the relations between Stephen and his family, between Bloom and his wife, between Stephen and Bloom and the Dedalus family—in fragments, as they are thrown out unexplained in the course of casual conversation, or as they lie embedded in the various strata of symbolic reference; and the same is true of all the allusions to Dublin life, history, and the external events of the twenty-four hours during which the novel takes place. In other words, all the factual background—so conveniently summarized for the reader in an ordinary novel—must be reconstructed from fragments, sometimes hundreds of pages apart, scattered through the book. As a result, the reader is forced to read *Ulysses* in exactly the same manner as he reads modern poetry—continually fitting fragments together and keeping allusions in mind until, by reflexive reference, he can link them to their complements.

Joyce intended, in this way, to build up in the reader's mind a sense of Dublin as a totality, including all the relations of the characters to one another and all the events which enter their consciousness. As the reader progresses through the novel, connecting allusions and references spatially, gradually becoming aware of the pattern of relationships, this sense was to be imperceptibly acquired; and, at the conclusion of the novel, it might almost be said that Joyce literally wanted the reader to become a Dubliner. For this is what Joyce demands: that the reader have at hand the same instinctive knowledge of Dublin life, the same sense of Dublin as a huge, surrounding organism, which the Dubliner possesses as a birthright. It is such knowledge which, at any one moment of time, gives him a knowledge of Dublin's past and present as a whole; and it is only such knowledge which might enable the reader, like the characters, to place all the references in their proper context. This, it should be realized, is practically the equivalent of saying that Joyce cannot be read—he can only be re-read. A knowledge of the whole is essential to an understanding of any part; but, unless one is a Dubliner, such knowledge can be obtained only after the book has been read, when all the references are fitted into their proper place and grasped as a unity. Although the burdens placed on the reader by this method of composition may seem insuperable, the fact remains that Joyce, in his unbelievably laborious fragmentation of narrative structure, proceeded on the assumption that a unified spatial apprehension of his work would ultimately be possible.

In a far more subtle manner than with Joyce and Flaubert, the same principle of composition is at work in Marcel Proust. Since Proust himself tells us that, before all else, his novel will have imprinted on it "a form which usually remains invisible, the form of Time," it may seem strange to speak of Proust in connection with spatial form. He has, almost invariably, been considered the novelist of time *par excellence*: the literary interpreter of that Bergsonian "real time" intuited by the sensibility, as distinguished from the abstract, chronological time of the conceptual intelligence. To stop at this point, however, is to miss what Proust himself considered the deepest significance of his work. Obsessed with the ineluctability of time,

Proust was suddenly visited by certain quasi-mystical experiences—described in detail in the last volume of his work, "Le temps retrouvé"—which, by providing him with a spiritual technique for transcending time, enabled him to escape what he considered to be time's domination. By writing a novel, by translating the transcendent, extra-temporal quality of these experiences to the level of esthetic form, Proust hoped to reveal their nature to the world—for they seemed to him a clue to the ultimate secrets of reality. And not only should the world learn about these experiences indirectly, by reading a descriptive account of them, but, through his novel, it would feel their impact on the sensibility as Proust himself had felt it.

To define the method by which this is accomplished, one must first understand clearly the precise nature of the Proustian revelation. Each such experience, Proust tells us, is marked by a feeling that "the permanent essence of things, usually concealed, is set free and our true self, which had long seemed dead but was not dead in other ways, awakes, takes on fresh life as it receives the celestial nourishment brought to it." This celestial nourishment consists of some sound, or odor, or other sensory stimulus, "sensed anew, simultaneously in the present and the past." But why should these moments seem so overwhelmingly valuable that Proust calls them celestial? Because, Proust observes, his imagination could only operate on the past; and the material presented to his imagination, therefore, lacked any sensuous immediacy. But, at certain moments, the physical sensations of the past came flooding back to fuse with the present; and, in these moments, Proust believed that he grasped a reality "real without being of the present moment, ideal but not abstract." Only in these moments did he attain his most cherished ambition—"to seize, isolate, immobilize for the duration of a lightning flash" what otherwise he could not apprehend, "namely: a fragment of time in its pure state." For a person experiencing this moment, Proust adds, the word "death" no longer has meaning. "Situated outside the scope of time, what could he fear from the future?"

The significance of this experience, though obscurely hinted at throughout the book, is made explicit only in the concluding pages which describe the final appearance of the narrator at the reception of the Princesse de Guermantes. The narrator decides to dedicate the remainder of his life to re-creating these experiences in a work of art; and this work will differ essentially from all others because, at its foundation, will be a vision of reality that has been refracted through an extra-temporal perspective. Viewing Proust as the last and most debilitated of a long line of neurasthenic esthetes, many critics have found in this decision to create a work of art merely the final step in his flight from the burdens of reality. Edmund Wilson, ordinarily so discerning, links up this view with Proust's ambition to conquer time, assuming that Proust hoped to oppose time by establishing something—a work of art—impervious to its flux; but this somewhat ingenuous interpretation scarcely does justice to Proust's own conviction, expressed with special intensity in the last volume of his work, that he was fulfilling a prophetic mission. It was not the work of art *qua* work of art that Proust cared about—his contempt for the horde of faddish scribblers was unbounded—but a work of art which should stand as a monument to his personal conquest of time. This his own work could do not simply because it was a work of art, but because it was at once the vehicle through which he conveyed his vision and the concrete substance of that vision shaped by a method which compels the reader to re-experience its exact effect.

The prototype of this method, like the analysis of the revelatory moment, occurs during the reception at the Princesse de Guermantes. After spending years in a sanatorium, losing touch almost completely with the fashionable world of the earlier volumes, the narrator comes out of seclusion to attend the reception. He finds himself bewildered by the changes in social position, and the even more striking changes in character and personality among his former friends. According to some socially-minded critics, Proust intended to paint here the invasion of French aristocratic society by the upper bourgeoisie, and the gradual breakdown of all social and moral standards caused by the First World War. No doubt this process is incidentally described at some length; but, as the narrator takes great pains to tell us, it is far from being the most important meaning of the scene. What strikes the narrator, almost with the force of a blow, is this: in trying to recognize old friends under the masks which, as he feels, the years have welded to them, he is jolted for the first time into a consciousness of the passage of time. When a young man addresses the narrator respectfully, instead of familiarly, as if he were an elderly gentleman, the narrator realizes suddenly that he has become an elderly gentleman; but for him the passage of time had gone unperceived up until that moment. To become conscious of time, the narrator begins to understand, it had first been necessary to remove himself from his accustomed environment—or, what amounts to the same thing, from the stream of time acting on that environment—and then to plunge back into the stream after a lapse of years. In so doing, the narrator found himself presented with two images—the world as he had formerly known it, and the world, transformed by time, that he now saw before him; and when these two images are juxtaposed, the narrator discovers, the passage of time is suddenly experienced through its visible effects. Habit, that universal soporific, ordinarily conceals the passage of time from those who have gone their accustomed ways: at any one moment of time the changes are so minute as to be imperceptible: "Other people," Proust writes, "never cease to change places in relation to ourselves. In the imperceptible, but eternal march of the world, we regard them as motionless in a moment of vision, too short for us to perceive the motion that is sweeping them on. But we have only to select in our memory two pictures taken of them at different moments, close enough together however for them not to have altered in themselves—perceptibly, that is to say—and the difference between the two pictures is a measure of the displacement that they have undergone in relation to us." By comparing these two images in a moment of time, the passage of time can be experienced concretely, in the impact of its visible effects on the sensibility, rather than as a mere gap counted off in numbers. And this discovery provides the narrator with a method which, in T. S. Eliot's phrase, is an "objective correlative" to the visionary apprehension of the fragment of "pure time" intuited in the revelatory moment.

When the narrator discovers this method of communicating his experience of the revelatory moment, he decides, as we have already said, to incorporate it in a novel. But the novel the narrator decides to write has just been finished by the reader; and its form is controlled by the method that the narrator has outlined in its concluding pages. The reader, in other words, is substituted for the narrator, and is placed by the author throughout the book in the same position as the narrator occupies before his own experience at the reception of the Princesse de Guermantes. This is done by the discontinuous presentation of character—a simple device which, nevertheless, is the clue to the form of Proust's vast structure. Every reader soon notices that Proust does not follow any of his characters through the whole course of his novel: they appear and re-appear, in various stages of their lives, but hundreds of pages sometimes go by between the time they are last seen and the time they re-appear; and when they do turn up again, the passage of time has invariably changed them in some decisive way. Instead of being submerged in the stream of time—which, for Proust, would be the equivalent of presenting a character progressively, in a continuous line of development—the reader is confronted with various snapshots of the characters "motionless in a moment of vision," taken at different stages in their lives; and the reader, in juxtaposing these images, experiences the effects of the passage of time exactly as the narrator had done. As he had promised, therefore, Proust does stamp his novel indelibly with the form of time; but we are now in a position to understand exactly what he meant by the promise.

To experience the passage of time, Proust learned, it was necessary to rise above it, and to grasp both past and present simultaneously in a moment of what he called "pure time." But "pure time," obviously, is not time at all—it is perception in a moment of time, that is to say, space. And, by the discontinuous presentation of character, Proust forces the reader to juxtapose disparate images of his characters spatially, in a moment of time, so that the experience of time's passage will be fully communicated to their sensibility. There is a striking analogy here between Proust's method and that of his beloved Impressionist painters; but this analogy goes far deeper than the usual comments about the "impressionism" of Proust's style. The Impressionist painters juxtaposed pure tones on the canvas, instead of mixing them on the palette, in order to leave the blending of colors to the eye of the spectator. Similarly, Proust gives us what might be called pure views of his characters—views of them "motionless in a moment of vision" in various phases of their lives—and allows the sensibility of the reader to fuse these views into a unity. Each view must be apprehended by the reader as a unit; and Proust's purpose is only achieved when these units of meaning are referred to each other reflexively in a moment of time. As with Joyce and the modern poets, we see that spatial form is also the structural scaffolding of Proust's labyrinthine masterpiece.

The name of Djuna Barnes is not unknown to those readers who followed, with any care, the stream of pamphlets, books, magazines, and anthologies that poured forth to enlighten America in the feverish days of literary expatriation. Miss Barnes, it is true, must always have remained a somewhat enigmatic figure even to the most attentive reader. Born in New York State, she spent most of her time abroad in England and France; and the glimpses one catches of her in the memoirs of the period are brief and unrevealing. She appears in the *Dial* from time to time with a drawing or a poem; she crops up now and again in some anthology of advance-guard writers—the usual agglomeration of people who are later to become famous, or to sink into the melancholy oblivion of frustrated promise. Before the publication of *Nightwood*, indeed, one might have been inclined to place her name in the latter group. For, while she has a book of short stories and an earlier novel to her credit, neither of them prepares one for the maturity of achievement so conspicuous in every line of her latest work.

Of the fantastical quality of her imagination, of the gift for imagery which, as T. S. Eliot has said, gives one a sense of horror and doom akin to Elizabethan tragedy; of the epigrammatic incisiveness of her phrasing and her penchant, also akin to the Elizabethans, for dealing with the more scabrous manifestations of human fallibility— of all these there is evidence in *Ryder*, Miss Barnes's first novel. But all this might well have resulted only in a momentary flare-up of capricious brilliance, whose radiance would have been as dazzling as it was insubstantial. *Ryder*, it must be confessed, is an anomalous creation from any point of view. Although Miss Barnes's unusual qualities gradually emerge from its kaleidoscope of moods and styles, these qualities are still, so to speak, held in solution, or at best placed in the service of a literary *jeu d'esprit*. Only in *Nightwood* do they finally crystallize into a definitive and comprehensible pattern.

Many critics—not least among them T. S. Eliot himself—have paid tribute to *Nightwood*'s compelling intensity, its head-and-shoulders superiority, simply as a stylistic phenomenon, to most of the works that currently pass for literature. But *Nightwood*'s reputation at present is similar, in many respects, to that of *The Waste Land* in 1922—it is known as a collection of striking passages, some of breathtaking poetic quality, appealing chiefly to connoisseurs of somewhat gamey literary items. Such a reputation, it need hardly be remarked, is not conducive to intelligent appreciation or understanding. Thanks to critics like F. R. Leavis, Cleanth Brooks, and F. O. Matthiessen, we are now able to approach *The Waste Land* as a work of art, rather than as a battleground for opposing poetic theories or as a curious piece of literary esoterica; and it is time that such a process should be at least begun for *Nightwood*.

Before dealing with *Nightwood* in detail, however, we must make certain broad distinctions between it and the novels already considered. While the structural principle of *Nightwood* is the same as in *Ulysses* and *A la recherche du temps perdu*—spatial form, obtained by means of reflexive reference—there are marked differences in technique that will be obvious to every reader. Taking an analogy from another art, we can say that these differences are similar to the differences between the work of Cézanne and the compositions of a later abstract painter like Braque. What characterizes the work of Cézanne, above all, is the tension between two conflicting but deeply-rooted tendencies: on the one hand, a struggle to attain esthetic form—conceived of by Cézanne as a self-enclosed unity of form-and-color harmonies—and, on the other hand, the desire to create this form through the recognizable depiction of natural objects. Later artists, abandoning Cézanne's efforts to achieve form in terms of natural objects, took over only his preoccupation with formal harmonies, omitting natural objects altogether or presenting them in some distorted manner.

Like Cézanne, Proust and Joyce accept the naturalistic principle, presenting their characters in terms of those commonplace details, those descriptions of circumstance and environment, that we have come to regard as verisimilar. At the same time, we have seen, they intended to control the ebullience of their naturalistic detail by the unity of spatial apprehension. But in *Nightwood*, as in the work of Braque and the later abstract painters, the naturalistic principle is totally abandoned: no attempt is made to convince us that the characters are actual flesh-and-blood human beings. We are asked only to accept their world as we accept an abstract painting or, to return to literature, as we accept a Shakespearian play—as an autonomous pattern giving us an individual vision of reality, rather than what we might consider its exact reflection.

To illustrate the transition that takes place in *Nightwood* let us examine an interesting passage from Proust, where the process can be caught at a rudimentary level. In describing Robert de Saint-Loup, an important character in the early sections of the novel, the narrator tells us that he could see concealed "beneath a courtier's smile his warrior's thirst for action—when I examined him I could see how closely the vigorous structure of his triangular face must have been modelled on that of his ancestors' faces, a face devised rather for an ardent bowman than for a delicate student. Beneath his fine skin the bold construction, the feudal architecture were apparent. His head made one think of those old dungeon keeps on which the disused battlements are still to be seen, although inside they have been converted into libraries." When the reader comes across this passage, he has already learned a considerable number of facts about Saint-Loup. He is, for one thing, a member of the Guermantes family, one of the oldest and most aristocratic in the French nobility and still the acknowledged leaders of Parisian society. Unlike their feudal ancestors, however, the Guermantes have no real influence over the internal affairs of France under the Third Republic. Saint-Loup, for another thing, is by way of being a family black sheep: seemingly uninterested in social success, a devoted student of Nietzsche and Proudhon, we are told that his head was full of "socialistic spoutings," and that he was "imbued with the most profound contempt for his caste." Knowing these facts from earlier sections of the novel, the reader accepts the passage quoted above simply as a trenchant summation of Saint-Loup's character. But so precisely do the images in this passage apply to everything the reader has learned about Saint-Loup, so exactly do they communicate the central impression of his personality, that it would be possible to derive a total knowledge of his character solely from the images without attaching them to a set of external social and historical details.

Images of this kind are commoner in poetry than in prose—more particularly, since we are speaking of character description, in dramatic poetry. In Shakespeare and the Elizabethans, descriptions of character are not "realistic" as we understand the word today: they are not a collection of circumstantial details whose bare conglomeration is assumed to form a definition. The dramatic poet, rather, defined both the physical and psychological aspects of character at one stroke, in an image or series of images. Here is Antony, for example, as Shakespeare presents him in the opening scene of *Antony and Cleopatra*:

> Nay, but this dotage of our general's
> O'erflows the measure: those his goodly eyes
> That o'er the files and musters of the war
> Have glow'd like plated Mars, now bend, now turn,
> The office and devotion of their view
> Upon a tawny front: his captain's heart,
> Which in the scuffles of great fights hath burst
> The buckles on his breast, reneges all temper,
> And is become the bellows and the fan
> To cool a gipsy's lust.

And then, to complete the picture, Antony is contemptuously called "the triple pillar of the world transformed into a strumpet's fool." Or, to take a more modern example, from a poet strongly influenced by the Elizabethans, here is the twentieth-century everyman:

> He, the young man carbuncular, arrives,
> A small house agent's clerk, with one bold stare,
> One of the low on whom assurance sits
> As a silk hat on a Bradford millionaire.

As Ramon Fernandez has remarked of similar character descriptions in the work of George Meredith, images of this kind analyze without dissociating; they describe character but, at the same time, hold fast to the unity of personality, without splintering it to fragments in trying to seize the secret of its integration.

Writing of this order, charged with symbolic overtones, piercing through the cumbrous mass of naturalistic detail to express the essence of character in an image, is the antithesis to what we are accustomed in the novel. Ordinary novels, as T. S. Eliot justly observes in his preface to *Nightwood*, "obtain what reality they have largely from an accurate rendering of the noises that human beings currently make in their daily simple needs of communication; and what part of a novel is not composed of these noises consists of a prose which is no more alive than that of a competent newspaper writer or government official." Miss Barnes abandons any pretensions to this kind of verisimilitude, just as modern artists have abandoned any attempt at naturalistic representation; and the result is a world as strange to the reader, at first sight, as the world of abstract art was to its first spectators. Since the selection of detail in *Nightwood* is governed, not by the logic verisimilitude, but by the demands of the *décor* necessary to enhance the symbolic significance of the characters, the novel has baffled even its most fascinated admirers. Perhaps we can clear up some of the mystery by applying our method of reflexive reference, instead of approaching the book, as most of its readers have done, expecting to find a coherent temporal pattern of narrative.

Since *Nightwood* lacks a narrative structure in the ordinary sense, it cannot be reduced to any sequence of action for purposes of explanation. One can, if one chooses, follow the narrator in Proust through the various stages of his social career; one can, with some difficulty, follow Leopold Bloom's epic journey through Dublin; but no such reduction is possible in *Nightwood*. As Dr. O'Connor remarks to Nora Flood, with his desperate gaiety, "I have a narrative, but you will be put to it to find it." Strictly speaking, the doctor is wrong—he has a static situation, not a narrative, and no matter how hard the reader looks he will find only the various facets of this situation explored from different angles. The eight chapters of *Nightwood* are like searchlights, probing the darkness each from a different direction, yet ultimately focusing on and illuminating the same entanglement of the human spirit. In the first four chapters we are introduced to each of the important persons—Felix Volkbein, Nora Flood, Robin Vote, Jenny Petherbridge, and Dr. O'Connor. The next three chapters are, for the most part, long monologues by the doctor, through which the developments of the earlier chapters begin to take on meaning. The last chapter, only a few pages long, has the effect of a coda, giving us what we have already come to feel is the only possible termination. And these chapters are knit together, not by the progress of any action—either physical action, or, as in a stream-of-consciousness novel, the act of thinking—but by the continual reference and cross-reference of images and symbols which must be referred to each other spatially throughout the time-act of reading.

Note

1. This discussion of the county-fair scene owes a good deal to Albert Thibaudet's *Gustave Flaubert,* probably the best critical study yet written on the subject. The quotation from Flaubert's letter is used by Thibaudet and has been translated from his book.

7

Technique as Discovery

MARK SCHORER

■

Like Joseph Frank, Mark Schorer turns from the kind of thematic criticism evident in Edmund Wilson's essay to a formalist criticism emphasizing the method of fictional creation. Schorer sets out to expose mistaken critical tendencies that "continue to regard [technique] as merely a means of organizing material which is 'given' rather than as the means of exploring and defining the values in an area of experience which, for the first time *then*, are being given." In other words, Schorer heartily agrees with the rather humorous question: "How do I know what I think until I have said it?" Without the technique that allows the author to "say" it, a work of fiction has no theme or values because they do not yet exist.

Recognizing that "technique," like "form," is a term too inclusive to be truly helpful to the critical enterprise, Schorer limits his usage to "the uses to which language, as language, is put to express the quality of the experience in question; and the uses of point of view not only as a mode of dramatic delimitation, but more particularly, of thematic definition." This essay, then, anticipates two major concerns of more recent criticism: point of view, the consideration of which has led to radical rereadings of such novels as *The Great Gatsby;* and language, which has increasingly been analyzed not only as the medium for the message but as the message itself. But it should be emphasized that Schorer's emphasis on technique, like Frank's does not mean that he abandons a concern for the themes and values embodied in a work of fiction; rather, as he claims, "technique alone objectifies the materials of art; hence technique alone evaluates those materials." And through the example of H. G. Wells's disparagement of an author's concern for technique, Schorer demonstrates how attention to technique produces the kind of "good novel" that Wilson defined, one that "find[s] expression for something which has never yet been expressed." "The virtue of the modern novelist," says Schorer, "—from James and Conrad on down—is not only that he pays so much attention to his medium, but that, when he pays most, he discovers through it a new subject matter, and a greater one." Schorer then echoes Virginia Woolf's recognition that to treat the subject matter of contemporary human nature authors must develop appropriate techniques that will not simply present their subjects but actually discover those very subjects through articulating them in fiction.

Mark Schorer (1908–1977), who taught for many years at the University of California, Berkeley, is well known for *Sinclair Lewis, An American Life* (1961), the standard biography of that author. He also published *William Blake: The Politics of Vision* (1959) and *The World We Imagine: Selected Essays* (1968), as well as several novels.

Modern criticism, through its exacting scrutiny of literary texts, has demonstrated with finality that in art beauty and truth are indivisible and one. The Keatsian overtones of these terms are mitigated and an old dilemma solved if for beauty we substitute form, and for truth, content. We may, without risk of loss, narrow them even more, and speak of technique and subject matter. Modern criticism has shown us that to speak of content as such is not to speak of art at all, but of experience; and that it is only when we speak of the *achieved* content, the form, the work of art as a work of art, that we speak as critics. The difference between content, or experience, and achieved content, or art, is technique.

When we speak of technique, then, we speak of nearly everything. For technique is the means by which the writer's experience, which is his subject matter, compels him to attend to it; technique is the only means he has of discovering, exploring, developing his subject, of conveying its meaning, and, finally, of evaluating it. And surely it follows that certain techniques are sharper tools than others, and will discover more; that the writer capable of the most exacting

"Technique as Discovery," by Mark Schorer, is reprinted from *The Hudson Review* 1.1 (1948) with permission of Mrs. Ruth Schorer.

technical scrutiny of his subject matter, will produce works with the most satisfying content, works with thickness and resonance, works which reverberate, works with maximum meaning.

We are no longer able to regard as seriously intended criticism of poetry which does not assume these generalizations; but the case for fiction has not yet been established. The novel is still read as though its content has some value in itself, as though the subject matter of fiction has greater or lesser value in itself, and as though technique were not a primary but a supplementary element, capable perhaps of not unattractive embellishments upon the surface of the subject, but hardly of its essence. Or technique is thought of in blunter terms from those which one associates with poetry, as such relatively obvious matters as the arrangement of events to create plot; or, within plot, of suspense and climax; or as the means of revealing character motivation, relationship, and development; or as the use of point of view, but point of view as some nearly arbitrary device for the heightening of dramatic interest through the narrowing or broadening of perspective upon the material, rather than as a means toward the positive definition of theme. As for the resources of language, these, somehow, we almost never think of as a part of the technique of fiction—language as used to create a certain texture and one which in themselves state and define themes and meanings; or language, the counters of our ordinary speech, as forced, through conscious manipulation, into all those larger meanings which our ordinary speech almost never intends. Technique in fiction, all this is a way of saying, we somehow continue to regard as merely a means to organizing material which is "given" rather than as the means of exploring and defining the values in an area of experience which, for the first time *then*, are being given.

Is fiction still regarded in this odd, divided way because it is really less tractable before the critical suppositions which now seem inevitable to poetry? Let us look at some examples: two well-known novels of the past, both by writers who may be described as "primitive," although their relative innocence of technique is of a different sort—Defoe's *Moll Flanders* and Emily Brontë's *Wuthering Heights;* and three well-known novels of this century—*Tono Bungay*, by a writer who claimed to eschew technique; *Sons and Lovers*, by a novelist who, because his ideal of subject matter ("the poetry of the immediate present") led him at last into the fallacy of spontaneous and unchangeable composition, in effect eschewed technique; and *A Portrait of the Artist as a Young Man*, by a novelist whose practice made claims for the supremacy of technique beyond those made by anyone in the past or by anyone else in the century.

Technique in fiction is, of course, all those obvious forms of it which are usually taken to be the whole of it, and many others; but for the present purposes, let it be thought of in two respects particularly: the uses to which language, as language, is put to express the quality of the experience in question; and the uses of point of view not only as a mode of dramatic delimitation, but more particularly, of thematic definition. Technique is really what T. S. Eliot means by "convention"—any selection, structure, or distortion, any form or rhythm imposed upon the world of action; by means of which—it should be added—our apprehension of the world of action is enriched or renewed. In this sense, everything is technique which is not the lump of experience itself, and one cannot properly say that a writer has no technique or that he eschews technique, for, being a writer, he cannot do so. We can speak of good and bad technique, of adequate and inadequate, of technique which serves the novel's purpose, or disserves.

———

In the prefatory remarks to *Moll Flanders*, Defoe tells us that he is not writing fiction at all, but editing the journals of a woman of notorious character, and rather to instruct us in the necessities and the joys of virtue than to please us. We do not, of course, take these professions seriously, since nothing in the conduct of the narrative indicates that virtue is either more necessary or more enjoyable than vice. On the contrary, we discover that Moll turns virtuous only after a life of vice has enabled her to do so with security; yet it is precisely for this reason that Defoe's profession of didactic purpose has interest. For the actual morality which the novel enforces is the morality of any commercial culture, the belief that virtue pays—in worldly goods. It is a morality somewhat less than skin deep, having no relation to motives arising from a sense of good and evil, least of all, of evil-*in*-good, but exclusively from the presence or absence of food, drink, linen, damask, silver, and timepieces. It is the morality of measurement, and without in the least intending it, *Moll Flanders* is our classic revelation of the mercantile mind: the morality of measurement, which Defoe has completely neglected to measure. He fails not only to evaluate this material in his announced way, but to evaluate it at all. His announced purpose is, we admit, a pious humbug, and he meant us to read the book as a series of scandalous events; and thanks to his inexhaustible pleasure in excess and exaggeration, this element in the book continues to amuse us. Long before the book has been finished, however, this element has also become an absurdity; but not half the absurdity as that which Defoe did not intend at all—the notion that Moll could live a rich and full life of crime, and yet, repenting, emerge spotless in the end. The point is, of course, that she has no moral being, nor has the book any moral life. Everything is external. Everything can be weighed, measured, handled, paid for in gold, or expiated by a prison term. To this, the whole texture of the novel testifies: the bolts of goods, the inventories, the itemized accounts, the landlady's bills, the lists, the ledgers: all this, which taken together comprises what we call Defoe's method of circumstantial realism.

He did not come upon that method by any deliberation: it represents precisely his own world of value, the importance of external circumstance to Defoe. The point of view of Moll is indistinguishable from the point of view of her creator. We discover the meaning of the novel (at unnecessary length, without economy, without emphasis, with almost none of the distortions or the advantages of art) in spite of Defoe, not because of him. Thus the book is not the true chronicle of a disreputable female, but the true allegory of an impoverished soul—the author's; not an anatomy of the criminal class, but of the middle class. And we read it as an unintended comic revelation of self and of a social mode. Because he had no adequate resources of technique to separate himself from his material, thereby to discover and to define the meanings of his material, his contribution is not to fiction but to the history of fiction, and to social history.

The situation in *Wuthering Heights* is at once somewhat the same and yet very different. Here, too, the whole novel turns upon itself, but this time to its estimable advantage; here, too, is a revelation of what is perhaps the author's secret world of value, but this time, through what may be an accident of technique, the revelation is meaningfully accomplished. Emily Brontë may merely have stumbled upon the perspectives which define the form and the theme of her book. Whether she knew from the outset, or even at the end, what she was doing, we may doubt; but what she did and did superbly we can see.

We can assume, without at all becoming involved in the author's life but merely from the tone of somnambulistic excess which is generated by the writing itself, that this world of monstrous passion, of dark and gigantic emotional and nervous energy, is for the author, or was in the first place, a world of ideal value; and that the book sets out to persuade us of the moral magnificence of such unmoral passion. We are, I think, expected, in the first place, to take at their own valuation these demonic beings, Heathcliff and Cathy: as special creatures, set apart from the cloddish world about them by their heightened capacity for feeling, set apart, even, from the ordinary objects of human passion as, in their transcendental, sexless relationship, they identify themselves with an uncompromising landscape and cosmic force. Yet this is absurd, as much of the detail that surrounds it ("Other dogs lurked in other recesses") is absurd. The novelist Emily Brontë had to discover these absurdities to the girl Emily; her technique had to evaluate them for what they were, so that we are persuaded that it is not Emily who is mistaken in her estimate of her characters, but they who are mistaken in their estimate of themselves. The theme of the moral magnificence of unmoral passion is an impossible theme to sustain, and what interests us is that it was device—and this time, mere, mechanical device—which taught Emily Brontë that, the needs of her temperament to the contrary, all personal longing and reverie to the contrary, perhaps—that this was indeed not at all what her material must mean as art. Technique objectifies.

To lay before us the full character of this passion, to show us how it first comes into being and then comes to dominate the world about it and the life that follows upon it, Emily Brontë gives her material a broad scope in time, lets it, in fact, cut across three generations. And to manage material which is so extensive, she must find a means of narration, points of view, which can encompass that material, and, in her somewhat crude concept of motive, justify its telling. So she chooses a foppish traveller who stumbles into this world of passionate violence, a traveller representing the thin and conventional emotional life of the far world of fashion, who wishes to hear the tale: and for her teller she chooses, almost inevitably, the old family retainer who knows everything, a character as conventional as the other, but this one representing not the conventions of fashion, but the conventions of the humblest moralism. What has happened is, first, that she has chosen as her narrative perspective those very elements, conventional emotion and conventional morality, which her hero and heroine are meant to transcend with such spectacular magnificence; and second, that she has permitted this perspective to operate throughout a long period of time. And these two elements compel the novelist to see what her unmoral passions come to. Moral magnificence? Not at all; rather, a devastating spectacle of human waste; ashes. For the time of the novel is carried on long enough to show Heathcliff at last an emptied man, burned out by his fever ragings, exhausted and will-less, his passion meaningless at last. And it goes even a little further, to Lockwood, the fop, in the graveyard, sententiously contemplating headstones. Thus in the end the triumph is all on the side of the cloddish world, which survives.

Perhaps not all on that side. For, like Densher at the end of *The Wings of the Dove*, we say, and surely Hareton and the second Cathy say, "We shall never be again as we were!" But there is more point in observing that a certain body of materials, a girl's romantic daydreams, have, through the most conventional devices of fiction, been pushed beyond their inception in fancy to their meanings, their conception as a written book—that they, that is, are not at all as they were.

Technique alone objectifies the materials of art; hence technique alone evaluates those materials. This is the axiom which demonstrates itself so devastatingly whenever a writer declares, under the urgent sense of the importance of his materials (whether these are autobiography, or social ideas, or personal passions)—whenever such a writer declares that he cannot linger with technical refinements. That art will not tolerate such a writer H. G. Wells handsomely proves. His enormous literary energy included no respect for the techniques of his medium, and his medium takes its revenge upon his bumptiousness. "I have never taken any very great pains about writing. I am outside the hierarchy of conscious and deliberate writers altogether. I am the absolute antithesis of Mr. James Joyce. . . . Long ago, living in close conversational proximity to Henry James, Joseph Conrad, and Mr. Ford Madox Hueffer, I escaped from under their immense artistic preoccupations by calling myself a journalist." Precisely. And he escaped—he disappeared—from literature into the annals of an era.

Yet what confidence! "Literature," Wells said, "is not jewelry, it has quite other aims than perfection, and the more one thinks of 'how it is done' the less one gets it done. These critical indulgences lead along a fatal path, away from every natural interest towards a preposterous emptiness of technical effort, a monstrous egotism of artistry, of which the later work of Henry James is the monumental warning. 'It,' the subject, the thing or the thought, has long since disappeared in these amazing works; nothing remains but the way it has been 'manipulated.' " Seldom has a literary theorist been so totally wrong; for what we learn as James grows for us and Wells disappears, is that without what he calls "manipulation," there *is* no "it," no "subject" in art. There is again only social history.

The virtue of the modern novelist—from James and Conrad down—is not only that he pays so much attention to his medium, but that, when he pays most, he discovers through it a new subject matter, and a greater one. Under the "immense artistic preoccupations" of James and Conrad and Joyce, the form of the novel changed, and with the technical change, analogous changes took place in substance, in point of view, in the whole conception of fiction. And the final lesson of the modern novel is that technique is not the secondary thing that it seemed to Wells, some external machination, a mechanical affair, but a deep and primary operation; not only that technique *contains* intellectual and moral implications, but that it *discovers* them. For a writer like Wells, who wished to give us the intellectual and the moral history of our times, the lesson is a hard one: it tells us that the order of intellect and the order of morality do not exist at all, in art, except as they are organized in the order of art.

Wells's ambitions were very large. "Before we have done, we will have all life within the scope of the novel." But that is where life already is, within the scope of the novel; where it needs to be brought is into novels. In Wells we have all the important topics in life, but no good novels. He was not asking too much of art, or asking that it include more than it happily can; he was not asking anything of it—as art, which is all that it can give, and that is everything.

A novel like *Tono Bungay*, generally thought to be Wells's best, is therefore instructive. "I want to tell—*myself*," says George, the hero, "and my impressions of the thing as a whole"—the thing as a whole being the collapse of traditional British institutions in the twentieth century. George "tells himself" in terms of three stages in his life which have rough equivalents in modern British social history, and this is, to be sure, a plan, a framework; but it is the framework of Wells's abstract thinking, not of his craftsmanship, and the primary demand which one makes of such a book as this, that means be discovered whereby the dimensions of the hero contain the experiences he recounts, is never met. The novelist flounders through a series of literary imitations—from an early Dickensian episode, through a kind of Shavian interlude, through a Conradian episode, to a Jules Verne vision at the end. The significant failure is in that end, and in the way that it defeats not only the entire social analysis of the bulk of the novel, but Wells's own ends as a thinker. For at last George finds a purpose in science. "I decided that in power and knowledge lay the salvation of my life, the secret that would fill my need; that to these things I would give myself."

But science, power, and knowledge are summed up at last in a destroyer. As far as one can tell Wells intends no irony, although he may here have come upon the essence of the major irony in modern history. The novel ends in a kind of meditative rhapsody which denies every value that the book had been aiming toward. For of all the kinds of social waste which Wells has been describing, this is the most inclusive, the final waste. Thus he gives us in the end not a novel, but a hypothesis; not an individual destiny, but a theory of the future; and not his theory of the future, but a nihilistic vision quite opposite from everything that he meant to represent. With a minimum of attention to the virtues of technique, Wells might still not have written a good novel; but he would at any rate have established a point of view and a tone which would have told us what he meant.

To say what one means in art is never easy, and the more intimately one is implicated in one's material, the more difficult it is. If, besides, one commits fiction to a therapeutic function which is to be operative not on the audience but on the author, declaring, as D. H. Lawrence did, that "One sheds one's sicknesses in books, repeats and presents again one's emotions to be master of them," the difficulty is vast. It is an acceptable theory only with the qualification that technique, which objectifies, is under no other circumstances so imperative. For merely to repeat one's emotions, merely look into one's heart and write, is also merely to repeat the round of emotional bondage. If our books are to be exercises in self-analysis, then technique must—and alone can—take the place of the absent analyst.

Lawrence, in the relatively late Introduction to his *Collected Poems*, made that distinction of the amateur between his "real" poems and his "composed" poems, between the poems which expressed his demon directly and created their own form "willy-nilly," and the poems which, through the hocus pocus of technique, he spuriously put together and could, if necessary, revise. His belief in a "poetry of the immediate present," poetry in which nothing is fixed, static, or final, where all is shimmeriness and impermanence and vitalistic essence, arose from this mistaken notion of technique. And from this notion, an unsympathetic critic like D. S. Savage can construct a case which shows Lawrence driven "concurrently to the dissolution of personality and the dissolution of art." The argument suggests that Lawrence's early, crucial novel, *Sons and Lovers*, is another example of meanings confused by an impatience with technical resources.

The novel has two themes: the crippling effects of a mother's love on the emotional development of her son; and the "split" between kinds of love, physical and spiritual, which the son develops, the kinds represented by two young women, Clara and Miriam. The two themes should, of course, work together, the second being, actually, the result of the first: this "split" is the "crippling." So one would expect to see the novel developed, and so Lawrence, in his famous letter to Edward Garnett, where he says that Paul is left at the end with the "drift towards death," apparently thought he had developed it. Yet in the last few sentences of the novel, Paul rejects his desire for extinction and turns towards "the faintly humming, glowing town," to life—as nothing in his previous history persuades us that he could unfalteringly do.

The discrepancy suggests that the book may reveal certain confusions between intention and performance.

The first of these is the contradiction between Lawrence's explicit characterizations of the mother and father and his tonal evaluations of them. It is a problem not only of style (of the contradiction between expressed moral epithets and the more general texture of the prose which applies to them) but of point of view. Morel and Lawrence are never separated, which is a way of saying that Lawrence maintains for himself in this book the confused attitude of his character. The mother is a "proud, *honorable* soul," but the father has a "small, *mean* head." This is the sustained contrast; the epithets are characteristic of the whole; and they represent half of Lawrence's feelings. But what is the other half? Which of these characters is given his real sympathy—the hard, self-righteous, aggressive, demanding mother who comes through to us, or the simple, direct, gentle, downright, fumbling, ruined father? There are two attitudes here. Lawrence (and Morel) loves his mother, but he also hates her for compelling his love; and he hates his father with the true Freudian jealousy, but he also loves him for what he is in himself, and he sympathizes more deeply with him because his wholeness has been destroyed by the mother's domination, just as his, Lawrence-Morel's, has been.

This is a psychological tension which disrupts the form of the novel and obscures its meaning, because neither the contradiction in style nor the confusion in point of view is made to right itself. Lawrence is merely repeating his emotions, and he avoids an austerer technical scrutiny of his material because it would compel him to master them. He would not let the artist be stronger than the man.

The result is that, at the same time that the book condemns the mother, it justifies her; at the same time that it shows Paul's failure, it offers rationalizations which place the failure elsewhere. The handling of the girl, Miriam, if viewed closely, is pathetic in what it signifies for Lawrence, both as man and artist. For Miriam is made the mother's scape-goat, and in a different way from the way that she was in life. The central section of the novel is shot through with alternate statements as to the source of the difficulty: Paul is unable to love Miriam wholly, and Miriam can love only his spirit. The contradictions appear sometimes within single paragraphs, and the point of view is never adequately objectified and sustained to tell us which is true. The material is never seen as material; the writer is caught in it exactly as firmly as he was caught in his experience of it. "That's how women are with me," said Paul. "They want me like mad, but they don't want to belong to me." So he might have said, and believed it; but at the end of the novel, Lawrence is still saying that, and himself believing it.

For the full history of this technical failure, one must read *Sons and Lovers* carefully and then learn the history of the manuscript from the book called *D. H. Lawrence: A Personal Record*, by one E. T., who was Miriam in life. The basic situation is clear enough. The first theme—the crippling effects of the mother's love—is developed right through to the end; and then suddenly, in the last few sentences, turns on itself, and Paul gives himself to life, not death. But all the way through, the insidious rationalizations of the second theme have crept in to destroy the artistic coherence of the work. A "split" would occur in Paul; but as the split is treated, it is superimposed upon rather than developed in support of the first theme. It is a rationalization made from it. If Miriam is made to insist on spiritual love, the meaning and the power of theme one are reduced; yet Paul's weakness is disguised. Lawrence could not separate the investigating analyst, who must be objective, from Lawrence, the subject of the book; and the sickness was not healed, the emotion not mastered, the novel not perfected. All this, and the character of a whole career, would have been altered if Lawrence had allowed his technique to discover the fullest meaning of his subject.

A Portrait of the Artist as a Young Man, like *Tono Bungay* and *Sons and Lovers*, is autobiographical, but unlike these it analyzes its material rigorously, and it defines the value and the quality of its experience not by appended comment or moral epithet, but by the texture of the style. The theme of *A Portrait*, a young artist's alienation from his environment, is explored and evaluated through three different styles and methods as Stephen Dedalus moves from childhood through boyhood into maturity. The opening pages are written in something like the stream of consciousness of *Ulysses*, as the environment impinges directly on the consciousness of the infant and the child, a strange, opening world which the mind does not yet subject to questioning, selection, or judgment. But this style changes very soon, as the boy begins to explore his surroundings, and as his sensuous experience of the world is enlarged, it takes on heavier and heavier rhythms and a fuller and fuller body of sensuous detail, until it reaches a crescendo of romantic opulence in the emotional climaxes which mark Stephen's rejection of domestic and religious values. Then gradually the style subsides into the austerer intellectuality of the final sections, as he defines to himself the outlines of the artistic task which is to usurp his maturity.

A highly self-conscious use of style and method defines the quality of experience in each of these sections, and, it is worth pointing out in connection with the third and concluding section, the style and method evaluate the experience. What has happened to Stephen is, of course, a progressive alienation from the life around him as he progressed in his initiation into it, and by the end of the novel, the alienation is complete. The final portion of the novel, fascinating as it may be for the developing aesthetic creed of Stephen-Joyce, is peculiarly bare. The life experience was not bare, as we know from *Stephen Hero;* but Joyce is forcing technique to comment. In essence, Stephen's alienation is a denial of the human environment; it is a loss; and the austere discourse of the final section, abstract and almost wholly without sensuous detail or strong rhythm, tells us of that loss. It is a loss so great that the texture of the notation-like prose here suggests that the end is really all an illusion, that when Stephen tells us and himself that he is going forth to forge in the smithy of his soul the uncreated conscience of his race, we are to infer from the very quality of the icy, abstract void he now inhabits, the implausibility of his aim. For *Ulysses* does not create the conscience of the race; it creates our consciousness.

In the very last two or three paragraphs of the novel, the style changes once more, reverts from the bare, notative kind to the romantic prose of Stephen's adolescence. "Away! Away! The spell of arms and voices: the white arms of roads, their promise of close embraces and the black arms of tall ships that stand against the moon, their tale of distant nations. They are held out to say: We are alone—come." Might one not say that the austere ambition is founded on adolescent longing? That the excessive intellectual severity of one style is the counterpart of the excessive lyric relaxation of the other? And that the final passage of *A Portrait* punctuates the illusory nature of the whole ambition?

For *Ulysses* does not create a conscience. Stephen, in *Ulysses*, is a little older, and gripped now by guilt, but he is still the cold young man divorced from the human no less than the institutional environment. The environment of urban life finds a separate embodiment in the character of Bloom, and Bloom is as lost as Stephen, though touchingly groping for moorings. Each of the two is weakened by his inability to reach out, or to do more than reach out to the other. Here, then, is the theme again, more fully stated, as it were in counterpoint.

But if Stephen is not much older, Joyce is. He is older as an artist not only because he can create and lavish his Godlike pity on a Leopold Bloom, but also because he knows now what both Stephen and Bloom mean, and *how much*, through the most brilliant technical operation ever made in fiction, they can be made to mean. Thus *Ulysses*, through the imaginative force which its techniques direct, is like a pattern of concentric circles, with the immediate human situation at its center, this passing on and out to the whole dilemma of modern life, this passing on and out beyond that to a vision of the cosmos, and this to the mythical limits of our experience. If we read *Ulysses* with more satisfaction than any other novel of this century, it is because its author held an attitude toward technique and the technical scrutiny of subject matter which enabled him to order, within a single work and with superb coherence, the greatest amount of our experience.[1]

Note

1 Part four of this essay has been omitted—editors.

8

Manners, Morals, and the Novel

LIONEL TRILLING

Lionel Trilling shares a concern similar to Edmund Wilson's in "The Historical Interpretation of Literature": the moral dimension of good literature. Trilling understands this dimension as constituting the entire historical and cultural context for each work of fiction. What he calls manners refers to "a culture's hum and buzz of implication," which can be heard in the background of any contemporaneous reading of a novel but is often lost when we read a novel from another time period or culture. Trilling focuses on American manners, beginning with the hypothesis "that our attitude toward manners is the expression of a particular conception of reality" and that "all literature tends to be concerned with the question of reality." According to Trilling the answer to that question lies in manners: "The novel, then, is a perpetual quest for reality, the field of its research being always the social world, the material of its analysis being always manners as the indication of the direction of man's soul."

From these observations Trilling concludes that such a novel of manners has not yet established itself in America with the key exceptions of Henry James's and William Faulkner's novels. Instead, American writers have concerned themselves with depicting reality through the portrayal of appearance, and the resulting literature has tended to substitute programmatic generalities for a rounded look at specific characters. In the novels of the 1930s and 1940s sociology has replaced psychology as a method of cultural analysis. The remedy, according to Trilling, lies in a renewed commitment to "moral realism." While recognizing that the novel is often an ungainly, flawed literary form, he states that "its greatness and its practical usefulness lay in its unremitting work of involving the reader himself in the moral life, inviting him to put his own motives under examination, suggesting that reality is not as his conventional education had led him to see it." It is particularly instructive to note the degree to which Trilling's remarks parallel those of Virginia Woolf, even as her emphasis is on form and his on subject matter. Yet both are concerned with human character and with how a focus on the individual is the best way to record the characteristics of an age. Schorer and Wilson would no doubt agree.

Lionel Trilling (1905–1975), who taught at Columbia University, was one of the important liberal voices in twentieth-century literary criticism. Many of his essays are collected in *The Liberal Imagination* (1950) (from which "Manners, Morals, and the Novel" is taken), *Beyond Culture* (1965), and *Sincerity and Authenticity* (1971).

The invitation that was made to me to address you this evening[1] was couched in somewhat uncertain terms. Time, place, and cordiality were perfectly clear, but when it came to the subject our hosts were not able to specify just what they wanted me to talk about. They wanted me to consider literature in its relation to manners—by which, as they relied on me to understand, they did not really mean *manners*. They did not mean, that is, the rules of personal intercourse in our culture; and yet such rules were by no means irrelevant to what they did mean. Nor did they quite mean manners in the sense of *mores*, customs, although, again, these did bear upon the subject they had in mind.

I understood them perfectly, as I would not have understood them had they been more definite. For they were talking about a nearly indefinable subject.

Somewhere below all the explicit statements that a people makes through its art, religion, architecture, legislation, there is a dim mental region of intention of which it is very difficult to become aware. We now and then get a strong sense of its existence when we deal with the past, not by reason of its presence in the past but by reason of its absence. As we read the great formulated monuments of the past, we notice that we are reading them without the accompaniment of something that always goes along with the formulated monuments of the present. The voice of multifarious intention and activity is stilled, all the buzz of implication which always surrounds us in the present, coming to us from what never gets fully stated, coming in the tone of greetings and the tone of quarrels, in slang and humor and popular songs, in the way children play, in the gesture the waiter makes when he puts down the plate, in the nature of the very food we prefer.

Some of the charm of the past consists of the quiet—the great distracting buzz of implication has stopped and we are left only with what has been fully phrased and precisely stated. And part of the melancholy of the past comes from our knowledge that the huge, unrecorded hum of implication was once there and left no trace—we feel that because it is evanescent it is especially human. We feel, too, that the truth of the great preserved monuments of the past does not fully appear without it. From letters and diaries, from the remote, unconscious corners of the great works themselves, we try to guess what the sound of the multifarious implication was and what it meant.

Or when we read the conclusions that are drawn about our own culture by some gifted foreign critic—or by some stupid native one—who is equipped only with a knowledge of our books, when we try in vain to say what is wrong, when in despair we say that he has read the books "out of context," then we are aware of the matter I have been asked to speak about tonight.

What I understand by manners, then, is a culture's hum and buzz of implication. I mean the whole evanescent context in which its explicit statements are made. It is that part of a culture which is made up of half-uttered or unuttered or unutterable expressions of value. They are hinted at by small actions, sometimes by the arts of dress or decoration, sometimes by tone, gesture, emphasis, or rhythm, sometimes by the words that are used with a special frequency or a special meaning. They are the things that for good or bad draw the people of a culture together and that separate them from the people of another culture. They make the part of a culture which is not art, or religion, or morals, or politics, and yet it relates to all these highly formulated departments of culture. It is modified by them; it modifies them; it is generated by them; it generates them. In this part of culture assumption rules, which is often so much stronger than reason.

The right way to begin to deal with such a subject is to gather together as much of its detail as we possibly can. Only by doing so will we become fully aware of what the gifted foreign critic or the stupid native one is not aware of, that in any complex culture there is not a single system of manners but a conflicting variety of manners, and that one of the jobs of a culture is the adjustment of this conflict.

But the nature of our present occasion does not permit this accumulation of detail and so I shall instead try to drive toward a generalization and a hypothesis which, however wrong they turn out to be, may at least permit us to circumscribe the subject. I shall try to generalize the subject of American manners by talking about the attitude of Americans toward the subject of manners itself. And since in a complex culture there are, as I say, many different systems of manners and since I cannot talk about them all, I shall select the manners and the attitude toward manners of the literate, reading, responsible middle class of people who are ourselves. I specify that they be reading people because I shall draw my conclusions from the novels they read. The hypothesis I propose is that our attitude toward manners is the expression of a particular conception of reality.

All literature tends to be concerned with the question of reality—I mean quite simply the old opposition between reality and appearance, between what really is and what merely seems. "Don't you *see?*" is the question we want to shout at Oedipus as he stands before us and before fate in the pride of his rationalism. And at the end of *Oedipus Rex* he demonstrates in a particularly direct way that he now sees what he did not see before. "Don't you *see?*" we want to shout again at Lear and Gloucester, the two deceived, self-deceiving fathers: blindness again, resistance to the clear claims of reality, the seduction by mere appearance. The same with Othello—reality is right under your stupid nose, how *dare* you be such a gull? So with Molière's Orgon— my good man, my honest citizen, merely *look* at Tartuffe and you will know what's what. So with Milton's Eve—"Woman, watch out! Don't you see—anyone can see—that's a *snake!*"

The problem of reality is central, and in a special way, to the great forefather of the novel, the great book of Cervantes, whose four hundredth birthday was celebrated in 1947. There are two movements of thought in *Don Quixote*, two different and opposed notions of reality. One is the movement which leads toward saying that the world of ordinary practicality *is* reality in its fullness. It is the reality of the present moment in all its powerful immediacy of hunger, cold, and pain, making the past and the future, and all ideas, of no account. When the conceptual, the ideal, and the fanciful come into conflict with this, bringing their notions of the past and the future, then disaster results. For one thing, the ordinary proper ways of life are upset—the chained prisoners are understood to be good men and are released, the whore is taken for a lady. There is general confusion. As for the ideal, the conceptual, the fanciful, or romantic—whatever you want to call it—it fares even worse: it is shown to be ridiculous.

Thus one movement of the novel. But Cervantes changed horses in midstream and found that he was riding Rosinante. Perhaps at first not quite consciously—although the new view is latent in the old from the very beginning—Cervantes begins to show that the world of tangible reality is not the real reality after all. The real reality is rather the wildly conceiving, the madly fantasying mind of the Don: people change, practical reality changes, when they come into its presence.

In any genre it may happen that the first great example contains the whole potentiality of the genre. It has been said that all philosophy is a footnote to Plato. It can be said that all prose fiction is a variation on the theme of *Don Quixote*. Cervantes sets for the novel the problem of appearance and reality: the shifting and conflict of social classes becomes the field of the problem of knowledge, of how we know and of how reliable our knowledge is, which at that very moment of history is vexing the philosophers and scientists. And the poverty of the Don suggests that the novel is born with the appearance of money as a social element—money, the great solvent of the solid fabric of the old society, the great generator of illusion. Or, which is to say much the same thing, the novel is born in response to snobbery.

Snobbery is not the same thing as pride of class. Pride of class may not please us but we must at least grant that it reflects a social function. A man who exhibited class pride—in the day when it was possible to do so—may have been puffed up about what he *was*, but this ultimately depended on what he *did*. Thus, aristocratic pride was based ultimately on the ability to fight and administer. No pride is without fault, but pride of class may be thought of as today we think of pride of profession, toward which we are likely to be lenient.

Snobbery is pride in status without pride in function. And it is an uneasy pride of status. It always asks, "Do I belong—do I really belong? And does he belong? And if I am observed talking to him, will it make me seem to belong or not to belong?" It is the peculiar vice not of aristocratic societies, which have their own appropriate vices, but of bourgeois democratic societies. For us the legendary strongholds of snobbery are the Hollywood studios, where two thousand dollars a week dare not talk to three hundred dollars a week for fear he be taken for nothing more than fifteen hundred dollars a week. The dominant emotions of snobbery are uneasiness, self-consciousness, self-defensiveness, the sense that one is not quite real but can in some way acquire reality.

Money is the medium that, for good or bad, makes for a fluent society. It does not make for an equal society but for one in which there is a constant shifting of classes, a frequent change in the personnel of the dominant class. In a shifting society great emphasis is put on appearance—I am using the word now in the common meaning, as when people say that "a good appearance is very important in getting a job." To appear to be established is one of the ways of becoming established. The old notion of the solid merchant who owns far more than he shows increasingly gives way to the ideal of signalizing status by appearance, by showing more than you have: status in a democratic society is presumed to come not with power but with the tokens of power. Hence the development of what Tocqueville saw as a mark of democratic culture, what he called the "hypocrisy of luxury"—instead of the well-made peasant article and the well-made middle-class article, we have the effort of all articles to appear as the articles of the very wealthy.

. And a shifting society is bound to generate an interest in appearance in the philosophical sense. When Shakespeare lightly touched on the matter that so largely preoccupies the novelist—that is, the movement from one class to another—and created Malvolio, he immediately involved the question of social standing with the problem of appearance and reality. Malvolio's daydreams of bettering his position present themselves to him as reality, and in revenge his enemies conspire to convince him that he is literally mad and that the world is not as he sees it. The predicament of the characters in *A Midsummer Night's Dream* and of Christopher Sly seems to imply that the meeting of social extremes and the establishment of a person of low class in the privileges of a high class always suggested to Shakespeare's mind some radical instability of the senses and the reason.

The characteristic work of the novel is to record the illusion that snobbery generates and to try to penetrate to the truth which, as the novel assumes, lies hidden beneath all the false appearances. Money, snobbery, the ideal of status, these become in themselves the objects of fantasy, the support of the fantasies of love, freedom, charm, power, as in *Madame Bovary*, whose heroine is the sister, at a three-centuries' remove, of Don Quixote. The greatness of *Great Expectations* begins in its title: modern society bases itself on great expectations which, if ever they are realized, are found to exist by reason of a sordid, hidden reality. The real thing is not the gentility of Pip's life but the hulks and the murder and the rats and decay in the cellarage of the novel.

An English writer, recognizing the novel's central concern with snobbery, recently cried out half-ironically against it. "Who cares whether Pamela finally exasperates Mr. B. into marriage, whether Mr. Elton is more or less than moderately genteel, whether it is sinful for Pendennis nearly to kiss the porter's daughter, whether young men from Boston can ever be as truly refined as middle-aged women in Paris, whether the District Officer's fiancée ought to see so much of Dr. Aziz, whether Lady Chatterley ought to be made love to by the gamekeeper, even if he was an officer during the war? Who cares?"

The novel, of course, tells us much more about life than this. It tells us about the look and feel of things, how things are done and what things are worth and what they cost and what the odds are. If the English novel in its special concern with class does not, as the same writer says, explore the deeper layers of personality, then the French novel in exploring these layers must start and end in class, and the Russian novel, exploring the ultimate possibilities of spirit, does the same—every situation in Dostoevski, no matter how spiritual, starts with a point of social pride and a certain number of rubles. The great novelists knew that manners indicate the largest intentions of men's souls as well as the smallest and they are perpetually concerned to catch the meaning of every dim implicit hint.

The novel, then, is a perpetual quest for reality, the field of its research being always the social world, the material of its analysis being always manners as the indication of the direction of man's soul. When we understand this we can understand the pride of profession that moved D. H. Lawrence to say, "Being a novelist, I consider myself superior to the saint, the scientist, the philosopher and the poet. The novel is the one bright book of life."

Now the novel as I have described it has never really established itself in America. Not that we have not had very great novels but that the novel in America diverges from its classic intention, which, as I have said, is the investigation of the problem of reality beginning in the social field. The fact is that American writers of genius have not turned their minds to society. Poe and Melville were quite apart from it; the reality they sought was only tangential to society. Hawthorne was acute when he insisted that he did not write novels but romances—he thus expressed his awareness of the lack of social texture in his work. Howells never fulfilled himself because, although he saw the social subject clearly, he would never take it with full seriousness. In America in the nineteenth century, Henry James was alone in knowing that to scale the moral and aesthetic heights in the novel one had to use the ladder of social observation.

There is a famous passage in James's life of Hawthorne in which James enumerates the things which are lacking to give the American novel the thick social texture of the English novel—no state; barely a specific national name; no sovereign; no court; no aristocracy; no church; no clergy; no army; no diplomatic service; no country gentlemen; no palaces; no castles; no manors; no old country houses; no parsonages; no thatched cottages; no ivied ruins; no cathedrals; no great universities; no public schools; no political society; no sporting class—no Epsom, no Ascot! That is, no sufficiency of means for the display of a variety of manners, no opportunity for the novelist to do his job of searching out reality, not enough complication of appearance to make the job interesting. Another great American novelist of very different temperament had said much the same thing some decades before: James Fenimore Cooper found that American manners were too simple and dull to nourish the novelist.

This is cogent but it does not explain the condition of the American novel at the present moment. For life in America has increasingly thickened since the nineteenth century. It has not, to be sure, thickened so much as to permit our undergraduates to understand the characters of Balzac, to understand, that is, life in a crowded country where the competitive pressures are great, forcing intense passions to express themselves fiercely and yet within the limitations set by a strong and complicated tradition of manners. Still, life here has become more complex and more pressing. And even so we do not have the novel that touches significantly on society, on manners. Whatever the virtues of Dreiser may be, he could not report the social fact with the kind of accuracy it needs. Sinclair Lewis is shrewd, but no one, however charmed with him as a social satirist, can believe that he does more than a limited job of social understanding. John Dos Passos sees much, sees it often in the great way of Flaubert, but can never use social fact as more than either backdrop or "condition." Of our novelists today perhaps only William Faulkner deals with society as the field of tragic reality and he has the disadvantage of being limited to a provincial scene.

It would seem that Americans have a kind of resistance to looking closely at society. They appear to believe that to touch accurately on the matter of class, to take full note of snobbery, is somehow to demean themselves. It is as if we felt that one cannot touch pitch without being defiled—which, of course, may possibly be the case. Americans will not deny that we have classes and snobbery, but they seem to hold it to be indelicate to take precise cognizance of these phenomena. Consider that Henry James is, among a large part of our reading public, still held to be at fault for noticing society as much as he did. Consider the conversation that has, for some interesting reason, become a part of our literary folklore. Scott Fitzgerald said to Ernest Hemingway, "The very rich are different from us." Hemingway replied, "Yes, they have more money." I have seen the exchange quoted many times and always with the intention of suggesting that Fitzgerald was infatuated by wealth and had received a salutary rebuke from his democratic friend. But the truth is that after a certain point quantity of money does indeed change into quality of personality: in an important sense the very rich *are* different from us. So are the very powerful, the very gifted, the very poor. Fitzgerald was right, and almost for that remark alone he must surely have been received in Balzac's bosom in the heaven of novelists.

It is of course by no means true that the American reading class has no interest in society. Its interest fails only before society as it used to be represented by the novel. And if we look at the commercially successful serious novels of the last decade, we see that almost all of them have been written from an intense social awareness—it might be said that our present definition of a serious book is one which holds before us some image of society to consider and condemn. What is the situation of the dispossessed Oklahoma farmer and whose fault it is, what situation the Jew finds himself in, what it means to be a Negro, how one gets a bell for Adano, what is the advertising business really like, what it means to be insane and how society takes care of you or fails to do so—these are the matters which are believed to be most fertile for the novelist, and certainly they are the subjects most favored by our reading class.

The public is probably not deceived about the quality of most of these books. If the question of quality is brought up, the answer is likely to be: no, they are not great, they are not imaginative, they are not "literature." But there is an unexpressed addendum: and perhaps they are all the better for not being imaginative, for not being literature—they are not literature, they are reality, and *in a time like this* what we need is reality in large doses.

When, generations from now, the historian of our times undertakes to describe the assumptions of our culture, he will surely discover that the word *reality* is of central importance in his understanding of us. He will observe that for some of our philosophers the meaning of the word was a good deal in doubt, but that for our political writers, for many of our literary critics, and for most of our reading public, the word did not open discussion but, rather, closed it. Reality, as conceived by us, is whatever is external and hard, gross, unpleasant. Involved in its meaning is the idea of power conceived in a particular way. Some time ago I had occasion to remark how, in the critical estimates of Theodore Dreiser, it is always being said that Dreiser has many faults but that it cannot be denied that he has great power. No one ever says "a kind of power." Power is assumed to be always "brute" power, crude, ugly, and undiscriminating, the way an elephant appears to be. It is seldom understood to be the way an elephant actually is, precise and discriminating; or the way electricity is, swift and absolute and scarcely embodied.

The word *reality* is a honorific word and the future historian will naturally try to discover our notion of its pejorative opposite, appearance, mere appearance. He will find it in our feeling about the internal; whenever we detect evidences of style and thought we suspect that reality is being a little betrayed, that "mere subjectivity" is creeping in. There follows from this our feeling about complication, modulation, personal idiosyncrasy, and about social forms, both the great and the small.

Having gone so far, our historian is then likely to discover a puzzling contradiction. For we claim that the great advantage of reality is its hard, bedrock, concrete quality, yet everything we say about it tends toward the abstract and it almost seems that what we want to find in reality is abstraction itself. Thus we believe that one of the unpleasant bedrock facts is social class, but we become extremely impatient if ever we are told that social class is indeed so real that it produces actual difference of personality. The very people who talk most about class and its evils think that Fitzgerald was bedazzled and Hemingway right. Or again, it might be observed that in the degree that we speak in praise of the "individual" we have contrived that our literature should have no individuals in it—no people, that is, who are shaped by our liking for the interesting and memorable and special and precious.

Here, then, is our generalization: that in proportion as we have committed ourselves to our particular idea of reality we have lost our interest in manners. For the novel this is a definitive condition because it is inescapably true that in the novel manners make men. It does not matter in what sense the word manners is taken—it is equally true of the sense which so much interested Proust or of the sense which interested Dickens or, indeed, of the sense which interested Homer. The Duchesse de Guermantes, unable to delay departure for the dinner party to receive properly from her friend Swann the news that he is dying but able to delay to change the black slippers her husband objects to; Mr. Pickwick and Sam Weller; Priam and Achilles—they exist by reason of their observed manners.

So true is this, indeed, so creative is the novelist's awareness of manners, that we may say that it is a function of his love. It is some sort of love that Fielding has for Squire Western that allows him to note the great, gross details which bring the insensitive sentient man into existence for us. If that is true, we are forced to certain conclusions about our literature and about the particular definition of reality which has shaped it. The reality we admire tells us that the observation of manners is trivial and even malicious, that there are things much more important for the novel to consider. As a consequence our social sympathies have indeed broadened, but in proportion as they have done so we have lost something of our power of love, for our novels can never create characters who truly exist. We make public demands for love, for we know that broad social feeling should be infused with warmth, and we receive a kind of public product which we try to believe is not cold potatoes. The reviewers of Helen Howe's novel of a few years ago, *We Happy Few*, thought that its satiric first part, an excellent comment on the manners of a small but significant segment of society, was ill-natured and unsatisfactory, but they approved the second part, which is the record of the heroine's self-accusing effort to come into communication with the great soul of America. Yet it should have been clear that the satire had its source in a kind of affection, in a real community of feeling, and told the truth, while the second part, said to be so "warm," was mere abstraction, one more example of our public idea of ourselves and our national life. John Steinbeck is generally praised both for his reality and his warmheartedness, but in *The Wayward Bus* the lower-class characters receive a doctrinaire affection in proportion to the suffering and sexuality which define their existence, while the ill-observed middle-class characters are made to submit not only to moral judgment but to the withdrawal of all fellow-feeling, being mocked for their very misfortunes and almost for their susceptibility to death. Only a little thought or even less feeling is required to perceive that the basis of his creation is the coldest response to abstract ideas.

Two novelists of the older sort had a prevision of our present situation. In Henry James's *The Princess Casamassima* there is a scene in which the heroine is told about the existence of a conspiratorial group of revolutionaries pledged to the destruction of all existing society. She has for some time been drawn by a desire for social responsibility; she has wanted to help "the people," she has longed to discover just such a group as she now hears about, and she exclaims in joy, "Then it's real, it's solid!" We are intended to hear the Princess's glad cry with the knowledge that she is a woman who despises herself, "that in the darkest hour of her life she sold herself for a title and a fortune. She regards her doing so as such a terrible piece of frivolity that she can never for the rest of her days be serious enough to make up for it." She seeks out poverty, suffering, sacrifice, and death because she believes that these things alone are real; she comes to believe that art is contemptible; she withdraws her awareness and love from the one person of her acquaintance who most deserves them, and she increasingly scorns whatever suggests variety and modulation, and is more and more dissatisfied with the humanity of the present in her longing for the more perfect humanity of the future. It is one of the great points that the novel makes that with each passionate step that she takes toward what she calls the real, the solid, she in fact moves further away from the life-giving reality.

In E. M. Forster's *The Longest Journey* there is a young man named Stephen Wonham who, although a gentleman born, has been carelessly brought up and has no real notion of the responsibilities of his class. He has a friend, a country laborer, a shepherd, and on two occasions he outrages the feelings of certain intelligent, liberal, democratic people in the book by his treatment of this friend. Once, when the shepherd reneges on a bargain, Stephen quarrels with him and knocks him down; and in the matter of the loan of a few shillings he insists that the money be paid back to the last farthing. The intelligent, liberal, democratic people know that this is not the way to act to the poor. But Stephen cannot think of the shepherd as the poor nor, although he is a country laborer, as an object of research by J. L. and Barbara Hammond; he is rather a reciprocating subject in a relationship of affection—as we say, a friend—and therefore liable to anger and required to pay his debts. But this view is held to be deficient in intelligence, liberalism, and democracy.

In these two incidents we have the premonition of our present cultural and social situation, the passionate self-reproachful addiction to a "strong" reality which must limit its purview to maintain its strength, the replacement by abstraction of natural, direct human feeling. It is worth noting, by the way, how clear is the line by which the two novels descend from *Don Quixote*—how their young heroes come into life with large preconceived ideas and are knocked about in consequence; how both are concerned with the problem of appearance and reality, *The Longest Journey* quite explicitly, *The Princess Casamassima* by indirection; how both evoke the question of the nature of reality by contriving a meeting and conflict of diverse social classes and take scrupulous note of the differences of manners. Both have as their leading characters people who are specifically and passionately concerned with social injustice and both agree in saying that to act against social injustice is right and noble but that to choose to act so does not settle all moral problems but on the contrary generates new ones of an especially difficult sort.

I have elsewhere given the name of moral realism to the perception of the dangers of the moral life itself. Perhaps at no other time has the enterprise of moral realism ever been so much needed, for at no other time have so many people committed themselves to moral righteousness. We have the books that point out the bad conditions, that praise us for taking progressive attitudes. We have no books that raise questions in our minds not only about conditions but about ourselves, that lead us to refine our motives and ask what might lie behind our good impulses.

There is nothing so very terrible in discovering that something does lie behind. Nor does it need a Freud to make the discovery. Here is a publicity release sent out by one of our oldest and most respectable publishing houses. Under the heading "What Makes Books Sell?" it reads, "Blank & Company reports that the current interest in horror stories has attracted a great number of readers to John Dash's novel . . . because of its depiction of Nazi brutality. Critics and readers alike have commented on the stark realism of Dash's handling of the torture scenes in the book. The publishers originally envisaged a woman's market because of the love story, now find men reading the book because of the other angle." This does not suggest a more than usual depravity in the male reader, for "the other angle" has always had a fascination, no doubt a bad one, even for those who would not themselves commit or actually witness an act of torture. I cite the extreme example only to suggest that something may indeed lie behind our sober, intelligent interest in moral politics. In this instance the pleasure in the cruelty is protected and licensed by moral indignation. In other instances moral indignation, which has been said to be the favorite emotion of the middle class, may be in itself an exquisite pleasure. To understand this does not invalidate moral indignation but only sets up the conditions on which it ought to be entertained, only says when it is legitimate and when not.

But, the answer comes, however important it may be for moral realism to raise questions in our minds about our motives, is it not at best a matter of secondary importance? Is it not of the first importance that we be given a direct and immediate report on the reality that is daily being brought to dreadful birth? The novels that have done this have effected much practical good, bringing to consciousness the latent feelings of many people, making it harder for them to be unaware or indifferent, creating an atmosphere in which injustice finds it harder to thrive. To speak of moral realism is all very well. But it is an elaborate, even fancy, phrase and it is to be suspected of having the intention of sophisticating the simple reality that is easily to be conceived. Life presses us so hard, time is so short, the suffering of the world is so huge, simple, unendurable—anything that complicates our moral fervor in dealing with reality as we immediately see it and wish to drive headlong upon it must be regarded with some impatience.

True enough: and therefore any defense of what I have called moral realism must be made not in the name of some highflown fineness of feeling but in the name of simple social practicality. And there is indeed a simple social fact to which moral realism has a simple practical relevance, but it is a fact very difficult for us nowadays to perceive. It is that the moral passions are even more willful and imperious and impatient than the self-seeking passions. All history is at one in telling us that their tendency is to be not only liberating but also restrictive.

It is probable that at this time we are about to make great changes in our social system. The world is ripe for such changes and if they are not made in the direction of greater social liberality, the direction forward, they will almost of necessity be made in the direction backward, of a terrible social niggardliness. We all know which of those directions we want. But it is not enough to want it, not even enough to work for it—we must want it and work for it with intelligence. Which means that we must be aware of the dangers which lie in our most generous wishes. Some paradox of our natures leads us, when once we have made our fellow men the objects of our enlightened interest, to go on to make them the objects of our pity, then of our wisdom, ultimately of our coercion. It is to prevent this corruption, the most ironic and tragic that man knows, that we stand in need of the moral realism which is the product of the free play of the moral imagination.

For our time the most effective agent of the moral imagination has been the novel of the last two hundred years. It was never, either aesthetically or morally, a perfect form and its faults and failures can be quickly enumerated. But its greatness and its practical usefulness lay in its unremitting work of involving the reader himself in the moral life, inviting him to put his own motives under examination, suggesting that reality is not as his conventional education has led him to see it. It taught us, as no other genre ever did, the extent of human variety and the value of this variety. It was the literary form to which the emotions of understanding and forgiveness were indigenous, as if by the definition of the form itself. At the moment its impulse does not seem strong, for there never was a time when the virtues of its greatness were so likely to be thought of as weaknesses. Yet there never was a time when its particular activity was so much needed, was of so much practical, political, and social use—so much so that if its impulse does not respond to the need, we shall have reason to be sad not only over a waning form of art but also over our waning freedom.

Note

1 This essay was read at the Conference on the Heritage of the English-speaking Peoples and Their Responsibilities, at Kenyon College, September 1947.

9

The Concept of Plot

R. S. CRANE

Here we reprint the first half of R. S. Crane's essay, "The Concept of Plot and the Plot of *Tom Jones*." Crane uses the plot of Henry Fielding's novel to make a case for not limiting the definition of plot to a strictly formal description of action but to include the moral dimension of action that concerns Edmund Wilson and Lionel Trilling. "We may say," he states, "that the plot of any novel or drama is the particular temporal synthesis effected by the writer of the elements of action, character, and thought that constitute the matter of his invention." On this basis Crane locates "plots of action, plots of character, and plots of thought," depending on which of these essential and interdependent elements governs the "particular temporal synthesis" of the individual work. Crane admits that many novels rely on the first kind of plot, that of action, which may account for the erroneous critical tendency to conceive of plot as simply an organization of action. In opposing a criticism that isolates and dissects the separate parts of the novel, he calls for one that synthesizes the essential elements that compose the dynamic relationship of action, character, and philosophy realized in any novel.

Further, beyond being interesting (James), beyond attending to character (Woolf), and beyond presenting a solution to a new problem (Wilson), the "more developed forms of imitative literature" (i.e., good novels) must also affect the reader as a result of the "particular ethical qualities manifested in their agents' actions and thoughts vis-à-vis the human situations in which they are engaged." For Crane, the "form of the plot," rather than being simply its temporal structure, depends upon the ethical superiority of its affective qualities, not simply upon its mimetic virtuosity, its honest treatment of character, or its stylistic finesse.

R. S. Crane (1886–1967), along with other faculty members at the University of Chicago, formed a critical movement known as Neo-Aristotelian because of its effort to base literary criticism on a new reading of Aristotle. In addition to contributing to *Critics and Criticism* (1952), from which this essay is drawn, Crane also wrote *The Language of Criticism and the Structure of Poetry* (1953) and *The Idea of the Humanities* (1967).

O f all the plots constructed by English novelists that of *Tom Jones* has probably elicited the most unqualified praise. There is "no fable whatever," wrote Fielding's first biographer, that "affords, in its solution, such artful states of suspense, such beautiful turns of surprise, such unexpected incidents, and such sudden discoveries, sometimes apparently embarrassing, but always promising the catastrophe, and eventually promoting the completion of the whole."[1] Not since the days of Homer, it seemed to James Beattie, had the world seen "a more artful epick fable." "The characters and adventures are wonderfully diversified: yet the circumstances are all so natural, and rise so easily from one another, and co-operate with so much regularity in bringing on, even while they seem to retard, the catastrophe, that the curiosity of the reader . . . grows more and more impatient as the story advances, till at last it becomes downright anxiety. And when we get to the end . . . we are amazed to find, that of so many incidents there should be so few superfluous; that in such variety of fiction there should be so great probability; and that so complex a tale should be perspicuously conducted, and with perfect unity of design."[2] These are typical of the eulogies that preceded and were summed up in Coleridge's famous verdict in 1834: "What a master of composition Fielding was! Upon my word, I think the Oedipus Tyrannus, The Alchemist, and Tom Jones, the three most perfect plots ever planned."[3] More recent writers have tended to speak less hyperbolically and, like Scott, to insist that "even the high praise due to the construction and arrangement of the story is inferior to that claimed by the truth, force, and spirit of the characters,"[4] but it is hard to think of any important modern discussion of the novel that does not contain at least a few sentences on Fielding's "ever-to-be-praised skill as an architect of plot."[5]

The question I wish to raise concerns not the justice of any of these estimates but rather the nature and critical adequacy of the conception of plot in general and of the plot of *Tom Jones* in particular that underlies most if not all of them. Now it is a striking fact that in all the more extended discussions of Fielding's masterpiece since 1749 the consideration of the plot has constituted merely one topic among several others, and a topic, moreover, so detached from the rest that once it is disposed of the consideration of the remaining elements of character, thought, diction, and narrative technique invariably proceeds without further reference to it. The characters are indeed agents of the story, but their values are assessed apart from this, in terms sometimes of their degrees of conformity to standards of characterization in literature generally, sometimes of the conceptions of morality they embody, sometimes of their relation to Fielding's experiences or prejudices, sometimes of their reflection, taken collectively, of the England of their time. The other elements are isolated similarly, both from the plot and from one another: what is found important in the thought, whether of the characters or of the narrator, is normally not its function as an artistic device but its doctrinal content as a sign of the "philosophy" of Fielding; the style and the ironical tone of the narrative are frequently praised, but solely as means to the general literary satisfaction of the reader; and, what is perhaps more significant, the wonderful comic force of the novel, which all have delighted to commend, is assumed to be independent of the plot and a matter exclusively of particular incidents, of the characters of some, but not all, of the persons, and of occasional passages of burlesque or witty writing.[6]

All this points to a strictly limited definition of plot as something that can be abstracted, for critical purposes, from the moral qualities of the characters and the operations of their thought. This something is merely the material continuity of the story considered in relation to the general pleasure we take in any fiction when our curiosity about the impending events is aroused, sustained, and then satisfied to a degree or in a manner we could not anticipate. A plot in this sense—the sense in which modern novelists pride themselves on having got rid of plot—can be pronounced good in terms simply of the variety of incidents it contains, the amount of suspense and surprise it evokes, and the ingenuity with which all the happenings in the beginning and middle are made to contribute to the resolution at the end. Given the definition, indeed, no other criteria are possible, and no others have been used by any of the critics of *Tom Jones* since the eighteenth century who have declared its plot to be one of the most perfect ever planned. They have uniformly judged it as interesting story merely—and this whether, as by most of the earlier writers, "the felicitous contrivance and happy extrication of the story" is taken to be the chief "beauty" of the novel or whether, as generally nowadays, preference is given to its qualities of character and thought. It is clearly of plot in no completer sense than this that Oliver Elton is thinking when he remarks that, although some "have cared little for this particular excellence, and think only of Partridge, timorous, credulous, garrulous, faithful, and an injured man; of Squire Western, and of the night at Upton, and of wit and humour everywhere," still "the common reader, for whom Fielding wrote, cares a great deal, and cares rightly, for plot; and so did Sophocles."[7]

When plot is conceived thus narrowly, in abstraction from the peculiar characters and mental processes of the agents, it must necessarily have, for the critic, only a relatively external relation to the other aspects of the work. That is why, in most discussions of *Tom Jones*, the critical treatment of the plot (as distinguished from mere summary of the happenings) is restricted to the kind of enthusiastic general appreciation of which I have given some examples, supplemented by more particular remarks on various episodes, notably those of the Man of the Hill and of Mrs. Fitzpatrick, which appear to do little to advance the action. The plot, in these discussions, is simply one of several sources of interest and pleasure afforded by a novel peculiarly rich in pleasurable and interesting things, and the problem of its relation to the other ingredients is evaded altogether. Occasionally, it is true, the question has been faced; but even in those critics, like W. L. Cross and Oliver Elton, who have made it most explicit, the formulas suggested never give to the plot of *Tom Jones* the status of more than an external and enveloping form in relation to which the rest of the novel is content. It is not, as they see it, an end but a means, and they describe it variously, having no language but metaphor for the purpose, as a "framework" in which character (which is Fielding's "real 'bill of fare' ") is "set"; as a device, essentially "artificial," for bringing on the stage "real men and women"; as a "mere mechanism," which, except now and then in the last two books, "does not obtrude," for keeping readers alert through six volumes.[8]

I do not believe, however, that it is necessary to remain content with this very limited and abstract definition of plot or with the miscellaneous and fragmentized criticism of works like *Tom Jones* that has always followed from it. I shall assume that any novel or drama not constructed on didactic principles[9] is a composite of three elements, which unite to determine its quality and effect—the things that are imitated (or "rendered") in it, the linguistic medium in which they are imitated, and the manner or technique of imitation; and I shall assume further that the things imitated necessarily involve human beings interacting with one another in ways determined by, and in turn affecting, their moral characters and their states of mind (i.e., their reasonings, emotions, and attitudes). If this is granted, we may say that the plot of any novel or drama is the particular temporal synthesis effected by the writer of the elements of action, character, and thought that constitute the matter of his invention. It is impossible, therefore, to state adequately what any plot is unless we include in our formula all three of the elements or causes of which the plot is the synthesis; and it follows also that plots will differ in structure according as one or another of the three causal ingredients is employed as the synthesizing principle. There are, thus, plots of action, plots of character, and plots of thought. In the first, the synthesizing principle is a completed change, gradual or sudden, in the situation of the protagonist, determined and effected by character and thought (as in *Oedipus* and *The Brothers Karamazov*); in the second, the principle is a completed process of change in the moral character of the protagonist, precipitated or molded by action, and made manifest both in it and in thought and feeling (as in James's *The Portrait of a Lady*); in the third, the principle is a completed process of change in the thought of the protagonist and consequently in his feelings, conditioned and directed by character and action (as in Pater's *Marius the Epicurean*). All these types of construction, and not merely the first, are plots in the meaning of our definition; and it is mainly, perhaps, because most of the familiar classic plots, including that of *Tom Jones*, have been of the first kind that so many critics have tended to reduce plot to action alone.[10]

If this is granted, we may go farther. For a plot, in the enlarged sense here given to the term, is not merely a particular synthesis of particular materials of character, thought, and action, but such a synthesis endowed necessarily, because it imitates in words a sequence of human activities, with a power to affect our opinions and emotions in a certain way. We are bound, as we read or listen, to form expectations about what is coming and to feel more or less determinate desires relatively to our expectations. At the very least, if we are interested at all, we desire to know what is going to happen or how the problems faced by the characters are going to be solved. This is a necessary condition of our pleasure in all plots, and there are many good ones—in the classics of pure detective fiction, for example, or in some modern psychiatric novels—the power of which depends almost exclusively on the pleasure we take in inferring progressively, from complex or ambiguous signs, the true state of affairs. For some readers and even some critics this would seem to be the chief source of delight in many plots that have obviously been constructed on more specific principles: not only *Tom Jones*, as we have seen, but *Oedipus* has been praised as a mystery story, and it is likely that much of Henry James's popularity is due to his remarkable capacity for provoking a superior kind of inferential activity. What distinguishes all the more developed forms of imitative literature, however, is that, though they presuppose this instinctive pleasure in learning, they go beyond it and give us plots of which the effects derive in a much more immediate way from the particular ethical qualities manifested in their agents' actions and thoughts vis-à-vis the human situations in which they are engaged. When this is the case, we cannot help becoming, in a greater or less degree, emotionally involved; for some of the characters we wish good, for others ill; and, depending on our inferences as to the events, we feel hope or fear, pity or satisfaction, or some modification of these or similar emotions. The peculiar power of any plot of this kind, as it unfolds, is a result of our state of knowledge at any point in complex interaction with our desires for the characters as morally differentiated beings; and we may be said to have grasped the plot in the full artistic sense only when we have analyzed this interplay of desires and expectations sequentially in relation to the incidents by which it is produced.

It is, of course, an essential condition of such an effect that the writer should so have combined his elements of action, character, and thought as to have achieved a complete and ordered whole, with all the parts needed to carry the protagonist, by probable or necessary stages, from the beginning to the end of his change: we should not have, otherwise, any connected series of expectations wherewith to guide our desires. In itself, however, this structure is only the matter or content of the plot and not its form; the form of the plot—in the sense of that which makes its matter into a definite artistic thing—is rather its distinctive "working or power," as the form of the plot in tragedy, for example, is the capacity of its unified sequence of actions to effect through pity and fear a catharsis of such emotions.

But if this is granted, then certain consequences follow for the criticism of dramas and novels. It is evident, in the first place, that no plot of this order can be judged excellent *merely* in terms of the unity of its action, the number and variety of its incidents, or the extent to which it produces suspense and surprise. These are but properties of its matter, and their achievement, even to a high degree, in any particular plot does not inevitably mean that the emotional effect of the whole will not still be diffused or weak. They are, therefore, necessary, but not sufficient, conditions of a good plot, the positive excellence of which depends upon the power of its peculiar synthesis of character, action, and thought, as inferable from the sequence of words, to move our feelings powerfully and pleasurably in a certain definite way.

But this power, which constitutes the form of the plot, is obviously, from an artistic point of view, the most important virtue any drama or novel can have; it is that, indeed, which most sharply distinguishes works of imitation from all other kinds of literary productions. It follows, consequently, that the plot, considered formally, of any imitative works is, in relation to the work as a whole, not simply a means—a "framework" or "mere mechanism"—but rather the final end which everything in the work, if that is to be felt as a whole, must be made, directly or indirectly, to serve. For the critic, therefore, the form of the plot is a first principle, which he must grasp as clearly as possible for any work he proposes to examine before he can deal adequately with the questions raised by its parts. This does not mean that we cannot derive other relevant principles of judgment from the general causes of pleasure operative in all artistic imitations, irrespective of the particular effect, serious or comic, that is aimed at in a given work. One of these is the imitative principle itself, the principle that we are in general more convinced and moved when things are "rendered" for us through probable signs than when they are given merely in "statement," without illusion, after the fashion of a scenario.[11] Critical judgments, valid enough if they are not taken absolutely, may also be drawn from considerations of the general powers of language as a literary medium, of the known potentialities or requirements of a given manner of representation (e.g., dramatic or narrative), and of the various conditions of suspense and surprise. We are not likely to feel strongly the emotional effect of a work in which the worse rather than the better alternatives among these different expedients are consistently chosen or chosen in crucial scenes. The same thing, too, can be said of works in which the thought, however clearly serving an artistic use, is generally uninteresting or stale, or in which the characters of the agents, though right enough in conception for the intended effect, are less than adequately "done" or fail to impress themselves upon our memory and imagination, or in which we perceive that the most has not been made of the possibilities implicit in the incidents. And there is also a kind of judgment, distinct from any of these, the object of which is not much the traits of a work that follow from its general character as an imitative drama or novel as the qualities of intelligence and moral sensibility in its author which are reflected in his conception and handling of its subject and which warrant us in ascribing "greatness," "seriousness," or "maturity" to some products of art and in denying these values to others no matter how excellent, in a formal sense, the latter may be.

Such criticism of parts in the light of general principles is indispensable, but it is no substitute for—and its conclusions, affirmative as well as negative, have constantly to be checked by—the more specific kind of criticism of a work that takes the form of the plot as its starting point and then inquires how far and in what way its peculiar power is maximized by the writer's invention and development of episodes, his step-by-step rendering of the characters of his people, his use and elaboration of thought, his handling of diction and imagery, and his decisions as to the order, method, scale, and point of view of his representation. . . .

Notes

1   Arthur Murphy (1762), quoted in Frederic T. Blanchard, *Fielding the Novelist: A Study in Historical Criticism* (New Haven, 1927), p. 161.

2   *Dissertations Moral and Critical* (1783), quoted in Blanchard, pp. 222–23.

3   Ibid., pp. 320–21.

4   Ibid., p. 327.

5   The phrase is Oliver Elton's in *A Survey of English Literature, 1730–1780*, vol. 1 (New York, 1928), p. 195. See also Wilbur L. Cross, *The History of Henry Fielding*, vol. 2 (New Haven, 1918), pp. 160–61; Aurelien Digeon, *Les Romans de Fielding* (Paris, 1923), pp. 210–16; Elizabeth Jenkins, *Henry Fielding* (London, 1947), pp. 57–58; and George Sherburn, in *A Literary History of England*, ed. Albert C. Baugh (New York and London, 1948), pp. 957–58; cf. his interesting introduction to the "Modern Library College Editions" reprint of *Tom Jones* (New York, 1950), pp. ix–x.

6   The explanation of this procedure lies, partly, in a still unwritten chapter in the history of criticism. When works of prose fiction became objects of increasing critical attention in the eighteenth century, it was natural that the new form should be discussed in terms of its obvious analogies, both positive and negative, to drama and epic and that critics of novels should avail themselves, consequently, of the familiar categories of "fable," "characters," "sentiments," and "language" which had been long established, in the neoclassical tradition, as standard devices for the analysis of tragedies, comedies, and heroic poems. In remote origin these distinctions derived from the four qualitative "parts" which Aristotle had shown to be common to tragedy and epic (cf. *Poetics* 5.1449b15ff.; 24.1459b8–11). In the course of their transmission to the eighteenth century, however—as a result partly of the influence of Horace and partly of a complex of more general causes operative from the beginnings of Aristotelian commentary in the Renaissance (see Crane, ed., *Critics and Criticism* [original ed.], pp. 319–48)—the analytical significance of the scheme had undergone a radical change. For Aristotle, concerned with the construction of poetic wholes that afford "peculiar pleasures" through their imitations of different species of human actions, the four terms had designated the essential elements upon the proper handling and combination of which, relative to the intended overall effect, the quality of a tragedy or epic necessarily depends. They are distinct parts in the sense of

being variable factors in the complex problem of composing works which, when completed, will produce their effects, synthetically, as organic wholes. Hence it is that in the *Poetics* they are treated, not discretely as coordinate topics, but hierarchically in a causal sequence of form-matter or end-means relationships in which plot is the most inclusive or architectonic of the four, subsuming all the others as its poetic matter; in which character, while subordinated materially to plot and effect, is similarly a formal or organizing principle with respect to thought and diction; in which thought, while functioning as matter relative to character, incident, and effect, is the form which immediately controls the choice and arrangement of language insofar as this is employed as a means to imitative rather than ornamental ends; and in which diction, though necessarily having a form of its own by virtue of its rhythmical, syntactical, and "stylistic" figuration, is the underlying matter which, as significant speech, at once makes possible all the other "parts" and is in turn, mediately or immediately, controlled by them. The nature of the four elements is such, in short, that, although a critic in his analysis of a given tragedy or epic may take any one of them as his primary object of attention, he can make no adequate judgment of the poet's success or failure with respect to it without bringing into his discussion all the others to which it is related, directly or indirectly, either as matter or as form.

Of this causal scheme only the general outlines survived in the doctrines of subsequent critics in the "Aristotelian" line. The distinction of the four parts was retained and, along with it, the substance of the rules Aristotle had formulated for their handling; what disappeared was precisely the rationale which in the *Poetics* had justified not only the rules but the discrimination, definition, and ordering of the parts themselves. In its place various new principles and schemes of analysis were substituted by different theorists and critics, the general tendency of which was to make of poetics a practical rather than a productive art and hence to reduce tragedy and epic to modes of ethical or rhetorical discourse designed to serve, each in its specialized way, the common purposes of all such discourse, namely, the delight and instruction of mankind. The consequence was that, although critics continued to distinguish aspects of tragedies and epics that corresponded roughly with the Aristotelian "parts" and although these served to determine the framework of the discussion at least in the most systematic treatises and essays, the discussion itself no longer turned on the nature and functional interrelations of the four parts as elements in an artistic synthesis of a particular kind but on the general qualities which the poet ought to aim at in each, in order to enhance its independent power of pleasing, moving, and edifying spectators or readers. And when this apparatus was carried over from the statement of tragic or epic theory to the practical criticism of tragedies or epics (as in Addison's papers on *Paradise Lost* or Pope's Preface to the *Iliad*), the disjunction of the four elements tended to become still more marked. They were no longer functional parts in an organic whole but so many relatively discrete loci of critical praise and blame; and critics could write *seriatim* of the beauties or defects in the fable, characters, sentiments, and language of a given tragedy or heroic poem without assuming any synthesizing principles more specific than the decorum of the genre or the necessity, for example, that the sentiments expressed should be consonant with the characters of the persons who uttered them (many illustrations of the procedure may be found in H. T. Swedenberg, Jr., *The Theory of the Epic in England, 1650–1800* [Berkeley and Los Angeles, 1944]; cf. the index under "Fable or action," "Characters," "Sentiments in the epic," and "Language of the epic").

It was at this stage in the history of the Aristotelian "parts" that they entered into the criticism, both general and applied, of modern prose fiction. See, for example, besides many notices of novels in the *Monthly Review* and the *Critical Review*, the anonymous *Critical Remarks on Sir Charles Grandison, Clarissa, and Pamela* (1754); Arthur Murphy's "Essay on the Life and Genius of Henry Fielding," in *The Works of Henry Fielding* (1762); James Beattie's "On Fable and Romance," in his *Dissertations* (1783); and John More's "View of the Commencement and Progress of Romance," in *The Works of Tobias Smollett* (1797). In spite of the general indifference of criticism since about 1750 to questions specific to the various poetic kinds, the tradition of method thus established has persisted, especially in academic circles, to the present day; its influence still lingers in the topical divisions of treatises or textbooks dealing with the technique of fiction; and it still provides the commonplaces of a good many "studies" of novelists and novels (e.g., the pages on *Tom Jones*, already referred to, in Elton's *Survey*). The undoubted deficiencies of the scheme (in its neoclassical degradation) as an instrument of critical analysis and judgment have not passed unnoticed in recent years, particularly among critics of the *Scrutiny* group, who point out, justly enough, that "plot" and "character" are treated in a fashion that abstracts them unduly from the continuum of the novelist's language through which alone they affect us. These critics, however, are usually content to offer, as a positive substitute for the traditional scheme, only a still more extreme reduction of Aristotle's principles, in which everything in the discussion of a novel is made to turn on the relations between diction, in the sense of the author's "verbal arrangements," and thought, in the sense of the "experience" which he communicates by imposing "the pattern of his own sensibility" on the reader through the medium of language. See, for example, Martin Turnell, "The Language of Fiction," *Times Literary Supplement*, August 19, 1949, pp. 529–31; reprinted in his *Novel in France* (New York, 1951).

7 Elton, *A Survey of English Literature*, I, 195.

8 Cross, *The History of Henry Fielding*, vol. 2, pp. 159–61; Elton, *A Survey of English Literature*, vol. 1, pp. 195–96.

9 See Crane, ed., *Critics and Criticism* (original ed.), pp. 588–92.

10 This accounts in large part, I think, for the depreciation of "plot" in E. M. Forster's *Aspects of the Novel*, and for his notion of a rivalry between "plot" and "character," in which one or the other may "triumph." For a view much

closer to that argued in this essay see Elizabeth Bowen, "Notes on Writing a Novel," *Orion* 2 (1945): 18ff.

11   The meaning and force of this will be clear to anyone who has compared in detail the text of *The Ambassadors* with James's preliminary synopsis of the novel (*The Notebooks of Henry James* [New York, 1947], pp. 372–415). See also the excellent remarks of Allen Tate, apropos of *Madame Bovary*, in his "Techniques of Fiction" (*Forms of Modern Fiction,* ed. William Van O'Connor [Minneapolis, 1948], esp. pp. 37–45).

10

Writing and the Novel

ROLAND BARTHES

■

Roland Barthes begins his critique of French literature with an assertion that "Narration, as a form common to both the Novel and to History, does remain, in general, the choice or the expression of an historical moment." Barthes attacks the concept that the nineteenth-century form of the chronologically narrated novel is synonymous with "writing." He notes that in French, the preterite form of the verb, "obsolete in spoken French," is used in writing literature and that its linguistic nature "calls for a sequence of events, that is, for an intelligible Narrative." According to Barthes, a grammatical structure, representing a particular mode of bourgeois perception, dominates the writing of novels. This structure presents an orderly, coherent view of history and life, but one that Barthes argues is false and misleading. The preterite, then, prevents the engagement of literature with the open-ended present, because it portrays the values of a particular class and period of history as universal values, just as the use of third-person narration presents an apparently authoritative and truthful narrator. (As Seymour Chatman demonstrates in his essay in this volume, the creation of nonnarrated stories and unreliable narrators subverts this convention.)

For Barthes, the novel is a temporary literary phenomenon, a product of bourgeois society challenged by the modernist efforts to write a new kind of novel: "Modernism begins with the search for a Literature which is no longer possible." As with a number of other French critics after World War II who were heavily influenced by Marxism and existentialism, for Barthes the novel was a product of bourgeois society. In order to fight that society one could not use the novel but had to proclaim its "death" and replace it with "writing"; i.e., other forms of literature that were not enslaved by the conventions of bourgeois narration. We may want to consider such a critique in light of the requirements for great literature proposed by Edmund Wilson and Mark Schorer. Can a historically determined form of literature, such as the "bourgeois novel," be used to express new experiences that have never before been expressed, including criticism of the very society that spawned the literary genre? Or must literature in its search for expressing the new reflect that discovery in new techniques of narration and characterization?

Roland Barthes, born in France in 1915, gained an extraordinary reputation as a brilliant, eclectic, and prolific cultural critic before his death in 1980. Identified with a number of critical movements, his method always remained uniquely individual, as in such works as *Writing Degree Zero* (1953; trans. 1967) (the source for this essay), *The Pleasure of the Text* (1973; trans. 1975), *S/Z* (1970; trans. 1974), *Mythologies* (1957; trans. 1972), and *Camera Lucida* (1980; trans. 1981).

The Novel and History have been closely related in the very century which witnessed their greatest development. Their link in depth, that which should allow us to understand at once Balzac and Michelet, is that in both we find the construction of an autarkic world which elaborates its own dimensions and limits, and organizes within these its own Time, its own Space, its population, its own set of objects and its myths.

This sphericity of the great works of the nineteenth century found its expression in those long recitatives, the Novel and History, which are, as it were, plane projections of a curved and organic world of which the serial story which came into being at that precise moment, presents, through its involved complications, a degraded image. And yet narration is not necessarily a law of the form. A whole period could conceive novels in letters, for instance; and another can evolve

"Writing and the Novel," originally published in French in 1953, is reprinted from Roland Barthes, *Writing Degree Zero*, English translation by Annette Lavers and Colin Smith. Translation copyright 1967 Jonathan Cape Ltd. Reprinted with permission of Hill and Wang, a division of Farrar, Straus & Giroux, Inc.

a practice of History by means of analyses. Therefore Narration, as a form common to both the Novel and to History, does remain, in general, the choice or the expression of an historical moment.

Obsolete in spoken French, the preterite, which is the cornerstone of Narration, always signifies the presence of Art; it is a part of a ritual of Letters. Its function is no longer that of a tense. The part it plays is to reduce reality to a point of time, and to abstract, from the depth of a multiplicity of experiences, a pure verbal act, freed from the existential roots of knowledge, and directed towards a logical link with other acts, other processes, a general movement of the world: it aims at maintaining a hierarchy in the realm of facts. Through the preterite, the verb implicitly belongs with a causal chain, it partakes of a set of related and oriented actions, it functions as the algebraic sign of an intention. Allowing as it does an ambiguity between temporality and causality, it calls for a sequence of events, that is, for an intelligible Narrative. This is why it is the ideal instrument for every construction of a world; it is the unreal time of cosmogonies, myths, History and Novels. It presupposes a world which is constructed, elaborated, self-sufficient, reduced to significant lines, and not one which has been sent sprawling before us, for us to take or leave. Behind the preterite there always lurks a demiurge, a God or a reciter. The world is not unexplained since it is told like a story; each one of its accidents is but a circumstance, and the preterite is precisely this operative sign whereby the narrator reduces the exploded reality to a slim and pure logos, without density, without volume, without spread, and whose sole function is to unite as rapidly as possible a cause and an end. When the historian states that the duc de Guise died on December 23rd, 1588, or when the novelist relates that the Marchioness went out at five o'clock,[1] such actions emerge from a past without substance; purged of the uncertainty of existence, they have the stability and outline of an algebra, they are a recollection, but a useful recollection, the interest of which far surpasses its duration.

So that finally the preterite is the expression of an order, and consequently of a euphoria. Thanks to it, reality is neither mysterious nor absurd; it is clear, almost familiar, repeatedly gathered up and contained in the hand of a creator; it is subjected to the ingenious pressure of his freedom. For all the great storytellers of the nineteenth century, the world may be full of pathos but it is not derelict, since it is a grouping of coherent relations, since there is no over-lapping between the written facts, since he who tells the story has the power to do away with the opacity and the solitude of the existences which made it up, since he can in all sentences bear witness to a communication and a hierarchy of actions and since, to tell the truth, these very actions can be reduced to mere signs.

The narrative past is therefore a part of a security system for Belles-Lettres. Being the image of an order, it is one of those numerous formal pacts made between the writer and society for the justification of the former and the serenity of the latter. The preterite *signifies* a creation: that is, it proclaims and imposes it. Even from the depth of the most sombre realism, it has a reassuring effect because, thanks to it, the verb expresses a closed, well-defined, substantival act, the Novel has a name, it escapes the terror of an expression without laws: reality becomes slighter and more familiar, it fits within a style, it does not outrun language. Literature remains the currency in use in a society apprised, by the very form of words, of the meaning of what it consumes. On the contrary, when the Narrative is rejected in favour of other literary genres, or when, within the narration, the preterite is replaced by less ornamental forms, fresher, more full-blooded and nearer to speech (the present tense or the present perfect), Literature becomes the receptacle of existence in all its density and no longer of its meaning alone. The acts it recounts are still separated from History, but no longer from people.

We now understand what is profitable and what is intolerable in the preterite as used in the Novel: it is a lie made manifest, it delineates an area of plausibility which reveals the possible in the very act of unmasking it as false. The teleology common to the Novel and to narrated History is the alienation of the facts: the preterite is the very act by which society affirms its possession of its past and its possibility. It creates a content credible, yet flaunted as an illusion; it is the ultimate term of a formal dialectics which clothes an unreal fact in the garb first of truth then of a lie denounced as such. This has to be related to a certain mythology of the universal typifying the bourgeois society of which the Novel is a characteristic product; it involves giving to the imaginary the formal guarantee of the real, but while preserving in the sign the ambiguity of a double object, at once believable and false. This operation occurs constantly in the whole of Western art, in which the false is equal to the true, not through any agnosticism or poetic duplicity, but because the true is supposed to contain a germ of the universal, or to put it differently, an essence capable of fecundating by mere reproduction, several orders of things among which some differ by their remoteness and some by their fictitious character.

It is thanks to an expedient of the same kind that the triumphant bourgeoisie of the last century was able to look upon its values as universal and to carry over to sections of society which were absolutely heterogeneous to it all the Names which were parts of its ethos. This is strictly how myths function, and the Novel—and within the Novel, the preterite—are mythological objects in which there is, superimposed upon an immediate intention, a second-order appeal to a corpus of dogmas, or better, to a pedagogy, since what is sought is to impart an essence in the guise of an artefact. In order to grasp the significance of the preterite, we have but to compare the Western art of the novel with a certain Chinese tradition, for instance, in which art lies solely in the perfection with which reality is imitated. But in this tradition no sign, absolutely nothing, must allow any distinction to be drawn between the natural and the artificial objects: this wooden walnut must not impart to me, along with the image of a walnut, the intention of conveying to me the art which gave birth to it. Whereas on the contrary this is what writing does in the novel. Its task is to put the mask in place and at the same time to point it out.

This ambiguous function disclosed in the preterite is found in another fact relating to this type of writing: the third person in the Novel. The reader will perhaps recall a novel by Agatha Christie in which all the invention consisted in concealing the murderer beneath the use of the first person of the narrative. The reader looked for him behind every "he" in the plot: he was all the time hidden under the "I." Agatha Christie knew perfectly well that, in the novel, the "I" is usually a spectator, and that it is the "he" who is the actor. Why? The "he" is a typical novelistic convention; like the narrative tense, it signifies and carries through the action of the novel; if the third person is absent, the novel is powerless to come into being, and even wills its own destruction. The "he" is a formal manifestation of the myth, and we have just seen that, in the West at least, there is no art which does not point to its own mask. The third person, like the preterite, therefore performs this service for the art of the novel, and supplies its consumers with the security born of a credible fabrication which is yet constantly held up as false.

Less ambiguous, the "I" is thereby less typical of the novel: it is therefore at the same time the most obvious solution, when the narration remains on this side of convention (Proust's work, for instance, purports to be a mere introduction to Literature), and the most sophisticated, when the "I" takes its place beyond convention and attempts to destroy it, by conferring on the narrative the spurious naturalness of taking the reader into its confidence (such is the guileful air of some stories by Gide). In the same way the use of the "he" in a novel involves two opposed systems of ethics: since it represents an unquestioned convention, it attracts the most conformist and the least dissatisfied, as well as those others who have decided that, finally, this convention is necessary to the novelty of their work. In any case, it is the sign of an intelligible pact between society and the author; but it is also, for the latter, the most important means he has of building the world in the way that he chooses. It is therefore more than a literary experiment: it is a human act which connects creation to History or to existence.

In Balzac for instance, the multiplicity of "he's," this vast network of characters, slight in terms of solid flesh, but consistent by the duration of their acts, reveals the existence of a world of which History is the first datum. The Balzacian "he" is not the end-product of a development starting from some transformed and generalized "I"; it is the original and crude element of the novel, the material, not the outcome, the creative activity: there is no Balzacian history prior to the history of each third person in the novels of Balzac. His "he" is analogous to Caesar's "he": the third person here brings about a kind of algebraic state of the action, in which existence plays the smallest possible part, in favour of elements which connect, clarify, or show the tragedy inherent in human relationships. Conversely—or at any rate previously—the function of "he" in the novel can be that of expressing an existential experience. In many modern novelists the history of the man is identified with the course of the conjugation:

starting from an "I" which is still the form which expresses anonymity most faithfully, man and author little by little win the right to the third person, in proportion as existence becomes fate, and soliloquy becomes a Novel. Here the appearance of the "he" is not the starting point of History, it is the end of an effort which has been successful in extracting from a personal world made up of humours and tendencies, a form which is pure, significant, and which therefore vanishes as soon as it is born thanks to the totally conventional and ethereal decor of the third person. This certainly was the course displayed in the first novels of Jean Cayrol, whose case can be taken as an exemplar. But whereas in the classics—and we know that where writing is concerned classicism lasts until Flaubert—the withdrawal of the biological person testifies to the establishment of essential man, in novelists such as Cayrol, the invasion of the "he" is a progressive conquest over the profound darkness of the existential "I": so true it is that the Novel, identified as it is by its most formal signs, is a gesture of sociability; it establishes Literature as an institution.

Maurice Blanchot has shown, in the case of Kafka, that the elaboration of the impersonal narrative (let us notice, apropos of this term, that the "third person" is always presented as a negative degree of the person) was an act of fidelity to the essence of language, since the latter naturally tends towards its own destruction. We therefore understand how "he" is a victory over "I," inasmuch as it conjures up a state at once more literary and more absent. None the less this victory is ceaselessly threatened: the literary convention of the "he" is necessary to the belittling of the person, but runs at every moment the risk of encumbering it with an unexpected density. For Literature is like phosphorus: it shines with its maximum brilliance at the moment when it attempts to die. But as, on the other hand, it is an act which necessarily implies a duration—especially in the Novel—there can never be any Novel independently of Belles-Lettres. So that the third person in the Novel is one of the most obsessive signs of this tragic aspect of writing which was born in the last century, when under the weight of History, Literature became dissociated from the society which consumes it. Between the third person as used by Balzac and that used by Flaubert, there is a world of difference (that of 1848): in the former we have a view of History which is harsh, but coherent and certain of its principles, the triumph of an order;

in the latter, an art which in order to escape its pangs of conscience either exaggerates conventions or frantically attempts to destroy them. Modernism begins with the search for a Literature which is no longer possible.

Thus we find, in the Novel too, this machinery directed towards both destruction and resurrection, and typical of the whole of modern art. What must be destroyed is duration, that is, the ineffable binding force running through existence: for order, whether it be that of poetic flow or of narrative signs, that of Terror or plausibility, is always a murder in intention. But what reconquers the writer is again duration, for it is impossible to develop a negative within time, without elaborating a positive art, an order which must be destroyed anew. So that the greater modern works linger as long as possible, in a sort of miraculous stasis, on the threshold of Literature, in this anticipatory state in which the breadth of life is given, stretched but not yet destroyed by this crowning phase, an order of signs. For instance, we have the first person in Proust, whose whole work rests on a slow and protracted effort towards Literature. We have Jean Cayrol, whose acquiescence to the Novel comes only as the very last stage of soliloquy, as if the literary act, being supremely ambiguous, could be delivered of a creation consecrated by society, only at the moment when it has at last succeeded in destroying the existential density of a hitherto meaningless duration.

The Novel is a Death; it transforms life into destiny, a memory into a useful act, duration into an orientated and meaningful time. But this transformation can be accomplished only in full view of society. It is society which imposes the Novel, that is, a complex of signs, as a transcendence and as the History of a duration. It is therefore by the obviousness of its intention, grasped in that of the narrative signs, that one can recognize the path which, through all the solemnity of art, binds the writer to society. The preterite and the third person in the Novel are nothing but the fateful gesture with which the writer draws attention to the mask which he is wearing. The whole of Literature can declare *Larvatus prodeo*[2] "As I walk forward, I point out my mask." Whether we deal with the inhuman experience of the poet, who accepts the most momentous of all breaks, that from the language of society, or with the plausible untruth of the novelist, sincerity here feels a need of the signs of false-hood, and of conspicuous falsehood in order to last and to be con-sumed. Writing is the product, and ultimately the source, of this ambiguity. This specialized language, the use of which gives the writer a glorious but none the less superintended function, evinces a kind of servitude, invisible at first, which characterizes any respon-sibility. Writing, free in its beginnings, is finally the bond which links the writer to a History which is itself in chains: society stamps upon him the unmistakable signs of art so as to draw him along the more inescapably in its own process of alienation.

Notes

1 The sentence which for Valéry epitomized the conventions of the novel.
2 *Larvatus prodeo* was the motto of Descartes.

11

What Makes a Short Story Short?

NORMAN FRIEDMAN

■■■■

Although much has been written about specific short stories, the question that Norman Friedman poses in his title remains one that vexes those critics who grapple with the short story as a separate literary genre. Friedman's essay, first published in 1958, has become a classic on the form of the short story, one that provides a starting point for nearly all other discussions that have followed it, as we shall see when we come to Suzanne Ferguson's essay, "Defining the Short Story." Friedman makes his first controversial point in claiming that the forms of the short story and the novel differ "in degree but not in kind." He then claims that "a short story may be short" because "the material itself may be of small compass; or the material, being of broader scope, may be cut for the sake of maximizing the artistic effect." In one the object treated, and in the other the manner of presentation, produces brevity. Friedman concludes that to determine the answer to the title question, a reader must consider several possibilities and, in essence, ask not what makes *the* short story or *all* short stories short, but what makes *this* short story short. Such an orientation depends necessarily upon the author's initial claim that short stories differ from novels in degree but not in kind.

Norman Friedman (b. 1925), professor of English at Queens College, at the City University of New York, is the author of *E. E. Cummings, The Art of His Poetry* (1960), *E. E. Cummings, The Growth of a Writer* (1964), *Logic, Rhetoric, and Style* (1963), and *Form and Meaning in Fiction* (1975).

The truth is that, just as in the other imitative arts one imitation is always of one thing, so in poetry the story, as an imitation of action, must represent one action, a complete whole. . . . Now a whole is that which has a beginning, middle, and end. A beginning is that which is not itself necessarily after anything else, and which has naturally something else after it; an end is that which is naturally after something itself, either as its necessary or usual consequent, and with nothing else after it; and a middle, that which is by nature after one thing and has also another after it.—Aristotle, *Poetics*, chapters 7 and 8.

Although the short story as a literary type gets a fair share of attention in classroom texts and writer's handbooks, it is still—tainted by commercialism and damned by condescension—running a poor fourth to poetry, drama, and novel-length fiction in the books and journals devoted to serious theoretical criticism. It is in the hope of making a beginning toward the evaluation of the short story as a worthy and noble art that I should like to attempt a frontal attack upon its basic problem—that of its shortness.

But it is not a question merely of defining "shortness," of fixing the upper and lower limits in terms of the number of words a work of fiction should have in order to be called a short story. Common sense tells us that, although the exact dividing lines cannot—and need not—be determined, we can pretty well distinguish, apart from marginal cases, between long, short, and medium fiction. We will not argue, then, about length in strictly quantitative terms, for most of us know what a short story is and can pull down from our shelves at a moment's notice a dozen anthologies containing stories of varying lengths—all called "short." To haggle over the borderlines is almost always fruitless, and that is one very good reason for not trying. I will simply assume without proof that the examples discussed in this

"What Makes a Short Story Short?" by Norman Friedman, is reprinted with permission from *Modern Fiction Studies* 4 (1958). Copyright 1958 Purdue Research Foundation, West Lafayette, Ind. 47907.

paper as specimens of the type are indeed commonly regarded as short stories.

Nor is it a question of defining a different form, if by form we mean, as we usually do, certain materials unified to achieve a given effect, for the materials and their organization in a short story differ from those in a novel in degree but not in kind. To say, as has frequently been done, that short is distinguished from long fiction by virtue of its greater unity is surely to beg several questions at once. A fossil survivor of Poe's aesthetic, this notion confuses wholeness with singleness, unity with intensity. If unity implies that all the parts are related by an overall governing principle, there is certainly no reason why a short story should have more unity than a novel, although it may naturally have fewer parts to unify—a matter we shall examine in due course.

Nor may we say that a short story cannot deal with the growth of character, as has also been frequently done, or that it focuses upon culminations rather than traces developments, because the simple fact is that many stories do portray a character in the process of changing—Hemingway's "The Short Happy Life of Francis Macomber," for example, or Faulkner's "Barn Burning." Similarly, there is no reason why a story cannot deal with a change in thought, as in Steele's "How Beautiful with Shoes," or with a change in fortune, as in Fitzgerald's "Babylon Revisited." (Of course, some stories *are* static, and we shall discuss them below.) Nor may we say that stories are more commonly organized around a theme than novels, for some are, as Shirley Jackson's "The Lottery," and some are not, as Edith Wharton's "The Other Two." A story may arouse suspense and expectation, pity, repugnance, hope, and fear, just as a novel may, and may resolve those emotions in a complete and satisfying way, just as a novel may.[1]

There is, of course, much truth in the approaches we have just touched upon, but none of them manages to include enough of the actual possibilities to be finally useful. Surely short stories contain fewer words than novels, but that measure is a misleading one because it centers on symptoms rather than causes; surely short stories may make a more singular impact upon the reader, but that is an effect having to do with questions other than simply unity as such; and just as surely a novel may deal at greater length with dynamic actions than a story, but there are ways in which a story may handle changes within its own sphere. Most of these principles, in brief, are too prescriptive. In order to understand how and why a short story gets to be short, therefore, I would like to propose a way of answering these questions which will apply to all examples of the type without prescribing beforehand what the characteristics of that type should be.

A story may be short, to begin with a basic distinction, for either or both of two fundamental reasons: the material itself may be of small compass; or the material, being of broader scope, may be cut for the sake of maximizing the artistic effect. The first reason has to do with distinctions as to the *object of* representation, while the second with distinctions as to the *manner* in which it is represented. We will thus discuss the size of the action (which may be large or small, and is not to be confused with the size of the *story,* which may be short or long), and its static or dynamic structure; and then the number of its parts which may be included or omitted, the scale on which it may be shown, and the point of view from which it may be told. A story may be short in terms of any one of these factors or of any combination, but for the sake of clarity and convenience we shall discuss them separately and give cross-references where necessary.

Elder Olson has provided us with a useful set of terms for discussing the question of size with some degree of clarity and precision.[2] A *speech,* he says, contains the continuous verbal utterance of a single character in a closed situation; the speaker is either talking to himself without interruption (soliloquy), or, if there are others present they neither reply nor make entrances and exits while he speaks (monologue). This is the kind of action shown in most short poems commonly called "lyric," as in Marvell's "To His Coy Mistress," for example, or Keats's "On First Looking Into Chapman's Homer," and many many others. A *scene* includes the continuous chain of utterance engendered between two or more speakers as one replies to the other (dialogue) in a closed situation, while an *episode* contains two or more such scenes centering around one main incident. A *plot,* finally, is a system of two or more such episodes. And a short story may conceivably encompass an action of any such size.

Naturally, a large action, such as the plot of *Great Expectations,* although unified in terms of its overall size, will contain smaller subactions, such as speeches, scenes, and episodes, unified in terms of *their* particular sizes; and these smaller subactions may be and often are detachable for certain purposes, as when an episode, for example, is extracted from a larger work for inclusion in an anthology. Actions of different sizes, that is to say, dovetail the smaller into the larger. The point is, however, that a speech, scene, or episode which is designed in itself to serve as the unifying basis of a single complete work must be fully independent, whereas in a larger work it is only partially so, necessarily containing elements binding it to what has gone before and what is to come after.

Why an author makes a certain initial choice regarding size we can only guess, except that he probably senses that he has a whole and complete action in itself and that this will suffice as a basis for separate treatment. This is a matter, then, of the original conception, and all that we can say is that a writer chooses to treat actions of different sizes because he feels, either by habit or deliberate choice or intuition or some combination, that any given one embodies all that is relevant to his purpose. An action of any given size, then, may be whole and complete in itself, and the smaller the action, the shorter its presentation may be.

The relevant parts of an action which is whole and complete, therefore, include those incidents which are needed to bring about and then display whatever necessary or probable consequences the writer wants to show his protagonist enacting or undergoing, and such other incidents as may be useful in casting these in their proper light. The size of that action, then, will depend upon what he wants his protagonist to do or suffer and upon how far back, correspondingly, he must go in the protagonist's experience to find those causes which are both necessary and sufficient to motivate and make credible that action. Clearly, a dynamic action will call into play a larger number of causes than a static one, and a more inclusive change will require a longer chain of causes than a less inclusive one. An action of whatever size is thus whole and complete whenever the delicate interlinkage of causes and effects encompasses whatever is enough to make that action both understandable and likely.

The speech is best suited, obviously, to render a single moment or a brief succession of moments in any given chain of cause and effect. An immediate response, whether static or dynamic, to an immediate stimulus is the special province of lyric poetry. In Housman's "With Rue My Heart Is Laden," for example, the speaker responds with an expression of sorrow to the fact that many of his friends are now dead, while in Frost's "Stopping by Woods" the speaker responds to the mysterious attraction of the dark and snowy woods by first yielding to their temptation and then by resisting it. In the first we have a single but complete moment of lamentation, while in the second we have a longer but equally complete succession of moments during the course of which the speaker makes up his mind about something, in the sense of choosing between alternatives. Either way, these particular actions are inherently small, and whatever is needed to make them clear and likely may therefore be encompassed in a rather short space.

As a result, such actions are rarely treated in fiction, even short fiction. We all know that the devices of the poetic art are especially capable of handling this sort of thing in an intensified manner, and that narrative prose, being especially flexible, is much more suited to larger actions where more has to be shown. I do know of two such actions in fiction, but they are the exceptions which prove the rule. Dorothy Parker's "A Telephone Call" presents a young lady in the throes of anxious anticipation as she awaits her boyfriend's belated phone call. And that is all there is to it: as far as we are concerned here, the entire story comprises her interior soliloquy as she waits for the phone to ring. E. B. White's "The Door" similarly presents practically nothing but the continuous mental states of its one and only character—presented sometimes indirectly by way of narration and sometimes directly by way of interior soliloquy—who is shown in a state of uncertainty and frustration regarding the contradictory values of modern civilization.

To present a single scene is much more feasible in short fiction, although even here pure examples are not as common as one might think. The best and clearest specimen with which I am familiar is Hemingway's "Hills Like White Elephants," which shows a young American couple waiting in an isolated train station in the valley of the Ebro for the express from Barcelona. Except for the waitress who brings them drinks, the story encompasses only the single and continuous interchange of dialogue which occurs between the man and woman as they wait. The point of this story, which deals with a static situation, is, I think, to reveal to us by degrees the causes of the girl's plight, and through that to arouse our pity. Apparently unmarried, these two are on their way to get the girl an abortion. This is not, however, the source of the story's pathos; it lies, rather, in the fact that as the conversation progresses it becomes evident that her lover has no real feeling for her and her incipient need to extend their relationship to its normal fruition. Since that is all we need to know to get this particular effect, and since it can all be done within the bounds of a single conversation, that is all Hemingway had to show to unify this particular story.

And it is done, of course, with consummate skill. We read toward the end, for example: "He did not say anything but looked at the bags against the wall of the station. There were labels on them from all the hotels where they had spent nights." From this small detail we are allowed to infer worlds about the situation of this couple— the shallowness of their relationship, its rootlessness, its transiency. This allusion to the immediate past, although not formally a part of the whole action being shown (since the causes of the pathos are shown as the scene itself progresses), helps to place the situation in its proper light in the reader's mind. And notice how artfully it has been incorporated into the fabric of the present scene itself without authorial intrusion.

The episode is an even more commonly found size in the short story—indeed, its frequency may warrant our calling it the typical sort of action dealt with by this art. Hemingway's "Ten Indians," for example, contains five scenes centered around Nick's discovery of his Indian sweetheart's infidelity, his subsequent depression, and his final forgetfulness of his sorrow. He is, after all, rather young to allow heartbreak to affect him for more than a few hours at a time. This is a dynamic action involving changes in thought and feeling, and therefore requires—other things being equal—a larger action than a single scene for the establishing of its chain of cause and effect. It does, however, all take place within the span of a few hours and each of its scenes leads up to or away from a single central incident: (1) Nick is driving home late one afternoon from a Fourth of July celebration in town with the Garners and they kid him about his Indian girlfriend; (2) they arrive at the Garners, unload the wagon and Nick strikes out for his own home; (3) Nick is walking home; (4) his father gives him supper and tells him how he saw Prudie "having quite a time" in the woods with another boy, causing Nick to feel bad; (5) Nick goes unhappily to bed, but awakens contentedly later in the night to the sound of the wind and the waves, having forgotten his sorrow.

Thus a scene or episode requires less space in the telling, other things being equal, than the plot.

Another question regarding size is whether the action involves a change, and if so, whether that change is major or minor, and simple or complex. I hope it is clear by now that a short story may be either static or dynamic, but, as we have seen, an action which is static normally requires fewer parts than one which is dynamic and will therefore normally be shorter in the telling. That is to say, a static story simply shows its protagonist in one state or another and includes only enough to reveal to the reader the cause or causes of which this state is a consequence, while a dynamic story brings its protagonist through a succession of two or more states and thus must include the several causal stages of which these states are the consequences. Thus a static story will normally be shorter than a dynamic one.

Therefore, although not all short stories are static, most static actions are likely to be found in short stories—static situations expanded and elaborated to novel-length are comparatively rare (Mrs. Dalloway is an example). And there is a similar general correlation between static and dynamic actions and their various sizes. To achieve in fiction a change in the protagonist in an independent speech or scene is possible but not likely, and to extend a static situation through an entire independent episode or complete plot is also possible but equally unlikely. I would say, as a rule, that most static actions comprise a scene or a small episode.

Another example of a static story, in addition to "White Elephants" already discussed, is Sean O'Faoláin's "Sinners," in which a Catholic clergyman's mental anguish over the lies of a servant girl at confession is revealed. He is first shown twitching irritably at her stories during the confession, and then crying out in positive vexation later when he happens to overhear her admitting her lies at confession to her mistress. His emotional state is announced, as it were, in the first phase of the story, and confirmed in the second phase (because of transitions there are slightly more than two scenes here). Thus the reader is made to see his frustration, and then to understand it as having ample justification. And, in order to achieve this effect, the writer showed as much as he needed, two scenes or so, and no more.

Of course, he could have continued on with this story to show us the canon going through a subsequent change in feeling for the better, in which case he would have had to introduce a whole new line of causes working in that direction, and thus could have lengthened it; but if he had merely gone on with the same sort of thing, he would have blundered in exceeding the needs of his effect. It is this effect and the amount of action required to achieve it which determine the shortness of this story, when considered in itself as an independent work.

"Francis Macomber," "Barn Burning," "How Beautiful with Shoes," "Babylon Revisited," and "The Death of Ivan Ilyich" are short stories which comprise, on the other hand, dynamic actions. In the first, a cowardly man becomes finally courageous in the face of danger; in the second, a young boy decides to oppose at last his father's vindictive destruction of their landlord's property; in the third, an ignorant mountain girl becomes aware that man can be more than an animal; in the fourth, a reformed drunkard is frustrated temporarily in his plans to regain his estranged daughter; and in the fifth, a dying man sees his empty life truthfully for the first time. But there is a difference regarding magnitude even among dynamic actions, for all but the last are minor changes, not in the sense that they are unimportant or that their consequences are not serious or far-reaching, but rather in the sense that they call into play and require for their representation only one phase of their protagonists' lives. Thus a minor change will normally require less space than a major one.

Here again there may be a general correlation between inclusiveness and the size of an action, for most minor changes will involve but an episode, while a major change will involve a complete plot. In this sense, "Ilyich" has more in common with *Great Expectations* than with the other stories just mentioned; indeed, it even covers more aspects of its protagonist's life than the Dickens novel. Some episodes, then, are static, and some are dynamic, but plots tend almost always to be dynamic. And one of the differences between a short story plot and a novel plot need not, as we shall see below, be a difference in the intrinsic size of their actions but rather in the manner in which their actions are shown. In this sense, "Ilyich" is of course much closer in length to a short story than to a novel.

On the other hand, there is no reason why an action covering several episodes may not involve merely a minor change. We have thus to distinguish, on the basis of inclusiveness, minor and major plots (and I suppose an episode may deal with a major change, but I do not think this is likely). Fitzgerald points to this distinction as he narrates the experiences of Dexter Green in "Winter Dreams": "It is with one of those denials [the mysterious prohibitions in which life indulges] and not with his career as a whole that this story deals." And again, toward the end of the story: "This story is not his biography, remember, although things creep into it which have nothing to do with those dreams he had when he was young. We are almost done with them and with him now." Fitzgerald is saying, in effect, that this particular story finds its unity in treating only as many episodes as are required to show the reader the causes of Dexter's infatuation with Judy Jones and his subsequent disillusionment in her and the youthful possibilities she stands for in his mind, and that Dexter's other experiences (probably his business ventures and the like) are not particularly relevant thereto. He has guided himself, in consequence, largely by this original choice in matters of where to begin and end, and how much to include and omit. It is this limitation as to what phases of the protagonist's life are relevant to a given change which accounts for the shortness of this story.

The action of *The Great Gatsby*, on the other hand, although it is strikingly similar in its general outlines, because it deals with Gatsby's entire life, is a major plot. The obsession of Gatsby with Daisy and what she represents to him, that is to say, consumes all aspects of his career, and indeed costs him his very life at the end. The disillusionment of Gatsby, therefore, cannot be understood except in terms of his life as a whole, and that is why his story takes longer to tell than Dexter's. To have added Dexter's other interests to "Winter Dreams" would have been just as bad an artistic mistake as to have omitted Gatsby's from *The Great Gatsby:* the former would have resulted in irrelevance, while the latter would have caused a lack of clarity. Indeed, some critics of the novel have argued that it is too short even as it is to produce the requisite sense of probability or necessity in the reader, but that is quite another matter. (A rather different complaint has been raised against *For Whom the Bell Tolls*, which seems to some critics too *long* in proportion to the size of its action.)

There is a second difference regarding magnitude among dynamic actions which cuts across the one just examined between major and minor changes. A simple change brings its protagonist gradually from one state to another without reversals and is thus, since it calls into play only a single line of causation, a smaller action than a complex change, which brings its protagonist from one state into another and then into a third state opposite from the second, and which thus calls into play several lines of causation. The former, having consequently fewer parts, may be shorter in the telling.

All of the dynamic actions discussed so far are examples of the complex type, while Conrad's "An Outpost of Progress" illustrates a simple change. The moral characters of Kayerts and Carlier, weak and shallow to begin with, deteriorate swiftly and surely when brought to the acid test of prolonged and intimate contact "with pure unmitigated savagery" in the heart of Africa. If a short story can deal with the development of character, it can also deal, apparently, with its degeneration. It is interesting to contrast this story with "The Heart of Darkness," for there, in making Kurtz a paragon of moral character *before* his surrender to the abyss, Conrad set himself a much harder job. But he also achieved more vivid results, because if the fall of Kayerts and Carlier is more probable, it is also by the same token less interesting. The second story, however, is almost three times longer than the first (the great length of "The Heart of Darkness," incidentally, may also be explained in terms of its ruminative narrator—a topic to which we shall return below).

Thus, because it requires more "doing," a dynamic action tends to be longer than a static one; a major change, because it includes perforce more aspects of the protagonist's life, tends to be longer than a minor change; and a complex change, because it has more parts, tends to be longer than a simple one. But our principles must be continually qualified at every point because, as we shall see, we are dealing with a set of independent variables. A story which should be long in one way may actually be short in another; a story involving a major change, for example, which should be longer than one involving a minor change, all other things being equal, may actually turn out to be shorter because those other things are not equal.

A short story may be short, then, because its action is inherently small. But, as has been indicated, a story may encompass a larger action and still be short. If a writer has decided to show a plot, that is to say, he has a further option as to the manner in which he shall do so. And here he will be guided by his desire to maximize the vividness of his effect on the one hand, and to achieve that effect with the greatest economy of means on the other. He may decide, to begin with, that although a given part of his plot is relevant, he may best omit it and leave it to inference.

Since this question of selection can be discussed only in terms of how much of the whole action is put before the reader, and since we have defined "whole action" only generally, it behooves us to pause long enough to fill in our conceptions here. A whole action is, as we have seen, an action of a certain size—whether a speech, scene, episode, or plot—containing whatever is relevant to bringing the protagonist by probable or necessary stages from the beginning, through the middle, and on to the end of a given situation.

The question now under examination concerns how many of these parts are actually shown to the reader and how many are merely alluded to or left to inference. In Steinbeck's "Flight," for example, a young and hitherto rather shiftless boy, as a result of his first visit alone to the city, is forced to prove himself a man—even to the point of facing death bravely. In the actual telling of the story, however, Steinbeck chose to omit the boy's trip to Monterey entirely, bringing it in only later when the boy returns and tells his mother what happened there before he sets out for the mountains.

We are dealing with a complex dynamic action: what are the parts required for such an action to achieve its proper effect?

A complex change involves bringing the protagonist from one state to another by means of a reversal. What is required for clarity and belief, therefore, is (1) a precipitating cause to bring him into his first state, (2) a counterplot action to represent the consequences of that state, (3) an inciting cause which will serve to bring him out of the counterplot and on toward the opposite state, (4) a progressive action to represent him in the process of change, and (5) a culmination where the process is completed.[3] A simple change, as we have seen, involves bringing the protagonist from one state to another without a reversal, and therefore requires only the last three parts outlined above. And similar principles regarding selection may be applied to static actions in terms of the single states and relevant causes which they reveal.

Let us see how this scheme works for "Flight": (1) the boy is sent to Monterey for medicine by his mother; (2) he dons his father's hat and rides his father's saddle, boasting of his newfound manhood, and in Monterey drinks too much wine and gets into a fight; (3) he kills a man and must now either face the consequences like a man or run and hide "like a chicken"; (4) he returns home, tells his mother what happened, prepares himself for his journey, and suffers untold hardships for four days among the mountains; and (5) he dies finally with honor by facing, in his last extremity, his pursuers and accepting their vengeance. Most of phase two and all of three are omitted. Why?

We may say in the first place that, because probability demands that the protagonist tell his mother what happened anyway, Steinbeck simply acted in the interests of economy by avoiding repetition. That, however, is a rather mechanical explanation, although pertinent enough in its own way. More importantly, we may infer that Steinbeck intended to leave us with feelings of mingled pity and admiration for this boy as his story unfolds—pity for his suffering and death, and admiration for the noble manner in which he suffers and dies. This being the case, we may infer further that he left out most of the counterplot and the inciting incident because, in his effort to arouse our sympathies, he wanted consciously to avoid showing us his protagonist acting senselessly, without thought, and fatefully. By omitting these portions he also impresses us more vividly with the startling contrast between immaturity and maturity in his protagonist's behavior from the time he leaves in the morning till the time he returns at night. He is thus free to concentrate the greater portion of the reader's attention upon the boy's suffering and nobility rather than upon his rashness and immaturity. We must still *know*, however, what happened in Monterey, why the boy is taking to the mountains, and in what light to regard these events. And this we get from the boy's narration to his mother: the very fact that he tells her without hesitation and evasion is a sign of his real manhood. He was insulted, and so he killed before he knew what he was doing. Thus his ultimate death is made acceptable on the one hand and admirable on the other.

An instructive contrast to Steinbeck's wisdom in this matter is provided by a television adaptation of this story which I happened to see some time ago. Faced with wholly different technical problems, the television writer sought to enlarge his script not only by including those parts of the action which were left out of the original but also by elaborating upon and expanding them. The young boy was shown in Monterey—it was fiesta time and he got mixed up with a girl—and we see him getting insulted and killing his man. The fiesta allowed the insertion (intrusion would be a better word) of some dance productions as well as of some flicker of romantic interest. The flight itself was handled as honestly as possible, but even there the limitations of the medium necessitated the awkward device of having the boy talk to himself as he suffered, since he was, of course, alone and the fictional narrator was denied his function. The overall effect was distracting, to say the least: the only really relevant parts are the insult and the murder, so that the dancing and the girl, even though they were trumped up as the causes of his being insulted, simply came to nothing in terms of the rest of the story, and even with the insult and the murder it was quite upsetting actually to see our young hero draw blood; and the subsequent effort to elicit our sympathies for his suffering in the mountains was correspondingly vitiated. Perhaps because of the brevity of the original and its corresponding dependence upon narrative flexibility, the dramatized version of "Flight" was doomed from the outset.

The point to be made here is that a story may be short not because its action is inherently small, but rather because the author has chosen—in working with an episode or plot—to omit certain of its parts. In other words, an action may be large in size and still be short in the telling because not all of it is there. These gaps may be at the beginning of the action, somewhere along the line of its development, at the end, or some combination. Correspondingly, an action may be longer in the telling because more than its relevant parts are included.

Once he has decided what parts, of those which are relevant, he will include, the writer has a second option as to the scale on which he will show them. A given action, that is, may be made longer in the telling by expanding its parts, or shorter by contracting. What this implies is that, of all the things which actually "occur" or are present in a given scene—such as spoken dialogue, interior soliloquy, gesture, physical movement, clothing, and background setting—he may unfold them step by step or he may sum them up and mention only the high points. The contracted scale abstracts retrospectively from the event what is needed to advance the story and presents it in a condensed manner, while the expanded scale tries to give the illusion that the whole thing is being shown directly and in detail even as it happens. The contracted scale tends to cover a long time-span of action in a relatively short space, while the expanded scale tends to cover a short timespan in a relatively long space. And all this is, of course, actually a question of degree.

Flexibility, however, is one of the prime virtues of the fictional medium, and most narratives, whether long or short, vary the scale of presentation to suit the effect. Economy and vividness guide the writer here as before, but now the principle of proportion also comes into play. Those parts of the action which are more important than the others—and this, of course, will be related in each case to the effect intended—should naturally be emphasized by means of an expanded representation, and those which are less important should be condensed.

Although the amount of fictional time covered in the action has, as we shall see, no necessary connection with the length of its treatment, we can say that there is a general correlation, and that a writer who deals with actions covering a small timespan will normally choose the lesser magnitudes within which to work. The rule of economy tells the writer that, if the substance of his story takes place within the space of an hour, then a single scene will do the job. Likewise, if it covers several hours, a day, or a week, then an episode will be called for; and if it covers months or years, then a plot is needed. Joyce's *Ulysses*, however, reverses this correlation by expanding a single day into a full-length novel comprising many episodes, which merely emphasizes once again that we are dealing with a set of independent variables.

Tolstoy's "Death of Ivan Ilyich," on the other hand, is as good an example of a whole and full-sized plot condensed down to the length of a short story—albeit a rather long one—as can be found. It contains twelve numbered sections of varying lengths and, with some backtracking, takes its protagonist all the way from his childhood to his death in late middle age, and includes his schooling, courtship, marriage, career, and children. The whole action culminates in Ivan's first and final awareness, as he dies, of the reality of death and consequently of the hollowness of his entire life up to that point. Clearly, in order for this change to strike the reader with the proper intelligibility and force, Ivan's entire life has to be shown. The impact, that is to say, of Ivan's discovery depends for its point upon a knowledge of how his life has been lived previously and in terms of what values and attitudes.

But "Ivan Ilyich" is short (relatively) because, although the whole plot and more is shown, it is shown largely on a condensed scale. Likewise *Ulysses*, although it covers so much smaller a timespan, is so much longer because its action is expanded to the last detail (apparently).

Economy is still the general principle in these cases, however. Even though Ivan's whole life must be shown, it is of such a repetitive and shallow character (which is exactly the point, of course) that to have shown it on a full scale would have bored the reader to extinction—although Tolstoy naturally does represent the more important parts of his plot on an expanded scale. Joyce, too, did what he had to do to get his effect, although it is of an altogether different sort. Since the work turns on the ironic contrast between man as he is and man as he would be, it is exactly the meanness and triviality of daily life which Joyce must emphasize. It follows, therefore, that an almost infinite expansion serves Joyce's purpose but would have hampered Tolstoy in the achievement of his.

Another instructive contrast between the two extremes is found in comparing "Ivan Ilyich," which utilizes, as we have seen, a high degree of contraction, with "White Elephants," which is almost as expanded as a single scene between two people covering thirty minutes or so can get. And the reasons for this difference should be clear by now: Tolstoy has a large action to show, but most of it is important only as it throws light upon the final few scenes; while Hemingway has only one scene to show, and show it he does. Thus a story may be short, even if it encompasses a large action, because much of its action is best shown on a contracted scale.

———————

We may consider, finally, how the choice of a point of view is related to the question of length.[4] If a writer decides, for example, to allow his narrator complete omniscience, then several things will naturally follow. His narrator may editorialize, as in *Tom Jones* or *War and Peace*, and this of course will add significantly to the bulk of the work. Or, given omniscience, his narrator may analyze his characters' motives and states of mind at some length, and such commentary and exposition will also increase the bulk of the work. This is the reason why Mann's "Disorder and Early Sorrow" seems to cover so much more ground at first sight than it actually turns out to encompass upon close study: although it takes almost two hours to read, it actually includes an action whose timespan runs only from afternoon to evening of one day. Because, however, the action is shown through a screen of exposition and commentary regarding the Professor's states of mind, and even though the external action itself is rarely, as a consequence, shown directly and on an expanded scale, the story—although short—is a lengthy one in proportion to the time covered in the action.

Omniscience involves, on the other hand, features favorable to brevity. That is, a narrator who exists over and above the action itself may exercise, as they say, wide discretionary powers in matters of scale and selection. Because he is bound by no "mortal" limitations, he can manipulate his material at will. Thus he may shift the scene of the action in time and place, and, more importantly for the question in hand, may omit and/or sum up parts of the action which do not merit more explicit and detailed treatment. In the long run, then, omniscience is characterized by its flexibility and is equally at home in novels and short stories alike.

A character narrator may also be given to commentary and speculation, as is Marlow in "Heart of Darkness," and this too may add to the bulk of the work. The dramatic point of view similarly, because it is committed by definition to an expanded scale, as on the stage, tends toward length. Thus, an author who chooses the dramatic method for a short story had best work with an action of small size to begin with or, dealing with a larger one, omit certain of its parts.

To sum up, a story may be short because its action is intrinsically small; or because its action, being large, is reduced in length by means of the devices of selection, scale, and/or point of view. No one can tell in advance that, if a story is short, it is short because it has a certain number of words, or because it has more unity, or because it focuses upon culmination rather than development. All we can do, upon recognizing its shortness, is to ask how and why, keeping balanced simultaneously in our minds the alternative ways of answering these questions and their possible combinations. And then we may win increased understanding and hence appreciation of the specific artistic qualities of this curious and splendid but vastly underrated art.

Notes

1 Cf. R. S. Crane, "The Concept of Plot and the Plot of *Tom Jones*," *Critics and Criticism: Ancient and Modern*, ed. R. S. Crane (Chicago, 1952) pp. 616–47; and Theodore A. Stroud, "A Critical Approach to the Short Story," *Journal of General Education* 9 (1956): 91–100. The present essay may be read as a companion to Stroud's.

2 See Olson, "An Outline of Poetic Theory," in Crane, ed., *Critics and Criticism*, pp. 546–66, esp. p. 560.

3 Similar terms and concepts are used by Paul Goodman in his *Structure of Literature* (Chicago, 1954), but in a slightly different way. I had arrived at my own position independently, before I read this brilliant but puzzling book.

4 See my "Point of View in Fiction: The Development of a Critical Concept," *PMLA* 70 (1955): 1160–84, for a full-length analysis of the varieties of this device.

12

Distance and Point-of-View:
An Essay in Classification

WAYNE BOOTH

Wayne Booth opens his essay by arguing that, while there have been many studies of narrative point of view in fiction, these have tended to be too descriptively particular or overtly prescriptive to generate useful guidelines for critical analysis. The former approach provides us with no terms to discuss the techniques of narrative point of view because they describe only individual works or artists; the latter provides too few terms because prescriptive critics reduce the "right" kind of narration to the techniques of which they approve. Frequently then, Booth charges, a work of fiction such as *Moby-Dick,* is criticized for "deviating" from the critic's model or is inadequately discussed because no terms exist to describe the narrative techniques actually employed.

Booth begins his discussion of specific terms by criticizing the too general use of the word "person." Beyond the phrases of "first-person" and "third-person," he argues, we need to consider such distinctions as *"dramatised* narrators and *undramatised* narrators"; we must also distinguish the "implied author" from the narrator. While explaining what he means by these distinctions, Booth also makes additional distinctions within these terms, such as one between dramatized narrators who are "mere *observers"* or *"narrator-agents."* He then discusses how "distance" pertains to the relationships among narrators and implied authors, narrators and readers, and implied authors and readers. Another crucial issue explored by Booth is that of reliable and unreliable narrators, a distinction that has caused major critical reassessments of such works as *The Great Gatsby* and *Huckleberry Finn.* Booth's exercise in classification, *The Rheoric of Fiction* (1961), upon which this essay is based, helped to initiate—along with structuralist approaches to literary analysis–a major revaluation of the function of narrative. This has in turn led to the development of an entire sphere of literary theory called narratology.

Wayne C. Booth (b. 1921) is professor of English at the University of Chicago. In addition to *The Rhetoric of Fiction,* a revised version of which was published in 1983, he has published numerous other works, including *A Rhetoric of Irony* (1974) and *Critical Understanding: The Powers and Limits of Pluralism* (1979).

> "But he [the narrator] little knows what surprises lie in wait for him, if someone were to set about analysing the mass of truth and falsehoods which he has collected here."—"Dr. S.," in *Confessions of Zeno*

Like other notions used in talking about fiction, point-of-view has proved less useful than was expected by the critics who first brought it to our attention. When Percy Lubbock hailed the triumph of Henry James's dramatic use of the "central intelligence," and told us that "the whole intricate question of method, in the craft of fiction," is governed by "the relation in which the narrator stands to the story," he might have predicted that many critics would, like E. M. Forster, disagree with him. But he could hardly have predicted that his converts would produce, in forty years of elaborate investigations of point-of-view, so little help to the author or critic who must decide whether this or that technique in a particular work is appropriate to this or that effect. On the one hand we have been given classifications and descriptions which leave us wondering why we have bothered to classify and describe; the author who counted the number of times the word "I" appears in each of Jane Austen's novels may be more obviously absurd than the innumerable scholars who have traced in endless detail the *"Ich-Erzählung,"* or *"erlebte Rede,"* or *"monologue intérieur"* from Dickens to Joyce or from James to Robbe-Grillet. But he is no more irrelevant to literary judgment. To describe particulars may be interesting but it is only the preliminary

"Distance and Point-of-View: An Essay in Classification," by Wayne C. Booth, is reprinted from *Essays in Criticism* 11 (1961) with permission of Wayne C. Booth.

to the kind of knowledge that might help us explain the success or failure of individual works.

On the other hand, our efforts at formulating useful principles have been of little more use because they have been overtly prescriptive. If to count the number of times "I" occurs tells us nothing about how many times "I" should occur, to formulate abstract appeals for more "showing" and less "telling," for less authorial commentary and more drama, for more realistic consistency and fewer arbitrary shifts which remind the reader that he is reading a book, gives us the illusion of having discovered criteria when we really have not. While it is certainly true that some effects are best achieved by avoiding some kinds of telling, too often our prescriptions have been for "the novel" entire, ignoring what James himself knew well: there are "5,000,000 ways to tell a story," depending on one's overall purposes. Too many Jamesians have tried to establish in advance the precise degree of realistic intensity or irony or objectivity or "aesthetic distance" his work should display.

It is true that dissenting voices are now heard more and more frequently, perhaps the most important being Kathleen Tillotson's recent inaugural lecture at The University of London, *The Tale and the Teller*. But the clichés about the superiority of dramatic showing over mere telling are still to be found everywhere: in scholarly journals, in the literary quarterlies, in the weekly reviews, in the latest book on how to read a novel, and in dust-jacket blurbs. "The author does not tell you directly but you find out for yourself from their [the characters] every word, gesture, and act," a Modern Library jacket tells us about Salinger's *Nine Stories*. That this is praise, that Salinger would be in error if he were found telling us anything directly, is taken for granted.

Since the novelist's choices are in fact practically unlimited, in judging their effectiveness we can only fall back on the kind of reasoning used by Aristotle in the *Poetics* : *if* such-and-such an effect is desired, *then* such-and-such points-of-view will be good or bad. We all agree that point-of-view is in some sense a technical matter, a means to larger ends; whether we say that technique is the artist's way of discovering his artistic meaning or that it is his way of working his will upon his audience, we still can judge it only in the light of the larger meanings or effects which it is designed to serve. Though we all at times violate our own convictions, most of us are convinced that we have no right to impose on the artist abstract criteria derived from other kinds of work.

But even when we have decided to put our judgments in the hypothetical "if-then" form, we are still faced with an overwhelming variety of choices. One of the most striking features of our criticism is the casual way in which we allow ourselves to reduce this variety, thoughtlessly, carelessly, to simple categories, the impoverishment of which is evident whenever we look at any existing novel. On the side of effect critics at one time had a fairly large number of terms to play with—terms like tragedy, comedy, tragi-comedy, epic, farce, satire, elegy, and the like. Though the neo-classical kinds were often employed in inflexible form, they did provide a frame of discourse which allowed the critic and artist to communicate with each other: "if the effect you want is what we have traditionally expected under the concept 'tragedy,' then your technique here is inadequate." If what we are working for is a first-rate comedy, Dryden tells us in "An Essay of Dramatic Poesy," then here are some rules we can count on; they may be difficult to apply, they may require painstaking discussion, and they will certainly require genius if they are to be made to work, but they can still be of help to artist and critic because they are based on an agreement about a recognised literary effect.

In place of the earlier kinds, we have generally substituted a criticism based on qualities that are supposed to be sought in all works. All novels are said to be aiming for a common degree of realistic intensity; ambiguity and irony are discussed as if they were always beauties, never blemishes. Point-of-view should always be used "consistently," because otherwise the realistic illusion will be destroyed.

When technical means are related to such simplified ends, it is hardly surprising that they are themselves simplified. Yet we all know that our experience of particular works is more complex than the simple terminology suggests. The prescriptions against "telling" cannot satisfy any reader who has experienced *Tom Jones*, *The Egoist*, *Light in August*, or *Ulysses* (the claim that the author does not address us directly in the last of these is one of the most astonishingly persistent myths in modern criticism). They explicitly contradict our experience of dozens of good novels of the past fifteen years which, like Joyce

Cary's posthumous *The Captive and the Free*, have rediscovered for us how lively "telling" can be. We all know, of course, that "too much" of the author's voice is, as Aristotle said, unpoetic. But how much is too much? Is there an abstract rule applicable to "the novel," quite aside from the needs of particular works or kinds?

Our experience with the great novels tells us that there is not. Most novels, like most plays, cannot be purely dramatic, entirely shown as taking place in the moment. There are always what Dryden called "relations," narrative summaries of action that takes place "off-stage." And try as we will to ignore the troublesome fact, "some parts of the action are more fit to be represented, some to be related." But related by whom? When? At what length? The dramatist must decide, and his decision will be based in large part on the particular needs of the work in hand. The novelist's case is different mainly in that he has more devices to choose from; he may speak with all of the voices available to the dramatist, and he may also choose—some would say he is also tempted by—some forms of telling not easily adapted to the stage.

Unfortunately our terminology for the author's many voices has been inadequate. If we name over three or four of the great narrators—say Cervantes' Cid Hamete Benengeli, Tristram Shandy, the "author" of *Middlemarch* and Strether in *The Ambassadors* (with his nearly effaced "author" using his mind as a reflector of events)—we find again that to describe any of them with conventional terms like "first-person" and "omniscient" tells us little about how they differ from each other, and consequently it tells us little about why they succeed while others, described in the same terms, fail. Some critics do, indeed, talk about the problem of "authority," showing that first-person tales produce difficulties in stories which do not allow any one person to know all that goes on; having made this point, which seems so obvious, they are often then driven to find fault with stories like *Moby-Dick*, in which the author allows his narrator to know of events that happen outside his designated sphere of authority.

We can never be sure that enriching our terms will improve our criticism. But we can be quite sure that the terms with which we have long been forced to work cannot help us in discriminating among effects too subtle—as are all actual literary effects—to be caught in such loose-meshed nets. Even at the risk of pedantry, then, it should be worth our while to attempt a richer tabulation of the forms the author's voice can take.

(1) Perhaps the most overworked distinction is that of "person." To say that a story is told in the first or the third person, and to group novels into one or the other kind, will tell us nothing of importance unless we become more precise and describe how the particular qualities of the narrators relate to specific desired effects. It is true that choice of the first person is sometimes unduly limiting; if the "I" has inadequate access to necessary information, the author may be led into improbabilities. But we can hardly expect to find useful criteria in a distinction that would throw all fiction into two, or at most three, heaps. In *this* pile we see *Henry Esmond*, "A Cask of Amontillado," *Gulliver's Travels*, and *Tristram Shandy*. In *that* we have *Vanity Fair*, *Tom Jones*, *The Ambassadors*, and *Brave New World*. But the commentary in *Vanity Fair* and *Tom Jones* is in the first person, often resembling more the intimate effect of *Tristram Shandy* than that of many third person works. And again, the effect of *The Ambassadors* is much closer to that of the great first-person novels, since Strether in large part "narrates" his own story, even though he is always referred to in the third person.

Further evidence that this distinction is ordinarily overemphasised is seen in the fact that all of the following functional distinctions apply to both first- and third-person narration alike.

(2) There are *dramatised* narrators and *undramatised* narrators. The former are always and the latter are usually distinct from the implied author who is responsible for their creation.

(*a*) *The Implied Author* (*the author's "second self"*). Even the novel in which no narrator is dramatised creates an implicit picture of an author who stands behind the scenes, whether as stage-manager, as puppeteer, or as an indifferent God, silently paring his fingernails. This implied author is always distinct from the "real man"—whatever we may take him to be—who creates a superior version of himself as he creates his work; any successful novel makes us believe in an "author" who amounts to a kind of "second self." This second self is usually a highly refined and selected version, wiser, more sensitive, more perceptive than any real man could be.

In so far as a novel does not refer directly to this author, there will be no distinction between him and the implied, undramatised narrator; for example, in Hemingway's *The Killers* there is no narrator other than the implicit second self that Hemingway creates as he writes.

(b) *Undramatised Narrators.* Stories are usually not as rigorously scenic as *The Killers;* most tales are presented as passing through the consciousness of a teller, whether an "I" or a "he." Even in drama much of what we are given is narrated by someone, and we are often as much interested in the effect on the narrator's own mind and heart as we are in learning what *else* the author has to tell us. When Horatio tells of his first encounter with the ghost in *Hamlet,* his own character, though never mentioned explicitly as part of the narrative event, is important to us as we listen. In fiction, as soon as we encounter an "I" we are conscious of an experiencing mind whose views of the experience will come between us and the event. When there is no such "I," as in *The Killers,* the inexperienced reader may make the mistake of thinking that the story comes to him unmediated. But even the most naïve reader must recognise that something mediating and transforming has come into a story from the moment that the author explicitly places a narrator into the tale, even if he is given no personal characteristics whatever.

One of the most frequent reading faults comes from a naïve identification of such narrators with the authors who create them. But in fact there is always a distinction, even though the author himself may not have been aware of it as he wrote. The created author, the "second self," is built up in our minds from our experience with all of the elements of the presented story. When one of those elements is an explicit reference to an experiencing narrator, our view of the author is derived in part from our notion of how the presented "I" relates to what he claims to present. Even when the "I" or "he" thus created is ostensibly the author himself—Fielding, Jane Austen, Dickens, Meredith—we can always distinguish between the narrator and the created author who presents him. But though the distinction is always present, it is usually important to criticism only when the narrator is explicitly dramatised.

(c) *Dramatised Narrators.* In a sense even the most reticent narrator has been "dramatised" as soon as he refers to himself as "I," or, like Flaubert, tells us that "we" were in the classroom when Charles Bovary entered. But many novels dramatise their narrators with great fullness.

In some works the narrator becomes a major person of great physical, mental, and moral vividness (*Tristram Shandy, Remembrance of Things Past*, and *Dr. Faustus*); in such works the narrator is often radically different from the implied author who creates him, and whose own character is built up in our minds partly by the way in which the narrator is made to differ from him. The range of human types that have been dramatised as narrators is almost as great as the range of other fictional characters—one must say "almost" because there are some characters who are unqualified to narrate or reflect a story.

We should remind ourselves that many dramatised narrators are never explicitly labelled as narrators at all. In a sense, every speech, every gesture, narrates; most works contain disguised narrators who, like Molière's *raisonneurs,* are used to tell the audience what it needs to know, while seeming merely to act out their roles. The most important unacknowledged narrators are however, the third-person "centres of consciousness" through whom authors filter their narrative. Whether such "reflectors," as James sometimes called them, are highly-polished, lucid mirrors reflecting complex mental experience, or the rather turbid, sense-bound "camera eyes" of much fiction since James, they fill precisely the function of avowed narrators.

> Gabriel had not gone with the others. He was in a dark part of the hall gazing up the staircase. A woman was standing near the top of the first flight, in the shadow also. He could not see her face but he could see the terra-cotta and salmon-pink panels of her skirt which the shadow made appear black and white. It was his wife. She was leaning on the banisters, listening to something. Gabriel was surprised at her stillness and strained his ear to listen also. But he could hear little save the noise of laughter and dispute on the front steps, a few chords struck on the piano and a few notes of a man's voice singing. . . . He asked himself what is a woman standing on the stairs in the shadow, listening to distant music, a symbol of.

The very real advantages of this method, for some purposes, have been a dominant note in modern criticism. Indeed, so long as our attention is on such qualities as naturalness and vividness, the advantages seem overwhelming. It is only as we break out of the fashionable assumption that all good fiction seeks these qualities in the same degree that we are forced to recognise disadvantages. The third-person reflector is only one mode among many, suitable for some effects but cumbersome and even harmful when other effects are desired.

(3) Among dramatised narrators, whether first-person or third-person reflectors, there are mere *observers* (the "I" of *Tom Jones*, *The Egoist*, *Troilus and Criseyde*), and there are *narrator-agents* who produce some measurable effect on the course of events (ranging from the minor involvement of Nick in *The Great Gatsby* to the central role of Tristram Shandy, Moll Flanders, Huckleberry Finn, and—in the third-person—Paul Morel in *Sons and Lovers*). Clearly any rules we might discover about observers may or may not apply to narrator-agents, yet the distinction is seldom made in talk about point-of-view.

(4) All narrators and observers, whether first or third-person, can relay their tales to us primarily as *scene* (*The Killers*, *The Awkward Age*), primarily as *summary* or what Lubbock called "picture" (Addison's almost completely non-scenic tales in *The Spectator*) or, most commonly, as a combination of the two.

Like Aristotle's distinction between dramatic and narrative manners, the somewhat different modern distinction between telling and showing does cover the ground. But the trouble is that it pays for broad coverage with gross imprecision. Narrators of all shapes and shades must either report dialogue alone or support it with "stage directions" and description of setting. But when we think of the radically different effect of a scene reported by Huck Finn and a scene reported by Poe's Montresor, we see that the quality of being "scenic" suggests very little about literary effect. And compare the delightful summary of twelve years given in two pages of *Tom Jones* (III, i), with the tedious showing of even ten minutes of uncurtailed conversation in the hands of a Sartre when he allows his passion for "durational realism" to dictate a scene when summary is called for. We can only conclude that the contrast between scene and summary, between showing and telling—indeed, between any two dialectical terms that try to cover so much ground—is not prescriptive or normative but loosely descriptive only. And as description, it is likely to tell us very little until we specify the kind of narrator who is providing the scene or the summary.

(5) Narrators who allow themselves to tell as well as show vary

greatly depending on the amount and kind of *commentary* allowed in addition to a direct relating of events in scene and summary. Such commentary can, of course, range over any aspect of human experience, and it can be related to the main business in innumerable ways and degrees. To treat of it as if it were somehow a single device is to ignore important differences between commentary that is merely ornamental, commentary that serves a rhetorical purpose but is not part of the dramatic structure, and commentary that is integral to the dramatic structure, as in *Tristram Shandy*.

(6) Cutting across the distinction between observers and narrator-agents of all these kinds is the distinction between *self-conscious narrators*, aware of themselves as writers (*Tom Jones, Tristram Shandy, Barchester Towers, The Catcher in the Rye, Remembrance of Things Past, Dr. Faustus*), and narrators or observers who rarely if ever discuss their writing chores (*Huckleberry Finn*) or who seem unaware that they are writing, thinking, speaking, or "reflecting" a literary work (Camus's *The Stranger*, Lardner's *Haircut*, Bellow's *The Victim*).

(7) Whether or not they are involved in the action as agents, narrators and third-person reflectors differ markedly according to the degree and kind of *distance* that separates them from the author, the reader, and the other characters of the story they relate or reflect. Such distance is often discussed under terms like "irony," or "tone," but our experience is in fact much more diverse than such terms are likely to suggest. "Aesthetic distance" has been especially popular in recent years as a catch-all term for any lack of identification between the reader and the various norms in the work. But surely this useful term should be reserved to describe the degree to which the reader or spectator is asked to forget the artificiality of the work and "lose himself" in it; whatever makes him aware that he is dealing with an aesthetic object and not real life increases "aesthetic distance," in this sense. What I am dealing with is more complex and more difficult to describe, and it includes "aesthetic distance" as one of its elements.

In any reading experience there is an implied dialogue among author, narrator, the other characters, and the reader. Each of the four can range, in relation to each of the others, from identification to complete opposition, on any axis or value or judgment; moral, intellectual, aesthetic, and even physical (does the reader who stammers react to the stammering of H. C. Earwicker as I do? Surely not). The elements usually discussed under "aesthetic distance" enter in of course; distance in time and space, differences of social class or conventions of speech or dress—these and many others serve to control our sense that we are dealing with an aesthetic object, just as the paper moons and other unrealistic stage effects of some modern drama have had an "alienation" effect. But we must not confuse these effects with the equally important effects of personal beliefs and qualities, in author, narrator, reader, and all others in the cast of characters. Though we cannot hope to deal with all of the varieties of control over distance that narrative technique can achieve, we can at least remind ourselves that we deal here with something more than the question of whether the author attempts to maintain or destroy the illusion of reality.

(a) The *narrator* may be more or less distant from the *implied author*. The distance may be moral (Jason versus Faulkner; the barber versus Lardner, the narrator versus Fielding in *Jonathan Wild*). It may be intellectual (Twain and Huck Finn, Sterne and Tristram Shandy in the matter of bigotry about the influence of noses, Richardson and Clarissa). It may be physical or temporal: most authors are distant from even the most knowing narrator in that they presumably know how "everything turns out in the end"; and so on.

(b) The *narrator* also may be more or less distant from the *characters* in the story he tells. He may differ, for example, morally, intellectually, and temporally (the mature narrator and his younger self in *Great Expectations* or *Redburn*), morally and intellectually (Fowler the narrator and Pyle the American in Greene's *The Quiet American*, both departing radically from the author's norms but in different directions), morally and emotionally (Maupassant's "The Necklace," and Huxley's "Nuns at Luncheon," in which the narrators affect less emotional involvement than Maupassant and Huxley clearly expect from the reader).

(c) The *narrator* may be more or less distant from the *reader's* own norms, e.g., physically and emotionally (Kafka's *The Metamorphosis*); morally and emotionally (Pinkie in *Brighton Rock*, the miser in Mauriac's *Knot of Vipers*; the many moral degenerates that modern fiction has managed to make into convincing human beings).

One of the standard sources of plot in modern fiction—often advanced in the name of repudiating plot—is the portrayal of narrators whose characteristics change in the course of the works they narrate. Ever since Shakespeare taught the modern world what the Greeks had overlooked in neglecting character change (compare *Macbeth* and *Lear* with *Oedipus*), stories of character development or degeneration have become more and more popular. But it was not until we had discovered the full uses of the third-person reflector that we found how to show a narrator changing *as he narrates*. The mature Pip, in *Great Expectations*, is presented as a generous man whose heart is where the reader's is supposed to be; he watches his young self move away from the reader, as it were, and then back again. But the third-person reflector can be shown, technically in the past tense but in effect present before our eyes, moving toward or away from values that the reader holds dear. The twentieth century has proceeded almost as if determined to work out all of the permutations and combinations on this effect: start far and end near; start near and end far; start far, move close, but lose the prize and end far; start near, like Pip, move away but see the light and return close; start far and move farther (many modern "tragedies" are so little tragic because the hero is too distant from us at the beginning for us to care that he is, like Macbeth, even further at the end); start near and end nearer. . . . I can think of no theoretical possibilities that haven't been tried; anyone who has read widely in modern fiction can fill in examples.

(*d*) The *implied author* may be more or less distant from the *reader*. The distance may be intellectual (the implied author of *Tristram Shandy*, not of course to be identified with Tristram, is more interested in and knows more about recondite classical lore than any of his readers), moral (the works of Sade), and so on. From the author's viewpoint, a successful reading of his book will reduce to zero the distance between the essential norms of his implied author and the norms of the postulated reader. Often enough there is very little distance to begin with; Jane Austen does not have to convince us that pride and prejudice are undesirable. A bad book, on the other hand, is often a book whose implied author clearly asks that we judge according to norms we cannot accept.

(*e*) The *implied author* (and reader) may be more or less distant from *other characters*, ranging from Jane Austen's complete approval of Jane Fairfax in *Emma* to her contempt for Wickham in *Pride and Prejudice*. The complexity that marks our pleasure in all significant literature can be seen by contrasting the kinds of distance in these two situations. In *Emma*, the *narrator* is non-committal toward Jane Fairfax, though there is no sign of disapproval. The *author* can be inferred as approving of her almost completely. But the chief *reflector, Emma,* who has the largest share of the job of narration, is definitely disapproving of Jane Fairfax for most of the way. In *Pride and Prejudice*, on the other hand, the narrator is non-committal toward Wickham for as long as possible, hoping to mystify us; the author is secretly disapproving; and the chief reflector, Elizabeth, is definitely approving for the first half of the book.

It is obvious that on each of these scales my examples do not begin to cover the possibilities. What we call "involvement" or "sympathy" or "identification," is usually made up of many reactions to author, narrators, observers, and other characters. And narrators may differ from their authors or readers in various kinds of involvement or detachment, ranging from deep personal concern (Nick in *The Great Gatsby*, MacKellar in *The Baster of Ballantrae*, Zeitblom in *Dr. Faustus*) to a bland or mildly amused or merely curious detachment (Waugh's *Decline and Fall*).

In talk about point-of-view in fiction, the most seriously neglected of these kinds of distance is that between the fallible or unreliable narrator and the implied author who carries the reader with him as against the narrator. If the reason for discussing point-of-view is to find how it relates to literary effects, then surely the moral and intellectual qualities of the narrator are more important to our judgment than whether he is referred to as "I" or "he," or whether he is privileged or limited, and so on. If he is discovered to be untrustworthy, then the total effect of the work he relays to us is transformed.

Our terminology for this kind of distance in narrators is almost hopelessly inadequate. For lack of better terms, I shall call a narrator *reliable* when he speaks for or acts in accordance with the norms of the work (which is to say, the implied author's norms), *unreliable* when he does not. It is true that most of the great reliable narrators indulge in large amounts of incidental irony, and they are thus "unreliable" in the sense of being potentially deceptive. But difficult irony is not sufficient to make a narrator unreliable. We should reserve the term unreliable for those narrators who are presented as if they spoke *throughout* for the norms of the book and who do not in fact do so.

Unreliability is not ordinarily a matter of lying, although deliberately deceptive narrators have been a major resource of some modern novelists (Camus's *The Fall*, Calder Willingham's *Natural Child*, etc.). It is most often a matter of what James calls *inconscience*; the narrator is mistaken, or he pretends to qualities which the author denies him. Or, as in *Huckleberry Finn*, the narrator claims to be naturally wicked while the author silently praises his virtues, as it were, behind his back.

Unreliable narrators thus differ markedly depending on how far and in what direction they depart from their author's norms; the older term "tone," like the currently fashionable "distance," covers many effects that we should distinguish. Some narrators, like Barry Lyndon, are placed as far "away" from author and reader as possible, in respect to every virtue except a kind of interesting vitality. Some, like Fleda Vetch, the reflector in James's *The Spoils of Poynton*, come close to representing the author's ideal of taste, judgment, and moral sense. All of them make stronger demands on the reader's powers of inference than does reliable narration.

(8) Both reliable and unreliable narrators can be *isolated*, unsupported or uncorrected by other narrators (Gully Jimson in *The Horse's Mouth*, Henderson in Bellow's *Henderson the Rain King*) or supported or corrected (*The Sound and the Fury*). Sometimes it is almost impossible to infer whether or to what degree a narrator is fallible; sometimes explicit corroborating or conflicting testimony makes the inference easy. Support or correction differs radically, it should be noted, depending on whether it is provided from within the action, so that the narrator-agent might benefit (Faulkner's *Intruder in the Dust*) or is simply provided externally, to help the reader correct or reinforce his own view *as against the narrator's* (Graham Greene's *The Power and the Glory*). Obviously the effects of isolation will be radically different in the two cases.

(9) Observers and narrator-agents, whether self-conscious or not, reliable or not, commenting or silent, isolated or supported, can be either *privileged* to know what could not be learned by strictly natural means or *limited* to realistic vision and inference. Complete privilege is what we usually call omniscience. But there are many kinds of privilege and very few "omniscient" narrators are allowed to know or show as much as their authors know.

We need a good study of the varieties of limitation and their function. Some limitations are only temporary, or even playful, like the ignorance Fielding sometimes imposes on his "I" (as when he doubts his own powers of narration and invokes the Muses for aid, e.g., *Tom Jones* XIII, i). Some are more nearly permanent but subject to momentary relaxation, like the generally limited, humanly realistic Ishmael in *Moby Dick*, who can yet break through his human limitations when the story requires (" 'He waxes brave, but nevertheless obeys; most careful bravery that!' murmured Ahab"—with no one present to report to the narrator). And some are confined to what their literal condition would allow them to know (first person, Huck Finn; third person, Miranda and Laura in Katherine Anne Porter's stories).

The most important single privilege is that of obtaining an inside view, because of the rhetorical power that such a privilege conveys upon a narrator. A curious ambiguity in our notions of "omniscience" is ordinarily hidden by our terminology. Many modern works that we usually classify as narrated dramatically, with everything relayed to us through the limited views of the characters, postulate fully as much omniscience in the silent author as Fielding claims for himself. Our roving visitation into the minds of sixteen characters in Faulkner's *As I Lay Dying*, seeing nothing but what those minds contain, may seem in one sense not to depend on an omniscient narrator. But this method is omniscience with teeth in it: the implied author demands our absolute faith in his powers of divination. We must never for a moment doubt that he knows everything about each of these sixteen minds, or that he has chosen correctly how much to show of each. In short the choice of the most rigorously limited point-of-view is really no escape from omniscience—the true narrator is as "unnaturally" all-knowing as he ever was. If evident artificiality were a fault—which it is not—modern narration would be as faulty as Trollope's.

Another way of suggesting the same ambiguity is to look closely at the concept of "dramatic" story-telling. The author can present his characters in a dramatic situation without in the least presenting them in what we normally think of as a dramatic manner. When Joseph Andrews, who has been stripped and beaten by thieves, is overtaken by a stage-coach, Fielding presents the scene in what by some modern standards must seem an inconsistent and undramatic mode. "The poor wretch, who lay motionless a long time, just began to recover his senses as a stage-coach came by. The postilion hearing a man's groans, stopped his horses, and told the coachman, he was certain there was a dead man lying in the ditch. . . . A lady, who heard what the postilion said, and likewise heard the groan, called eagerly to the coachman to stop and see what was the matter. Upon which he bid the postilion alight, and look into the ditch. He did so, and returned, 'That there was a man sitting upright, as naked as ever he was born.'" There follows a splendid description, hardly meriting the name of *scene*, in which the selfish reactions of each passenger are recorded. A young lawyer points out that they might be legally liable if they refuse to take Joseph up. "These words had a sensible effect on the coachman, who was well acquainted with the person who spoke them; and the old gentleman above mentioned, thinking the naked man would afford him frequent opportunities of showing his wit to the lady, offered to join with the company in giving a mug of beer for his fare; till partly alarmed by the threats of the one, and partly by the promises of the other, and being perhaps a little moved with compassion at the poor creature's condition, who stood bleeding and shivering with the cold, he at length agreed." Once Joseph is in the coach, the same kind of indirect reporting of the "scene" continues, with frequent excursions, however superficial, into the minds and hearts of the assembly of fools and knaves, and occasional guesses when complete knowledge seems inadvisable. If to be dramatic is to show characters dramatically engaged with each other, motive clashing with motive, the outcome depending upon the resolution of motives, then this scene is dramatic. But if it is to give the impression that the story is taking place by itself, with the characters existing in a dramatic relationship vis-à-vis the spectator, unmediated by a narrator and decipherable only through inferential matching of word to word and word to deed, then this is a relatively undramatic scene.

On the other hand, an author can present a character in this latter kind of dramatic relationship with the reader without involving that character in any internal drama at all. Many lyric poems are dramatic in this sense and totally undramatic in any other. "That is no country for old men—" Who says? Yeats, or his "mask," says. To whom? To us. How do we know that it is Yeats and not some character as remote from him as Caliban is remote from Browning in "Caliban upon Setebos"? We infer it as the dramatised statement unfolds; the need for the inference is what makes the lyric *dramatic* in this sense. Caliban, in short, is dramatic in two senses; he is in a dramatic situation with other characters and he is in a dramatic situation over-against us. Yeats, or if we prefer "Yeats's mask," is dramatic in only one sense.

The ambiguities of the word dramatic are even more complicated in fiction that attempts to dramatise states of consciousness directly. Is *A Portrait of the Artist as a Young Man* dramatic? In some respects, yes. We are not told about Stephen. He is placed on the stage before us, acting out his destiny with only disguised helps or comments from his author. But it is not his actions that are dramatised directly, not his speech that we hear unmediated. What is dramatised is his mental record of everything that happens. We see his consciousness at work on the world. Sometimes what it records is itself dramatic, as when Stephen observes himself in a scene with other characters. But the report itself, the internal record, is dramatic in the second sense only. The report we are given of what goes on in Stephen's mind is a monologue uninvolved in any modifying dramatic context. And it is an *infallible* report, even less subject to critical doubts than the typical Elizabethan soliloquy. We accept, by convention, the claim that what is reported as going on in Stephen's mind really goes on there, or in other words, that Joyce knows how Stephen's mind works. "The equation of the page of his scribbler began to spread out a widening tail, eyed and starred like a peacock's; and, when the eyes and stars of its indices had been eliminated, began slowly to fold itself together again. The indices appearing and disappearing were eyes opening and closing; the eyes opening and closing were stars . . ." Who says so? Not Stephen, but the omniscient, infallible author. The report is direct, and it is clearly unmodified by any "dramatic" context—that is, unlike a speech in a dramatic scene, we do not suspect that the report has here been in any way aimed at an effect on anyone but the reader. We are thus in a dramatic relation with Stephen only in a limited sense—the sense in which a lyrical poem is dramatic.

Indeed if we compare the act of reporting in *Tom Jones* with the act of reporting in *Portrait*, the former is in one sense considerably more dramatic; Fielding dramatises himself and his telling, and even though he is essentially reliable we must be constantly on our toes in comparing word to word and word to deed. "It is an observation sometimes made, that to indicate our idea of a simple fellow, we say, he is easily to be seen through: nor do I believe it a more improper denotation of simple book. Instead of applying this to any particular performance, we choose rather to remark the contrary in this history, where the scene opens itself by small degrees; and he is a sagacious reader who can see two chapters before him." Our running battle to keep up with these incidental ironies in Fielding's narration is matched, in *Portrait*, with an act of absolute, unquestioning credulity.

We should note finally that the author who eschews both forms of artificiality, both the traditional omniscience and the modern manipulation of inside views, confining himself to "objective" surfaces only, is not necessarily identical with the "undramatised author" under (2) above. In *The Awkward Age*, for example, James allows himself to comment frequently, but only to conjecture about the meaning of surfaces; the author is dramatised, but dramatised as partially ignorant of what is happening.

(10) Finally, narrators who provide inside views differ in the depth and the axis of their plunge. Boccaccio can give inside views, but they are extremely shallow. Jane Austen goes relatively deep morally, but scarcely skims the surface psychologically. All authors of stream-of-consciousness narration attempt to go deep psychologically, but some of them deliberately remain shallow in the moral dimension. We should remind ourselves that any sustained inside view, of whatever depth, temporarily turns the character whose mind is shown into a narrator; inside views are thus subject to variations in all of the qualities we have described above, and most importantly in the degree of unreliability. Generally speaking, the deeper our plunge, the more unreliability we will accept without loss of sympathy. The whole question of how inside views and moral sympathy interrelate has been seriously neglected.

Narration is an art, not a science, but this does not mean that we are necessarily doomed to fail when we attempt to formulate principles about it. There are systematic elements in every art, and criticism of fiction can never avoid the responsibility of trying to explain technical successes and failures by reference to general principles. But the question is that of where the general principles are to be found. Fiction, the novel, point-of-view—these terms are not in fact subject to the kind of definition that alone makes critical generalisations and rules meaningful. A given technique cannot be judged according to its service to "the novel," or "fiction," but only according to its success in particular works or kinds of work.

It is not surprising to hear practising novelists report that they have never had help from critics about point-of-view. In dealing with point-of-view the novelist must always deal with the individual work: which particular character shall tell this particular story, or part of a story, with what precise degree of reliability, privilege, freedom to comment, and so on. Shall he be given dramatic vividness? Even if the novelist has decided on a narrator who will fit one of the critic's classifications—"omniscient," "first-person," "limited omniscient," "objective," "roving," "effaced," and so on—his troubles have just begun. He simply cannot find answers to his immediate, precise, practical problems by referring to statements that the "omniscient is the most flexible method," or "the objective the most rapid or vivid," or whatever. Even the soundest of generalisations at this level will be of little use to him in his page-by-page progress through his novel. As Henry James's detailed records show, the novelist discovers his narrative technique as he tries to achieve for his readers the potentialities of his developing idea. The majority of his choices are consequently choices of degree, not kind. To decide that your narrator shall not be omniscient decides practically nothing. The hard question is, just how *inconscient* shall he be? To decide that you will use first-person narration decides again almost nothing. What kind of first-person? How fully characterised? How much aware of himself as a narrator? How reliable? How much confined to realistic inference, how far privileged to go beyond realism? At what points shall he speak truth and at what points utter no judgment or even utter falsehood?

There are no doubt *kinds* of effect to which the author can refer—e.g., if he wants to make a scene more amusing, poignant, vivid, or ambiguous, or if he wants to make a character more sympathetic or more convincing, such-and-such practices may be indicated. But it is not surprising that in his search for help in his decisions, he should find the practice of his peers more helpful than the abstract rules of the textbooks: the sensitive author who reads the great novels finds in them a storehouse of precise examples, examples of how *this* effect, as distinct from all other possible effects, was heightened by the proper narrative choice. In dealing with the types of narration, the critic must always limp behind, referring constantly to the varied practice which alone can correct his temptations to overgeneralise.

13

The Lyrical Novel: Retrospect and Prognosis

RALPH FREEDMAN

In this essay, the concluding chapter of *The Lyrical Novel: Studies in Herman Hesse, Andre Gide, and Virginia Woolf* (1963), Ralph Freedman explores the similarities and differences between "lyrical fiction" and more conventional novels. He sees both as addressing the "confrontation between self and world," with the lyrical novel turning the "I" of lyric poetry into "the protagonist, who refashions the world through his perceptions and renders it as a form of the imagination." Freedman's description suggests that the lyrical novel does not depend upon what R. S. Crane might call a "plot of action." But while Virginia Woolf would probably claim that her novels rely on a "plot of character," Freedman would define them as having a "plot of thought." Woolf might argue that her plots revolve around the development of character as an end in itself, while Freedman would argue that such development is a means to an end—such an end being the display of a specific character's perceptual reconfiguration of the world.

What might be of equal interest are the ways in which the lyrical novel is influenced by and uses the techniques of lyric poetry, including "spatial form" and the construction of narrative around a single metaphor. Freedman provides a historical overview of the lyrical novel's development and defines the thematic purposes that would require that such a form be established. He concludes by suggesting that even though the lyrical novel has entered a period of decline, it will remain an alternative genre that "has been an immensely fertile corrective for the conventional novel." In considering genre, then, we must ask whether or not there is a "conventional" center of novelistic production from which other forms of fiction depart and return, which they react against and influence, but which they cannot escape or replace. If there is such a center, is it simply the product of history and convention?

Ralph Freedman (b. 1920) has taught for a number of years in the Department of Comparative Literature at Princeton University. In addition to *The Lyrical Novel*, he has published *Herman Hesse: Pilgrim of Crisis, a Biography* (1978).

The types of lyrical fiction we have examined share a similar approach to the novel's traditional confrontation between self and world. The "I" of the lyric becomes the protagonist, who refashions the world through his perceptions and renders it as a form of the imagination. The poetic imagination of the lyrical novelist, however, functions differently from that of his conventional *confrère*. The world he creates from the materials given to him in experience becomes a "picture"—a disposition of images and motifs—of relations which in the ordinary novel are produced by social circumstance, cause and effect, the schemes fashioned by chronology. At the same time, lyricism in the novel assumes a significance which it does not possess in verse. Whether he addresses an audience, a beloved, or himself, the lyric poet, too, speaks on the occasion of a situation or an object: Laura's hair, a Grecian Urn, a Golden Bird. But in the novel, as, surely, in epic poetry, the extended narrative introduces a further dimension. The lyrical process expands because the lyrical "I" is also an experiencing protagonist. The poet's stance is turned into an epistemological act.

The exploitation of awareness as such is, of course, no prerogative of lyrical fiction. Self-conscious narrators, who modify or deform the worlds they observe, have populated novels from Richardson and Sterne to Conrad and Henry James. Some of their novels appear to be lyrical; others do not. The selective mind of the narrator or hero may deform its world to achieve a greater penetration of society or a more pervasive analysis of character, or, like Moréas's clown, it may

"The Lyrical Novel: Retrospect and Prognosis" is reprinted from Ralph Freedman, *The Lyrical Novel*, with permission of Princeton University Press, copyright 1963.

draw a mask that bears the features of a suffering humanity. We observed in the lyrical novel how the protagonists rearranged their perceptions, how they dissolved outward forms or reproduced them in various arrangements that created the effect of poems. These trans-mutations of perceptions into images of "artifice" can be pictorial; as in many romantic novels, the protagonists' knowledge may be caught in sequences of pictures or encounters "mirroring" an ideal. But they can also reproduce the unconscious impulse or a deliberately shaped interior monologue, as in many novels since the eighteen-eighties. They can depict figures and objects within the texture of prose poetry, or they can constitute intellectually contrived metaphors. In such novels communication is sometimes difficult, especially when the forms are too private or too strained in their meanings—Djuna Barnes's *Nightwood* might be an example. But occasionally the shifts in perspective induced by the lyrical mode can make communication easier. The metaphor on which the narrative is constructed may be readily understood by the audience and hence the peculiar slant given to observed reality may seem welcome and familiar as, for instance, in poetic folk tales or in novels like Hesse's *Demian*.

The contribution of lyrical fiction has been this peculiar way of looking at perception. Narrative by definition deals with man and world; it has done so since Odysseus's epic encounters. Leaving aside the drama, which must cope with this problem in a different way (involved as it is with visual effects, staging, incidents, audience re-sponse, etc.), the engagements of a knowing self in the world are the novel's mark of distinction. But the novelist has many different ways at his disposal to express this relationship. He can ask how a hero relates to the historical process, to environment and ideas; he can inquire into the reciprocal relations of man and society, man and man. But novels can also ask these questions differently: how does the mind know its world? what is the functional relationship between the inner and the outer? what is the relationship of awareness or knowledge to human conduct and choice? This is how Stendhal, Flau-bert, and, above all, Henry James, addressed themselves to their craft. And this is also the dominant mood in the lyrical novel.

Lyrical fiction, then, is a special instance of the novel of awareness. Yet the lyrical novel has also remained a distinct genre. In Germany, as we have had occasion to notice, it has remained to this day a potent survivor of romanticism; in France, it produced that fruitful fusion of the psychological investigation of consciousness with the aesthetic purposes of *poésie pure*, which has had a crucial effect on the novel of the mind. If it is more useful to describe the engagement of lyrical fiction in epistemological rather than in psychological terms, its distinctive quality lies nonetheless elsewhere. It must be found, not in the modes of apprehension, but in the way images are formed. The characteristic differentiating lyrical from nonlyrical fiction is portraiture, the halting of the flow of time within constellations of images or figures. In this fashion, the lyrical novel has continued to project a unique quality and has been a most influential genre, at least up to the present.

———————

The lyrical novel, then, is closely related to the evolution of the narrative genre as a whole. In its range from narrative to poetry, it has utilized compounds of both its elements, although, as they endure the stresses and strains between types of narration and designs of imagery, lyrical novels preserve a poetic approach. But the questions remain why so early in the evolution of a genre this type of aboriginal "anti-novel" should have developed and why its peculiar way of illuminating human awareness should have shown such persistence.

In the eighteenth century, the "poetic" manner of *Werther* and *A Sentimental Journey* had been prompted by a desire to penetrate to the substance of emotion underlying the behavior of characters. The form most suitable for achieving this purpose seemed to be the sentimental novel, which had been invigorated by the work of Richardson. In *Tristram Shandy*, the emphasis on sensibility was combined with a bizarre displacement of reality, a disruption of logical continuity, a creation of unexpected effects. It is easy to see why this work should have transcended its immediate context and should have become significant for the poetic inspirations of lyrical novelists. The romance and the Gothic tale, too, introduced a realm of fantasy which came to nourish the romantic strand of the lyrical novel. But the romance, as it was understood in the eighteenth century, was ill suited for the purpose of catching the essence of feeling. Rather, in novels such as Beckford's *Vathek* or Walpole's *Castle of Otranto*, it caught a weird rearrangement of the world. It took a nineteenth-century sensibility to see such shifts in the normal expectations of the real as forms of the poetic imagination, to experience man's pilgrimage through the world as Coleridge viewed his Mariner's symbolic quest.

The rationale for turning toward lyrical fiction was generally different among German romantic writers from that of their predecessors in England and elsewhere. Although these novelists were still concerned with rendering feelings, their main interest was the role of the hero as the poet's ideal image. In novels like *Hyperion* and *Heinrich von Ofterdingen*, the hero actually functions as the poet's "I." Many of these writers were indeed also poets, but they often believed that the novel was a superior form, a *Gesamtkunstwerk*, in which they most completely fulfilled their poetic function. The impetus toward the form came from a feeling of dissatisfaction with the supposed realism of the classical novels of the eighteenth century. The medieval romance and *Don Quixote*, or Sterne's novels of sensibility, appealed to them as more meaningful. Of course, not all German romantic fiction was lyrical, but the ideal of the novel coincided with that of lyrical prose narrative. The poet's *persona* was to approach the transcendental seer; time-bound reality was accordingly deformed into poetic imagery.

The French symbolists came to the same conclusions from a similar sense of dissatisfaction. But the naïve reaction against the "mercantilistic spirit" of most eighteenth-century English fiction, as it had been expressed by the German romantics, was no longer possible following a century that had seen the development of the novel from Balzac and Flaubert to the Goncourts and Zola. Here the break became most decisive for world literature, for it is mostly through symbolist efforts in the novel—Villiers de l'Isle Adam, Rémy de Gourmont, Édouard Dujardin, Huysmans, and especially Maeterlinck—that the impulse of romantic aestheticism was spread throughout the literary world. Schopenhauer's aesthetics and philosophy, the practice of Novalis and E. T. A. Hoffmann, had helped mold a new "romantic" novel which now appeared in a rather different guise. If the German romantics had thought of the novel as a comprehensive genre, a "super-poetry," the French symbolists believed that poetry was the more satisfactory form and sought to adapt the methods of poetry to prose narrative. The romantic emphasis on the mind (as a way of knowing and allegorizing reality) was now more closely connected with consciousness, and the rendering of the unconscious became an important means of portrayal. Other methods, as we have seen, are concerned with the more violent distortions of life to suit the poetic emotion, the rendering, however bizarre, of a situation, a theme, a perception or inner life as a concrete image from which the self is ultimately withdrawn.

Both the German romantic and the French symbolist conceptions of the lyrical novel, then, had been conditioned by dissatisfactions with conventions that seemed inadequate: the realism of the eighteenth century and nineteenth-century naturalism. Similarly, in the twentieth century the lyrical novel emerged as a reaction against a prevailing mood. Apparent in both poetry and prose, this reaction was produced by the writer's awareness of his role as an heir of the romantic exile. Modern writing has perpetuated the nineteenth-century ambivalence between hero and world and its emphasis on the self's isolation. At the same time, the novel has expanded its scope, especially in view of the increasingly restricted audience of poetry, and has approached, in its comprehensiveness of content and its variety of techniques, an almost romantic breadth. Poetic sensibilities, sharpened by methods inherited from romantic and symbolist writers, could legitimately choose the novel as a form in which man's awareness is mirrored as poetry.

Although lyrical writing is a rather specialized genre, it bears deep implications for modern writing as a whole. But if, beneath its enormous variety of individual forms, we notice a certain uniformity of purpose, the peculiarities of literary as well as historical traditions in each country produced considerable variations in the critical acceptance of the genre. In some national literatures a lyrical form appears to be more welcome than in others; a fashion which is conventional in one country may be *outré* in another. We have seen that there has been a secure place for romantic lyrical fiction in German literature. The reasons for the relative prominence of lyrical novels in Germany and in German-speaking countries are complex, but are partly discerned in the national history of the novel. For if we exempt the rather halting beginnings of the eighteen century, German prose narrative owes its chief impetus to romanticism and to the model of Goethe's *Wilhelm Meister*, which, though not itself lyrical, is a rather "un-novelistic" kind of novel that easily lent itself to allegorical distortions.

Lyrical fiction is not pervasive in the French novel, but, from Chateaubriand and Nerval to the twentieth century, it has always been a viable alternative. We may recall that the prose poem had developed since the early nineteenth century into an embryonic lyrical novel which stressed at first, not the hallucinations or vagaries of the unconscious, but the precise dispositions of images related to the poet or to his *persona*. Indeed, whatever its hesitant public may have thought of this hybrid form, the prose poem is a uniquely French contribution. But even in full-length fiction, Rivière's impassioned, if one-sided, debate with symbolism in his "Roman d'aventure" attests to the importance of the lyrical genre for French writers. Aestheticism in the novel—its original connection with "pure poetry"—has reinforced the exploration of awareness which has so often characterized French fiction. Nor is the hospitality to lyricism confined to the early interest in consciousness, an interest which has been much commented upon in discussions of Dujardin, Valéry Larbaud, and, of course, Proust. From Gide to Maurice Blanchot's *L'Arrêt de mort* we encounter various efforts to recast imaginatively a world of perception into poetic forms. For all these tendencies, however, French lyrical fiction has still been a far less oppressive heritage than a corresponding tradition has been for German writers.

Perhaps because of the accident of Bloomsbury, surely because of the stature of Virginia Woolf and the importance of Joyce, there has been a recent flowering of lyrical fiction in England, despite a notorious inhospitality to the genre in the English literary tradition. None of the traditional romantic forms of the novel (early or late) had been taken seriously as valid lyrical modes. For reasons connected with the unique role played by the English novel as middle class entertainment, an aestheticist or poetic approach to a form held to be reserved for a portrait of society was frowned upon by influential arbiters of literary taste. If not poetry, at least the novel seemed inviolably English, whose norms had been set by Fielding, Thackeray, and Trollope. To be sure, even George Eliot, certainly Meredith, Hardy, and Conrad, had in some ways strayed from the narrow path of this tradition, but none so much as to question its basic outlines. Despite poetic rebels like Emily Brontë or D. H. Lawrence, there remained a formidable barrier to lyricism in fiction. New vistas were opened only when experimentations with language were identified with a new psychology of the novel.

The stream of consciousness, nourished partly by the backwash of symbolism of the early nineteen-hundreds and partly by the rise of psychoanalysis as an exciting new discipline, offered possibilities for poetic fiction which were whole-heartedly exploited by several experimental writers in English. But it seems pertinent to observe that this way of looking at reality (unlike, for example, that of the romantic picaresque or the aetheticist prose poem) was still rooted in a native tradition: the associationist doctrines of the seventeenth- and eighteenth-century British empiricists which had found their most sublime literary echo in Laurence Sterne. For Dorothy Richardson, the stream of consciousness was not yet a lyrical mode; for Joyce it had become more than lyricism. Perhaps Virginia Woolf was one of the few typical poetic novelists in England to find a wide audience, because, far-fetched as her poetry was for the uninitiated reader, she was so deeply steeped in her national tradition, in the literary history of her country, and especially in the basic purpose of the novel that she combined lyricism with a type of narrative that still revealed the qualities of traditional English fiction. It is one of her greatest triumphs and paradoxes that in *The Waves* she achieved her purest lyricism precisely as she accomplished her most objective novel of manners.

This paradox has remained a legacy of the lyrical novel in England which has communicated itself to our day. Beyond Virginia Woolf, Joyce's *Finnegans Wake* had reached perhaps the apex of the "novel as poem"—without a commitment to traditional forms of narrative—but, like most of Joyce's seminal work, its quality as a lyrical novel in our sense is open to question. Perhaps the most uniquely lyrical novel to come from this ferment of the nineteen-twenties and thirties has been Djuna Barnes's *Nightwood*. Obviously owing a great deal to Joyce, this novel tries to maintain the form and even the plot of narrative but to convert them into poetic imagery. Extravagantly praised by T. S. Eliot as a novel which appeals to the reader as a poem, this book seems to avoid both the pitfall of pure poetry and that of plain psychologizing. The world is transformed into the soliloquists' images (including those of the author) from which character and action are made to emerge. Yet Djuna Barnes was never fully accepted in spite of her esoteric emulators. To be successful in English, a lyrical novel must be capable of maintaining itself as a "novel of fact." With the demise of Bloomsbury, lyrical fiction has entered upon a new phase.

———

At present we confront a paradox in the fortunes of the lyrical novel. At a time when narrative has evolved toward a greater penetration of the self, the lyrical novel, which has fostered this condition, has undergone a decline. This is not to say that the lyrical novel is finished. It is merely to suggest that following its great importance in the first half of this century as a response to the naturalistic novel, a hiatus in its influence has occurred. Nevertheless, its methods have had a lasting effect. Whatever its difficulties, the lyrical novel developed a new orientation toward experience: internal without being necessarily subjective; reflective without being essayistic; pictorial or musical without abandoning the narrative framework of the novel. All these qualities have entered current fiction, but they have nourished a different, if related strand in prose narrative.

The new concern with awareness implies a different sort of involvement from that of the lyrical novelists we have so far considered. Awareness is neither the idealistic portrait of the world within the mind nor the act of consciousness as such. "I" and "other" are opposed; by measuring itself against that which is "other," the self obtains its identity. A famous novel of awareness and action—Malraux's *La Condition humaine*—dramatizes this relationship. It is illuminated by the opening scene in which Ch'en faces the sleeping body of his intended victim. Self confronts "other"; in a foreknowledge of the murder, the assassin is intensely aware of the noises in the street; at the same time he already senses the yielding flesh against the point of his dagger. There is nothing lyrical in this confrontation. The knife has replaced the eye, the contact of blade and flesh the pictorial *blason* embodied by a mind. Yet the situation defines the man, the victim, the place, and the human condition as surely as would have a poetic image. Although in its date of composition, *La Condition humaine* is closer to *Les Faux-Monnayeurs* and *The Waves* than to contemporary fiction, it suggests a technique which so-called "existentialist" novels—like Sartre's *La Nausée*—have refined. Rather than blending self and world into imagery, it renders them in a narrative contest.

Albert Camus was similarly involved with the self and its appropriate stance toward an independent world; his techniques, more than Malraux's or Sartre's, approach those of the lyrical novel. His evocative fiction is connected with imagistic portraits of life. This is especially true of *L'Étranger*, in which, as in a lyric, sensuous imagery depicts a moral point. Yet even here the hero's awareness continuously dissociates, separates itself from its objects. The alienation of the theme is also revealed in the form. It would stretch the point to suggest that *La Peste* and *La Chute* are lyrical novels. But the fact remains that, especially in his earlier work, Camus's sensibility draws men and objects into patterns of imagery, whereas Sartre, even in his experimental *Le Sursis*, relies largely on the design of the realistic novel.

More recently, the novel of awareness has gone an even more diversified way. Nathalie Sarraute (like Blanchot) seems close to a lyrical genre, but the work of a writer such as Alain Robbe-Grillet typifies a new spirit, which, however, would have been unthinkable without the "lyrical" generation before him. In *Le Voyeur*, he uses precisely the epistemological situation favored by the lyrical novelist, but, instead of deforming the image aesthetically, he turns the method in on itself. Outward appearances are not illuminated by apprehension; rather, a distinct world of objects gradually reveals a character, a situation, an act. This type of novel has been made possible by the fiction of "abstract lyricism" Gide had perfected, which is based on a sensitive denuding of external life.

In England, as we noted earlier, lyricism has again reverted to a minor role, yet Virginia Woolf had a lasting effect even on those who most strongly rejected her. For she achieved what Jane Austen could not: an exploration of the quality of experience which required a concept of the imagination that had been nurtured by the nineteenth century. Her technical achievement left its mark on the new partially "symbolic," partially "epistemological" novel—that of Iris Murdoch, for example, and of William Golding. Golding especially reflects an awareness of a lyrical mode which occasionally he even approached. His *Pincher Martin* dramatizes in a gigantic concluding image the struggle between the "inner" and the "outer" which had concerned Virginia Woolf. In this momentary vision of a dying sailor, the "mouth" and the "center"—consciousness and its awareness—are engaged in a terrifying dialogue which culminates in the vision of God as a Mariner in his Sea Boots. Naturally, Golding does not epitomize English fiction, which is also prominently represented by Joyce Cary and C. P. Snow (who have hewn a path back to the tradition of Trollope and Thackeray); nor is his work comparable to that of Graham Greene, who has called upon different conventions altogether. Recently, we have even witnessed in the fiction of Lawrence Durrell a return to the lyrical novel in larger dimensions. The success of Durrell's *Alexandria Quartet* (more even than his accomplishment as a writer) has shown that lyricism in the novel is by no means dead. But Golding has revealed most clearly what lyrical fiction can, at its best, contribute to a contemporary writer even as he rejects its conventions and its indrawn concern with sensibility.

Even in German-speaking countries a turn away from the lyricism of the romantic novel has materialized. Not that Germany has lacked naturalistic novels, didactic novels, novels of political tracts, and realistic novels of education, but its fiction has been somehow infected by the virus of romanticism which few novels have escaped. Such different writers of the first half of the century as Heinrich Mann, Stefan Zweig, Alfred Döblin, Klabund, Rudolf Binding, and even Franz Kafka and Robert Musil, have been beset in some fashion by a romantic form such as the legend, the episodic quest, or the imagistic portrait of the self. Thomas Mann seemed sometimes oppressed by this heritage as by a burden, although often (as, for example in *Doktor Faustus*, which occasionally even borders on lyrical fiction) it forced him to create with great intensity and depth. Kafka's work, too, employs many conventions of romantic lineage, but his philosophical rationale moved him in an opposite direction. The Kafkaesque nightmare is based on an interaction of self and world similar to Dostoevsky's. He emphasized relations between man and the furnishings of a distorted physical world. Yet there remains an intimate kinship between Kafka's "engagement" of mind and "other" and a lyrical mode based on their union in imagery. Significantly, Kafka admired the Swiss writer Robert Walser, who was a lyricist *par excellence*, delicate in the imagery and poetic movements of his narratives, yet who also produced bizarre reconstructions of everyday reality with which Kafka felt an immediate kinship.

The situation confronting the German novelist is somewhat different from that faced by his fellow writers in England or France. Since lyricism has always been an accepted tradition in the German novel, it has been part of the "establishment." The writer searching for new forms of expression is not likely to find it exciting or fresh; he is more disposed than others, perhaps, to expunge traces of its influence rather than to absorb them. This attitude, directed particularly at the "transcendental" lyricism of the German novel, was summarily expressed by a Swiss writer of the new generation, Friedrich Duerrenmatt, when he began in his introduction to *Die Panne:*

> Are real stories still possible, stories for writers? If the writer does not want to tell about himself, romanticize, poeticize, universalize his ego; if he feels no inclination to talk about his hopes and failures, no matter how truthfully, or of the ways he sleeps with women . . . ; if he does not want this, but prefers to decently keep personal matters to himself, to work the material before him like a sculptor his stone, shaping and developing it, and hoping thereby to gain something of the classicist's faculty of not falling too readily into despair, . . . —if this is his endeavor, then writing becomes a far more difficult and lonely as well as a more senseless occupation.[1]

In its many different forms, from the poetic image of the ego to the enactment of consciousness, the lyrical novel emerges as a genre to be overcome as well as to be used. It has been an immensely fertile corrective for the conventional novel, and yet, compared to more concrete explorations of life such as *Le Rouge et le noir* or *The Brothers Karamazov*, it has always suffered from a certain anemia. But no detailed examinations of conscience, no discussions of motives, sensibilities, or realistic portraits of manners can make up for the intensely inward projection of experience in which the lyrical novel excels. Few other forms allow the author, or his *persona*, to penetrate so directly into the very act of knowledge and to represent it in immediately accessible portraiture. The limitations of this approach are obvious enough: an underemphasis on character and an overemphasis on image, dream-like encounter, or allegory. The excitement created by the plot is largely absent and the excitement instilled by the expectations of the lyrical process does not usually make up for it. Nevertheless, at its best the lyrical novel can be a voyage of discovery onto a strange subterranean sea in which the lyrical mood—abbreviated, even truncated in verse—is acted out in worlds of fiction populated by an imagery of figures, emblazoned by an imagery of scenes.

Note

1 Friedrich Duerrenmatt, *Traps*, trans. Richard Winston and Clara Winston (New York: Knopf, 1960), pp. 3–4. Original edition, *Die Panne*, in *Die Arche* (Zurich: Peter Schifferli, 1956).

14

Marxist Aesthetics and
Literary Realism

GEORG LUKÁCS

In this excerpt from the preface to *Studies in European Realism* (1948; trans. 1950), Georg Lukács presents a Marxist analysis of European fiction, declaring Marxists to be "jealous guardians of our classical heritage in their aesthetics." They are able to evaluate the historical role of this heritage in the dialectical development of human culture, unlike "modern thinkers" who reject "the idea that there is any such thing as an unchanged general line of development." Lukács's purpose in studying the nineteenth-century realists, however, is less to emphasize their place in the world's cultural heritage than to defend "realism" as the highest form of fictional creation. Lukács claims a unique value for "realism" in literary production, one similar to Lionel Trilling's "moral realism." "Realism," he says, "is the recognition of the fact that a work of literature can rest neither on a lifeless average, as the naturalists suppose, nor on an individual principle which dissolves its own self into nothing."

Lukács argues that great literature must "depict the most important turning-points" of "the social and historical task humanity has to solve" (i.e., revolution). It can do this only by means of "realism," which enables it to create "types" that represent "the organic, indissoluble connection between man as a private individual and man as a social being, as a member of a community." Lukács does not claim, however, that a "great realist" must necessarily believe in Marxism and revolution. Conservative realists (Balzac) can be considered greater writers than left-wing naturalists (Zola) because the great realists "all have in common that they penetrate deeply into the great universal problems of their time and inexorably depict the true essence of reality as they see it." Lukács concludes his essay with a spirited defense of Russian realism, arguing that "never in all its history did mankind so urgently require a realist literature as it does to-day." While we may agree with Lukács's belief in literature's positive role in cultural development, we should ask whether only one form of literature can play such a role; and, in fact, whether "realist" fiction has actually played that role in any historical period.

Georg Lukács (1885–1971), a leading Marxist literary theorist, was born in Budapest. He returned there from Moscow after World War II to become professor of aesthetics at the University of Budapest. Although *Studies in European Realism* was the first of his Marxist books to be translated into English, his pre-Marxist work, *The Theory of the Novel* (1920; trans. 1971), is perhaps the best known of his translated criticism.

The Marxist philosophy of history is a comprehensive doctrine dealing with the necessary progress made by humanity from primitive communism to our own time and the perspectives of our further advance along the same road as such it also gives us indications for the historical future. But such indications— born of the recognition of certain laws governing historical development—are not a cookery book providing recipes for each phenomenon or period; Marxism is not a Baedeker of history, but a signpost pointing the direction in which history moves forward. The final certainty it affords consists in the assurance that the development of mankind does not and cannot finally lead to nothing and nowhere.

Of course, such generalizations do not do full justice to the guidance given by Marxism, a guidance extending to every topical problem of life. Marxism combines a consistent following of an unchanging direction with incessant theoretical and practical allowances for the deviousness of the path of evolution. Its well-defined philosophy of history is based on a flexible and adaptable acceptance and analysis of historical development. This apparent duality—which is in re-

"Marxist Aesthetics and Literary Realism" is reprinted from Georg Lukács, *Studies in European Realism* (1950), trans. Edith Bone, with permission of Grosset and Dunlap, copyright 1964.

ality the dialectic unity of the materialist worldview—is also the guiding principle of Marxist aesthetics and literary theory.

Those who do not know Marxism at all or know it only superficially or at second-hand, may be surprised by the respect for the classical heritage of mankind which one finds in the really great representatives of this doctrine and by their incessant references to that classical heritage. Without wishing to enter into too much detail, we mention as an instance, in philosophy, the heritage of Hegelian dialectics, as opposed to the various trends in the latest philosophies. "But all this is long out of date," the modernists cry. "All this is the undesirable, outworn legacy of the nineteenth century," say those who—intentionally or unintentionally, consciously or unconsciously—support the Fascist ideology and its pseudo-revolutionary rejection of the past, which is in reality a rejection of culture and humanism. Let us look without prejudice at the bankruptcy of the very latest philosophies; let us consider how most philosophers of our day are compelled to pick up the broken and scattered fragments of dialectic (falsified and distorted in this decomposition) whenever they want to say something even remotely touching its essence about present-day life; let us look at the modern attempts at a philosophical synthesis and we shall find them miserable, pitiful caricatures of the old genuine dialectic, now consigned to oblivion.

It is not by chance that the great Marxists were jealous guardians of our classical heritage in their aesthetics as well as in other spheres. But they do not regard this classical heritage as a reversion to the past; it is a necessary outcome of their philosophy of history that they should regard the past as irretrievably gone and not susceptible of renewal. Respect for the classical heritage of humanity in aesthetics means that the great Marxists look for the true highroad of history, the true direction of its development, the true course of the historical curve, the formula of which they know; and because they know the formula they do not fly off at a tangent at every hump in the graph, as modern thinkers often do because of their theoretical rejection of the idea that there is any such thing as an unchanged general line of development.

For the sphere of aesthetics this classical heritage consists in the great arts which depict man as a whole in the whole of society. Again it is the general philosophy (here: proletarian humanism) which determines the central problems posed in aesthetics. The Marxist philosophy of history analyses man as a whole, and contemplates the history of human evolution as a whole, together with the partial achievement, or non-achievement of completeness in its various periods of development. It strives to unearth the hidden laws governing all human relationships. Thus the object of proletarian humanism is to reconstruct the complete human personality and free it from the distortion and dismemberment to which it has been subjected in class society. These theoretical and practical perspectives determine the criteria by means of which Marxist aesthetics establish a bridge back to the classics and at the same time discover new classics in the thick of the literary struggles of our own time. The ancient Greeks, Dante, Shakespeare, Goethe, Balzac, Tolstoy all give adequate pictures of great periods of human development and at the same time serve as signposts in the ideological battle fought for the restoration of the unbroken human personality.

Such viewpoints enable us to see the cultural and literary evolution of the nineteenth century in its proper light. They show us that the true heirs of the French novel, so gloriously begun early in the last century, were not Flaubert and especially not Zola, but the Russian and Scandinavian writers of the second half of the century. The present volume contains my studies of French and Russian realist writers seen in this perspective.

If we translate into the language of pure aesthetics the conflict (conceived in the sense of the philosophy of history) between Balzac and the later French novel, we arrive at the conflict between realism and naturalism. Talking of a conflict here may sound a paradox to the ears of most writers and readers of our day. For most present-day writers and readers are used to literary fashions swinging to and fro between the pseudo-objectivism of the naturalist school and the mirage-subjectivism of the psychologist or abstract-formalist school. And inasmuch as they see any worth in realism at all, they regard their own false extreme as a new kind of near-realism or realism. Realism however is not some sort of middle way between false objectivity and false subjectivity, but on the contrary the true, solution-bringing third way, opposed to all the pseudo-dilemmas engendered by the wrongly-posed questions of those who wander without a chart in the labyrinth of our time. Realism is the recognition of the fact that a work of literature can rest neither on a lifeless average, as the naturalists suppose, nor on an individual principle which dissolves its own self into nothingness. The central category and criterion of realist literature is the type, a peculiar synthesis which organically binds together the general and the particular both in characters and situations. What makes a type a type is not its average quality, not its mere individual being, however profoundly conceived; what makes it a type is that in it all the humanly and socially essential determinants are present on their highest level of development, in the ultimate unfolding of the possibilities latent in them, in extreme presentation of their extremes, rendering concrete the peaks and limits of men and epochs.

True great realism thus depicts man and society as complete entities, instead of showing merely one or the other of their aspects. Measured by this criterion, artistic trends determined by either exclusive introspection or exclusive extraversion equally impoverish and distort reality. Thus realism means a three-dimensionality, an all-roundness, that endows with independent life characters and human relationships. It by no means involves a rejection of the emotional and intellectual dynamism which necessarily develops together with the modern world. All it opposes is the destruction of the completeness of the human personality and of the objective typicality of men and situations through an excessive cult of the momentary mood. The struggle against such tendencies acquired a decisive importance in the realist literature of the nineteenth century. Long before such tendencies appeared in the practice of literature, Balzac had already prophetically foreseen and outlined the entire problem in his tragi-comic story *Le Chef d'Oeuvre Inconnu*. Here experiment on the part of a painter to create a new classic three-dimensionality by means of an ecstasy of emotion and colour quite in the spirit of modern impressionism, leads to complete chaos. Fraunhofer, the tragic hero, paints a picture which is a tangled chaos of colours out of which a perfectly modelled female leg and foot protrude as an almost fortuitous fragment. Today a considerable section of modern artists has given up the Fraunhofer-like struggle and is content with finding, by means of new aesthetic theories, a justification for the emotional chaos of their works.

The central aesthetic problem of realism is the adequate presentation of the complete human personality. But as in every profound philosophy of art, here, too, the consistent following-up to the end of the aesthetic viewpoint leads us beyond pure aesthetics: for art, precisely if taken in its most perfect purity, is saturated with social and moral humanistic problems. The demand for a realistic creation of types is in opposition both to the trends in which the biological being of man, the physiological aspects of self-preservation and procreation are dominant (Zola and his disciples) and to the trends which sublimate man into purely mental, psychological processes. But such an attitude, if it remained within the sphere of formal aesthetic judgments, would doubtless be quite arbitrary, for there is no reason why, regarded merely from the point of view of good writing, erotic conflict with its attendant moral and social conflicts should be rated higher than the elemental spontaneity of pure sex. Only if we accept the concept of the complete human personality as the social and historical task humanity has to solve; only if we regard it as the vocation of art to depict the most important turning-points of this process with all the wealth of the factors affecting it; only if aesthetics assign to art the role of explorer and guide, can the content of life be systematically divided up into spheres of greater and lesser importance; into spheres that throw light on types and paths and spheres that remain in darkness. Only then does it become evident that any description of mere biological processes—be these the sexual act or pain and sufferings, however detailed and from the literary point of view perfect it may be—results in a levelling-down of the social, historical, and moral being of men and is not a means but an obstacle to such essential artistic expression as illuminating human conflicts in all their complexity and completeness. It is for this reason that the new contents and new media of expression contributed by naturalism have led not to an enrichment but to an impoverishment and narrowing-down of literature.

Apparently similar trains of thought were already put forward in early polemics directed against Zola and his school. But the psychologists, although they were more than once right in their concrete condemnation of Zola and the Zola school, opposed another no less false extreme to the false extreme of naturalism. For the inner life of man, its essential traits and essential conflicts can be truly portrayed only in organic connection with social and historical factors. Separated from the latter and developing merely its own immanent dialectic, the psychologist trend is no less abstract, and distorts and impoverishes the portrayal of the complete human personality no less than does the naturalist biologism which it opposes.

It is true that, especially regarded from the viewpoint of modern literary fashions, the position in respect of the psychologist school is at the first glance less obvious than in the case of naturalism. Everyone will immediately see that a description in the Zola manner of, say, an act of copulation between Dido and Aeneas or Romeo and Juliet would resemble each other very much more closely than the erotic conflicts depicted by Virgil and Shakespeare, which acquaint us with an inexhaustible wealth of cultural and human facts and types. Pure introspection is apparently the diametrical opposite of naturalist levelling-down, for what it describes are quite individual, non-recurring traits. But such extremely individual traits are also extremely abstract, for this very reason of non-recurrence. Here, too, Chesterton's witty paradox holds good, that the inner light is the worst kind of lighting. It is obvious to everyone that the coarse biologism of the naturalists and the rough outlines drawn by propagandist writers deform the true picture of the complete human personality. Much fewer are those who realize that the psychologists' punctilious probing into the human soul and their transformation of human beings into a chaotic flow of ideas destroy no less surely every possibility of a literary presentation of the complete human personality. A Joyce-like shoreless torrent of associations can create living human beings just as little as Upton Sinclair's coldly calculated all-good and all-bad stereotypes.

Owing to lack of space this problem cannot be developed here in all its breadth. Only one important and at present often neglected point is to be stressed here because it demonstrates that the live portrayal of the complete human personality is possible only if the writer attempts to create types. The point in question is the organic, indissoluble connection between man as a private individual and man as a social being, as a member of a community. We know that this is the most difficult question of modern literature today and has been so ever since modern *bourgeois* society came into being. On the surface the two seem to be sharply divided and the appearance of the autonomous, independent existence of the individual is all the more pronounced, the more completely modern *bourgeois* society is developed.

It seems as if the inner life, genuine "private" life, were proceeding according to its own autonomous laws and as if its fulfillments and tragedies were growing ever more independent of the surrounding social environment. And correspondingly, on the other side, it seems as if the connection with the community could manifest itself only in high-sounding abstractions, the adequate expression for which would be either rhetoric or satire.

An unbiased investigation of life and the setting aside of these false traditions of modern literature leads easily enough to the uncovering of the true circumstances, to the discovery which had long been made by the great realists of the beginning and middle of the nineteenth century and which Gottfried Keller expressed thus: "Everything is politics." The great Swiss writer did not intend this to mean that everything was immediately tied up with politics: on the contrary, in his view—as in Balzac's and Tolstoy's—every action, thought, and emotion of human beings is inseparably bound up with the life and struggles of the community, i.e., with politics; whether the humans themselves are conscious of this, unconscious of it, or even trying to escape from it, objectively their actions, thoughts, and emotions nevertheless spring from and run into politics.

The true great realists not only realized and depicted this situation—they did more than that, they set it up as a demand to be made on men. They knew that this distortion of objective reality (although, of course, due to social causes), this division of the complete human personality into a public and a private sector was a mutilation of the essence of man. Hence they protested not only as painters of reality, but also as humanists, against this fiction of capitalist society however unavoidable this spontaneously formed superficial appearance. If as writers, they delved deeper in order to uncover the true types of man, they had inevitably to unearth and expose to the eyes of modern society the great tragedy of the complete human personality.

In the works of such great realists as Balzac we can again find a third solution opposed to both false extremes of modern literature, exposing as an abstraction, as a vitiation of the true poesy of life, both the feeble commonplaces of the well-intentioned and honest propagandist novels and the spurious richness of a preoccupation with the details of private life.

This brings us face to face with the question of the topicality today of the great realist writers. Every great historical period is a period of transition, a contradictory unity of crisis and renewal, of destruction and rebirth; a new social order and a new type of man always come into being in the course of a unified though contradictory process. In such critical, transitional periods the tasks and responsibility of literature are exceptionally great. But only truly great realism can cope with such responsibilities; the accustomed, the fashionable media of expression, tend more and more to hamper literature in fulfilling the tasks imposed by history. It should surprise no one if from this point of view we turn against the individualistic, psychologist trends in literature. It might more legitimately surprise many that these studies express a sharp opposition to Zola and Zolaism.

Such surprise may be due in the main to the fact that Zola was a writer of the left and his literary methods were dominant chiefly, though by no means exclusively, in left-wing literature. It might appear, therefore, that we are involving ourselves in a serious contradiction, demanding on the one hand the politicization of literature and on the other hand attacking insidiously the most vigorous and militant section of left-wing literature. But this contradiction is merely apparent. It is, however, well suited to throw light on the true connection between literature and *Weltanschauung*.

The problem was first raised (apart from the Russian democratic literary critics) by Engels, when he drew a comparison between Balzac and Zola. Engels showed that Balzac, although his political creed was legitimist royalism, nevertheless inexorably exposed the vices and weakness of royalist feudal France and described its death agony with magnificent poetic vigour. This phenomenon, references to which the reader will find more than once in these pages, may at the first glance again—and mistakenly—appear contradictory. It might appear that the *Weltanschauung* and political attitude of serious great realists are a matter of no consequence. To a certain extent this is true. For from the point of view of the self-recognition of the present and from the point of view of history and posterity, what matters is the picture conveyed by the work; the question to what extent this picture conforms to the views of the authors is a secondary consideration.

This, of course, brings us to a serious problem of aesthestics. Engels, in writing about Balzac, called it "the triumph of realism";

it is a problem that goes down to the very roots of realist artistic creation. It touches the essence of true realism: the great writer's thirst for truth, his fanatic striving for reality—or expressed in terms of ethics: the writer's sincerity and probity. A great realist such as Balzac, if the intrinsic artistic development of situations and characters he has created comes into conflict with his most cherished prejudices or even his most sacred convictions, will, without an instant's hesitation, set aside these his own prejudices and convictions and describe what he really sees, not what he would prefer to see. This ruthlessness towards their own subjective world-picture is the hall-mark of all great realists, in sharp contrast to the second-raters, who nearly always succeed in bringing their own *Weltanschauung* into "harmony" with reality, that is forcing a falsified or distorted picture of reality into the shape of their own world-view. This difference in the ethical attitude of the greater and lesser writers is closely linked with the difference between genuine and spurious creation. The characters created by the great realists, once conceived in the vision of their creator, live an independent life of their own: their comings and goings, their development, their destiny is dictated by the inner dialectic of their social and individual existence. No writer is a true realist—or even a truly good writer, if he can direct the evolution of his own characters at will.

All this is however merely a description of the phenomenon. It answers the question as to the ethics of the writer: what will he do if he sees reality in such and such a light? But this does not enlighten us at all regarding the other question: what does the writer see and how does he see it? And yet it is here that the most important problems of the social determinants of artistic creation arise. In the course of these studies we shall point out in detail the basic differences which arise in the creative methods of writers according to the degree to which they are bound up with the life of the community, take part in the struggles going on around them or are merely passive observers of events. Such differences determine creative processes which may be diametrical opposites; even the experience which gives rise to the work will be structurally different, and in accordance with this the process of shaping the work will be different. The question whether a writer lives within the community or is a mere observer of it, is determined not by psychological, not even by typological factors; it is the evolution of society that determines (not automatically, not fatalistically, of course), the line the evolution of an author will take. Many a writer of a basically contemplative type has been driven to an intense participation in the life of the community by the social conditions of his time; Zola, on the contrary, was by nature a man of action, but his epoch turned him into a mere observer and when at last he answered the call of life, it came too late to influence his development as a writer.

But even this is as yet only the formal aspect of this problem, although no longer the abstractly formal. The question grows essential and decisive only when we examine concretely the position taken up by a writer. What does he love and what does he hate? It is thus that we arrive at a deeper interpretation of the writer's true *Weltanschauung*, at the problem of the artistic value and fertility of the writer's world-view. The conflict which previously stood before us as the conflict between the writer's world-view and the faithful portrayal of the world he sees, is now clarified as a problem within the *Weltanschauung* itself, as a conflict between a deeper and a more superficial level of the writer's own *Weltanschauung*.

Realists such as Balzac or Tolstoy in their final posing of questions always take the most important, burning problems of the community for their starting-point; their pathos as writers is always stimulated by those sufferings of the people which are the most acute at the time; it is these sufferings that determine the objects and direction of their love and hate and through these emotions determine also what they see in their poetic visions and how they see it. If, therefore, in the process of creation their conscious world-view comes into conflict with the world seen in their vision, what really emerges is that their true conception of the world is only superficially formulated in the consciously held world-view and the real depth of their *Weltanschauung*, their deep ties with the great issues of their time, their sympathy with the sufferings of the people can find adequate expression only in the being and fate of their characters.

No one experienced more deeply than Balzac the torments which the transition to the capitalist system of production inflicted on every section of the people, the profound moral and spiritual degradation which necessarily accompanied this transformation on every level of society. At the same time Balzac was also deeply aware of the fact that this transformation was not only socially inevitable, but at the same time progressive. This contradiction in his experience Balzac attempted to force into a system based on a Catholic legitimism and tricked out with Utopian conceptions of English Toryism. But this system was contradicted all the time by the social realities of his day and the Balzacian vision which mirrored them. This contradiction itself clearly expressed, however, the real truth: Balzac's profound comprehension of the contradictorily progressive character of capitalist development.

It is thus that great realism and popular humanist are merged into an organic unity. For if we regard the classics of the social development that determined the essence of our age, from Goethe and Walter Scott to Gorki and Thomas Mann, we find *mutatis mutandis* the same structure of the basic problem. Of course every great realist found a different solution for the basic problem in accordance with his time and his own artistic personality. But they all have in common that they penetrate deeply into the great universal problems of their time and inexorably depict the true essence of reality as they see it. From the French Revolution onwards the development of society moved in a direction which rendered inevitable a conflict between such aspirations of men of letters and the literature and public of their time. In this whole age a writer could achieve greatness only in the struggle against the current of everyday life. And since Balzac the resistance of daily life to the deeper tendencies of literature, culture, and art has grown ceaselessly stronger. Nevertheless there were always writers who in their life-work, despite all the resistance of the day, fulfilled the demand formulated by Hamlet: "to hold the mirror up to nature," and by means of such a reflected image aided the development of mankind and the triumph of humanist principles in a society so contradictory in its nature that it on the one hand gave birth to the ideal of the complete human personality and on the other hand destroyed it in practice.

The great realists of France found worthy heirs only in Russia. All the problems mentioned here in connection with Balzac apply in an even greater measure to Russian literary development and notably to its central figure Leo Tolstoy. It is not by chance that Lenin (without having read Engels's remarks about Balzac) formulated the Marxist view of the principles of true realism in connection with Tolstoy.

Hence there is no need for us to refer to these problems again here. There is all the more need, however, to call attention to the erroneous conceptions current in respect of the historical and social foundations of Russian realism, errors which in many cases are due to deliberate distortion or concealment of facts. In Britain, as everywhere else in Europe, the newer Russian literature is well known and popular among the intelligent reading public. But as everywhere else, the reactionaries have done all they could to prevent this literature from becoming popular; they felt instinctively that Russian realism, even if each single work may not have a definite social tendency, is an antidote to all reactionary infection.

Only if we have a correct aesthetic conception of the essence of Russian classical realism can we see clearly the social and even political importance of its past and future fructifying influence on literature. With the collapse and eradication of Fascism a new life has begun for every liberated people. Literature has a great part to play in solving the new tasks imposed by the new life in every country. If literature is really to fulfill this role, a role dictated by history, there must be as a natural prerequisite, a philosophical and political rebirth of the writers who produce it. But although this is an indispensable prerequisite, it is not enough. It is not only the opinions that must change, but the whole emotional world of men; and the most effective propagandists of the new, liberating, democratic feeling are the men of letters. The great lesson to be learnt from the Russian development is precisely the extent to which a great realist literature can fructifyingly educate the people and transform public opinion. But such results can be achieved only by a truly great, profound, and all-embracing realism. Hence, if literature is to be a potent factor of national rebirth, it must itself be reborn in its purely literary, formal, aesthetic aspects as well. It must break with reactionary, conservative traditions which hamper it and resist the seeping-in of decadent influences which lead into a blind alley.

In these respects the Russian writers' attitude to life and literature is exemplary, and for this, if for no other reason, it is most important to destroy the generally accepted reactionary evaluation of Tolstoy, and, together with the elimination of such false ideas, to understand the human roots of his literary greatness. And what is most important of all: to show how such greatness comes from the human and artistic identification of the writer with some broad popular movement. It matters little in this connection what popular movement it is in which the writer finds this link between himself and the masses; that Tolstoy sinks his roots into the mass of the Russian peasantry, and Gorki of the industrial workers and landless peasants. For both of them were to the bottom of their souls bound up with the movements seeking the liberation of the people and struggling for it. The result of such a close link in the cultural and literary sphere was then and is to-day that the writer can overcome his isolation, his relegation to the role of a mere observer, to which he would otherwise be driven by the present state of capitalist society. He thus becomes able to take up a free, unbiased, critical attitude towards those tendencies of present-day culture which are unfavourable to art and literature. To fight against such tendencies by purely artistic methods, by the mere formal use of new forms, is a hopeless undertaking, as the tragic fate of the great writers of the West in the course of the last century clearly shows. A close link with a mass movement struggling for the emancipation of the common people does, on the other hand, provide the writer with the broader viewpoint, with the fructifying subject-matter from which a true artist can develop the effective artistic forms which are commensurate with the requirements of the age, even if they go against the superficial artistic fashions of the day.

These very sketchy remarks were required before we could express our final conclusion. Never in all its history did mankind so urgently require a realist literature as it does today. And perhaps never before have the traditions of great realism been so deeply buried under a rubble of social and artistic prejudice. It is for this reason that we consider a revaluation of Tolstoy and Balzac so important. Not as if we wished to set them up as models to be imitated by the writers of our day. To set an example means only: to help in correctly formulating the task and studying the conditions of a successful solution. It was thus that Goethe aided Walter Scott, and Walter Scott aided Balzac. But Walter Scott was no more an imitator of Goethe than Balzac was of Scott. The practical road to a solution for the writer lies in an ardent love of the people, a deep hatred of the people's enemies and the people's own errors, the inexorable uncovering of truth and reality, together with an unshakable faith in the march of mankind and their own people towards a better future.

There is to-day in the world a general desire for a literature which could penetrate with its beam deep into the tangled jungle of our time. A great realist literature could play the leading part, hitherto always denied to it, in the democratic rebirth of nations. If in this connection we evoke Balzac in opposition to Zola and his school, we believe that we are helping to combat the sociological and aesthetical prejudices which have prevented many gifted authors from giving their best to mankind. We know the potent social forces which have held back the development of both writers and literature: a quarter-century of reactionary obscurantism which finally twisted itself into the diabolical grimace of the Fascist abomination.

Political and social liberation from these forces is already an accomplished fact, but the thinking of the great masses is still bedevilled by the fog of reactionary ideas which prevents them from seeing clearly. This difficulty and dangerous situation puts a heavy responsibility on the men of letters. But it is not enough for a writer to see clearly in matters political and social. To see clearly in matters of literature is no less indispensable and it is to the solution of these problems that this book hopes to bring its contribution.

15

Literary Fiction and Reality

FRANK KERMODE

Frank Kermode begins this chapter from *The Sense of an Ending* (1966) by using Robert Musil's narrative experimentation to demonstrate the modernist dilemma about the relationship of fiction and reality. Kermode states that the novel "is the central form of literary art" and that "its history is an attempt to evade the laws of what Scott called 'the land of fiction'—the stereotypes which ignore reality, and whose remoteness from it we identify as absurd." Strangely enough, as fiction has moved away from the "realistic" presentation of the nineteenth century, it has attempted more and more radically to represent how reality is perceived and experienced. And, Kermode adds, each new stage of experimentation creates laws of narration that must be broken by the next generation, just as, for Virginia Woolf, the Georgians broke the laws of the Edwardians. He believes that even if the novelist aspires "to live in reality unprotected by myth, [he] has to allow room for different versions of reality, including what some call mythical and some call absolute."

Kermode explores the conflict that modern writers face through an analysis of Jean Paul Sartre's *La Nausée*. He observes that despite his commitment to an existentialist reality, Sartre must engage in fictional creation because "it is by his fiction that we know he is free." Furthermore, writing a novel in itself is an act of fictionality because it puts the events described into an artificial form, or structure, that does not exist in the real world. No matter how one may attempt to write a contingent, open-ended, and incomplete work of fiction in order to mirror reality, the novel still comes to an end, even if it merely breaks off on the last page before the binding. Kermode concludes that in the very act of struggling against the forms and patterns of the "old" novel, the contemporary generation, like its predecessors, finds itself reimposing fictional structure on the formless reality it seeks to render. Kermode seems to be suggesting that the difference between novelists past and present has to do more with the fact that modern novelists seem not to believe in a universe that has form and purpose rather than because there are deficiencies in the contemporary novel as an artform.

Frank Kermode (b. 1919), one of the best known and most prolific contemporary critics, has published such works as *The Classic: Literary Images of Permanence and Change* (1975), *The Genesis of Secrecy: On the Interpretation of Narrative* (1979), *The Art of Telling: Essays on Fiction* (1983), and, most recently, *Forms of Attention* (1985).

A dissonance
in the valence of Uranium
led to the discovery

Dissonance
(if you're interested)
leads to discovery

—W. C. Williams, *Paterson* IV (On the Curies)

Towards the beginning of his novel *The Man Without Qualities*, Robert Musil announces that "no serious attempt will be made to . . . enter into competition with reality." And yet it is an element in the situation he cannot ignore. How good it would be, he suggests, if one could find in life the simplicity inherent in *narrative order*. "This is the simple order that consists in being able to say: 'When that had happened, then this happened.' What puts our mind at rest is the simple sequence, the overwhelming variegation of life now represented in, as a mathematician would say, a unidimensional order." We like the illusions of this sequence, its acceptable appearance of causality: "it has the look of necessity." But the look is illusory; Musil's hero Ulrich has "lost this elementary narrative ele-

"Literary Fiction and Reality" is reprinted from *The Sense of an Ending: Studies in the Theory of Fiction,* by Frank Kermode, by permission of Oxford University Press, Inc., copyright 1967.

ment" and so has Musil. *The Man Without Qualities* is multidimensional, fragmentary, without the possibility of a narrative end. Why could he not have his narrative order? Because "everything has now become non-narrative." The illusion would be too gross and absurd.

Musil belonged to the great epoch of experiment; after Joyce and Proust, though perhaps a long way after, he is the novelist of early modernism. And as you see he was prepared to spend most of his life struggling with the problems created by the divergence of comfortable story and the non-narrative contingencies of modern reality. Even in the earlier stories he concerned himself with this disagreeable but necessary dissociation; in his big novel he tries to create a new genre in which, by all manner of dazzling devices and metaphors and stratagems, fiction and reality can be brought together again. He fails; but the point is that he had to try, a sceptic to the point of mysticism and caught in a world in which, as one of his early characters notices, no curtain descends to conceal "the bleak matter-of-factness of things."

I have spoken in my earlier talks about the operation of clerical scepticism on other kinds of fiction, and you may have felt somewhat sceptical of *my* fictions; but now, when I have to speak of it as a factor in the changing condition of literary fiction, I see that all I shall be doing is to give a large emphasis to what is commonplace. In speaking of a continual attempt on the part of the clerisy to relate, by frequent alteration, an inherited paradigm to a changed sense of reality, we may strain the attention of hearers so long as we speak of physics or law or theology, but as soon as the subject is the novel the argument drops into a perfectly familiar context.

It happens that in our phase of civility, the novel is the central form of literary art. It lends itself to explanations borrowed from any intellectual system of the universe which seems at the time satisfactory. Its history is an attempt to evade the laws of what Scott called "the land of fiction"—the stereotypes which ignore reality, and whose remoteness from it we identify as absurd. From Cervantes forward it has been, when it has satisfied us, the poetry which is "capable," in the words of Ortega, "of coping with present reality." But it is a "realistic poetry" and its theme is, bluntly, "the collapse of the poetic" because it has to do with "the barbarous, brutal, mute, meaningless reality of things." It cannot work with the old hero, or with the old laws of the land of romance; moveover, such new laws and customs as it creates have themselves to be repeatedly broken under the demands of a changed and no less brutal reality. "Reality has such a violent temper that it does not tolerate the ideal even when reality itself is idealized." Nevertheless, the effort continues to be made. The extremest revolt against the customs or laws of fiction—the anti-novels of Fielding or Jane Austen or Flaubert or Natalie Sarraute—creates its new laws, in their turn to be broken. Even when there is a profession of complete narrative anarchy, as in some of the works I discussed last week, or in a poem such as *Paterson*, which rejects as spurious whatever most of us understand as form, it seems that time will always reveal some congruence with a paradigm—provided always that there is in the work that necessary element of the customary which enables it to communicate at all.

I shall not spend much time on matters so familiar to you. Whether, with Lukács, you think of the novel as peculiarly the resolution of the problem of the individual in an open society—or as relating to that problem in respect of an utterly contingent world; or express this in terms of the modern French theorists and call its progress a necessary and "unceasing movement from the known to the unknown"; or simply see the novel as resembling the other arts in that it cannot avoid creating new possibilities for its own future—however you put it, the history of the novel is the history of forms rejected or modified, by parody, manifesto, neglect, as absurd. Nowhere else, perhaps, are we so conscious of the dissidence between inherited forms and our own reality.

There is at present some good discussion of the issue not only in French but in English. Here I have in mind Iris Murdoch, a writer whose persistent and radical thinking about the form has not as yet been fully reflected in her own fiction. She contrasts what she calls "crystalline form" with narrative of the shapeless, quasi-documentary kind, rejecting the first as uncharacteristic of the novel because it does not contain free characters, and the second because it cannot satisfy that need of form which it is easier to assert than to describe; we are at least sure that it exists, and that it is not always illicit. Her argument is important and subtle, and this is not an attempt to restate it; it is enough to say that Miss Murdoch, as a novelist, finds much difficulty in resisting what she calls "the consolations of form" and in that degree damages the "opacity," as she calls it, of character. A novel has this (and more) in common with love, that it is, so to speak, delighted with its own inventions of character, but must respect their uniqueness and their freedom. It must do so without losing the formal qualities that make it a novel. But the truly imaginative novelist has an unshakable "respect for the contingent"; without it he sinks into fantasy, which is a way of deforming reality. "Since reality is incomplete, art must not be too afraid of incompleteness," says Miss Murdoch. We must not falsify it with patterns too neat, too inclusive; there must be dissonance. "Literature must always represent a battle between real people and images." Of course it must also have form; but as Mrs. Byatt says in her valuable book on Miss Murdoch, the novelist seems to feel some "metaphysical regret" about this.

Here, in a subtle philosophical novelist, is what I crudely call the dilemma of fiction and reality. When Miss Murdock herself succeeds in writing a novel which contains opaque, impenetrable persons in a form which nowhere betrays a collapse from the strict charities of the imagination into the indulgent mythologies of fantasy, we shall have more evidence that the history of the novel is a history of anti-novels.

This, one might add, is likely to be true, even when the good novelist makes no obviously revolutionary proposals. He might even reject the anti-novel as such, and yet possess the power to make constitutional changes so profound that no proclamation of reform could be more effective. There is, for example, Mrs. Spark; her reality is not the brutal chaos of which Ortega speaks, but a radically noncontingent reality to be dealt with in purely novelistic terms, and so related to novels that only a profound virtuosity is needed to make this apparent. In her new novel, which is a work of profound virtuosity, she not only makes these assumptions about the novel, but also considers anti-novels. After all, they exist; and with the panache she reserves for her most deeply serious statements, she includes a sample of one. It is a transcript of a dull day in the Eichmann trial, a day of pure contingency, and yet, under the pressure of the novel's higher reality, it becomes the "desperate heart" not only of the trial but of the book. The *nouveau roman*, with its deliberately limited, solipsistic realism, is given meaning by inclusion in a higher form. The relation of fiction and reality is uniquely reimagined. And thus the new, even if it restates the old, requires us to undergo the characteristic experience of serious modern fiction, a radical re-appraisal of this relation. In short, the novelist, though he may aspire—in the language of Tillich—to live in conditions of reality unprotected by myth, has to allow room for different versions of reality, including what some call mythical and some call absolute. Also we find that there is an irreducible minimum of geometry—of humanly needed shape or structure—which finally limits our ability to accept the mimesis of pure contingency.

But having stressed what Mrs. Spark has in common with other researchers into novelistic form, one needs also to point out a deep difference of mood. Those deep and delightful concordances assume or assert that the world itself is a land of fiction, a divine fiction which is the supreme fiction because absolutely if strangely true; and that contingencies, under the pressure of imagination, resolve themselves into beautiful, arbitrary, and totally satisfying images of this benign arrangement. Few, I suppose, will nowadays claim empirical knowledge of such concord. Mrs. Spark is certainly one who believes that form is a matter of *recherche*, as the French are always saying; but that having found it you have a right to be consoled by it, for the good reason that it is authentic, and reflects, however imperfectly, a universal plot, an enchanting order of beginning, middle, and end, concords so apt and unexpected that you laugh or weep when you stumble on them; peripeteias so vast and apparently uncontrolled that nothing in the literature of comedy or tragedy can do more than faintly image them. All, rightly seen, is riches, and sin is behovely; "all's well that ends well, still the fine's the crown." This is not, after all, quite the world of those who seek "the courage to be" and to strip reality of the protection of myth. We are all poor; but there is a difference between what Mrs. Spark intends by speaking of "slender means," and what Stevens called our poverty or Sartre our need, *besoin*. The poet finds his brief, fortuitous concords, it is true: not merely "what will suffice," but "the freshness of transformation," the "reality of decreation," the "gaiety of language." The novelist accepts need, the difficulty of relating one's fictions to what one knows about the nature of reality, as his *donnée*.

It is because no one has said more about this situation, or given such an idea of its complexity, that I want to devote most of this talk to Sartre and the most relevant of his novels, *La Nausée*. As things go now it isn't of course very modern; Robbe-Grillet treats it with amused reverence as a valuable antique. But it will still serve for my purposes. This book is doubtless very well known to you; I can't undertake to tell you much about it, especially as it has often been regarded as standing in an unusually close relation to a body of philosophy which I am incompetent to expound. Perhaps you will be charitable if I explain that I shall be using it and other works of Sartre merely as examples. What I have to do is simply to show that *La Nausée* represents, in the work of one extremely important and representative figure, a kind of crisis in the relation between fiction and reality, the tension or dissonance between paradigmatic form and contingent reality. That the mood of Sartre has sometimes been appropriate to the modern demythologized apocalypse is something I shall take for granted; his is a philosophy of crisis, but his world has no beginning and no end. The absurd dishonesty of all prefabricated patterns is cardinal to his beliefs; to cover reality over with eidetic images—illusions persisting from past acts of perception, as some abnormal children "see" the page or object that is no longer before them—to do this is to sink into *mauvaise foi*. This expression covers all comfortable denials of the undeniable—freedom—by myths of necessity, nature, or things as they are. Are all the paradigms of fiction eidetic? Is the unavoidable, insidious, comfortable enemy of all novelists *mauvaise foi*?

Sartre has recently, in his first instalment of autobiography, talked with extraordinary vivacity about the role-playing of his youth, of the falsities imposed upon him by the fictive power of words. At the beginning of the Great War he began a novel about a French private who captured the Kaiser, defeated him in single combat, and so ended the war and recovered Alsace. But everything went wrong. The Kaiser, hissed by the *poilus*, no match for the superbly fit Private Perrin, spat upon and insulted, became "somehow heroic." Worse still, the peace, which should instantly have followed in the real world if this fiction had a genuine correspondence with reality, failed to occur. "I very nearly renounced literature," says Sartre. Roquentin, in a subtler but basically similar situation, has the same reaction. Later, Sartre would find again that the hero, however assiduously you use the pitchfork, will recur, and that gaps, less gross perhaps, between fiction and reality will open in the most close-knit pattern of words. Again, the young Sartre would sometimes, when most identified with his friends at the *lycée*, feel himself to be "freed at last from the sin of existing"—this is also an expression of Roquentin's, but Roquentin says it feels like being a character in a novel.

How can novels, by telling lies, convert existence into being? We see Roquentin waver between the horror of contingency and the fiction of *aventures*. In *Les Mots* Sartre very engagingly tells us that he *was* Roquentin, certainly, but that he was Sartre also, "the elect, the chronicler of hells" to whom the whole novel of which he now speaks so derisively was a sort of *aventure*, though what was represented within it was "the unjustified, brackish existence of my fellow-creatures." All this is good fun, but it is only another way of talking about a problem which, in a different mood he saw to be serious, namely, the relation between fictions as we use them in our existential crises, and fictions as we construct them in books.

Novels, says Sartre, are not life, but they owe their power upon us, as upon himself as an infant, to the fact that they are somehow like life. In life, he once remarked, "all ways are barred and nevertheless we must act. So we try to change the world; that is, to live *as if* the relations between things and their potentialities were governed not by deterministic processes but by magic." The *as if* of the novel consists in a similar negation of determinism, the establishment of an accepted freedom by magic. We make up *aventures*, invent and ascribe the significance of temporal concords to those "privileged moments" to which we alone award their prestige, make our own human clocks tick in a clockless world. And we take a man who is by definition *de trop*, and create a context in which he isn't.

The novel is a lie only as our quotidian inventions are lies. The power which goes to its making—the imagination—is a function of man's inescapable freedom. This freedom, in Mary Warnock's words, "expresses itself in his ability to see things which are *not*." It is by his fiction that we know he is free. It is not surprising that Sartre as ontologist, having to describe many kinds of fictive behaviour, invents stories to do so, thus moving into a middle ground between life and novel. The stories in *L'Etre et le néant* of the girl with her seducer, the waiter who plays the role of waiter, are inventions exemplary of *mauvaise foi;* only in their being related by an explicit philosophical argument, and in their not being related by anything that could be called a plot, do they differ from the story of the lighthouse, or of the sick café proprietor, in *La Nausée*. But of course this single difference is a very great one, and we need to be as clear as possible about it. In a word, it is literary form, something quite different from the form of philosophical discourse. For example, Sartre admired *L'Etranger* because it did not contain a single superfluous episode or image; suppose your novel is about a man as necessarily *de trop*, it must make him and itself the very reverse of that.

This is one reason why *La Nausée* is so challenging. One of the criteria in which we habitually judge novels is that by which Sartre judged Camus's book—by its transfiguration, as it were, of the contingent. But Sartre's novel needs to give very full representation to the horror of contingency; to say, in Miss Murdoch's word, that Sartre "respects" it gives a very pale notion of the role of contingency as antagonist in *La Nausée*. And deep in the imagery of the book there is a radical representation of this war between what is *de trop* and what must not be *de trop*. Contingency is nauseous and viscous; it has been suggested that the figure is ultimately sexual. This is unformed matter, *materia, matrix*; Roquentin's is ultimately the form-giving male role. He experiences reality in all its contingency, without benefit of human fiction; he resolves to make a fiction. Between his experience and his fiction lies Sartre's book. In so far as it gives structure and form to the metaphysical beliefs expressed in the treatise, it both represents and belies them. Sartre noted of Maurice Blanchot's work that a metaphysic looks different in and out of the water of a novel, and in his own case he cannot avoid this; the novel itself has a hand in the game, and may insist on meanings and relations which the treatise denies or confutes. This is what form does; somewhere along the line it will join what Sartre calls "bad faith." There may be an irony in Roquentin's decision to attempt a novel "beautiful and hard as steel" but is a way of talking about Sartre's own attempt to include contingency in a form which is, in so far as it succeeds, the destroyer of contingency. The novel has, for all that may be said in theory against such a possibility, "*a priori* limitations."

That this is so, and that Sartre's novel demonstrates it, we can see by looking at some of the doctrine that seems in some degree falsified by its appearance in novel form. Take, for example, Sartre's pronouncements on the past—how would they show in a novel? Existentialist man, who has total responsibility for his actions, has no relevant past. He is in a world which he not only never made, but which was never made at all. His world is a chaos without potentiality, and he himself is purely potential nothingness; in the world "all is act"; potentiality is purely human. To see the thing *pour soi*, as Roquentin does in the park, is to be nauseously aware that "all is fullness": *mes yeux ne rencontraient jamais que du plein*. When the tree shuddered in the wind, the shudder was not "a passing from potency to act; it was a thing." But the world a novel makes (and *La Nausée* makes) is unlike the world of our common experience because it is created and because it has the potency of a humanly imaginative creation. For Aristotle the literary plot was analogous to the plot of the world in that both were eductions from the potency of matter. Sartre denies this for the world, and specifically denies, in the passage just referred to, that without potentiality there is no change. He reverts to the Megaric view of the matter, which Aristotle took such trouble to correct. But this is not our affair. The fact is that even if you believe in a Megaric world there is no such thing as a Megaric novel; not even *Paterson*. Change without potentiality in a novel is impossible, quite simply; though it is the hopeless aim of the cut-out writers, and the card-shuffle writers. A novel which really implemented this policy would properly be a chaos. No novel can avoid being in some sense what Aristotle calls "a completed action." This being so, all novels imitate a world of potentiality, even if this implies a philosophy disclaimed by their authors. They have a fixation on the eidetic imagery of beginning, middle, and end, potency and cause.

Novels, then, have beginnings, ends, and potentiality, even if the world has not. In the same way it can be said that whereas there may be, in the world, no such thing as character, since a man is what he does and chooses freely what he does—and in so far as he claims that his acts are determined by psychological or other predisposition he is a fraud, *lâche*, or *salaud*—in the novel there can be no just representation of this, for if the man were entirely free he might simply walk out of the story, and if he had no character we should not recognize him. This is true in spite of the claims of the doctrinaire *nouveau roman* school to have abolished character. And Sartre himself has a powerful commitment to it, though he could not accept the Aristotelian position that it is through character that plot is actualized. In short, novels have characters, even if the world has not.

What about time? It is, effectively, a human creation, according to

Sartre, and he likes novels because they concern themselves only with human time, a faring forward irreversibly into a virgin future from ecstasy to ecstasy, in his world, from *kairos* to *kairos* in mine. The future is a fluid medium in which I try to actualize my potency, though the end is unattainable; the present is simply the *pour-soi*, "human consciousness in its flight out of the past into the future." The past is bundled into the *en-soi*, and has no relevance. "What I was is not the foundation of what I am, any more than what I am is the foundation of what I shall be." Now this is not novel-time. The faring forward is all right, and fits the old desire to know what happens next; but the denial of all causal relation between disparate *kairoi*, which is after all basic to Sartre's treatment of time, makes form impossible, and it would never occur to us that a book written to such a recipe, a set of discontinuous epiphanies, should be called a novel. Perhaps we could not even read it thus: the making of a novel is partly the achievement of readers as well as writers, and readers would constantly attempt to supply the very connections that the writer's programme suppresses. In all these ways, then, the novel falsifies the philosophy.

In Simone de Beauvoir's autobiography there is an account of her telling Ramon Fernandez and Adamov about the novel she is working on, *L'Invitée*. She claims that it is "a real novel, with a beginning, a middle, and an end." And real novels do have these. A truly Sartrean novel would be nothing but a discontinuous unorganized middle. And it would be entirely undetermined. But in practice it cannot be so. "I provided Marcel with a wife," says Mlle de Beauvoir, "whom I used as a foil." Similarly Sartre, in his trilogy (*Les Chemins de la liberté*), determines many things, for instance, that Lola shall possess the money Matthieu needs for Marcelle's abortion. Here is a piece of virtually nineteenth-century plotting. There is nothing quite so crude in *La Nausée*, but it has its necessary share of contrivance or "faking."

The novel, then, provides a reduction of the world different from that of the treatise. It has to lie. Words, thoughts, patterns of word and thought, are enemies of truth, if you identify that with what may be had by phenomenological reductions. Sartre was always, as he explains in his autobiography, aware of their being at variance with reality. One remembers the comic account of this antipathy in Iris Murdoch's *Under the Net*, one of the few truly philosophical novels in English; truth would be found only in a silent poem or a silent novel. As soon as it speaks, begins to be a novel, it imposes causality and concordance, development, character, a past which matters and a future within certain broad limits determined by the project of the author rather than that of the characters. They have their choices, but the novel has its end.[1]

It sounds good to say that the novelist is free; that, like the young man who asked Sartre whether he should join the Resistance or stay with his mother, he can be told "You are free, therefore choose; that is to say, invent." We may even agree that until he has chosen he will not know the reasons for his choice. But there is in practice this difference between the novelist and the young man as Sartre sees him: the young man will always be free in just this degree; whether he stays with his mother or not, his decision will not be relevant to his next decision. But the novelist is not like that; he is more Thomist than Sartrean, and every choice will limit the next. He has to collaborate with his novel; he grows in bad faith. He is a world in which past, present, and future are related inextricably.

That Sartre is not unaware of this difficulty we can, I think, gather from some of the things he has said about novels. The attack on Mauriac, and on the novels of the past, is founded upon a conviction that they are dishonestly determinate. The characters in a Christian novel, he says, ought surely to be "centres of indeterminacy" and not the slaves of some fake omniscience. It is by the negation of such formalism that we may make literature a liberating force. "There is nothing else to spiritualize, nothing else to renew, but this multi-coloured and concrete world with its weight, its opacity, its zones of generalization, and its swarms of anecdotes." A novel which tackles these qualities will have no eidetic form, no concordance suggesting false absolutes. Those that have, Mauriac's, for instance, are manipulated, belong to an obsolete world-style, replace reality by myth. But when Sartre comes upon L'Etranger, its discontinuous present "eliminating all the significant links which are also part of the experience," he says that it is not a novel because, among other things, it lacks "development"; though he admires it for its economy of organization. Yet "development" surely implies continuity and a mimesis of the actualization of potency; and organization is form. He has later attacked the nouveau roman, which offers, one would have thought, a view of reality congenial to him, on the ground that it is formalistic. It is very difficult to sort this out, but it seems clear enough that what is not taken into account is the novel itself, the collaborator from which neither writer nor reader can free himself, the source of all the falsifying eidetic images.

Let me give one more example of the pressure of these eidetic images, by saying a word about the hero. Robbe-Grillet complains that Sartre failed to do what he intended in *La Nausée:* he names but does not characterize contingency, and is classically connected and chronological; and he lets Roquentin become a kind of hero. Now the images of tragedy and the hero surely do brood over existentialist thought in general; it has been said that the existentialist choice is an adaptation of Christian eschatology, and we should add to that category the eschatological type of the hero. This is why Kott can speak of transferring tragedy and its heroes into the mode of absurdity; accepting his anguish in freedom, the existentialist man repeats the gestures of the tragic hero in a context which is not tragic but absurd. In the novel of Camus, for example, Meursault—the man who "without any heroics, accepts to die for the truth" as the author puts it—is a gratuitous murderer and not a gratuitous victim; but in many ways he is clearly and literally an Antichrist, with the tradition of Christian heroism rendered absurd in him; we might say the careful meaninglessness of his life is exactly antithetical to the fullness of the concordances found in the life of Jesus. Sartre gives to his anti-hero, in the anguish of freedom, a burden of responsibility which looks absurd in the monstrous world of contingency, but is precisely the burden that we recognize in other literature as tragic: "when a man commits himself to anything, fully realizing that he is not only choosing what he will be, but is thereby at the same time a legislator deciding for the whole of mankind—in such a moment he cannot escape from the sense of profound and complete responsibility." This is the hero in a world where existence precedes essence, and where, "in the present, one is foresaken." And as Sartre himself clearly sees, to think of a man thus is to think of him as the hero of a novel. If you put such a man in a novel he will in some irreducible measure be shadowed by the eidetic image of the Hero. Like the Kaiser, beaten up by the superbly fit Private Perrin, he becomes *somehow* heroic.

I hope I have now made it clear why I thought it best, in speaking of the dissonances between fiction and reality in our own time, to concentrate on Sartre. His hesitations, retractions, inconsistencies, all proceed from his consciousness of the problems: how do novelistic differ from existential fictions? How far is it inevitable that a novel give a novel-shaped account of the world? How can one control, and how make profitable, the dissonances between that account and the account given by the mind working independently of the novel?

For Sartre it was ultimately, like most or all problems, one of freedom. For Miss Murdoch it is a problem of love, the power by which we apprehend the opacity of persons to the degree that we will not limit them by forcing them into selfish patterns. Both of them are talking, when they speak of freedom and love, about the imagination. The imagination, we recall, is a form-giving power, an esemplastic power; it may require, to use Simone Weil's words, to be preceded by a "decreative" act, but it is certainly a maker of orders and concords. We apply it to all forces which satisfy the variety of human needs that are met by apparently gratuitous forms. These forms console; if they mitigate our existential anguish it is because we weakly collaborate with them, as we collaborate with language in order to communicate. Whether or no we are predisposed towards acceptance of them, we learn them as we learn a language. On one view they are "the heroic children whom time breeds / Against the first idea," but on another they destroy by falsehood the heroic anguish of our present loneliness. If they appear in shapes preposterously false we will reject them; but they change with us, and every act of reading or writing a novel is a tacit acceptance of them. If they ruin our innocence, we have to remember that the innocent eye sees nothing. If they make us guilty, they enable us, in a manner nothing else can duplicate, to submit, as we must, the show of things to the desires of the mind.

I shall end by saying a little more about La Nausée, the book I chose because, although it is a novel, it reflects a philosophy it must, in so far as it possesses novel form, belie. Under one aspect it is what Philip Thody calls "an extensive illustration" of the world's contingency and the absurdity of the human situation. Mr. Thody adds that it is the novelist's task to "overcome contingency"; so that if the illustration were too extensive the novel would be a bad one. Sartre himself provides a more inclusive formula when he says that "the final aim of art is to reclaim the world by revealing it as it is, but as if it had its source in human liberty." This statement does two things. First, it links the fictions of art with those of living and choosing. Secondly, it means that the humanizing of the world's contingency cannot be achieved without a representation of that contingency. This representation must be such that it induces the proper sense of horror at the utter difference, the utter shapelessness, and the utter inhumanity of what must be humanized. And it has to occur simultaneously with the *as if*, the act of form, of humanization, which assuages the horror.

This recognition, that form must not regress into myth, and that contingency must be formalized, makes *La Nausée* something of a model of the conflicts in the modern theory of the novel. How to do justice to a chaotic, viscously contingent reality, and yet redeem it? How to justify the fictive beginnings, crises, ends; the atavism of character, which we cannot prevent from growing, in Yeats's figure, like ash on a burning stick? The novel will end; a full close may be avoided, but there will be a close: a fake fullstop, an "exhaustion of aspects," as Ford calls it, an ironic return to the origin, as in *Finnegans Wake* and *Comment c'est*. Perhaps the book will end by saying that it has provided the clues for another, in which contingency will be defeated, the novel Marcel can write after the experience described in *Le Temps retrouvé*, or Roquentin at the end of *La Nausée*.

But Roquentin's book is only a part of Sartre's book; if there is here a true novel, an agent of human freedom, it must be Sartre's, not Roquentin's, which we shall never be able to read. And evidently Sartre knew about the fallacy of imitative form: his book, though it surrounds the hero with images of formlessness, inhumanity, nausea, must not itself be formless or viscous or inhuman, any more than it may repeat the formal presumptuousness of the nineteenth-century novel or the arrogant omniscience of Mauriac. It works somewhere between these extremes; in the homely figure of George Eliot, it is the candle that makes a pattern of the random scratches on the looking-glass. This pattern is so humanly important that, humanly speaking, contingency is merely its material; Robbe-Grillet, thinking of this, remembers Mallarmé's remark that the world exists *pour aboutir à un livre*. And yet the contingency must be there, or our *as if* will be mere fantasy and unrelated to the basic human task of imaginative self-invention.

Sartre began *La Nausée* as an episodic work, and Roquentin's practices reflect this; but the need for structure grew imperious; it is not enough to write *comme les petites filles*. Something begins that must have a consonant end: *quelque chose commence pour finir*. There will be order. The first title of the book was *Melancholia*, after the Dürer engraving. Melancholy is not only an illness; she is also the patroness of creativity. Alone and desperate among all those discrete objects—plane and sphere, knife, goat, balance, irregular solid—she will discover an order. This discovery follows the experience of contingency; and it can never be achieved without imagination, simply by raking among the ashes of the *en-soi*, the dump of the past. That is why Roquentin, when we first encounter him, is a historian. He practises the study of that from which art enables us to escape. We observe his mounting disgust, and finally he rejects M. Rollebon. The association of this historical worthy with the loathsomeness of contingency is inexplicit, achieved by one of those counterfeitings which are the logic of novels, in which collocation represents more than contingency. "M. de Rollebon m'assomme. Je me lève. Je remue dans cette lumière pâle; je la vois changer sur mes mains et sur la manche de ma veste: je ne peux pas assez dire comme elle me dégoûte." "M. de Rollebon bores me. I get up. I move through this pale light; I see it change on my hands and on the sleeve of my coat: I cannot begin to say how much it disgusts me." How then is he to contain, to transfigure reality? Not by the pathetic mechanical method of the Autodidact, whose alphabetical assimilation of knowledge simply grinds the meaningless ash of contingency even finer; not by the fictions of the *salauds* as he sees them in the art gallery, or of the doctor, who uses conventions as a protection against the anguish of his own freedom. It has to be done by a fiction which is not fraudulent.

Such a fiction is the song, "Some of these days." This frail piece is human, creates a human duration, destroys the disorder and the dead time of the world. It contains nothing that is merely a happening; its moments, such as they are, are *aventures*. This is what is needed. There are other hints of the same transfiguration: a card-game has its *aventures*, a life may be looked upon as having them, and indeed as having a structure of them, so that it comes to resemble a novel. . . . But when Roquentin experiences the metaphysical hangover that comes from indulgence in such thoughts, he tells himself to "beware of literature." The *as if* of the novel is not so easily to be applied to life. In life there are no beginnings, those "fanfares of trumpets" which imply structures "whose outlines are lost in the mist." In a novel the beginning implies the end: if you seem to begin at the beginning, "It was a fine evening in 1922. I was a notary's clerk in Marommes," you are in fact beginning at the end; all that seems fortuitous and contingent in what follows is in fact reserved for a later benefaction of significance in some concordant structure. This, Roquentin reminds himself, and the young Sartre had reminded himself, distinguishes novels from life, and represents the danger of arguments which confound the two. By a very imaginative piece of faking, Sartre obliquely illustrates the point in the passage where an "actual" conversation in a restaurant is counterpointed against a conversation in *Eugénie Grandet*. They belong to different orders of life and time. So, too, when Roquentin on his Sunday walk feels that for once here is *aventure*, what he says is that this gives him a sense of being which is proper not to life but to art: "Il arrive que je suis moi et que je suis ici . . . je suis heureux comme un héros de roman." Faced with a perfectly ordinary choice of life, the sense of living in a novel at once deserts him. But of course he *is* living in a novel. Thus does Sartre hold together the contingent and the structure of "adventures" in a dissonance that leads to discovery.

The faking by which this is done—I use E. M. Forster's word, which means something beneficent—is not the faking of the cowards and the *salauds*. A French critic would here think of Gide rather than Forster, and Claude-Edmonde Magny distinguishes between "cheating"—which is what the artist does—and "counterfeit cheating" the cheating in bad faith of the *salauds*. The novelist cheats by arranging collocations which, since he is meeting us in a context which we both understand as we might understand the nature and the rules of a game, we shall not regard as fortuitous, in which we shall discover point and rhythm. *La Nausée*, like any other novel, has a great many such contrivances. Finding, like Roquentin, that the root of the tree is "beneath all explanation," we invent, because we are free, what has the qualities to satisfy the desires of the mind: a circle, says Roquentin, but he might have said a novel. There are no circles in reality, and no novels. When Anny gave Roquentin the kiss which sealed a relationship, she was sitting in a patch of nettles. If life were "like a work of art" this would not occur; the interesting thing about *La Nausée* as an enquiry into novel-form is, of course, that the nettles are there. If the world of words is to have value, if it is to be distinguished from the protective fictions of the *salauds* and the nineteenth-century novelists, the nettles must be there.

Why, then, choose, as the leading instance of the satisfactions of art, the song "Some of these days"? This, of course, is another piece of faking. The song is a minimal work of art, the tiniest conceivable check to contingency. In its three-minute compass the authors made themselves like heroes of a novel, says Roquentin: "they washed themselves of the sin of existing." They created artificial beginning and end, a duration minute but human in which all, between those points, is ordered, and so in a fiction challenges and negates the pure being of the world. If existentialism is a humanism, so is this song, and so is the novel. Fredric Jameson shows us that *La Nausée* is full of fake beginnings and endings; individual sentences are apocalyptically charged by fictive ends; and as the narrative develops the final end begins to exert a gravitational pull over the adventures and the non-adventures which are thus given the status of adventures, and so finally distinguish the work from a non-human nature. Finally there is no "facticity," the novel is non-contingent. Otherwise it would be a babble of unforeshortened dialogue, a random stubbing of cigarettes, a collection of events without concordance. Unlike works which belong wholly to the land of fiction, *La Nausée* represents a world of which this might be said. Its form has elements of the eidetic, but upon such images are superimposed new images of contingency. Thus the inherited form is made, for a time at any rate, acceptable to those whose life behind the screen of words has not entirely closed their eyes to the nature of the world. The form of *La Nausée* is an instructive dissonance between humanity and contingency; it discovers a new way of establishing a concord between the human mind and things as they are.

When I say that this is characteristic of modern fiction I do not of course mean that the association of consciousness with nothingness, and of being with a random and agitated meaninglessness, a disgusting evil paste, is a necessary intellectual position. What is radically characteristic in Sartre's general position is his treatment of fiction as deeply distrusted and yet humanly indispensable. In the novel, where there is an inescapable element of the counterfeit, and an inescapable inheritance of eidetic images, this mistrust of the indispensable produces that continuous *recherche* of which the new theorists speak; the *recherche* itself is not new; though it has been speeded up it is a permanent feature of the genre, which has always been threatened on one side from the need to mime contingency and from the other by the power of form to console. In short, the pressures which require its constant alteration are anguish and bad faith. As to the latter, it proceeds from an uncritical or cowardly adherence to the paradigms. Yet they cannot be dispensed with; and what may seem the necessary impurity of the result is refined by further research. How can we, in a necessarily impure medium, wash ourselves of the sin of existing? Hence the rigour of the theorists, hence novels in which the reader is the only character, and the time so precisely his time that the duration of the book is measured by the time he takes to read it, as the duration of the film *Marienbad* is the ninety minutes passed in watching it.

Extreme rigour could, I suppose, destroy the paradigms and so destroy the novel. I admit that of all the claims made by Robbe-Grillet the most baffling, to me, is that in this new realism the ordinary reader can at last find himself. He repeats this claim in a recent interview printed in *Le Monde* (7–13 October, 1965). "My intention is to make a popular cinema and a popular literature. . . . I've rediscovered in me the entire arsenal of the popular imagination." "Hum!" says the interviewer. I myself find the tone of Sartre's novel to be deeper than that of the books which are in some sense its progeny, if only because he understood that even when the *donnée* is that nothing is given, still not everything can be new. His hero, his beginning and end, his concords, are not in this sense new; they grow in the shadow of earlier beginnings, ends and concords, earlier heroes; had there been no novels in the world to condemn, *La Nausée* could not have been thought of, and it may be that *L'Etre et le néant* could not have been thought of, either.

La Nausée, as I say, has its progeny. The research has gone on. Michel Butor, for example, says that the novel is "developing within itself those elements which will show how it is related to the rest of reality, and how it illuminates reality; the novelist is beginning to know what he is doing, and the novel to say what it is." This again seems very characteristic of the stage of "research" we have reached, the use of fictions for the exploration of fiction. As to reality, this neo-realist (a term which is puzzling, when you think that it is applied not only to Butor but to C. P. Snow) takes nothing for granted. "Never," says Mr. Peter Brooks, "never has the novel been so thoroughly about itself, yet never has it been so engaged with reality." This is probably excessive; it is a way of calling *L'Emploi du temps* the great modern novel. I should not claim this even for *La Nausée;* but both will be among the books our successors will examine when they consider how little, or perhaps how much, we were, in our day, muddled about the question of what, in our crisis, we could take on trust from the past; and how, being so morbidly aware of the nature and motive of our mendacity, we understood the relations between fiction and reality.

Note

1 There is a remarkable passage in Ortega y Gasset's London essay "History as a System" (in *Philosophy and History*, ed. Klibansky and Paton, 1936) which very clearly states the issues more notoriously formulated by Sartre. Ortega is discussing man's duty to make himself. "I invent projects of being and doing in the light of circumstance. This alone I come upon, this alone is given me: circumstance. It is too often forgotten that man is impossible without imagination, without the capacity to invent for himself a conception of life, to 'ideate' the character he is going to be. Whether he be original or a plagiarist, man is the novelist of himself. . . . Among . . . possibilities I must choose. Hence, I am free. But, be it well understood, I am free *by compulsion*, whether I wish to be or not. . . . To be free means to be lacking in constitutive identity, not to have subscribed to a determined being, to be able to be other than what one was . . ." This "constitutive instability" is the human property lacking in the novels condemned by Sartre and Murdoch. Ortega differs from Sartre on the use of the past; but when he says that his free man is, willy-nilly, "a second-hand God," creating his own entity, he is very close to Sartre, who says that to be is to be like the hero in a novel. In one instance the eidetic image is of God, in the other of the Hero.

16

Plot in the Modern Novel

J. ARTHUR HONEYWELL

Beginning with a discussion of R. S. Crane's definition of plot, J. Arthur Honeywell develops an analysis of plot in the modern novel by contrasting it with the standard structure of eighteenth- and nineteenth-century British fiction. In particular, Honeywell stresses the changing treatment of temporal progression. In order to have a coherent structure, a novel must contain a "temporal progression" that meets three criteria: one, "it must have a definite beginning and a definite ending"; two, it "must somehow be sequential, that is, each event must arise out of preceding events and give rise to succeeding events"; three, "the events which make up the progression must all be somehow related in the more general sense of all belonging to the same 'world' or the same 'vision of reality.'" Although each condition must be present to ensure coherence, novelists usually emphasize one of the three, with the result that we can "distinguish three distinct kinds of plot."

Honeywell argues that eighteenth-century authors tended to organize their plots around "definite beginnings and endings," while in the nineteenth century, "novelists began to subordinate the problem of beginnings and endings to the problem of constructing a logical sequence of events, a sequence in which no event occurred without a reason or cause." In such novels attention shifts from the resolution of events to the forces and laws that govern situations and the "necessary" or logical outcome of such situations; but with the rise of modernism the focus shifts again. Twentieth-century plots are organized around a progression not so much through time as from "appearance" to "reality." Honeywell explains the initial difficulty we have in reading many modern novels by arguing that for authors "to construct plots which achieve a temporal synthesis by means of a movement from appearance to reality they must start by plunging the reader into the appearances . . . and let him discover for himself as he reads the structures of reality which gradually emerge."

J. Arthur Honeywell (b. 1928) is professor of philosophy at Skidmore College. In addition to "Plot in the Modern Novel" (1968), he has published essays on literature, poetics, ethics, and philosophy in such journals as *Ethics, New Scholasticism,* and the *Journal of Aesthetics and Art Criticism.*

Perhaps the clearest way to give a general indication of the nature of plot in the modern novel is to start by discussing briefly the concept of plot itself. In "The Concept of Plot and the Plot of *Tom Jones,*" one of the few recent attempts to develop the idea of plot as a central critical concept, R. S. Crane gives a short history of the term and then defines plot as "the particular temporal synthesis effected by the writer of the elements of action, character, and thought that constitute the matter of his invention."[1] This definition can serve as a starting point, since a brief analysis of the notion of plot as the temporal synthesis of the materials of the novel will reveal some of the possibilities of plot development and, by contrast with the other possibilities, how plot operates in many modern novels.

If plot is thought of as a temporal synthesis, then obviously it has two central characteristics. First, it operates as an organizing and unifying principle. It provides the synthesis which insures that the materials of a novel are experienced as all cohering into one unified object—the novel itself in its wholeness. Secondly, it operates in time. Since the experience of reading a novel is a temporal process and since the plot is the organization of this temporal process, the plot of a novel inevitably has the quality of developing in time. This raises the question of how temporal syntheses can be achieved.

For any temporal progression to be experienced as a significant and organized whole, three requirements must in some way be met. First,

"Plot in the Modern Novel," by J. Arthur Honeywell, originally appeared in *Critical Approaches to Fiction,* ed. Shiv Kumar and Keith McKean. Reprinted with permission of McGraw-Hill Book Co., copyright 1968.

it must have a definite beginning and a definite ending. Otherwise, the progression cannot be distinguished from what went before and what comes after and so cannot be either conceived or experienced as a single thing. Secondly, the progression must somehow be sequential, that is, each event must arise out of preceding events and give rise to succeeding events. If this is not accomplished, then the result is a mixture of progressions rather than a single temporal progression. Thirdly, the events which make up the progression must all be somehow related in the more general sense of all belonging to the same "world" or the same "vision of reality." That is, there must be a general context which encompasses both the beginning and ending and the sequence of events and gives to them their significance. Otherwise there is no possibility of conceiving of or experiencing the events as parts of a coherent whole; they would be merely fortuitous results of random causal interactions having no meaningful interrelations. Although each of these requirements must somehow be met in any novel (or, in special cases where unusual effects are desired, must be deliberately neglected), it is usually the case that novelists place their emphasis on one of the three and subordinate the other two. As a result, it is possible to distinguish three distinct kinds of plot.

Novelists of the eighteenth century tended to construct their plots around definite beginnings and endings. The temporal progression of their novels was a movement from a natural starting point to a definitive ending—an ending of the "happy ever after" variety if the novel had a comic structure. The synthesis was that provided by a single action which moved, usually by way of reversals and discoveries, from a natural beginning point to a natural ending. This is the kind of plot which Aristotle analyzes in the *Poetics* and with which Professor Crane is concerned in his analysis of the plot of *Tom Jones*. One of the problems of constructing a plot of this kind is that of achieving the sense of finality which the ending requires, and eighteenth-century novelists tended to solve this problem with some variation of "poetic justice." The action is brought to a stage in which the good characters, after a period of difficulties, achieve on a permanent basis the conditions which insure their happiness and the bad characters are placed in conditions which insure their suffering. The major distinction which results is that between tragic and comic plots, although many variations of these two modes are possible. When the final and permanent happiness of the central characters is of a worldly sort, as in *Tom Jones* and *Humphry Clinker*, the action forms a comic plot. When the final and permanent happiness of the central character is of an other-worldly variety and is the result of worldly misfortune and death, as in *Clarissa*, the action forms a tragic plot. It follows also that plots of this kind require a certain kind of characterization. Most important, the central agents must be clearly characterized as virtuous, and thus deserving of happiness, or evil, and thus deserving of suffering. Only when this is done can the ending be constructed to provide that sense of justness which makes it definitive and final. Thus Fielding, Richardson, and Smollett all take pains to construct characters who are either virtuous or evil and to make the distinctions clear to their readers.

Early in the nineteenth century, most clearly with the novels of Sir Walter Scott, the fashion began to change. Novelists began to subordinate the problem of beginnings and endings to the problem of constructing a logical sequence of events, a sequence in which no event occurred without a reason or cause. The temporal progression of their novels tended to become a clearly articulated causal sequence from one state of affairs to another—in its more extreme form a "slice of life" in which both beginning and ending were arbitrary. The synthesis was achieved by establishing a single causal sequence in which each event is shown to be an effect of previous causes and the cause of subsequent effects. No longer are endings distinguished by their finality: rather they tend to become open-ended or at least ambiguous in terms of justice. Characteristic endings of this sort are those of *The Red and the Black, Crime and Punishment, Madame Bovary, The Return of the Native,* and *The Ambassadors.* The central problem of constructing plots of this sort is that of achieving the sense of causal or rational sequence which provides the organization of the events, and novelists tended to solve this problem by placing a specific type of character in a specific set of conditions and then letting the logic of the situation work itself out to its rational conclusion. What is important is not the ending but the insight into the operation of the causal laws and influences which condition human affairs. The major distinction which results is that between the realistic novel and the romance. When the set of conditions established is patterned on the details of ordinary life and the characters are presented as being for the most part passively influenced by these conditions, the novel tends toward the realistic or naturalistic mode. When, on the other hand, the set of conditions established includes the supernatural or at least the abnormal and the characters are presented as being active in manipulating or responding to these conditions, then the novel tends toward the mode of romance. The requirements of characterization also change. Central characters no longer have to be clearly virtuous or the reverse, but they do have to have clearly defined motives based on clearly defined passions and modes of behavior. Only with such characters can the causal sequence be made explicit. Characters such as Julian Sorel, Raskolnikov, Emma Bovary, Becky Sharp, Eustacia Vye, and Strether, although none are unambiguously virtuous or evil, are all constructed around passions and rules of action which bring them into conflict with the conditions surrounding them. The causal sequence is such that an ending of the final, "happy ever after" variety is inconceivable for any of the characters mentioned. Even death does not achieve the sense of finality and justness which Richardson manages in *Clarissa*, mainly because the conditions which make the death a logical conclusion are presented as still operating, whereas in *Clarissa* Richardson both eliminates the conditions which cause Clarissa's death and makes it clear that Clarissa achieves the supreme happiness of eternal bliss.

During the first two decades of the present century the fashion in plot development began changing again. Novelists lost interest in constructing logical or rational sequences and turned to the third possibility, that of structuring the events of the novel so as to present a coherent "world" or vision of reality. When the reader starts a novel like *Ulysses*, he is immediately confronted with a great variety of what appear to be incongruous, contradictory, and inconsequential facts. As he reads structural relations begin to emerge which tie the various facts together and give them significance. By the time he has finished, if not the first then the second or third reading, these structural relations are so firmly established that most of the facts have acquired significance and even the incongruities and contradictions can be seen to have meaning, to be a part of the reality of the world of the novel. The temporal progression of plots of this kind can then be described as a movement from appearance—the maze of apparently unrelated facts—to reality—the structural relations which, when apprehended, give significance and meaning to the facts. The synthesis is that established by the structural relations which emerge as the novel progresses and which are firmly established as the "reality" of the world of the novel by the time the novel ends.

An early example of this kind of plot is that of *The Good Soldier* by Ford Madox Ford. The novel begins with Dowell, the narrator, looking back at events of his past life which in his naiveté he has totally misunderstood. He has seen only the appearance of these events and has been blind to their real significance. The progression of the novel is that of Dowell's attempt to make sense of these past events. He fits together apparently unrelated facts, resolves apparent contradictions, gains insight into the motivation of the people involved, changes his evaluations of people and events, so that by the end of the novel he has a better insight into the realities of these past events than any of the other characters involved and has himself changed from being naive to being realistic. The reader, following Dowell's train of thought throughout the novel, moves in a similar way from the superficial appearances of the facts to an understanding of the realities of the situation and so of the real significance of the facts.

It should be stated at once that the fact that modern novelists tend to share basic assumptions about the construction of plots does not preclude a great diversity in the application of those assumptions. Like the novelists of the eighteenth and nineteenth centuries, they have achieved a wide variety of plot development within the limits of their shared assumptions. The central problem of constructing modern plots is that of establishing the structural relations which give coherence and significance to the at first apparently unrelated facts and which thus express a specific view of reality. But the patterns which emerge as structures of reality can take many forms. They can be universal patterns or archetypes which are presented as structuring the affairs of men at all times and places. Such archetypes are present in *Ulysses* (as the title itself suggests), *Finnegans Wake*, many of the novels of Thomas Mann, and other novels based upon mythical patterns. They can be social and institutional patterns which make sense of otherwise incongruous and inexplicable events. In *Absalom, Absalom!*, for example, the facts of the Sutpen story become significant and intelligible only as the social patterns of the South emerge during the course of the novel. In *The Good Soldier*, it is the sense of the social realities of Edwardian England which emerges as the facts of Dowell's story become intelligible. Or the structure of reality can be found in the subtle nuances and feelings, often incongruous and without rationale, which pervade even an ordinary mind on an ordinary day. The novels of Virginia Woolf and Nathalie Sarraute explore patterns of this kind. When the mind becomes less ordinary, such nuances become the feeling of nausea in the presence of existence explored by Sartre or the ironies and paradoxes of the life of the imagination explored by Nabokov in *Pale Fire.* The structure of reality, finally, can be found in underlying psychological patterns basic to the nature of men. The novels of D. H. Lawrence explore the degradations and victories of the psyche as it struggles to realize its true nature, while Lawrence Durrell's *Alexandria Quartet* makes use of the psychological complexities and patterns taken by love in modern society. Even this short list gives some indication of the diversity of structures which can be found to give coherence and significance to the "facts" of the human condition.

Since the time of Aristotle, the concept of plot has been associated with the concepts of discovery and reversal. There are discoveries and reversals in the better modern plots, but their nature is different from those used in the plots of earlier centuries. In eighteenth-century plots, formed as they were around a unified action, the appropriate kind of reversal was a reversal in the line of action from a movement toward one state of fortune to a movement toward another. In *Tom Jones*, for example, near the end of the novel the action seems to be moving unalterably toward Tom's disgrace and death when, as a result of certain discoveries, the line of action reverses itself completely and moves quickly to the highest state of fortune for Tom that he, or the reader, can imagine. The discoveries appropriate to such reversals of fortune consists of such things as the discovery of identity, of character, or of past events. In *Tom Jones* the discovery that Blifil had, in the past, concealed the evidence of Tom's parentage leads to the discovery of Tom's identity. This, in turn, leads to the recognition of Tom's virtuous character. This sequence of discoveries initiates the reversal of the action leading to Tom's final good fortune. Richardson, in *Clarissa*, handles reversals differently, but they are still reversals of the line of action. He constructs his plot around frequent changes of direction as Clarissa, and along with her the reader, given the changing information at her disposal, alternatively sees the action as moving toward good fortune or bad. The resulting constant fluctuation between hope and fear is central to the interest of the reader. The discoveries appropriate to these reversals are those made by Clarissa as she observes the actions and estimates the character of Lovelace and the other agents in a position to help or harm her.

Nineteenth-century plots, formed as they were around a causal sequence resulting from an opposition between the central characters and their surroundings, turned on reversals of intention and moral maxims. Typically the central character starts with one intention and one set of moral maxims, discovers that actions based on them lead to untenable conflicts with his surroundings, and ends by changing his intentions and his maxims. In *Crime and Punishment*, for example, Raskolnikov starts with the intention of improving the condition of men by murdering the old woman and with the utilitarian maxims he associates with such an intention. The act of murder, based on these convictions, leads to conflicts which were unforeseen and which soon become untenable. The reversal is completed in the last chapter where, sent to Siberia after his confession and trial, he is seen in the process of adopting convictions of a religiously humanitarian nature, convictions quite the reverse of those he held at the beginning. The discovery appropriate to such a reversal is generally the discovery of aspects of the surroundings left out of account by the original intention and maxims. In Raskolnikov's case it is the discovery of the religious side of life, in particular the sense of a more than merely utilitarian aspect to justice and mercy, which initiates his confession and subsequent reversal of convictions. In *The Ambassadors* the reversal and discovery take the same general form. Strether has come to Europe with the maxims of capitalistic New England and the intention of bringing Chad home. He gradually discovers aspects of Parisian life, in particular the aesthetic side of human life, which the New England maxims failed to take into account. Finding his original convictions untenable, he reverses his intention—he urges Chad to stay in Paris—and adopts a new maxim—that of gaining nothing for himself at the expense of other people—one he now sees as the reverse of the New England maxims.

Twentieth-century plots are formed around a movement from appearance to reality constituted by the emergence of structural patterns which give coherence and intelligibility to facts previously seen as unrelated and incongruous. These plots turn on reversals of perspective and reversals of valuation. What generally happens is that events and characters seen at one point in the novel in one perspective are seen at a later point in a different and often opposed perspective. The result of the reversal of perspective is often a reversal of valuation. In *The Good Soldier*, for example, Dowell (and the reader) at the beginning see Florence, Leonora, and Edward in the perspective of the superficial social conventions of Edwardian England. Since Edward is seen to have broken the conventions in such a way as to injure the others, he is evaluated as of relatively bad character while the two women are judged to be relatively innocent. By the end of the novel, as a result of the fuller understanding of the facts by Dowell (and the reader), these three characters are seen in another and more adequate perspective, a perspective centering on private virtues and motives rather than public conventions, with the result that Edward is now evaluated as relatively innocent and even virtuous in some ways and the two women are judged to be primarily guilty of the misfortunes which have affected them all. The discovery appropriate to this kind of reversal is the discovery of the realities of the situation. In *The Good Soldier* it is the discovery of the private lives and characters of the agents behind the public facade.

The same general type of reversal and discovery operates in a different manner in a novel like *Ulysses*. In *Ulysses* the title suggests at the beginning the perspective in which to evaluate Bloom; he is to be judged against Ulysses, a traditional hero. Seen in this perspective, Bloom is at first evaluated as a timid, inept, ignorant, vulgar, and overly docile character, lacking all the virtues of a traditional hero like Ulysses. As the reader follows Bloom through his day in Dublin, however, seeing him respond to the various episodes of the day and learning more about his private attitudes and convictions, the perspective and the evaluation tend to change. Judged not against the traditional hero but against the other Dubliners whom he meets during the day as he responds to the challenges of modern urban life, Bloom begins to be seen as something of a hero himself and to share with Ulysses some qualities—qualities such as curiosity, tolerance, a sense of adventure, a regard for wife and children—which many of his compatriots do not possess. He becomes a typical modern anti-hero.

One of the problems presented by a difficult novel like *Ulysses* is that most readers have been unable to perceive the reversal of perspective and evaluation during the first reading, which means they have been unable to follow the plot. Indeed the early critical judgments tended to see only the negative side of Bloom's character, his appearance of lacking all the qualities prominent in the traditional hero. It is only in recent years that critical opinion has recognized in Bloom the modern versions of some of the traditional heroic virtues found in Ulysses.

The concept of the anti-hero suggests some of the problems of characterization in modern novels resulting from the requirements of the new kind of plot. If the movement from appearance to reality is to involve a reversal of perspective and evaluation, then characters must be so constructed as to have two main aspects: a public side, that which is most apparent from the few facts in the reader's possession during the early parts of the novel, and a private side, that which emerges as the reader acquires more insight into the realities of the character and his situation. If the reversal of evaluation is to be pronounced, then the private side must be different from and even opposed to the public side. In terms of the publicly accepted and traditional conventions, Bloom is a nobody; in terms of his private aspirations and convictions, he is something of a modern hero. This doubling of character is itself a source of many of the apparent contradictions and incongruities which occur in modern novels and which have given it a reputation for obscurity.

The character of the anti-hero fits perfectly the requirements of modern plots. The anti-hero is a character who, judged by the publicly recognized conventions and standards of morality and importance and the traditional appearances of heroism, is evaluated as a person of no social importance, as often engaging in morally reprehensible actions, and as lacking all the qualities associated with the heroic. But the anti-hero also has a private side. When, as a result of the reader's insight into the realities of the world of the novel, he is judged in the perspective of more realistically grounded standards of morality and importance and the realities rather than the appearances of heroism, a reversed evaluation is made in which he becomes, in his own way, moral, important, and heroic. This is not to say that all modern novels contain anti-heroes, but this mode of characterization fits the plot requirements so well that it is often used. This is why many modern

novels are filled with characters existing on the outskirts of their society, characters who reject positions of social importance, who ignore
the precepts of conventional morality, and who scoff at the traditional heroic postures. This also suggests the reason why in many
modern novels the characters who hold the conventionally important
public positions—the generals, priests, ministers, doctors, psychia-
trists, government officials, and in general the leaders of society—
often turn out in the end to be despicable characters lacking any true
sense of morality and justice, any real importance on the personal or
familial level, and any real heroism. In these cases the reversal of
evaluation is working in the opposite direction, moving from high to
low rather than from low to high.

One of the reasons why many modern novels have been called experimental is because the new type of plot has required innovations in
technique. In nineteenth-century novels the reader is introduced immediately to the causal influences operating in the novel, since only
then can he follow with understanding the causal sequence as it progresses. This requires narrative methods which follow the causal sequence of the story in its temporal progression. In modern novels, on
the other hand, the reader must not be introduced immediately to the
causal influences operating in the story, for it is his gradual insight
into these influences as they emerge from the welter of facts that constitutes the plot of the novel. The new methods of narration were devised to achieve this gradual emergence of significance.

One procedure often used is the separation of the sequence of the
presentation of the story from the story itself and its causal sequences.
In *The Good Soldier,* for example, the story told is that of the complex
affair involving Dowell, Edward, Florence, Leonora, and Nancy. The
presentation of the story, on the other hand, consists of Dowell's attempt to make sense of the affair after the events have occurred. The
result is that the causal sequence of the story itself is broken up as
Dowell jumps backward and forward in time in his attempt to understand the significance of the facts he has to work with. The temporal
movement of the presentation of the story follows a line of increasing
significance and meaning, not the line of causal influences in the story
itself. Such a method of narration is perfectly adapted to plots which
move on a line of increasing significance and understanding from ap-

pearance to reality. *Absalom, Absalom!* uses similar methods. The Sutpen story is what is presented, but the presentation is done by Quentin and Shreve long after Sutpen has been dead and follows a line of increasing understanding rather than the line of causal influences.

Another procedure is the use of the stream of consciousness technique to record the events in the mind of one or more characters during short periods of time. In *Mrs. Dalloway*, for example, the reader is presented with events in Clarissa Dalloway's consciousness during a single day. The story being presented, however, includes many past events which Mrs. Dalloway remembers during that day. Similar techniques are used in a more complex way in *Ulysses* and *The Sound and the Fury*. The effect of all these techniques is to break up the causal sequence of the story and to allow the facts to emerge in such a way that the reader is involved in a movement of increasing understanding of the realities of the story.

One consequence of modern plots and their techniques is that the reader is involved in the plot to an unusual degree. The reader is presented with what seem to be contradictory and inconsequential facts; there is no narrator who understands the story and who can tell the reader what standards of morality are operating in the novel, what constitutes good or bad fortune for the characters, or what the cause and effect relations are. It is the job of the reader to actively contribute to the plot by seeking for the significant relations between the facts and by grasping the resulting patterns of reality as they emerge from the facts. In particular, he must, on the basis of the evidence he has, work out for himself the moral standards, the sources of happiness and suffering, and the operative causes in the world of each novel.

This analysis of modern plots and their consequences for characterization and methods of narration should explain why many modern novels are difficult to read and present the appearance of obscurity. It is not that modern novelists are interested in difficulty or obscurity for their own sake. It is rather that in order to construct plots which achieve a temporal synthesis by means of a movement from appearance to reality they must start by plunging the reader into the appearances, into the midst of seemingly unrelated, contradictory, incongruous, inconsequential, and even fantastic facts, and let him discover for himself as he reads the structures of reality which gradually emerge, if the reading is successful, to give meaning to the facts and coherence to the novel.

Note

1   R. S. Crane, "The Concept of Plot and the Plot of *Tom Jones*," in *Critics and Criticism; Ancient and Modern*, ed. R. S. Crane (Chicago: University of Chicago Press, 1952), p. 620.

17

The Concept of Point of View

MITCHELL A. LEASKA

In his essay on narrative point of view, Mitchell A. Leaska states that three major possibilities are open to the novelist. The first is omniscient narration, in which the author "may borrow, at will, the point of view of any of one or another character and observe things from that person's angle of perspective." The narrator may either *tell* the story or *dramatize* it, but in either case, the author establishes "a mediatory distance between the reader and the story."

Leaska sees modern fiction as tending toward the dramatic and less than omniscient perspectives, his second possibility. One form of limited narration is that of a "first-person observer," which emphasizes the narrator's personality and realiability. A variation is the "first-person narrator-participant," who is an actor in the development of the plot. This further narrows the perspective on events, because the narrator's own behavior affects his interpretation of actions. Another variation is that of "the third-person voice." Like first-person narration, "it does not permit of any direct account of the inner states of the characters under observation except in terms of surmise." Third-person narration, however, does not mean that the story is presented from a point of view outside the fiction. Leaska suggests that "perhaps the surest index to discovering the author's choice of vantage point is to consider the character on whom he focuses the reader's attention and on that character's relationship to the action of the story."

The third possibility abolishes the narrator altogether and confronts "the reader directly with the mental experience of a character" (Seymour Chatman discusses such stories later in this volume). "Non-narrated" stories may present a single perception of experience or "multiple inner points of view," but both preclude narrative summary. Leaska succinctly explains the difference between this method and that of omniscient narration: "While in the omniscient-author-point-of-view novel, the author looks into the minds of his characters and relates to the reader what is going on there, the information is presented as *he* sees and interprets it, rather than as his people see it. . . . In the multiple-point-of-view novel, however, the mental contents—the thoughts, feelings and perceptions of the *persona*—are rendered as they seem and feel to him." The character's inner mental processes are not filtered by any interpreting voice; instead, the responsibility for filtering, interpreting, and, in some cases, organizing the perceptions into a coherent plot devolves upon the reader.

Mitchell A. Leaska (b. 1934) is professor of English at New York University. In addition to writing *Virginia Woolf's Lighthouse* (1970), from which this essay is excerpted, he is also the author of *The Voice of Tragedy* (1963) and *The Novels of Virginia Woolf: From Beginning to End* (1977).

The question of who shall narrate the story or through whose eyes the reader shall see is one which every writer of the novel has had to face. The question does not seem to have been an especially vexing one to novelists of the past. But since the beginning of the modern novel—more specifically, since Henry James—with a more vigorous determination to achieve a greater reality of both the inner and the outer life to reveal the whole of experience, the choice of the angle or angles of narration, through which the story is to be transmitted, has created a great deal of difficulty and concern among literary craftsmen, artists, and critics alike.

In his critical prefaces, now collected as *The Art of the Novel* (1934), James was deeply concerned with problems of literary method, particularly the method of narrative presentation through a single consciousness—the "central intelligence" or the "sentient centre" or the

"The Concept of Point of View" is reprinted from Mitchell A. Leaska, *Virginia Woolf's Lighthouse*. Copyright 1970 Columbia University Press. Reprinted with permission of Mitchell A. Leaska.

"reflector," as he variously called it. Drawing principally from James's prefaces, Percy Lubbock, in *The Craft of Fiction* (1921), coherently formulated James's concepts about point of view—concepts which, since Lubbock, have become fairly rigid and consequently transmuted, by later critics of fiction, to a somewhat dogmatic statement of theory.

Wayne C. Booth, however, in his study, *The Rhetoric of Fiction* (1961), in re-examining these earlier critical interpretations of method and procedure, has, by carefully pointing out weaknesses and fallacies in the doctrine, made perhaps the most significant single attempt at revising and modifying so important a concept as point of view. This critical evolution notwithstanding, however, it is important to recognize that as pioneer in and practitioner of the theory of point of view, Henry James was an advance guard of the new psychological fiction.

As every storyteller knows, a tale conceived in a particular way has certain affective potentialities over a reader's feelings and attitudes. But just how that tale is presented to the reader will determine whether those affective potentialities either become vivid or remain lifeless on the page. A useful way of considering point of view as a technical problem is to think of a novelist presenting his story as if he were a motion-picture director filming a script. The question to arise first is what angle or what combinations and variations of angles of vision will most effectively project the story for the viewer. After settling this question, the director must decide when to move the camera up close and when to increase the distance between the viewer and the viewed; when to reveal a scene slowly and when to quicken the pace; how to effect transitions smoothly from one angle to another so as to create a sense of continuity; whether to unfold the story chronologically or scramble the sequence while simultaneously building up a sense of relatedness and integration. All of these, and many more, are problems which must be dealt with if the story is to be transmitted intelligibly, vividly, and—most important—persuasively. The choices made will be determined, ultimately, by the choice of the angle or angles of vision.

Generally, for the novelist there are three broad possibilities open. The first of these is the point of view of the *omniscient narrator*. According to Beckson and Ganz, the omniscient view enables the writer to present the inner thoughts and feelings of his characters. Godlike, he may survey from his Olympian position past and present so that the reader may come to know more of his imaginative world than any single character in it. In *Ulysses,* for example, a work that employs shifting points of view, Joyce reveals the inner thoughts of his three major characters through the stream of consciousness . . . and presents actions, unknown to the individual characters, going on in various parts of Dublin. Moreover, the omniscient author may sometimes openly comment on the behavior of his characters, as in Thackeray's *Vanity Fair. . . .*[1]

In omniscient narration, the author tells the story *after* it has happened. Moreover, the omniscient narrator may borrow, at will, the point of view of any of one or another character and observe things from that person's angle of perspective; and he may, with authorial responsibility, at other times, choose to abridge some part of the story, or comment on it, or take a panoramic view of it.

The opening lines from three different novels will illustrate the general tenor of omniscient narration:

from Hardy's *The Mayor of Casterbridge:*

One evening of late summer, before the present century had reached its thirteenth year, a young man and woman, the latter carrying a child, were approaching the large village of Weydon-Priors, in Upper Wessex, on foot. They were plainly but not ill clad, though the thick hoar of dust which had accumulated on their shoes and garments from an obviously long journey lent a disadvantageous shabbiness to their appearance just now.

from Jane Austen's *Pride and Prejudice:*

It is a truth universally acknowledged that a single man in possession of a good fortune must be in want of a wife.

However little known the feelings or views of such a man may be on his first entering a neighborhood, this truth is so well fixed in the minds of the surrounding families, that he is considered as the rightful property of some one or other of their daughters.

from Tolstoy's *Anna Karenina:*

> Happy families are all alike; every unhappy family is unhappy in its own way.[2]

One of the distinguishing features of an omniscient narrator is his power not only to inform the reader of the ideas and emotions of his characters, but also to reveal, in varying degrees, his own biases, whether by overt authorial intrusions or by the way in which he generalizes about life, morals, manners, and so on. This method of narration may very often be editorial in attitude; that is, the author not only reports ideas and events, but he criticizes and passes judgments on them as well.

I have been describing the omniscient narrator as primarily *telling* the story rather than dramatizing it. And in so far as *telling* is concerned, I have tried to emphasize the fact that summary narrative (as this mode of telling is often called) is characterized, in part, by the general manner in which events are reported; by the indefinite period of time such events cover; by the variety and freedom of locations where such events occur; by the tendency of the author-narrator to editorialize, to criticize, and, openly, even to judge.

The omniscient narrator, however, with all the latitude of storytelling he assumes, may choose to *dramatize*, to *show* the reader rather than to tell him. The method is theatrical, "objectified," as it were. When the omniscient narrator chooses to have his characters— no one of their consciousnesses, now, open to view—act and speak equally before the reader, the authorial voice becomes neutral, the point of view impersonal, detached—"detached," that is, *only as it is possible in any work of fiction.*

When the author subdues his own vociferous presence, he, in a sense, forces the reader to deduce, from all the details he has seen and heard, his own generalizations as to what is going on and what his own attitude should be towards the spectacle placed before him. Because the reader, if he is to respond appropriately, requires from the scene the transmission of considerable data, one natural consequence of the stratagem is the presentation of a *specific* temporal and spatial framework capable of containing the concrete details and enclosing the dialogue—all of which are the *sine qua non* of the dramatic mode.

Because Flaubert favoured this impersonal stance of omniscient narrator, two scenes from *Madame Bovary* will serve to illustrate— the first, primarily dialogue; the second, primarily detail:

> He took her hand, and this time she did not withdraw it.
>
> "First prize for all-round farming!" cried the chairman.
>
> "Just this morning, for example, when I came to your house . . ."
>
> "To Monsieur Bizet, of Quincampoix."
>
> "Did I have any idea that I'd be coming with you to the show?"
>
> "Seventy francs!"
>
> "A hundred times I was on the point of leaving, and yet I followed you and stayed with you . . ."
>
> "For the best manures."
>
> ". . . as I'd stay with you tonight, tomorrow, every day, all my life!"
>
> "To Monsieur Caron, of Argueil, a gold medal!"
>
> "Never have I been so utterly charmed by anyone . . ."
>
> "To Monsieur Bain, of Givry-Saint-Martin!"
>
> ". . . so that I'll carry the memory of you with me . . ."
>
> "For a merino ram . . ."
>
> "Whereas you'll forget me; I'll vanish like a shadow."
>
> "To Monsieur Belot, of Notre-Dame . . ."
>
> "No, though! Tell me it isn't so! Tell me I'll have a place in your thoughts, in your life!"
>
> "Hogs: a tie! To Messieurs Leherisse and Cullembourg, sixty francs!"
>
> Rodolphe squeezed her hand, and he felt it all warm and trembling in his, like a captive dove that longs to fly away; but then, whether in an effort to free it, or in response to his pressure, she moved her fingers.
>
> "Oh! Thank God! You don't repulse me! How sweet, how kind! I'm yours; you know that now! Let me see you! Let me look at you!"
>
> A gust of wind coming in the windows ruffled the cloth on the

table; and down in the square all the tall headdresses of the peasant women rose up like fluttering white butterfly wings. (part 2, chapter 8)

But it was above all at mealtime that she could bear it no longer—in that small ground-floor room with its smoking stove, its squeaking door, its sweating walls and its damp floor tiles. All the bitterness of life seemed to be served up to her on her plate; and the steam rising from the boiled meat brought gusts of re-vulsion from the depths of her soul. Charles was a slow eater; she would nibble a few hazel-nuts, or lean on her elbow and draw lines on the oilcloth with the point of her table knife. (part 1, chapter 9)[3]

One important rhetorical function effected by the dramatic mode is to persuade the reader that he sees and ultimately judges for himself. This, in itself, has a great deal of appeal for the reader because a sense of immediacy has been achieved. It follows that if *showing*, unat-tended by authorial commentary and overt direction, effects a sense of immediacy, then one further difference between the narrative method and the dramatic is that in the narrative the distance between the story and the reader is considerably greater than it is in the dra-matic, in which the very effect of impersonal presentation creates a more personal involvement of the reader with the story.

Suffice it to say, that in omniscient narration, the author has many advantages of dealing with both the story and the character in various descriptive and developmental ways. But one salient characteristic prevails with omniscient narration: namely, the author's readiness to place himself between the reader and the story to clarify a point, to make a confident interpretation of what otherwise might remain am-biguous and bothersome, and so on. And while no twentieth-century reader should be disturbed when something is made clear for him, if he is sufficiently conscious of some of the subtleties which obtain in all omniscience, he may become more alert as a reader when he begins to realize that even when the author is presenting something dramati-cally, he renders the scene through his own eyes rather than through the eyes of his characters—thus creating, however tenuous, a media-tory distance between the reader and the story.

The evolution towards direct presentation in the novel marks the chain of events in the course of which the novelist relinquishes some of his possible points of view; and by so doing, he also surrenders many sources of information which were available to him as an omniscient author. As he deprives himself of the privilege of commentary when he resorts to presenting his story dramatically, so the author denies himself any direct pronouncements in his fictional proceedings when he bequeaths his tale to a narrator who is either an observer or a participant in the story.

If the novelist chooses as his narrator a *first-person observer*, he restricts himself to some extent in that the narrator, as the observer, no longer has access to the inner states of the characters involved and, therefore, can report only what he witnessed or has genuinely discovered or, in extreme cases, has drawn inferences from. He may even guess. But he is not allowed entry into the minds of the principal characters of his story. The narrator-observer, moreover, although he views the story from what Friedman calls the "wandering periphery,"[4] like the omniscient narrator, is given the prerogative of presenting his material at any given point either as summary narrative or as scene. Thus the distances or variations in distance established between the reader and the story will, for the most part, be determined by the narrator's choice and manipulation of his modes of presentation—that is, whether by the narrative mode or the dramatic.

Because the narrator-observer, in reporting his story, is simultaneously interpreting that story, the reader's response to it and to his interpretation of it will inevitably be influenced by the impression he gets of the narrator, himself. It is necessary, therefore, to notice how, either before introducing the narrator or by endowing him with special self-evident characteristics such as honesty, perceptiveness, et cetera, the author persuades the reader that the narrator is worthy of his attention and trust.

Joseph Conrad in *Heart of Darkness,* for example, prepares us for Marlow's tale:

> The yarns of seamen have a direct simplicity, the whole meaning of which lies within the shell of a cracked nut. But Marlow was not typical (if his propensity to spin yarns be excepted), and to

him the meaning of an episode was not inside like a kernel but outside, enveloping the tale which brought it out only as a glow brings out a haze, in the likeness of one of these misty halos that sometimes are made visible by the spectral illumination of moonshine.

When there is no preparation, when the reader has no way of knowing about the narrator except from the process of his "acting himself out," there is apt to be trouble. One of Henry James's least popular novels, *The Sacred Fount*, is a good example. The story is an account of a weekend party at a place called Newmarch; and it is told by an unnamed narrator who spends his entire time there trying to fathom the relationships between some of the guests. Very early in the novel, we learn that he sees close human relationships as a depletion of one individual for the enrichment of the other—metaphorically, as a "sacred fount" being drained.

From the very beginning, the reader is trapped in the consciousness of the narrator: there is no prelude or introductory information about him given from some other source. As a result, the reader is to the very end helplessly confined to only the evidence which the narrator chooses to furnish. And since he makes no bid for our sympathy in his rather unengaging search for depleted characters, we are at a loss as to how credible a witness he is. It takes no profound analysis to discover that the narrator is given to flights of fantasy; that he keeps a good deal of emotional distance between himself and others; that his drive for intellectual superiority is compulsive; and that he is obsessed with the notion that he is capable of "reading into mere human things an interest so much deeper than mere human things were in general prepared to supply." In fact, he reports what other characters in the story say of him: "You're abused by a fine fancy"; "You over-estimate the penetration of others"; ". . . people have such a notion of what you embroider on things that they're rather afraid to commit themselves or to lead you on"; and so on.

The reader, if he has managed to maintain enough interest to finish the novel, discovers at the end that nothing has been solved; in fact, nothing has actually happened that needs to be solved except for evaluating the narrator's ornate and highly suspect ruminations. Perhaps one of the surest pleasures to be derived from the work, either by the student of James or by the psychological critic, is in deducing the character and personality of an extremely complex and ambiguous narrator, because in this short novel James has pushed the impersonal aspect of the point-of-view method almost to the limits of absurdity. It is, therefore, small wonder that *The Sacred Fount* has never found either a wide or an enthusiastic reading public.

The long shelf of fiction is filled with stories told by *first-person narrator-participants;* that is, by narrators who have been actively involved in the events and reported, in their own voice, the story from a point in time *after* the experience itself. Moll Flanders, Huckleberry Finn, Jane Eyre, Claudius, Holden Caulfield, David Copperfield mention only a few of these narrators who are also principal participants in the stories they tell. Quite often these narrators speak in the first-person voice, because that voice gives an impression of being livelier and more direct; and confidence can be more quickly established than with the use of the third-person voice.

When the "I" is used, however, the author denies himself more channels of information. More than that, he must surrender some of the vantage points the narrator-observer enjoyed from his "wandering periphery." Now the narrator-participant is centrally involved in the action, with his angle of perspective fixed at the centre of the experience he relates. In so far as concerns the source of his information, he is limited to his own thoughts, feelings, and perceptions. As Moll Flanders, for example, says very early in her "History and Misfortunes":

> This is too near the first hours of my life for me to relate anything of myself but by hearsay; 'tis enough to mention that, as I was born in such an unhappy place, I had no parish to have recourse to for my nourishment in my infancy; nor can I give the least account how I was kept alive, other than that, as I have been told, some relation of my mother took me away, but at whose expense, or by whose direction, I know nothing at all of it.

In subtler pieces of fiction however, the limitations set on available information are convincingly overcome by a narrator's capacity to speculate and to draw inferences. For example, Conrad works around the problem in the opening pages of *The Secret Sharer:* "On my right hand there were lines of fishing stakes *resembling* a *mysterious* system of half-submerged bamboo fences, *incomprehensible* in its division of the domain of tropical fishes, and *crazy* of aspect *as if* abandoned forever. . . . To the left a group of barren islets, *suggesting* ruins of stone walls, . . . *There must have been* some glare in the air. . . .[5]

But the narrator-participant angle of view can offer problems to the reader. For one of the liveliest debates in contemporary criticism, we need only look at the conflicting interpretations given to the governess' story in James's *The Turn of the Screw*. The problem arises, among other things, from the fact not only that James has kept her impersonal, to the extent of leaving her unnamed—very much the same as the narrator in *The Sacred Fount*—but also that the reader's introduction to her by Douglas, the outer and indeed very favourable frame of reference, tends to cast her in a most auspicious light—a setting in which we are prepared even before meeting her to accept as absolute truth her testimony of the ghastly happenings at Bly.

But when readers' opinions of the governess range from that of a sexually repressed psychotic to that of an "honourable and fearless lady," as Rebecca West thinks of her, it is no longer a question of a reader's alertness or stupidity: it is rather more an issue of James's having willfully obscured his narrator-participant ("lucid reflector" seems inappropriate in this instance). The result is that few of us, as Booth remarks, "feel happy with a situation in which we cannot decide whether the subject is two evil children as seen by a naïve but well-meaning governess or two innocent children as seen by a hysterical, destructive governess."[6]

It is ironic that of all novelists, it was Henry James who, in a letter to H. G. Wells, concerning the dangers of first-person narration, called it that "accursed autobiographic form which puts a premium on the loose, the impoverished, the cheap and the easy. Save in the fantastic and the romantic . . . it has no authority, no persuasive or convincing force. . . ."

Although thus far I have dealt exclusively with first-person narrator-observers and participants, a narrator—whether an observer or a participant—is employed very often, and as effectively, with the *third-person* voice. The method of narrator-observer, with no "I" to alert the reader that an experiencing mind is mediating between him and the event, is a subtle device which frequently causes the inexperienced reader to think that the fictional material is coming to him directly. Even though the author may give his narrator no personal characteristics, there are certainly effects which are produced by the undramatized narrator's tonal characteristics and the attitude he projects towards what he is reporting.

In this method of narration, everything depends directly on the presentation of background, external action, gesture, and speech. Since the method tends to transmit the story as a dramatic presentation of objective scenes, a sense of detachment and impersonality may be created. It shares, moreover, one basic limitation with the first-person narrator-observer: namely, that it does not permit of any direct account of the inner states of the characters under observation except in terms of surmise.

Because Hemingway creates perhaps the most rigorously impersonal stories by means of the undramatized narrator, the following passage from his short story, "Soldier's Home," will serve to illustrate:

> . . . He had tried so to keep his life from being complicated. Still, none of it had touched him. He had felt sorry for his mother and she had made him lie. He would go to Kansas City and get a job and she would feel all right about it. There would be one more scene maybe before he got away. He would not go down to his father's office. He would miss that one. He wanted his life to go smoothly. It had just gotten going that way. Well, that was all over now, anyway. He would go over to the schoolyard and watch Helen play indoor baseball.

When the *narrator-participant* is rendered in the *third person*, the unsuspecting reader, again, may confuse it with omniscient narration. D. H. Lawrence's *Sons and Lovers*, for example, is frequently thought of as narrated by the author; but if one stopped to consider where the fictional ballast lay, he would soon realize that the story, with the exception of the first three chapters, comes filtered almost entirely through Paul Morel, and it is his story—told in the third-person voice. Perhaps the surest index to discovering the author's choice of vantage point is to consider the character on whom he focuses the reader's attention and on that character's relationship to the action of the story. In the case of the third-person narrator-participant, if the selected character has no relation to a particular event, or if some occurrence is of no interest to him or is beyond his understanding, then no report of it is made.

Henry James's *The Ambassadors* is a worthy example of third-person-participant narration. In his discussion of that novel, Percy Lubbock says that James does not "tell the story of Strether's mind; he makes it tell itself, he dramatizes it."[7] He says further that everything in that work is rendered objectively: "whether it is a page of dialogue or a page of description nobody is addressing us, nobody is reporting his impression to the reader. The impression is enacting itself in the endless series of images that play over the outspread expanse of the man's mind and memory."[8] Perhaps the most important assertion Lubbock makes in his discussion of this Jamesian novel is that the presentation in time is integral to the objective method, because it requires the reader to "live" through the experience with the character—and at *his* pace.

Equally significant in the objective method is that it forces the reader to organize the story for himself, to make of it what he will. The French critic, Ramon Fernandez, suggests this aspect when he describes the novel as a "representation of events which take place in time, a representation submitted to the conditions of apparition and development of these events."[9]

The third-person-narrator-participant method is particularly effective in *The Ambassadors* not only because the reader's sympathies are likely to be given up to Strether very early in the work, but also because the full awareness of his desires pitted against the restrictions of his conscience—the internal struggle dramatically depicted in the novel—is a conflict known to everyone at one time or another. *The Ambassadors* is, moreover, a perfect example of James's success in the fusion of form and content, because as a work of art it is an eloquent testimony of the dictum which occupies the very centre of James's aesthetic of the novel: and that is, to show something intensely, it must be shown from the appropriate angle of vision.

Finally, narrator-observers and participants, whether first person or third, have the privilege, at any given point, of summarizing the narrative or of presenting it dramatically, thereby modulating at will the distance between the reader and the story, by technical means. What is important here (as with omniscient narration) is the fact that distance—which in aesthetic terms is inversely proportional to involvement or sympathy or identification (critical terminology is inadequate on this point)—is ultimately the result of the author's or the narrator's or the character's effect on the reader. It makes no difference whether the voice is "I" or "he" or "she" or "we." The intellectual and moral and emotional qualities of the narrator, in the last analysis, will be more important in molding a reader's experience and judgment than the person of the voice. Our delight with Moll Flanders, our disapproval of Wickham in *Pride and Prejudice,* our pity for Anna Karenina, our disgust with Kafka's country doctor, our aversion to Faulkner's Jason Compson should indicate that the achievement of a literary effect has no fast or fixed rubric.

———————

So long as there is a narrator, someone is mediating between the reader and the story. The next step in the direction of objectification is effected by doing away with the narrator altogether and dramatizing the inner state of a *persona* by *direct mental transmission;* that is, by confronting the reader directly with the mental experience of a character. One vivid example which illustrates direct transmission is found in James Joyce's *A Portrait of the Artist as a Young Man:*

> . . . When would he be like the fellows in Poetry and Rhetoric? They had big voices and big boots and they studied trigonometry. That was very far away. First came the vacation and then the next term and then again the vacation. It was like a train going in and out of tunnels and that was like the boys eating in the refectory when you opened and closed the flaps of the ears. Term, vacation; tunnel, out; noise, stop. How far away it was! It was better to go to bed to sleep. Only prayers in the chapel and then bed. (Chapter I)

So thoroughly has Joyce given us the novel in terms of Stephen Dedalus, and so purged is the text of his own authorial presence, that readers coming to the work for the first time accept the fictional material to the extent that they frequently find themselves making only those value judgments which are shared by the narrator himself: for example, they share the profound seriousness with which he views himself; they accept the somewhat debauched version of aesthetic theory he offers; and they marvel, as much as Stephen himself, at his own artistry.[10]

When the mental atmospheres of two or more *personae* are presented, we have what might be called *multiple inner points of view*. The method of presentation—similar to that of a single consciousness—is almost entirely in the direction of scene, both of an inner view of the mind and of an outer view by means of speech and action. Erich Auerbach calls the method the "multipersonal representation of consciousness"[11] and points out that one of the possibilities of the multiple-consciousness method is its "obscuring and even obliterating the impression of an objective reality completely known to the author."[12] Discussing a passage from Virginia Woolf's *To the Lighthouse*, Professor Auerbach observes that Mrs. Woolf presents herself "to be someone who doubts, wonders, hesitates, as though the truth about her characters were not better known to her than it is to them or to the reader."[13] The statement is extremely significant in that it has to do not only with the author's attitude towards reality, but also, and more important, with the relationship between the form of the novel and how that form defines and communicates its meaning. This aspect will be discussed later in considerable detail.

In the multiple-point-of-view method, when a descriptive detail is necessary, it is supplied by way of "stage direction," as Norman Friedman calls it, or it is given through the thoughts and utterances of the *personae* themselves.

When the novelist maintains the third-person angle throughout, as does Virginia Woolf, in both *Mrs. Dalloway* and *To the Lighthouse*, one might legitimately ask how precisely this differs from an omniscient-author-point-of-view novel. The difference, though often not susceptible to detection, is chiefly this: While in the omniscient-author-point-of-view novel, the author looks into the minds of his characters and relates to the reader what is going on there, the information is presented as *he* sees and interprets it, rather than as his people see it. Moreover, in the traditional omniscient novel, the information is narrated as though it had already occurred. In the multiple-point-of-view novel (as I shall refer to it hereafter), however, the mental contents—the thoughts, feelings, and perceptions of the *persona*—are rendered as they seem and feel to him. In addition, the mental states are presented scenically as if the settings or situations which evoked those states were happening *now* before the reader, at the time of the reading. In brief, life is presented as it seems to the fictional people who are living it. As a consequence, the physical appearance of a character, what he does, what he thinks and feels—in short, all the fictional data—are communicated through the consciousness of someone present.

Notes

1 Karl Beckson and Arthur Ganz, *A Reader's Guide to Literary Terms* (New York, 1960), p. 162.
2 Translated by Constance Garnett.
3 Translated by Francis Steegmuller.
4 Norman Friedman, "Point of View in Fiction: The Development of a Critical Concept," PMLA 70 (December 1955): 1160–84; reprinted in Robert Scholes, ed., *Approaches to the Novel* (San Francisco, 1961), p. 130.
5 Italics are mine.
6 Wayne C. Booth, *The Rhetoric of Fiction* (Chicago, 1961), p. 346.
7 Percy Lubbock, *The Craft of Fiction* (London, 1921), p. 147.
8 Ibid., p. 170.
9 *Messages;* cited in Edwin Muir, *The Structure of the Novel* (London, 1928), pp. 119–20.
10 Booth, *The Rhetoric of Fiction*, pp. 323–36. For a detailed account of Joyce's method, see the unpublished dissertation by Erwin R. Steinberg, "The Stream-of-Consciousness Technique in James Joyce's *Ulysses*," (New York University, 1956).
11 Erich Auerbach, *Mimesis: The Representation of Reality in Western Literature*, trans. Willard Trask (New York, 1953), p. 474.
12 Ibid., p. 472.
13 Ibid.

18

The Concept of Character
in Fiction

WILLIAM H. GASS

William Gass begins his discussion by claiming that "great character is the most obvious single mark of great literature. . . . A great character has an endless interest; its fascination never wanes." Character must be a constant source of new discovery, not only for the reader who picks up a novel for the first time, but also for the one who returns to the same novel for pleasure. Citing Aristotle as a case in point, Gass observes that character has not always been a major concern of critics or authors. Now, however, that character has become a focus of attention, does that mean that critics and authors have come to understand what constitutes a character and its relationship to reality? Gass thinks not. While many critics still follow Aristotle in upholding mimesis, Gass assures us that character is not "a mirror or a window onto life."

Having defined what character is *not* in the first part of his essay, Gass defines what it *is* in the third part (we have omitted the second part—eds.): "Characters are those primary substances to which everything else is attached." Here Gass breaks through the stereotype that "character" means *person,* by suggesting that it can also refer to natural objects, symbols, and even ideas. Gass observes paradoxically that, while we invariably think of characters as people, the proper names given to characters are initially the emptiest words used in a novel—"Mr. Smith" means nothing without description. Often, however, authors help us by providing proper names that are really descriptive words, such as Mr. Cashmore, and then reinforce their descriptions through the sounds they employ as well as the connotations of the common words used in proper names. It is this investiture of a fictional creation with verbal detail that makes characters not "a mirror or a window onto life," but a creation of language, which "freed from existence, can shine like essence, and purely Be." If we accept this nonmimetic concept of character, we might want to ask ourselves how it affects our view of Virginia Woolf's concern for "Mrs. Brown" or Lionel Trilling's concern for a "moral realism." Before answering that question, however, we might first want to decide whether or not we believe that art is mimetic. Georg Lukács, for instance, would no doubt condemn Gass's rejection of mimesis as another form of bourgeois decay.

William H. Gass (b. 1924) has taught philosophy at Washington University, St. Louis, for many years. He is well known as a novelist and literary critic, having produced such works as *Omensetter's Luck* (1966), *In the Heart of the Heart of the Country* (1968), and *Fiction and the Figures of Life* (1970), from which this essay is taken.

I have never found a handbook on the art of fiction or the stage, nor can I imagine finding one, that did not contain a chapter on the creation of character, a skill whose mastery, the author of each manual insists, secures for one the inner secrets of these arts: not, mind you, an easy thing: rather as difficult as the whole art itself, since, in a way, it *is* the whole art: to fasten in the memory of the reader, like a living presence, some bright human image. All well and good to paint a landscape, evoke a feeling, set a tempest loose, but not quite good enough to nail an author to his immortality if scheming Clarence, fat, foul-trousered Harry, or sweetly terraced Priss do not emerge from the land they huff and rage and eat in fully furnished out by Being; enough alive, indeed, to eat and huff in ours—dear God, more alive than that!—sufficiently enlarged by genius that they threaten to eat up and huff down everything in sight.

Talk about literature, when it is truly talk about something going on in the pages, if it is not about ideas, is generally about the people in it, and ranges from those cries of wonder, horror, pleasure, or surprise, so readily drawn from the innocently minded, to the annotated stammers of the most erudite and nervous critics. But it is all the same. Great character is the most obvious single mark of great literature. The rude, the vulgar, may see in Alyosha nothing more than the image of a modest, God-loving youth; the scholar may perceive through this demeanor a symbolic form; but the Alyosha of the untutored is somehow more real and present to him than the youth on his street whom he's known since childhood, loving of his God and modest too, equally tried, fully as patient; for in some way Alyosha's visionary figure will take lodging in him, make a model for him, so to reach, without the scholar's inflationary gifts, general form and universal height; whereas the neighbor may merely move away, take cold, and forget to write. Even the most careful student will admit that fiction's fruit survives its handling and continues growing off the tree. A great character has an endless interest; its fascination never wanes. Indeed it is a commonplace to say so. Hamlet. Ahab. Julien Sorel. Madame Bovary. There is no end to their tragedy. Great literature is great because its characters are great, and characters are great when they are memorable. A simple formula. The Danish ghost cries to remember him, and obediently—for we are gullible and superstitious clots—we do.

It hasn't always been a commonplace. Aristotle regarded character as a servant of dramatic action, and there have been an endless succession of opinions about the value and function of characters since— all dreary—but the important thing to be noted about nearly every one of them is that whatever else profound and wonderful these theories have to say about the world and its personalities, characters are clearly conceived as living outside language. Just as the movie star deserts herself to put on some press agent's more alluring fictional persona, the hero of a story sets out from his own landscape for the same land of romance the star reached by stepping there from life. These people—Huckleberry Finn, the Snopeses, Prince Myshkin, Pickwick, Molly Bloom—seem to have come to the words of their novels like a visitor to town . . . and later they leave on the arm of the reader, bound, I suspect, for a shabbier hotel, and dubious entertainments.

However, Aristotle's remark was a recommendation. Characters ought to exist for the sake of the action, he thought, though he knew

they often did not, and those who nowadays say that given a sufficiently powerful and significant plot the characters will be dominated
by it are simply answered by asking them to imagine the plot of
Moby-Dick in the hands of Henry James, or that of *Sanctuary* done
into Austen. And if you can persuade them to try (you will have no
success), you may then ask how the heroes and the heroines come
out. The same disastrous exercise can be given those who believe that
traits make character like definitions do a dictionary. Take any set
of traits you like and let Balzac or Joyce, Stendhal or Beckett, loose
in a single paragraph to use them. Give your fictional creatures qualities, psychologies, actions, manners, moods; present them from without or from within; let economics matter, breeding, custom, history;
let spirit wet them like a hose: all methods work, and none do. The
nature of the novel will not be understood at all until this is: *from
any given body of fictional text, nothing necessarily follows, and anything plausibly may.* Authors are gods—a little tinny sometimes but
omnipotent no matter what, and plausible on top of that, if they can
manage it.[1]

Though the handbooks try to tell us how to create characters, they
carefully never tell us we are making images, illusions, imitations.
Gatsby is not an imitation, for there is nothing he imitates. Actually,
if he were a copy, an illusion, sort of shade or shadow, he would not
be called a character at all. He must be unique, entirely himself, as if
he had a self to be. He is required, in fact, to act *in character*, like a
cat in a sack. No, theories of character are not absurd in the way
representational theories are; they are absurd in a grander way, for
the belief in Hamlet (which audiences often seem to have) is like the
belief in God—incomprehensible to reason—and one is inclined to
seek a motive: some deep fear or emotional need.

There are too many motives. We pay heed so easily. We are so
pathetically eager for this other life, for the sounds of distant cities
and the sea; we long, apparently, to pit ourselves against some trying
wind, to follow the fortunes of a ship hard beset, to face up to murder
and fornication, and the somber results of anger and love; oh, yes,
to face up—*in books*—when on our own we scarcely breathe. The
tragic view of life, for instance, in Shakespeare or in Schopenhauer,
Unamuno, Sartre, or Sophocles, is not one jot as pure and penetrat-
ingly tragic as a pillow stuffed with Jewish hair, and if we want to

touch life where it burns, though life is what we are even now awash with—futilely, stupidly drawing in—we ought not to back off from these other artifacts (wars, pogroms, poverty: men make them, too). But of course we do, and queue up patiently instead to see Prince Hamlet moon, watch him thrust his sword through a curtain, fold it once again into Polonius, that foolish old garrulous proper noun. The so-called life one finds in novels, the worst and best of them, is nothing like actual life at all, and cannot be; it is not more real, or thrilling, or authentic; it is not truer, more complex, or pure, and its people have less spontaneity, are less intricate, less free, less full.[2]

It is not a single cowardice that drives us into fiction's fantasies. We often fear that literature is a game we can't afford to play—the product of idleness and immoral ease. In the grip of that feeling it isn't life we pursue, but the point and purpose of life—its facility, its use. So Sorel is either a man it is amusing to gossip about, to see in our friends, to puppet around in our dreams, to serve as our more able and more interesting surrogate in further fanciful adventures; or Sorel is a theoretical type, scientifically profound, representing a deep human strain, and the writing of *The Red and the Black* constitutes an advance in the science of—what would you like? sociology?

Before reciting a few helpless arguments, let me suggest, in concluding this polemical section, just how absurd these views are which think of fiction as a mirror or a window onto life—as actually creative of living creatures—for really one's only weapon against Tertullians is ridicule.

There is a painting by Picasso which depicts a pitcher, candle, blue enamel pot. They are sitting, unadorned, upon the barest table. Would we wonder what was cooking in that pot? Is it beans, perhaps, or carrots, a marmite? The orange of the carrot is a perfect complement to the blue of the pot, and the genius of Picasso, neglecting nothing, has surely placed, behind that blue, invisible disks of dusky orange, which, in addition, subtly enrich the table's velvet brown. Doesn't that seem reasonable? Now I see that it must be beans, for above the pot—you can barely see them—are quaking lines of steam, just the lines we associate with boiling beans . . . or is it blanching pods? Scholarly research, supported by a great foundation, will discover that exactly such a pot was used to cook cassoulet in the kitchens of Charles the Fat . . . or was it Charles the Bald? There's a dissertation in that. And this explans the dripping candle standing by the pot. (Is it dripping? no? a pity. Let's go on.) For isn't Charles the Fat himself that candle? Oh no, some say, he's not! Blows are struck. Reputations made and ruined. Someone will see eventually that the pot is standing on a table, not a stove. But the pot has just come from the stove, it will be pointed out. Has not Picasso caught that vital moment of transition? The pot is too hot. The brown is burning. Oh, not *this* table, which has been coated with resistant plastic. Singular genius—blessed man—he thinks of everything.

Here you have half the history of our criticism in the novel. Entire books have been written about the characters in Dickens, Trollope, Tolstoy, Faulkner. But why not? Entire books have been written about God, his cohorts, and the fallen angels.

A character, first of all, is the noise of his name, and all the sounds and rhythms that proceed from him. We pass most things in novels as we pass things on a train. The words flow by like the scenery. All is change.[3] But there are some points in a narrative which remain relatively fixed; we may depart from them, but soon we return, as music returns to its theme. Characters are those primary substances to which everything else is attached. Hotels, dresses, conversations, sausage, feelings, gestures, snowy evenings, faces—each may fade as fast as we read of them. Yet the language of the novel will eddy about a certain incident or name, as Melville's always circles back to Ahab and his wedding with the white whale. Mountains are characters in Malcolm Lowry's *Under the Volcano*, so is a ravine, a movie, mescal, or a boxing poster. A symbol like the cross can be a character. An idea or a situation (the anarchist in *The Secret Agent*, bomb ready in his pocket), or a particular event, an obsessive thought, a decision (Zeno's, for instance, to quit smoking), a passion, a memory, the weather, Gogol's overcoat—anything, indeed, which serves as a fixed point, like a stone in a stream or that soap in Bloom's pocket, functions as a character. Character, in this sense, is a matter of degree, for the language of the novel may loop back seldom, often, or incessantly. But the idea that characters are like primary substances has to be taken in a double way, because if any thing becomes a character simply to the degree the words of the novel qualify it, it also loses some of its substance, some of its primacy, to the extent that it, in turn, qualifies something else. In a perfectly organized novel, every word would ultimately qualify one thing, like the God of the metaphysician, at once the subject and the body of the whole.[4] Normally, characters are fictional human beings, and thus are given proper names. In such cases, to create a character is to give meaning to an unknown X; it is *absolutely* to *define;* and since nothing in life corresponds to these Xs, their reality is borne by their name. They *are,* where it *is.*

Most of the words the novelist uses have their meanings already formed. Proper names do not, except in a tangential way. It's true that Mr. Mulholland could not be Mr. Mull, and Mr. Cashmore must bear, as best he can, the curse of his wealth forever, along with his desire for gain. Character has a special excitement for a writer (apart from its organizing value) because it offers him a chance to give fresh meaning to new words. A proper name begins as a blank, like a wall or a canvas, upon which one might paint a meaning, perhaps as turbulent and mysterious, as treacherous and vast, as Moby Dick's, perhaps as delicate, scrupulous, and sensitive as that of Fleda Vetch.

I cannot pause here over the subject of rhythm and sound, though they are the heartbeat of writing, of prose no less than poetry.

> Their friend, Mr. Grant-Jackson, a highly preponderant pushing person, great in discussion and arrangement, abrupt in overture, unexpected, if not perverse, in attitude, and almost equally acclaimed and objected to in the wide midland region to which he had taught, as the phrase was, the size of his foot—their friend had launched his bolt quite out of the blue and had thereby so shaken them as to make them fear almost more than hope.[5]

Mr. Grant-Jackson is a preponderant pushing person because he's been made by *p*'s, and the rhythm and phrasing of James's writing here prepares and perfectly presents him to us. Certainly we cannot think of Molly Bloom apart from her music, or the gay and rapid Anna Livia apart from hers.

If one examines the texture of a fiction carefully, one will soon see that some words appear to gravitate toward their subject like flies settle on sugar, while others seem to emerge from it. In many works this logical movement is easily discernible and very strong. When a character speaks, the words seem to issue from him and to be acts of his. Description first forms a *nature,* then allows that nature to *perform.* We must be careful, however, not to judge by externals. Barkis says that Barkis is willing, but the expression *functions* descriptively to qualify Barkis, and it is Dickens's habit to treat speech as if it were an attribute of character, like tallness or honesty, and not an act. On the other hand, qualities, in the right context, can be transformed into verbs. Later in the book don't we perceive the whiteness of the whale as a design, an intention of Moby Dick's, like a twist of his flukes or the smashing of a small boat?

Whether Mr. Cashmore was once real and sat by James at someone's dinner table, or was instead the fabrication of James's imagination,[6] as long as he came into being from the world's direction he once existed outside language. The task of getting him in I shall call the problem of rendering. But it must be stressed (it cannot be stressed too severely) that Mr. Cashmore may never have had a model, and may never have been imagined either, but may have come to be in order to serve some high conception (a Mr. Moneybags) and represent a type, not just himself, in which case he is not a reality *rendered,* but a universal *embodied.*[7] Again, Mr. Cashmore might have had still other parents. Meanings in the stream of words before his appearance might have suggested him, dramatic requirements may have called him forth, or he may have been the spawn of music, taking his substance from rhythm and alliteration. Perhaps it was all of these. In well-regulated fictions, most things are *over-determined.*

So far I have been talking about the function of a character in the direct stream of language, but there are these two other dimensions, the rendered and the embodied, and I should like to discuss each briefly.

If we observe one of J. F. Powers' worldly priests sharpening his eye for the pin by putting through his clerical collar, the humor, with all *its* sharpness, lives in the situation, and quite incidentally in the words.[8] One can indeed imagine Powers thinking it up independently of any verbal formula. Once Powers had decided that it would be funny to show a priest playing honeymoon bridge with his housekeeper, then his problem becomes the technical one of how best to accomplish it. What the writer must do, of course, is not only render the scene, but render the scene inseparable from its language, so that if the idea (the chaste priest caught in the clichés of marriage) is taken from the situation, like a heart from its body, both die. Far easier to render a real cornfield in front of you, because once that rendering has reached its page, the cornfield will no longer exist for literary purposes, no one will be able to see it by peering through your language, and consequently there will be nothing to abstract from your description. But with a "thought up" scene or situation, this is not the case. It comes under the curse of story. The notion, however amusing, is not literary, for it might be painted, filmed, or played. If we inquire further and ask why Powers wanted such a scene in the first place, we should find, I think, that he wanted it in order to embody a controlling "idea"—at one level of abstraction, the worldliness of the church, for instance. If he had nuns around a kitchen table counting the Sunday take and listening to the Cubs, *that* would do it. Father Burner beautifully embodies just such a controlling idea in Powers' celebrated story "The Prince of Darkness." Both rendering and embodying involve great risks because they require working into a scientific order of words what was not originally there. Any painter knows that a contour may only more or less enclose his model, while a free line simply and completely is. Many of the model's contours may be esthetically irrelevant, so it would be unwise to follow them. The free line is subject to no such temptations. Its relevance can be total. As Valéry wrote: There are no details in execution.

Often novelists mimic our ordinary use of language. We report upon ourselves; we gossip. Normally we are not lying; and our language, built to refer, actually does. When these selfsame words appear in fiction, and when they follow the forms of daily use, they create, quite readily, that dangerous feeling that a real Tietjens, a real Nickleby, lives just beyond the page; that through that thin partition we can hear a world at love.[9] But the writer must not let the reader out; the sculptor must not let the eye fall from the end of his statue's finger; the musician must not let the listener dream. Of course, he will; but let the blame be on himself. High tricks are possible: to run the eye rapidly along that outstretched arm to the fingertip, only to draw it up before it falls away in space; to carry the reader to the very edge of every word so that it seems he must be compelled to react as though to truth as told in life, and then to return him, like a philosopher liberated from the cave, to the clear and brilliant world of concept, to the realm of order, proportion, and dazzling construction . . . to fiction, where characters, unlike ourselves, freed from existence, can shine like essence, and purely Be.

Notes

1 This has already been discussed in "Philosophy and the Form of Fiction." In "Mirror, Mirror," I complain that Nabokov's omnipotence is too intrusive. [The essays to which Gass refers in all of these notes appear in W. H. Gass, *Fiction and The Figures of Life*.]

2 I treat the relation of fiction to life in more detail in "In Terms of the Toenail: Fiction and the Figures of Life." The problem is handled in other ways in "The Artist and Society," "Even if, by All the Oxen in the World," and "The Imagination of an Insurrection."

3 Of course nothing prevents a person from feeling that life is like this. See "A Spirit in Search of Itself."

4 There is no reason why every novel should be organized in this way. This method constructs a world according to the principles of Absolute Idealism. See "Philosophy and the Form of Fiction."

5 Henry James, "The Birthplace."

6 Some aspects of this imagination are dealt with in "The High Brutality of Good Intentions," and "In The Cage."

7 See "Philosophy and the Form of Fiction."

8 I enlarge on this aspect of Powers's work in "The Bingo Game at the Foot of the Cross."

9 See "The Medium of Fiction."

19

Time and Narrative in
A la recherche du temps perdu

GÉRARD GENETTE

■■■■

Gérard Genette outlines here the critical method he employs in *Narrative Discourse: An Essay in Method* (1972; trans. 1980). Genette is concerned in *Narrative Discourse* with what he considers the three main problems of narrative discourse: time, mode, and voice. This essay focuses exclusively on the problem of time, which the author subdivides into three parts: "the temporal *order* of the events that are being told and the pseudo-temporal order of the narrative," "the *duration* of the events and the duration of the narrative," and "the *frequency* of repetition between the events and the narrative, between history and story."

As Genette observes, literary narratives have in fact tended *not* to relay a plot in the chronological order in which the story's events occur. Epics tend to begin in the middle of things and then relate earlier events through flashbacks, while novels also use flashforwards. Genette identifies various elements of the narrative reshuffling of chronology and suggests some of the functions they serve. Flashbacks, for example, may either fill previous blank spaces in the narrative or serve as retrospections, emphasizing the importance of an event through repetition. Genette suggests, however, that such identifications can mislead the reader unless we also take duration into account. For example, Genette discovers that, as Marcel Proust's novel proceeds, more and more narrative ellipses occur, and an increasing number of pages are given over to episodes of decreasing chronological duration, resulting in an "increasing discontinuity of the narrative."

The third problem that concerns Genette is frequency. While the "singular narrative"—one that tells about each event once—is used most frequently, "repetitive narratives," which repeat key episodes or information at various points in the text, also exist. A third type is the "iterative narrative," in which "a single narrative assertion covers several recurrences of the same event or, to be more precise, of several analogical events considered only with respect to what they have in common." Genette focuses his attention on Proust and temporal structure precisely because, as Joseph Frank argues, modern literature, by breaking with traditional conceptions of chronology and narration, has learned to exploit alternative temporal ordering to create new ways for the reader to experience literature and, hence, perceive reality.

Gérard Genette (b. 1930) is a French critic and rhetorician whose *Narrative Discourse* has been recognized as a major document of French structuralism. His criticism has been published in French in the three-volume *Figures* (1966–1972), from which *Narrative Discourse* and *Figures of Literary Discourse* (1982) have been translated, as well as *Mimologiques* (1976) and *Palimpsestes* (1982).

I suggest a study of *narrative discourse* or, in a slightly different formulation, of *narrative (récit) as discourse (discours)*. As a point of departure, let us accept the hypothesis that all narratives, regardless of their complexity or degree of elaboration— and Proust's *A la recherche du temps perdu*, the text I shall be using as an example, reaches of course a very high degree of elaboration— can always be considered to be the development of a verbal statement such as "I am walking," or "He will come," or "Marcel becomes a writer." On the strength of this rudimentary analogy, the problems of narrative discourse can be classified under three main headings: the categories of *time* (temporal relationships between the narrative [story] and the "actual" events that are being told [history]); of *mode* (relationships determined by the distance and perspective of the narrative with respect to the history); and of *voice* (relationships between the narrative and the narrating agency itself: narrative situation, level of narration, status of the narrator and of the recipient, etc.). I shall deal only, and very sketchily, with the first category.

The time-category can itself be divided into three sections: the first concerned with the relationships between the temporal *order* of the events that are being told and the pseudotemporal order of the narrative; the second concerned with the relationships between the *duration* of the events and the duration of the narrative; the third dealing with relationships of *frequency* of repetition between the events and the narrative, between history and story.

Order

It is well known that the folk-tale generally keeps a one-to-one correspondence between the "real" order of events that are being told and the order of the narrative, whereas literary narrative, from its earliest beginnings in Western literature, that is, in the Homeric epic, prefers to use the beginning *in medias res*, generally followed by an explanatory flashback. This chronological reversal has become one of the formal *topoi* of the epic genre. The style of the novel has remained remarkably close to its distant origin in this respect: certain beginnings in Balzac, as in the *Duchesse de Langeais* or *César Birotteau*, immediately come to mind as typical examples.

From this point of view, the *Recherche*—especially the earlier sections of the book—indicates that Proust made a much more extensive use than any of his predecessors of his freedom to reorder the temporality of events.

The first "time," dealt with in the six opening pages of the book, refers to a moment that cannot be dated with precision but that must take place quite late in the life of the protagonist: the time at which Marcel, during a period when, as he says, "he often used to go to bed early," suffered from spells of insomnia during which he relived his own past. The first moment in the organization of the narrative is thus far from being the first in the order of the reported history, which deals with the life of the hero.

The second moment refers to the memory relived by the protagonist during his sleepless night. It deals with his childhood at Combray, or, more accurately, with a specific but particularly important moment of this childhood: the famous scene that Marcel calls "the drama of his going to bed," when his mother, at first prevented by Swann's visit from giving him his ritualistic good-night kiss, finally gives in and consents to spend the night in his room.

The third moment again moves far ahead, probably to well within the period of insomnia referred to at the start, or a little after the end of this period: it is the episode of the *madeleine*, during which Marcel recovers an entire fragment of his childhood that had up till then remained hidden in oblivion.

This very brief third episode is followed at once by a fourth: a second return to Combray, this time much more extensive than the first in temporal terms since it covers the entire span of the Combray childhood. Time segment (4) is thus contemporary with time segment (2) but has a much more extensive duration.

The fifth moment is a very brief return to the initial state of sleeplessness and leads to a new retrospective section that takes us even further back into the past, since it deals with a love experience of Swann that took place well before the narrator was born.

There follows a seventh episode that occurs some time after the last events told in the fourth section (childhood at Combray): the story of Marcel's adolescence in Paris and of his love for Gilberte. From then on, the story will proceed in more closely chronological order, at least in its main articulations.

A la recherche du temps perdu thus begins with a zigzagging movement that could easily be represented by a graph and in which the relationship between the time of events and the time of the narrative could be summarized as follows: $N(\text{arrative}) \ 1 = H(\text{istory}) \ 4$; $N_2 = H_2$; $N_3 = H_4$; $N_4 = H_2$; $N_5 = H_4$; $N_6 = H_1$ (Swann's love); $N_7 = H_3$. We are clearly dealing with a highly complex and deliberate transgression of chronological order. I have said that the rest of the book follows a more continuous chronology in its main patterns, but this large-scale linearity does not exclude the presence of a great number of anachronisms in the details: *retrospections*, as when the story of Marcel's stay in Paris during the year 1914 is told in the middle of his later visit to Paris during 1916; or *anticipations*, as when, in the last pages of *Du Côté de chez Swann*, Marcel describes what has become of the Bois de Boulogne at a much later date, the very year he is actually engaged in writing his book. The transition from the

Côté des Guermantes to *Sodome et Gomorrhe* is based on an interplay of anachronisms: the last scene of *Guermantes* (announcing the death of Swann) in fact takes place later than the subsequent first scene of *Sodome* (the meeting between Charlus and Jupien).

I do not intend to analyze the narrative anachronisms in detail but will point out in passing that one should distinguish between *external* and *internal* anachronisms, according to whether they are located without or within the limits of the temporal field defined by the main narrative. The external anachronisms raise no difficulty, since there is no danger that they will interfere with the main narrative. The internal anachronisms, on the contrary, create a problem of interference. So we must subdivide them into two groups, according to the nature of this relation. Some function to fill in a previous or later blank (ellipsis) in the narrative and can be called *completive* anachronisms, such as the retrospective story of Swann's death. Others return to a moment that has already been covered in the narrative: they are *repetitive* or apparently redundant anachronisms but fulfill in fact a very important function in the organization of the novel. They function as *announcements* (in the case of prospective anticipations) or as *recalls* (when they are retrospective). Announcements can, for example, alert the reader to the meaning of a certain event that will only later be fully revealed (as with the lesbian scene at Montjouvain that will later determine Marcel's jealous passion for Albertine). Recalls serve to give a subsequent meaning to an event first reported as without particular significance (as when we find that Albertine's belated response to a knock on the door was caused by the fact that she had locked herself in with Andrée), or serve even more often to alter the original meaning—as when Marcel discovers after more than thirty years' time that Gilberte was in love with him at Combray and that what he took to be a gesture of insolent disdain was actually meant to be an advance.

Next to these relatively simple and unambiguous retrospections and anticipations, one finds more complex and ambivalent forms of anachronisms: anticipations within retrospections, as when Marcel remembers what used to be his projects with regard to the moment that he is now experiencing; retrospections within anticipations, as when the narrator indicates how he will later find out about the episode he is now in the process of telling; "announcements" of events that have already been told anticipatively or "recalls" of events that took place earlier in the story but that have not yet been told; retrospections that merge seamlessly with the main narrative and make it impossible to identify the exact status of a given section, etc. Finally, I should mention what is perhaps the rarest but most specific of all instances: structures that could properly be called *achronisms*, that is to say, episodes entirely cut loose from any chronological situation whatsoever. These occurrences were pointed out by J. P. Houston in a very interesting study published in *French Studies*, January 1962, entitled "Temporal Patterns in *À la recherche du temps perdu*." Near the end of *Sodome et Gomorrhe*, as Marcel's second stay at Balbec draws to a close, Proust tells a sequence of episodes not in the order in which they took place but by following the succession of roadside-stops made by the little train on its journey from Balbec to La Raspelière. Events here follow a geographical rather than a chronological pattern. It is true that the sequence of places still depends on a temporal event (the journey of the train), but this temporality is not that of the "real" succession of events. A similar effect is achieved in the composition of the end of *Combray*, when the narrator successively describes a number of events that took place on the Méséglise way, at different moments, by following the order of their increasing distance from Combray. He follows the temporal succession of a walk from Combray to Méséglise and then, after returning to his spatial and temporal point of departure, tells a sequence of events that took place on the Guermantes way using exactly the same principle. The temporal order of the narrative is not that of the actual succession of events, unless it happens to coincide by chance with the sequence of places encountered in the course of the walk.

I have given some instances of the freedom that Proust's narrative takes with the chronological order of events, but such a description is necessarily sketchy and even misleading if other elements of narrative temporality such as duration and frequency are not also taken into account.

Duration

Generally speaking, the idea of an isochrony between narrative and "history" is highly ambiguous, for the narrative unit which, in literature, is almost always a narrative text cannot really be said to possess a definite duration. One could equate the duration of a narrative with the time it takes to read it, but reading-times vary considerably from reader to reader, and an ideal average speed can only be determined by fictional means. It may be better to start out from a definition in the form of a relative quantity, and define isochrony as a uniform projection of historical time on narrative extension, that is, number of pages per duration of event. In this way, one can record variations in the speed of the narrative in relation to itself and measure effects of acceleration, deceleration, stasis, and ellipsis (blank spaces within the narrative while the flow of events keeps unfolding).

I have made some rather primitive calculations of the relative speed of the main narrative articulations, measuring on the one hand the narrative of the *Recherche* by number of pages and on the other hand the events by quantity of time. Here are the results.

The first large section, *Combray* or Marcel's childhood, numbers approximately 180 pages of the Pléiade edition and covers about ten years (let me say once and for all that I am defining the duration of events by general consensus, knowing that it is open to question on several points). The next episode, Swann's love-affair with Odette, uses approximately 200 pages to cover about two years. The Gilberte episode (end of *Swann*, beginning of *Jeunes filles en fleurs*) devotes 160 pages to a duration that can be evaluated at two or three years. Here we encounter an ellipsis involving two years of the protagonist's life and mentioned in passing in a few words at the beginning of a sentence. The Balbec episode numbers 300 pages for a three-month-long time-span; then the lengthy section dealing with life in Paris society (*Côté de Guermantes* and beginning of *Sodome et Gomorrhe*) takes up 750 pages for two and a half years. It should be added that considerable variations occur within this section: 110 pages are devoted to the afternoon party at Mme. de Villeparisis's that lasts for about two hours, 150 pages to the dinner of nearly equal length at the Duchesse de Guermantes's, and 100 pages to the evening at the Princesse de Guermantes's. In this vast episode of 750 pages for two and a half years, 360 pages—nearly one-half—are taken up by less than ten hours of social life.

The second stay at Balbec (end of *Sodome*) covers approximately six months in 380 pages. Then the Albertine sequence, reporting the hero's involvement with Albertine in Paris (*La Prisonnière* and the beginning of *La Fugitive*), requires 630 pages for an eighteen-month period, of which 300 deal with only two days. The stay in Venice uses 35 pages for a few weeks, followed by a section of 40 pages (astride *La Fugitive* and *Le Temps retrouvé*) for the stay in Tansonville, the return to the country of Marcel's childhood. The first extended ellipsis of the *Recherche* occurs here; the time-span cannot be determined with precision, but it encompasses approximately ten years of the hero's life spent in a rest-home. The subsequent episode, situated during the war, devotes 130 pages to a few weeks, followed by another ellipsis of ten years again spent in a rest-home. Finally, the concluding scene, the party at the Princesse de Guermantes's, devotes 190 pages to a two- or three-hour-long reception.

What conclusions can be derived from this barren and apparently useless enumeration? First of all, we should note the extensive shifts in relative duration, ranging from one line of text for ten years to 190 pages for two or three hours, or from approximately one page per century to one page per minute. The second observation refers to the internal evolution of the *Recherche* as a whole. It could be roughly summarized by stressing, on the one hand, the gradual slowing down of the narrative achieved by the insertion of longer and longer scenes for events of shorter and shorter duration. This is compensated for, on the other hand, by the presence of more and more extensive ellipses. The two trends can be easily united in one formula: increasing discontinuity of the narrative. As the Proustian narrative moves toward its conclusion, it becomes increasingly discontinuous, consisting of gigantic scenes separated from each other by enormous gaps. It deviates more and more from the ideal "norm" of an isochronic narrative.

We should also stress how Proust selects among the traditional literary forms of narrative duration. Among the nearly infinite range of possible combinations of historical and narrative duration, the literary tradition has made a rather limited choice that can be reduced to the following fundamental forms: (1) the *summary*, when the narrative duration is greatly reduced with respect to the historical duration; it is well known that the summary constitutes the main connective tissue in the classical *récit*; (2) the dramatic scene, especially the dialogue, when narrative and historical time are supposed to be nearly equal; (3) the narrative *stasis*, when the narrative discourse continues while historical time is at a standstill, usually in order to take care of a description; and (4) *ellipsis*, consisting of a certain amount of historical time covered in a zero amount of narrative. If we consider the *Recherche* from this point of view, we are struck by the total absence of summarizing narrative, which tends to be absorbed in the ellipses, and by the near-total absence of descriptive stasis: the Proustian descriptions always correspond to an actual observation-time on the part of the character; the time-lapse is sometimes mentioned in the text and is obviously longer than the time it takes to read the description (three-quarters of an hour for the contemplation of the Elstir paintings owned by the Duc de Guermantes, when the description takes only four or five pages of the text). The narrative duration is not interrupted—as is so often the case with Balzac—for, rather than *describing*, Proust *narrates* how his hero perceives, contemplates, and experiences a given sight; the description is incorporated within the narrative and constitutes no autonomous narrative form. Except for another effect with which I shall deal at some length in a moment, Proust makes use of only two of the traditional forms of narrative duration: scene and ellipsis. And since ellipsis is a zero point of the text, we have in fact only one single form: the scene. I should add, however, without taking time to develop a rather obvious observation, that the narrative function of this traditional form is rather strongly subverted in Proust. The main number of his major scenes do not have the purely dramatic function usually associated with the classical "scene." The traditional economy of the novel, consisting of summarizing and nondramatic narrative alternating with dramatic scenes, is entirely discarded. Instead, we find another form of alternating movement toward which we must now direct our attention.

Frequency

The third kind of narrative temporality, which has in general received much less critical and theoretical attention than the two previous ones, deals with the relative frequency of the narrated events and of the narrative sections that report them. Speaking once more very schematically, the most obvious form of narration will tell once what happens once, as in a narrative statement such as: "Yesterday, I went to bed early." This type of narrative is so current and presumably normal that it bears no special name. In order to emphasize that it is merely one possibility among many, I propose to give it a name and call it the *singulative* narrative (*récit singulatif*). It is equally possible to tell several times what happened several times, as when I say: "Monday I went to bed early, Tuesday I went to bed early, Wednesday I went to bed early," etc. This type of anaphoric narrative remains singulative and can be equated with the first, since the repetitions of the story correspond one-to-one to the repetitions of the events. A narrative can also tell several times, with or without variations, an event that happened only once, as in a statement of this kind: "Yesterday I went to bed early, yesterday I went to bed early, yesterday I tried to go to sleep well before dark," etc. This last hypothesis may seem *a priori* to be a gratuitous one, or even to exhibit a slight trace of senility. One should remember, however, that most texts by Alain Robbe-Grillet, among others, are founded on the repetitive potential of the narrative: the recurrent episode of the killing of the centipede, in *La Jalousie*, would be ample proof of this. I shall call *repetitive* narrative this type of narration, in which the story-repetitions exceed in number the repetitions of events. There remains a last possibility. Let us return to our second example: "Monday, Tuesday, Wednesday," etc. When such a pattern of events occurs, the narrative is obviously not reduced to the necessity of reproducing it as if its discourse were incapable of abstraction or synthesis. Unless a deliberate stylistic effect is aimed for, even the simplest narration will choose a formulation such as "every day" or "every day of the week" or "all week long." We all know which of these devices Proust chose for the opening sentence of the *Recherche*. The type of narrative in which a single narrative assertion covers several recurrences of the same event or, to be more precise, of several analogical events considered only with respect to what they have in common, I propose to call by the obvious name of *iterative* narrative (*récit itératif*).

My heavy-handed insistence on this notion may well seem out of place, since it designates a purely grammatical concept without literary relevance. Yet the quantitative amount and the qualitative function of the iterative mode are particularly important in Proust and have seldom, to my knowledge, received the critical attention they deserve. It can be said without exaggeration that the entire Combray episode is essentially an iterative narrative, interspersed here and there with some "singulative" scenes of salient importance such as the motherly good-night kiss, the meeting with the Lady in the pink dress (a retrospective scene), or the profanation of Vinteuil's portrait at Montjouvain. Except for five or six such scenes referring to a single action and told in the historical past (*passé défini*), all the rest, told in the imperfect, deals with what used to happen at Combray regularly, ritualistically, every night or every Sunday, or every Saturday, or whenever the weather was good or the weather was bad, etc. The narrative of Swann's love for Odette will still be conducted, for the most part, in the mode of habit and repetition; the same is true of the story of Marcel's love for Swann's daughter Gilberte. Only when we reach the stay at Balbec in the *Jeunes filles en fleurs* do the singulative episodes begin to predominate, although they remain interspersed with numerous iterative passages: the Balbec outings with Mme. de Villeparisis and later with Albertine, the hero's stratagems at the beginning of *Guermantes* when he tries to meet the Duchess every morning, the journeys in the little train of the Raspelière (*Sodome*, II), life with Albertine in Paris (the first eighty pages of *La Prisonnière*) the walks in Venice (*La Fugitive*), not to mention the iterative treatment of certain moments within the singulative scenes, such as the conversations about genealogy during the dinner at the Duchess's, or the description of the aging guests at the last Guermantes party. The narrative synthesizes these moments by reducing several distinct occurrences to their common elements: "the *women* were like this . . . the *men* acted like that; *some* did this, *others* that," etc. I shall call these sections *internal iterations*, in contrast with other, more common passages, in which a descriptive-iterative parenthesis begins in the middle of a singulative scene to convey additional information needed for the reader's understanding and which I shall call *external iterations*. An example would be the long passage devoted, in the middle of the first Guermantes dinner, to the more general and therefore necessarily iterative description of the Guermantes wit.

The use of iterative narrative is by no means Proust's invention; it is one of the most classical devices of fictional narrative. But the frequency of the mode is distinctively Proustian, a fact still underscored by the relatively massive presence of what could be called *pseudo-iterations*, scenes presented (mostly by the use of the imperfect tense) as if they were iterative, but with such a wealth of precise detail that no reader can seriously believe that they could have taken place repeatedly in this way, without variations. One thinks for example of some of the conversations between Aunt Léonie and her maid Françoise that go on for page after page, or of conversations in Mme. Verdurin's or Mme. Swann's salon in Paris. In each of these cases, a singular scene has arbitrarily, and without any but grammatical change, been converted into an iterative scene, thus clearly revealing the trend of the Proustian narrative toward a kind of inflation of the iterative.

It would be tempting to interpret this tendency as symptomatic of a dominant psychological trait: Proust's highly developed sense of habit and repetition, his feeling for the *analogy* between different moments in life. This is all the more striking since the iterative mode of the narrative is not always, as in the Combray part, based on the repetitive, ritualistic pattern of a bourgeois existence in the provinces. Contrary to general belief, Proust is less aware of the specificity of moments than he is aware of the specificity of places; the latter is one of the governing laws of his sensibility. His moments have a strong tendency to blend into each other, a possibility which is at the root of the experience of spontaneous recollection. The opposition between the "singularity" of his spatial imagination and, if I dare say so, the "iterativity" of his temporal imagination is nicely illustrated in the following sentence from *Swann*. Speaking of the Guermantes landscape, Proust writes: "[Its] specificity would *at times*, in my dreams, seize upon me with almost fantastical power" ("le paysage dont *parfois*, la nuit dans mes rêves, l'individualité m'étreint avec une puissance presque fantastique"). Hence the highly developed sense of *ritual* (see, for example, the scene of the Saturday luncheon at Combray) and, on the other hand, the panic felt in the presence of irregularities of behavior, as when Marcel, at Balbec, wonders about the complex and secret law that may govern the unpredictable absences of the young girls on certain days.

But we must now abandon these psychological extrapolations and turn our attention to the technical questions raised by the iterative narration.

Every iterative sequence can be characterized by what may be called its *delimitation* and its *specification*. The delimitation determines the confines within the flow of external duration between which the iterative sequence, which generally has a beginning and an end, takes place. The delimitation can be vague, as when we are told that "from a certain year on, Mlle. Vinteuil could never be seen alone" (I, 147), or precise, defined—a very rare occurrence in Proust—by a specific date, or by reference to a particular event, as when the break between Swann and the Verdurins puts an end to an iterative sequence telling of Swann's encounters with Odette and starts off a new sequence. The specification, on the other hand, points out the recurring periodicity of the iterative unit. It can be indefinite (as is frequently the case in Proust who introduces an iterative statement by such adverbs of time as "sometimes," "often," "on certain days," etc.) or definite, when it follows an absolute and regular pattern such as: "every day," "every Sunday," etc. The pattern can also be more irregular and relative, as when the walks toward Méséglise are said to take place in bad or uncertain weather, or the walks toward Guermantes whenever the weather is good. Two or more specifications can of course be juxtaposed. "Every summer" and "every Sunday" combine to give "every Sunday in the summer," which is the iterative specification of much of the Combray section.

The interplay between these two dimensions of the iterative narrative varies and enriches a temporal mode threatened, by its very nature, by a degree of abstraction. Provided it has a certain length, an iterative section can very closely resemble an ordinary narrative, except for some grammatical traits. Yet it goes without saying that a narrative such as "Sunday at Combray" that would retain only events that *all* Sundays have in common would run the risk of becoming as dryly schematic as a stereotyped time-schedule. The monotony can be avoided by playing on the internal delimitations and specifications.

Internal delimitations: for instance, the diachronic caesura brought about by the story of the encounter with the "Lady in the pink dress" in the narration of Marcel's Sunday afternoon readings: this encounter will bring about a change of locale, after the quarrel between Marcel's parents and Uncle Adolphe has put the latter's room out of bounds. Another instance would be the change of direction in the hero's dreams of literary glory after his first encounter with the Duchess in the church of Combray. The single scene, in those instances, divides the iterative sequence into a *before* and an *after*, and so diversifies it into two subsequences which function as two *variants*.

Internal specifications: I mentioned the good weather/bad weather pattern which introduces a definite specification in the iterative series of the Sunday walks and determines the choice between Guermantes and Méséglise. Most of the time, however, the iterative narrative is diversified in indefinite specifications introduced by "sometimes . . ." or "one time . . . some other time . . . ," etc. These devices allow for a very flexible system of variations and for a high degree of particularization, without leaving the iterative mode. A characteristic example of this technique occurs toward the end of the *Jeunes filles en fleurs* in a description of Albertine's face (I, 946–47). The iterative mode, indeed, applies just as well to the descriptive as to the narrative passages; half of Proust's descriptions make use of this mode:

> *Certains jours,* mince, le teint gris, l'air maussade, une transparence violette descendant obliquement au fond de ses yeux comme il arrive quelquefois pour la mer, elle semblait éprouver une tristesse d'exilée. *D'autres jours,* sa figure plus lisse engluait les désirs à sa surface vernie et les empêchait d'aller au delà; *à moins que* je ne la visse tout à coup de côté, car ses joues mates comme une blanche cire à la surface étaient roses par transparence, ce qui donnait tellement envie de les embrasser, d'atteindre ce teint différent qui se dérobait. *D'autres fois,* le bonheur baignait ces joues d'une clarté si mobile que la peau, devenue fluide et vague, laissait passer comme des regards sous-jacents qui la faisaient paraître d'une autre couleur, mais non d'une autre matière, que les yeux; *quelquefois,* sans y penser, quand on regardait sa figure ponctuée de petits points bruns et où flottaient seulement deux taches plus bleues; C'était comme on eût fait d'un oeuf de chardonneret, *souvent* comme d'une agate opaline travaillée et polie à deux places seulement où, au milieu de la pierre brune, luisaient, comme les ailes

transparentes d'un papillon d'azur, les yeux où la chair devient miroir et nous donne l'illusion de nous laisser, plus qu'en les autres parties du corps, approcher de l'âme. Mais *le plus souvent* aussi elle était plus colorée, et alors plus animée: *quelquefois* seul était rose, dans sa figure blanche, le bout de son nez, fin comme celui d'une petite chatte sournoise avec qui l'on aurait eu envie de jouer; *quelquefois* ses joues étaient si lisses que le regard glissait comme sur celui d'une miniature sur leur émail rose, que faisait encore paraître plus délicat, plus intérieur, le couvercle entr'ouvert et superposé de ses cheveux noirs; *il arrivait que* le teint de ses joues atteingnît le rose violacé du cyclamen, et *parfois* même, quand elle était congestionnée ou fiévreuse, et donnant alors l'idée d'une complexion maladive qui rabaissait mon désir à quelque chose de plus sensuel et faisait exprimer à son regard quelque chose de plus pervers et de plus malsain, la sombre pourpre de certaines roses d'un rouge presque noir; et chacune de ces Albertin était différente, comme est différente chacune des apparitions de la danseuse dont sont transmutées les couleurs, la forme, le caractère, selon les jeux innombrablement variés d'un projecteur lumineux. (Italics added)[1]

On certain days, slim, with grey cheeks, a sullen air, a violet transparency falling obliquely from her such as we notice sometimes on the sea, she seemed to be feeling the sorrows of exile. *On other days* her face, more sleek, caught and glued my desires to its varnished surface and prevented them from going any farther; *unless* I caught a sudden glimpse of her from the side, for her dull cheeks, like white wax on the surface, were visibly pink beneath, which made me anxious to kiss them, to reach that different tint, which thus avoided my touch. *At other times* happiness bathed her cheeks with a clarity so mobile that the skin, grown fluid and vague, gave passage to a sort of stealthy and sub-cutaneous gaze, which made it appear to be of another colour but not of another substance than her eyes; *sometimes*, instinctively, when one looked at her face punctuated with tiny brown marks among which floated what were simply two larger, bluer stains, it was like looking at the egg of a goldfinch—or *often* like an opalescent agate cut and polished in two places only, where, from the heart of the brown stone, shone like the transparent wings of a sky-blue butterfly her eyes, those features in which the flesh becomes a mirror and gives us the illusion that it allows us, more than through the other parts of the body, to approach the soul. But *most often of all* she shewed more colour, and was then more animated; *sometimes* the only pink thing in her white face was the tip of her nose, as finely pointed as that of a mischievous kitten with which one would have liked to stop and play; *sometimes* her cheeks were so glossy that one's glance slipped, as over the surface of a miniature, over their pink enamel, which was made to appear still more delicate, more private, by the enclosing though half-opened case of her black hair; *or it might happen that* the tint of her cheeks had deepened to the violet shade of the red cyclamen, and, *at times, even,* when she was flushed or feverish, with a suggestion of unhealthiness which lowered my desire to something more sensual and made her glance expressive of something more perverse and un-wholesome, to the deep purple of certain roses, a red that was almost black; and each of these Albertines was different, as in every fresh appearance of the dancer whose colours, form, character, are transmitted according to the innumerably varied play of projected limelight. (I, 708; italics added)

The two devices (internal delimitation and internal specification) can be used together in the same passage, as in this scene from *Combray* that deals in a general way with returns from walks. The general statement is then diversified by a delimitation (itself itera-tive, since it recurs every year) that distinguishes between the begin-ning and the end of the season. This second sequence is then again diversified by a single indefinite specification: "certains soirs. . . ." The following passage is built on such a system; very simple but very productive:

Nous rentrions *toujours* de bonne heure de nos promenades, pour pouvoir faire une visite à ma tante Léonie avant le dîner. *Au commencement de la saison,* où le jour finit tôt, quand nous arrivions rue du Saint-Esprit, il y avait encore un reflet du couchant sur les vitres de la maison et un bandeau de pourpre au fond des bois du Calvaire, qui se reflétait plus loin dans l'étang, rougeur qui, accompagnée souvent d'un froid assez vif, s'associait, dans mon esprit, à la rougeur du feu au-dessus duquel rôtissait le poulet qui ferait succéder pour moi au plaisir poétique donné par la promenade, le plaisir de la gourmandise, de la chaleur et du repos. *Dans l'été, au contraire*, quand nous rentrions le soleil ne se couchait pas encore; et pendant la visite que nous faisions chez ma tante Léonie, so lumière qui s'abaissait et touchait la fenêtre, était arrêtée entre les grands rideaux et les embrasses, divisée, ramifiée, filtrée, et, incrustant de petits morceaux d'or le bois de citronnier de la commode, illuminait obliquement la chambre avec la délica-tesse qu'elle prend dans les sous-bois. Mais, *certains jours forts rares*, quand nous rentrions, il y avait bien longtemps que la commode avait perdu ses incrustations momentanées, il n'y avait plus, quand nous arrivions rue du Saint-Esprit, nul reflet de couchant étendu sur les vitres, et l'étang au pied du calvaire avait perdu sa rougeur, quelquefois il était dèjà couleur d'opale, et un long rayon de lune, qui allait en s'élargissant et se fendillait de toutes les rides de l'eau, le traversait tout entier. (I, 133; italics added)

We used *always* to return from our walks in good time to pay aunt Léonie a visit before dinner. *In the first weeks of our Combray holidays*, when the days ended early, we would still be able to see, as we turned into the Rue du Saint-Esprit, a re-flection of the western sky from the windows of the house and a band of purple at the foot of the Calvary, which was mir-rored further on in the pond; a fiery glow which, accompa-nied often by a cold that burned and stung, would associate itself in my mind with the glow of the fire over which, at that very moment, was roasting the chicken that was to furnish me, in place of the poetic pleasure I had found in my walk, with the sensual pleasures of good feeding, warmth and rest. *But in summer*, when we came back to the house, the sun would not have set; and while we were upstairs paying our visit to aunt Léonie its rays, sinking until they touched and lay along her window-sill, would there be caught and held by the large inner curtains and the bands which tied them back to the wall, and split and scattered and filtered; and then, at last, would fall upon and inlay with tiny flakes of gold the lemonwood of her chest-of-drawers, illuminating the room in their passage with the same delicate, slanting, shadowed beams that fall among the boles of forest trees. *But on some days, though very rarely,* the chest-of-drawers would long since have shed its momentary adornments, there would no longer, as we turned into the Rue du Saint-Esprit, be any reflection from the western sky burning along the line of window-panes; the pond beneath the Calvary would have lost its fiery glow, sometimes indeed had changed already to an opalescent pallor, while a long ribbon of moonlight, bent and broken and broadened by every ripple upon the water's surface, would be lying across it, from end to end. (I, 102; italics added)

Finally, when all the resources of iterative particularization have been exhausted, two devices remain. I have already mentioned pseudo-iteration (as in the conversations between Françoise and Aunt Léonie); this is admittedly a way of cheating or, at the very least, of stretching the reader's benevolence to the limit. The second device is more honest—if such ethical terminology can have any sense in the world of art—but it represents an extreme case leading out of the actually iterative mode: in the midst of an iterative section the narrator mentions a particular, singular occurrence, either as illustration, or example, or, on the contrary, as an exception to the law of repetition that has just been established. Such moments can be introduced by an expression such as "thus it happened that . . ." ("c'est ainsi que . . .") or, in the case of an exception, "this time however . . ." ("une fois pourtant . . ."). The following passage from the *Jeunes filles* is an example of the first possibility: "*At times,* a kind gesture of one [of the girls] would awaken within me an expansive sympathy that replaced, for a while, my desire for the others. *Thus it happened that* Albertine, one day . . ." etc. (I, 911).[2] The famous passage of the Martinville clock towers is an example of the second possibility. It is explicitly introduced as an exception to the habitual pattern: generally, when Marcel returns from walks, he forgets his impressions and does not try to interpret their meaning. "This time, however" (the expression is in the text), he goes further and composes the descriptive piece that constitutes his first literary work. The exceptional nature of an event is perhaps even more explicitly stressed in a passage from *La Prisonnière* that begins as follows: "*I will put aside*, among the days during which I lingered at Mme. de Guermantes's, one day that was marked by a small incident . . . ," after which the iterative narrative resumes: "*Except for this single incident*, everything went *as usual* when I returned from the Duchess's . . ." (III, 54 and 55).[3]

By means of such devices, the singulative mode merges, so to speak, with the iterative section and is made to serve it by positive or negative illustrations, either by adhering to the code or by transgressing it—which is another way of recognizing its existence.

The final problem associated with iterative temporality concerns the relationship between the duration or, rather, the internal diachrony of the iterative unit under consideration, and the external diachrony, that is, the flow of "real" and necessarily singulative time between the beginning and the end of the iterative sequence. A unit such as "sleepless night," made up of a sequence that stretches over several years, may very well be told in terms of its own duration from night to morning, without reference to the external passage of years. The typical night remains constant, except for internal specifications, from the beginning to the end of the sequence, without being influenced by the passage of time outside the particular iterative unit. This is, in fact, what happens in the first pages of the *Recherche*. However, by means of internal delimitations, the narrative of an iterative unit may just as readily encompass the external diachrony and narrate, for example, "a Sunday at Combray" by drawing attention to changes in the dominical ritual brought about by the passage of years: greater maturity of the protagonist, new acquaintances, new interests, etc. In the Combray episodes, Proust very skillfully plays upon these possibilities. J. P. Houston claimed that the narrative progresses simultaneously on three levels: with the duration of the day, of the season, and of the years. Things are perhaps not quite as clear and systematic as Houston makes them out to be, but it is true that, in the Sunday scenes, events taking place in the afternoon are of a later date than those taking place in the morning and that, in the narration of the walks, the most recent episodes are assigned to the longest itineraries. For the reader, this creates the illusion of a double temporal progression, as if the hero were a naïve little boy in the morning and a sophisticated adolescent at night, aging several years in the course of a single day or a single walk. We are touching here upon the outer limits of the iterative narrative mode.

Thus Proust appears to substitute for the *summary*, which typifies the classical novel, another form of synthesis, the iterative narrative. The synthesis is no longer achieved by acceleration, but by analogy and abstraction. The rhythm of Proust's narrative is no longer founded, as in the classical *récit*, on the alternating movement of dramatic and summarizing sections, but on the alternating movement of iterative and singular scenes. Most of the time, these alternating sections overlay a system of hierarchical subordinations that can be revealed by analysis. We already encountered two types of such systems: an iterative-explanatory section that is functionally dependent on an autonomous singular episode: the Guermantes wit (iterative) in the midst of a dinner at the duchess's (singular): and a singular-illustrative section dependent on an autonomous iterative sequence (in the scenes used as illustrations or exceptions). The hierarchical systems of interdependence can be more complex, as when a singular scene illustrates an iterative section that is itself inserted within another singulative scene: this happens, for example, when a particular anecdote (such as Oriane's wordplay on Taquin le Superbe) is used to illustrate the famous Guermantes wit: here we have a singulative element (Taquin le Superbe) within an iterative sequence (Guermantes wit) itself included in a singulative scene (dinner at Oriane de Guermantes's). The description of these structural relationships is one of the tasks of narrative analysis.

If often happens that the relationships are less clear and that the Proustian narrative fluctuates between the two modes without visible concern for their respective functions, without even seeming to be aware of the differences. Some time ago, Marcel Vigneron pointed out confusions of this sort in the section dealing with Marcel's love for Gilberte at the Champs-Elysées: an episode would start off in the historical past (*passé défini*), continue in the imperfect, and return to the historical past, without any possibility for the reader to determine whether he was reading a singular or an iterative scene. Vigneron attributed these anomalies to last-minute changes in the manuscript made necessary by publication. The explanation may be correct, but it is not exhaustive, for similar discrepancies occur at other moments in the *Recherche* when no such considerations of expediency can be invoked. Proust probably at times forgets what type of narrative he is using; hence, for example, the very revealing sudden appearance of a historical past within a pseudo-iterative scene (I, 104, 722). He was certainly also guided by a secret wish to set the narrative forms free from their hierarchical function, letting them play and "make music" for themselves, as Proust himself said of Flaubert's ellipses. Hence the most subtle and admirable passages of all, of which J. P. Houston has mentioned a few, in which Proust passes from an iterative to a singular passage or uses an almost imperceptible modulation—such as an ambiguous imperfect of which it is impossible to know whether it functions iteratively or singularly, or the interposition of directly reported dialogue without declarative verb and, consequently, without determined mode, or a page of commentary by the narrator, in the present tense—to achieve the opposite effect; such a modulation, lengthily developed and to all appearances carefully controlled, serves as a transition between the first eighty pages of *La Prisonnière* that are in an iterative mode, and the singulative scenes that follow.

I have particularly stressed the question of narrative frequency because it has often been neglected by critics and by theoreticians of narrative technique, and because it occupies a particularly prominent place in the work of Marcel Proust. A paper that deals so sketchily and provisionally with a single category of narrative discourse cannot hope to reach a conclusion. Let me therefore end by pointing out that, together with the daring manipulations of chronology I have mentioned in the first part of my paper and the large-sized distortions of duration described in the second, Proust's predilection for an iterative narrative mode and the complex and subtle manner in which he exploits the contrasts and relations of this mode with a singulative discourse combine to free his narrative forever from the constraints and limitations of traditional narration. For it goes without saying that, in an iterative temporality, the order of succession and the relationships of duration that make up classical temporality are from the very beginning subverted or, more subtly and effectively, *perverted*. Proust's novel is not only what it claims to be, a novel of time lost and recaptured, but also, perhaps more implicitly, a novel of controlled, imprisoned, and bewitched time, a part of what Proust called, with reference to dreams, "the formidable game it plays with Time" ("le jeu formidable qu'il fait avec le Temps").

Notes

1 All citations are from the Pléiade edition of *A la recherche du temps perdu*. The English version of this passage and of the passage on [pp. 292–93] is from the translation by C. K. Scott Moncrieff, published by Random House. Translations in the text are by Paul De Man.

2 "*Parfois* une gentille attention de telle ou telle éveillait en moi d'amples vibrations qui éloignaient pour un temps le désir des autres. *Ainsi un jour Albertine* . . ."

3 "*Je mettrai à part*, parmi ces jours ou je m'attardai chez Mme. de Guermantes, un qui fût marqué par un petit incident . . ."; "*Sauf cet incident unique*, tout se passair *normalement* quand je remontais de chez la duchesse . . ."

20

The Literary Motif:
A Definition and Evaluation

WILLIAM FREEDMAN

William Freedman takes a common but often vaguely defined critical term, "literary motif," and attempts to develop a comprehensive definition. He begins with a standard definition: "a theme, character, or verbal pattern which recurs in literature or folklore" and which may recur in a number of works or a single work; he then emphasizes that a motif may appear as a "verbal pattern" and may "act symbolically." In regard to being a verbal pattern, a motif, "although it may appear as something described, perhaps even more often forms part of the description." Thus, unlike a symbol, it may recur in a work without using the same object, image, or word each time. Freedman cites the repetition of varying references to money, finance, and economics in some of Henry James's and F. Scott Fitzgerald's novels. According to Freedman, a motif will fall into "one or more of three principal categories: cognitive, affective (or emotive), and structural." In addition, a motif must recur with sufficient frequency to make it recognizable, and its appearance must be avoidable or unlikely, so that it stands out from the general descriptive background.

Having established the appearance of a "motif," Freedman provides five criteria for evaluating its effectiveness: frequency, avoidability and unlikelihood, significance of context, the degree of the relevance and coherence of the motif as a whole, and—for those motifs that function symbolically—its appropriateness to what it symbolizes. After producing a working definition, Freedman discusses the literary value of the motif and its key contribution to artistic complexity: "the motif is a complex of separate parts subtly reiterating on one level what is taking place on another. It thus multiplies levels of meaning and interest." This evaluation is based on the premise "that subtlety, richness, and complexity are desirable qualities in a work of art," a premise that echoes James's belief that a work of fiction is only required to be "interesting." In this context, we may want to ask whether—just as it is possible for a work of fiction to be enhanced by complexity—it is possible for a work of fiction to be weakened by attempting too much subtlety and complexity, thereby sacrificing thematic content for artistic form.

William Freedman taught for many years at Brooklyn College. In 1969 he emigrated to Israel to become senior lecturer in English at the University of Haifa. In addition to "The Literary Motif" (1971), he has published essays on fiction, particularly American Jewish fiction, in such journals as *Modern Fiction Studies* and the *Mississippi Quarterly.*

Since the rise of the New Criticism in the Thirties, a criticism preoccupied with the work-in-itself and consequently with literary technique, there has been a steadily increasing flow of critical essays primarily concerned with language. One important phase of this study of language has been the attempt to discover clusters or families of related words or phrases that, by virtue of their frequency and particular use, tell us something about the author's intentions, conscious or otherwise. Mark Schorer, concerning himself only with families of metaphors, terms them "metaphoric substructures."[1] Reuben Brower, also mainly concerned with recurrent images or metaphors, terms them "continuities."[2] But although most critics have concentrated primarily on the metaphoric members of these language families, it seems obvious that the literal components, in conjunction with the figurative, form a larger unit that may prove more revealing still. And when we combine the literal and the figurative into a single family unit, we emerge with what is perhaps most accurately called the literary "motif."

Although there has been much discussion of the function of motifs in specific works, so far as I know there has been nothing approaching a detailed analysis of the device. I should like, therefore, to at-

"The Literary Motif: A Definition and Evaluation," by William Freedman, is reprinted with permission of the editors of *Novel* 5 (Winter 1971).

tempt such an analysis, a description of what the literary motif is and how it functions. And when I have done that I should like then to examine the question of its literary value. It is a fairly automatic critical assumption that to demonstrate the existence of an elaborate motif in a given work is to demonstrate something that enhances the value of that work. I agree. But at the same time I think it advisable to inquire into the reasons behind this widespread assent. It is not enough to show that an author has employed a motif or that one has found its way into his work without at least inquiring why or if its presence is an asset.

Perhaps as useful a starting point as any is the entry under "motif" in one of the standard literary dictionaries:

> A theme, character, or verbal pattern which recurs in literature or folklore. . . . A motif may be theme which runs through a number of different works. The motif of the imperishability of art, for example, appears in Shakespeare, Keats, Yeats, and many other writers. A recurring element within a single work is also called a motif. Among the many motifs that appear and reappear in Joyce's *Ulysses*, for example, are Plumtree's Potted Meat, the man in the brown mackintosh, and the one-legged sailor.[3]

My concern is with the latter part of this description, with the motif as it is employed within a single work. The statement in the *Reader's Guide* supplies a reasonable start toward a more complete definition of this kind of motif by accounting fairly well for the literal use of motifs, the repetition for emphasis of a self-contained, self-explanatory theme or the like. But it leaves much to be said. For one thing, it fails to make clear that the motif in a single work, like that which runs through many different works, may take the form of a verbal pattern. And it may be a family or, to borrow a term from Kenneth Burke, an "associational cluster," rather than merely a single, unchanging element. Second, it does not take into account what is perhaps the primary function of the motif as it is most often used and discussed, namely, to act symbolically. This description, in other words, does not encompass the money or finance motifs in James's *The Wings of the Dove* and *The Golden Bowl*, or Fitzgerald's *The Great Gatsby* and *Tender is the Night*. The language of money, finance, and economics is indeed recurrent in these novels. But it recurs for a reason. Viewed collectively, this language refers to something outside itself, namely, the economic preoccupation of the society or some of its members. The motif, then, tells the reader something—to establish a convenient separation—about the action of the story (either its total structure or the events), the minds of the characters, the emotional import or the moral or cognitive content of the works. It tells him subtly what the incidents perhaps tell him bluntly. It is, in short, symbolic.

But this is not the same as saying that each instance of this language is a symbol, for two major lines of differentiation distinguish the symbolic motif from the symbol. First, the symbol may occur singly. The motif is necessarily recurrent and its effect cumulative. For this reason Steinbeck's symbolic turtle, which appears on the opening pages of *The Grapes of Wrath* and synecdochically foreshadows the movements and spirit of the Okies, is a symbol and not a motif. But if we were to find scattered throughout the book frequent references to, say, a turtle-neck sweater which Tom Joad is never without or frequent reiterations of remarks to the effect that Ma Joad is hard-shelled or slow as a tortoise but equally persistent, then in this "associational cluster" we would have the makings of a motif. Here each reference to turtles, tortoises, or to things turtle-like or tortoise-like would not necessarily be a symbol, for each reference would not always be a thing or event, but often only a symbolic way of talking about a thing or event.

This takes us to the second distinction. A symbol is something described; it is an event or it is a thing. It may be Melville's white whale or the mode of Ahab's death; it may be the New Testament's cross or the crucifixion of Christ upon it; or it may be the scarlet letter or little Pearl's peculiar reactions to it. But it is always a thing or event described. A motif, on the other hand, although it may appear as something described, perhaps even more often forms part of the description. It slips, as it were, into the author's vocabulary, into the dialogue, and into his imagery, often even at times when the symbolized referent is not immediately involved. For example, in our hypothetical case, Tom Joad's turtle-neck sweater or Ma Joad's figurative hard shell might be referred to even when their perseverance is not at issue. Or, to cite a real example, Dreiser makes constant reference in *Sister Carrie* to Carrie's "dull little round" and Hurstwood's "exclusive circle" well before the question of circularity and futile, repetitive striving arises. The motif prepares us for the time when it will.

The motif, then, may become a part of the total perspective, pervading the book's atmosphere and becoming an important thread in the fabric of the work. Such permeation is achieved, for example, by the motif of circularity in *Sister Carrie*,[4] by the machine and animal motifs in *The Grapes of Wrath*,[5] by the isolation motif (doors, gates, fences, and so forth) in *The Sound and the Fury*,[6] and by the music motif in Sterne's *A Sentimental Journey*, to name but a very few of many.

The motif is not a symbol, but it may be symbolic. When it is, it acquires this character cumulatively and either by its relationship to the action (whether it be the total shape of the action or simply one or more of the events), to one or more of the characters, to the affective or cognitive content of the work, or to any combination of these possibilities. Whether the motif is symbolic or literal, however, it is through its service to one or more of these same aspects of the work that it achieves its purpose, and the motif therefore generally falls into one or more of three principal categories: cognitive, affective (or emotive), and structural. A motif may contribute to only one of these three aspects of the work. The motif of commerce and property in Austen's *Persuasion*, as an instance, is primarily cognitive. It serves to reveal to the reader the "social fact" that most characters in the novel measure value entirely in arithmetical and economic terms. Most motifs, however, relate to more than one of these aspects, although one may be of paramount importance. The motif of circularity in *Sister Carrie* is perhaps chiefly cognitive. It underscores Dreiser's presentation of the circular futility of human striving. But since this point is made largely by means of a repetitive circular patterning of the events of the novel, the motif relates to and underscores the novel's structure as well as its cognitive content. Although the chief function of the music motif in *A Sentimental Journey* is its enrichment of the emotive quality of the work, it is importantly related to both the cognitive content and structure as well. In *Tristram Shandy* it underscores the emotive quality, the structure and the cognitive content of the work, but principally its structure.

Two factors are indispensable to the establishment of a motif. The first is the frequency with which it recurs. The recurrence of references to finance in only two or three, or even five or ten, instances in a novel the size of, say, *The Golden Bowl,* would hardly constitute a motif. It might well be nothing more than coincidence or necessity. Obviously no specific numbers of references can possibly be fixed as requisite to the motif. That will vary with each work. But members of the family of references should occur often enough to indicate that purposiveness rather than merely coincidence or necessity is at least occasionally responsible for their presence. They should pervade the atmosphere sufficiently to assure that they will be at least subliminally felt.

Second is the avoidability and unlikelihood of the particular uses of a motif, or of its appearance in certain contexts, or of its appearance at all. References to hats in a novel about a milliner, for example, are all but unavoidable. Consequently, more than mere frequency of occurrence is required if hats are to function as a motif. This is not to say that their appearance or use must be unlikely to the point of inappropriateness. Quite the contrary, appropriateness is a basic test of efficacy. What I do mean is that the contexts in which the references appear or the uses to which they are put (extraliteral uses, for example) do not *demand* references from the field of the motif. In a novel about a milliner, a man's home, automobile, or other articles of clothing might serve equally well as indices of character, social status, or the like. The repeated use of hats to these symbolic purposes may, however, make these and other references to hats unexplainable as anything other than instances of a motif.

Assuming we have discovered a motif in a given work, our next concern is to measure its effectiveness. Five basic factors determine the efficacy of a motif. The first is again frequency. All other factors being equal and within limits to be adumbrated below, the greater the frequency with which instances of a motif recur the deeper the impression it is likely to make on the reader. The effect, of course, will also be increased the more extensive the individual references are. One need hardly be told that an extended metaphor or episode involving the motif subject is more likely to catch the reader's attention than a passing reference.

The second factor is again avoidability and unlikelihood. Clearly the more uncommon a reference is in a given context, the more likely it is to strike the reader, consciously or subconsciously, and the greater will be its effect. A reader might pass unnoticingly over a reference to a drummer, for example. But he is not so likely to remain unaffected by a metaphor that compares the impulse to pity to a musical instrument, a very common sort of metaphor in *A Sentimental Journey* and *Tristram Shandy*. For both of these criteria a qualification is needed. There would seem to be a law of diminishing returns here, the efficacy of the motif beginning to decline at the point where unlikelihood begins to shade into unsuitability or frequency into tedious repetition. Maximum power will therefore probably be achieved at the degree of frequency and improbability just short of this negative tendency, a point that varies from work to work.

A third factor determining the potency of a motif is the significance of the contexts in which it occurs. A motif that appears at most or all of the climactic points of a work, particularly if the symbolized referent of the motif is in the fore at these points, has greater effect than one that occurs only in less central passages, particularly if these passages do not overtly concern the tenor of the motif. The fact that the crucial event in the Benjy section of *The Sound and the Fury*—his misunderstood abuse of the passing schoolgirl—results from Benjy's opening the accidentally unlocked gate and that the crucial event in the Jason section concerns the stealing of the money he has locked in a strongbox, which he keeps in a dresser drawer inside a closet of his locked room, combines with the general pervasiveness of the motif of isolation and confinement to make that motif an important factor in the book and to ensure the fulfillment of its purpose.

A fourth factor is the degree to which all instances of the motif are relevant to the principal end of the motif as a whole and to which they fit together into a recognizable and coherent unit. If a unified effect is to be produced it will hardly be achieved by a motif in which all the parts are related only remotely and ramify into a variety of unrelated purposes: the closer the association between the components of the cluster the more unified their effect. The finance motif in *Tender Is the Night* is rendered more effective by the fact that its components point almost exclusively to the corrosive powers of money (as with Dick Diver's "emotional bankruptcy") rather than to several other possible qualities not related to the intended effect of either the motif or the work as a whole.

The fifth and final factor, which concerns only those motifs whose function is symbolic, is the appropriateness of the motif to what it symbolizes. Obviously a motif of circularity is more appropriate to a book about the circular repetitiveness of human fortune and behavior and the circular, futile strivings of the ill-equipped dreamer, as in *Sister Carrie*, than to one about, say, a love triangle. And again *The Sound and the Fury* is a good example. Constant references to doors, fences, gates, and the like are patently appropriate as symbolic representations of the Compsons' physical and spiritual isolation.

A possible criticism of the reader or critic who seems to find a motif in every cupboard is the observation that in certain instances the references seem virtually unavoidable. One may claim, for instance—and quite rightly—that James could hardly have written a novel like *The Golden Bowl* without alluding frequently to matters of finance. In the light of what has been said so far, however, this seems to me no very damaging accusation. If the reader can show satisfactorily that the presence of the motif is at least sometimes quite easily avoidable, that its overall frequency is greater than sheer coincidence or necessity might produce, that the separate members of the family or cluster operate together to a common end, and that they are singularly appropriate to a given aspect of the work in hand, he has, I think, shown both the existence and efficacy of a motif in that work. It is then virtually inevitable that the cumulative force of the motif, acting by association, must at least to some extent suffuse every occurrence of it, however unavoidable or insignificant any one may appear independently.

Perhaps now I may hazard a definition. A motif, then, is a recurrent theme, character, or verbal pattern, but it may also be a family or associational cluster of literal or figurative references to a given class of concepts or objects, whether it be animals, machines, circles, music, or whatever. It is generally symbolic—that is, it can be seen to carry a meaning beyond the literal one immediately apparent; it represents on the verbal level something characteristic of the structure of the work, the events, the characters, the emotional effects or the moral or cognitive content. It is presented both as an object of description and, more often, as part of the narrator's imagery and descriptive vocabulary. And it indispensably requires a certain minimal frequency of recurrence and improbability of appearance in order both to make itself at least subconsciously felt and to indicate its purposiveness. Finally, the motif achieves its power by an appropriate regulation of that frequency and improbability, by its appearance in significant contexts, by the degree to which the individual instances work together toward a common end or ends and, when it is symbolic, by its appropriateness to the symbolic purpose or purposes it serves.

    But what of the literary value of a motif? What, if anything, does it contribute to the work it graces and to the reader's appreciation of that work? Everyone who writes about literature of course hopes that the nature and value of his efforts are self-evident. In most critical studies (book reviews and biographical and bibliographical notes usually excepted) this hope takes the form of an implicit syllogism that goes something like this: All works, or at least the one or ones here under consideration, are better if they possess a certain attribute or attributes or can be understood in certain terms. This book has these attributes or can be understood in these terms. Therefore, this is a better book than was previously supposed. As I've said, this syllogism is almost always implicit and only the minor premise is expressed in writing. In many cases the hidden assumptions might not be completely acceptable were they brought into the open, and although it is in such cases that exposure is most useful I think something may be gained by exposing even quite widely held evaluative assumptions in order that the reader may be a bit clearer about just what he is agreeing to.

Purely descriptive studies need not take a rear seat in the critical bus. The writer performs a worthwhile function when he attempts no more than to elucidate what he sees in the work, when he seeks to increase the reader's understanding of a work of art. The discovery of the motif should be as valuable—or at least nearly so—to the reader who sees no additional artistic merit accruing to the book as a result of the addition of this new information as it is to the reader who thinks it a better book therefore. If that hypothetical reader can be led to better understand what is going on in a given literary work, even to better understand why he does not like it, I think it will have been worth the effort. Nevertheless, let it be admitted that I do attach value to the motif. How widespread the approval of a well-handled motif in literature really is would seem to be a question for the pollsters. But while I can speak only for myself, I think it would be generally agreed that the discovery in a given work of a motif adequately fulfilling the criteria suggested above tends to enhance appreciation and alter judgment as well as increase understanding. The question then is "Why?" In what sense may we justifiably consider "motif" as a value term?

I think it is plain that unlike such terms as, say, "unity," or "order," "motif" is not an aesthetic primitive. That is to say our approval of the motif seems to derive by implication from several more fundamental premises or axioms. One such premise and one possible explanation of what I believe to be its acceptability as a term of implicit approbation may be found in Kenneth Burke's exaltation of the synecdoche. The synecdoche, as he defines it, is "the figure of speech wherein the part is used for the whole, the whole for the part, the container for the thing contained, the cause for the effect, the effect for the cause, etc."[7] Since the symbolic motif is basically microcosmic, since it is a part of a literary work that may often stand for the whole, it performs, I think, a synecdochic function. Consequently it may justly derive some of its appeal from that which Burke discovers in the synecdoche. "The more I examine both the structure of poetry and the structure of human relations outside of poetry," says Burke, "the more I become convinced that this is the 'basic' figure of speech, and that it occurs in many modes besides that of the formal trope" (pp. 23–24). As Burke points out, "we use the same word for sensory, artistic and political representation": our sensory abstractions "represent" the tree; the colors and forms in a painting "represent" the society as a whole. The fetish, the scapegoat, and perhaps above all the name are further instances of symbolic representatives of the whole. Clearly, then, the symbolic representation of a whole or of other parts by a single part forms an indispensable part of both the way we see things and the way we communicate them. This helps at least partially to explain why the literary motif, a subtle and elaborate variation of this figure in a work of art, would be likely to attract our interest and approval.

As I have defined it, the motif is a complex of separate parts subtly reiterating on one level what is taking place on another. It thus multiplies levels of meaning and interest. A second premise from which our approval of the motif may be derived, then, is that subtlety, richness, and complexity are desirable qualities in a work of art. This generalization does not always hold, for doubtless there are times when the barest simplicity is preferable. Nevertheless, we do take pleasure in at least a certain degree of subtlety, richness, and complexity. We say that *King Lear* is a greater achievement than any of Shakespeare's sonnets, and that Beethoven's Ninth Symphony is a greater achievement than his Second Piano Sonata, and one of the reasons is complexity. The reasons for complexity's hold upon us are not far to seek. Complication involves us more continually, more deeply, and more completely. It brings, as Coleridge said poetry must, "the whole soul of man into activity." But this is familiar stuff. Less often remarked (which is to say, I have never seen it mentioned) is the possible role of anthropomorphism. Spinoza once observed that if triangles had the power of intellectual conception they would conceive a triangular god. It seems equally likely that our attraction to complexity and its correlatives stems at least partially from the fact that the human organism is itself a highly subtle complex of parts functioning, to our own endless wonder, toward a single end: life. Clearly, human behavior and human relationships are no less complex. If, therefore, art is to function as an "imitation of life" (in whichever of the almost endless ways one might choose to interpret that phrase) and if it is to satisfy man's anthropomorphic inclinations and desires, complexity must be a part of it. So pervasive are these inclinations that the whole of organismic physics, the physics that was dominant from Aristotle through Newton and that to a certain extent persists to this day, has an anthropomorphic base; that is, it is based on the analogy between the human organism and the universe.[8] And just as anthropomorphism has served as a foundation for man's attempt to interpret the universe, so has it exerted an important influence on matters of desire and preference, although the anthropomorphic view of God and the universe is also, as more recent physics has shown, very likely a matter of preference as well as an attempt at understanding. Anthropomorphism has been suggested, for example, as a possible explanation for man's demonstrable affinity for symmetry in art and architecture. It seems to me at least as applicable to his preference for the qualities of richness and complexity.

Since all of the works cited here are novels and since the motif is chiefly a novelist's tool, it seems worthy of note that in two of the most useful definitions of the novel, or of a particular kind of novel, complexity occupies a central place. For Henry Fielding in his famous Preface to *Joseph Andrews*, a comic romance—his term for the kind of novel he claimed to be writing and whose status he hoped to insure—"is a comic epic poem in prose: differing from comedy, as the serious epic from tragedy: its action being more extended and comprehensive; containing a much larger circle of incidents, and introducing a greater variety of characters." Two centuries later Ian Watt, defining in retrospect the genre as a whole, has this to say:

> Formal realism . . . is the narrative embodiment of a premise that Defoe and Richardson accepted very literally, but which is implicit in the novel form in general: the premise, or primary convention, that the novel is a full and authentic report of human experience, and is therefore under an obligation to satisfy its reader with such details of the story as the individuality of the actors concerned, the particulars of the times and places of their actions, details which are presented through a more largely referential use of language than is common in other literary forms.[9]

Watt's definition of the novel and Fielding's definition of his own kind of novel and of the form as he hoped it would evolve have very little in common. For as Watt makes clear it was the tradition of formal realism, not that of Fielding's classicism and polished artificiality, that finally won out. Nevertheless, although they agree in little else, they both insist on complexity. The principle of plenitude seems to apply to products of human no less than divine creation.

Perhaps one may sum up the value of the motif in the combination of its intellectual and affective appeals. Intellectually, since the motif usually points to a skillful author capable of subtlety and complexity, it first of all enhances the reader's respect for that author. This increased respect, I think, becomes inextricable from his impression of the work. We may not like to admit it—and admittedly all may not feel it—but for many of us the wonder we feel in the presence of, say, the genius of Shakespeare translates into increased appreciation of every evidence of that genius. I am prepared to suggest that the discovery that the tragedies are, after all, the issue of that infinite conglomeration of monkeys would in some degree diminish our response and appreciation. We are, at bottom, quite in love with ourselves as a species and are awed by what some of us, at least, can do. "Did one of us do that?" we wonder. And the fact that one of us did makes us love it all the more. We love the sign for what it points to as well as for what it is.

Second, and perhaps more basically, subtlety and complexity are themselves abundant sources of literary enjoyment and appreciation for reasons already discussed. And third, the motif appeals to whatever analytic interests we may have, to our sheer delight in discovering a technique and in watching it work both on its own and as a spoke in a well-oiled wheel. Affectively, assuming that the emotional effect or effects sought by any work are worth eliciting at all, it follows that the reinforcement of those effects on various levels, particularly the enrichment of the overall effect by means of a part, can only add scope and depth to the reading experience.

A final word about the motif, not as a literary device but as part of a critical approach. The kind of approach to fiction I have tried to outline here, it seems to me, performs that uncommon but useful coalescing function of bringing together under one roof the all too often disassociated schools of criticism. In its concentration on language, technique, and the text itself, the method is perhaps primarily what is generally called "New Critical." But in so far as it also investigates the possibility of authorial intention and awareness and, more important, the meaning of the motif to the contemporary audience and its probable effect on the given work's first readers, it attempts to make use of the abundant fruits of biographical and historical analysis as well.

Notes

1 Mark Schorer, "Fiction and the 'Matrix of Analogy,'" *Kenyon Review* 11 (1949): 539–60.

2 Reuben Brower, *The Fields of Light: An Experiment in Critical Reading* (New York: Oxford University Press, 1962). See particularly pp. 13, 14, 52–56, 103–17, 124–26, 148–50, 157–59, 161–63.

3 Karl Beckson and Arthur Ganz, *A Reader's Guide to Literary Terms* (New York: Noonday Press, 1960), p. 129.

4 William Freedman, "A Look at Dreiser as Artist: The Motif of Circularity in *Sister Carrie,*" *Modern Fiction Studies* 8 (1962): 384–92.

5 Robert J. Griffin and William Freedman, "Machines and Animals: Pervasive Motifs in *The Grapes of Wrath,*" *JEGP* 62 (1963): 569–80.

6 Freedman, "Techniques of Isolation in *The Sound and the Fury, Mississippi Quarterly* 15 (1961): 21–26.

7 Kenneth Burke, *The Philosophy of Literary Form: Studies in Symbolic Action* (rev. ed.; New York: Vintage Books, 1957), pp. 22–23.

8 In *Philosophy of Science* (Englewood Cliffs, N.J.: Prentice-Hall, 1957), p. 119, Philipp Frank points out that "Newton explained the planetary motions by an analogy with the behavior of human beings, just as Aristotelian physics did." Similarly, Auguste Comte, in *Positive Philosophy* (trans. Harriett Martineau [London: George Bell & Sons, 1896]), book 3, chapter 1 remarks that "The spirit of all theological and metaphysical philosophy consists in conceiving all phenomena as analogous to the only one which is known through immediate consciousness—Life."

9 Ian Watt, *The Rise of the Novel* (Berkeley and Los Angeles: University of California Press, 1959), p. 32.

21

Introduction to the Study
of the Narratee

GERALD PRINCE

Gerald Prince defines the narratee as "someone whom the narrator addresses," and as a "someone" who has been critically neglected. He argues that critical treatments of topics pertinent to the narratee have generally been subsumed in discussions of the narrator. But perhaps this is also due to a tendency to view listeners, readers, or narratees as passive recipients of the story rather than as active participants, as Mikhail Bakhtin would define them.

Prince suggests that we can find a phenomenal diversity of narratees in fiction and demonstrates the important differences between a narratee and the "real reader," "virtual reader," and "ideal reader." In order to describe the diversity of narratees, Prince creates a minimal portrait, that of "the zero-degree narratee," and observes how various fictions alter this "zero-degree" through certain narrative signals, as when the narrator of *Le Père Goriot* defines the narratee as white. Prince points out that the narrator may discuss such qualities in passages addressed to or overheard by the reader, rather than the narratee. But, as Prince emphasizes, "nevertheless, the portrait of a narratee emerges above all from the narrative addressed to him."

Having said this, Prince classifies fictional narratees according to types: (1) no one in particular, (2) a named or identified party who is not a character in the story, and (3) a character in the story. In the latter case, the narratee-character might play no other role than that of listener or might more actively participate in the plot. In either case, narratee-characters can either be affected by the stories related to them or remain unaffected. Furthermore, they can be essential, in that only a certain type of narratee will allow the story to be told, or interchangeable. Finally, they can be either listeners or readers.

After discussing their various functions, Prince concludes by claiming that "the narratee is one of the fundamental elements of all narration." Whether or not we agree with this claim, we can see the critical benefits to be gained from analyzing narratees. These benefits arise in part from perceiving fiction as a dialogue that occurs between author and reader and among narrator, characters, and narratee, rather than as a message simply received. Such perceptions recognize the recipients of fictional utterances, both internal and external to the text, as more active constructors of meaning than has been generally acknowledged.

Gerald Prince (b. 1941), professor of French at the University of Pennsylvania, is author of *A Grammar of Stories: An Introduction* (1973) and *Narratology: The Form and Functioning of Narrative* (1982).

Allow narration, whether it is oral or written, whether it recounts real or mythical events, whether it tells a story or relates a simple sequence of actions in time, presupposes not only (at least) one narrator but also (at least) one narratee, the narratee being someone whom the narrator addresses. In a fiction-narration—a tale, an epic, a novel—the narrator is a fictive creation as is his narratee. Jean-Baptiste Clamence, Holden Caulfield, and the narrator of *Madame Bovary* are novelistic constructs as are the individuals to whom they speak and for whom they write. From Henry James and Norman Friedman to Wayne C. Booth and Tzvetan Todorov, numerous critics have examined the diverse manifestations of the narrator in fictive prose and verse, his multiple roles and his importance.[1] By contrast, few critics have dealt with the narratee and none to date has undertaken an in-depth study;[2] this neglect persists despite the lively interest raised by Benveniste's fine articles on dis-

"Introduction to the Study of the Narratee," by Gerald J. Prince, originally appeared in *Poetique* 14 (1973) and was translated by Francis Mariner for *Reader-Response Criticism*, ed. Jane P. Tompkins (Baltimore: Johns Hopkins University Press, 1980). It is reprinted here with permission of Gerald Prince.

course (*le discours*), Jakobson's work on linguistic functions, and the evergrowing prestige of poetics and semiology.

Nowadays, any student minimally versed in the narrative genre differentiates the narrator of a novel from its author and from the novelistic *alter ego* of the author and knows the difference between Marcel and Proust, Rieux and Camus, Tristram Shandy, Sterne the novelist, and Sterne the man. Most critics, however, are scarcely concerned with the notion of the narratee and often confuse it with the more or less adjacent notions of receptor (*récepteur*), reader, and arch-reader (*archilecteur*). The fact that the word *narratee* is rarely employed, moreover, is significant.

This lack of critical interest in narratees is not inexplicable. Indeed, their study has been neglected, more than likely, because of a characteristic of the narrative genre itself; if the protagonist or dominant personality of a narration often assumes the role of the narrator and affirms himself as such (Marcel in *A la recherche du temps perdu*, Roquentin in *La Nausée*, Jacques Revel in *L'Emploi du temps*), there is no hero who is above all a narratee—unless one includes narrators who constitute their own narratee,[3] or perhaps a work like *La Modification*. Besides, it should not be forgotten that the narrator, on a superficial if not a profound level, is more responsible than his narratee. If the caliph should become tired and stop listening, Scheheracharacteristics. Finally, many problems of poetic narrative that might have been approached from the angle of the narratee have already been studied from the point of view of the narrator; after all, the individual who relates a story and the person to whom the story is told are more or less interdependent in any narration.

Whatever the case may be, narratees deserve to be studied. Major storytellers and novelists, as well as the less important, bear out this point. The variety of narratees found in fictive narrations is phenomenal. Docile or rebellious, admirable or ridiculous, ignorant of the events related to them or having prior knowledge of them, slightly naive as in *Tom Jones*, vaguely callous as in *The Brothers Karamazov*, narratees rival narrators in their diversity. Moreover, many novelists have in their own way examined the distinctions that should be maintained between the narratee and the receptor or between the narratee and the reader. In a detective novel by Nicholas Blake, for example, and in another by Philip Loraine, the detective succeeds in solving the crime when he realizes that the narratee and the receptor are not the same. In addition, there is no want of narratives that underscore the importance of the narratee, *A Thousand and One Nights* providing an excellent illustration. Scheherazade must exercise her talent as a storyteller or die, for as long as she is able to retain the attention of the caliph with her stories, she will not be executed. It is evident that the heroine's fate and that of the narration depend not only upon her capabilities as a storyteller, but also upon the humor of the narratee. If the caliph should become tired and stop listening. Scheherazade will die and the narrative will end.[4] The same fundamental situation can be found in the encounter of Ulysses with the Sirens,[5] as well as in a more recent work. Like Scheherazade, the hero of *La Chute* has a desperate need for a certain type of narratee. In order to forget his own guilt, Jean-Baptiste Clamence must find someone who will listen to him and whom he will be able to convince of everyone's guilt. He finds this someone at the Mexico City Bar in Amsterdam and it is at that moment that his narrative account begins.

The Zero-Degree Narratee

In the very first pages of *Le Père Goriot*, the narrator exclaims: "That's what you will do, you who hold this book with a white hand, you who settle back in a well-padded armchair saying to yourself: perhaps this is going to be amusing. After reading about old Goriot's secret misfortunes, you'll dine with a good appetite attributing your insensitivity to the author whom you'll accuse of exaggeration and poetic affectation." This "you" with white hands, accused by the narrator of being egotistical and callous, is the narratee. It's obvious that the latter does not resemble most readers of *Le Père Goriot* and that consequently the narratee of a novel cannot be automatically identified with the reader: the reader's hands might be black or red and not white; he might read the novel in bed instead of in an armchair; he might lose his appetite upon learning of the old merchant's unhappiness. The reader of a fiction, be it in prose or in verse, should not be mistaken for the narratee. The one is real, the other fictive. If it should occur that the reader bears an astonishing resemblance to the narratee, this is an exception and not the rule.

Neither should the narratee be confused with the virtual reader. Every author, provided he is writing for someone other than himself, develops his narrative as a function of a certain type of reader whom he bestows with certain qualities, faculties, and inclinations according to his opinion of men in general (or in particular) and according to the obligations he feels should be respected. This virtual reader is different from the real reader: writers frequently have a public they don't deserve. He is also distinct from the narratee. In *La Chute*, Clamence's narratee is not identical to the reader envisioned by Camus: after all, he's a lawyer visiting Amsterdam. It goes without saying that a virtual reader and a narratee can be alike, but once again it would be an exception.

Finally, we should not confuse the narratee with the ideal reader, although a remarkable likeness can exist between the two. For a writer, an ideal reader would be one who would understand perfectly and would approve entirely the least of his words, the most subtle of his intentions. For a critic, an ideal reader would perhaps be one capable of interpreting the infinity of texts that, according to certain critics, can be found in one specific text. On the one hand, the narratees for whom the narrator multiplies his explanations and justifies the particularities of his narrative are numerous and cannot be thought of as constituting the ideal readers dreamed up by a novelist. We need only think of the narratees of *Le Père Goriot* and *Vanity Fair*. On the other hand, these narratees are too inept to be capable of interpreting even a rather restricted group of texts within the text.

If narratees are distinct from real, virtual, or ideal readers,[6] they very often differ from each other as well. Nonetheless, it should be possible to describe each one of them as a function of the same categories and according to the same models. It is necessary to identify at least some of these characteristics as well as some of the ways in which they vary and combine with each other. These characteristics must be situated with reference to a sort of "zero-degree" narratee, a concept which it is now time to define.

In the first place, the zero-degree narratee knows the tongue (*langue*) and the language(s) (*langage[s]*) of the narrator. In his case, to know a tongue is to know the meanings (*dénotations*)—the signifieds as such and, if applicable, the referents—of all the signs that constitute it; this does not include knowledge of the connotations (the subjective values that have been attached to them). It also involves a perfect mastery of grammar but not of the (infinite) paragrammatical possibilities. It is the ability to note semantic (and/or syntactic ambiguities and to be able to resolve these difficulties from the context. It is the capacity to recognize the grammatical incorrectness or oddness of any sentence or syntagm—by reference to the linguistic system being used.[7]

Beyond this knowledge of language, the zero-degree narratee has certain faculties of reasoning that are often only the corollaries of this knowledge. Given a sentence or a series of sentences, he is able to grasp the presuppositions and the consequences.[8] The zero-degree narratee knows narrative grammar, the rules by which any story is elaborated.[9] He knows, for example, that a minimal complete narrative sequence consists in the passage from a given situation to the inverse situation. He knows that the narrative possesses a temporal dimension and that it necessitates relations of causality. Finally, the zero-degree narratee possesses a sure memory, at least in regard to the events of the narrative about which he has been informed and the consequences that can be drawn from them.

Thus, he does not lack positive characteristics. But he also does not want negative traits. He can thus only follow a narrative in a well-defined and concrete way and is obliged to acquaint himself with the events by reading from the first page to the last, from the initial word to the final word. In addition, he is without any personality or social characteristics. He is neither good nor bad, pessimistic nor optimistic, revolutionary nor bourgeois, and his character, his position in society, never colors his perception of the events described to him. Moreover, he knows absolutely nothing about the events or characters mentioned and he is not acquainted with the conventions prevailing in that world or in any other world. Just as he doesn't understand the connotations of a certain turn of phrase, he doesn't realize what can be evoked by this or that situation, this or that novelistic action. The consequences of this are very important. Without the assistance of the narrator, without his explanations and the information supplied by him, the narratee is able neither to interpret the value of an action nor to grasp its repercussions. He is incapable of determining the morality or immorality of a character, the realism or extravagance of a description, the merits of a rejoinder, the satirical intention of a tirade. And how would he be able to do so? By virtue of what experience, what knowledge, or what system of values?

More particularly, a notion as fundamental as verisimilitude only counts very slightly for him. Indeed, verisimilitude is always defined in relation to another text, whether this text be public opinion, the rules of a literary genre, or "reality." The zero-degree narratee, however, is acquainted with no texts and in the absence of commentary, the adventures of Don Quixote would seem as ordinary to him as those of Passemurailles (an individual capable of walking through walls) or of the protagonists of *Une Belle Journée*.[10] The same would hold true for relations of implicit causality. If I learn in *La Légende de Saint Julien l'Hospitalier* that "Julien believes he has killed his father and faints," I establish a causal relationship between these two propositions founded upon a certain commonsense logic, my experience of the world, and my knowledge of certain novelistic conventions. We are, moreover, aware that one of the mechanisms of the narrative process "is the confusion of consecutiveness and consequence, what comes *after* being read in the narrative as *caused by*. . . ."[11] But the narratee with no experience and no common sense does not perceive relations of implicit causality and does not fall victim to this confusion. Finally, the zero-degree narratee does not organize the narrative as a function of the major codes of reading studied by Roland Barthes in *S/Z*. He doesn't know how to unscramble the different voices that shape the narration. After all, as Barthes has said: "The code is a convergence of quotations, a structural mirage . . . the resulting units . . . made up of fragments of this something which always has *already* been read, seen, done, lived: the code is the groove of this *already*. Referring back to what has been written, that is, to the Book (of culture, of life, of life as culture), the code makes the text a prospectus of this Book."[12] For the zero-degree narratee, there is no *already*, there is no Book.

The Signals of the Narratee

Every narratee possesses the characteristics that we have enumerated except when an indication to the contrary is supplied in the narration intended for him: he knows, for example, the language employed by the narrator, he is gifted with an excellent memory, he is unfamiliar with everything concerning the characters who are presented to him. It is not rare that a narrative might deny or contradict these characteristics: a certain passage might underline the language-related difficulties of the narratee, another passage might disclose that he suffers from amnesia, yet another passage might emphasize his knowledge of the problems being discussed. It is on the basis of these deviations from the characteristics of the zero-degree narratee that the portrait of a specific narratee is gradually constituted.

Certain indications supplied by the text concerning a narratee are sometimes found in a section of the narrative that is not addressed to him. One has only to think of *L'Immoraliste*, the two *Justines*, or *Heart of Darkness* to verify that not only the physical appearance, the personality, and civil status of a narratee can be discussed in this fashion, but also his experience and his past. These indications may precede the portion of the narrative intended for the narratee, or may follow, interrupt, or frame it. Most often, they confirm what the rest of the narration has revealed to us. At the beginning of *L'Immoraliste*, for example, we learn that Michel has not seen his narratees for three years and the story he tells them quickly confirms this fact. Nonetheless, sometimes these indications contradict the narrative and emphasize certain differences between the narratee as conceived by the narrator and as revealed by another voice. The few words spoken by Doctor Spielvogel at the end of *Portnoy's Complaint* reveal that he is not what the narrative has led us to believe.[13]

Nevertheless, the portrait of a narratee emerges above all from the narrative addressed to him. If we consider that any narration is composed of a series of signals directed to the narratee, two major categories of signals can be distinguished. On the one hand there are those signals that contain no reference to the narratee or, more precisely, no reference differentiating him from the zero-degree narratee. On the other hand, there are those signals that, on the contrary, define him as a specific narratee and make him deviate from the established norms. In *Un Coeur simple* a sentence such as "She threw herself on the ground" would fall into the first category; this sentence reveals nothing in particular about the narratee while still permitting him to appreciate the sorrow of Félicité. On the contrary, a sentence such as "His entire person produced in her that confusion into which we are all thrown by the spectacle of extraordinary men" not only records the reactions of the heroine in the presence of M. Bourais, but also informs us that the narratee has experienced the same feelings in the presence of extraordinary individuals. By interpreting all signals of the narration as a function of the narratee, we can obtain a partial reading of the text, but a well-defined and reproducible reading. By regrouping and studying the signals of the second category, we can reconstruct the portrait of the narratee, a portrait more or less distinct, original, and complete depending upon the text considered.

The signals belonging to the second category are not always easy to recognize or to interpret. In fact, if many of them are quite explicit, others are much less so. The indications supplied on the narratee at the beginning of *Le Père Goriot* are very clear and present no problem: "That's what you will do, you who hold this book with a white hand, you who settle back in a well-padded armchair. . . ." But the first two sentences of *The Sun Also Rises* present more difficulty. Jake does not explicitly state that, according to his narratee, to say that a man has been a boxing champion is to express admiration for him. It is enough for him to imply this: "Robert Cohn was once middleweight boxing champion of Princeton. Do not think that I am very much impressed by that as a boxing title, but it meant a lot to Cohn." A greater number of indications concerning this or that narratee are even more indirect. Obviously, any indication, whether explicit or indirect, should be interpreted on the basis of the text itself, using as a guide the language employed, its presuppositions, the logical consequences that it entails, and the already established knowledge of the narratee.

The signals capable of portraying the narratee are quite varied and one can easily distinguish several types that are worth discussing. In the first place, we should mention all passages of a narrative in which the narrator refers directly to the narratee. We retain in this category statements in which the narrator designates the narratee by such words as "reader" or "listener" and by such expressions as "my dear" or "my friend." In the event that the narration may have identified a specific characteristic of the narratee, for example, his profession or nationality, passages mentioning this characteristic should also be considered in this first category. Thus, if the narratee is a lawyer, all information concerning lawyers in general is pertinent. Finally, we should retain all passages in which the addressee is designated by second-person pronouns and verb forms.

Besides those passages referring quite explicitly to the narratee, there are passages that, although not written in the second person, imply a narratee and describe him. When Marcel in *A la recherche du temps perdu* writes: "Besides, most often, we didn't stay at home, we went for a walk," the "we" excludes the narratee. On the contrary, when he declares: "Undoubtedly, in these coincidences which are so perfect, when reality withdraws and applies itself to what we have dreamt about for so long a time, it hides it from us entirely," the "we" includes the narratee.[14] Often an impersonal expression or an indefinite pronoun can only refer to the narratee: "But, the work completed, perhaps one will have shed a few tears *intra muros* and *extra*."

Then again, there are often numerous passages in a narrative that, though they contain apparently no reference—even an ambiguous one—to a narratee, describe him in greater or lesser detail. Accordingly, certain parts of a narrative may be presented in the form of questions or pseudo-questions. Sometimes these questions originate neither with a character nor with the narrator who merely repeats them. These questions must then be attributed to the narratee and we should note what excites his curiosity, the kinds of problems he would like to resolve. In *Le Père Goriot*, for example, it is the narratee who makes inquiries about the career of M. Poiret: "What had he been? But perhaps he had been employed at the Ministry of Justice. . . ." Sometimes, however, the narrator addresses questions to the narratee himself, some of whose knowledge and defenses are thus revealed in the process. Marcel will address a pseudo-question to his narratee asking him to explain the slightly vulgar, and for that reason surprising, behavior of Swann: "But who has not seen unaffected royal princesses . . . spontaneously adopt the language of old bores? . . ."

Other passages are presented in the form of negations. Certain of these passages are no more the extension of a given character's statement than they are the response to a given narrator's question. It is rather the beliefs of the narratee that these passages contradict, his preoccupations that are attacked, and his questions that are silenced. The narrator of *Les Faux-Monnayeurs* vigorously rejects the theory advanced by the narratee to explain Vincent Molinier's nocturnal departures: "No, it was not to his mistress that Vincent Molinier went each evening." Sometimes a partial negation can be revelatory. In *A la recherche du temps perdu*, the narrator, while believing that the narratee's conjectures about the extraordinary suffering of Swann are well-founded, at the same time finds them insufficient: "This suffering which he felt resembled nothing he had ever thought possible. Not only because in his hours of deepest doubt he had rarely imagined anything so painful, but because even when he imagined this thing, it remained vague, uncertain. . . ."

There are also passages that include a term with demonstrative significance that instead of referring to an anterior or ulterior element of the narrative, refers to another text, to extra-textual experience (*hors-texte*) known to the narrator and his narratee. "He looked at the tomb and there buried his final tear as a young man . . . one of those tears which though they fall to the earth flow upward to the heavens." From these few lines, the narratee of *Le Père Goriot* recognizes the kind of tears buried by Rastignac. He has certainly already heard about them, without a doubt he has seen them, perhaps he has shed some himself.

Comparisons or analogies found in a narration also furnish us with information more or less valuable. Indeed, the second term of a comparison is always assumed to be known better than the first. On this basis, we can assume that the narratee of *The Gold Pot*, for example, has already heard the bursting of thunder ("The voice faded like the faraway muffled rumbling of thunder"), and we can accordingly begin the partial reconstruction of the type of universe with which he is familiar.

But perhaps the most revelatory signals and at times the most difficult to grasp and describe in a satisfactory way are those we shall call—for lack of a more appropriate term—*over-justifications* (*sur-justifications*). Any narrator more or less explains the world inhabited by his characters, motivates their acts, and justifies their thoughts. If it occurs that these explanations and motivations are situated at the level of meta-language, meta-commentary, or meta-narration, they are over-justifications. When the narrator of *La Chartreuse de Parme* advises the narratee that at La Scala "it's customary for visits to the boxes to last only twenty minutes or so," he is only thinking about supplying the narratee with information necessary for the understanding of the events. On the other hand, when he asks to be excused for a poorly phrased sentence, when he excuses himself for having to interrupt his narrative, when he confesses himself incapable of describing well a certain feeling, these are over-justifications that he employs. Over-justifications always provide us with interesting details about the narratee's personality, even though they often do so in an indirect way; in overcoming the narratee's defenses, in prevailing over his prejudices, in allaying his apprehensions, they reveal them.

The narratee's signals—those that describe him as well as those that only provide him with information—can pose many problems for the reader who would wish to classify them in order to arrive at a portrait of the narratee or a certain reading of the text. It's not simply a question of their being sometimes difficult to notice, to grasp, or to explain, but in certain narratives, one can find contradictory signals. Sometimes they originate with a narrator who wishes to amuse himself at the expense of the narratee or underscore the arbitrariness of the text; often the world presented is a world in which the principles of contradiction known to us don't exist or are not applicable; finallly, the contradictions—the entirely obvious ones—often result from the different points of view that the narrator strives to reproduce faithfully. Nonetheless it occurs that not all contradictory data can be entirely explained in this fashion. In these cases, they should be attributed to the author's ineptness—or temperament. In many pornographic novels, in the worst as well as in the best, the narrator, like the heroes of *La Cantatrice chauve*, will first describe a character as having blond hair, large breasts, and a bulging stomach and then on the following page will speak with as much conviction of her black hair, her flat stomach, and her small breasts. Coherence is certainly not an imperative for the pornographic genre in which a wild variation is the rule rather than the exception. It nonetheless remains that in these cases, it is difficult—if not impossible—to interpret the semantic material presented to the narratee.

Sometimes it is the signals describing the narratee that form a strangely disparate collection. Indeed, every signal relating to a narratee need not continue or confirm a preceding signal or announce a signal to follow. There are narratees who change much as narrators do or who have a rich enough personality to embrace various tendencies and feelings. But the contradictory nature of certain narratees does not always result from a complex personality or a subtle evolution. The first pages of *Le Père Goriot* indicate that a Parisian narratee would be able to appreciate "the particularities of this scene full of local observations and color." But these opening pages contradict what they have just asserted in accusing the narratee of insensitivity and in judging him guilty of mistaking reality for fiction. This contradiction will never be resolved. On the contrary, other contradictions will be added and it will become more and more difficult to know whom the narrator addresses. A case of ineptitude? Perhaps Balzac does not worry about technical details and sometimes commits errors which in a Flaubert or a Henry James would be shocking. But this is a revelatory instance of ineptitude: Balzac, who is obsessed with problems of identity—these problems are certainly very important in *Le Père Goriot*—does not manage to decide who will be his narratee.

Despite the questions posed, the difficulties raised, the errors committed, it is evident that the kinds of signals used, their respective numbers, and their distribution determine to a certain extent the different types of narrative.[15] Narratives in which explanations and motivations abound (*Don Quixote* and *Tristram Shandy*, *Les Illusions perdues* and *Le Temps retrouvé*) are very different from those in which explanations and motivations play a limited role (*The Killers*, *The Maltese Falcon*, *La Jalousie*). The former are often by narrators who find the dimension of discourse (*discours*) more important than that of narrative (*récit*) or who are acutely aware of the gratuitousness—and even the falseness—of any narrative or of a certain type of narrative and consequently try to exorcise it. The latter are produced by narrators who feel perfectly at ease in the narrative (*récit*) or who, for different reasons, wish to be transported from their usual surroundings. Moreover, explanations and motivations can present themselves for what they are or, on the other hand, can dissimulate their nature by disguising themselves more or less completely. A narrator of Balzac or Stendhal does not hesitate to declare the necessity of explaining a thought, an act, or a situation. "We are obliged at this point to interrupt for a moment the story of this bold undertaking in order to supply an indispensable detail which will explain in part the duchess's courage in advising Fabrice upon this quite dangerous flight." But Flaubert's narrators—in particular after *Madame Bovary*—often play upon ambiguity and we no longer know exactly if one sentence explains another or if it merely follows or precedes it: "He assembled an army. It became bigger. He became famous. He was sought after." Explanations can also be presented in the form of uni-

versal rules or general laws as in Balzac and Zola or can avoid as much
as possible all generality as in the novels of Sartre and Simone de
Beauvoir. Explanations can contradict or confirm one another, be
repeated or used a single time, appear only at strategic moments or
occur anywhere in the narrative. Each time a different type of narration is constructed.

Classification of Narratees

Thanks to the signals describing the narratee, we are able to
characterize any narration according to the type of narratee to whom
it is addressed. It would be useless, because too long, too complicated,
and too imprecise, to distinguish different categories of narratees according to their temperament, their civil status, or their beliefs. On
the other hand, it would be comparatively easy to classify narratees
according to their narrative situation, to their position in reference
to the narrator, the characters, and the narration.

Many narrations appear to be addressed to no one in particular:
no character is regarded as playing the role of narratee and no narratee is mentioned by the narrator either directly ("Without a doubt,
dear reader, you have never been confined in a glass bottle") or indirectly ("We could hardly do otherwise than pluck one of its flowers
and present it to the reader"). Just as a detailed study of a novel such
as *L'Education sentimentale* or *Ulysses* reveals the presence of a narrator who tries to be invisible and to intervene as little as possible in
the course of the events, so too a thorough examination of a narration
that appears to have no narratee—the two works mentioned above as
well as *Sanctuary*, *L'Etranger*, and *Un Coeur simple*—permits his discovery. The narrator of *Un Coeur simple*, for example, does not refer
a single time to a narratee in an explicit manner. In his narrative,
nonetheless, there are numerous passages indicating more or less
clearly that he is addressing someone. It is thus that the narrator identifies the individuals whose proper names he mentions: "Robelin, the
farmer from Geoffosses . . . Liébard, the farmer from Touques . . .
M. Bourais, a former lawyer." It cannot be for himself that he identifies Robelin, Liébard, or M. Bourais; it must be for his narratee.
Moreover, the narrator often resorts to comparisons in order to

describe a character or situate an event, and each comparison defines more precisely the type of universe known to the narratee. Finally, the narrator sometimes refers to extra-textual experiences ("that confusion into which we are all thrown by the spectacle of extraordinary men"), which provide proof of the narratee's existence and information about his nature. Thus, even though the narratee may be invisible in a narration, he nonetheless exists and is never entirely forgotten.

In many other narrations, if the narratee is not represented by a character, he is at least mentioned explicitly by the narrator. The latter refers to him more or less frequently and his references can be quite direct (*Eugene Onegin, The Gold Pot, Tom Jones*) or quite indirect (*The Scarlet Letter, The Old Curiosity Shop, Les Faux-Monnayeurs*). Like the narratee of *Un Coeur simple*, these narratees are nameless and their role in the narrative is not always very important. Yet because of the passages that designate them in an explicit manner, it is easy to draw their portrait and to know what their narrator thinks of them. Sometimes, in *Tom Jones*, the narrator supplies so much information about his narratee, takes him aside so often, lavishes his advice upon him so frequently, that the latter becomes as clearly defined as any character.

Often instead of addressing—explicitly or implicitly—a narratee who is not a character, the narrator recounts his story to someone who is (*Heart of Darkness, Portnoy's Complaint, Les Infortunes de la vertu*). This character can be described in a more or less detailed manner. We know practically nothing about Doctor Spielvogel in *Portnoy's Complaint*, except that he is not lacking in perspicacity. On the other hand, in *Les Infortunes de la vertu*, we are informed about all of Juliette's life.

The narratee-character might play no other role in the narrative than that of narratee (*Heart of Darkness*). But he might also play other roles. It is not rare, for example, for him to be at the same time a narrator. In *L'Immoraliste*, one of the three individuals listening to Michel writes a long letter to his brother. In this letter, he repeats the story told to him by his friend, entreats his brother to shake Michel from his unhappiness, and records his own reactions to the narrative as well as the circumstances that led to his being present at its telling. Sometimes the narratee of a story can be at the same time its narrator.

He doesn't intend the narration to be for anyone other than himself. In *La Nausée*, for example, as in most novels written in the form of a diary, Roquentin counts on being the only reader of his journal.

Then again, the narratee-character can be more or less affected, more or less influenced by the narrative addressed to him. In *Heart of Darkness*, the companions of Marlow are not transformed by the story that he recounts to them. In *L'Immoraliste*, the three narratees, if they are not really different from what they were before Michel's account, are nonetheless "overcome by a strange feeling of malaise." And in *La Nausée*, as in many other works in which the narrator constitutes his own narratee, the latter is gradually and profoundly changed by the events he recounts for himself.

Finally, the narratee-character can represent for the narration someone more or less essential, more or less irreplaceable as a narratee. In *Heart of Darkness*, it's not necessary for Marlow to have his comrades on the *Nellie* as narratees. He would be able to recount his story to any other group; perhaps he would be able to refrain from telling it at all. On the other hand, in *L'Immoraliste*, Michel wished to address his friends and for that reason gathered them around him. Their presence in Algeria holds out hope: they will certainly not condemn him, they will perhaps understand him, and they will certainly help him get over his current situation. And in *A Thousand and One Nights*, to have the caliph as narratee is the difference between life and death for Scheherazade. If he refuses to listen to her, she will be killed. He is thus the only narratee whom she can have.

Whether or not he assumes the role of character, whether or not he is irreplaceable, whether he plays several roles or just one, the narratee can be a listener (*L'Immoraliste*, *Les Infortunes de la vertu*, *A Thousand and One Nights*) or a reader (*Adam Bede*, *Le Père Goriot*, *Les Faux-Monnayeurs*). Obviously, a text may not necessarily say whether the narratee is a reader or a listener. In such cases, it could be said that the narratee is a reader when the narration is written (*Hérodias*) and a listener when the narration is oral (*La Chanson de Roland*).

. . . We could probably think of other distinctions or establish other categories, but in any case, we can see how much more precise and more refined the typology of narrative would be if it were based not only upon narrators but also upon narratees. The same type of narrator can address very different types of narratees. Thus, Louis (*Le Noeud de vipères*), Salavin (*Journal de Salavin*), and Roquentin (*La Nausée*) are three characters who all keep a journal and who are very conscious of writing. But Louis changes narratees several times before deciding to write for himself; Slavin does not regard himself as the sole reader of his journal; and Roquentin writes exclusively for himself. Then again, very different narrators can address narratees of the same type. The narrators of *Un Coeur simple* and *La Condition humaine* as well as Meursault in *L'Etranger* all address a narratee who is not a character, who doesn't know them and who is not familiar with the individuals presented in the text nor with the events recounted.

Nonetheless, it is not only for a typology of the narrative genre and for a history of novelistic techniques that the notion of the narratee is important. Indeed, this notion is more interesting, because it permits us to study better the way in which a narration functions. In all narrations, a dialogue is established between the narrator(s), the narratee(s), and the character(s).[16] This dialogue develops—and consequently the narration also—as a function of the distance separating them from each other. In distinguishing the different categories of narratees, we have already used this concept, but without dwelling upon it too much: it is clear that a narratee who has participated in the events recorded is, in one sense, much closer to the characters than a narratee who has never even heard of them. But the notion of distance should be generalized. Whatever the point of view adopted—moral, intellectual, emotional, physical—narrator(s), narratee(s), and character(s) can be more or less close to each other ranging from the most perfect identification to the most complete opposition.

. . . As there are often several narrators, several narratees, and several characters in a text, the complexity of the rapports and the variety of the distances that are established between them can be quite significant. In any case, these rapports and these distances determine to a great extent the way in which certain values are praised and others are rejected in the course of a narration and the way in which certain events are emphasized and others are nearly passed over in silence. They determine as well the tone and the very nature of the narration. In *Les Cloches de Bâle*, for example, the tone changes completely—and cannot but change—once the narrator decides to proclaim his friendship for the narratee and to speak to him more honestly and more directly than he had previously: abandoning romantic extravagance, he becomes quasi-documentary; leaving behind false detachment, he becomes brotherly. On the other hand, many ironic effects in narration depend upon the differences existing between two images of the narratee or between two (groups of) narratees (*Les Infortunes de la vertu, Werther*), upon the distance existing between narrator and narratee on the one hand and character on the other (*Un Amour de Swann*), or yet again upon the distance existing between narrator and narratee (*Tom Jones*). The complexity of a situation results sometimes from the instability of the distances existing between the narrator, the narratee, and the characters. If Michel's guilt—or innocence—is not clearly established, it is partly because several times he shows himself capable of overcoming the distance separating him from his friends, or, if one prefers, because his friends are unsure of how much distance to put between themselves and him. . . .

The Narratee's Functions

The type of narratee that we find in a given narrative, the relations that tie him to narrators, characters, and other narratees, the distances that separate him from ideal, virtual, or real readers partially determine the nature of this narrative. But the narratee exercises other functions that are more or less numerous and important and are more or less specific to him. It will be worth the effort to enumerate these functions and to study them in some detail.

The most obvious role of the narratee, a role that he always plays in a certain sense, is that of relay between the narrator and the reader(s), or rather between the author and the reader(s). Should certain values have to be defended or certain ambiguities clarified, this can easily be done by means of asides addressed to the narratee. Should the importance of a series of events be emphasized, should one reassure or make uneasy, justify certain actions or underscore their arbitrariness, this can always be done by addressing signals to the narratee. In *Tom Jones*, for example, the narrator explains to the narratee that prudence is necessary for the preservation of virtue, an explanation that allows us to judge better his hero, virtuous but imprudent: "Prudence and circumspection are necessary even to the best men. . . . It is not enough that your designs, nay, that your actions, are intrinsically good, you must take care they shall appear so." Likewise, we know that although Legrandin is a snob, he is not lying when he protests against snobbery because Marcel says quite clearly to his narratee: "And indeed, that doesn't mean that Legrandin was not sincere when he inveighed against snobs." Indeed, the mediation doesn't always operate that directly: thus, narrator-narratee relations are sometimes developed in the ironic mode and the reader cannot always interpret literally the statements of the former to the latter. There exist other conceivable relays than direct and explicit asides addressed to the narratee, other possibilities of mediation between authors and readers. Dialogues, metaphors, symbolic situations, allusions to a particular system of thought or to a certain work of art are some of the ways of manipulating the reader, guiding his judgments, and controlling his reactions. Moreover, those are the methods preferred by many modern novelists, if not the majority of them; perhaps because they accord or seem to accord more freedom to the reader, perhaps because they oblige him to participate more actively in the development of the narrative, or perhaps simply because they satisfy a certain concern for realism. The role of the narratee as mediator is rather reduced in these cases. Everything must still pass via the narratee since everything—metaphors, allusions, dialogues—is still addressed to him; but nothing is modified, nothing is clarified for the reader by this passage. Whatever the advantages may be of this type of mediator it should nonetheless be recognized that from a certain point of view, direct and explicit statements by the narrator to the narratee are the most economical and the most effective sort of mediation. A few sentences suffice to establish the true significance of an unexpected act or the true nature of a character; a few words suffice to facilitate the interpretation of a complex situation. Although we can question indefinitely Stephen's esthetic maturity in *Portrait of the Artist as a Young Man* or the significance of a particular act in *A Farewell to Arms*, we always know exactly—or almost always—according to the text, what to think of Fabrice and la Sanseverina or of the intrigues of Mlle. Michonneau.[17]

Besides the function of mediation, the narratee exercises in any narration a function of characterization. . . . In the case of narrator-characters, the function of characterization is important although it can be reduced to a minimum even here: because he is at a distance from everything and from himself, because his strangeness and solitude depend upon this distance, Meursault would not know how to engage in a true dialogue with his narratee and, thus, cannot be described by this dialogue. Nonetheless, the relations that a narrator-character establishes with his narratee reveal as much—if not more—about his character than any other element in the narrative. In *La Religeuse*, Sister Suzanne, because of her conception of the narratee and her asides addressed to him, emerges as much less naive and much more calculating and coquettish than she would like to appear.

 . . . Moreover, the relations between the narrator and the narratee in a text may underscore one theme, illustrate another, or contradict yet another. Often the theme refers directly to the narrative situation and it is the narration as theme that these relations reveal. In *A Thousand and One Nights*, for instance, the theme of narration as life is emphasized by the attitude of Scheherazade toward the caliph and vice versa: the heroine will die if her narratee decides not to listen to her any more, just as other characters in the narrative die because he will not listen to them: ultimately, any narrative is impossible without a narratee. But often, themes that do not concern the narrative situation—or perhaps concern it only indirectly—reveal the positions of the narrator and the narratee in relation to each other. In *Le Père Goriot*, the narrator maintains relations of power with his narratee. From the very beginning, the narrator tries to anticipate his narratee's objections, to dominate him, and to convince him. All means are used: the narrator coaxes, entreats, threatens, derides, and in the final analysis we suspect that he succeeds in getting the better of his narratee. In the last part of the novel, when Vautrin has been put in prison and Goriot is advancing more and more quickly toward death, the narrator rarely addresses his narratee. This is because the narrator has won the battle. He is now sure of his effects, of his domination, and he need no longer do anything but recount the story. This sort of war, this desire for power, can be found at the level of the characters. On the level of the events as well as on the level of narration, the same struggle takes place.

 If the narratee contributes to the thematic of a narrative, he is also always part of the narrative framework, often of a particularly concrete framework in which the narrator(s) and narratee(s) are all characters (*Heart of Darkness, L'Immoraliste, The Decameron*). The effect is to make the narrative seem more natural. The narratee like the narrator plays an undeniable *verisimilating (vraisemblabilisant)* role. Sometimes this concrete framework provides the model by which a work or narration develops. In *The Decameron* or in *L'Heptameron*, it is expected that each of the narratees will in turn become a narrator. More than a mere sign of realism or an index of verisimilitude, the narratee represents in these circumstances an indispensable element for the development of the narrative.

. . . Finally it sometimes happens that we must study the narratee in order to discover a narrative's fundamental thrust. In *La Chute*, for example, it is only by studying the reactions of Clamence's narratee that we can know whether the protagonist's arguments are so powerful that they cannot be resisted, or whether, on the contrary, they constitute a skillful but unconvincing appeal. To be sure, the narratee doesn't say a single word throughout the entire novel and we don't even know if Clamence addresses himself or someone else: we only understand, from the narrator's remarks, that his narratee, like himself, is a bourgeois, in his forties, a Parisian, familiar with Dante and the Bible, a lawyer. . . . Nevertheless, this ambiguity emphasizing the essential duplicity of the protagonist's world does not represent a problem for the reader who would wish to discover the way in which Clamence is judged in the novel: whatever the identity of the narratee may be, the only thing that counts is the extent of his agreement with the theses of the hero. The latter's discourse shows evidence of a more and more intense resistance on the part of his interlocutor. Clamence's tone becomes more insistent and his sentences more embarrassed as his narrative progresses and his narratee escapes him. Several times in the last part of the novel he even appears seriously shaken. If at the end of *La Chute* Clamence is not defeated, he certainly has not been triumphant. If his values and his vision of the world and men are not entirely false, neither are they incontestably true. There are perhaps other professions than that of judge-penitent and there are perhaps other acceptable ways to live than Clamence's.

The narratee can, thus, exercise an entire series of functions in a narrative: he constitutes a relay between the narrator and the reader, he helps establish the narrative framework, he serves to characterize the narrator, he emphasizes certain themes, he contributes to the development of the plot, he becomes the spokesman for the moral of the work. Obviously, depending upon whether the narrator is skillful or inept, depending upon whether or not problems of narrative technique interest him, and depending upon whether or not his narrative requires it, the narratee will be more or less important, will play a greater or lesser number of roles, will be used in a way more or less subtle and original. Just as we study the narrator to evaluate the economy, the intentions, and the success of a narrative, so too we should examine the narratee in order to understand further and/or differently its mechanisms and significance.

The narratee is one of the fundamental elements of all narration. The thorough examination of what he represents, the study of a narrative work as constituted by a series of signals addressed to him, can lead to a more sharply delineated reading and a deeper characterization of the work. The study can lead also to a more precise typology of the narrative genre and a greater understanding of its evolution. It can provide a better appreciation of the way a narrative functions and a more accurate assessment of its success from a technical point of view. In the final analysis, the study of the narratee can lead us to a better understanding not only of the narrative genre but of all acts of communication.

Notes

1   See, for example, Henry James, *The Art of Fiction and Other Essays*, ed. Morris Roberts (New York: Oxford University Press, 1948); Norman Friedman, "Point of View in Fiction: The Development of a Critical Concept," *PMLA* 70 (December 1955): 1160–84; Wayne C. Booth, *The Rhetoric of Fiction* (Chicago: University of Chicago Press, 1961); Tzvetan Todorov, "Poetique," in Oswald Ducrot et al., *Qu'est-ce que le structuralisme?* (Paris: Seuil, 1968), pp. 97–166; and Gérard Genette, *Figures*, vol. 3 (Paris: Seuil, 1972).

2   See, among others, Walker Gibson, "Authors, Speakers, Readers, and Mock Readers," *College English* 9 (February 1950): 265–69; Roland Barthes, "Introduction à l'analyse structurale des récits," *Communications* 8 (1966): 18–19; Tzvetan Todorov, "Les Categories du récit litteraire," *Communications* 8 (1966): 146–47; Gerald Prince, "Notes Towards a Categorization of Fictional

'Narratees,' " *Genre* 4 (March 1971): 100–105; and Genette, *Figures*, vol. 3 pp. 265–67.

3 In a certain sense, every narrator is his own narratee. But most narrators have other narratees as well.

4 See Tzvetan Todorov, "Les Hommes-récits," in *Poetique de la prose* (Paris: Seuil, 1971), pp. 78–91.

5 See Tzvetan Todorov, "Le Récit primitif," in ibid., pp. 66–77.

6 For convenience' sake, we speak (and will speak often) of readers. It is obvious that a narratee should not be mistaken for a listener—real, virtual, or ideal.

7 This description of the linguistic capabilities of the zero-degree narratee nonetheless raises many problems. Thus, it is not always easy to determine the meaning(s) (*dénotation*[s]) of a given term and it becomes necessary to fix in time the language (*langue*) known to the narratee, a task that is sometimes difficult when working from the text itself. In addition, the narrator can manipulate a language in a personal way. Confronted by certain idiosyncrasies that are not easy to situate in relation to the text, do we say that the narratee experiences them as exaggerations, as errors, or on the contrary do they seem perfectly normal to him? Because of these difficulties and many others as well, the description of the narratee and his language cannot always be exact. It is, nevertheless, to a large extent reproducible.

8 We use these terms as they are used in modern logic.

9 See in this regard, Gerald Prince, *A Grammar of Stories: An Introduction* (The Hague: Mouton, 1973). A formal description of the rules followed by all narratives can be found in this work.

10 On verisimilitude, see the excellent *Communications* 11 (1968).

11 Barthes, "Introduction à l'analyse structurale des récits," p. 10. It should be noted that while this confusion has been very much exploited, it is not at all necessary for the development of a narrative.

12 Roland Barthes, *S/Z* (Paris: Seuil, 1970), pp. 27–28.

13 We should undoubtedly distinguish the "virtual" narratee from the "real" narratee in a more systematic manner. But this distinction would perhaps not be very helpful.

14 Note that even an "I" can designate a "you."

15 See, in this regard, Gérard Genette, "Vraisemblance et motivation," in his *Figures*, vol. 2 (Paris: Seuil, 1969).

16 We follow here in modifying the perspective, Booth, *The Rhetoric of Fiction*, pp. 155ff.

17 See Wayne C. Booth, ibid.

22

Realism Reconsidered

GEORGE LEVINE

▬▬

Observing that " 'realism' seems to be a term from which there is no escaping in discussions of fiction, even now," George Levine sets out to redefine fictional realism. He notes that the term did not arise until the mid-nineteenth century, and that its short life has produced the strong counterreactions of modernism and the "self-consciously anti-realistic litera-ture" of postmodernism, both of which are reactions against the idealist Victorian portrayal of reality. Levine argues, however, that despite its anti-realistic surface, "the idea that literature should be describing reality or truth is implicitly present still" in modern fiction.

To understand this apparent discrepancy between a commitment to re-ality and a rejection of realism, we must first distinguish between realism as a historical literary method and realism as an ideal. Understood in the first sense, realism "reflects both inherited conventions and a way of look-ing at the world, a metaphysic, as it were. It implies certain assumptions about the nature of the real world, assumptions which need not be made explicit in any realistic text but which certainly constitute a ground of meaning." By "a ground of meaning," Levine means that a fiction may be viewed as realistic in terms related to the author's effort to render observ-able details accurately, or in terms of the audience's comparison of the fiction's content with its own perception of social reality. When speaking of realism, Levine argues, we are therefore talking about how a work's con-tent relates to a "dominant and shared notion of reality in operation," de-veloped in contrast to "older and currently unsatisfying" conventions, and a consensus that "moral value" inheres in "the representation of that reality."

In order to move beyond this consensual conception of reality, Levine proposes ten assumptions to guide his discussion of realism, the paramount one, repeated first and last, being that "all fiction is fiction." This dictum can be understood as asserting that the beauty of art arises from imaginative lying: "The emphasis on lying should remind us of how much our admiration of great fictions depends not on their recording of life but on their creation of it through language and of how deeply all fiction is indebted to literature and its tradition." Levine carefully qualifies this remark by adding that "the pressures on literary form come not only from literary tradition but from the form of each writer's belief in the nature of reality." The issue, then, lies not in whether literature creates reality or reality creates literature, but in understanding how the two influence and alter each other, as in the case of the modernists, who both encouraged and reflected a rejection of Victorian values.

George Levine (b. 1931) is professor of English at Rutgers University. In addition to editing several books, he is author of *The Boundaries of Fiction: Carlyle, Macaulay, Newman* (1968) and *The Realistic Imagination: English Fiction from Frankenstein to Lady Chatterley* (1981).

Realism would seem now to be a tired subject, and to revive it is to risk repetition and boredom. Unfortunately, however, the word "realism" is only tired, not dead, and whatever it refers to seems also more or less alive; certainly the problems raised by its meaning in literary contexts persist. In England there has been a continuous tradition of realistic writing, most recently in self-conscious repudiation of various modes of modernism, and in a very recent book David Lodge comes close to insisting on the almost precise overlap between realism and the novel as a form. Since, moreover, his point is to prove that the novel is not dead, he is also obliged to prove that realism, too, lives.[1] In any case, "realism" seems to be a term from which there is no escaping in discussions of fiction, even now.

"Realism Reconsidered," by George Levine, is reprinted from *The Theory of the Novel: New Essays*, ed. John Helperin, by permission of Oxford University Press, Inc., copyright 1974.

It is, of course, a commonplace of criticism that "realism" is an elusive word, that it has been recklessly and carelessly used; but despite some very serious efforts, it has been impossible, finally, either to provide it with a consistently precise definition or to banish it. Even to argue that it describes a kind of phantom, something that is not and never has been, is to affirm a fairly comfortable position which has long since lost its shock value.[2] But it is important to note that the word has a relatively short history in English, appearing for the first time somewhere in the middle of the nineteenth century; and it developed, for the purposes of English fiction, on an analogy with French fiction.[3] And the very fiction it was used to describe—that, for instance, of Thackeray, or Mrs. Gaskell, or George Eliot—is regarded by modern artists as profoundly unrealistic in the sense that it surrendered to the happy ending and to coincidence, that it consistently omitted certain aspects of reality, that it tended to assume an intelligible universe.[4]

Part of the modern growth of self-consciously anti-realistic literature and criticism has surely been the result of a rejection of Victorian conceptions of reality, but the idea that literature should be describing reality or truth is implicitly present still. The most interesting fiction of our day frequently seems to be game-playing, to be enjoying—as in Borges, Barth, and Nabokov—the possibilities of language and pleasures of literary parody. But the games themselves, while suggesting powerfully the writers' consciousness of the way verbal structures intervene between us and reality, provide for us new possibilities of reality. Reality has become problematic in ways the Victorians could only barely imagine, yet much of the energy of modern fiction comes from sources similar to those which directed earlier realism: from a conscious rejection of the notions of reality implicit in earlier fictions and from a sense of the limits of the power of language to render reality at all. The method of Robbe-Grillet, as he himself has made clear, is an attempt to get more precise about reality as it is experienced by human consciousness.[5] With this notion of changing realities in mind, we can, moreover, make some sense of Erich Auerbach's treatment of Virginia Woolf as a great culmination of the tradition of literary realism.

Most of the confusions about the word "realism," I would argue, come from an initial confusion between an historically definable literary method and a more general (perhaps inescapable) attempt to be faithful to the real. Since reality is both inexhaustible and perpetually changing to human consciousness, the word "realism" had no chance of a stable meaning. Despite all its dangers, the word has the one virtue of forcing us to wrestle with some of the central problems of criticism and of art.

The question it poses initially is, not so simply, whether literature in any sense describes the real, extra-literary world. And that question, of course, leads to others: is it the function of literature to record reality or to illuminate, even create, new possibilities? What value can there be in a mere record of reality? Is it possible to render reality when perception can never be pure and the medium of language seems inevitably to influence its subject?[6] How can one judge literature on the basis of its fidelity to the real when the real itself is so elusive and variable? Questions like these are the province of philosophy and aesthetics, but they must enter into criticism, and they certainly underlie most of our assumptions of value. Every literary generation has to struggle with them, though I do not propose here to do so directly. Although much of what I say will remain at a high and dangerous level of abstraction, what I want to do here is help toward the development of a critical approach to fiction which will at once deal with our immediate or naive sense that fiction is somehow like life, that appropriate terms of judgment can be found in the comparison of fiction to what really happens in life, that the novel is the most mixed of literary forms and therefore the one most responsive to extra-literary pressures, and with our more literary awareness of fiction as a structure of language working out from earlier structures and profoundly limited by the medium of language itself.

My bias, then, is historical, and I am convinced that criticism of fiction would profit from a fuller and more precise sense both of the traditions of the novel and of the changes in sensibility and perception which have affected those traditions. In its only even relatively precise sense, realism is an historical phenomenon, a literary method (or methods) rather than a literary or metaphysical ideal. Obviously, the second notion influenced the first, and historically speaking it is fair to say that writers thought that in adopting realism as a technique they were in fact moving closer to the truth. What is interesting here is that at one point in European history writers should have become so self-conscious about truth-telling in art (which I take to imply the growth of doubt about art in society) that they were led to raise truth-telling to the level of doctrine and to imply that previous literatures had not been telling it. Surely this is an important development in intellectual and cultural history, but surely, too, criticism is misled which works on the assumption that realistic novels—those of George Eliot, say—represent real life more accurately than do the narratives of Milton, or Melville, or even Fielding.

So extraordinary a book as Auerbach's *Mimesis* can itself be taken as fostering the confusion by implying that Western literature has been moving constantly toward a finer and finer approximation to reality. If we read the book in that way, we can fall into the trap of assuming that there is some sort of absolute reality toward which artistic consciousness, in a kind of Hegelian dialectical movement, is progressively moving. Auerbach's great value lies not in his treatment of Virginia Woolf as the greatest "realist" because her techniques most precisely record the nature of psychological reality and the flux of experience, but in his wonderful treatment of the various styles of writers as they attempt to deal with new versions of reality, and in his implied assumption that the language of each writer creates the new reality. Perhaps the most fruitful approach to the problem is suggested by E. H. Gombrich's *Art and Illusion*,[7] a book which deals with the way in which artistic creation and audience perception are controlled by the conventions for the representation of reality within art and society. Artists have taught us to *see* differently; the way we see is culturally conditioned, so that lines suggesting depth to us may seem mere lines to those living in a different culture.[8]

Realism, like any literary method, reflects both inherited conventions and a way of looking at the world, a metaphysic, as it were. It implies certain assumptions about the nature of the real world, assumptions which need not be made explicit in any realistic text but which certainly constitute a ground of meaning. Among other things, it has, surely, implied that ordinariness is more real—at least more representative and therefore truthful—than heroism, that people are morally mixed rather than either good or bad, that the firmest realities are objects rather than ideas or imaginings. English realism, the type with which I will be most directly concerned, tended, moreover, to assume that the real is both meaningful and good, while French realism has consistently tended away from such moral assumptions to lead more directly to the notion of an indifferent universe and to that even more specialized kind of realism, naturalism.

Whatever the specific assumptions, one way to deal with the problem of realism is to locate those assumptions and to identify the conventions (including, in particular, assumptions about how literature ought to be affecting its audience). When a literary method comes to be called realistic it tends to imply several things: first, that there is a dominant and shared notion of reality in operation, upon which the writer and his audience can rely; second, that this notion is self-consciously replacing an older and currently unsatisfying one which is open to parody and rejection; third, that there is moral value (to be debated by those who continue to defend the older notion) in the representation of that reality. This obviously leads to confusions because the argument seems not to be about the nature of literary technique but about the nature of reality. Such confusion is redoubled by literary debates over whether, even if the artist's version of reality is accurate, the recording of that reality is rightfully the function of art. Much nineteenth-century criticism of realistic writers—of such different ones as George Eliot and Zola—was precisely of this kind. As Linda Nochlin suggests, such criticism assumed that writers "were doing no more than mirroring every-day reality. These statements derived from the belief that perception could be 'pure' and unconditioned by time or place."[9]

Just as realism implies certain metaphysical or quasi-metaphysical assumptions, so does criticism of it. In order to proceed with my argument, I need at this point to make clear as well as I can the assumptions upon which my analysis will—more or less ingenuously—be based. For economy's sake, I lay them out in propositional form, although they have not the rigor of philosophical argument. I do intend them as a coherent and gradually developing argument but believe it possible to accept some of the propositions without accepting all that precede or follow. I should, furthermore, preface them with two qualifying remarks: first, that the ideas apply most directly to the classical tradition of the nineteenth-century English novel (although I do believe them applicable, with some qualifications, to all fiction);

and second, that like all truisms mine appear to me to be debatable or, at least, occasionally to disguise what is moot by leaving key words incompletely defined. At the risk then of either banality or obfuscation, let me begin.

1. All fiction is fiction.
2. All fiction emerges from the consciousness of the individual writer and is therefore shaped in the way that consciousness perceives.
   2a. The writer's consciousness will necessarily be deeply involved in the shared assumptions of his culture and in at least some of the traditions of fictional form.[10]
   2b. The writer's perceptions as well as his language will be largely controlled by these assumptions in combination with his private psychological needs.
3. The basic materials of fiction are words, and words are the means by which each consciousness constructs and orders its world and by which each private world is made shareable.
   3a. Words, as implied in 2a, are invested with the assumptions and history of the culture.
   3b. Words inevitably carry not only the burden of description (and perception) but the burden of value. A change in language implies a change both in perceptions and values—and, concomitantly, a change in the forms of fiction.
4. The fundamental form of fiction is, therefore, the working out in language of the possibilities imaginable by the writer in the direction of the most complete shareable fulfillment of his values.
   4a. Mimetic language, the language of "realistic" fiction, explores not only the possibilities of what is but the possibilities of what should be (as limited by the shareable assumptions implicit in the language, the culture, and the writer's mind).
   4b. Insofar as the descriptive and prescriptive tendencies of language and fiction are separable, the descriptive tends toward disorder, the prescriptive toward order, the one to integrity of detail, the other to coherence of design.[11]
5. The predominating energy in most fiction, however discursive, episodic, or apparently formless, is not the representation of reality but the shaping of the rendered experience. It is, in other words, formal, and manifests itself traditionally in plot, but also—

as new critical analyses have suggested—in patterns of imagery, motifs, relationships.[12]

6. If romance can be stipulatively defined as a form in which pattern dominates over plausibility, in which the central figure achieves the fullest possible freedom from the limitations of a restricting context, in which ideal values are worked out and shown to be viable, romance is the underlying form of most fiction, whatever its ostensible mode.

6a. Romance is the translation of the writer's perceptions into narrative, i.e., the imposition of form on experience.

6b. The imposition of form on experience is the mode by which literary conventions are transmitted. Curiously, the most intense and personal feelings and perceptions tend to take the most formally recognizable shapes. In Frye's convincing paradoxical formulation: "It has been a regular rule that the uninhibited imagination, in the structural sense, produces highly conventional art."[13]

6c. Romance is also the mode by which the particular psychic needs of the writer are most directly placed, as imaginative projections, in narrative.

7. Although novels may aspire to create the illusion of reality and to tell the truth, the most fruitful direct approach to fiction is through a focus on romance elements, the romance being the generator of form.

8. Form in any given novel is meaning since it determines the relations of the surface elements.

9. Patterning is the distinctive quality of fiction and of language, the material of fiction; and patterning is a reflection of the translation of experience into mind and feeling.

9a. There is no such thing as raw experience, since that implies some kind of experience undisturbed and unmodified—by mind or feeling.

9b. Fictional language differs from non-fictional rather in the degree to which engagement imposes meaning than in any formal way. Realism attempts to create the illusion of nonfiction as the writer struggles to come to terms with, as Frye puts it, "things as they are and not as the story-teller would like them to be for his convenience."[14]

10. All fiction is fiction.

Such abstract speculation on truth, reality, and perception is likely to miss out on the most obvious fact about fiction—its special power to amuse and engage us through narrative, to arouse expectations and provide satisfying resolutions.[15] And it is for this reason, among others, that I have insisted on the fictionality of fiction. Fiction is shaping, giving precedence to form over reality and even plausibility, when necessary.[16] It is the working out of imaginings and desires and needs, and its form is an expression of these. Traditionally, literature was taken as being both sweet and useful, *dulce et utile*. But the realist aesthetic tends to subsume both of these under the heading "form" as opposed to that of "truth." And a good part of the energy of English realist art was devoted to attempting to make it possible to combine the sweet and useful with the truthful.

By the end of the nineteenth century the difficulty of such an enterprise was clear. Oscar Wilde's wonderfully satiric and intelligent dialogue "The Decay of Lying" is a rich assertion of my rather more pallid propositions 4 through 4b, an attack on the conventions of realism dominating at the time and a recognition of an apparent incompatibility between form (coherence of design) and truth (integrity of detail). "What Art really reveals to us is Nature's lack of design," says Vivian.[17] The whole dialogue comes to equate imagination with lying, or, to put the better face on it, lying with imagination. It argues that what we value in art is the lying, not the mundane recording of a patternless and unattractive universe. "It is always the unreadable that occurs," Vivian says.[18] In this and the companion dialogue, "The Artist as Critic," Wilde suggests how the liar actually creates reality for us, although he would never allow himself so solemn a formulation. Wilde (or Vivian) goes on to suggest the virtues (heaven help us) of lying, and in so doing links together—beautifully for my purposes—the notion of entertainment, lying, imagination, and creativity:

> For the aim of the liar is simply to charm, to delight, to give pleasure. He is the very basis of civilized society, and without him a dinner party, even at the mansions of the great, is as dull as a lecture at the Royal Society. . . . Nor will he be welcomed by society alone. Art, breaking from the prison-house of real-

ism, will run to greet him, and will kiss his false, beautiful lips, knowing that he alone is in possession of the great secret of all her manifestations, the secret that Truth is entirely and absolutely a matter of style; while Life—poor, probable, uninteresting human life—tired of repeating herself for the benefit of Mr. Herbert Spencer, scientific historians, and the compilers of statistics in general, will follow meekly after him, and try to produce, in her own simple and untutored way, some of the marvels of which he talks.[19]

This is no joke.

The emphasis on lying should remind us of how much our admiration of great fictions depends not on their recording of life but on their creation of it through language and of how deeply all fiction is indebted to literature and its traditions: "Art," says Wilde, "finds her own perfection within, and not outside of, herself. She is not to be judged by any external standard of resemblance. She is a veil rather than a mirror."[20] This is a happier way of putting Frye's assertion that "Literary shape cannot come from life; it comes only from literary tradition."

At the very least, these ideas seem valid in arguing that fiction is not to be judged "by any external standard of resemblance." Much of the weakness of criticism of the great novels in the central tradition of nineteenth-century realistic fiction is a result of the tendency to judge by such an external standard. We can see quite clearly now that disparagement of the "spontaneous combustion" episode in *Bleak House* because such things do not happen, or of the fairy-tale quality of *Jane Eyre* because it is mere wish-fulfillment, is entirely beside the point of the special qualities of those books. To criticize in this way is to equate "realism" with "truth," and with "truth" as we happen to define it. Surely, the relation between art and truth is more complicated and interesting than that.

Of course, it will not do to dismiss entirely the mimetic element in the language of realism and simply to assimilate realism to romance. Frye is surely oversimplifying when he says that "literary shape cannot come from life," even though he means here overall structure rather than local detail. The pressures on literary form come not only from literary tradition but from the form of each writer's belief in the nature of reality. That this form is culturally influenced does not mean that it is exclusively shaped by literature—as witness, for example, the literary effects of *The Origin of Species*. The realistic method does develop out of conventions of empiricism. In her extremely interesting qualification of the views of Gombrich, Linda Nochlin, accepting our view that realism is an historically locatable technique rather than a direct expression of truth, points out that "if one takes the opposition between convention and empirical observation in art as a relative rather than an absolute criterion, one can see that in Realism the role played by observation is greater, that by convention smaller."[21] As an example, she shows how Constable, though he based his paintings of clouds partly on the work of Alexander Cozzens, an eighteenth-century engraver, nevertheless painted clouds as *he* saw them, and they are readily identifiable as to type, where Cozzens's clouds are not. I would argue, moreover, that the commitment to what was taken as observed reality significantly reshaped the larger structures and subject matters of fiction.

Yet patterning remains the distinctive quality of fiction, and it is with this patterning that novelists must, finally, come to terms, even if one of their initial motives is the telling of truth. For the truth must be the truth as they see it and in a mode whose traditions themselves entail a shape. The history of the novel in English from Defoe to the present reveals the dominance of "lying" in the convention of realism itself. Realism has been only one of the novel's modes, though a central mode, and its pressures have led the novelist to struggle—through all its transformations—to deal with "things as they are" rather than as he "would like them to be for his own convenience." But the struggle was never quite won because the obstacles realism itself created to the writers' imaginative needs led, inevitably, to its abandonment or at least radical revision. There developed a recognition, which we can see in Hardy, Conrad, Virginia Woolf, and others around the turn of the century, that things as they are are themselves a convention, and that the convention was a peculiarly painful one.

Notes

1 David Lodge, *The Novelist at the Crossroads* (London, 1971), p. 4.
2 For a discussion of the confusions surrounding the word realism see Erich Heller, "The Realistic Fallacy," *Listener* 53 (May 19, 1955): 188–89. Reprinted

in George Becker, *Documents of Literary Realism* (Princeton, 1967). Heller suggests the emptiness of the word, as does my "Realism, or, In Praise of Lying: Some Nineteenth Century Novels," *College English* 31 (January 1970): 355–65.

3 The word seems to have been borrowed from the French in the 1850s. See Richard Stang, *The Theory of the Novel in England, 1850–1870* (New York, 1959), p. 145; and two essays to which Stang alludes, R. G. Davis, "The Sense of the Real in English Fiction," *Comparative Literature* 3 (Summer 1951): 200–217; and "Balzac and His Writings," *Westminster Review* 60 (July 1853): 199–214. The latter essay still seems to assume a naive realism, but its brief discussion of the term is useful in suggesting—correctly—the close connection between realism and romanticism.

4 The most obvious and popular recent example of the attitude is in John Fowles's *The French Lieutenant's Woman;* but, of course, while rejecting naive notions of realism and insisting instead on imaginative reality, Fowles exploits Victorian realistic techniques and writes a new best-seller.

5 Alain Robbe-Grillet, *Pour un nouveau roman* (Paris, 1955). At one point he says, "Tous les écrivains pensent être realistes," and after a brief discussion he argues that "on doit conclure que tous ont raison" (p. 135).

6 See Linda Nochlin, *Realism* (Harmondsworth, Middlesex, 1971): "The commonplace notion that Realism is a 'styleless' or transparent style, a mere simulacrum or mirror image of visual reality, is another barrier to its understanding as an historical and stylistic phenomenon. This is a gross simplification, for Realism was no more a mere mirror of reality than any other style, and its relation *qua* style to phenomenal data—the donée—is as complex and difficult as that of Romanticism, the Baroque or Mannerism" (p. 14).

7 Ernst Gombrich, *Art and Illusion* (London, 1960). No summary can begin to cope with the argument of this brilliant book. Some of its orientation, however, is suggested by one key sentence: "Art is born of art, not of nature" (p. 21).

8 Linda Nochlin's book (see n. 6, above) is in part an attempt to qualify Gombrich's argument by showing that although realism is conventional, it differs from other conventions in its commitment to empirical truth: "It was not until the nineteenth century that contemporary ideology came to equate belief in the facts with the total content of belief itself; it is in this the crucial difference lies between nineteenth century Realism and all its predecessors" (p. 45).

9 Nochlin, *Realism*, p. 14.

10 See Lucien Goldmann, *The Human Sciences and Philosophy*, trans. Hayden White and Robert Anchor (London, 1969): "Every manifestation is the work of its individual author and expresses his thought and way of feeling, but these ways of thinking and feeling are not independent entities with respect to the actions and behaviour of other men. They exist and may be understood only in terms of their inter-subjective relations which give them their whole tenor and richness" (p. 128). See also Henry James, "The Art of Fic-

tion," in Leon Edel, ed., *The House of Fiction* (London, 1957): "A novel is in its broadest definition a personal, a direct impression of life." Gombrich, however, writes, "If art were only, or merely, an expression of personal vision, there could be no history of art" (p. 4).

11   On points 4a and 4b Northrop Frye's essay "Myth, Fiction, and Displacement," in *Fables of Identity* (New York, 1963), is particularly helpful, and I should confess to a deep debt to its arguments, which have provoked (in both senses) much of my most recent thinking on the subject. Frye argues that "the realistic writer soon finds that the requirements of literary form and plausible content always fight against each other" (p. 36). The entire essay brilliantly explores the difference between imagination as a creative and structural power and imagination as a reproductive power, between "recognition of credibility, fidelity to experience," in fiction, and "recognition of the identity of total design." In Frye's terms, art "deals, not with the world that man contemplates, but with the world that man creates" (p. 31). When art " 'imitates' nature it assimilates nature to human forms," a point not very different from the one that I am making. But Frye makes too sharp a distinction between literature and life by making too sharp a distinction between credibility and coherence.

12   Complicated qualifications would have to be made here because recent developments in fiction have self-consciously rejected or parodied the traditions of the great realistic novels of the nineteenth century. My major concern here is with the classical novel, from Richardson to Lawrence, but I would be prepared to argue that even for fictions like those of Nabokov, Barth, Butor, or Robbe-Grillet, this assertion is applicable.

13   Frye, "Myth, Fiction, and Displacement," p. 27.

14   Ibid.

15   See Sheldon Sacks, *Fiction and the Shape of Belief* (Chicago, 1964). Sacks discusses the way in which genre imposes directions on narrative structure.

16   The traditional English realistic novel tended to work itself out so that the audience's aroused expectations would be satisfied by at least some rough poetic justice, usually distributed by virtue of appropriate coincidences. As an aspect of a changing vision of reality, the fiction of writers so different as Hardy and Zola tended, whether by coincidence or circumstantially realistic patterning, to make the absence of poetic justice precisely the aesthetic point of their fictions. The revised reality produced a revised aesthetic with its own kind of perversely satisfying resolutions and satisfactions. See Kenneth Graham's discussion of Zola as a romancer in *English Criticism of the Novel 1865–1900* (London, 1965), pp. 56–61.

17   "The Decay of Living," reprinted in Richard Ellmann, ed., *The Artist as Critic: Critical Writings of Oscar Wilde* (New York, 1968), p. 290.

18   Ellmann, ibid., p. 292.

19   Ibid., p. 305.

20   Ibid., p. 319.

21   Nochlin, *Realism*, p. 18.

23

Approach to the Novella
through Its Forms

MARY DOYLE SPRINGER

In *Forms of the Modern Novella* (1975), Mary Doyle Springer has written one of the few works in English devoted exclusively to that genre. In this, the first chapter of her book, Springer begins by asserting that the novella has been the subject of little theoretical discussion, even though the form has been practiced by such prominent modern authors as Henry James, William Faulkner, James Joyce, and Leo Tolstoy. Like Suzanne Ferguson, Springer also argues with Norman Friedman's remarks on the short story, particularly his willingness to lump novellas such as Tolstoy's *The Death of Ivan Ilyich* together with short stories. For Springer, the term "short novel" describes a flawed work in which form and content remain at odds, whereas "novella" is a form that lies, in length, between the short story and the novel, but is one that unites form and content. While a novella's length can easily be defined by recourse to word counts, this fact explains little about its "qualities," those "formal purposes" that produce a work of 15,000 to 50,000 words. Accordingly, for Springer, "the novella is its own genre by means of taking its own forms," which she outlines in this chapter and then discusses in the rest of her book. Springer wishes to help critical readers learn "to ask the right questions about a novella," rather than to judge it with questions more pertinent to the short story or the novel.

Mary Doyle Springer (b. 1918) is professor of English at St. Mary's College, Moraga, Calif., and also author of *A Rhetoric of Literary Character: Some Women of Henry James* (1978).

It must soon become apparent that a short novel is something in itself, neither a lengthily written short story nor the refurbished attempt at a novel sent out into the world with its hat clapped on at the eightieth page.—Howard Nemerov

"Kinds" are the very life of literature, and truth and strength come from the complete recognition of them, from abounding to the utmost in their respective senses and sinking deep into their consistency. . . . The confusion of kinds is the inelegance of letters and the stultification of values. . . . —Henry James

We propose to consider poems as unique existent things the structural principles of which are to be discovered, rather than as embodiments of general truths about the structure of poetry already adequately known.—R. S. Crane

What is a novella? And how would an answer to that question enhance our understanding and appreciation of those works we call novellas, or "short novels"? It will be my purpose in this and succeeding chapters to respond to these two questions, and to show that the answers can reflect understanding on modern fictional works of all sizes.

The Desert Area of Novella Theory, with Pious Hopes for a Better Future

In recent years there has been a strong show of critical interest in developing a theory of prose fiction, especially of the novel. There now exists works of the first importance defining forms of the novel, considering closely its separate formal elements, and studying how some of these elements are related to its rhetorical or emotional effects.[1] The short story, too, has begun to receive extensive formal consideration.[2] Curiously, the serious study of the novella remains an almost desert area. Readers have long been pleased with whatever it is that this genre has especially to offer (witness the recent proliferation of paperback anthologies of novellas). Yet, except for occasional brief thematic treatment,[3] several historical and technical studies limited to the German *novelle*,[4] and the admirable historical work of Gerald Gillespie on terminology,[5] critics generally offer only introductory commentary which avoids the task of defining the novella in more than a few words, or else they ignore it altogether as a separate entity.

Theorists of the short story usually attend to the questions of length and of magnitude as though no works existed to enlighten their comparisons except short stories at the one extreme and long novels at the other. But the novella does not, when it is ignored, fade away and refuse to make trouble. Ignoring it as a separate genre can lead to strange, if not insupportable, formal judgments about some of these longer works. Speaking of Conrad's *Heart of Darkness*, one critic accounts for length partly on grounds that Marlow is simply "given to commentary and speculation"; and he treats Tolstoy's novella, *The Death of Ivan Ilyich*, as a condensation down to a short story—"albeit a rather long one"—of a life too boring to be expanded into a long novel.[6] In the case of short stories, the necessity of trying to incorporate into the discussion only a few of what I would separate out as novellas helps tempt the critic into niceties of classification which are sometimes helpful, sometimes overelaborate (the most ardent lover of formal distinctions may tire under such classifications as "painful" lined up against "tragedy" and "pathos," with subclasses of "romantic pathos" and "caustic pathos").[7]

Yet, when analysis does not serve to gather in longer works, there results a kind of gap in nature. Elizabeth Bowen speaks of the short story as "free from the *longueurs* of the novel and also exempt from the novel's conclusiveness—too often forced and false."[8] Where does this leave the novella: free as the short story, or stricken with conclusiveness like the novel?

That the novella has some existence of its own, more palpable than a phantom occupying shadowy space between a short story and a novel, is recognized mainly by the two groups who bump up against the question most conspicuously: writers of novellas, and editors of both novella anthologies and short-story anthologies.

Martha Foley, perhaps the best-known anthologist of American short stories, claims to have sat down with her predecessor, Edward O'Brien, who founded the *Best American Short Stories* annual series, and made a considered decision to "be responsible for the introduction of the word novella into the English language," mainly because she detested the term "novelette," which was "used in the sense of a condensed novel, a digest." O'Brien, it developed, had a handy acquaintance with an editor of the *Oxford English Dictionary*, whom he persuaded to include the word "novella." The story turns out somewhat unhappily: Martha Foley admits that the meaning of the word is still "often distorted" in dictionaries. The degree of clarity that she herself supplies can be left to my reader's judgment of the following imaginary dialogue she conducts with herself about definitions of the genres of prose fiction. When she asks herself "What *is* a short story?" the answer is: "I wish I knew. . . . A short story is a story that is not too long." And "if it is very long and interesting, I suppose it could be called a novel." Next question: "What about the novella?" Her answer: "It is a beautiful form of writing, longer than a short story, shorter than a novel, which authors love. Many editors, including myself, have to forgo it because of space limitations."[9]

Editors of novella anthologies seem to depend mainly on practice, or on custom, to define their choices. Thus, neither reader nor editor is surprised when he finds collected together such long-accepted "short novels" as Mann's *Death in Venice*, Dostoevsky's *Notes From Underground*, James's *Daisy Miller*, Joyce's *The Dead*, Kafka's *The Metamorphosis*, Melville's *Bartleby the Scrivener*, *Benito Cereno*, and *Billy Budd*. The difficulty arises when the editor necessarily departs from previous anthologies to make some choices not ordinarily encountered. At that point he seems to feel an implicit question which he does not wish to answer simply in terms of length or taste: "What definition of the novella accounts for the choice of these works as belonging under that title?" Under the relatively safe shelter of an "introduction" (which by custom can raise questions without providing full answers), the problem is taken up with minimal seriousness, and never with any scope which would begin to match the attention that has enlightened the study of the short story and of the novel.[10]

I should like to pause here at the outset of my discussion to agree with Foley and O'Brien that the term "novella" is the most useful one. My reasons are two: (1) I wish to stress both the dignity and separate identity of the novella—my whole purpose will be to help describe that identity; (2) the term is increasingly appearing as common currency—one sees it in film credits, in indexes of critical articles such as those provided by the Modern Language Association, and one hears it used among teachers and students of literature. As Percy Lubbock long ago pointed out, we are in need of a common language for discussing literature. One contradiction that must be faced is, that despite the above evidence favoring a public choice of the term novella, an overwhelming number of anthologies are titled with the term "short novels." I am convinced that this is because, in the absence of a concentrated empirical study of what factors define the novella as a distinct genre, the easiest way is to fall back more or less unconsciously into an assumption that Martha Foley recognized to be false, namely, that these works are condensations or digests of what might have been long novels if they had not ended as "short novels."

That there exist in literature such condensations of what should have been long novels is undoubted. But I believe that the key to understanding genre is to understand that such works are, in the relation of their size to their formal purposes, flawed. They are works whose architecture as a whole (though some of its parts may have beauty) has failed. There is a need to recognize that each genre is defined by its own special powers, and that these are not simply a matter of degree—that is, of the same powers expanded or contracted. If I am right in this, Vladimir Nabokov is treating the matter too casually when he says that the writer of novellas operates by "diminishing large things and enlarging small ones." As Mark Schorer puts it:

> The "possible" for the novel is different from the "possible" for the short story. The distinction is relative, and does not help very much to define either *genre*. Is it not necessary to look further, to ask whether the difference in unity between a short story and a novel is not rather one of kind than of degree? Do we not all the time read novels that we feel should have been short stories, and short stories that should have been novelettes, at least?

Is it not that the unity of a novel can encompass one kind of thing and the unity of a short story another kind?[11]

The answer to these questions is clearly "yes," except that the "kind" in each of these genres is so various that I would use the plural and speak of "kinds" or "forms" that each of these genres can encompass.

John Galsworthy, though he does not think the matter through to an answer as Schorer does, produces a vivid metaphor to elucidate the problem:

What dictates the size of the bottle into which we pour our wine—or vinegar? Certainly not deliberate resolution, for then one would have written nothing but stories of from ten to thirty thousand words. . . . The whole thing is a puzzle. Why should one have to write a novel when a certain figure, incident or idea takes possession of the imagination; a short story about a second incident or figure; and a tale of medium length around a third? I cannot answer; but I am convinced that he is in luck to whom the unseen hander-out of bottles offers the pint.[12]

A genre called, increasingly often, the "novella" does exist in terms, not simply of length, but of some kinds of things it does and in terms of some kinds of beauties which only the "pint" size contains—all of this intuited, when not clearly expressed, by both critics and authors.

Henry James, in his preface to *The Lesson of the Master*, clarifies the connection that exists between the length of fiction and its "organic form." He gives an obviously delighted account of what happened to him at the foundation of "the small square lemon-coloured quarterly" called "The Yellow Book":

I was invited, and all urgently, to contribute to the first number, and was regaled with the golden truth that my composition might absolutely assume, might shamelessly parade in, its own organic form. It was disclosed to me, wonderfully, that—so golden the air pervading the enterprise—any projected contribution might conform, not only unchallenged but by this circumstance itself the more esteemed, to its true intelligible nature. For any idea I might wish to express I might have space, in other words, elegantly to express it—an offered license that, on the spot, opened up the millennium to the "short story." One had so often known this product to struggle, in one's hands, under the rude prescription of brevity at any cost, with the opposition so offered to its really becoming a story, that my friend's emphasized indifference to the arbitrary limit of length struck me, I remember, as the fruit of the finest artistic intelligence.[13]

James makes it quite clear that by opening up "the millennium to the 'short story' " he does not simply mean enlarging the short story and giving it a chance to breathe but rather that a distinct other genre which he calls the "nouvelle" is being given a new chance at separate existence and formal identity. He goes on to say:

We had been at one—that we already knew—on the truth that the forms of wrought things, in this order, *were*, all exquisitely and effectively, the things; so that, for the delight of mankind, form might compete with form and might correspond to fitness; might, that is, in the given case, have an inevitability, a marked felicity. Among forms, moreover, we had had, on the dimensional ground—for length and breadth—our ideal, the beautiful and blest *nouvelle*; the generous, the enlightened hour for which appeared thus at last to shine. It was under the star of the *nouvelle* that, in other languages, a hundred interesting and charming results . . . had been, all economically, arrived at. . . . It had taken the blank misery of our Anglo-Saxon sense of such matters to organise, as might be said, the general indifference to this fine type of composition. In that dull view a "short story" was a "short story," and that was the end of it. Shades and differences, varieties and styles, the value above all of the idea happily *developed*, languished, to extinction, under the hard-and-fast rule of the "from six to eight thousand words"—when, for one's benefit, the rigour was a little relaxed. For myself, I delighted in the shapely *nouvelle*.

We have not yet really recovered from "the dull view that a 'short story' was a 'short story,' and that was the end of it." We seem to have missed a kind of turning point in genre. To escape our still blank Anglo-Saxon sensibility, it seems useful to re-read James employing such words for the novella as "blest and beautiful," and also "shapely"—as though, if we were only to look, we might see what shapes it had, and thus appreciate its blessedness and beauty.

In a *Paris Review* interview another master of the genre, Katherine Anne Porter, seems to intuit some comparative definition of the "short novel" when she says, "A novel is really like a symphony, you know, where instrument after instrument has to come in at its own time, and no other. I tried to write it [*Ship of Fools*] as a short novel . . . but it just wouldn't confine itself."[14] Thomas Mann, in the preface to his "short stories" describes the same kind of difficulty when he says, "*Death in Venice* proved persistent well beyond the terminus which I had fixed for it."

Length as Essence, and How Little that Helps

In the notebooks of Henry James it is suggested that he may have excluded a story from the collected edition of his works because it "did not justify its length of twenty-five thousand words."[15] Another time, what James called an "awfully good possibility" in a story idea grew to an "unwieldy thirty-six thousand word tale." The question is again very like the one of confinement or persistence raised by Porter and Mann. How do works go about justifying their length or, conversely, show themselves unwieldy? It is clear in all these cases that an author cannot safely choose length arbitrarily, since there are some things which a novella does better than a short story and better than a novel.

The length of the novella ought, in my view, simply to be accepted empirically: a count of any anthology of novellas (except, of course, anthologies that make no distinction that excludes short stories) will attest to a common length between 15,000 and 50,000 words. The kinds of works which are now recognized as novellas began to arise in the nineteenth century, with its publication habits as described in the quote from James above, and novella length has been as arbitrary as a magazine editor's rejection slip based on space: that is, authors have sometimes proceeded under the necessity of doing what *can* be done once length is enforced. Editors and publishers are probably as responsible as authors for the common count that causes E. M. Forster (in *Aspects of the Novel*) to say that literary works "when they contain 50,000 words or more, are called novels"—once again an empirical statement of fact which does not begin the discussion of novel forms but does carry some seeds of that discussion within it. A significant story is told of Howells (as editor) proposing a story idea to Henry James, which James refused because he "had quickly seen that he couldn't manage what he wanted within the limit of fifty thousand words."[16] Howell's limit is nothing but a fact of space—James's refusal, and its bases, are the subject of our real interest.

I would, if I could, avoid strict length limits, for they suggest something we are bound to feel is ridiculous, namely, that five hundred words over a certain length causes a short story to become a novella, and five hundred words less than a certain length causes a novel to become a novella—thus once more connecting all three as though they were merely extensions or reductions of each other.

My preference, in discussing word limits, would be to speak of "a fiction of a certain length" with no more, and no less, mystery than when one speaks of "a woman of a certain age"; one knows she must have certain qualities unavailable either to youth or to old age, and we do not have to specify the exact number of pages in her book of life in order to know that. What the defining *qualities* of such a woman are, becomes the matter of much greater interest if one wants truly to know and appreciate her. And I wish to call sharp attention to the plural, "qualities," for it suggests what I shall hold to be centrally true of the novella: that it is not itself a single form, in the sense of being capable of realizing only one kind of affective power. As Gerald Gillespie concludes from his historical study, "The theorist dealing with the *novella* should always remember that, ultimately, *novellas* exist in the plural. This caution prevents blind concentration of attention on some specific example, some 'model' *novella* in the singular."[17] Let us assume as demonstrable, then, that *the novella is a prose fiction of a certain length (usually 15,000 to 50,000 words), a length equipped to realize several distinct formal functions better than any other length.*

The achievement I hope for will be a definition of the novella less by what it is (I have just said that what it *is* is simply a length of prose fiction), than by describing what it does: a series of formal functions which can best be achieved at that length, functions which cause authors intuitively or consciously to choose that length.

Stated another way, my central problem has by now defined itself rather clearly as a question of what Aristotle called "magnitude," and it is a problem susceptible of solution by formal theoretical modes that derive from Aristotle's thought on poetry. In the *Poetics* he calls that work beautiful which has "as much magnitude as is in accordance with what is likely or necessary."[18] Though his discussion is limited to the length of tragic plots, we can take for granted that "likely or necessary" can be extended to a discussion of that length which would be suitable, or "necessary," to the realization of *any* affective power, be that power tragic, comic, serious, didactic, satiric, or some subclass of these.

Authors must, then, discover the length appropriate to their formal purpose; if not, they risk failure of that purpose. In the aesthetics of short fiction, as in that of all the other arts, the right size for a work is not necessarily its actual size—it is possible to say that a statue is too tall, or a story too short. This is, of course, what James meant when he spoke, in the preface cited above, of stories having "languished, to extinction, under the hard-and-fast rule of the 'from six to eight thousand words.'" To say that editors, for their own publication needs, have forced modern authors to operate at certain lengths, often arbitrary and precise, is not to credit editors with defining the genres of prose fiction. It says, rather, that editors have either caused authors' formal purposes to languish fatally, or forced them into formal purposes particular to a certain length. It points to the converse of the argument I have been making: an author restrained by a short-story length will tend to restrict himself to certain kinds of formal purposes which can be most effectively realized at that length. Because James's formal purposes were very often understood by him to be appropriate to the novella length, he felt squeezed.

When I turn to the discussion of formal purposes, I enter an area of indebtedness too great to be covered in a footnote, to theorists of prose fiction whose concepts and method also derive from, and are logical extensions of, Aristotle's *Poetics*, chief among them Sheldon Sacks, R. S. Crane, Wayne Booth, and Elder Olson. All careful readers intuitively perceive that fictional works depend for their coherence on certain general, as well as particular, formal principles (it is a remarkable experience to watch students apprehend this unaided), but Sheldon Sacks has brought this intuition into conscious theory and method in the seminal first chapter of his book *Fiction and the Shape of Belief*. There Sacks delineates three major informing principles discoverable in prose fictions: *actions, apologues,* and *satires*. Since I expect to show that subforms of these are some of the forms which define the novella, it seems important to describe them.

All fiction consists in setting characters into some kind of motion, conflict, or action, but Sacks reserves the term *"Action"* for the kind of "unstable relations" between characters that are tightly plotted in order to be resolved into either a tragic, comic, or serious effect. *"Apologue"* makes use of the characters and what happens to them to maximize "the truth of a statement or statements," a principle which other critics variously call "allegory," "parable," or sometimes "fable." *"Satire"* takes its usual meaning: that informing principle whereby all parts of the fiction cohere in the purpose of ridiculing objects in the world outside the story.

As principles of wholeness, Sacks insists, these forms are "mutually exclusive," so that if we wish to understand, for example, a story which is formally an apologue, we must not confuse it with the kind of stories which formally are actions—thus whose ends are not primarily didactic—or the appreciation of the whole may be lost.

Everywhere that I employ the word "form" in my discussion I shall understand the term as Kenneth Burke, in *The Philosophy of Literary Form*, minimally defines it: "The functioning of a structure to achieve a certain purpose," be that purpose ridicule, the centering on the truth of a statement, or the realization of a tragic, comic, or serious resolution of an action where the characters themselves are our chief concern. And I would enlarge upon Burke's definition by adding the stress that R. S. Crane lays on form as tightly connected in every case to potential feeling (*dynamis*), whether a feeling of ridiculousness (satire), a feeling that a statement is true (apologue), or a feeling for the fate of characters (action): "Form as we conceive it is simply that which gives definite shape, emotional power, and beauty to the materials of man's experience out of which the writer has composed his work."[19]

In no case will I employ the word "form" to mean merely structure without that final "emotional power" of which the structure is only one cause: the power of a story being comparable to the "capacity to cut" in W. K. Wimsatt's metaphor of the poem as a carpenter's saw: "The goodness of a saw, its capacity to cut, is determined by the steel fashioned in a certain shape."[20]

And, just as form does not mean structure alone, neither will I employ it to mean weights and measures of parts separate from their formal power. In a discussion of Katherine Anne Porter's *Noon Wine* as it relates to genre, one critic describes the novella as "more ambitious than the short story. It introduces more characters, more fictional time, more motifs, more settings, and more revelatory moments."[21] What distinguishes it from the long novel, in this view, is simply compression of novelistic elements—a court trial is "recollected, not dramatized," and one gets "a sense of the passage of time without the drama of an extended action" that would be offered in a novel. Once more, the novella is reduced to definition that is too single (general) and relative: "more" items than a short story, less drama than a novel.

A Beginning Tour of Novella Forms, and How Much They Might Help

The novella is its own genre by means of taking its own forms. Chapter by chapter, I plan to discuss each of several formal functions for which that "certain" novella word-limit seems necessary, together with a discussion of the devices that fulfill these functions, so that we may recognize and enjoy them appropriately when we come upon them again in other novellas than the ones I shall choose to analyze. Lest my reader feel he is constantly waiting for late guests to arrive at the party so that he can see what the whole congregation looks like, it seems proper to begin by briefly listing some of those functions which the novella seems definitely to achieve.

1. *The serious "plot of character,"*[22] wherein the action is resolved to serious effect in three variations of this plot: (a) simply revealing the character (Colette's *Julie de Carneilhan*); (b) showing the character in the process of learning (Porter's *Old Mortality*); and (c) the character not only learning but beginning to profit from what he learns (Mann's *Tonio Kröger*). In long novels, characters not only learn but complete their process of change in a complexity of inter-

action with other characters (James's *Portrait of a Lady*). When the focus is on a single character revelation, or on a single isolated learner, the novella is an appropriate length for that function.

2. *The degenerative or pathetic tragedy*, of which Mann's *Death in Venice* is a prime example. It consists in the relentless, relatively simple (in plot), and swift degeneration of a central character into unrelieved misery or death. Its relentlessness and the depth of the misery expand it beyond the single episode which often characterizes the short story.

3. *Satire* which, whether loosely plotted (James's *The Death of the Lion*) or an episodic structure of the Gulliver kind (Vonnegut's *Cat's Cradle*), chooses the novella length because the object of ridicule is a single one rather than a compendium of the follies of mankind.

4. *Apologue.* In order to demonstrate that apologues are a prominent form in novellas (authors seem to undertake very long prose apologues only at the risk of failure, for reasons I shall try to suggest), I plan to undertake a description of the literary signals that help distinguish modern prose fiction apologues from actions. Here the ordinary reader's intuition can often be trusted better than the judgment of the practical critic who has trained himself to find a "theme" in every action, thus tending to turn his discussion away from centrally absorbing characters, and by this ignoring the form he is really dealing with. What a pity if such initial preconceptions should cause us to talk about *Death in Venice* as an example of civic corruption rather than attend to the unhappy fate of Aschenbach. In order to maintain the examination of theme where it is truly useful, namely, in those works whose organic unity depends on a theme or statement, we need to know how to recognize such works. The problem is a real one for modern literature; Aesop's fables presented themselves with their moral statements tacked on clearly at the end, and old allegories revealed themselves with characters who were personified abstractions (when Christian ploughs through the Slough of Despond, we know what he is formally about, as distinct from Aschenbach), but modern apologues "look like" other stories at first glance.

5. *The Example*, a subclass of apologue often dealing with a single character in incidents which are not plotted to aim at our feelings for the particular character but instead to make use of our feelings

for didactic ends, for exposing this character through his actions, as one example of a large human type. Thus, the implicit statement of this type of apologue always begins in the same way: "It is like this to be . . ." (Crane's *Maggie: A Girl of the Streets*). As in the action plot of character, the concentration on a single character accounts in part for the novella length.

Once I have suggested, in the examination of a number of novellas, that the novella functions most often to achieve these several particular kinds of forms, perhaps I shall automatically have answered the question of what makes a novella short-but-not-so-short-as-a-short-story yet much less lengthy than a novel, and a genre independent of those other two. And, if the generalizations of this chapter should prove valid in the actual examination of the multitudes of novellas, they may lead to still another generalization. Apologues and plots of character are thought-provoking, serious forms; and novellas exist also in the realm of limited tragedy. If these predominate as the major types of the novella, they may be asking us to pay attention to the possibility that the novella lends itself especially to the serious or restrainedly tragic, seldom or never to the comic, though parts are often comic*al* in the service of satire and other forms. A remark by one anthology editor, that the novella is a "literary genre which specializes in themes that remind men of their own frailty,"[23] led me to take a count of several other collections. None contained a novella whose principle of coherence could be called comedy.

Comedy is, of course, slippery of definition in modern criticism. Ten years after *Wise Blood* first appeared, Flannery O'Connor prefaced it with an introduction calling it a "comic novel about a Christian *malgré lui,* and as such, very serious." Indeed, once one accepts the Christian assumptions of this novella, even Hazel Motes's death is a "happy" ending. So also *The Violent Bear It Away* is comedy, its comic expectations built "with a certainty sunk in despair" around a boy protagonist who is "trudging into the distance in the bleeding stinking mad shadow of Jesus." If this is comedy in some intellectual formal sense, it feels like something much harsher. The expense (given our dour expectations in real life) of making plausible a truly joyful ending is probably reserved by its necessities to the long novel—and perhaps to novels of an earlier era which was still hopeful enough to represent life not as it is but more as it might be.

Notes

1   A list of works on the novel that I have found most helpful appears in my selected bibliography. In the area of formal relations in the novel I find particularly useful the work of Sheldon Sacks on the general types of prose fictions: *Fiction and the Shape of Belief* (Berkeley: University of California Press, 1964); Wayne Booth on the rhetoric of narrative modes: *The Rhetoric of Fiction* (Chicago: University of Chicago Press, 1961); the articles on various novel elements collected by Philip Stevick, ed., in *The Theory of the Novel* (New York: Free Press, 1967).

2   Austin McGiffert Wright, *The American Short Story in the Twenties* (Chicago: University of Chicago Press, 1961), and Eugene Current-Garcia and Walton R. Patrick, eds., *What Is the Short Story?* (Chicago: Scott, Foresman, 1961).

3   Howard Nemerov, "Composition and Fate in the Short Novel," *Graduate Journal* 5, no. 2 (Winter 1963): 375–91. This article contains insights into a number of individual novellas but treats the genre primarily as a "middle term," dependent for its visibility on "slighting" qualities of the other terms, short story and novel. Further, by treating novellas thematically ("appearance and reality," "freedom and necessity," "madness and sanity," all bound up in a main theme of "identity") Nemerov fails of his purpose to define the novella as "something in itself," especially something distinct from the long novel and its "problems of philosophy."

4   Edwin K. Bennett and H. M. Waidson, *A History of the German Novelle* (Cambridge: Cambridge University Press, 1965); John M. Ellis, *Narration in the German Novelle* (Cambridge: Cambridge University Press, 1974). These works attempt novella theory but are basically skeptical of achieving it: "One must be content with approximations; difficulties only arise if one seeks the abstract 'die Novelle'" (Ellis, p. 10). Their skepticism (conscious or unconscious) derives from their methods, in that these critics ignore the possibility of holistic forms governed by the length of the stories and turn instead to consideration of narrative techniques, "thematic complexity," and historical influences on the writer—all interesting considerations which cannot, however, advance the distinction between the novella and the novel because they manifest themselves in both.

Despite my examination of works by Mann and Kafka, I am moved to think my study has little to do with the German *novelle*, of which it is affirmed that its length may vary between "a few pages" and "over four hundred pages" (Bennett and Waidson, p. 1). At this latitude, Waidson is certainly right to say that "short story may merge into Novelle, Novelle

into novel" (p. 245), and any attempt at generic definition is automatically
blocked. Neither skepticism nor latitude, however, seems to kill the intuition
of these critics that the "middle length" *is* something that could be defined
if one could only find the most fruitful theoretical framework for the discussion. My book came into being because I believe formalism is that
framework.

5 Gerald Gillespie, "Novella, Nouvelle, Novelle, Short Novel?—A Review of
   Terms," a two-part article in *Neophilologus* 51, no. 2 (April 1967): 119–27,
   and no. 3 (July 1967): 225–29. Gillespie properly sees this detailed historical
   study of terms as a "first step toward any discussion of form." I am indebted
   to him for saving me that step, and for concluding with an encouraging
   invitation: "The establishment of a qualitative definition [of the novella] is
   a worthwhile task for English criticism."

6 Norman Friedman, "What Makes A Short Story Short?" *Modern Fiction
   Studies* 4 (1958): 103–17.

7 Wright, *The American Short Story*, chapter on "Pathos."

8 Elizabeth Bowen, "The Short Story," in *The Faber Book of Modern Stories*
   (London: Faber and Faber, 1937), p. 15.

9 Martha Foley, ed., *The Best American Short Stories 1968* (Boston: Houghton
   Mifflin, 1968), pp. xi–xii.

10 The best of such anthology introductions are those by Ronald Paulson, ed.,
   for *The Novelette Before 1900* and for *The Modern Novelette* (both from
   Englewood Cliffs, N.J.: Prentice-Hall, 1965).

11 Mark Schorer, ed., *The Story* (New York: Prentice-Hall, 1950), p. 432.

12 Quoted by Edward Weeks, ed., in *Great Short Novels* (Garden City, N.Y.:
   Doubleday Doran, 1941), Foreword, p. viii.

13 Henry James, *The Art of the Novel* (New York: Charles Scribner's Sons,
   1948), p. 219.

14 "Katherine Anne Porter," *Writers at Work*, The Paris Review Interviews,
   2d ser. (New York: Viking Press, 1963), p. 162.

15 F. O. Matthiessen and Kenneth Murdock, eds., *The Notebooks of Henry
   James* (New York: Oxford University Press, 1947), p. 66.

16 F. O. Matthiessen, *Henry James, The Major Phase* (New York: Oxford University Press, 1963), p. 133.

17 Gillespie, "Novella," p. 225.

18 *Poetics*, trans. and ed. Kenneth A. Telford (Chicago: Henry Regnery, 1961),
   p. 16.

19 R. S. Crane, *The Languages of Criticism and the Structure of Poetry* (Toronto: University of Toronto Press, 1953), p. 189.

20 Quoted by David Lodge, *Language of Fiction* (New York: Columbia University Press, 1966), p. 34 n.

21 M. M. Liberman, " 'Noon Wine,' Henry James, and the Novella," in *Katherine Anne Porter's Fiction* (Detroit: Wayne State University Press, 1971),
   p. 56.

22 The term is R. S. Crane's ("The Concept of Plot and the Plot of *Tom Jones*,"

in Crane, ed., *Critics and Criticism* [Chicago: University of Chicago Press, 1952], p. 620). Crane usefully points out that the traditional view of plot as a change in action is too limited to cover what plot often does in modern fiction, namely, produce change not only in "action" but in "thought," or "character," as well—and that these can be distinct types of plot unity.

23 William Wasserstrom, ed., *The Modern Short Novel* (New York: Holt, Rinehart and Winston, 1965), pp. x–xi.

24

Discourse: Nonnarrated Stories

SEYMOUR CHATMAN

In his structuralist work *Story and Discourse: Narrative Structure in Fiction and Film* (1978), Seymour Chatman poses a crucial distinction between types of narrative statements: "Is the statement directly presented to the audience or is it mediated by someone—the someone we call the narrator?" Direct presentation assumes that the audience overhears the statement. Mediated narration, on the other hand, assumes a more or less express communication from narrator to audience. Because the latter kind of narrative statement predominates in works of fiction it has received a great deal of study, as some of the previous essays attest, but the nonnarrated story has received far less attention. Chatman's purpose is not to focus on what he calls "nonnarrated stories," but to introduce their existence as a possible means by which an author may present a story. In the course of a brief overview of the differences among "Real Author, Implied Author, Narrator, Real Reader, Implied Reader, and Narratee," Chatman concludes that "only the implied author and implied reader are immanent to a narrative, the narrator and narratee are optional."

Unlike Wayne Booth in his discussion of point of view, Chatman distinguishes between point of view and narrative voice: "Point of view is the physical place or ideological situation or practical life-orientation to which narrative events stand in relation. Voice, on the contrary, refers to the speech or other overt means through which events and existents are communicated to the audience." Thus, "the perspective and the expression need not be lodged in the same person." As a result of this distinction, we can understand the possibility of a nonnarrated story having a particular point of view, such as that of a single character, without having an identifiable narrative voice, since the story is directly presented to the audience. Chatman's distinction enables us to make sharper critical differentiations among the components comprising the expression, or "discourse," of the fiction's content, or "story."

Seymour Chatman (b. 1928) is professor of rhetoric at the University of California, Berkeley. He has also published *A Theory of English Meter* (1965) and *The Later Style of Henry James* (1972), as well as editing books on linguistics and literature.

Silence is become his mother tongue.—Oliver Goldsmith, *The Good-Natured Man*

Every narrative—so this theory goes—is a structure with a content plane (called "story") and an expression plane (called "discourse"). . . . The expression plane is the set of narrative statements, where "statement" is the basic component of the form of the expression, independent of and more abstract than any particular manifestation—that is, the expression's substance, which varies from art to art. A certain posture in the ballet, a series of film shots, a whole paragraph in a novel, or only a single word—any of these might manifest a single narrative statement. I have proposed that narrative statements are of two kinds—process and stasis—corresponding to whether the deep narrative (not the surface linguistic) predicate is in the mode of existence (IS) or action (DOES).

Crosscutting this dichotomy is another: Is the statement directly presented to the audience or is it mediated by someone—the someone we call the narrator? Direct presentation presumes a kind of overhearing by the audience. Mediated narration, on the other hand, presumes a more or less express communication from narrator to audience. This is essentially Plato's distinction between *mimesis* and *diegesis*,[1] in modern terms between showing and telling. Insofar as there is telling, there must be a teller, a narrating voice.

"Discourse: Nonnarrated Stories" is reprinted from Seymour Chatman, *Story and Discourse: Narrative Structure in Fiction and Film*. Copyright 1978 Cornell University. Reprinted with permission of Cornell University Press.

The teller, the transmitting source, is best accounted for, I think, as a spectrum of possibilities, going from narrators who are least audible to those who are most so. The label affixed to the negative pole of narratorhood is less important than its reality in the spectrum. I say "nonnarrated"; the reader may prefer "minimally narrated," but the existence of this kind of transmission is well attested.

The narrator's presence derives from the audience's sense of some demonstrable communication. If it feels it is being told something, it presumes a teller. The alternative is a "direct witnessing" of the action. Of course, even in the scenic arts like drama and the ballet, pure mimesis is an illusion. But the degree of possible analogy varies. The main question is how the illusion is achieved. By what convention does a spectator or reader accept the idea that it is "as if" he were personally on the scene, though he comes to it by sitting in a chair in a theater or by turning pages and reading words. Authors may make special efforts to preserve the illusion that events "literally unfold before the reader's eyes," mostly by restricting the kinds of statements that can occur.

To understand the concept of narrator's voice (including its "absence") we need to consider three preliminary issues: the interrelation of the several parties to the narrative transaction, the meaning of "point of view" and its relation to voice, and the nature of acts of speech and thought as a subclass of the class of acts in general. These topics form a necessary prolegomena to the analysis of narrator's voice, upon which any discussion of narrative discourse rests.

Real Author, Implied Author, Narrator, Real Reader, Implied Reader, Narratee

That it is essential not to confuse author and narrator has become a commonplace of literary theory. As Monroe Beardsley argues, "the speaker of a literary work cannot be identified with the author—and therefore the character and condition of the speaker can be known by internal evidence alone—unless the author has provided a pragmatic context, or a claim of one, that connects the speaker with himself."[2] But even in such a context, the speaker is not the author, but the "author" (quotation marks of "as if"), or better the "author"-narrator, one of several possible kinds.

In addition, there is a demonstrable third party, conveniently dubbed, by Wayne Booth, the "implied author":

> As he writes, [the real author] creates not simply an ideal, impersonal "man in general" but an implied version of "himself" that is different from the implied authors we meet in other men's works. . . . Whether we call this implied author an "official scribe," or adopt the term recently revived by Kathleen Tillotson—the author's "second self"—it is clear that the picture the reader gets of this presence is one of the author's most important effects. However impersonal he may try to be, his reader will inevitably construct a picture of the official scribe.[3]

He is "implied," that is, reconstructed by the reader from the narrative. He is not the narrator, but rather the principle that invented the narrator, along with everything else in the narrative, that stacked the cards in this particular way, had these things happen to these characters, in these words or images. Unlike the narrator, the implied author can *tell* us nothing. He, or better, *it* has no voice, no direct means of communicating. It instructs us silently, through the design of the whole, with all the voices, by all the means it has chosen to let us learn. We can grasp the notion of implied author most clearly by comparing different narratives written by the same real author but presupposing different implied authors. Booth's example: the implied author of *Jonathan Wild* "is by implication very much concerned with public affairs and with the effects of unchecked ambition on the 'great men' who attain to power in the world," whereas the implied author "who greets us on page one of *Amelia*" conveys rather an "air of sententious solemnity."[4] The implied author of *Joseph Andrews,* on the contrary, sounds "facetious" and "generally insouciant." Not merely the narrator but the whole design of *Joseph Andrews* functions in a tone quite different from that of *Jonathan Wild* or *Amelia.* Henry Fielding created three clearly different implied authors.

The distinction is particularly evident in the case of the "unreliable narrator" (another of Booth's happy coinages). What makes a narrator unreliable is that his values diverge strikingly from that of the implied author's; that is, the rest of the narrative—"the norm of the work"—conflicts with the narrator's presentation, and we become suspicious of his sincerity or competence to tell the "true version." The unreliable narrator is at virtual odds with the implied author; otherwise his unreliability could not emerge.

The implied author establishes the norms of the narrative, but Booth's insistence that these are moral seems unnecessary. The norms are general cultural codes, whose relevance to story we have already considered. The real author can postulate whatever norms he likes through his implied author. It makes no more sense to accuse the real Céline or Montherlant of what the implied author causes to happen in *Journey to the End of the Night* or *Les Jeunes Filles* than to hold the real Conrad responsible for the reactionary attitudes of the implied author of *The Secret Agent* or *Under Western Eyes* (or, for that matter, Dante for the Catholic ideas of the implied author of the *Divine Comedy*). One's moral fibre cannot really be "seduced" by wily implied authors. Our acceptance of their universe is aesthetic, not ethical. To confound the "implied author," a structural principle, with a certain historical figure whom we may or may not admire morally, politically, or personally would seriously undermine our theoretical enterprise.[5]

There is always an implied author, though there might not be a single real author in the ordinary sense: the narrative may have been composed by committee (Hollywood films), by a disparate group of people over a long period of time (many folk ballads), by random-number generation by a computer, or whatever.[6]

The counterpart of the implied author is the *implied reader*—not the flesh-and-bones you or I sitting in our living rooms reading the book, but the audience presupposed by the narrative itself. Like the implied author, the implied reader is always present. And just as there may or may not be a narrator, there may or may not be a *narratee*.[7] He may materialize as a character in the world of the work: for example, the someone listening to Marlow as he unfolds the story of Jim or Kurtz. Or there may be no overt reference to him at all, though his presence is felt. In such cases the author makes explicit the desired audience stance, and we must give him the benefit of the doubt if we are to proceed at all. The narratee-character is only one device by which implied author informs the real reader how to perform as implied reader, which *Weltanschauung* to adopt. The narratee-character tends to appear in narratives like Conrad's whose moral texture is particularly complex, where good is not easily distinguished from evil. In narratives without explicit narratees, the stance of the implied reader can only be inferred, on ordinary cultural and moral terms. Thus, Hemingway's "The Killers" does not permit us to assume that we too are members of the Mob; the story just will not work if we do. Of course, the real reader may refuse his projected role at some ultimate level—nonbelievers do not become Christians just to read *The Inferno* or *Paradise Lost*. But such refusal does not contradict the imaginative or "as if" acceptance of implied readership necessary to the elementary comprehension of the narrative.

It is as necessary to distinguish among narratees, implied readers (parties immanent to the narrative), and real readers (parties extrinsic and accidental to the narrative) as it is among narrator, implied author, and real author. The "you" or "dear reader" who is addressed by the narrator of *Tom Jones* is no more Seymour Chatman than is the narrator Henry Fielding. When I enter the fictional contract I add another self: I become an implied reader. And just as the narrator may or may not ally himself with the implied author, the implied reader furnished by the real reader may or may not ally himself with a narratee. In *Tom Jones* or *Tristram Shandy* the alliance is reasonably close; in *Les Liaisons dangereuses* or *Heart of Darkness* the distance is great.

The situation of the narratee is parallel to that of the narrator: he ranges from a fully characterized individual to "no one." Again, "absence" or "unmarkedness" is put in quotation marks: in some sense every tale implies a listener or reader, just as it implies a teller. But the author may, for a variety of reasons, leave these components unmentioned, indeed, go out of his way to suggest that they do not exist.

We can now diagram the whole narrative-communication situation as follows:

Narrative text

| Real author | - - → | Implied author | →(Narrator)→(Narratee)→ | Implied reader | - - → | Real reader |

The box indicates that only the implied author and implied reader are immanent to a narrative, the narrator and narratee are optional (parentheses). The real author and real reader are outside the narrative transaction as such, though, of course, indispensable to it in an ultimate practical sense. . . .

Point of View and Its Relation to Narrative Voice

It is the task of narrative theory, like any theory, to deal with the ambiguities and unclarities of terms passed down to it. To understand the concept of narrator's voice—including the case where one is "not" (or minimally) present—we must first distinguish it from "point of view," one of the most troublesome of critical terms. Its plurisignification must give pause to anyone who wishes to use it in precise discussion. At least three senses can be distinguished in ordinary use: (a) literal: through someone's eyes (perception); (b) figurative: through someone's world view (ideology), conceptual system, *Weltanschauung*, etc.); (c) transferred: from someone's interest-vantage (characterizing his general interest, profit, welfare, well-being, etc.). The following sentences will illustrate these distinctions: (a) From John's point of view, at the top of Coit Tower, the panorama of the San Francisco Bay was breath-taking. (b) John said that from his point of view, Nixon's position, though praised by his supporters, was somewhat less than noble. (c) Though he didn't realize it at the time, the divorce was a disaster from John's point of view. In the first sentence, "The panorama of the Bay" is reported as actually seen by John; he stands at the center of a half-circle of vision. Let us call that his *perceptual* point of view. In the second, there is no reference to his actual physical situation in the real world but to his attitudes or conceptual apparatus, his way of thinking, and how facts and impressions are strained through it. We can call that his *conceptual* point of view. In the third, there is no reference to John's mind at all, either to perceptual or conceptual powers. Since John is unaware of the mentioned consequences, he is not "seeing," in either the actual or the figurative sense; the term then is a simple synonym for "as far as John is concerned." Let us call this his *interest* point of view. What is confusing is that "point of view" may thus refer to an *action* of some kind—perceiving or conceiving—or to a *passive state*—as in the third sense.

Now texts, any kind of text, even ordinary conversation, may entail one or any combination of these senses. A simple description of an experiment or an explorer's account of a new island may convey only the literal perceptions of the author, but it may also entail his *Weltanschauung*, or his practical interests. A philosophical treatise on abstract issues does not usually entail perceptual point of view, but may express quite eloquently the author's personal interests in the matter, along with his ideology.

When we turn to narrative texts, we find an even more complicated situation, since as we have seen there is no longer a single presence, as in expository essays, sermons, political speeches, and so on, but two—character and narrator—not to speak of the implied author. Each of these may manifest one or more kinds of point of view. A character may literally perceive a certain object or event; and/or it may be presented in terms of his conceptualization; and/or his interest in it may be invoked (even if he is unconscious of that interest).[8]

Thus the crucial difference between "point of view" and narrative voice: point of view is the physical place or ideological situation or practical life-orientation to which narrative events stand in relation. Voice, on the contrary, refers to the speech or other overt means through which events and existents are communicated to the audience. Point of view does *not* mean expression; it only means the perspective in terms of which the expression is made. *The perspective and the expression need not be lodged in the same person.*[9] Many combinations are possible. Consider just literal, that is perceptual, point of view. Events and existents may be perceived by the narrator and recounted by him in his own first person: "I felt myself fall down the hill" or "I saw Jack fall down the hill" (in the first case, the narrator is protagonist, in the second, witness). Or the point of view may be assigned to a character who is not the narrator: then the separate narrating voice may or may not make itself heard—"Mary, *poor dear*, saw Jack fall down the hill" versus "Mary saw Jack fall down the hill." Or the event may be presented so that it is not clear who, if anyone, perceived it (or perception is not an issue): "Jack fell down the hill."

The "camera eye" names a convention (an "illusion of mimesis") which pretends that the events just "happened" in the presence of a neutral recorder. To call such narrative transmission "limited third person" is wrong because it specifies only the point of view, not the narrative voice. It is necessary to distinguish between "limited third person point of view voiced by a covert narrator," "limited third person point of view voiced by an overt narrator," and so on.

Perception, conception, and interest points of view are quite independent of the manner in which they are expressed. When we speak of "expression," we pass from point of view, which is only a perspective or stance, to the province of narrative voice, the medium through which perception, conception, and everything else are communicated. Thus point of view is *in* the story (when it is the character's), but voice is always outside, in the discourse. From *A Portrait of the Artist as a Young Man*: "A few moments [later] he found himself on the stage amid the garish gas and the dim scenery." The perceptual point of view is Stephen's, but the voice is the narrator's. Characters' perceptions need not be articulated—Stephen is not saying to himself the *words* "garish gas and dim scenery"; the words are the narrator's. This is a narrator's report. But in " 'He shivered a little, and I beheld him rise slowly as if a steady hand from above had been pulling him out of the chair by the hair' " (*Lord Jim*), not only the voice, but the perceptual point of view is the narrator's, Marlow's, not Jim's. And in "Coffin now. Got here before us, dead as he is. Horse looking round at it with his plume skewways. Dull eye: collar tight on his neck, pressing on a bloodvessel or something. Do they know what they cart out here every day?" ("Hades," *Ulysses*), the perceptual point of view is Leopold Bloom's, and so are the words, but he is no narrator. He is not telling a narratee anything. Indeed, he is not speaking even to himself: the convention argues that he is directly perceiving the coffin and the nag's dull eye, and nothing more. There *is* no narrator.

In all these cases the character perceives: his senses are directed outward upon the story-world. But when that perception is reported, as in the first two examples, there is necessarily presupposed another act of "seeing" with an independent point of view, namely that of the narrator, who has "peered into" the character's mind (metaphors are inevitable) and reports its contents from his *own* point of view. Can this kind of point of view be called "perceptual"? The word sounds strange, and for good reason. It makes sense to say that the character is literally perceiving something within the world of the work ("homodiegetically," as Genette would say). But what the narrator reports from his perspective is almost always outside the story (heterodiegetic), even if only retrospective, that is, temporally distant. Typically, he is looking back at his own earlier perception-as-a-character. But that looking-back is a conception, no longer a perception. The completely external narrator presents an even more purely conceptual view. He never *was* in the world of the work: discourse-time is not a later extension of story-time. He did not "perceive" in the same direct or diegetic sense that any character did. Literally speaking, he cannot have "seen" anything in that other world.

Thus the use of terms like "view" and "see" may be dangerously metaphorical. We "see" issues in terms of some cultural or psychological predisposition; the mechanism is entirely different from that which enables us to see cats or automobiles. Though it is true that preconceptions of various sorts affect our strictly physiological vision too (people may not see what is literally before their noses because they have compelling personal reasons not to), there remains an essential difference between perceptions and conceptions. Further, the narrator's is second-order or heterodiegetic conceptualizing *about* the story—as opposed to the first-order conceptualizing of a character within the story. These distinctions most clearly emerge where the two conflict, where the narrator is operating under a clearly different set of attitudes than those of the character. Then the narrator's conceptual point of view (except when he is unreliable) tends to override the character's, despite the fact that the latter maintains the center of interest and consciousness. An example is Conrad's *The Secret Agent:* the narrator is clearly unsympathetic to Verloc. Or, more precisely, the character has a conceptual point of view undermined by the narrator's manner of depicting it. Verloc's ideology (such as it is) reeks of indolence; the narrator carefully picks words to so characterize it. For example, Verloc does not simply stay in bed, he "wallows" in it. But the narrator (like all Conrad's narrators) is on the side of vigorous achievement. Similarly, he tells us that Verloc "remained undisturbed by any sort of aesthetic doubt about his appearance." From the narrator's conceptual point of view, implicitly communicated, Verloc's physical messiness is reprehensible and a clear analogue to moral sloth and political dishonesty. Or consider the difference between Verloc's and the narrator's attitudes toward female psychology. Verloc's unpleasant encounter with Mr. Vladimir brings him home in a towering rage. Forgetting that his wife is mourning the death of her brother, for which he is responsible, he is disappointed that she does not soothe him. Yet, immediately, he realizes that she is "a woman of few words." But his notion of his relationship with her, his conceptual point of view, is paraphrased in the narrator's superior diction: "[Winnie's] reserve, expressing in a way their profound confidence in each other, introduced at the same time a certain element of vagueness into their intimacy." Though the "profound confidence in each other" is the narrator's expression, not Verloc's, whose verbal style we know to be less elegant, it can only be Verloc's sentiment. His complacency, of course, turns out suicidal.

Disparity between the character's point of view and the narrator's expression of it need not entail ironic opposition. The narrator may verbalize neutrally or even sympathetically what (for reasons of youth, lack of education and intelligence, and so on) the character cannot articulate. This is the whole structural principle of James's *What Maisie Knew*. Maisie's uncertainly about when next she will visit her mother is expressed thusly: "Mama's roof, however, had its turn, this time, for the child, of appearing but remotely contingent. . . ." Clearly these are not phrases in Maisie's vocabulary. We accept them only because a sensitive little girl might have feelings that somehow matched the narrator's elegant terms. That is, we can "translate" into more childlike verbiage—for instance, "I don't expect to be at Mama's again very soon." The diction is sanctioned only by the convention of the "well-spoken narrator."

"Point of view" expressing someone's interests is even more radically distanced, since there is not even a figurative "seeing." The subject may be completely unconscious that events work for or against his interests (welfare, success, happiness). The identification of interest point of view may follow the clear specification of the character's perceptual and conceptual points of view. Once they are established, we continue identifying with his interests, by a process of inertia, even if he is unaware of something. In *The Ambassadors*, the narrator speaks of Maria Gostrey's powers of "pigeon-holing her fellow mortals": "She was as equipped in this particular as Strether was the reverse, and it made an opposition between them which he might well have shrunk from submitting to if he had fully suspected it." The narrator informs us of aspects of Maria's character that Strether does not know, yet it makes perfect sense to say that the sentence is "from his point of view." The focus of attention remains on him. Maria's traits are significant only in their implications for him—even though he is not aware of them.

Access to a character's consciousness is the standard entree to his point of view, the usual and quickest means by which we come to identify with him. Learning his thoughts insures an intimate connection. The thoughts are truthful, except in cases of willful self-deception. Unlike the narrator, the character can only be "unreliable" to himself.

At the same time, interest point of view can be established quite independently. The point of view may reside in a character who is "followed" in some sense, even if there is no reference at all to his thinking. If Jack and Peter are in the first scene, and Jack and Mary in the second, and Jack and Joseph in the third, we identify with Jack simply because he is the one continually on the scene. This has nothing to do with whether or not we care for him on human or other grounds.

The notion of interest point of view is not very meaningfully applied to an external narrator. His only interest is to get the narrative told. Other sorts of interest arise only if he is or was also a character. Then he may use the narrative itself as vindication, expiation, explanation, rationalization, condemnation, or whatever. There are hundreds of reasons for telling a story, but those reasons are the narrator's, not the implied author's, who is without personality or even presence, hence without motivation other than the purely theoretical one of constructing the narrative itself. The narrator's vested interests may be so marked that we come to think of him as unreliable.

The different points of view usually combine, but in important and interesting cases, they do not. Consider "autobiographical" or first-person narration, as in *Great Expectations*. The protagonist-as-narrator reports things from the perceptual point of view of his younger self. His ideology on the other hand tends to be that of his older self. The narrator is older and wiser for his experiences. In other narratives the ideology may not change; the narrator may exhibit substantially the same traits as characterized his earlier self. Where the narrator is a different person than the hero, he may present his own ideology, against which he judges his hero's actions, either overtly, as in *Tom Jones,* or covertly and inferentially, as in *The Ambassadors.* The narrator may utilize a perceptual point of view possible to no character, for example when he describes a bird's-eye view, or a scene with no one present, or what the character did *not* notice.

Notes

1 These terms are revived by Gérard Genette in "Frontieres du recit," *Communications* 8 (1966).

2 In *Aesthetics* (New York, 1958), p. 240. Cf. Walker Gibson, "Authors, Speakers, Readers, Mock Readers," *College English* 11 (1950): 265–69; and Kathleen Tillotson, *The Tale and the Teller* (London, 1959).

3 *Rhetoric of Fiction,* pp. 70–71.

4 Ibid., p. 72.

5 There is an interesting discussion of the question in Susan Suleiman, "Ideological Dissent from Works of Fiction: Toward a Rhetoric of the *Roman a these,*" *Neophilologus* (April 1976): 162–77. Suleiman thinks that the implied author, as well as the narrator, can be unreliable, and thus we can accept imaginatively a narrative that we reject ideologically.

6 Christian Metz, *Film Language: A Semiotics of the Cinema.* Trans. Michael Taylor (Oxford University Press, 1974), p. 20.

7 The term was first coined, so far as I know, by Gerald Prince, "Notes Toward a Categorization of Fictional 'Narratees,'" *Genre* 4 (1971): 100–105. Booth's "postulated reader" is what I call the implied reader.

8 Another ambiguity of "point of view" was recognized by Sister Kristin Morrison in "James's and Lubbock's Differing Points of View," *Nineteenth-Century Fiction* 16 (1961): 245–56. Lubbock and his followers used the term in the sense of the narrative perspective of the speaker (the narrator), while James usually used it in the sense of the perspective of the knower or reader. Boris Uspensky in *Poetics of Composition,* trans. Valentina Zavarin and Susan Wittig (Berkeley, 1974), ch. 1, distinguishes various kinds of point of view along lines similar to mine. Some alternatives to "point of view" have been proposed: for instance, James's "central consciousness," Allen Tate's "post of observation," and Todorov's "*vision*" (derived from Jean Pouillon). The latter two continue the confusion between cognition and interest.

9 For example a recent article misreads "Eveline" by confusing character's point of view and narrator's voice (Clive Hart, "Eveline," in *James Joyce's Dubliners: Critical Essays* [London, 1969], p. 51). The author argues that Eveline is shallow and incapable of love—which may be true—but supports

his argument with questionable evidence: "She over-dramatizes her association with Frank, calls it an 'affair' and him her 'lover'; she thinks of herself in pulp-literature terms as 'unspeakably' weary. But most obvious of all is the strong note of falsity in the language of the passage in which she re-asserts her choice to leave: 'As she mused the pitiful vision of her mother's life laid its spell on the very quick of her being. . . .' Dublin has so para-lysed Eveline's emotions that she is unable to love, can think of herself and her situation only by means of a series of tawdry cliches." Surely the ob-jectionable words are not Eveline's but the narrator's. It is he who is parody-ing pulp-literature sentimentality in tawdry cliches (as does the narrator of the "Nausicaa" section of *Ulysses*). Eveline may indeed feel maudlin senti-ments, but "mused," "pitiful vision," "very quick of her being" are not in her vocabulary.

25

Towards a Feminist Poetics

ELAINE SHOWALTER

■■■■

Elaine Showalter argues here that at the end of the 1970s "feminist criticism [was] the most isolated and the least understood" of all the current approaches to English studies. After citing a number of reasons for this situation, she divides feminist criticism into two major types: the first, which she names feminist critique, "is concerned with *woman as reader.* . . . Its subjects include the images and stereotypes of women in literature, the omissions and misconceptions about women in criticism, and the fissures in male-constructed literary history"; the second, which she names gynocritics, is concerned with *"woman as writer*—with the woman as the producer of textual meaning, with the history, themes, genres and structures of literature by women."

Having defined these two types, Showalter proceeds to demonstrate their methods, taking up first a feminist critique of Thomas Hardy's *The Mayor of Casterbridge.* She points out that one of the problems with feminist critique is that much of its analysis "is male-oriented," focusing on the "stereotypes of women, the sexism of male literary critics, and the limited roles women play in literary history." In contrast, "the programme of gynocritics is to construct a female framework for the analysis of women's literature." Also, unlike feminist critique, gynocriticism has a strongly interdisciplanary orientation using feminist research within a broad array of other disciplines. Showalter's examples include discussions of recent American gynocritical scholarship, as well as gynocritical evaluations of the feminist authors Elizabeth Barrett Browning and Muriel Spark. She then raises perhaps the most controversial issue of feminist criticism: Is there a distinct women's writing, even a women's language, what the French feminists call *écriture feminine?* Showalter discusses her conception of three historical stages in women's writing: "Feminine, Feminist, and Female," along with the varieties of theoretical approaches found in feminist criticism, such as Marxism and structuralism. Showalter concludes by asserting that feminist criticism is here to stay and by inviting her male colleagues to participate in its continuing discoveries and revaluations of literature.

Elaine Showalter (b. 1941), a major feminist critic, is professor of English at Princeton University. Her books include *A Literature of Their Own: British Women Novelists from Brontë to Lessing* (1977) and *The Female Malady: Women, Madness, and Culture in England, 1830–1980* (1985). She has also edited *Women's Liberation and Literature* (1971) and *The New Feminist Criticism* (1985).

In 1977, Leon Edel, the distinguished biographer of Henry James, contributed to a London symposium of essays by six male critics called *Contemporary Approaches to English Studies.* Professor Edel presented his essay as a dramatised discussion between three literary scholars who stand arguing about art on the steps of the British Museum:

> There was Criticus, a short, thick-bodied intellectual with spectacles, who clung to a pipe in his right hand. There was Poeticus, who cultivated a Yeatsian forelock, but without the eyeglasses and the ribbon. He made his living by reviewing and had come to the B.M. to look up something or other. Then there was Plutarchus, a lean and lanky biographer wearing a corduroy jacket.

As these three gentlemen are warming to their important subject, a taxi pulls up in front of them and releases "an auburn-haired young woman, obviously American, who wore ear-rings and carried an armful of folders and an attaché case." Into the Museum she dashes, leaving the trio momentarily wondering why femininity requires brain-

"Towards a Feminist Poetics," by Elaine Showalter, first appeared in *Women Writing & Writing About Women,* ed. Mary Jacobus, Barnes and Noble, 1979. Copyright 1979 Elaine Showalter. Reprinted with permission of Barnes and Noble Books.

work. They are still arguing when she comes out, twenty-one pages later.[1]

I suppose we should be grateful that at least one woman—let us call her Critica—makes an appearance in this gathering, even if she is not invited to join the debate. I imagine that she is a feminist critic—in fact if I could afford to take taxis to the British Museum, I would think they had perhaps seen me—and it is pleasing to think that while the men stand gossiping in the sun, she is inside hard at work. But these are scant satisfactions when we realise that of all the approaches to English studies current in the 1970s, feminist criticism is the most isolated and the least understood. Members of English departments who can remember what Harold Bloom means by *clinamen*, and who know the difference between Tartu and Barthian semiotics, will remark that they are against feminist criticism and consequently have never read any. Those who have read it, often seem to have read through a glass darkly, superimposing their stereotypes on the critical texts. In his introduction to Nina Auerbach's subtle feminist analysis of *Dombey and Son* in the *Dickens Studies Annual*, for example, Robert Partlow discusses the deplorable but nonexistent essay of his own imagining:

> At first glance, Nina Auerbach's essay . . . might seem to be a case of special pleading, another piece of women's lib propaganda masquerading as literary criticism, but it is not quite that . . . such an essay could have been . . . ludicrous . . . it could have seen dark phallic significance in curving railroad-tracks and upright church pews—but it does not.[2]

In contrast to Partlow's caricature (feminist criticism will naturally be obsessed with the phallus), there are the belligerent assumptions of Robert Boyers, in the winter 1977 issue of the influential American quarterly *Partisan Review*, that it will be obsessed with destroying great male artists. In "A Case Against Feminist Criticism," Boyers used a single work, Joan Mellen's *Women and Their Sexuality in the New Film* (1973), as an example of feminist deficiency in "intellectual honesty" and "rigour." He defines feminist criticism as the "insistence on asking the same questions of every work and demanding ideologically satisfactory answers to those questions as a means of evaluating it," and concludes his diatribe thus:

Though I do not think anyone has made a credible case for feminist criticism as a viable alternative to any other mode, no one can seriously object to feminists continuing to try. We ought to demand that such efforts be minimally distinguished by intellectual candour and some degree of precision. This I have failed to discover in most feminist criticism.[3]

Since his article makes its "case" so recklessly that Joan Mellen brought charges for libel, and the *Partisan Review* was obliged to print a retraction in the following issue, Boyers hardly seems the ideal champion to enter the critical lists under the twin banners of honesty and rigour. Indeed, his terminology is best understood as a form of intimidation, intended to force women into using a discourse more acceptable to the academy, characterised by the "rigour" which my dictionary defines as strictness, a severe or cruel act, or "state of rigidity in living tissues or organs that prevents response to stimuli." In formulating a feminist literary theory, one ought never to expect to appease a Robert Boyers. And yet these "cases" cannot continue to be settled, one by one, out of court. The absence of a clearly articulated theory makes feminist criticism perpetually vulnerable to such attacks, and not even feminist critics seem to agree what it is that they mean to profess and defend.

A second obstacle to the articulation of a feminist critical practice is the activist's suspicion of theory, especially when the demand for clarification comes from sources as patently sexist as the egregiously named Boyers and Mailers of the literary quarterlies. Too many literary abstractions which claim to be universal have in fact described only male perceptions, experiences, and options, and have falsified the social and personal contexts in which literature is produced and consumed. In women's fiction, the complacently precise and systematising male has often been the target of satire, especially when his subject is Woman. George Eliot's impotent structuralist Casaubon is a classic instance, as is Mr. Ramsay, the self-pitying philosopher in Virginia Woolf's *To the Lighthouse*. More recently Doris Lessing's Professor Bloodrot in *The Golden Notebook* lectures confidently on orgasm in the female swan; as Bloodrot proceeds, the women in the audience rise one by one and leave. What women have found hard to take in such male characters is their self-deception, their pretence to objectivity, their emotion parading as reason. As Adrienne Rich comments in *Of Woman Born*, "the term 'rational' relegates to its opposite term all that it refuses to deal with, and thus ends by assuming itself to be purified of the nonrational, rather than searching to identify and assimilate its own surreal or nonlinear elements."[4] For some radical feminists, methodology itself is an intellectual instrument of patriarchy, a tyrannical Methodolatry which sets implicit limits to what can be questioned and discussed. "The God Method," writes Mary Daly,

> is in fact a subordinate deity, serving higher powers. These are social and cultural institutions whose survival depends upon the classification of disruptive and disturbing information as non-data. Under patriarchy, Method has wiped out women's questions so totally that even women have not been able to hear and formulate our own questions, to meet our own experiences.[5]

From this perspective, the academic demand for theory can only be heard as a threat to the feminist need for authenticity, and the visitor looking for a formula he or she can take away without personal encounter is not welcome. In the United States, where Women's Studies programmes offer degree options in nearly 300 colleges and universities, there are fears that feminist analysis has been co-opted by academia, and counter-demands that we resist the pressure to assimilate. Some believe that the activism and empiricism of feminist criticism is its greatest strength, and point to the flourishing international women's press, to new feminist publishing houses, and to writing collectives and manifestos. They are afraid that if the theory is perfected, the movement will be dead. But these defensive responses may also be rationalisations of the psychic barriers to women's participation in theoretical discourse. Traditionally women have been cast in the supporting rather than the starring roles of literary scholarship. Whereas male critics in the twentieth century have moved to centre-stage, openly contesting for primacy with writers, establishing coteries and schools, speaking unabashedly (to quote Geoffrey Hartman) of their "pen-envy,"[6] women are still too often translators, editors, hostesses at the conference and the Festschrift, interpreters; to congratulate ourselves for working patiently and anonymously for the coming of Shakespeare's sister, as Virginia Woolf exhorted us to do in 1928, is in a sense to make a virtue of necessity. In this essay, therefore, I would like to outline a brief taxonomy, if not a poetics, of feminist criticism, in the hope that it will serve as an introduction to a body of work which needs to be considered both as a major contribution to English studies and as part of an interdisciplinary effort to reconstruct the social, political, and cultural experience of women.

Feminist criticism can be divided into two distinct varieties. The first type is concerned with *woman as reader*—with woman as the consumer of male-produced literature, and with the way in which the hypothesis of a female reader changes our apprehension of a given text, awakening us to the significance of its sexual codes. I shall call this kind of analysis the *feminist critique,* and like other kinds of critique it is a historically grounded inquiry which probes the ideological assumptions of literary phenomena. Its subjects include the images and stereotypes of women in literature, the omissions and misconceptions about women in criticism, and the fissures in male-constructed literary history. It is also concerned with the exploitation and manipulation of the female audience, especially in popular culture and film; and with the analysis of woman-as-sign in semiotic systems. The second type of feminist criticism is concerned with *woman as writer*—with woman as the producer of textual meaning, with the history, themes, genres and structures of literature by women. Its subjects include the psychodynamics of female creativity; linguistics and the problem of a female language; the trajectory of the individual or collective female literary career; literary history; and, of course, studies of particular writers and works. No term exists in English for such a specialised discourse, and so I have adapted the French term *la gynocritique:* "gynocritics" (although the significance of the male pseudonym in the history of women's writing also suggested the term "georgics").

The feminist critique is essentially political and polemical, with theoretical affiliations to Marxist sociology and aesthetics; gynocritics is more self-contained and experimental, with connections to other modes of new feminist research. In a dialogue between these two positions, Carolyn Heilbrun, the writer, and Catherine Stimpson, editor of the American journal *Signs: Women in Culture and Society,* compare the feminist critique to the Old Testament, "looking for the sins and errors of the past," and gynocritics to the New Testament, seeking "the grace of imagination." Both kinds are necessary, they explain, for only the Jeremiahs of the feminist critique can lead us out of the "Egypt of female servitude" to the promised land of the feminist vision. That the discussion makes use of these Biblical metaphors points to the connections between feminist consciousness and conversion narratives which often appear in women's literature; Carolyn Heilbrun comments on her own text, "when I talk about feminist criticism, I am amazed at how high a moral tone I take."[7]

The Feminist Critique: Hardy

Let us take briefly as an example of the way a feminist critique might proceed, Thomas Hardy's *The Mayor of Casterbridge*, which begins with the famous scene of the drunken Michael Henchard selling his wife and infant daughter for five guineas at a country fair. In his study of Hardy, Irving Howe has praised the brilliance and power of this opening scene:

> To shake loose from one's wife; to discard that drooping rag of a woman, with her mute complaints and maddening passivity; to escape not by a slinking abandonment but through the public sale of her body to a stranger, as horses are sold at a fair; and thus to wrest, through sheer amoral wilfulness, a second chance out of life—it is with this stroke, so insidiously attractive to male fantasy, that *The Mayor of Casterbridge* begins.[8]

It is obvious that a woman, unless she has been indoctrinated into being very deeply identified indeed with male culture, will have a different experience of this scene. I quote Howe first to indicate how the fantasies of the male critic distort the text; for Hardy tells us very little about the relationship of Michael and Susan Henchard, and what we see in the early scenes does not suggest that she is drooping, complaining, or passive. Her role, however, is a passive one; severely constrained by her womanhood, and further burdened by her child, there is no way that *she* can wrest a second chance out of life. She cannot master events, but only accommodate herself to them.

What Howe, like other male critics of Hardy, conveniently overlooks about the novel is that Henchard sells not only his wife but his child, a child who can only be female. Patriarchal societies do not readily sell their sons, but their daughters are all for sale sooner or later. Hardy wished to make the sale of the daughter emphatic and central; in early drafts of the novel Henchard has two daughters and sells only one, but Hardy revised to make it clearer that Henchard is symbolically selling his entire share in the world of women. Having severed his bonds with this female community of love and loyalty, Henchard has chosen to live in the male community, to define his human relationships by the male code of paternity, money, and legal contract. His tragedy lies in realising the inadequacy of this system, and in his inability to repossess the loving bonds he comes desperately to need.

The emotional centre of *The Mayor of Casterbridge* is neither Henchard's relationship to his wife, nor his superficial romance with Lucetta Templeman, but his slow appreciation of the strength and dignity of his wife's daughter, Elizabeth-Jane. Like the other women in the book, she is governed by her own heart—man-made laws are not important to her until she is taught by Henchard himself to value legality, paternity, external definitions, and thus in the end to reject him. A self-proclaimed "woman-hater," a man who has felt at best a "supercilious pity" for womankind, Henchard is humbled and "unmanned" by the collapse of his own virile façade, the loss of his mayor's chain, his master's authority, his father's rights. But in Henchard's alleged weakness and "womanishness," breaking through in moments of tenderness, Hardy is really showing us the man at his best. Thus Hardy's female characters in *The Mayor of Casterbridge*, as in his other novels, are somewhat idealised and melancholy projections of a repressed male self.

As we see in this analysis, one of the problems of the feminist critique is that it is male-oriented. If we study stereotypes of women, the sexism of male critics, and the limited roles women play in literary history, we are not learning what women have felt and experienced, but only what men have thought women should be. In some fields of specialisation, this may require a long apprenticeship to the male theoretician, whether he be Althusser, Barthes, Macherey, or Lacan; and then an application of the theory of signs or myths or the unconscious to male texts or films. The temporal and intellectual investment one makes in such a process increases resistance to questioning it, and to seeing its historical and ideological boundaries. The critique also has a tendency to naturalise women's victimisation, by making it the inevitable and obsessive topic of discussion. One sees, moreover, in works like Elizabeth Hardwick's *Seduction and Betrayal*, the bittersweet moral distinctions the critic makes between women merely betrayed by men, like Hetty in *Adam Bede*, and the heroines who make careers out of betrayal, like Hester Prynne in *The Scarlet Letter*. This comes dangerously close to a celebration of the opportunities of victimisation, the seduction of betrayal.[9]

Gynocritics and Female Culture

In contrast to this angry or loving fixation on male literature, the programme of gynocritics is to construct a female framework for the analysis of women's literature, to develop new models based on the study of female experience, rather than to adapt male models and theories. Gynocritics begins at the point when we free ourselves from the linear absolutes of male literary history, stop trying to fit women between the lines of the male tradition, and focus instead on the newly visible world of female culture. This is comparable to the ethnographer's effort to render the experience of the "muted" female half of a society, which is described in Shirley Ardener's collection, *Perceiving Women*.[10] Gynocritics is related to feminist research in history, anthropology, psychology, and sociology, all of which have developed hypotheses of a female subculture including not only the ascribed status, and the internalised constructs of femininity, but also the occupations, interactions and consciousness of women. Anthropologists study the female subculture in the relationships between women, as mothers, daughters, sisters, and friends; in sexuality, reproduction, and ideas about the body; and in rites of initiation and passage, purification ceremonies, myths, and taboos. Michelle Rosaldo writes in *Woman, Culture, and Society*,

> the very symbolic and social conceptions that appear to set women apart and to circumscribe their activities may be used by women as a basis for female solidarity and worth. When men live apart from women, they in fact cannot control them, and unwittingly they may provide them with the symbols and social resources on which to build a society of their own.[11]

Thus in some women's literature, feminine values penetrate and undermine the masculine systems which contain them; and women have imaginatively engaged the myths of the Amazons, and the fantasies of a separate female society, in genres from Victorian poetry to contemporary science fiction.

In the past two years, pioneering work by four young American feminist scholars has given us some new ways to interpret the culture of nineteenth-century American women, and the literature which was its primary expressive form. Carroll Smith-Rosenberg's essay "The Female World of Love and Ritual" examines several archives of letters between women, and outlines the homosocial emotional world of the nineteenth century. Nancy Cott's *The Bonds of Womanhood: Woman's Sphere in New England 1780–1835* explores the paradox of a cultural bondage, a legacy of pain and submission, which none the less generates a sisterly solidarity, a bond of shared experience, loyalty and compassion. Ann Douglas's ambitious book, *The Feminization of American Culture,* boldly locates the genesis of American mass culture in the sentimental literature of women and clergymen, two allied and "disestablished" post-industrial groups. These three are social historians; but Nina Auerbach's *Communities of Women: An Idea in Fiction* seeks the bonds of womanhood in women's literature, ranging from the matriarchal households of Louisa May Alcott and Mrs. Gaskell to the women's schools and colleges of Dorothy Sayers, Sylvia Plath, and Muriel Spark. Historical and literary studies like these, based on English women, are badly needed; and the manuscript and archival sources for them are both abundant and untouched.[12]

Gynocritics: Elizabeth Barrett Browning and Muriel Spark

Gynocritics must also take into account the different velocities and curves of political, social, and personal histories in determining women's literary choices and careers. "In dealing with women as writers," Virginia Woolf wrote in her 1929 essay, "Women and Fiction," "as much elasticity as possible is desirable; it is necessary to leave oneself room to deal with other things besides their work, so much has that work been influenced by conditions that have nothing whatever to do with art."[13] We might illustrate the need for this completeness by looking at Elizabeth Barrett Browning, whose versenovel *Aurora Leigh* (1856) has recently been handsomely reprinted by the Women's Press. In her excellent introduction Cora Kaplan defines Barrett Browning's feminism as romantic and bourgeois, placing its faith in the transforming powers of love, art, and Christian charity. Kaplan reviews Barrett Browning's dialogue with the artists and radicals of her time; with Tennyson and Clough, who had also written poems on the "woman question"; with the Christian Socialism of Fourier, Owen, Kingsley, and Maurice; and with such female predecessors as Madame de Staël and George Sand. But in this exploration of Barrett Browning's intellectual milieu, Kaplan omits discussion of the male poet whose influence on her work in the 1850s would have been most pervasive: Robert Browning. When we understand how susceptible women writers have always been to the aesthetic standards and values of the male tradition, and to male approval and validation, we can appreciate the complexity of a marriage between artists. Such a union has almost invariably meant internal conflicts, self-effacement, and finally obliteration for the women, except in the rare cases—Eliot and Lewes, the Woolfs—where the husband accepted a managerial rather than a competitive role. We can see in Barrett Browning's letters of the 1850s the painful, halting, familiar struggle between her womanly love and ambition for her husband and her conflicting commitment to her own work. There is a sense in which she *wants* him to be the better artist. At the beginning of the decade she was more famous than he; then she notes with pride a review in France which praises him more; his work on *Men and Women* goes well; her work on *Aurora Leigh* goes badly (she had a young child and was recovering from the most serious of her four miscarriages). In 1854 she writes to a woman friend, "I am behind hand with my poem . . . Robert swears he shall have his book ready in spite of everything for print when we shall be in London for the purpose, but, as for mine, it must wait for the next spring I begin to see clearly. Also it may be better not to bring out the two works together." And she adds wryly, "If mine were ready I might not say so perhaps."[14]

Without an understanding of the framework of the female subculture, we can miss or misinterpret the themes and structures of women's literature, fail to make necessary connections within a tradition. In 1852, in an eloquent passage from her autobiographical essay "Cassandra," Florence Nightingale identified the pain of feminist awakening as its essence, as the guarantee of progress and free will. Protesting against the protected unconscious lives of middle-class Victorian women, Nightingale demanded the restoration of their suffering: "Give us back our suffering, we cry to Heaven in our hearts— suffering rather than indifferentism—for out of suffering may come the cure. Better to have pain than paralysis: A hundred struggle and drown in the breakers. One discovers a new world."[15] It is fascinating to see how Nightingale's metaphors anticipate not only her own medical career, but also the fate of the heroines of women's novels in the nineteenth and twentieth centuries. To waken from the drugged, pleasant sleep of Victorian womanhood was agonising; in fiction it is much more likely to end in drowning than in discovery. It is usually associated with what George Eliot in *Middlemarch* calls "the chill hours of a morning twilight," and the sudden appalled confrontation with the contingencies of adulthood. Eliot's Maggie Tulliver, Edith Wharton's Lily Barth, Olive Schreiner's Lyndall, Kate Chopin's Edna Pontellier wake to worlds which offer no places for the women they wish to become; and rather than struggling they die. Female suffering thus becomes a kind of literary commodity which both men and women consume. Even in these important women's novels—*The Mill on the Floss, Story of an African Farm, The House of Mirth*—the fulfillment of the plot is a visit to the heroine's grave by a male mourner.

According to Dame Rebecca West, unhappiness is still the keynote of contemporary fiction by English women.[16] Certainly the literary landscape is strewn with dead female bodies. In Fay Weldon's *Down Among the Women* and *Female Friends*, suicide has come to be a kind of domestic accomplishment, carried out after the shopping and the washing-up. When Weldon's heroine turns on the gas, "she feels that she has been half-dead for so long that the difference in state will not be very great." In Muriel Spark's stunning short novel of 1970, *The Driver's Seat*, another half-dead and desperate heroine gathers all her force to hunt down a woman-hating psychopath, and persuade him to murder her. Garishly dressed in a purposely bought outfit of clashing purple, green and white—the colours of the suffragettes (and the colours of the school uniform in *The Prime of Miss Jean Brodie*)—

Lise goes in search of her killer, lures him to a park, gives him the knife. But in Lise's careful selection of her death-dress, her patient pursuit of her assassin, Spark has given us the devastated postulates of feminine wisdom: that a woman creates her identity by choosing her clothes, that she creates her history by choosing her man. That, in the 1970s, Mr. Right turns out to be Mr. Goodbar, is not the sudden product of urban violence, but a latent truth which fiction exposes. Spark asks whether men or women are in the driver's seat, and whether the power to choose one's destroyer is women's only form of self-assertion. To label the violence or self-destructiveness of these painful novels as neurotic expressions of a personal pathology, as many reviewers have done, is to ignore, Annette Kolodny suggests, "the possibility that the worlds they inhabit may in fact be real, or true, and for them the only worlds available, and further, to deny the possibility that their apparently 'odd' or unusual responses may in fact be justifiable or even necessary."[17]

But women's literature must go beyond these scenarios of compromise, madness, and death. Although the reclamation of suffering is the beginning, its purpose is to discover the new world. Happily, some recent women's literature, especially in the United States, where novelists and poets have become vigorously involved in the women's liberation movement, has gone beyond reclaiming suffering to its reinvestment. This newer writing relates the pain of transformation to history. "If I'm lonely," writes Adrienne Rich in "Song,"

> it must be the loneliness
> of waking first, of breathing
> dawn's first cold breath on the city
> of being the one awake
> in a house wrapped in sleep[18]

Rich is one of the spokeswomen for a new women's writing which explores the will to change. In her recent book, *Of Woman Born: Motherhood as Experience and Institution*, Rich challenges the alienation from and rejection of the mother that daughters have learned under patriarchy. Much women's literature in the past has dealt with "matrophobia" or the fear of becoming one's mother.[19] In Sylvia Plath's *The Bell Jar*, for example, the heroine's mother is the target for the novel's most punishing contempt. When Esther announces to her therapist that she hates her mother, she is on the road to recovery. Hating one's mother was the feminist enlightenment of the fifties and sixties; but it is only a metaphor for hating oneself. Female literature of the 1970s goes beyond matrophobia to a courageously sustained quest for the mother, in such books as Margaret Atwood's *Surfacing*, and Lisa Alther's recent *Kinflicks*. As the death of the father has always been an archetypal rite of passage for the Western hero, now the death of the mother as witnessed and transcended by the daughter has become one of the most profound occasions of female literature. In analysing these purposeful awakenings, these reinvigorated mythologies of female culture, feminist criticism finds its most challenging, inspiriting, and appropriate task.

Women and the Novel: The "Precious Specialty"

The most consistent assumption of feminist reading has been the belief that women's special experience would assume and determine distinctive forms in art. In the nineteenth century, such a contribution was ambivalently valued. When Victorian reviewers like G. H. Lewes, Richard Hutton, and Richard Simpson began to ask what the literature of women might mean, and what it might become, they focused on the educational, experiential, and biological handicaps of the woman novelist, and this was also how most women conceptualised their situation. Some reviewers, granting women's sympathy, sentiment, and powers of observation, thought that the novel would provide an appropriate, even a happy, outlet for female emotion and fantasy. In the United States, the popular novelist Fanny Fern understood that women had been granted access to the novel as a sort of repressive desublimation, a harmless channel for frustrations and drives that might otherwise threaten the family, the Church and the State. Fern recommended that women write as therapy, as a release from the stifling silence of the drawing-room, and as a rebellion against the indifference and insensitivity of the men closest to them:

> Look around, and see innumerable women, to whose barren and loveless lives this would be improvement and solace, and I say to them, write! write! It will be a safe outlet for thoughts

and feelings that maybe the nearest friend you have has never dreamed had place in your heart and brain . . . it is not *safe* for the women of 1867 to shut down so much that cries out for sympathy and expression, because life is such a maelstrom of business or folly or both that those to whom they have bound themselves, body and soul, recognize only the needs of the former. . . . One of these days, when that diary is found, when the hand that penned it shall be dust, with what amazement and remorse will many a husband or father exclaim, I never knew my wife or my child until this moment.[20]

Fern's scribbling woman spoke with fierce indirectness to the male audience, to the imagined husband or father; her purpose was to shock rather than to please, but the need to provoke masculine response was the controlling factor in her writing. At the turn of the century, members of the Women Writers Suffrage League, an important organisation of novelists and journalists, began to explore the psychological bondage of women's literature and its relationships to a male-dominated publishing industry. Elizabeth Robins, the first president of the League, a novelist and actress who had starred in early English productions of Ibsen, argued in 1908 that no woman writer had ever been free to explore female consciousness:

> The realization that she had access to a rich and as yet unrifled storehouse may have crossed her mind, but there were cogent reasons for concealing her knowledge. With that wariness of ages which has come to be instinct, she contented herself with echoing the old fables, presenting to a man-governed world puppets as nearly as possible like those that had from the beginning found such favour in men's sight.
>
> Contrary to the popular impression, to say in print what she thinks is the last thing the woman-novelist or journalist is so rash as to attempt. There even more than elsewhere (unless she is reckless) she must wear the aspect that shall have the best chance of pleasing her brothers. Her publishers are not women.[21]

It was to combat this inhibiting commercial monopoly that nineteenth-century women began to organise their own publishing houses, beginning with Emily Faithfull's Victoria Press in the 1870s, and reaching a peak with the flourishing suffrage presses at the beginning of this century. One of the most fervent beliefs of the Women Writers Suffrage League was that the "terra incognita" of the female psyche would find unique literary expression once women had overthrown male domination. In *A Room of One's Own*, Virginia Woolf argued that economic independence was the essential precondition of an autonomous women's art. Like George Eliot before her, Woolf also believed that women's literature held the promise of a "precious speciality," a distinctly female vision.

Feminine, Feminist, Female

All of these themes have been important to feminist literary criticism in the 1960s and 1970s but we have approached them with more historical awareness. Before we can even begin to ask how the literature of women would be different and special, we need to reconstruct its past, to rediscover the scores of women novelists, poets and dramatists whose work has been obscured by time, and to establish the continuity of the female tradition from decade to decade, rather than from Great Woman to Great Woman. As we recreate the chain of writers in this tradition, the patterns of influence and response from one generation to the next, we can also begin to challenge the periodicity of orthodox literary history, and its enshrined canons of achievement. It is because we have studied women writers in isolation that we have never grasped the connections between them. When we go beyond Austen, the Brontës, and Eliot, say, to look at a hundred and fifty or more of their sister novelists, we can see patterns and phases in the evolution of a female tradition which correspond to the developmental phases of any subcultural art. In my book on English women writers, *A Literature of Their Own*, I have called these the Feminine, Feminist, and Female stages.[22] During the Feminine phase, dating from about 1840 to 1880, women wrote in an effort to equal the intellectual achievements of the male culture, and internalised its assumptions about female nature. The distinguishing sign of this period is the male pseudonym, introduced in England in the 1840s, and a national characteristic of English women writers. In addition to the famous names we all know—George Eliot, Currer, Ellis, and Acton Bell—dozens of other women chose male pseudonyms as a way of coping with a double literary standard. This masculine disguise goes well beyond the title page; it exerts an irregular pressure on the narrative, affecting tone, diction, structure, and characterisation. In contrast to the English male pseudonym, which signals such clear self-awareness of the liabilities of female authorship, American women during the same period adopted super-feminine, little-me pseudonyms (Fanny Fern, Grace Greenwood, Fanny Forester), disguising behind these nominal bouquets their boundless energy, powerful economic motives, and keen professional skills. It is pleasing to discover the occasional Englishwoman who combines both these techniques, and creates the illusion of male authorship with a name that contains the encoded domestic message of femininity—such as Harriet Parr, who wrote under the pen name "Holme Lee." The feminist content of feminine art is typically oblique, displaced, ironic, and subversive; one has to read it between the lines, in the missed possibilities of the text.

In the Feminist phase, from about 1880 to 1920, or the winning of the vote, women are historically enabled to reject the accommodating postures of femininity and to use literature to dramatise the ordeals of wronged womanhood. The personal sense of injustice which feminine novelists such as Elizabeth Gaskell and Frances Trollope expressed in their novels of class struggle and factory life become increasingly and explicitly feminist in the 1880s, when a generation of New Women redefined the woman artist's role in terms of responsibility to suffering sisters. The purest examples of this phase are the Amazon Utopias of the 1890s, fantasies of perfected female societies set in an England or an America of the future, which were also protests against male government, male laws, and male medicine. One author of Amazon Utopias, the American Charlotte Perkins Gilman, also analysed the preoccupations of masculine literature with sex and war, and the alternative possibilities of an emancipated feminist literature. Gilman's Utopian feminism carried George Eliot's idea of the "precious speciality" to its matriarchal extremes. Comparing her view of sisterly collectivity to the beehive, she writes that

> the bee's fiction would be rich and broad, full of the complex tasks of comb-building and filling, the care and feeding of the young. . . . It would treat of the vast fecundity of motherhood,

the educative and selective processes of the group-mothers, and the passion of loyalty, of social service, which holds the hives together.[23]

This is Feminist Socialist Realism with a vengeance, but women novelists of the period—even Gilman, in her short stories—could not be limited to such didactic formulas, or such maternal topics.

In the Female phase, ongoing since 1920, women reject both imitation and protest—two forms of dependency—and turn instead to female experience as the source of an autonomous art, extending the feminist analysis of culture to the forms and techniques of literature. Representatives of the formal Female Aesthetic, such as Dorothy Richardson and Virginia Woolf, began to think in terms of male and female sentences, and divide their work into "masculine" journalism and "feminine" fictions, redefining and sexualising external and internal experience. Their experiments were both enriching and imprisoning retreats into the celebration of consciousness; even in Woolf's famous definition of life: "a luminous halo, a semi-transparent envelope surrounding us from the beginning of consciousness to the end,"[24] there is a submerged metaphor of uterine withdrawal and containment. In this sense, the Room of One's Own becomes a kind of Amazon Utopia, population 1.

Feminist Criticism, Marxism and Structuralism

In trying to account for these complex permutations of the female tradition, feminist criticism has tried a variety of theoretical approaches. The most natural direction for feminist criticism to take has been the revision, and even the subversion of related ideologies, especially Marxist aesthetics and structuralism, altering their vocabularies and methods to include the variable of gender. I believe, however, that this thrifty feminine making-do is ultimately unsatisfactory. Feminist criticism cannot go around forever in men's ill-fitting hand-me-downs, the Annie Hall of English studies; but must, as John Stuart Mill wrote about women's literature in 1869, "emancipate itself from the influence of accepted models, and guide itself by its own impulses"[25]—as, I think, gynocritics is beginning to do. This is not to deny the necessity of using the terminology and techniques of our profession. But when we consider the historical conditions in which critical ideologies are produced, we see why feminist adaptations seem to have reached an impasse.

Both Marxism and structuralism see themselves as privileged critical discourse, and pre-empt the claim to superior places in the hierarchy of critical approaches. A key word in each system is "science"; both claim to be sciences of literature, and repudiate the personal, fallible, interpretative reading. Marxist aesthetics offers a "science of the text," in which the author becomes not the creator but the producer of a text whose components are historically and economically determined. Structuralism presents linguistically based models of textual permutations and combinations, offering a "science of literary meaning," a grammar of genre. The assimilation of these positivist and evangelical literary criticisms by Anglo-American scholarship in the past fifteen years is not—I would argue—a spontaneous or accidental cultural phenomenon. In the Cold War atmosphere of the late 1950s, when European structuralism began to develop, the morale of the Anglo-American male academic humanist was at its nadir. This was the era of Sputnik, of scientific competition with the Soviet Union, of government money flowing to the laboratories and research centres. Northrop Frye has written about the plight of the male intellectual confronting

> the dismal sexist symbology surrounding the humanities which he meets everywhere, even in the university itself, from freshman classes to the president's office. This symbology, or whatever one should call it, says that the sciences, especially the physical sciences, are rugged, aggressive, out in the world doing things, and so symbolically male, whereas the literatures are narcissistic, intuitive, fanciful, staying at home and making the home more beautiful but not doing anything serious and are therefore symbolically female.[26]

Frye's own *Anatomy of Criticism*, published in 1957, presented the first postulates of a systematic critical theory, and the "possibility of literary study's attaining the progressive, cumulative qualities of science."[27]

The new sciences of the text based on linguistics, computers, genetic structuralism, deconstructionism, neo-formalism and deformalism, affective stylistics, and psychoaesthetics, have offered literary critics the opportunity to demonstrate that the work they do is as manly and aggressive as nuclear physics—not intuitive, expressive, and feminine, but strenuous, rigorous, impersonal, and virile. In a shrinking job market, these new levels of professionalisation also function as discriminators between the marketable and the marginal lecturer. Literary science, in its manic generation of difficult terminology, its establishment of seminars and institutes of post-graduate study, creates an élite corps of specialists who spend more and more time mastering the theory, less and less time reading the books. We are moving towards a two-tiered system of "higher" and "lower" criticism, the higher concerned with the "scientific" problems of form and structure, the "lower" concerned with the "humanistic" problems of content and interpretation. And these levels, it seems to me, are now taking on subtle gender identities, and assuming a sexual polarity—hermeneutics and hismeneutics. Ironically, the existence of a new criticism practised by women has made it even more possible for structuralism and Marxism to strive, Henchard-like, for systems of formal obligation and determination. Feminists writing in these modes, such as Hélène Cixous and the women contributors to *Diacritics*, risk being allotted the symbolic ghettoes of the special issue or the back of the book for their essays.

It is not only because the exchange between feminism, Marxism, and structuralism has hitherto been so one-sided, however, that I think attempts at syntheses have so far been unsuccessful. While scientific criticism struggles to purge itself of the subjective, feminist criticism is willing to assert (in the title of a recent anthology) *The Authority of Experience*.[28] The experience of women can easily disappear, become mute, invalid, and invisible, lost in the diagrams of the structuralist or the class conflict of the Marxists. Experience is not emotion; we must protest now as in the nineteenth century against the equation of the feminine with the irrational. But we must also recognise that the questions we most need to ask go beyond those that science can answer. We must seek the repressed messages of women in history, in anthropology, in psychology, and in ourselves, before we can locate the feminine not-said, in the manner of Pierre Macherey, by probing the fissures of the female text.

Thus the current theoretical impasse in feminist criticism, I believe, is more than a problem of finding "exacting definitions and a suitable terminology," or "theorizing in the midst of a struggle." It comes from our own divided consciousness, the split in each of us. We are both the daughters of the male tradition, of our teachers, our professors, our dissertation advisers, and our publishers—a tradition which asks us to be rational, marginal, and grateful; and sisters in a new women's movement which engenders another kind of awareness and commitment, which demands that we renounce the pseudo-success of token womanhood, and the ironic masks of academic debate. How much easier, how less lonely it is, not to awaken—to continue to be critics and teachers of male literature, anthropologists of male culture, and psychologists of male literary response, claiming all the while to be universal. Yet we cannot will ourselves to go back to sleep. As women scholars in the 1970s we have been given a great opportunity, a great intellectual challenge. The anatomy, the rhetoric, the poetics, the history, await our writing.

I am sure that this divided consciousness is sometimes experienced by men, but I think it unlikely that many male academics would have had the division in themselves as succinctly and publicly labelled as they were for me in 1976 when my official title at the University of Delaware was Visiting Minority Professor. I am deeply aware of the struggle in myself between the professor, who wants to study major works by major writers, and to mediate impersonally between these works and the readings of other professors—and the minority, the woman who wants connections between my life and my work, and who is committed to a revolution of consciousness that would make my concerns those of the majority. There have been times when the Minority wishes to betray the Professor, by isolating herself in a female ghetto; or when the Professor wishes to betray the Minority by denying the troubling voice of difference and dissent. What I hope is that neither will betray the other, because neither can exist by itself. The task of feminist critics is to find a new language, a new way of reading that can integrate our intelligence and our experience, our reason and our suffering, our scepticism and our vision. This enterprise should not be confined to women; I invite Criticus, Poeticus, and Plutarchus to share it with us. One thing is certain: feminist criticism is not visiting. It is here to stay, and we must make it a permanent home.

Notes

I wish to thank Nina Auerbach, Kate Ellis, Mary Jacobus, Wendy Martin, Adrienne Rich, Helen Taylor, Martha Vicinus, Margaret Walters, and Ruth Yeazell for sharing with me their ideas on feminist criticism.

1 Leon Edel, "The Poetics of Biography," in Hilda Schiff, ed., *Contemporary Approaches to English Studies* (London, 1977), p. 38. The other contributors to the symposium are George Steiner, Raymond Williams, Christopher Butler, Jonathan Culler, and Terry Eagleton.

2 Robert Partlow, *Dickens Studies Annual*, vol. 5 (Carbondale: Southern Illinois University Press, 1976), pp. xiv–xv. Nina Auerbach's essay is called "Dickens and Dombey: A Daughter After All."

3 Robert Boyers, "A Case Against Feminist Criticism," *Partisan Review* 44 (Winter 1977): 602, 610.

4 Adrienne Rich, *Of Woman Born: Motherhood as Experience and Institution* (New York, 1977), p. 62.

5 Mary Daly, *Beyond God the Father: Towards a Philosophy of Women's Liberation* (Boston, 1973), pp. 12–13.

6 Geoffrey Hartman, *The Fate of Reading* (Chicago, 1975), p. 3.

7 "Theories of Feminist Criticism," in Josephine Donovan, ed., *Feminist Literary Criticism: Explorations in Theory* (Lexington, 1976), pp. 64, 68, 72.

8 Irving Howe, *Thomas Hardy* (London, 1968), p. 84. For a more detailed discussion of this problem see my essay "The Unmanning of the Mayor of Casterbridge," in Dale Kramer, ed., *Critical Approaches to Hardy* (London, 1979).

9 Elizabeth Hardwick, *Seduction and Betrayal* (New York, 1974).

10 Shirley Ardener, ed., *Perceiving Women* (London, 1975).

11 "Women, Culture, and Society: A Theoretical Overview," in Louise Lamphere and Michelle Rosaldo, eds., *Women, Culture and Society* (Stanford, 1974), p. 39.

12 Carroll Smith-Rosenberg, "The Female World of Love and Ritual: Relations Between Women in Nineteenth-Century America," *Signs: Journal of Women in Culture and Society* 1 (Autumn 1975): 1–30; Nancy Cott, *The Bonds of Womanhood* (New Haven, 1977); Ann Douglas, *The Feminization of American Culture* (New York, 1977); Nina Auerbach, *Communities of Women* (Cambridge, Mass., 1978).

13 "Women and Fiction," in Virginia Woolf, *Collected Essays*, vol. 2 (London, 1967), p. 141.

14 Peter N. Heydon and Philip Kelley, eds., *Elizabeth Barrett Browning's Letter to Mrs. David Ogilvy* (London, 1974), p. 115.

15 "Cassandra," in Ray Strachey, ed., *The Cause* (London, 1928), p. 398.

16 Rebecca West, "And They All Lived Unhappily Ever After," *TLS* (July 26, 1974): 779.

17 Annette Kolodny, "Some Notes on Defining a 'Feminist Literary Criticism,'" *Critical Inquiry* 2 (1975): 84. For an illuminating discussion of *The Driver's Seat*, see Auerbach, *Communities of Women*, p. 181.

18 Adrienne Rich, *Diving into the Wreck* (New York, 1973), p. 20.

19 The term "matrophobia" has been coined by Lynn Sukenick; see Rich, *Of Woman Born*, pp. 235ff.

20 Quoted in Ann Douglas Wood, "The 'Scribbling Women' and Fanny Fern: Why Women Wrote," *American Quarterly* 23 (1971): 3–24.

21 Elizabeth Robins, *Woman's Secret*, WSPU pamphlet in the collection of the Museum of London, p. 6. Jane Marcus is preparing a full-length study of Elizabeth Robins.

22 Elaine Showalter, *A Literature of Their Own: British Women Novelists from Brontë to Lessing* (Princeton, New Jersey, 1977).

23 Charlotte Perkins Gilman, *The Man-made World* (London, 1911), pp. 101–2.

24 Woolf, "Modern Fiction," in *Collected Essays*, vol. 2, p. 106.

25 J. S. Mill, *The Subjection of Women* (London, 1869), p. 133.

26 Northrop Frye, "Expanding Eyes," *Critical Inquiry* 2 (1975): 201–2.

27 Robert Scholes, *Structuralism in Literature: An Introduction* (New Haven, 1974), p. 118.

28 Lee Edwards and Arlyn Diamond, eds., *The Authority of Experience* (Amherst, Mass., 1977).

Reading as Construction

TZVETAN TODOROV

▬▬▬▬

Tzvetan Todorov addresses a critical space he sees existing between the study of readers in "their social, historical, collective, or individual variability" and "the image of the reader . . . as character or as 'narratee.'" He defines this space as "the domain of the logic of reading," and he analyzes the reading of "so-called representative texts." According to Todorov, such reading "unfolds as a construction" because we tend to view the text as representing reality and we imaginatively create an appropriate world for that reality. Todorov is not concerned with arguing about the relationship of text and reality, but with answering the question: "How does a text get us to construct an imaginary world?" He employs a linguistic and structuralist method to answer this question, beginning by distinguishing between referential and nonreferential sentences, and arguing that readers use only the referential as construction material. Todorov then outlines how the narrative parameters of "time, point of view, and mode" serve different construction functions, their roles being reinforced by repetition, which enables the reader to "construct *one* event from *many* accounts."

Why is it so important to establish the concept of reading as construction? Todorov notes that no two readings of a novel are identical because each reader does not *receive* the novel's image of the universe, but *creates* his or her own image from partial and composite information. Part of the difference between two readers' readings results from the distinction between *signification* and *symbolization*. In the first, the reader is told of an event; in the second we are given clues, symbols, and implications that must be interpreted. We can see the validity of this distinction if we stop for a moment and consider how our reading of a work changes from the interpretations we make along the way to the interpretation we make at the end, when we reevaluate earlier symbolization in the context of the overall story. Todorov argues that just as readers construct different readings, so too the text may furnish us with readings through its characters or narrator. He calls this "construction as theme" and cites detective novels as an example: "a Watson figure constructs like the reader, but a Sherlock Holmes constructs better." As we can see from this example, not all constructions provided within a text need be helpful ones; some may purposely mislead the reader. Such a distinction helps us understand that while no single reading can be said to be "correct," not all readings construct their interpretations equally well or fully.

Tzvetan Todorov, born in 1939 in Sofia, Bulgaria, is professor of aesthetics at the Centre National de la Recherche Scientifique, Paris. He is the author of numerous books, among them *The Fantastic* (1970; trans. 1973), *Symbolism and Interpretation* (1978; trans. 1983), *Mikhail Bakhtin: The Dialogical Principle* (1981; 1984), and *The Conquest of America: The Question of the Other* (1982; trans. 1984).

What is omnipresent is imperceptible. Nothing is more commonplace than the reading experience, and yet nothing is more unknown. Reading is such a matter of course that, at first glance, it seems there is nothing to say about it.

In literary studies, the problem of reading has been posed from two opposite perspectives. The first concerns itself with readers, their social, historical, collective, or individual variability. The second deals with the image of the reader as it is represented in certain texts: the reader as character or as "narratee." There is, however, an unexplored area situated between the two: the domain of the logic of reading. Although it is not represented in the text, it is nonetheless anterior to individual variation.

There are several types of reading. I shall pause here to discuss one

"Reading as Construction," by Tzvetan Todorov, originally appeared in *The Reader in the Text: Essays on Audience and Interpretation*, ed. Susan R. Suleiman and Inge Crosman. Reprinted with permission of Princeton University Press, copyright 1980.

of the more important ones: the one we usually practice when we read classical fiction or, rather, the so-called representative texts. This particular type of reading, and only this type, unfolds as a construction.

Although we no longer refer to literature in terms of imitation, we still have trouble getting rid of a certain way of looking at fiction; inscribed in our speech habits, it is a vision through which we perceive the novel in terms of representation, or the transposition of a reality that exists prior to it. This attitude would be problematic even if it did not attempt to describe the creative process. When it refers to the text itself, it is sheer distortion. What exists first and foremost is the text itself, and nothing but the text. Only by subjecting the text to a particular type of reading do we construct, from our reading, an imaginary universe. Novels do not imitate reality; they create it. The formula of the pre-Romantics is not a simple terminological innovation; only the perspective of construction allows us to understand thoroughly how the so-called representative text functions.

Given our framework, the question of reading can be restated as follows: How does a text get us to construct an imaginary world? Which aspects of the text determine the construction we produce as we read? And in what way? Let us begin with basics.

Referential Discourse

Only referential sentences allow construction to take place; not all sentences, however, are referential. This fact is well known to linguists and logicians, and we need not dwell on it.

Comprehension is a process different from construction. Take for example the following two sentences from *Adolphe:* "Je la sentais meilleure que moi; je me méprisais d'être indigne d'elle. C'est un affreux malheur que de n'être aimé quand on aime; mais c'en est un bien grand d'être aimé avec passion quand on n'aime plus."[1] The first sentence is referential: it evokes an event (Adolphe's feelings); the second sentence is not referential; it is a maxim. The difference between the two is marked by grammatical indices: the maxim requires a third-person present-tense verb, and contains no anaphores (words referring to preceding segments of the same discourse).

A sentence is either referential or nonreferential; there are no intermediary stages. However, the words that make up a sentence are not all alike in this respect; depending on the lexical choice, the results will be very different. Two independent oppositions seem pertinent here: the affective versus the nonaffective, and the particular versus the general. For example, Adolphe refers to his past as "au milieu d'une vie très dissipée." This remark evokes perceptible events but in an extremely general way. One could easily imagine hundreds of pages describing this very same fact. Whereas in the other sentence, "Je trouvais dans mon père, non pas un censeur, mais un observateur froid et caustique, qui souriait d'abord de pitié, et qui finissait bientôt la conversation avec impatience,"[2] we have a juxtaposition of affective versus nonaffective events: a smile, a moment of silence, are observable facts; pity and impatience are suppositions (justified, no doubt) about feelings to which we are denied direct access.

Normally, a given fictional text will contain examples of all these speech registers (although we know that their distribution varies according to period, schools of thought, or even as a function of the text's global organization). We do not retain nonreferential sentences in the kind of reading I call reading as construction (they belong to another kind of reading). Referential sentences lead to different types of construction depending on their degree of generality and on the affectivity of the events they evoke.

Narrative Filters

The characteristics of discourse mentioned thus far can be identified outside of any context: they are inherent in the sentences themselves. But in reading, we read whole texts, not just sentences. If we compare sentences from the point of view of the imaginary world which they help to construct, we find that they differ in several ways or, rather, according to several parameters. In narrative analysis, it has been agreed to retain three parameters: time, point of view, and mode. Here again, we are on relatively familiar ground (which I have already dealt with in my book, *Poétique*); now it is simply a question of looking at the problems from the point of view of reading.

Mode. Direct discourse is the only way to eliminate the differences between narrative discourse and the world which it evokes: words are identical to words, and construction is direct and immediate. This is not the case with nonverbal events, nor with transposed discourse.

At one point, the "editor" in *Adolphe* states: "Notre hôte, qui avait causé avec un domestique napolitain, qui servait cet étranger [i.e., Adolphe] sans savoir son nom, me dit qu'il ne voyageait point par curiosité, car il ne visitait ni les ruines, ni les sites, ni les monuments, ni les hommes."[3] We can imagine the conversation between the editor-narrator and the host, even though it is unlikely that the former used words (be it in Italian) identical to those which follow the "he told me that" formula. The construction of the conversation between the host and the servant, which is also evoked, is far less determined; thus we have more freedom if we want to construct it in detail. Finally, the conversations and the other activities common to Adolphe and the servant are completely vague; only a general impression is given.

The remarks of a fictional narrator can also be considered as direct discourse, although on a different (higher) level. This is especially the case if, as in *Adolphe*, the narrator is represented in the text. The maxim, which we previously excluded from reading as construction, becomes pertinent here—not for its value as an "énoncé" (i.e., a statement) but as "énonciation" (i.e., an utterance, implying a speaker and his circumstances). The fact that Adolphe as narrator formulates a maxim on the misery of being loved tells us something about his character, and therefore about the imaginary universe of which he is a part.

Time. The time of the fictional world ("story" time) is ordered chronologically. However, the sentences in the text do not, and as a rule cannot, absolutely respect this order; the reader undertakes therefore, unconsciously, the task of chronological reordering. Similarly, certain sentences evoke several events which are distinct yet similar ("iterative narrative"); in these instances we reestablish the plurality of the events as we construct.

Point of view. The "vision" we have of the events evoked by the text clearly determines our work of construction. For example, in the case of a positively slanted vision, we take into consideration (1) the event recounted, and (2) the attitude of the person who "sees" the event.

Furthermore, we know how to distinguish between information that a sentence gives concerning its object, and the information it gives concerning its subject; thus the "editor" of *Adolphe* can only think of the latter, as he comments on the story we have just read: "Je hais cette vanité qui s'occupe d'elle-même en racontant le mal qu'elle a fait, qui a la prétention de sa faire plaindre en se décrivant, et qui, planant indestructible au milieu des ruines, s'analyse au lieu de se repentir."[4] The editor constructs the subject of the narrative (Adolphe the narrator), and not its object (Adolphe the character, and Ellénore).

We usually do not realize just how repetitive, or rather how redundant, fiction is; we could, in fact, state almost categorically that each event is narrated at least twice. For the most part, these repetitions are modulated by the filters mentioned above: at one point a conversation may be reproduced in its entirety; at another, it may be alluded to briefly; action may be observed from several different points of view; it can be recounted in the future, in the present, and in the past. In addition, all these parameters can be combined.

Repetition plays an important role in the process of construction. We must construct *one* event from *many* accounts of it. The relationship between these different accounts varies, ranging from total agreement to downright contradiction. Even two identical accounts do not necessarily produce the same meaning (a good example of this is seen in Coppola's film *The Conversation*). The functions of these repetitions are equally varied: they help to establish the facts as in a police investigation, or to disprove the facts. Thus in *Adolphe,* the fact that the same character expresses contradictory views on the same subject at two different times which are quite close to each other, helps us to understand that states of mind do not exist in and of themselves, but rather in relationship to an interlocutor, to a partner. Constant himself expressed the law of this universe in the following manner: "L'objet qui nous échappe est nécessairement tout différent de celui qui nous poursuit."[5]

Therefore, if the reader is to construct an imaginary universe through his reading of the text, the text itself must be referential; in the course of reading, we let our imagination go to work, filtering the information we receive through the following types of questions: To what extent is the description of this universe accurate (mode)? When did the events take place (time)? To what extent is the story distorted by the various "centers of consciousness" through whom it is told (vision)? At this point, however, the job of reading has only begun.

Signification and Symbolization

How do we know what happens as we read? Through introspection; and if we want to confirm our own impressions, we can always have recourse to other readers' accounts of their own reading. Nevertheless, two accounts of the same text will never be identical. How do we explain this diversity? By the fact that these accounts describe, not the universe of the book itself, but this universe as it is transformed by the psyche of each individual reader. The stages of this transformation can be diagrammed as follows:

1. The author's account   4. The reader's account
          ↓   ↑

2. The imaginary universe   3. The imaginary universe
   evoked by the author   →   constructed by the reader

We could question whether there really is a difference between stages 2 and 3, as is suggested by the diagram. Is there such a thing as nonindividual construction? It is easy to show that the answer must be positive. Everyone who reads *Adolphe* knows that Ellénore first lived with the Comte de p[xxx], that she left him, and went to live with Adolphe; they separated; she later joined him in Paris, etc. On the other hand, there is no way to establish with the same certainty whether Adolphe is weak or merely sincere.

The reason for this duality is that the text evokes facts according to two different modes, which I shall call signification and symbolization. Ellénore's trip to Paris is *signified* by the words in the text. Adolphe's (ultimate) weakness is *symbolized* by other factors in the imaginary universe, which are themselves signified by words. For example, Adolphe's inability to defend Ellénore in social situations is signified; this in turn symbolizes his inability to love. Signified facts are *understood:* all we need is knowledge of the language in which the text is written. Symbolized facts are *interpreted;* and interpretations vary from one subject to another.

Consequently, the relationship between stages 2 and 3, as indicated above, is one of symbolization (whereas the relationship between stages 1 and 2, or 3 and 4, is one of signification). In any case, we are not dealing with a single or unique relationship, but rather a heterogeneous ensemble. First, we always abbreviate as we read: stage 4 is (almost) always shorter than stage 1, whence stage 2 is richer than stage 3. Secondly, we often make mistakes. In both cases, studying the relationship between stages 2 and 3 leads to psychological projection: the transformations tell us about the reading subject. Why does he remember (or even add) certain facts and not others? But there are other transformations which provide information about the reading process itself, and these are the ones that will be our main concern here.

It is hard for me to say whether the situation I observe in the most varied kinds of fiction is universal or whether it is historically and culturally determined. Nevertheless, it is a fact that in every case, symbolization and interpretation (the movement from stage 2 to stage 3) imply the determinism of action. Would reading other texts, lyrical poems for example, require an effort of symbolization based on other presuppositions (e.g., universal analogy)? I do not know; the fact remains that in fiction, symbolization is based on the acknowledgement, either implicit or explicit, of the principle of causality. The questions we address, therefore, to the events that constitute the mental image of stage 2 are the following: What is their cause? What is their effect? We then add their answers to the mental image that constitutes stage 3.

Let us admit that this determinism is universal; what is certainly not universal is the form it takes in a given case. The simplest form, although one that we rarely find in our culture as a reading norm, consists in constructing another fact of the same type. A reader might say to himself, "If John killed Peter (a fact present in the story), it's because Peter slept with John's wife (a fact absent from the story)." This type of reasoning, characteristic of courtroom procedures, is not applied seriously to the novel; we assume that the author has not cheated and that he has provided (has signified) all the information we need to understand the story (*Armance* is an exception). The same is true as concerns effects or aftereffects: many books are sequels to others and tell the consequences of events in the imaginary universe represented in the first text; nevertheless, the content of the second book is generally not considered inherent in the first. Here again, reading practices differ from everyday habits.

When we read, we usually base our constructions upon another kind of causal logic; we look for the causes and consequences of a particular event elsewhere, in elements unlike the event itself. Two types of causal construction seem most frequent (as Aristotle already noted): the event is perceived as the consequence (and/or the cause) either of a character trait or of an impersonal or universal law. *Adolphe* contains numerous examples of both types of interpretation, and they are integrated into the text itself. Here is how Adolphe describes his father: "Je ne me souviens pas, pendant mes dix-huit premières années, d'avoir eu jamais un entretien d'une heure avec lui. . . . Je ne savais pas alors ce que c'etait que la timidité."[6] The first sentence signifies a fact (the absence of lengthy conversations). The second makes us consider this fact as symbolic of a character trait—timidity: if the father behaves in this way, it is because he is timid. The character trait is the cause of the action. Here is an example of the second case: "Je me dis qu'il ne fallait rien précipiter, qu'Ellénore était trop peu préparée à l'aveu que je méditais, et qu'il valait mieux attendre encore. Presque toujours, pour vivre en repos avec nous-mêmes, nous travestissons en calculs et en systèmes nos impuissances ou nos faiblesses: cela satisfait cette portion de nous qui est, pour ainsi dire, spectatrice de l'autre."[7] Here, the first sentence describes the event, and the second provides the reason—a universal law of human behavior, not an individual character trait. We might add that this second type of causality is dominant in *Adolphe:* the novel illustrates psychological laws, not individual psychologies.

After we have constructed the events that compose a story, we begin the task of reinterpretation. This enables us to construct not only the "personalities" of the characters but also the novel's underlying system of values and ideas. A reinterpretation of this type is not arbitrary; it is controlled by two series of constraints. The first is contained in the text itself: the author need but take a few moments to teach us how to interpret the events he evokes. This was the case in the passages from *Adolphe* cited earlier: once he has established a few deterministic interpretations, Constant can forgo naming the cause of the subsequent events; we have learned his lesson, and we shall continue to interpret in the way he has taught us. Such explicit interpretations have a double function: on the one hand, they tell us the reason behind a particular fact (exegetic function); on the other hand, they initiate us into the author's own system of interpretation, the one that will operate throughout the course of the text (meta-exegetic function).

The second series of constraints comes from the cultural context. If we read that so-and-so has cut his wife up into little pieces, we do not need textual indications to conclude that this is truly a cruel deed. These cultural constraints, which are nothing but the common-places of a society (its "set" of probabilities), change with time. These changes permit us to explain why interpretations differ from one period to another. For example, since extramarital love is no longer considered proof of moral corruption, we have trouble under-standing the condemnations heaped upon so many fictional heroines of the past.

Human character and ideas: such entities are symbolized through action, but they can be signified as well. This was precisely the case in the passages from *Adolphe* quoted earlier: action symbolized shy-ness in Adolphe's father. Later, however, Adolphe signified the same thing, saying: My father was shy; that is also true of the general maxim. Human character and ideas can thus be evoked in two ways: directly and indirectly. During the course of his construction, the reader will compare the various bits of information obtained from each source and will find that they either tally or do not. The relative proportion of these two types of information has varied greatly during the course of literary history, as goes without saying: Hem-ingway did not write like Constant.

We must, however, differentiate between human character con-structed in this way and the characters in a novel as such: not every character has a character, so to speak. The fictional character is a segment of the spatio-temporal universe represented in the text, nothing more; he/she comes into existence the moment referential linguistic forms (proper names, certain nominal syntagms, personal pronouns) appear in the text regarding an anthropomorphic being. In and of itself the fictional character has no content: someone is identified without being described. We can imagine—and there ex-ist—texts where the fictional character is limited to just that: being the agent of a series of actions. But, as soon as psychological determinism appears in the text, the fictional character becomes endowed with character: he acts in a certain way, *because* he is shy, weak, courageous, etc. There is no such thing as character without determinism of this type.

The construction of character is a compromise between difference and repetition. On the one hand, we must have continuity: the reader must construct the *same* character. This continuity is already given in the identity of the proper name, which is its principal function. At this point, any and all combinations become possible: all actions might illustrate the same character trait, or the behavior of a particular character might be contradictory, or he might change the circumstances of his life, or he might undergo profound character modification. . . . So many examples come to mind that it is not necessary to mention them. Here again the choices are more a function of the history of styles than of the idiosyncrasies of individual authors.

Character, then, can be an effect of reading; there exists a kind of reading to which every text can be subjected. But in fact, the effect is not arbitrary; it is no accident that character exists in the eighteenth- and nineteenth-century novel and not in Greek tragedy or the folktale. A text always contains within itself directions for its own consumption.

Construction as Theme

One of the difficulties in studying reading is due to the fact that reading is so hard to observe: introspection is uncertain, psycho-sociological investigation is tedious. It is therefore with a kind of relief that we find the work of construction represented in fiction itself, a much more convenient place for study.

Construction appears as a theme in fiction simply because it is impossible to refer to human life without mentioning such an essential activity. Based on the information he receives, every character must construct the facts and the characters around him; thus, he parallels exactly the reader who is constructing the imaginary universe from his own information (the text, and his sense of what is probable); thus, reading becomes (inevitably) one of the themes of the book.

The thematics of reading can, however, be more or less emphasized, more or less exploited as a technique in a given text. In *Adolphe*, it is only partially the case: only the ethical undecidability of action is emphasized. If we want to use fiction to study construction, we must choose a text where construction appears as one of the principal themes. Stendhal's *Armance* is a perfect example.

The entire plot of the novel is, in fact, subjugated to the search for knowledge. Octave's erroneous construction functions as the novel's point of departure: based upon Armance's behavior (an interpretation deducing a character trait from an action), Octave believes that Armance is too concerned with money. This initial misunderstanding is barely settled when it is followed by a second one, symmetrical to but the reverse of the first: Armance now believes that Octave is too concerned with money. This initial mix-up establishes the pattern of the constructions that follow. Next, Armance correctly constructs her feelings for Octave, but it takes Octave ten chapters before he discovers that his feelings for Armance are called *love*, not *friendship*. For five chapters Armance believes that Octave doesn't love her; Octave believes that Armance doesn't love him during the book's fifteen main chapters; the same misunderstanding is repeated toward the end of the novel. The characters spend all their time searching for the truth, in other words, constructing the facts and the events around them. The tragic ending of the love relationship is not caused by impotence, as has often been said, but by ignorance. Octave commits suicide because of an erroneous construction: he believes that Armance doesn't love him anymore. As Stendhal says suggestively, "Il manquait de pénétration et non pas de caractère."[8]

We can see from this brief summary that several aspects of the construction process can vary. One can be agent or patient, a sender or receiver of information; one can even be both. Octave is an agent when he pretends or reveals, a patient when he learns or is mistaken. It is also possible to construct a fact ("first-level" construction), or someone else's construction of that same fact ("second-level" construction). Thus, Armance rejects the idea of marrying Octave when she contemplates what others might think of her. "Je passerais dans le monde pour une dame de compagnie qui a séduit le fils de la maison. J'entends d'ici ce que dirait Mme. la duchesse d'Ancre et même les femmes les plus respectables, par exemple la marquise de Seyssins qui voit dans Octave un époux pour l'une de ses filles."[9] Octave likewise rejects the idea of suicide when he envisions the possible constructions of others. "Si je me tue, Armance sera compromise; toute la société recherchera curieusement pendant huit jours les plus petites circonstances de cette soirée; et chacun de ces messieurs qui étaient présents sera autorisé à faire un récit différent."[10]

What we learn above all in *Armance* is the fact that a construction can be either right or wrong; if all right constructions are alike (they are the "truth"), wrong constructions vary, as do the reasons behind them: flaws in the transmitted information. The simplest type is the case of total ignorance: until a certain point in the plot, Octave hides the very existence of a secret concerning him (active role); Armance is also unaware of its existence (passive role). Afterwards, the existence of the secret may be learned, but without any additional information; the receiver may then react by inventing his own "truth" (Armance suspects Octave of having killed someone). Illusion constitutes yet a further degree of faulty information: the agent does not dissemble, but misrepresents; the patient is not ignorant or unknowing, but is in error. This is the most prevalent situation in the novel: Armance camouflages her love for Octave, claiming she will marry someone else; Octave thinks that Armance feels only friendship toward him. One may be both agent and victim of the travesty; thus Octave hides from himself the fact that he loves Armance. Finally, the agent can reveal the truth, and the patient can apprehend it.

Ignorance, imagination, illusion, and truth: here are at least three stages through which the search for knowledge passes before leading a character to a definitive construction. Obviously, the same stages are possible in the reading process. Normally, the construction represented in the text is isomorphic to the one that takes the text as its point of departure. What the characters don't know, the reader doesn't know either; of course, other combinations are possible as well. In the detective novel, a Watson figure constructs like the reader, but a Sherlock Holmes constructs better: the two roles are equally necessary.

Other Readings

The flaws in the reading construction do not in any way undermine its existence: we do not stop constructing because of insufficient or erroneous information. On the contrary, defects such as these only intensify the construction process. Nevertheless, it is possible that construction does not occur, and that other types of reading supersede it.

Discrepancies between readings are not necessarily found where we might expect. For example, there does not seem to be a big difference between construction based on a literary text and construction based on a referential but nonliterary text. This resemblance was implied in the propositions I advanced in the previous section; in other words, the construction of characters (from nonliterary material) is analogous to the reader's construction (from the text of a novel). "Fiction" is not constructed any differently from "reality." Both the historian and the judge, the former on the basis of written documents, the latter on that of oral testimony, reconstitute the facts; in principle, they do not proceed differently from the reader of *Armance;* this does not mean there are no differences as far as details are concerned.

A more difficult question, beyond the scope of this study, concerns the relationship between construction based on verbal information and construction based on other perceptions. From the smell of roast lamb, we construct the roast; similarly for a sound, a view, etc. Piaget calls this phenomenon "the construction of reality." In these instances the differences may be much greater.

We do not have to stray very far from the novel to find material requiring another type of reading. There are many literary texts, nonrepresentative texts, that do not lead to any construction at all. Several types can be distinguished here. The most obvious is a specific type of poetry, generally called lyric poetry, which does not describe events, which evokes nothing exterior to it. The modern novel, in turn, requires a different reading; the text is still referential, but construction does not occur because, in a certain sense, it is undecidable. This effect is obtained by a dismantling of any one of the mechanisms necessary for construction as we have described them. To take just one example: we have seen that a character's identity was a function of the identity and inambiguity of his name. Suppose now that, in a text, the same character is evoked successively by several different names, first "John," then "Peter," then "the man with the black hair," then "the man with the blue eyes," without any indication of co-reference between the two expressions; or, suppose again that "John" designates not one, but three or four characters; each time, the result is the same: construction is no longer possible because the text is representatively undecidable. We see the difference here between such impossibility of construction and the defective constructions mentioned earlier: we shift from the misunderstood to the unknowable. This modern literary practice has its counterpart outside of literature: schizophrenic discourse. Schizophrenic discourse preserves its representative intention, yet through a series of inappropriate procedures (which I have tried to classify elsewhere) it renders construction impossible.

This is not the place to study other types of reading; noting their place beside reading as construction will suffice. To perceive and describe reading as construction is all the more necessary, given that the individual reader, far from being aware of the theoretical nuances it exemplifies, reads the same text in several ways at the same time, or at different times. His activity is so natural to him that it remains imperceptible. Therefore, it is necessary to learn how to construct reading—whether it be as construction or as deconstruction.

Notes

1 "I felt that she was better than I; I scorned myself for being unworthy of her. It is a terrible misfortune not to be loved when one loves; but it is a far greater misfortune to be loved passionately when one no longer loves." All translations from *Adolphe* and *Armance* by Susan Suleiman.

2 "I found in my father not a censor, but a cold and caustic observer who would first smile in pity and soon finish the conversation with impatience."

3 "Our host, who had chatted with a Neapolitan servant who attended on that stranger [i.e., Adolphe] without knowing his name, told me that he was not at all traveling out of curiosity, for he visited neither the ruins, nor the natural sites, nor the monuments, nor his fellow-men."

4 "I hate that vanity which is preoccupied only with recounting the evil it has done, which has the pretension of inspiring pity by describing itself, and which, hovering indestructibly above the ruins, analyzes itself instead of repenting."

5 "The object that escapes us is of necessity altogether different from the one that pursues us."

6 "I cannot recall, during the first eighteen years of my life, ever having had an hour's conversation with him. . . . I did not know then what timidity was."

7 "I told myself that I mustn't be overhasty, that Ellénore was not sufficiently prepared for the confession I was planning and that it was better to wait some more. Almost always, to live in peace with ourselves, we hide our weaknesses and impotence beneath the guise of calculations and systems: this satisfies the part of ourselves which is, as it were, the spectator of the other."

8 "He lacked penetration, not character."

9 "The world would regard me as a lady's companion who seduced the son of the house. I can already hear what the duchesse d'Ancre would say, or even more respectable women like the marquise de Seyssins, who sees in Octave a husband for one of her daughters."

10 "If I kill myself, Armance will be compromised. All of society will spend a week in tracking down the most minute circumstances of this evening; and every one of these gentlemen who were present will be authorized to give a different account of what happened."

27

The Literature of Replenishment

JOHN BARTH

John Barth states that "The Literature of Replenishment" (1980) is "meant as a companion and corrective" to "The Literature of Exhaustion" (1967). In the earlier essay Barth took a pessimistic view of late modernist literature. In "The Literature of Replenishment," he takes a more positive view of what he calls postmodernist literature. Barth begins by naming some of postmodernism's practitioners, such as himself, William Gass, John Hawkes, Donald Barthelme, Robert Coover, Thomas Pynchon, and Kurt Vonnegut, Jr. But even providing a list proves troublesome, much less attempting a definition. By its very nature, the term "postmodernism" requires some agreement about "modernism": a literary mode from which "postmodernism" proceeds and against which it reacts.

Barth attempts to define his term by beginning with Gerald Graff's delineation of modernism and discussing the ways in which postmodernism departs from it. The key to understanding modernism is "that one cardinal preoccupation of the modernists was the problematics, not simply of language, but of the medium of literature." For Barth, modernism was a repudiation of what Roland Barthes calls "bourgeois" fiction, and while postmodernism in part repudiates that repudiation, literature cannot simply consist of a movement of negations. Instead, Barth states: "My ideal postmodernist author neither merely repudiates nor merely imitates either his twentieth-century modernist parents or his nineteenth-century premodernist grandparents. . . . The ideal postmodernist novel will somehow rise above the quarrel between realism and irrealism, formalism and 'contentism,' pure and committed literature, coterie fiction and junk fiction." He ends his essay with the hope that postmodernist fiction may eventually be recognized as "a literature of replenishment."

John Barth (b. 1930), who teaches English and creative writing at Johns Hopkins University, has been hailed as one of America's leading "postmodernists," having published such novels as *Giles Goat-Boy* (1966), *The End of the Road* (1967), *The Sot-Weed Factor* (1967), and, more recently, *Sabbatical: A Romance* (1982), as well as numerous short stories.

The word is not yet in our standard dictionaries and encyclopedias, but since the end of World War II, and especially in the United States in the latter 1960s and the 1970s, "postmodernism" has enjoyed a very considerable currency, particularly with regard to our contemporary fiction. There are university courses in the American postmodernist novel; at least one quarterly journal is devoted exclusively to the discussion of postmodernist literature; at the University of Tübingen last June (1979), the annual meeting of the Deutsche Gesellshaft für Amerikastudien took as its theme "America in the 1970s," with particular emphasis on American postmodernist writing. Three alleged practitioners of that mode—William Gass, John Hawkes, and myself—were even there as live exhibits. The December annual convention of the Modern Language Association, just held in San Francisco, likewise scheduled a symposium on "the self in postmodernist fiction," a subtopic that takes the larger topic for granted.

From all this, one might innocently suppose that such a creature as postmodernism, with defined characteristics, is truly at large in our land. So I myself imagined when, in preparation for the Tübingen conference, and in response to being frequently labeled a postmodernist writer, I set about to learn what postmodernism is. I had a sense of *déjà vu*: About my very first published fiction, a 1950 undergraduate effort published in my university's quarterly magazine, a graduate-student critic wrote: "Mr. Barth alters that modernist

"The Literature of Replenishment," originally published in the *Atlantic*, January 1980, is reprinted from John Barth, *The Friday Book*, by permission of The Putnam Publishing Group. Copyright 1984 John Barth.

dictum, 'the plain reader be damned': He removes the adjective." Could that, I wondered now, be postmodernism?

What I quickly discovered is that while some of the writers labeled as postmodernists, myself included, may happen to take the label with some seriousness, a principal activity of postmodernist critics (also called "metacritics" and "paracritics"), writing in postmodernist journals or speaking at postmodernist symposia, consists in disagreeing about what postmodernism is or ought to be, and thus about who should be admitted to the club—or clubbed into admission, depending upon the critic's view of the phenomenon and of particular writers.

Who are the postmodernists? By my count, the American fictionists most commonly included in the canon, besides the three of us at Tübingen, are Donald Barthelme, Robert Coover, Stanley Elkin, Thomas Pynchon, and Kurt Vonnegut, Jr. Several of the critics I read widen the net to include Saul Bellow and Norman Mailer, different as those two writers would appear to be. Others look beyond the United States to Samuel Beckett, Jorge Luis Borges, and the late Vladimir Nabokov as engendering spirits of the "movement"; others yet insist upon including the late Raymond Queneau, the French "new novelists" Nathalie Sarraute, Michel Butor, Alain Robbe-Grillet, Robert Pinget, Claude Simon, and Claude Mauriac, the even newer French writers of the *Tel Quel* group, the Englishman John Fowles, and the expatriate Argentine Julio Cortázar. Some assert that such filmmakers at Michelangelo Antonioni, Federico Fellini, Jean-Luc Godard, and Alain Resnais are postmodernists. I myself will not join any literary club that doesn't include the expatriate Colombian Gabriel García Márquez and the semi-expatriate Italian Italo Calvino, of both of whom more presently. Anticipations of the "postmodernist literary aesthetic" have duly been traced through the great modernists of the first half of the twentieth century—T. S. Eliot, William Faulkner, André Gide, James Joyce, Franz Kafka, Thomas Mann, Robert Musil, Ezra Pound, Marcel Proust, Gertrude Stein, Miguel de Unamuno, Virginia Woolf—through *their* nineteenth-century predecessors—Alfred Jarry, Gustave Flaubert, Charles Baudelaire, Stéphane Mallarmé, and E. T. A. Hoffmann—back to Laurence Stern's *Tristram Shandy* (1767) and Miguel de Cervantes's *Don Quixote* (1615).

On the other hand, among certain commentators the sifting gets exceedingly fine. Professor Jerome Klinkowitz of Northern Iowa, for

example, hails Barthelme and Vonnegut as the exemplary "postcon-
temporaries" of the American 1970s and consigns Pynchon and myself to some 1960ish outer darkness. I regard the novels of John
Hawkes as examples of fine late modernism rather than of postmodernism (and I admire them no less for that). Others might regard
most of Bellow, and Mailer's *The Naked and the Dead*, as comparatively *pre*modernist, along with the works of such more consistently
traditionalist American writers as John Cheever, Wallace Stegner,
William Styron, or John Updike, for example (the last of whom,
however, Ihab Hassan calls a modernist), or those of most of the
leading British writers of this century (as contrasted with the Irish),
or those of many of our contemporary American women writers of
fiction, whose main literary concern, for better or worse, remains the
eloquent issuance of what the critic Richard Locke has called "secular
news reports." Even among the productions of a given writer, distinctions can be and often are invoked. Joyce Carol Oates writes all
over the aesthetical map. John Gardner's first two published novels
I would call distinctly modernist works; his short stories dabble in
postmodernism; his polemical nonfiction is aggressively reactionary.
Italo Calvino, on the other hand, began as an Italian new-realist (in
The Path to the Nest of Spiders, 1947) and matured into an exemplary postmodernist (with e.g., *Cosmicomics*, 1965, and *The Castle
of Crossed Destinies*, 1969) who on occasion rises, sinks, or merely
shifts to modernism (e.g., *Invisible Cities*, 1972). My own novels
and stories seem to me to have both modernist and postmodernist
attributes, even occasional premodernist attributes.

One certainly does have a sense of having been through this before. Indeed, some of us who have been publishing fiction since the
1950s have had the interesting experience of being praised or damned
in that decade as existentialists and in the early 1960s as black
humorists. Had our professional careers antedated the Second World
War, we would no doubt have been praised or damned as modernists,
in the distinguished company listed above. Now we are praised or
damned as postmodernists.

Well, but what *is* postmodernism? When one leaves off the mere
recitation of proper names, and makes due allowance for the differences among any given author's works, do the writers most often
called postmodernist share any aesthetic principles or practices as

significant as the differences between them? The term itself, like "post-impressionism," is awkward and faintly epigonic, suggestive less of a vigorous or even interesting new direction in the old art of storytelling than of something anticlimactic, feebly following a very hard act to follow. One is reminded of the early James Joyce's fascination with the word *gnomon* in its negative geometrical sense: the figure that remains when a parallelogram has been removed from a similar but larger parallelogram with which it shares a common corner.

My Johns Hopkins colleague Professor Hugh Kenner, though he does not use the term postmodernist, clearly feels that way in his study of American modernist writers (*A Homemade World*, 1975): After a chapter on William Faulkner entitled "The Last Novelist," he dismisses Nabokov, Pynchon, and Barth with a sort of sigh. The late John Gardner goes even farther in his tract *On Moral Fiction* (1978), an exercise in literary kneecapping that lumps modernists and postmodernists together without distinction and consigns us all to Hell with the indiscriminate fervor characteristic of late converts to the right. Irving Howe (*The Decline of the New*, 1970) and George P. Elliott (*The Modernist Deviation*, 1971) would applaud— Professor Howe perhaps less enthusiastically than Professor Elliott. Professor. Gerald Graff of Northwestern University, writing in *Tri-Quarterly* in 1975, takes a position somewhat similar to Kenner's, as the titles of two of his admirable essays make clear: "The Myth of the Postmodernist Breakthrough" (*Tri-Quarterly* 26) and "Babbitt at the Abyss" (*Tri-Quarterly* 33). Professor Robert Alter of Berkeley, in the same magazine, subtitles *his* essay on postmodernist fiction "reflections on the aftermath of modernism." Both critics proceed to a qualified sympathy for what they take to be the postmodernist program (as does Professor Ihab Hassan of the University of Wisconsin-Milwaukee in his 1971 study *The Dismemberment of Orpheus: Towards a Postmodern Literature*), and both rightly proceed *from* the premise that that program is in some respects an extension of the program of modernism, in other respects a reaction against it. The term *postmodernism* clearly suggests both; any discussion of it must therefore either presume that modernism in its turn, at this hour of the world, needs no definition—surely everybody knows what modernism is!—or else must attempt after all to define or redefine that predominant aesthetic of Western literature (and music, painting, sculpture, architecture, and the rest) in the first half of this century.

Professor Alter takes the former course: His aforementioned essay opens with the words: "Over the past two decades, as the high tide of modernism ebbed and its masters died off . . ." and proceeds without further definition to the author's reflections upon the ensuing low tide. Professor Graff, on the other hand, borrowing from Professor Howe, makes a useful quick review of the conventions of literary modernism before discussing the mode of fiction which, in his words, "departs not only from realistic conventions but from modernist ones as well."

It is good that he does, for it is not only *post*modernism that lacks definition in our standard reference books. My *Oxford English Dictionary* attests *modernism* to 1737 (Jonathan Swift, in a letter to Alexander Pope) and *Modernist* to 1588, but neither term in the sense we mean. My *American Heritage Dictionary* (1973) gives as its fourth and last definition of *modernism* "the theory and practice of modern art," a definition which does not take us very far into our American Heritage. My *Columbia Encyclopedia* (1975) discusses modernism only in the theological sense—the reinterpretation of Christian doctrine in the light of modern psychological and scientific discoveries—and follows this with an exemplary entry on *el modernismo,* a nineteenth-century Spanish literary movement which influenced the "Generation of '98" and inspired the *ultraísmo* of which Jorge Luis Borges was a youthful exponent. Neither my *Reader's Encyclopedia* (1950) nor my *Reader's Guide to Literary Terms* (1960) enters *modernism* by any definition whatever, much less *postmodernism*.

Now, as a working writer who cut his literary teeth on Eliot, Joyce, Kafka, and the other great modernists, and who is currently branded as a postmodernist, and who in fact has certain notions, no doubt naïve, about what that term might conceivably mean if it is to describe anything very good very well, I am grateful to the likes of Professor Graff for not regarding his categories as self-defining. It is quite one thing to compare a line of Verdi or Tennyson or Tolstoy with a line of Stravinsky or Eliot or Joyce and to recognize that you have put the nineteenth century behind you: "Happy families are all alike; every unhappy family is unhappy in its own way" (Leo Tolstoy, *Anna Karenina*, tr. Constance Garnett). ". . . riverrun, past Eve's and Adam's, from swerve of shore to bend of bay, brings us by a commodius vicus of recirculation back to Howth Castle and Environs" (James Joyce, *Finnegans Wake*). It is quite another thing to characterize the differences between those two famous opening sentences, to itemize the aesthetic principles—premodernist and modernist—from which each issues, and then to proceed to a great *post*modernist opening sentence and show where its aesthetics resemble and differ from those of its parents, so to speak, and those of its grandparents, respectively: "Many years later, as he faced the firing squad, Colonel Aureliano Buendia was to remember that distant afternoon when his father took him to discover ice" (Gabriel García Márquez, *One Hundred Years of Solitude*, tr. Gregory Rabassa).

Professor Graff does not do this, exactly, though no doubt he could if pressed. But I shall borrow his useful checklist of the characteristics of modernist fiction, add a few items to it, summarize as typical his and Professor Alter's differing characterizations of *post*modernist fiction, disagree with them respectfully in some particulars, and then fall silent, except as a storyteller.

The ground motive of modernism, Graff asserts, was criticism of the nineteenth-century bourgeois social order and its world view. Its artistic strategy was the self-conscious overturning of the conventions of bourgeois realism by such tactics and devices as the substitution of a "mythical" for a "realistic" method and the "manipulation of conscious parallels between contemporaneity and antiquity" (Graff is here quoting T. S. Eliot on James Joyce's *Ulysses*); also the radical disruption of the linear flow of narrative, the frustration of conventional expectations concerning unity and coherence of plot and character and the cause-and-effect "development" thereof, the deployment of ironic and ambiguous juxtapositions to call into question the moral and philosophical "meaning" of literary action, the adoption of a tone of epistemological self-mockery aimed at the naïve pretensions of bourgeois rationality, the opposition of inward consciousness to rational, public, objective discourse, and an inclination to subjective distortion to point up the evanescence of the objective social world of the nineteenth-century bourgeoisie.

This checklist strikes me as reasonable, if somewhat depressing from our historical perspective. I would add to it the modernists' insistence, borrowed from their romantic forebears, on the special, usually alienated role of the artist in his society, or outside it: James Joyce's priestly, self-exiled artist-hero; Thomas Mann's artist as charlatan, or mountebank; Franz Kafka's artist as anorexic, or bug. I would add too, what is no doubt implicit in Graff's catalogue, the modernists' foregrounding of language and technique as opposed to straightforward traditional "content": We remember Thomas Mann's remark (in *Tonio Kröger*, 1903), ". . . what an artist talks *about* is never the main point"; a remark which echoes Gustave Flaubert's to Louise Colet in 1852—". . . what I could like to do . . . is write a book about nothing . . ."—and which anticipates Alain Robbe-Grillet's *obiter dictum* of 1957: ". . . the genuine writer has nothing to say . . . He has only a way of speaking." Roland Barthes sums up this fall from innocence and ordinary content on the part of modernist literature in *Writing Degree Zero* (1953): ". . . the whole of literature, from Flaubert to the present day, became the problematics of language."

This is French hyperbole: It is enough to say that one cardinal preoccupation of the modernists was the problematics, not simply of language, but of the medium of literature.

Now, for Professor Alter, Professor Hassan, and others, *post-*modernist fiction merely emphasizes the "performing" self-consciousness and self-reflexiveness of modernism, in a spirit of cultural subversiveness and anarchy. With varying results, they maintain, postmodernist writers write a fiction that is more and more about itself and its processes, less and less about objective reality and life in the world. For Graff, too, postmodern fiction simply carries to its logical and questionable extremes the antirationalist, antirealist, antibourgeois program of modernism, but with neither a solid adversary (the bourgeois having now everywhere co-opted the trappings of modernism and turned its defiant principles into mass-media kitsch) nor solid moorings in the quotidian realism it defines itself against. From this serious charge Graff exempts certain postmodernist satire, in particular the fiction of Donald Barthelme, Saul Bellow, and Stanley Elkin, as managing to be vitalized by the same kitschy society that is its target.

I must say that all this sounds persuasive to me—until I examine more closely what I'm so inclined to nod my head yes to.

It goes without saying that critical categories are as more or less fishy as they are less or more useful. I happen to believe that just as an excellent teacher is likely to teach well no matter what pedagogical theory he suffers from, so a gifted writer is likely to rise above what he takes to be his aesthetic principles, not to mention what *others* take to be his aesthetic principles. Indeed, I believe that a truly splendid specimen in whatever aesthetic mode will pull critical ideology along behind it, like an ocean liner trailing seagulls. Actual artists, actual texts, are seldom more than more or less modernist, postmodernist, formalist, symbolist, realist, surrealist, politically committed, aesthetically "pure," "experimental," regionalist, internationalist, what have you. The particular work ought always to take primacy over contexts and categories. On the other hand, art lives in human time and history, and general changes in its modes and materials and concerns, even when not obviously related to changes in technology, are doubtless as significant as the changes in a culture's general attitudes, which its arts may both inspire and reflect. Some are more or less trendy and superficial, some may be indicative of more or less deep malaises, some perhaps healthy correctives of or reactions against such malaises. In any case, we can't readily discuss what artists aspire to do and what they end up doing except in terms of aesthetic categories, and so we should look further at this approximately shared impulse called postmodernism.

In my view, if it has no other and larger possibilities than those noted by, for example, Professors Alter, Graff, and Hassan, then postmodernist writing is indeed a kind of pallid, last-ditch decadence, of no more than minor symptomatic interest. There is no lack of actual texts illustrative of this view of the "postmodernist breakthrough"; but that is only to remind us that what Paul Valéry remarked of an earlier generation applies to ours as well: "Many ape the postures of modernity, without understanding their necessity." In my view, the proper program for postmodernism is neither a mere extension of the modernist program as described above, nor a mere intensification of certain aspects of modernism, nor on the contrary a wholesale subversion or repudiation of either modernism or what I'm calling premodernism: "traditional" bourgeois realism.

To go back a moment to our catalogue of the field-identification marks of modernist writing: Two other conspicuous ones are not yet there acknowledged, except by implication. On the one hand, James Joyce and the other great modernists set very high standards of artistry, no doubt implicit in their preoccupation with the special remove of the artist from his or her society. On the other hand, we have their famous relative difficulty of access, inherent in their anti-linearity, their aversion to conventional characterization and cause-and-effect dramaturgy, their celebration of private, subjective experience over public experience, their general inclination to "metaphoric" as against "metonymic" means. (But this difficulty is *not* inherent, it is important to note, in their high standards of craftsmanship.)

From this relative difficulty of access, what Hassan calls their aristocratic cultural spirit, comes of course the relative unpopularity of modernist fiction, outside of intellectual circles and university curricula, by contrast with the fiction of, say, Dickens, Twain, Hugo, Dostoevsky, Tolstoy. From it comes also and notoriously the engenderment of a necessary priestly industry of explicators, annotators, allusion-chasers, to mediate between the text and the reader. If we need a guide, or a guidebook, to steer us through Homer or Aeschylus, it is because the world of the text is so distant from our own, as it presumably was not from Aeschylus's and Homer's original audiences. But with *Finnegans Wake* or Ezra Pound's *Cantos* we need a guide because of the inherent and immediate difficulty of the text. We are told that Bertolt Brecht, out of socialist conviction, kept on his writing desk a toy donkey bearing the sign *Even I must understand it;* the high modernists might aptly have put on their desks a professor-of-literature doll bearing, unless its specialty happened to be the literature of high modernism, the sign *Not even I can understand it.*

I do not say this in deprecation of these great writers and their sometimes brilliant explicators. If modernist works are often forbidding and require a fair amount of help and training to appreciate, it does not follow that they are not superbly rewarding, as climbing Mount Matterhorn must be, or sailing a small boat around the world. To return to our subject: Let us agree with the commonplace that the rigidities and other limitations of nineteenth-century bourgeois realism, in the light of turn-of-the-century theories and discoveries in physics, psychology, anthropology, technology, etc., prompted or fueled the great adversary reaction called modernist art—which came to terms with our new ways of thinking about the world at the frequent expense of democratic access, of immediate or at least ready delight, and often of political responsibility (the politics of Eliot, Joyce, Pound, Nabokov, and Borges, for example, are notoriously inclined either to nonexistence or to the far right). But in North America, in western and northern Europe, in the United Kingdom, in Japan, and in some of Central and South America, at least, these nineteenth-century rigidities are virtually no more. The modernist aesthetic is in my opinion unquestionably the characteristic aesthetic of the first half of our century—and in my opinion it *belongs* to the first half of our century. The present reaction against it is perfectly understandable and to be sympathized with, both because the modernist coinages are by now more or less debased common currency and because we really don't *need* more *Finnegans Wakes* and *Pisan Cantos*, each with its staff of tenured professors to explain it to us.

But I deplore the artistic and critical cast of mind that repudiates the whole modernist enterprise as an aberration and sets to work as if it hadn't happened; that rushes back into the arms of nineteenth-century middle-class realism as if the first half of the twentieth century hadn't happened. It *did* happen: Freud and Einstein and two world wars and the Russian and sexual revolutions and automobiles and airplanes and telephones and radios and movies and urbanization, and now nuclear weaponry and television and microchip technology and the new feminism and the rest, and except as readers there's no going back to Tolstoy and Dickens. As the Russian writer Evgeny Zamyatin was already saying in the 1920s (in his essay *On Literature, Revolution, and Entropy*): "Euclid's world is very simple, and Einstein's world is very difficult; nevertheless, it is now impossible to return to Euclid's."

On the other hand, it is no longer necessary, if it ever was, to repudiate *them*, either: the great premodernists. If the modernists, carrying the torch of romanticism, taught us that linearity, rationality, consciousness, cause and effect, naïve illusionism, transparent language, innocent anecdote, and middle-class moral conventions are not the whole story, then from the perspective of these closing decades of our century we may appreciate that the contraries of those things are not the whole story either. Disjunction, simultaneity, irrationalism, anti-illusionism, self-reflexiveness, medium-as-message, political olympianism, and a moral pluralism approaching moral entropy—these are not the whole story either.

A worthy program for postmodernist fiction, I believe, is the synthesis or transcension of these antitheses, which may be summed up as premodernist and modernist modes of writing. My ideal postmodernist author neither merely repudiates nor merely imitates either his twentieth-century modernist parents or his nineteenth-century premodernist grandparents. He has the first half of our century under his belt, but not on his back. Without lapsing into moral or artistic simplism, shoddy craftsmanship, Madison Avenue venality, or either false or real naïveté, he nevertheless aspires to a fiction more democratic in its appeal than such late-modernist marvels (by my definition) as Beckett's *Texts for Nothing* or Nabokov's *Pale Fire*. He may not hope to reach and move the devotees of James Michener and Irving Wallace—not to mention the great mass of television-addicted non-readers. But he *should* hope to reach and delight, at least part of the time, beyond the circle of what Mann used to call the Early Christians: professional devotees of high art.

I feel this in particular for practitioners of the novel, a genre whose historical roots are famously and honorably in middle-class popular culture. The ideal postmodernist novel will somehow rise above the quarrel between realism and irrealism, formalism and "contentism," pure and committed literature, coterie fiction and junk fiction. Alas for professors of literature, it may not need as much *teaching* as Joyce's or Nabokov's or Pynchon's books, or some of my own. On the other hand, it will not wear its heart on its sleeve, either; at least not its whole heart. (In a recent published exchange between William Gass and John Gardner, Gardner declares that he wants everybody to love his books; Gass replies that he would no more want his books to be loved by everybody than he'd want his daughter to be loved by everybody, and suggests that Gardner is confusing love with promiscuity.) My own analogy would be with good jazz or classical music: One finds much on successive listenings or close examination of the score that one didn't catch the first time through; but the first time through should be so ravishing—and not just to specialists—that one delights in the replay.

Lest this postmodern synthesis sound both sentimental and impossible of attainment, I offer two quite different examples of works which I believe approach it, as perhaps such giants as Dickens and Cervantes may be said to anticipate it. The first and more tentative example (it is not meant to be a blockbuster) is Italo Calvino's *Cosmicomics* (1965): beautifully written, enormously appealing space-age fables—"perfect dreams," John Updike has called them—whose materials are as modern as the new cosmology and as ancient as folktales, but whose themes are love and loss, change and permanence, illusion and reality, including a good deal of specifically Italian reality. Like all fine fantasists, Calvino grounds his flights in local, palpable detail: Along with the nebulae and the black holes and the lyricism, there is a nourishing supply of pasta, bambini, and good-looking women sharply glimpsed and gone forever. A true postmodernist, Calvino keeps one foot always in the narrative past—characteristically the Italian narrative past of Boccaccio, Marco Polo, or Italian fairy tales—and one foot in, one might say, the Parisian structuralist present; one foot in fantasy, one in objective reality, etc. It is appropriate that he has, I understand, been chastized from the left by the Italian communist critics and from the right by the Italian Catholic critics; it is symptomatic that he has been praised by fellow authors as divergent as John Updike, Gore Vidal, and myself. I urge everyone to read Calvino at once, beginning with *Cosmicomics* and going right on, not only because he exemplifies my postmodernist program, but because his fiction is both delicious and high in protein.

An even better example is Gabriel García Márquez's *One Hundred Years of Solitude* (1967): as impressive a novel as has been written so far in the second half of our century and one of the splendid specimens of that splendid genre from any century. Here the synthesis of straightforwardness and artifice, realism and magic and myth, political passion and nonpolitical artistry, characterization and caricature, humor and terror, are so remarkably sustained that one recognizes with exhilaration very early on, as with *Don Quixote* and *Great Expectations* and *Huckleberry Finn*, that one is in the presence of a masterpiece not only artistically admirable, but humanly wise, lovable, literally marvelous. One had almost forgotten that new fiction could be so *wonderful* as well as so merely important. And the question whether my program for postmodernism is achievable goes happily out the window, like one of García Márquez's characters on flying carpets. Praise be to the Spanish language and imagination! As Cervantes stands as an exemplar of premodernism and a great precursor of much to come, and Jorge Luis Borges as an exemplar of *dernier cri* modernism and at the same time as a bridge between the end of the nineteenth century and the end of the twentieth, so Gabriel García Márquez is in that enviable succession: an exemplary post-modernist and a master of the storyteller's art.

A dozen years ago I published in these pages a much-misread essay called "The Literature of Exhaustion," occasioned by my admiration for the stories of Señor Borges and by my concern, in that somewhat apocalyptic place and time, for the ongoing health of narrative fiction. (The time was the latter 1960s; the place Buffalo, N.Y., on a university campus embattled by tear-gassing riot police and tear-gassed Vietnam War protesters, while from across the Peace Bridge in Canada came Professor Marshall McLuhan's siren song that we "print-oriented bastards" were obsolete.) The simple burden of my essay was that the forms and modes of art live in human history and are therefore subject to used-upness, at least in the minds of significant numbers of artists in particular times and places: in other words, that artistic conventions are liable to be retired, subverted, transcended, transformed, or even deployed against themselves to generate new and lively work. I would have thought that point unexceptionable. But a great many people—among them, I fear, Señor Borges himself—mistook me to mean that literature, at least fiction, is *kaput;* that it has all been done already; that there is nothing left for contemporary writers but to parody and travesty our great predecessors in our exhausted medium—exactly what some critics deplore as post-modernism.

That is not what I meant at all. Leaving aside the celebrated fact that, with *Don Quixote,* the novel may be said to *begin* in self-transcendent parody and has often returned to that mode for its refreshment, let me say at once and plainly that I agree with Borges that literature can never be exhausted, if only because no single literary text can ever be exhausted—its "meaning" residing as it does in its transactions with individual readers over time, space, and language. I like to remind misreaders of my earlier essay that written literature is in fact about 4,500 years old (give or take a few centuries depending on one's definition of literature), but that we have no way of knowing whether 4,500 years constitutes senility, maturity, youth, or mere infancy. The number of splendid sayable things—metaphors for the dawn or the sea, for example—is doubtless finite; it is also doubtless very large, perhaps virtually infinite. In some moods we writers may feel that Homer had it easier than we, getting there early with his rosy-fingered dawn and his wine-dark sea. We should console ourselves that one of the earliest extant literary texts (an Egyptian papyrus of ca. 2000 B.C., cited by Walter Jackson Bate in his 1970 study *The Burden of the Past and the English Poet*) is a complaint by the scribe Khakheperresenb that he has arrived on the scene too late: "Would I had phrases that are not known, utterances that are strange, in new language that has not been used, free from repetition, not an utterance that has grown stale, which men of old have spoken."

What my essay "The Literature of Exhaustion" was really about, so it seems to me now, was the effective "exhaustion" not of language or of literature, but of the aesthetic of high modernism: that admirable, not-to-be-repudiated, but essentially completed "program" of what Hugh Kenner has dubbed "the Pound era." In 1966–67 we scarcely had the term *postmodernism* in its current literary-critical usage—at least I hadn't heard it yet—but a number of us, in quite different ways and with varying combinations of intuitive response and conscious deliberation, were already well into the working out, not of the next-best thing after modernism, but of the *best next* thing: what is gropingly now called postmodernist fiction; what I hope might also be thought of one day as a literature of replenishment.

28

Time Sequence in Spatial Fiction

IVO VIDAN

Ivo Vidan builds on Joseph Frank's conception of spatial form in order to examine "whether the very handling of the sequential character of a story can also produce spatial form or be a dominant contributory factor to it." Vidan makes a key distinction between earlier works and more modern ones: the former provide the connections between events and time periods, while the latter often rely on "collocation and juxtaposition" that require "the reader to construct a meaning out of seemingly loose elements." Thus, according to Vidan, modern works provide a greater freedom for "subjective interpretation"; or, in terms of Tzvetan Todorov's argument, spatial form encourages a greater variety of constructed readings than do more traditional forms.

Through a discussion of Joseph Conrad's *Lord Jim*, Vidan analyzes the relationship of chronological sequence and spatial form and the effect it has on reading. He concludes that "the natural sequence of occurrences has been transmuted into the simultaneous existence of the human quandary in which chronological stages and links and continuities lose significance: time has turned into space." Having established criteria for defining a work with spatial form, Vidan subdivides such works into four groups: "novels with a continuous fable that develops in an ascertainable way," "novels of subjective exploration that share many facets of lyrical organization largely based on the stream-of-consciousness technique," "the multivolume (or multipart) novel in which the examination of spatial form involves the temporal parallelism between the semiautonomous parts," and, "the novel of indeterminate sequentiality."

Vidan discusses only the first group in detail. He then defines three types of narrative organization within this group: "works making up a complex unity of narrative strata, internally connected through thematic recurrence," "works based on connections between narrative and memory," and, "works depending for their effect on the way in which separate strands of the narrative are collocated." He concludes his essay by suggesting that the twentieth century has witnessed a progression of effects beginning with the first of the four categories he outlined and developing toward the fourth, indeterminate sequentiality, in recent postmodernist fiction. We might want to ask ourselves whether such experimentation, particularly toward indeterminate, or open-ended forms represents a retreat from mimesis or an advance, as Virginia Woolf might perceive it, toward a more accurate rendering of reality and perception.

Ivo Vidan is professor of English and American literature at the University of Zagreb, Yugoslavia. He has published several books in Serbo-Croatian, such as *The Unreliable Narrator* and *The Stream of Consciousness Novel*, as well as essays in English on Conrad, nineteenth-century American literature, and comparativist topics.

In attacking pictorial poetry and allegorical painting, Lessing's *Laocoön*, says Joseph Frank, offered "a new approach to aesthetic form." Criticism, "instead of prescribing rules for art, was to explore the necessary laws by which art governs itself."[1]

Frank's own seminal concept of spatial form in modern literature develops, paradoxically, from Lessing's polarization between the spatial and the temporal arts. To insist on simultaneity in the perception of a literary work—a poem or a novel—may seem once again to confuse the natural media of artistic expression. Yet the non-naturalistic tendency in modern art, Frank shows, reduces perspectives to surfaces, and motion to a moment of stasis, and transforms "the historical imagination into myth" (p. 60). Sequentiality, which is the chief intrinsic convention of literature, therefore loses its axiomatic status. The development of a story or indeed of any complex utter-

"Time Sequence in Spatial Fiction," by Ivo Vidan, originally appeared in *Spatial Form in Narrative*, ed. Jeffrey R. Smitten and Ann Daghistany. Reprinted with permission of Cornell University Press, copyright 1981.

ance in time may seem to be the arrangement that spontaneously follows the nature of things. Our age, however, has become aware that the quiddity of an art need not overlap with the mode of its natural presentation. In Russia the so-called Formalist school produced in the twenties the concept of literariness, the purpose of which was to create a focus for research into the means of construction, the devices making up what is "literary" in a work of literature.[2] If the "subject" and the "fable" of a novel or story do not coincide,[3] this is because the author, in Henry James's phrase, did the thing in the way "that shall make it undergo most doing"[4] or, in Formalist terms, because a process of "defamiliarization" made the work "literary."[5]

It has been shown that the masters of apparently traditional, carelessly organized narration—Dostoevsky and Tolstoy—did not produce "loose and baggy monsters," but carefully structured, highly patterned art constructs. It has even been argued that the concept of spatial form fully applies to books like *Crime and Punishment*. This certainly extends the notion to works that, apart from containing "reflexive reference" or "linkages"[6] on the level of words or imagery, depend as large wholes primarily upon sinewy articulate plots.

But can the plot itself, or simply the story, be considered a factor of spatiality, of simultaneous perceptibility? Or is the plot rather the guarantee of continuous sequential organization, making the story a product primarily dominated by natural temporality irrespective of chronological loopings, twists of perspective, or mechanical shuffling of time units?

Formalists such as Victor Shklovsky have often touched upon the distortions of the natural passage of time in narrative construction. Yet time as a medium of perception, a necessary medium for the apprehension of the work in its natural continuities (with all their digressions), remains outside their field of interest. Literary "science," as they understand it, deals with architectonics and texture, not with effects, with the subjective correlative of the construct in the perceiver's mind.

Spatial form in fiction is obviously a matter of effect. If certain requirements are met, it is produced in the process of reading that necessarily takes place in a segment of mechanical time. Frank himself, however, emphasized only the thematic organization and the function of reflexive references and juxtapositions, and did not discuss the relationship of time sequences in the inner organization of fiction. The idea of spatial form is usually associated with the novel as a poem or as a composition dominated by the recurrence and juxtaposition of verbal motifs, operative words, and key themes. There the recurrent elements produce spatiality in spite of all the variations, development, semantic shifts, whether we deal with the radiating "lighthouse" or a punning "throw away." But "verbal space acquires consistency as the stylistic rendering of the text becomes apparent: reiteration, allusion, parallelism, and contrast relate some parts of the narration to others, and the construction imposes itself on the reader through the action constituted by the reading."[7] What I will examine is whether the very handling of the sequential character of a story can also produce spatial form or be a dominant contributory factor to it. If so, then what are the requirements for such a form to appear? And what different models in the history of fiction can one adduce as evidence?

Having defined the aim of my inquiry, a further, basic question has to be put: can one in principle distinguish novels dominated by spatial form from those that are not? In order to understand later sections of any narrative, we must connect their content with that of the earlier sections, thereby establishing reflexive reference on the level of events, character features, etc. But the reflexive reference here is in the mind that constructs the story out of verbal signals, not necessarily in the reiteration of verbal signals. The sequential consistency makes the story easy to follow, and we are aware that here, too, we are dealing with a system of mutual relationships.

But there is a difference between traditional narrative wholes and more modern works, where on the one hand the story develops through chronological looping, and on the other the organization is not merely that of a story but of significant image patterns, of collocation and juxtaposition. In these latter ones a tendency is at work to expect the reader to construct a meaning out of seemingly loose elements. The story may still be comparatively simple or, again, it may be as difficult as it is in the most allusive works of the novel-as-poem type. In any case, we have encountered a tendency to rely on a subjective construction of meaning rather than on a fixed model opposed to that in traditional narrative.

The process by which a work of literature becomes knowledge is analyzed by the Polish philosopher Roman Ingarden in his *Vom Erkennen des literarischen Kunstwerks*.[8] This phenomenological thinker sees the work as a schematic construct to which its many cases of individual concretization have to be opposed. These concretizations are the result of each individual reading. The work is thus intersubjectively accessible and at the same time reproducible. These qualities relate it to the reading community, which means that the work allows itself to be surveyed from many individual angles: what remains in the mind is always a condensed Gestalt rather than the book or a complete part of the book that has been perused.

The very notion of spatial form may correspond to such a subjectively envisaged generalized shape. We may agree that there is no difference in principle between the way in which a traditional novel evolves into a Gestalt and that in which the more modern types create themselves in the reader's total perception. Yet there is something that distinguishes from the traditional model not only novels which grow on the principle of an organized system of imagery, but also those which have a distorted chronology. There is wider room for subjective interpretation, for deliberate construction.

Perhaps one can speak of spatial form in both cases, because consecutive narration has been broken up or distorted by the authorial voice or a fictional narrator, or complicated by internal or external relationships between two or more voices. In any case, the inner time continuity does not proceed in its natural order and is instead problematized both by the order substituted for it and by the way the reader's consciousness experiences this problematization. This requires that the story should be felt as being not spontaneously related, but deliberately organized through the medium of an implied narrator, or several narrators, or one personalized narrator.

Joseph Frank sees spatial form as a twentieth-century mode, and it is therefore symbolic that *Lord Jim*, published in the year that divides the nineteenth century from the twentieth, should be such a characteristic case in point. We might understand Jim as a young man whose life takes the form of an adventure story. Yet what, then, is the meaning of Marlow's presence in the story? Marlow is in the story in order to undergo the process of achieving an understanding of Jim. Primarily the book presents not a story or the portraiture or delineation of character, but a partial, tentative, ambiguous *assessment* of a character, which opens a range of possible interpretations.

The interaction between narrator and protagonist creates three levels of narration: Marlow's story to his audience, Jim's encounters and indirect contacts with Marlow, and Jim's experiences before and between his meetings with Marlow. At the moment Marlow begins speaking about Jim, the narrative on the other two levels has not been finished. In addition, the ultimate authorial voice, which related the first four chapters, takes over briefly between the two long Marlovian sequences.

The time scheme to which these four levels simultaneously contribute is necessarily intricate, and more so since, apart from Marlow's encounters with Jim, there are tributary stories or informative observations by many episodic characters and witnesses. Thus on levels two and three the partial stories coming from various sources build up a complex unity. The structure of *Lord Jim* has often been described and analyzed, and though one could find occasion to add to the existing comments of details in the story and to the critical explanation of their function in the whole, we should here concentrate on one question: should *Lord Jim* be seen and evaluated in terms of spatial form?

If it is impossible to answer this question without hesitation, this may be due not only to scholarly scruples against making statements about a work before it has been examined, but also to the fact that to apply the very notion of spatial form to an individual work may depend on our subjective evaluation of certain relevant elements in the work. Thus spatial form cannot be objectively ascertained but only felt as being intrinsically present or not. If this is so, what value does the notion actually possess? But perhaps one should not hurry with one's speculative conclusions. Let us instead look at the work under scrutiny.

Lord Jim was started by Conrad as a short story that was not to exceed 20 to 30 thousand words.[9] He thought of it more along the lines of "Youth" than of *Heart of Darkness*.[10] But though it became very long, it can still be considered as something short of a novel—a story of a developing personality or of a relationship between persons. Arthur Symons saw it as a plotless study in temperament.[11] This judgment can be compared with a statement by Conrad in a letter to his publisher that the reader "is following the development of *one* situation, only *one* really from beginning to end" so that the work did not really have "chapters in the usual sense each carrying the action a step further or embodying a whole episode." The divisions were meant to be no more than a device to enable the reader's attention to rest.[12] Yet Conrad himself said in an earlier letter that the story fell into two parts.[13] He also complained that its structure was "a little loose"[14] and called it in the Author's Note "a free and wandering tale." Despite the work's seemingly episodic composition, the modern reader can see it as a well-integrated whole: there are Jim's three jumps, which define the story that is the external concomitant of the psychological and moral issue; the parallel situations, like Jim's failure and Brierly's suicide; Jim's analogies with Brown; the pattern of his behavior on the *Patna* and at Patusan; and the consistency with which he assumes the consequences of his actions.

What, then, is the function of the complex time scheme? Does it make for this situational unity or does it work toward its disintegration? As has been mentioned, the real complexity of the time scheme is vertical rather than horizontal. Through the greatest part of the book three strata of time seem to be involved at each particular moment: the time of Marlow's actual narration, the time of his experience or interview with Jim or some subordinate character, and the time to which Marlow and his partner refer in their conversation. The frequent general reflections and the associations that direct the transition from one set of circumstances involved in Jim's story to another belong to the nearest and highest time level: to Marlow's actual narration, which has a chronological continuity. On the lowest level, all single items form their own continuity together. Thus Jim's personal history and Marlow's narration both proceed evenly. The shuffling occurs only in the middle stratum through the backslidings and foreshortenings occasioned by the vagrancy of Marlow's mind as he is telling the story. An effect of the time looping is that an exact chronology of events is sometimes impossible to establish, although its general outline becomes clear once we start to sort out details. "The novel is made up of recurrences in which each part of the story has already happened repeatedly when the reader first encounters it, either in someone's mind, or in someone's telling, or in the way it repeats other similar events in the same person's life or in the lives of others."[15] The actual order in time has been suppressed through the actual juxtaposition of episodes, minor incidents, and analytical recallings: the effect is one of simultaneous relevance. Sequence is transposed into coexistence.

This unconventional composition is profoundly motivated in a mimetic sense: this is how an articulate sailor might actually spin a yarn. Yet, like one of Yeats's Byzantine nightingales—artifacts that imitate natural birds—this novel is a highly contrived narrative structure, one that uses a number of sophisticated narrative devices in order to imitate reality.

The temporal succession could be analyzed at every associative link in Marlow's narration, and it could be demonstrated that the association is produced on the basis of analogy or of contrast, or of progress in time with an elision of insignificant phases. The important fact is that the sequence of events can be put into chronological order, though the text would have to be altered after such an operation. What would the story itself lose? Probably the effect upon the reader of Jim's personality, and of Marlow's experience of that personality and its fortune. One important aspect of the particular effect achieved by Conrad's art is the contemporaneity, the coexistence, the simultaneity of the relevance of all the details in that subtle and tenuously interconnected history. The natural sequence of occurrences has been transmuted into the simultaneous existence of the human quandary in which chronological stages and links and continuities lose significance: time has turned into space.

One might perhaps challenge the validity of such a simplification, but it would be fair to admit its comparative justification if, for instance, we glance at Conrad's preceding Marlow story, *Heart of Darkness* (1899). The chronology of the inner narrative in that work is not distorted; it is, in fact, perfectly regular, though one or two narrative hints as to the future effect of certain experiences intensify the atmosphere of expectation. *Heart of Darkness* is an account of progression in space and its accompanying insight into the nature of things. In spite of the spatial organization of a network of linkages, the overall effect is one of movement, even of history, not of permanence and independence from transmission in time!

The texture of both works contains a number of recurrent, thematically significant images, the shorter fiction certainly not fewer than the longer one. It follows that the particular spatial effect of *Lord Jim* must depend on the way in which the story has been handled. It might be that the form of *Lord Jim* was dictated by the fact that a narrator is coping with the crisis in another person's life and is speculating about its meaning. In *Heart of Darkness* the narrator's experience itself is the object of attention, and in order to keep its outlines clear, the historical method may have been incumbent. But it is impossible to substantiate the connection between the narrative focus and chronology.

What is more, Conrad's last Marlow novel, *Chance* (1912), in spite of its even more intricate structure (which removes the core of the story from the reader by yet another intermediate narrator), does not strike us as a spatial construct. Compared to *Lord Jim*, the apparatus of the narrator in *Chance* is, in fact, multiplied, and the object under observation is not so much a single hero as a particular situation involving more than one character. Most of the characters have a double role: they play a part in the story, but in addition every one of them communicates, more or less directly, his own observation about some stage of the story. Envisaged from the angle of structure, the relationship between Marlow and Jim is, in comparison, much simpler. Marlow's discoveries and his meditations coincide with the revelation of Jim's characters and his inner adventures. In *Chance* the relationship between the narrators themselves, that is, between characters only indirectly or partly connected with the central situation, is minutely observed and elaborated in detail, so that it practically becomes a subject for a separate novel. Therefore, the basic story, which unites all the characters, does not coincide with the history of its detection and comprehension. It takes a long time before it is realized that the former story has an autonomous course and that it is more than a pretext for an investigation of the character and behavior of the narrators and interpreters themselves. From this opposite angle, the narrators look as if they are parts of a superimposed machinery blurring the view and preventing access to the moral core of the story. Thus there appears to be a tension between content and form, substance and method.

Marlow's own procedure in *Chance* is not the same as that in *Lord Jim*. The story does not come to him in the course of his normal engagements; rather, it unfolds as evidence produced in a precisely established series of auditory sessions. What he does is rationally to reconstruct the case for Flora, to ascertain the facts from which her state of mind can be judiciously inferred; but in *Lord Jim* he participates in Jim's plight by feeling that he himself is personally involved, through the universal significance of what Jim does.

The irrelevance of the method in *Chance* in relation to the subject matter becomes obvious beyond any doubt in the second part of the book. Here Marlow is no longer a direct witness but merely retells, in an omniscient third-person manner, what he was told by Powell. In both parts, then, the method by which Marlow conducts his inquiry and by which he reproduces it must be intellectual and aloof. The whole book appears to be a misdirected effort to grasp and present a human situation which, being outside the scope of the author's most intimate moral preoccupations as well as his personal experiences, fascinated but did not temperamentally appeal to him. He uses it for a sentimental reassessment of some basic values in which he always wanted to believe: the moral superiority of the disciplined frankness of sea life against the suffocating complications on shore.

This lengthy analysis of the faults of a pretentious failed novel indicates that a necessary element for the achievement of the effect of spatiality—that is, the simultaneous significance of a novel in its total extension—may be the quality of realization, of illumination, of an intuitive awareness of its noumenal quality: the vision of significance that informs the whole story. This vision is present in *Heart of Darkness* too, yet it is experienced as being prepared in stages and then, at a moment of sudden insight, illuminates the path covered as well as the journey back and its consequences: "It was the farthest point of navigation and the culminating point of my experience. It seemed somehow to throw a kind of light on everything about me—and into my thoughts."[16]

My own reluctance to attribute spatiality as a dominating form to *Heart of Darkness* despite its texture and its admirably integrated set of symbols suggests that spatial form is a subjective category the application of which depends on individual appreciation. Does the work in question strike one more as an image of a complex *situation* or as that of an *enfolding* process?

If, according to the argument that has been put forward, *Heart of Darkness* basically does not belong to spatial fiction, this concept would apply even less to a novel like *Crime and Punishment*. Reflexive reference is not enough to create "spatial" fiction. What is needed is a way in which the temporal sequentiality of the story is neutralized by an appropriate abandonment of chronological presentation. *Lord Jim* appears to satisfy this requirement, though lack of space prevents me from demonstrating it at greater length.

In examining the function of time sequence in the creation of spatial form, the criteria established in studying *Lord Jim* may be applied to other novels to which this concept can be attributed. For heuristic purposes they may be divided into four groups:

1. Novels with a continuous fable that develops in an ascertainable way, however intricate their story might be. The intricacies in the composition are due to the narrator's difficulties in achieving psychological insight and coordinating the various characters' judgments, and even more to inescapable ambiguities that arise continually in the act of understanding. *Lord Jim* may be considered as a prototype in this group, and as interesting variants Ford's *The Good Soldier* and Faulkner's *Absalom, Absalom!* deserve separate study. An important subdivision in this group consists of works with an apparently comparable but basically simpler time structure, of which several will be briefly considered.

2. The novels of subjective exploration that share many facets of lyrical organization largely based on the stream-of-consciousness technique. The process of narration is not commented upon even in its omniscient portions. Instead, a large portion of the story coincides with the time-looping vagrancy of the characters' minds. The underlying story has no intrinsic significance, and the symbolic values that one feels in the text are due to the thematic interplay of connotations. This is true both of works based entirely on regular syntactic and lexical conjunctions, however personal and original, and of those relying largely on fragmentation, punning, and other types of verbal play. Proust and Joyce can be mentioned as extreme examples of the two possibilities, and theirs are the works usually cited as typical of spatial form in fiction.

3. The multivolume (or multipart) novel in which the examination of spatial form involves the temporal parallelism between the semi-autonomous parts that go into the production of one novel (like Faulkner's *The Sound and the Fury*) or an integrated series (like

Durrell's *Alexandria Quartet*). Each part in itself may belong to any of the other types or may not be spatial at all.

4. The novel of indeterminate sequentiality. This group includes many works belonging to the French *nouveau roman* and a large variety of experimental fiction that can be related to this structurally fascinating avant-garde tendency.

Some interesting and important works will share features of more than one group, and two, as models of different types, will be described later: a French one, Claude Simon's *Flanders Road*, and one from Latin America, *The Green House* by the Peruvian author Mario Vargas Llosa.

To deal with the problems of time sequence in all the four groups would far exceed the space at my disposal. It will be necessary to restrict this study to the first group, the only one in which the actual sequence of events, as played against the layers of fictional time in the organized narration, is in itself a key to the work's spatial organization.

How close Ford Madox Ford's *Good Soldier* (1915) is to *Lord Jim* becomes apparent when one considers a book Ford wrote even later, *Joseph Conrad: A Personal Remembrance* (1924). He maintains that that book is "a novel exactly on the lines of the formula that Conrad and the writer [i.e. Ford] evolved."[17] If you write of a character, "you must first get him in with a strong impression, and then work backwards and forwards over his past." According to his and Conrad's ideas, he maintains, a novel was to be "the rendering of an Affair. . . . the whole novel was to be an exhaustion of aspects," the end of the novel revealing "the psychological significance of the whole" (p. 137). The novel, as he had written a few years earlier, should render "one embroilment, one set of embarrassments, one human coil, one psychological progression."[18]

These general principles have obviously been extracted from the very techniques of *Lord Jim* and *The Good Soldier*. The cautious narrator is only one item in the complex structure of relativity—the gradual, subjectively directed revelation of fact. *The Good Soldier* is a more homogeneously woven pattern, a less dramatically evolving structure, than Conrad's, devoid as it is of Conradian bold strokes of unfrustrated melodrama. The narration, however, elaborates a human embroilment just as difficult to explicate as that of *Lord Jim*. Hesi-

tatingly, groping for facts, it gradually establishes circumstantial justification for the action and the narrator's experience of it. The rhythm
of events, the unity of occurrence, and the illumination that arises
cause the novel to be *one* total impression of the kind that Conrad's
work has been said to be.

The structure of relationships in *The Good Soldier* is perhaps not
subtler but is certainly even more complicated than that of Conrad's
novel. There is not just one axis of a give-and-take relationship between narrator and hero but a "little four-square coterie"[19] in which
the narrator has an equal share. The relationship between any two of
these characters is in constant flux, since with each of Ashburnham's
new love affairs the relationships toward his wife, his mistress, and
his mistress's husband are modified, and new tensions among the rest
of the group are introduced. Imperceptive, naive, even somewhat obtuse, the narrator, Dowell, in his "moral flabbiness"[20] is not—like
Marlow—the author's persona, who shares the author's values and
contributes to the overall pattern and its very limitations. Seemingly
erratic, the novel is beautifully composed: as in *Lord Jim*, the initial
narrative situation is not chronologically the last one from which an
ultimate retrospective can be given. Basically the story moves through
"piecework chronology,"[21] but each stage is part of a rich arabesque
of forward-pointing and backward-amplifying hints. Though the presentation is by no means static, it achieves at each moment some kind
of omnitemporal quality: all its phases coexist simultaneously in the
created novelistic space.

Absalom, Absalom! (1936) belongs to the same category of
spatial fiction as *Lord Jim* and *The Good Soldier*, but it constitutes a
different model, one in which the method of the earlier novels is even
more radically exemplified; and the notion of spatiality is as justified
as is possible in narrative works. For *Absalom, Absalom!* presents a
process of interpretation and discovery conducted by several narrators and not simply by one. Shreve and Quentin receive information
and opinions from Mr. Compson and from Rose Caulfield and integrate them with their own speculation, conjecture, and imaginative
reconstruction, and fill in the gaps.

Like the other two novels, this one contains an important development toward its very end, a development that takes place after the main part of the narrators' compound discourse has already been performed. Thus the very end of the novel coincides with a thematic thrust that somehow illuminates all the preceding action and lends it meaning. The main hero, Sutpen, is removed from almost all of the narrators' direct experience, and we know him less intimately than Jim or even Ashburnham. The layers of narration are more numerous than in the preceding spatial novels (for example, the experience of Sutpen, Rosa's story, Mr. Compson's comment, Quentin's retelling, Shreve's interpretation). Despite the fact that each narrator has a distinct tone or style (some of which have been associated by critics with different cultural epochs), the collective result of this mutual complementary effect appears as a unique story with a radically fragmented time scheme and a great deal of repetition with variation. A situation will be suddenly revealed and on later occasions returned to several times. Gradually it will be accounted for within the context of other situations, earlier and later.

Thus the narration shuttles to and fro, joining together events from all stages of the story; its general movement with its accompanying piecemeal interpretation and detection has been called a "circling in." The feeling of concentration is heightened by the fact that all that occurs takes place in a few houses or a few estates, within one narrow geographic region and during a definite period of historical crisis. Since the historical facts and atmosphere are psychologically relevant and directly motivate the behavior of characters, the story is an examination not only of Sutpen's relationships but also of the nature and meaning of the South as a cultural and historical entity. The biblical title and classical references contribute to the timeless significance of this historically circumscribed set of events.

The spatial quality of *Absalom, Absalom!* is created even by the novel's theme: the rise and fall of a mighty house as a metaphor of the historical destiny of the South. The story is informed by a philosophical vision: the central event that gives meaning to the South is the Civil War, and its moral core is the ambivalent feeling about the racial relationships that necessarily involve the guilt of self-aware oppressors. The mechanism of cause and effect loses its sequential character and is seen as a dynamic copresence of both poles. Any moment in the story can be felt as pointing to the past and as being pregnant with its own consequences. The fate of Jim and the tenuous contacts of the couples in *The Good Soldier* make simple stories compared to the complex interlinked relationships among narrators and actants—each person assuming both functions as we review layer upon layer in each situation in the story.

It would be possible to tell the story in linear form, but then the meaning of this copresence of events would be lost. Faulkner's narrative method is functionally related to his imagination and his vision of man. The story as it exists covers up the minor contradictions (slips by the author?), conflicting assertions, and inconsistencies that it contains. Yet to say that "any attempted summary of the plot of *Absalom* is . . . necessarily impossible" is itself an unnecessary exaggeration, even though the motives for Henry's killing of Bon are unclear. "Always the novel returns to one basic question: did Thomas Sutpen's second son kill the first because he had a quadroon mistress, or because the marriage to his sister would be incestuous, or because of the miscegenation?"[22] The story as it is told allows for this mystery to remain unknown because its three motifs radiate throughout the mores and the manners of the Faulknerian South far beyond the confines of this novel: they are a central knot in the spatial organization of *Absalom, Absalom!*

The logic of its specific form—and of the Modernist view of the complex of history—can be illuminated by a highly interesting external parallel: the structure of *Wuthering Heights* (1847). The function of Heathcliff is analogous to that of Sutpen, and the interconnections of the two narrators' accounts (those of Nelly Dean—ancestress of Rosa Caulfield!—and Mr. Lockwood) point toward a source of Faulkner's inspiration. There is, however, an important difference between the two novels: the fortunes of the two main generations are, in Emily Brontë's novel, never as completely entangled as they are in Faulkner's; a mellowed wisdom and a coming to terms with life is finally brought about—some kind of human growth and progress is effected, and it can be followed through the stages of Mr. Lockwood's sensible report. Heathcliff's Gothic demonism—parallel to Sutpen's—does not prevent conjectures from getting answered and the puzzling situations from being accounted for. This is why *Wuthering Heights*—a most unusual nineteenth-century novel, though in style and sensibility definitely belonging to the Romantic wake—does not create the kind of spatial form that we see in the beginning with *Lord Jim,* in spite of its superficial similarities in chronological distortion and interlocked narrative strands.

Side by side with this line one encounters throughout twentieth-century fiction works in which the story has a broken-up chronology, though it is simpler to follow than that of *Wuthering Heights*. Essentially they allow us to study spatial form in narrative in a purer form than do the more difficult examples that we have discussed, where leitmotifs and subjective narrative perspectives somewhat obscure the problem of pure narrative sequence. A model example of research in that illuminating category of spatial fiction is Jeffrey R. Smitten's examination of Conrad's *Secret Agent* (1907).[23] It is a novel that deserves the same attention as *Nostromo* (1904), which Albert J. Guerard sees as "a more radical example of spatial form than *Lord Jim*." His reason is that *Nostromo* does not pretend to be "the oral narrative of a free wandering memory."[24]

This means that the difficulties, even the possible arbitrariness of the author's handling of chronology, should be a quality in itself, and yet Guerard complains of the technical clumsiness in this "great but radically defective novel" (p. 203). Most of its several beginnings take place in the harbor of Sulaco, and so the moment when their various incidents happen blend in the reader's mind. "The Custom House is the solid immovable object on which the novel nearly founders" (p. 207). Yet "it could be argued . . . that the chronological dislocations and distortions of emphasis may reflect a theory of history as repetitive yet inconsecutive, devoid of reason, refusing to make sense. The method would then reflect the material in an extreme example of organic or imitative form" (p. 215). The very concentration of the action through many historical changes in a precisely delineated, narrow geographical area gives the reader the impression that the book is spatially organized.

The example of *Nostromo* seems to corroborate the opinion implied earlier in this essay that in novels where spatiality depends on the handling of the story more than on recurring thematic imagery, the term "spatial form" will largely be used impressionistically. And yet, again, the effect of worthwhile spatial organization cannot depend merely on a shuffling of chronology. Fitzgerald used retrospect creatively in *The Great Gatsby* (1925), though modeling the novel loosely on *Lord Jim* and *Heart of Darkness*, thus bringing about a less extreme innovation. In the first and still reprinted version of *Tender Is the Night* (1934)—a work less concentrated and elliptic—the retrospective composition seemed to the author to spoil the story line of the process of Dick Diver's degeneration and of the hourglass symmetry in the development of the two main characters.

When the author presents a story without intermediate narrators, the reader is more aware of the actual story line than when the story is conveyed in what is presented as the natural order in a narrator's mind. This can be illustrated by a novel in which the involuted order of sequences is explicitly demonstrated by the dates in the chapter headings, as it is in Aldous Huxley's *Eyeless in Gaza* (1934). The number of points in time that are presented is limited: the situations beginning on certain dates in 1902, 1912, 1926, 1933, and 1934 develop over the ensuing days or even months. Huxley's narrative is not as fluid as Conrad's, Ford's, or Faulkner's in the novels considered before; it is clear at each point whether we are reading a third-person account, a diary, or a direct confession. The story is one of linear growth, but there are five lines starting at different moments in historical time, each gradually developing. Glancing at the chapter headings, the reader knows that there are several strands removed in time and intermixed chronologically, but running parallel to one another. It is soon realized that an awareness of Anthony Beavis's relative maturity and of his opinions at each stage is necessary if we are to perceive the theme and its meaning.

But why the simultaneous development from the five initial points? And do they make for a unified field of coexisting strands of action, for spatial form? Indeed they do, because Anthony's embracing of mysticism—his growing insight and its ensuing commitment—is seen as part of one unique human situation: instead of a *Bildungsroman* we have an account of a pacifistic revelation that begins from various focuses that eventually fall into one. The technique, carefully calculated by its rationalistic author, works well, but one has the feeling that a single linear story would not have been utterly dissimilar from what Huxley actually achieved. The significance of its spatial effect should not be underrated, but it cannot be put in the same category with that of *Nostromo*, let alone *Lord Jim*, *The Good Soldier*, and *Absalom, Absalom!*

When, however, in Malcolm Lowry's *Under the Volcano* (1947) the action is concentrated within twenty-four hours, in a narrow area topographically and culturally reminiscent of *Nostromo*, its frequent retrospectives pertinent to the mood and behavior of the characters in the present produce authentic spatial form: this is a tragedy—displaying the last stage in the fall of the hero—with a unity of time, place, and action; but it is also a symbolic narrative that has been very consciously structured. In Robert Penn Warren's *All the King's Men* (1946), we are back with the fictional technique of narrator-toward-protagonist, as in Conrad, Ford, and Faulkner, but the verbal patterns are less taut and an abundance of realistic circumstantiality allows easier reading. The presentation of private lives in terms of public and political issues, of individual destiny in terms of historical significance, with the additional dimension of a parable from the past added: the Faulknerian inspiration contributes to our seeing the narrative interconnections as much more than technical adroitness. The retrospective telling with its gaps and significant detours makes the consequences and ultimate insights completely absorb the initial causes. However, the more relaxed the technique is and the more it concedes to traditional telling, the less fully does it seem to impress us as a spatial construct, and this applies to the whole series discussed.

On the basis of the foregoing analysis, one can speak of three types of narrative organization which, through their handling of time sequence, create spatial fiction with a continuous, ascertainable fable:

1. Works making up a complex unity of narrative strata, internally connected through thematic recurrence. The problem of interpreting what is recalled and narrated becomes itself one of the work's main themes (*Lord Jim, The Good Soldier, Absalom, Nostromo*).

2. Works based on connections between narrative and memory, where what is revealed in the retrospective portions becomes part of current memory (*Under the Volcano, All the King's Men*). The novels by Conrad, Ford, and Faulkner that belong to the first type also possess the characteristic feature of this one, while Warren's work partly possesses theirs.

3. Works depending for their effect on the way in which separate strands of the narrative are collocated. *Eyeless in Gaza* is a spatial fiction thanks to the author's handling of separate time sections on

what is essentially one and the same level of narrative. This feature occurs in other types of work, too, but plays a minor role in producing the effect of spatiality.

Though the handling of time in all three types is based on some aberration from linear temporality, the actual quantity of chronological looping is not decisive for the production of spatial form. Nor does it matter whether the time shifts belong to the sequential rhythm of the authorial voice or to the way in which personalized narrators relate the story. What is decisive is whether the order and relationship of time sequences functionally contribute to the impact of the novel's totality. In addition, a novel of this group, if it is to be experienced as spatial, must result in some kind of vision, an insight of universal relevance, perhaps in what Conrad means when he says through his narrator in *Under Western Eyes*—a novel not far from the spatial quality of some of those that we have discussed—that some "moral discovery . . . should be the object of every tale."[25] But this discovery—its structural significance has already been pointed out, in connection with *Heart of Darkness*—is not merely moral; it is deeper and more compelling. Smitten, in the context of his discussion of *The Secret Agent*, speaks of "an artistic pattern which resolves itself in a final stasis of illumination embracing at once all portions of the narrative."[26] In the present analysis this quality has not been stressed, for it has been frequently pointed out in earlier critical assessments of the works under consideration. It is a quality that these spatial fictions share with those we have called the novel-as-poem (Woolf, Proust, etc.). Smitten refers us to Robert Scholes and Robert Kellogg, according to whom in the twentieth century "plots began to be developed which were based on rearranging time so that the resolution became not so much a stasis of concluded action as a stasis of illumination."[27] Yet if the traditional novel ends in a stasis of concluded action and the novel-as-poem in a stasis of illumination, the spatial novel based on a continuous fable and on nonlinear narrative time achieves its resolution through both kinds of stasis.

———

In conclusion, let us briefly sum up our main findings. Spatial form in fiction is achieved either through a network of recurring motifs (when there is no continuing developing social or physical action in the forefront—basically this includes the mental action of reminiscence and anticipation), or through a pattern of forward-and-backward moving in time that plays against the chronological order of events. The two types do not exclude each other, but whereas Joseph Frank and most critics of modern literature have closely studied the first, we have tried here to concentrate on a general overview of the other.

Lord Jim was taken as a provisional general model. It has been shown that a narrative focus is important for the establishment of the nonchronological account of events, and that a basic situation radiating some kind of noumenous significance can be said to embody the main themes of such works.

It might be possible to define this group as spatial novels with a continuous story. Other types of spatial fiction I have classified in three further categories. Their features might now be briefly outlined in the light of the preceding analysis of the first and, genetically, earliest group.

In the second category belong works usually associated with the stream-of-consciousness method, though these seem to present only a special case within a somewhat large basic category or group that also includes Proust. Since no meaningful continuous story line can be worked out even when the recurring motifs are examined for that purpose, the stream-of-consciousness technique or the roaming memory by itself lends such works the status of spatial fiction. Yet since their spatiality does not depend on the story level, one would not apply to them the statement by Scholes and Kellogg that within twentieth-century narrative the achievement of a stasis of illumination means that "the missing pieces of the temporal jigsaw puzzle" are "all finally in place and the picture therefore complete."[28]

A third category consists of works made up of seemingly autonomous parts that roughly coincide in time but coexist in some kind of tension due to the different points of view and the ensuing different interpretations of facts. Chronology—and its distortions within such a cycle and its separate sections—is a significant aspect of the general perspective of these novels and the interrelationship of their parts.

The most radical experiments with time seem, however, to belong to the fourth category, which includes a wealth of new fictional structures thought out mainly in France or inspired by French technical innovations. In such works it is impossible to put events into any kind of even incomplete chronological order. The events described repeat themselves with variations: the actual level of fictional reality cannot be distinguished from illusions, remembrances, imaginings—so events themselves become recurring motifs, disturbing and misleading. This fourth group, except for the more extreme ambiguity of the motifs in it, is spatial in the sense of the stream-of-consciousness group but without the kind of symbolic reverberation that would give metaphoric significance to the action. The indeterminacy and lack of significance of the actual order may be an indication that spatial narrative fiction is dying into some new category for which the traditional genre names, like "novel" or "story," are no longer adequate.

The larger part of this essay has dealt with fiction in which the sequence of events is played against the layers of fictional time in the organized narration. This in itself is a key to the spatial organization of such works. These novels belong to a historical model that follows the traditional type of sequential fiction, usually realistic, occasionally with elements of fantasy. In literature in English we can identify its beginnings with the incipient Modernism of Conrad and see it achieve its culmination with Faulkner. Variations, inspired especially by Faulkner, occur later; examples range from Claude Simon in France to Mario Vargas Llosa in Peru. The spatial organization of new fictional forms that developed between and after the two world wars depends on what seems to be a logical extension of the principle commanding the spatial functioning of earlier types. One difference between the two main types has, however, to be recognized. When the attribute of spatiality is applied to works of the *Lord Jim* type, it seems largely to depend on a subjective interpretation of particular literary effects produced by the juxtaposition of distinct time segments and the repeated resumption of particular situations. More objectively evident signs of spatiality occur in the Modernist and post-Modernist use of collocation and juxtaposition of verbal motifs.[29]

Notes

1 Joseph Frank, "Spatial Form in Modern Literature," in his *The Widening Gyre: Crisis and Mastery in Modern Literature* (New Brunswick: Rutgers University Press, 1963), pp. 7, 8.

2 Ewa M. Thompson, *Russian Formalism and Anglo-American New Criticism* (The Hague: Mouton, 1971), p. 93.

3 "Tomashevsky creates an opposition between the sequence of events referred

to by the narrative and the way these events are presented in the story. 'The *fable* would seem to consist of a collection of narrative motifs in their chronological sequence, moving on from individual cause to effect, whereas the *subject* represents the same collected motifs, but in the specific order of occurrence which they are assigned to in the text. As for the fable, it is of little importance that the reader should become aware of an event in any particular part of the story, or that this event should be communicated to him directly by the author himself, inside the reported story of one of the characters in the main story or by way of marginal references. On the other hand, every narrative motif which is presented has an important role to play in the subject.'" Tzvetan Todorov, "Some Approaches to Russian Formalism," in *Russian Formalism*, ed. Stephen Bann and John E. Bowlt (Edinburgh: Scottish Academic Press, 1973), p. 15. The same article quotes also different but related definitions of the terms "fable" and "subject."

4   Henry James, "The New Novel," in *Selected Literary Criticism*, ed. Morris Shapira (New York: Horizon, 1964), p. 331.

5   Thompson, *Russian Formalism*, p. 26.

6   James M. Curtis, "Spatial Form as the Intrinsic Genre of Dostoevsky's Novels," *Modern Fiction Studies* 18 (1972): 140, 144.

7   Ricardo Gullon, "On Space in the Novel," trans. Rene de Costa, *Critical Inquiry* 2 (1975): 12.

8   Ingarden, *Vom Erkennen des literarischen Kunstwerks* (Tubingen: M. Niemeyer, 1968); English version: *The Cognition of the Literary Work of Art*, trans. Ruth Ann Crowley and Kenneth R. Olson (Evanston: Northwestern University Press, 1973).

9   Letter to Edward Garnett, May 1898, in *Letters from Conrad, 1895 to 1924*, ed. Edward Garnett (London: Nonesuch Press, 1928), p. 130. See also the letter to David Meldrum, February 1899, in *Joseph Conrad: Letters to William Blackwood and David S. Meldrum*, ed. William Blackburn (Durham: Duke University Press, 1958), p. 54.

10   Letter to William Blackwood, August 22, 1899, in Blackburn, *Joseph Conrad*, p. 63.

11   Arthur Symons, *Notes on Joseph Conrad* (London: Myers, 1925), p. 34.

12   Letter to William Blackwood, July 18, 1900, in Blackburn, *Joseph Conrad*, p. 106.

13   Letter to Edward Garnett, June 1899, in Garnett, *Letters from Conrad*, p. 151.

14   Letter to William Blackwood, August 22, 1899, in Blackburn, *Joseph Conrad*, p. 63.

15   J. Hillis Miller, "The Interpretation of *Lord Jim*," in *The Interpretation of Narrative: Theory and Practice*, ed. Morton W. Bloomfield (Cambridge: Harvard University Press, 1970), p. 223.

16   Joseph Conrad, *Heart of Darkness* (Harmondsworth: Penguin, 1975), p. 11.

17   Ford Madox Ford, *Joseph Conrad: A Personal Remembrance* (Boston: Little, Brown, 1924), p. 136.

18   Ford Madox Ford, *Thus to Revisit* (London: Chapman and Hall, 1921), p. 44.

19 Ford Madox Ford, *The Good Soldier* (Harmondsworth: Penguin, 1946), p. 13.

20 H. Wayne Schow, "Ironic Structure in *The Good Soldier*," *English Literature in Transition* 18 (1975): 210.

21 Ibid., p. 207.

22 Floyd C. Watkins, "What Happens in *Absalom, Absalom!*?" *Modern Fiction Studies* 13 (1967): 80.

23 Jeffrey R. Smitten, "Flaubert and the Structure of *The Secret Agent*: A Study in Spatial Form," in *Joseph Conrad: Theory and World Fiction*, ed. Wolodymyr T. Zyla and Wendell M. Aycock (Lubbock: Texas Tech Press, 1974), pp. 151–66.

24 Guerard, *Conrad the Novelist* (New York: Athenaeum, 1967), p. 210.

25 Conrad, *Under Western Eyes* (London: Dent, 1947), p. 67.

26 Smitten, "Flaubert and the Structure of *The Secret Agent*," p. 164.

27 Robert Scholes and Robert Kellogg, *The Nature of Narrative* (New York: Oxford University Press, 1966), p. 235.

28 Scholes and Kellogg, *The Nature of Narrative*, p. 235.

29 A discussion of Claude Simon's *Flanders Road* and Mario Vargas Llosa's *The Green House* has been omitted—editors.

Defining the Short Story:
Impressionism and Form

SUZANNE C. FERGUSON

Suzanne C. Ferguson begins by recognizing that critical theory in the 1980s remains at cross-purposes over how to define the short story as a discrete literary form. Is it one variant of prose fiction, like the novel, or is it a separate genre? Like Norman Friedman, Ferguson believes that "the main formal characteristics of the modern novel and the modern short story are the same," but the *modern* short story is even more heavily influenced by turn-of-the-century impressionism than the novel, and, hence, is more obviously distinct from earlier short fiction than is the modern novel from its prose precursors. But Ferguson, unlike Friedman, claims that in one specific element—plot—the modern short story is apparently unlike the modern novel. This claim depends in part upon the establishment of sufficient literary conventions known to the competent reader that enable the author to produce "elliptical plots" and "metaphorical plots" without rendering the short story incomprehensible. Ferguson builds her contention about short story plot in part upon Joseph Frank's distinction between spatially and temporally organized fictions, describing the modern short story as "a manifestation of impressionism rather than a discrete genre." But, like Friedman, Ferguson emphasizes this point in order to lead readers away from abstract generic debates and toward engagement with individual stories.

Suzanne C. Ferguson (b. 1939) is professor and chair of English at Wayne State University. She has authored *The Poetry of Randall Jarrell* (1971), edited *Critical Essays on Randall Jarrell* (1983), and coedited *Literature and the Visual Arts in Contemporary Society* (1986).

That there is no large and distinguished corpus of short story theory because the short story does not exist as a discrete and independent genre is a hypothesis—repugnant to many, of course—that ought to be taken seriously on occasion, if only to contemplate the perspective the hypothesis provides. "Intuition" or even "experience" may tell us that the "short story" exists, but defining it has proven surprisingly resistant to critical effort. A 1976 anthology, Charles May's *Short Story Theories*,[1] demonstrates the problematic situation. Short stories are defined in terms of unity (Poe, Brander Matthews, and others), techniques of plot compression (A. L. Bader, Norman Friedman, L. A. G. Strong), change or revelation of character (Theodore Stroud), subject (Frank O'Connor), tone (Gordimer), "lyricism" (Moravia), but there is no single characteristic or cluster of characteristics that the critics agree absolutely distinguishes the short story from other fictions. Thomas Gullason begins by lambasting Poe's formulas for "unity of effect" as "destructive," but ends up praising the short story for its "compact impact," which comes from "distillation" and "telescoping."[2] Norman Friedman's valiant effort to discover "What Makes a Short Story Short?" leaves the distinct impression that it is a short story because it is—well—a *short* story.[3]

A structuralist conception of fiction[4] tends to confirm the suspicion that there may be no rational way to distinguish "short story" from other narratives in the same mimetic mode: *all* stories, short and long, have certain required properties of narrativity—characters, place, events, a "beginning, middle, and an end," and coherence among the parts. All stories can be reduced to minimal statements of the required elements or expanded by the inclusion of optional developments in the narrative chain, as long as they maintain a discoverable coherence in their interrelationships. Like the sentence, the story has "slots" where various elements may be inserted; beyond a basic minimum of noun phrase plus verb phrase or existent plus event (character plus action), both the sentence and the story may be almost infinitely expanded. *Tristram Shandy* and *Ulysses* suggest an extreme range of options for the extrapolation of simple narrative sequences into long and complex ones. Similar expansion could be applied to any story, from "The Town Mouse and the Country Mouse" to "Indian Camp"; but of course the "best" short stories give us a sense of the inevitability of each sentence and persuade us that they are as complete as possible, that any addition or deletion would destroy their aesthetic wholeness. Whereas the omission of an entire sentence from Aesop's "The Town Mouse and the Country Mouse" would likely jeopardize its narrative coherence, we might add several without destroying its elegant symmetry or its moral. Indeed, its basic structure is the foundation of a number of nineteenth-century novels. We might remove one or more sentences from "The Fall of the House of Usher" or even (sacrilege!) "Araby"—providing we chose carefully—without altering its theme or quality for most readers.

What accounts, then, for the persistent notion that the "modern" short story is a new genre, something different from the tale and sketch that preceded it? In fact, the modern short story shows all the same shifts in sensibility and technique that affected the novel and the long story (or nouvelle) around the end of the nineteenth century, but these changes "look" different in the short story precisely because it is physically short. The main formal characteristics of the modern novel and the modern short story are the same: (1) limitation and foregrounding of point of view, (2) emphasis on presentation of sensation and inner experience, (3) the deletion or transformation of several elements of the traditional plot, (4) increasing reliance on metaphor and metonymy in the presentation of events and existents, (5) rejection of chronological time ordering, (6) formal and stylistic economy, and (7) the foregrounding of style. All these elements are associated with the literary movement called impressionism, or, more specifically in fiction, the tradition of Flaubert. I will argue that, just as impressionism dominates the mainstream of the novel in the late nineteenth and early twentieth centuries, so it does that of the short story. But the short story, because it has fewer "optional" narrative elements in its structural "slots," manifests its formal allegiances to impressionism even more obviously than does the novel and, consequently, seems more radically different from earlier short fiction than the impressionist novel seems different from the realistic novel that preceded it.

Let me take the characteristics in the order listed above, briefly illustrating each one. The limiting of point of view to that of a character or characters in the narrative and the emphasis on the presentation of sensation and inner experience are inextricably related. The same impulses that turned nineteenth-century philosophy away from positivism and toward phenomenology turned writers to the representation of experience *as* experienced by individuals. The importance of this philosophical shift in the interpretation of reality cannot be over-estimated in an attempt to understand what happened to writers' representations of reality. Imitation of how things "feel" or "seem" to the characters became the preferred subject of fiction rather than the imitation of "how things are" in the "real" world. Where the characters' attitudes and responses had always been a part of a more comprehensive view of the world, the subjectivity of "reality" now became the prevailing mode of understanding, and the exploration of subjectivity became the elusive "object" of fictional imitation.

In the impressionist short story, even more than in the impressionist novel, the author conceals himself, presenting the entire narrative from a point of view within the story, that of the characters' subjective experience of events, their "impressions," by using either first-person narration or the Jamesian "method of the central intelligence." This emphasis on subjectivity inevitably affects the typical themes of modern fiction: alienation, isolation, solipsism, the quest for identity and integration. The characters, the experiencing subjects, are seen as isolated from other experiencing subjects, with only rare moments of communion or shared experience possible to them. Frank O'Connor's contention that the modern short story deals with outsiders, lonely individuals cut off from society, is true,[5] but that theme is equally typical of modern novels.

The preoccupation of impressionist authors with epistemological themes is another outgrowth of subjectivism, for when all we have in the world is our own experience of it, all received knowledge becomes suspect, and the very nature of knowledge becomes problematic. This uncertainty affects the concept of plot: the Aristotelian intertwining of knowledge with action is unraveled; protagonists become passive observers; the "absence" which impels the plot is absence of knowledge of some truth that could go beyond the merely personal to achieve a general validity. It is often the reader, rather than the character, who must directly confront the possibility that we cannot know anything for certain, that the processes we follow in search of truth may yield only fictions.[6]

Like the limiting of point of view and the theme of alienation, the quest for knowledge about reality is common to impressionist novels as well as short stories. In longer works of the earlier twentieth century, however, these features are usually less prominent than in shorter works because of the long works' elaboration of plot and character, their density of specification, and the like. Comparison of *Ulysses* with "The Dead" and of "The Dead" with "An Encounter" or "The Sisters" will clarify this contention. The theme of quest for reliable, transpersonal knowledge about the world is present in all three "genres"—novel, nouvelle, story—but there are complementary or ancillary themes in the longer works, along with multiplication of episodes in the plot, proliferation of detail in descriptions, and, in *Ulysses*, the diversification of styles in the texture of the work. Although all these factors actually do manifest the theme of the quest to define reality, the reader tends to be less aware of the theme as such and more engrossed in the richness of the longer works' texture. The compactness and focus of the short stories makes the theme more readily apparent.

It is in the realm of plot that the modern short story is most different from earlier short fiction and in which it appears to be most different from the novel. The deemphasis of physical action in impressionist fiction (or the disjunction of physical action from thought and feeling), which leaves adjustments of thought or feeling as the true "events" of the plot, makes the articulation of plot in many cases obscure. A related problem is the increasing expectation of the writers that their readers will have internalized the elements of traditional plots so thoroughly that the writers can presume readers will supply missing elements. The deletion of expected elements of the plot—from any "slot" in the story—is the hallmark of the late nineteenth- and early twentieth-century short story. There are two basic methods of deletion: that in which elements are simply omitted, which results in what I call "elliptical" plots, and that in which unexpected, dissonant existents or events are substituted for the omitted elements, which yields "metaphoric" plots.

Elliptical plots may omit the exposition and never get back to it (as in "Cat in the Rain" or "Hills Like White Elephants"); or pass over what would ordinarily be "dramatized" or extensively reported parts of the middle, episodes that develop the plot conflict (Kipling stories such as "Love O' Women" and "Mrs. Bathurst," or Faulkner's "A Rose for Emily"); or leave out closure (Chekhov's "On the Road" and many others). Impressionist novels more rarely begin *in medias res* without going back to fill in the beginning at some later point in the narrative, and they almost never omit important stages of the middle, because one of the basic principles of the novel is to develop and elaborate. Elements left out at their "normal" chronological point in the narrative sequence turn up elsewhere (as in *The Good Soldier*).

To understand the notion of "elliptical" plots, it is helpful to look at some actual stories and propose for them "hypothetical" plots that might form the "natural" or "deep structure" bases of the narratives. (By hypothetical plot I mean something more specifically formulable than the bare-bones structuralist "fabula": a counter-story, with a beginning, middle, and end, that tells "what happened" in chronological order.) In "Clay" a hypothetical plot is the story of Maria's life from the time when she had a "home" with Alphy and Joe's family, through the breakup of the family and her making a new "home" in the laundry, to the time of the actual story, at the end of which she (perhaps unconsciously) acknowledges her desolation, her "homelessness." The reader must to some extent construct this hypothetical plot in order for the actual story to seem meaningful. The act of constructing a hypothetical plot is what we ask students to perform when we ask them, "Who is Maria?"; "What is her relation to Alphy and Joe?"; "Why does she live at the laundry?"; "How do we know she won't get married?"; and the like.[7]

The actual plot of "Clay" deletes expository material and neglects to provide episodes showing Maria's desire for a home and family to which she could belong. The past when she had a sort of home is referred to in only a few phrases, and the bleakness of her life in the laundry is seen only obliquely in Maria's deliberately optimistic view of herself in the role of "peacemaker" to the unruly laundresses. This actual plot consists of three episodes, two of them developing tension and the third climactic. Maria prepares for the All Hallows party, hoping to reconcile Joe and Alphy and thus restore the conditions of a past in which she was relatively happy; she travels to the party, buying a piece of cake as an "offering" and losing it en route because of the distraction of a man flirting with her; after causing some distress at the party because of her concern at losing the cake, she is rejected (tricked) by an unthinking neighbor girl and consoled by the appreciation of her wishful song. The parts of the hypothetical plot that are omitted are represented metonymically by the episodes Joyce has written. Maria's experience at the party is representative of her life, or so we interpret the story.

In "Eveline," the darling of structuralist analysts, a hypothetical plot might be said to begin with Eveline's loss of her mother's love (through death), to run through her opportunity to find a new love with Frank, and to end with her acknowledgment that she cannot throw off the bonds of habit that link her, without love, to her father and her home. Here the actual plot begins after Eveline has been offered the chance to escape but before she rejects it. Both "Clay" and "Eveline" begin almost at the crisis of the traditional, "hypothetical" plot. Eveline is on the brink of an action that would change her life; Maria has her plan to reconcile the brothers. Eveline cannot act; Maria is deflected. For Eveline there is a tumult, inevitable (though untold) recognition; for Maria there is a simple retreat. Only the reader recognizes that Maria means little to Joe's family, that her future is not to reconcile and reunite the family but to move on alone into death.

In both stories, the exposition and earlier stages of conflict are alluded to in the protagonists' memories, but only the climaxes are dramatized. Although aesthetic closure is achieved in "Eveline" in the concluding images of the inundating sea, and in "Clay" in Maria's rendition of "I Dreamt that I Dwelt in Marble Halls" and Joe's reaction to it, the themes keep on unraveling into the futureless future beyond the end of the stories. The sense of a double plot in all such stories is strong; we recognize a story that has not been fully told lying behind the one that *is* told. Reading the stories, we become detectives, piecing together the main elements of the hypothetical plots in order to rationalize the actual plots.

In addition to stories in which parts of the plot are omitted, there are stories in which the elements of the hypothetical plot are represented at the surface level by sets of images or events—often trivial and unrelated to each other—that are analogous to and substitutes for events in the hypothetical plot; that is, they stand in relation to the theme of the story as the chain of events does in a normal plot, and the chain of events is left implicit. These I call "metaphoric" plots. "Ivy Day in the Committee Room" and "The Gambler, the Nun, and the Radio" are extreme examples. The surface events of these stories are disconnected and of little apparent significance, but they suggest a deep level at which themes of profound human import are developed.

The theme of "Ivy Day" is the debasement of Parnell's ideals in the behavior of his nominal followers. The conversation in the Committee Room exemplifies the dishonor while it implicitly evokes the image of Parnell and his struggle to give the Irish political freedom, an image the reader must remember independently of what is told in the actual story. Seen in retrospect, each separate, fragmentary episode is a small betrayal. As we read the story, however, we gather up seemingly random threads: the rejection of the old by the young, the chicaneries and temporizing of the political hacks, the disreputable activities of the clergy. A sort of climax is achieved in the plan to welcome Edward VII—opposite to Parnell, the "uncrowned king"— to Ireland on an official visit, although he represents not only English domination but womanizing, the pretext on which Parnell—the faithful lover of another man's wife—was brought down. The episodes of the plot are not only metaphoric in this case but ironic: the day that is meant to honor Parnell dishonors his memory. Joe Hynes's poem, banal but sincere, is the best a sorry lot can do to retrieve past heroism, and the popping corks of stout bottles complete the humans' feeble salute.

In Hemingway's story, the figures of the gambler and the nun are protagonists of auxiliary elliptical narratives within the actual plot, and they and the radio are vehicles of metaphors whose tenor is the theme of a general quest for the "opium of the people." Mr. Frazer, who plays the radio and contemplates the gambler and the nun, is in some obscure way the protagonist of another story of which we know too few details even to hypothesize a plot, as well as of the actual story, whose ironies bring him to a conclusion about the meaninglessness of experience and the nature of the opiums of the people.

Without our sense of how traditional plots work, these stories would simply be accounts of "what happened"; they seem to lack the obligatory coherence of existent and event of ordinary narrative. The disorder is of course intentional, and it imitates the surface disorder of the world in which we seek coherence. Combining our intuitive knowledge of "storiness" with a symbolic reading of the actual events and characters, we find the narrative element in the works and perceive them as short stories rather than random accounts of unrelated characters and happenings. A long impressionist fiction that would depend so heavily upon the reader's intensive interpretation of symbolic incidents and figures for the basis of its narrative sequence seems unworkable, and I am unable to name one. Metaphoric episodes or subplots are relatively common, however: the French architect episode in *Absalom, Absalom!*, the excursion to "M———" in *The Good Soldier*, and the owl-eyed man scenes of *The Great Gatsby* suggest themselves. The stylistic vagaries of *Ulysses* function similarly, although like other, later novels, *Ulysses* has already gone beyond the boundaries of impressionism in so many ways that one should probably not include it here. Instead of asking the reader to measure a subjective view against a traditional, "realistic" view, postimpressionist fiction denies the existence of the latter altogether.

Elliptical and metaphoric plots affirm Joseph Frank's conception of a spatially rather than a temporally organized form in modern fiction. In focusing on the crisis of a hypothetical narrative, or in representing that narrative only in figures or analogues, such plots devaluate temporal sequence and the chain of cause and effect. The deemphasis of the orderly unfolding of an action through time is closely related to the emergence of "epiphany" as an ordering device. The notion of single "moments" of experience as determiners of the quality of a whole life appears to be mystical in origin, and in secular literature it goes back at least to Wordsworth, but it has become characteristic of modern fiction both as an item of belief and a structural principle. In the modern novel, we move from epiphany to epiphany, or in Woolf's image, along a series of small revelations, "matches struck unexpectedly in the dark."[8] In the short story, we frequently see only one such privileged moment, which takes the place of the traditional "turning point," the climax of the plot. Not much actual dramatized time passes, although in the memory and fantasy of the characters large reaches of "time" may be covered. The narrator of "A Rose for Emily" tells his story after Emily's funeral, and his "epiphany" takes place when someone picks an iron-grey hair from her pillow, but the "story" covers many years in the life of Miss Emily Grierson, not just or not even most importantly the moment of her death. The actual plot unfolds the story of the town's discovery; but the more interesting story is the hypothetical plot the reader must puzzle out and restore to its "natural" chronology in order to understand the actual story. Time is as malleable here as in *The Sound and the Fury* or *Absalom, Absalom!*, but we are not so much concerned with its operations. Nevertheless, we must make a conscious effort to restore chronology in order to understand Miss Emily's story. In the foregrounding of time and in the temporal displacements between the hypothetical and actual plots, "A Rose for Emily" is an extreme case of the deviousness of many modern stories, which overtly seem to disdain temporal order but covertly remind us how time-bound we are.

The use of setting in impressionist fiction is also different from that in earlier fiction. Insofar as impressionism is an extension of realism in its sensational, experiential aspect, settings are established through the use of detail to give verisimilitude. That these details are chosen as much or more to reflect the mood of the characters perceiving them as to convey a location for the action and the characters' social standing marks a significant difference between realism and impressionism. Drawing upon the romantic (even Gothic) tradition, impressionist settings are frequently used metaphorically to substitute for representation of action or analysis. The fragmentary description of the house, street, and alleys that forms the beginning of "Araby" has to convey more than just the location of the events; it must stand in place of hypothetical episodes in which the boy's character would be developed in the context of his family and his larger social environment; it must convey his class, his situation, his innocence, his predilection for romance: in short, his sensibility and his *need* to engage in some meaningful action. These initial paragraphs, though they record no specific events, substitute for the exposition of a traditional plot.

In the modern novel, setting is used for similar purposes, but in most novels it supplements rather than replaces other kinds of character and plot development. Although it is often difficult, even for purposes of analysis, to separate "setting" from some aspects of "characterization,"[9] it is probably true that setting is a more significant factor in the modern story than in the nouvelle and novel in terms of proportion of discourse space allotted to it.

Techniques of limiting point of view, constructing elliptical or metaphoric plots, using representative details for setting and character development go hand in hand with the impressionists' attention to stylistic economy and the foregrounding of style. In transforming the plot by deletion and substitution, writers also made their language more economical: dense with meaning as it is in poetry. From Flaubert forward, impressionist fiction foregrounds style in the emphasis on rhythmic prose, exact diction, and a high reliance on figures, particularly simile and metaphor. The author may disappear as commentator on the action, but he calls attention to himself through the special "signature" of his style.

Stylistic foregrounding has both negative and positive effects: although Hemingway's and Faulkner's highly mannered styles may grow tedious, even self-parodic, in their novels, in the stories they are a force for cohesiveness, imparting a special coloration or atmosphere that binds the often disparate events and characters together. Though Joyce said he wrote *Dubliners* in a style of "scrupulous meanness," few readers would agree; the beauty of Joyce's style, applied to the squalor of the subject, gives these stories their classic quality. By and large—except for Lawrence—the great short story writers have reputations as outstanding stylists, and much of the praise for their style, in terms of its "jewelling" or "polish," arises from a sense of the care lavished in the search for *le mot juste* by writers from Poe to Kipling, Joyce, Mansfield, Hemingway, Faulkner, Porter, Welty, both O'Connors, O'Faolain, Updike. The attribution of "lyricism" to the story also comes in large measure from the attention to style, the deliberation that is so apparent in manipulating diction, figuration, and syntactic and phonemic patterning to achieve precise tonal effects.

Even the association of the short story with certain national traditions—French, Russian, Irish, and American—can be seen to be linked with its impressionist elements rather than a particular national "gift." Turgenev and Chekhov, among the Russians, display in particular the foregrounding of setting, the reduction of physical action, and the elevation of mood changes to the status of plots; a recent book, in fact, treats Chekhov with James as an impressionist.[10] Among the French, Maupassant is preeminent in the short story; his techniques of compression and suggestion come directly from Flaubert, not from a tradition of the short story. Though Crane and James are the first Americans properly to be called impressionist writers, Poe and Hawthorne foreshadow impressionist techniques in the focus on inner states, the substitution of setting for action, and the use of fallible, ambivalent narrators in first-person (Poe) and third-person (Hawthorne) in both long and short fiction. George Moore follows Turgenev, Joyce follows Moore and Flaubert, in changing the mainstream of Irish short fiction from anecdote to impression.

What has made the modern short story seem distinct from the novel, in addition to the different distribution and proportion of narrative elements, is finally a matter of prestige. Given the emphasis on its status as a work of art and the insistence by many turn-of-the-century writers on stylistic elegance (a sure sign of "high" art!), the story began to be read more intensively. The deletion of traditional plot elements also demanded a more attentive reading, one in which the reader is conscious of narrative technique and style as keys to meaning. As the story became more obviously artful, its artistry was the more remarked in criticism. James and Wells thought in terms of a "golden age" or "millennium" of the short story, and writers began to establish reputations solely on the basis of their short fiction.

The idea that a "true" short story grew out of some older, amateurish form of the early nineteenth century is not borne out by the evidence. Although earlier there is a finer line between "popular" and highbrow stories, and though much nineteenth-century short fiction belongs to the specialized subgenres more characteristic of popular than serious fiction, the mainstream short story of the nineteenth century is as likely to deal with the same concerns as the novel of its time as the modern story and the modern novel are apt to deal with modern concerns. Brevity, however, is not well suited to the vision of Victorian fiction, in which men and women move through a complex society, posing goals and working toward them with greater or less success. One can imagine a short story about Dorothea Brooke or Willoughby, but not a very impressive one. Thus, though coherent and competently written, few Victorian short stories are of much interest to the modern reader.

In bringing to a close this sketch of the relations between impressionist conceptions and techniques and the forms of early modern fiction, I would like to focus on a point implicit in much of the rest of my argument. Comparison of nineteenth-century short and long fictions with their modern counterparts reveals one final way in which short stories seem different from longer ones in their formal identities. The less we are occupied with verisimilitude, with physical action, with extended characterization, the more obvious it is that the element which binds the whole *into* a whole is what readers perceive as a governing *theme* and often express as "the author's intention": in old-fashioned stories, the "moral." This "semantic" aspect of the story we abstract from its lexical aspect—the events, existents, and authorial commentary—as we see that organized in the syntactic aspect—plot, temporal ordering. Theme is what readers constitute as they study the significance and relationships of the various elements and locate the "storiness" emerging from the often obscure system the author provides. In realistic literature, the interplay of character and action in the plot is the primary vector of theme. In the modern, impressionist short story, in which plot is frequently suppressed, in which characterization is often achieved by having the characters perceive something or somebody "other" rather than acting or being themselves described by an implied author, in which setting may displace event, and in which the very sentence structures or figurative language may imply relationships not otherwise expressed, the readers' ability to recognize a theme is paramount to their acceptance of the work as belonging to the genre, "story." Oddly, this kind of narrative, whose most typical epistemology assumes the privacy of truth in individual experience, becomes the genre in which the readers' abstraction of theme—the statement of an interpretation—is a major factor in their differentiating it from other kinds of narrative. The moral is no longer an easily abstractable truism verified by an implied author, but a complex and hardly won proposition whose validity remains conditional and implicit, unconfirmed by the authorial voice, giving the story both "unity of effect" and a certain vagueness or mystery.

In attempting to show that the "modern short story" is a manifestation of impressionism rather than a discrete genre, I have cited many of the same characteristics that others have observed in arguing that the short story *is* a genre. That the short story *seems* very different from the novel in its plot, in the proportions of action to setting and character, or in the prominence of theme over vicarious experience, I concede, yet the context of impressionism seems to me a more comprehensive vantage point from which to interpret these differences than that of genre.

Any perspective, of genre or mode, is only a starting point in the interpretation and assimilation of a literary work. The complex adjustments in reading process we make in going from "The Town Mouse and the Country Mouse," Grimms' fairy tales, or "Wandering Willie's Tale" to "The Jolly Corner" or "The Gambler, the Nun, and the Radio" are considerable: greater, I would argue, than those we make in going from *The Good Soldier* or *To the Lighthouse* to "Soldier's Home" or "Ivy Day in the Committee Room." (Those who argue from a generic perspective would likely agree.) Nevertheless, our knowledge of Aesop or a fairy tale or Scott's tale—or any of the stories we heard as children or read in adolescence, no matter how crude or cheap—provide us with the basic knowledge of the fictional codes that we need to begin reading sophisticated modern short stories and their longer relatives. The question "What is a short story?" or even "What is an impressionist short story?" is probably not as important a question in the long run as other, specific questions we might ask about the relations of long and short stories, popular and highbrow stories, hypothetical and actual plots, or stories and reality. The object of such criticism is not, finally, to find generic or modal boxes to put stories into, but to open the boxes and let stories out for more illuminating scrutiny.

Notes

1 Charles E. May, ed., *Short Story Theories* (Athens: Ohio University Press, 1976).
2 Thomas Gullason, "The Short Story: An Underrated Art," in May, *Short Story Theories*, pp. 20–21, 30.
3 Norman Friedman, "What Makes a Short Story Short?" in May, *Short Story Theories*, pp. 131–46.

4 Beginning with V. K. Propp in *Morphology of the Folktale* (1928) and re-
   affirmed in later structuralist critics such as Claude Bremond and A. J.
   Greimas in *Communications* 8 (1966): 28–59 and 60–76; Roland Barthes,
   "An Introduction to the Structural Analysis of Narrative," trans. Lionel
   Duisit in *NLH* 6 (1975): 237–72; Seymour Chatman, *Story and Discourse*
   (Ithaca, N.Y.: Cornell University Press, 1978), pp. 43–48.

5 Frank O'Connor, from *The Lonely Voice* (1963), reprinted in May, *Short
   Story Theories*, pp. 86–89.

6 The fictionality of all (subjective) truth becomes an obsession in postmodern
   writing; it is a given in the work of Borges, Robbe-Grillet, Pynchon, and
   others, rather than an intuition against which the characters struggle, as in
   impressionist fiction.

7 These are types of questions it would be pointless to ask about the characters in Borges or Barthelme, or even in such a relatively conservative postmodern story as Pynchon's "Entropy," for these characters *have* no "other"
   existence; the tie with a "real" world, in which we might imagine the characters as acting and suffering, is broken.

8 Virginia Woolf, *To the Lighthouse* (New York: Harcourt, Brace and World,
   1955), p. 240.

9 Chatman, *Story and Discourse*, pp. 138–45.

10 Peter Stowell, *Literary Impressionism, James and Chekhov* (Athens: University of Georgia Press, 1980).

30

Breaking the Sentence;
Breaking the Sequence

RACHEL BLAU DUPLESSIS

In her feminist analysis of women's writing Rachel Blau DuPlessis builds on the work of Virginia Woolf, from whom the title of this essay is taken: "Mary is tampering with the expected sequence. First she broke the sentence; now she has broken the sequence." For DuPlessis, this statement describes "a poetics of rupture and critique" that defines much of the literature written by women. For her, the breaking of the sentence indicates the rejection of "the structuring of the female voice by the male voice, female tone and manner by male expectations, female writing by male emphasis, female writing by existing conventions of gender. . . . Breaking the sentence is a way of rupturing language and tradition sufficiently to invite a female slant, emphasis, or approach." Women have been well represented as objects and characters in fiction, but DuPlessis, along with Woolf, argues that they have been underrepresented as subjects and authors.

DuPlessis argues further that, in addition to "breaking the sentence," the woman's voice in literature has also embarked on "breaking the sequence" in order to be heard. The "sequence" is the approved forms for fictional creation, the canonical genres recognized as "good" literature. In DuPlessis's words, "breaking the sequence is a rupture in habits of narrative order, that expected story told when 'love was the only possible interpreter' of women's textual lives." She suggests that this broken sequence can take the shape of "delegitimating the specific narrative and cultural orders of nineteenth-century fiction—the emphasis on successful or failed romance, the subordination of quest to love, the death of the questing female, the insertion into family life." In twentieth-century writing it can be seen as two major oscillations, one in "the gendering process" and the other in "the hegemonic process"—or, as we might say, in the domains of sexuality and power. DuPlessis analyzes the first oscillation through a radical critique of Freudianism. The second she analyzes through a discussion of feminist social theories, including a concept of women's development of a "double-consciousness," which arises from their marginal position as a muted group in patriarchal societies. In addition, then, to exploring the efforts of female writers to create an authentic "women's voice" through disrupting accepted norms, DuPlessis introduces us to feminist criticism, psychology, and social theory.

Rachel Blau DuPlessis (b. 1941) is associate professor of English and director of Women's Studies at Temple University. She is author of *American Women* (1972), *Writing Beyond the Ending: Narrative Strategies of Twentieth-Century Women Writers* (1985), from which this excerpt is taken, and *H.D., The Career of That Struggle* (1986).

> I am almost sure, I said to myself, that Mary Carmichael is playing a trick on us. For I feel as one feels on a switchback railway when the car, instead of sinking, as one has been led to expect, swerves up again. Mary is tampering with the expected sequence. First she broke the sentence; now she has broken the sequence. . . . Perhaps she had done this unconsciously, merely giving things their natural order, as a woman would, if she wrote like a woman. But the effect was somehow baffling; one could not see a wave heaping itself, a crisis coming round the next corner. . . . For whenever I was about to feel the usual things in the usual places, about love, about death, the annoying creature twitched me away, as if the important point were just a little further on.—Virginia Woolf, *A Room of One's Own* (1929)
>
> . . . *Charlotte was gazing up into the dark eyes of Redmond. "My darling," he breathed hoarsely. Strong arms lifted her, his warm lips pressed her own. . . .*
>
> That was the way it was supposed to go, that was the way it had always gone before, but somehow it no longer felt right. I'd taken a wrong turn somewhere; there was something, some fact or clue, that I had overlooked.—Margaret Atwood, *Lady Oracle* (1976)

One approach to the feminist criticism of these modern writers is suggested in an analysis of "Mary Carmichael's first novel, *Life's Adventure*," a work and author invented by Virginia Woolf and explicated in *A Room of One's Own*.[1] This is a novel by the last of the series of ancestral mothers alluded to in the Elizabethan ballad of the Four Marys, which forms a frame for the essay. The first two are Mary Beton, with her legacy of money, and Mary Seton, who provides "room"—institutional and psychological space. Both are necessary for Mary Carmichael, the modern author, and all of them express the baffled and unmentioned Mary Hamilton, from the ages when women had no way to dissent, except through infanticide and anonymous song. Woolf scrutinizes this novel's style, plot, and purpose with a diffident casualness, finding "some fact or clue" of great importance: "Mary is tampering with the expected sequence. First she broke the sentence; now she has broken the sequence" (*AROO*, 85). In these matching statements are telescoped a poetics of rupture and critique.

The sentence broken is one that expresses "the ridicule, the censure, the assurance of inferiority" about women's cultural ineptitude and deficiencies.[2] To break the sentence rejects not grammar especially, but rhythm, pace, flow, expression: the structuring of the female voice by the male voice, female tone and manner by male expectations, female writing by male emphasis, female writing by existing conventions of gender—in short, any way in which dominant structures shape muted ones. For a woman to write, she must experiment with "altering and adapting the current sentence until she writes one that takes the natural shape of her thought without crushing or distorting it" (*G&R*, 81).[3]

At first it appeared as if Mary Carmichael would not be able to break this sentence and create her own. Her style was jerky, short, and terse, which "might mean that she was afraid of something; afraid of being called 'sentimental' perhaps; or she remembers that women's writing has been called flowery and so provides a superfluity of thorns . . ." (*AROO*, 85). Here she overcompensated for female-ness in deference to existing conventions.

But eventually, facing gender in an authentic way, the writer pro-duces "a woman's sentence," the "the psychological sentence of the feminine gender," which "is used to describe a woman's mind by a writer [Dorothy Richardson] who is neither proud nor afraid of any-thing that she may discover in the psychology of her sex."[4] The sen-tence is "psychological" not only because it deepens external realism with a picture of consciousness at work but also because it involves a critique of her own consciousness, saturated as it is with discourses of dominance.

There is nothing exclusively or essentially female about "the psy-chological sentence of the feminine gender," because writers of both sexes have used that "elastic" and "enveloping" form. But it is a "woman's sentence" because of its cultural and situational function, a dissension stating that women's minds and concerns have been neither completely nor accurately produced in literature as we know it. Breaking the sentence is a way of rupturing language and tradition sufficiently to invite a female slant, emphasis, or approach. Similarly there is nothing innately gendered about the signifier "I," yet in *A Room of One's Own* the speaker's "I" is both female and plural—"a woman's voice in a patriarchal literary tradition"—and another "I," shadowing the page, is "polished, learned, well-fed," an explicitly male subject speaking of and from dominance.[5]

Woolf's "woman's sentence," then, has its basis not in biology, but rather in cultural fearlessness, in the attitude of critique—a dissent from, a self-conscious marking of, dominant statement. It can be a stress shifting, the kind of realignment of emphasis noted by Nancy Miller, following Luce Irigaray: "an italicized version of what passes for the neutral or standard face . . . a way of marking what has al-ready been said. . . ."[6]

A "woman's sentence" is Woolf's shorthand term for a writing un-afraid of gender as an issue, undeferential to male judgment while not unaware of the complex relations between male and female. A "woman's sentence" will thus be constructed in considered indiffer-ence to the fact that the writer's vision is seen as peculiar, incompe-tent, marginal. So Woolf summarizes "the first great lesson" mastered by Mary Carmichael: "she wrote as a woman, but as a woman who has forgotten that she is a woman . . ." (AROO, 96). The doubled emphasis on woman, yet on forgetting woman, is a significant maneuver, claiming freedom from a "tyranny of sex" that is nonetheless palpable and dominant, both negated and affirmed.[7]

In both A Room of One's Own and the related "Women and Fiction," Woolf criticizes women for "resenting the treatment of [their] sex and pleading for its rights," because, in her view, this threatens the poise a writer achieves by the transcending of "indignation" on the one hand and "resignation" on the other, the "too masculine" here and the "too feminine" there.[8] This movement between complicity and critique expresses Woolf's version of a doubled dynamic that is, as we shall see momentarily, characteristic of other women writers.[9]

What binds these writers is their oppositional stance to the social and cultural construction of gender.[10] This opposition has a number of origins. Perhaps the most suggestive is that of marginality in two arenas.[11] When a female writer is black (Alice Walker, Zora Neale Hurston, Gwendolyn Brooks, Toni Morrison), colonial (Olive Schreiner, Doris Lessing, Jean Rhys), Canadian (Margaret Atwood), of working-class origin (Tillie Olsen, Marge Piercy), of lesbian or bisexual orientation (H.D., Virginia Woolf, Adrienne Rich, Joanna Russ), or displaced and déclassé (Dorothy Richardson), double marginalization can be produced. Either it compels the person to negate any possibility for a critical stance, seeking instead "conformity and inclusion" because the idea of an authoritative center is defensively affirmed, or it enlivens the potential for critique by the production of an (ambiguously) nonhegemonic person, one in marginalized dialogue with the orders she may also affirm.[12]

The woman writers studied here are further unified by their interested dissent from androcentric culture in nonfictional texts: essay, memoir, polemic, and social study. The texts will be seen, case by case, to contribute to their fictional elaborations and narrative stances.[13] Hence while hardly all of the writers would describe themselves as feminists, and some, indeed, resist that term, one may assert that any female cultural practice that makes the "meaning production process" itself "the site of struggle" may be considered feminist.[14] These authors are "feminist" because they construct a variety of oppositional strategies to the depiction of gender institutions in narrative. A writer expresses dissent from an ideological formation by attacking elements of narrative that repeat, sustain, or embody the values and attitudes in question. So after breaking the sentence, a rupture with the internalization of the authorities and voices of dominance, the woman writer will create that further rupture which is a center for this book: breaking "the sequence—the expected order" (*AROO*, 95).

Breaking the sequence is a rupture in habits of narrative order, that expected story told when "love was the only possible interpreter" of women's textual lives (*AROO*, 87). In her study of *Life's Adventure*, Woolf notes that the novelist Mary Carmichael alludes to "the relationship that there may be between Chloe and Roger," but this is set aside in favor or another bond, depicted "perhaps for the first time in literature" (*AROO*, 84, 86). "Chloe liked Olivia. They shared a laboratory together," begins Woolf (*AROO*, 87). The romance names with the allusions to Shakespearean transvestite characters are very suggestive, especially as opposed to the firmly heterosexual "Roger," with a whole history of slang behind him. One of these women is married, with children; the other is not. Their work—finding a cure for pernicious anemia—may suggestively beef up women's weakness of nerve with a good dose of female bonding.

The ties between Chloe and Olivia may be homosocial or, given the subsequent sexual-cultural metaphor of exploring the "serpentine cave" of women, they may be lesbian.[15] In either case, Woolf clearly presents a nonheterosexual relation nourished by the healthy vocation of women. She is also eloquent about the meaning of these changes. The women's friendship, based on their work life, will be "more varied and lasting because it will be less personal" (*AROO*, 88). "Personal" is Woolf's word (in essays throughout the twenties) for the privatization and exclusiveness that is part of the script of heterosexual romance. So the tie between Chloe and Olivia, a model for modern women writers, makes a critique of heterosexuality and the love plot, and offers (Woolf implies) a stronger and more positive sense of female quest. One is no longer allowed to "feel the usual things in the usual places, about love, about death" (*AROO*, 95). So breaking the sequence can mean delegitimating the specific narrative and cultural orders of nineteenth-century fiction—the emphasis on successful or failed romance, the subordination of quest to love, the death of the questing female, the insertion into family life. "The important point . . . just a little further on" that Mary Carmichael pushes her reader to see might be such narrative strategies as reparenting, female bonding, including lesbian ties, mother-child dyads, brother-sister pairs, familial transpositions, the multiple individual, and the transpersonal protagonist.

This study is also designed to suggest what elements of female identity would be drawn on to make plausible the analytic assumption that there is a women's writing with a certain stance toward narrative.[16] The narrative strategies of twentieth-century writing by women are the expression of two systemic elements of female identity—a psychosexual script and a sociocultural situation, both structured by major oscillations. The oscillations occur in the gendering process and in the hegemonic process. Oscillation is a swinging between two positions, a touching of two limits, or, alternately, a fluctuation between two purposes, states, centers, or principles. The narrative strategies I will present here all take basic elements of female identity, such as the gendering sequence, and realign their components.

The possibilities for heterosexual love and romance take shape in the object relations within the family, that is, in the ties of kinship forged between child and parent, and in the processes of gendering, all given very complete cultural and social support. As we know, there is a sequence that assists these arrangements—a psychosexual script that is one of our first dramas. The occasion of our "learning the rules of gendering and kinship" and the apparatus for the production of sexual personality is, of course, the oedipal crisis.[17]

Freudian theory, postulating the telos of "normal femininity" as the proper resolution of the oedipal crisis, bears an uncanny resemblance to the nineteenth-century endings of narrative, in which the female hero becomes a heroine and in which the conclusion of a valid love plot is the loss of any momentum of quest. The pitfalls to be avoided by a woman seeking normal femininity are very consistent with the traits of the female hero in narrative: defiance, activity, selfishness, heroic action, and identification with other women. For Freudian theory puts a high premium on female passivity and narcissism and on the "end" of husband, home, and male child. As for quest or individual aspiration, Freud poignantly realizes that the achievement of femininity has left "no paths open to [a woman] for further development; . . . [it is] as though, in fact, the difficult development which leads to femininity had exhausted all the possibilities of the individual."[18] By the repressions and sacrifices involved in becoming feminine, quest is at a dead end—a sentiment that we have seen replicated in narrative endings.

The "original bisexuality" or "bisexual disposition" of every individual is the major starting point for this account.[19] The oedipal crisis is a social process of gendering that takes "bisexual, androgynous," libidinally active, and ungendered infants and produces girls and boys, giving to the male future social and sexual domination, and to the female future domesticated status within the rules of the sex-gender system of its society.[20] Thus gender is a product. That there must be some kind of passage of an infant "into a social human being" is not at issue. It will involve the "[dialectical] process of struggle with and ultimate supersession (including integration) of symbolic figures of love, desire, and authority." As this citation from Ortner proposes, the theoretical possibility that the oedipal crisis is historically mutable must not be overlooked.[21] The drama might unfold with some alternate figures and some alternate products or emphases.

Another major element of the oedipal crisis for girls is the requisite shift of object choice from "phallic" or preoedipal mother—the mother of power—to a heterosexual object, the father. Little boys must shift generations, but not genders, in their object choice. The reason for the female shift has been contested. Freud postulated that a girl will turn from her mother, sometimes with hatred and hostility, when the mother is discovered to be bereft of the genital marker of male power. In feminist revisions of Freud, this revelation, called "penis envy" by Freud, has been viewed as the delivery of knowledge well beyond the perception of sheer genital difference, the shock of learning a whole array of psychosocial rules and orders valorizing maleness.

To Freud, the girl's tasks in the oedipal drama involve the repression of what he calls the "little man" inside her, that active, striving, clitoral self, and the repression of love for her mother, a person of her own sex. Yet even the Freudian account somewhat reluctantly presents a recurring tension between the oedipal and preoedipal phases for the female, whereas in most males (as far as the theory tells) the oedipus complex has a linear and cumulative movement. Freud has found that "Regressions to fixations at these pre-oedipal phases occur very often; in many women we actually find a repeated alternation of periods in which either masculinity or femininity has obtained the upper hand."[22] So the oedipal crisis can extend over years and follow an individual woman right into adulthood. Or, to say it another way, the "feminine" or "correct" resolution of women's gender identity comes easily unstuck and cannot be counted on.

A further elaboration of the oedipal crisis in women is available in Nancy Chodorow's analysis of mothering as a key institution in the social and psychic reproduction of gender. In her view, in the development of a girl, the preoedipal attachment to the mother is never entirely given up; it persists in coloring oedipalization, in shaping problems and issues of the female ego (boundlessness and boundary problems, "lack of separation or differentiation"), and in its influence on both the fact and the way that women mother. So while the gendering process is the "arena" where the goal of heterosexuality is "negotiated," it is also where the mother-daughter dyad and female bonding are affirmed.[23]

The narrative and cultural implications of this neo-Freudian picture of gendering are staggering. With no easy or one-directional passage to "normal femininity," women as social products are characterized by unresolved and continuous alterations between allegiance to males and to females, between heterosexuality and female-identified, lesbian, or bisexual ties. The "original bisexuality" of the individual female is not easily put to rest or resolved by one early tactical episode; rather the oscillation persists and is reconstituted in her adult identity. Further, the emotional rhythms of female identity involve repeated (and possibly even stimultaneous) articulations of these two principles or states, which are taken (ideologically) as opposing poles.[24]

Twentieth-century women writers undertake a reassessment of the processes of gendering by inventing narrative strategies, especially involving sequence, character, and relationship, that neutralize, minimize, or transcend any oversimplified oedipal drama. This occurs by a recognition in various elements of narrative of the "bisexual oscillation" in the psychic makeup of characters, in the resolutions of texts, in the relationships portrayed. In twentieth-century narratives, effort is devoted to depicting masculine and feminine sides in one character—in Woolf's androgyny and in similar procedures in Richardson. Original bisexuality is extended the length of a character's life in H.D. and in Woolf. Women writers readjust the maternal and paternal in ways that unbalance the univocal sequence of object choices. This is why some female quest plots, like *To the Lighthouse* and *The Four-Gated City*, loop backward to mother-child attachments. Narratives of twentieth-century women, notably their *Künstlerromane*, may invent an interplay between the mother, the father, and the hero, in a "relational triangle."[25] These changes are often accompanied by pointed remarks about the plots, characters, and situations once expected in narrative: gender polarization, patrisexual romantic love, the arrest of female quest, the "happy ending"—remarks that, as we shall see, underline the self-consciousness of this critique of narrative scripts and the psychosexual drama that forms them.[26]

These representations of gendering could be achieved irrespective of whether any of the authors were aware of the exact terms of Freudian theory, although no doubt a number were, or whether they explicitly connected their narratives to any aspect of Freud's position (something that does occur in Woolf's *Orlando*, in H.D.'s *Helen in Egypt* and *Tribute to Freud*, and in Doris Lessing's *The Golden Notebook*).[27] For women artists, this sense of "remaining in the Oedipus situation for an indefinite period" would not have to be consciously understood.[28] One may simply postulate that the habit of living with an "unresolved" oedipus complex would lead the bearer to a greater identification of the unstable elements, greater intuitive knowledge of these components of one's interior life.

Indeed, Freud suggests a massive slippage of effectiveness, so that the learning of the rules of gender may need a good deal of extrafamilial reinforcement, especially where the girl is concerned. The formation of the superego—the acceptance of social rules, including those governing gender—is the result of "educative influences, of external intimidation threatening loss of love."[29] That is, education as an institution of gender, and culture as a whole, including literary products like narrative, channel the girl into dominant structures of the sex-gender system. The romance plot in narrative thus may be seen as a necessary extension of the processes of gendering, and the critique of romance that we find in twentieth-century female authors, as part of the oppositional protest lodged against both literary culture and a psychosexual norm.

The psychosexual oscillation of the gendering process, so distinctly theorized, interacts with another systemic aspect of female identity, which shows the same wavering, dialogic structure: a sociocultural oscillation of hegemonic processes. In the social and cultural arena, there is a constant repositioning between dominant and muted, hegemonic and oppositional, central and colonial, so that a woman may be described as (ambiguously) nonhegemonic or, with equal justice but less drama, as (ambiguously) hegemonic if her race, class, and sexuality are dominant. Virginia Woolf envisions this oscillating consciousness in *A Room of One's Own*. "It [the mind] can think back through its fathers or through its mothers, as I have said that a woman writing thinks back through her mothers. Again if one is a woman one is often surprised by a sudden splitting off of consciousness, say in walking down Whitehall, when from being the natural inheritor of that civilization, she becomes, on the contrary, outside of it, alien and critical" (*AROO*, 101). Note how Woolf passes from the oedipal-preoedipal division in object relations to the social oscillation, suggesting the relation of both processes to female identity. The debate between inheritor and critic is a movement between deep identification with dominant values and deep alienation from them. Whitehall, a street in London, is a synechdoche for British civil service and administrative agreements that endure beyond changes in specific governments, and thus is a metaphor for broad sociocultural agreement.

The shifting into alternative perspectives is taken by Woolf as a phenomenon peculiarly resonant for a woman. Her use of the word *natural* as opposed to the word *critical* sums the process up. *Natural* is what every ideology happily claims it is; the beliefs, social practices, sense of the self are second nature, assumed. The word *critical*, however, has the force of a severe and transgressive dissent from cherished mental structures and social practices. This contradictory quiver, this social vibrato creates a critical sensibility: dissent from the culture by which women are partially nourished, to which they are connected.

A major originating moment of Woolf's "outsider's feeling" came, significantly enough, in her confrontation at the turn of the century

with the banal but forceful social and romantic expectations represented by George Duckworth, her half-brother and self-appointed
substitute parent. At issue was her green dress, unconventionally
made of upholstery fabric. From the moment of his anger at her
appearance, from her as yet muted defiance, Woolf crystallizes that
hegemonic set: proper dress, patterned feminine behavior, "tea table
training," the absolute necessity for romance, the "patriarchal machinery" creating rigid, polarized male and female personalities. What
astonished Woolf most was the female role of passive, appreciative
spectator and the acrobatic—almost Swiftean—jumping through
hoops demanded of males; the whole "circus" or "required act" was
accomplished with no irony or critical questioning.[30]

Many commentators on women as a group and on female identity
have isolated as systemic some kind of dual relationship to the definitions offered by various dominant forces. Simone de Beauvoir sees
the female child "hesitating between the role of *object, Other*, which
is offered to her, and the assertion of her liberty" as subject.[31] John
Berger argues that the "social presence" of women and their ingenuity in living in "the keeping of men" have created "two con-
stituent yet always distinct elements of her identity as a woman":
the "surveyor and the surveyed."[32] The "duality of women's position
in society" is Gerda Lerner's explanation for the fact that women as
a group can be both victims and upholders of the status quo:
"Women live a duality—as members of the general culture and as
partakers of women's culture."[33] Nancy Cott similarly views "wom-
en's group consciousness as a subculture uniquely divided against
itself by ties to the dominant culture."[34] Sheila Rowbotham describes
the war of parts of the self, given the attitudes of the dominant group
on the Left. "One part of ourselves mocked another, we joined in the
ridicule of our own aspirations. . . . Part of us leapt over into their
world, part of us stayed at home. . . . We were never all together
in one place, we were always in transit, immigrants into alien terri-
tory."[35] And Alice Walker, in "In Search of Our Mothers' Gardens,"
cites Woolf's *A Room of One's Own* to come to terms with the "contrary instincts" in certain work by black women from Phillis Wheatley to Zora Neale Hurston.[36] In sum, women writers as women nego-
tiate with divided loyalties and doubled consciousness, both within
and without a social and cultural agreement. This, in conjunction with

the psychosexual oscillation, has implications for "sentence" and "sequence"—for language, ideology, and narrative.

Later in her career, Woolf continued her analysis of the source of women's sociocultural oscillation. In *Three Guineas*, Woolf finds that women's structural position enables them to take an adversarial stance to institutions of dominance. Women, she argues, are basically outsiders, formed by their nondominant ("unpaid for") education, as they observe the privileges of maleness and the sacrifices exacted from women themselves for those privileges. The lived experience of women and men even from the same social class differs so greatly that their world views and values are irreconcilably distinct: "though we look at the same things, we see them differently."[37]

Constituting a separate group within their social class, women should capitalize on this built-in zone of difference to think of themselves as an interested, coherent political bloc: an actual Society of Outsiders. They can and should refuse male society and its values (militarism, hierarchy, authoritarianism) even as they enter formerly all-male professions. And women have, Woolf is certain, less chance than men for being apologists for political, economic, and social oppression so intense that—her central point—the patriarchal politics of bourgeois liberalism is on a continuum with fascism and the authoritarian state. Being already outsiders, women should turn its negative markers ("poverty, chastity, derision, freedom from unreal loyalties") into positive markers of difference, and turn their marginal status to political advantage and analytic power (*TG*, 78).

The function of *Three Guineas* is to drive a politically motivated wedge of analysis and polemic between dominant and muted, inheritor and critic, class and gender allegiances, to try to convince educated women no longer to cooperate with the politics of their class. Indeed, in 1940 Woolf argued that women are in a position to make cross-class alliances with working-class men and women because their identification as "commoners, outsiders" will override apparent class distinctions.[38]

Yet the shift to the imperative mode and the call for a vow in *Three Guineas* betray the fact that women are not purely and simply Outsiders; otherwise one would not have to exhort them to remain so. They are, however, less integrated into the dominant orders than are men of their class. Women are a muted or subordinate part of a hegemonic process. Raymond Williams suggests that seeing hegemonic processes would be a way of visualizing culture to credit the internal debate between affirmation and critique. Hegemony includes a relationship in conflictual motion between the ideologies and practices of a dominant class or social group and the alternative practices, which may be either residual or emergent, of the muted classes or groups. Any set of hegemonic assumptions—notions orthodox in a given society and historical era—are "deeply saturating" and pervasive, "organized and lived," woven into the most private areas of our lives.[39] Still the hegemonic is always in motion, being "renewed, recreated, defended and modified."[40] These hegemonic processes are a site for both sociocultural reproduction and sociocultural dissent. The debate that women experience between the critic and the inheritor, the outsider and the privileged, the oppositional and the dominant is a major example of a hegemonic process, one whose results are evident in both social and narrative texts. Constantly reaffrmed as outsiders by others and sometimes by themselves, women's loyalties to dominance remain ambiguous, for they are not themselves in control of the processes by which they are defined.

Issues of control of voice and definition, then, allow Edwin Ardener's otherwise more static model to offer a complementary set of terms to define gender relations: the articulate or dominant men and then the nondominant or muted women. The latter term recalls the muted sonority of a musical instrument—the sound different, tamped down, repressed, but still speaking, with the speech bearing the marks of partial silencing. Interestingly, giving voice to the voiceless and making visible the invisible are two prime maneuvers in feminist poetics. As Ardener would gloss this, "The muted structures are 'there' but cannot be 'realized' in the language of the dominant structure."[41] To depict these relationships, Ardener posits two almost overlapping circles, one standing for dominant vision, the other for muted. The larger uncontested space where the circles overlap is shared by men and women in a given society as parallel inhabitants of main culture. The tiny crescent-shaped band left over for women is their zone of difference. Visualizing the relationship between dominant and muted in this fashion suggests that women can oscillate between the two parts of the circle that represents them, between difference and dominance.

The concept of a "double-consciousness" that comes from one's oscillation between a main and a muted position is not, nor could it ever be, a way of describing women exclusively, but it offers a way of seeing the identity of any group that is at least partially excluded from or marginal to the historically current system of meaning, value, and power.[42] Feminist criticism, then, may be said to begin with W. E. B. DuBois, postulating for blacks this double consciousness, born in negotiation with hegemonic processes.

Ellen Moers analyzed distinctive female stances based not on innate or essential femininity but on the shared cultural experiences of secondary status—constraints on travel, education, social mediations of childhood and motherhood—and reflected in particular uses of certain cultural tropes, such as the Gothic, the monster, the landscape.[43] This postulate was given forceful statement by Elaine Showalter: that women are parallel to other minority groups in their subcultural position "relative to a dominant society" and that this position leads to a unity of "values, conventions, experiences and behaviors" from which women draw and to which they respond with various fictional and biographical strategies.[44] Following Showalter's emphasis on formal and biographical strategies of response, Sandra Gilbert and Susan Gubar pose a repeated and reinvoked struggle as the master plot for women of the nineteenth century: in a dynamic generational confrontation in which dominant culture is the father and women are either sage daughters or mad wives in relation to patriarchal power. A nineteenth-century woman writer is the site of an internalized cultural debate: her own rage that she cannot speak and her culture's rage that she can. This contradiction is resolved in a powerful fictional motif: the madwoman, in whom expression struggles with repression.[45]

Where a reading of twentieth-century materials necessarily differs from the nineteenth-century texts most profoundly analyzed by Showalter and Gilbert and Gubar is that, by the twentieth century, middle-class women are technically—on paper—rather more part of the economic world, rather less legally and politically circumscribed than they were in the nineteenth. This changed position does not alter the negotiation process, but it does mean that women have an interior identification with dominant values (traditionally expressed as a rejection of female specialness) as well as an understanding of muted alternatives. Dominant and muted may be more equally balanced opponents in the twentieth century than in the nineteenth.

Mary Jacobus has also noted, and made central to her analysis of women's writing, the split between alien critic and inheritor that I have taken as a key text for this book. Jacobus further argues that, given this situation, "at once within culture and outside it," a woman writer must simultaneously "challenge the terms and work within them."[46] This precisely parallels my argument—that woman is neither wholly "subcultural" nor, certainly, wholly main-cultural, but negotiates differences and sameness, marginality and inclusion in a constant dialogue, which takes shape variously in the various authors, but with one end—a rewriting of gender in dominant fiction. The two processes in concert—the gendering and the hegemonic process—create mutual reinforcement for the double consciousness of women writers. This is the social and sexual basis of the poetics of critique.[47]

All forms of dominant narrative, but especially romance, are tropes for the sex-gender system as a whole.[48] Given the ideological and affirmative functions of narrative, it is no surprise that the critique of story is a major aspect of the stories told by twentieth-century women writers. . . .[49]

Notes

1 Virginia Woolf, *A Room of One's Own* (New York: Harcourt, Brace and World, 1957); abbreviated in the text as *AROO*. The epigraphs come from pp. 85 and 95.

2 Virginia Woolf, "Women and Fiction" (1929), in *Granite and Rainbow* (New York: Harcourt, Brace, 1958), p. 80; abbreviated as *G&R*.

3 The sentence is further qualified as being "too loose, too heavy, too pompous for a woman's use" (*G&R*, 81). A parallel, but slightly softened, statement about the sentence is found in *AROO*, p. 79, and an elaboration in the 1923 review of Dorothy Richardson, "Romance and the Heart," reprinted in *Contemporary Writers: Essays on Twentieth Century Books and Authors* (New York: Harcourt Brace Jovanovich, 1965), pp. 123–25. Working with these passages, Josephine Donovan also notes that the differences between "male" and "female" sentences exist in the tone of authority, the declaration of the insider in one, the under-the-surface life in the other, which rejects the authoritarian. Donovan also links Woolf's achievements in subjective realism to her critique of gender ideologies in narrative. "Feminist Style Criticism," in *Images of Women in Fiction: Feminist Perspectives*, ed. Susan Koppelman

Cornillon (Bowling Green: Bowling Green University Popular Press, 1972), pp. 339–52. A further note on the analysis of Woolf's "sentence." In this study as a whole, I am carefully (too?) agnostic on the subject of those actual disruptions of syntax, grammar, and words more characteristic of, say, Gertrude Stein; however, what Julia Kristeva calls the semiotic and symbolic registers may be another oscillation of dominant discourse in dialogue with marginality.

4   Richardson, "Romance and the Heart," pp. 124–25.

5   This is Nelly Furman's argument. "Textual Feminism," in *Women and Language in Literature and Society*, ed. Sally McConnell-Ginet, Ruth Borker, and Nelly Furman (New York: Praeger, 1980), pp. 50–51.

6   Nancy Miller, "Emphasis Added: Plots and Plausibilities in Women's Fiction," *PMLA* 96, no. 1 (January 1981): 38.

7   Woolf, "Women Novelists," reprinted in *Contemporary Writers*, p. 25.

8   Woolf, *Granite and Rainbow*, p. 80.

9   Here in the twenties, Woolf holds in conflictive tension her materialist and idealist views of writing. She argues that through art one may—indeed one must—transcend the cultural conditions of one's own formation. So in *A Room of One's Own*, Woolf combines a materialist analysis of the conditions that determine a woman's identity and capacity for work and an idealist vision of androgyny, a unity of the warring and unequal genders in luminous serenity. This point is made by Michele Barrett in her introduction to a collection of essays by Virginia Woolf, *Women and Writing* (New York: Harcourt Brace Jovanovich, 1979), pp. 20, 22.

10 For example, Woolf compared living with the institutions of gender as they are to living in "half-civilized barbarism," a slap at the meliorism of liberal ideology. Reply to "Affable Hawk" from the *New Statesman* of 1920, in *The Diary of Virginia Woolf, Volume Two: 1920–1924*, ed. Anne Olivier Bell and Andrew McNeillie (New York: Harcourt Brace Jovanovich, 1978), p. 342.

11 Carolyn G. Heilbrun points toward the role of double determining when she suggests that "to be a feminist one had to have an experience of being an outsider more extreme than merely being a woman." *Reinventing Womanhood* (New York: W. W. Norton, 1979), pp. 20–24. Adrienne Rich describes the tension leading to a doubled vision: "Born a white woman, Jewish or of curious mind / —twice an outsider, still believing in inclusion—" *A Wild Patience Has Taken Me This Far* (New York: W. W. Norton, 1981), p. 39.

12 Myra Jehlen, "Archimedes and the Paradox of Feminist Criticism," *Signs* 6, no. 4 (Summer 1981): 594. Jehlen makes this point about nineteenth-century American women, attempting to explain the literature of sentiment and limited challenge that they produced. "In this society, women stand outside any of the definitions of complete being; hence perhaps the appeal to them of a literature of conformity and inclusion." "(Ambiguously) nonhegemonic" from my essay "For the Etruscans: Sexual Difference and Artistic Production—the Debate over a Female Aesthetic," in *The Future of Difference*, ed. Hester Eisenstein and Alice Jardine (Boston: G. K. Hall, 1980). A further develop-

ment of the phrase "(ambiguously) nonhegemonic" is found in Margaret Homans, " 'Her Very Own Howl': The Ambiguities of Representation in Recent Women's Fiction," *Signs* 9, no. 2 (Winter 1983): 186–205. Homans suggests that "there is a specifically gender-based alienation from language" visible in thematic treatments of language in women's fiction, which derives from "the special ambiguity of women's simultaneous participation in and exclusion from a hegemonic group," p. 205.

13 For example, Olive Schreiner, *Women and Labour*; Charlotte Perkins Gilman, *The Man-Made World; or, Our Androcentric Culture* and *Women and Economics*; Virginia Woolf, *Three Guineas, A Room of One's Own*, and various essays; H.D., *Tribute to Freud, End to Torment*, and *The Gift*; Dorothy Richardson, essays on women; Adrienne Rich, *Of Woman Born* and *On Lies, Secrets and Silence*; Tillie Olsen, *Silences*; Doris Lessing, *A Small Personal Voice*; Alice Walker, *In Search of Our Mothers' Gardens*.

14 Annette Kuhn, *Women's Pictures: Feminism and Cinema* (London: Routledge and Kegan Paul, 1982), p. 17. The first chapter is a sterling exposition of feminist analysis of culture.

15 In the course of her research on the draft of *A Room of One's Own*, Alice Fox communicated to Jane Marcus that Woolf originally, wittily left a blank unfilled by the word *laboratory*. "Then she wrote that she was afraid to turn the page to see what they shared, and she thought of the obscenity trial for a novel." The allusion made and excised is to the contemporaneous trial of *The Well of Loneliness*; the implication that Woolf handled differently in her published text is that homophobic censorship and self-censorship alike conspire to mute discussion of relational ties between women. Jane Marcus, "Liberty, Sorority, Misogyny," in *The Representation of Women in Fiction*, ed. Carolyn G. Heilbrun and Margaret R. Higonnet (Baltimore: Johns Hopkins University Press, 1983), p. 82.

16 Elaine Showalter proposed "that the specificity of women's writing [is] not . . . a transcient by-product of sexism but [is] a fundamentally and continually determining reality." "Feminist Criticism in the Wilderness," *Critical Inquiry* 8, no. 2 (Winter 1981): 205.

17 Gayle Rubin, "The Traffic in Women: Notes on the 'Political Economy' of Sex," in *Toward an Anthropology of Women*, ed. Rayna [Rapp] Reiter (New York: Monthly Review Press, 1975): pp. 157–210.

18 Sigmund Freud, "The Psychology of Women" (1933), in *New Introductory Lectures on Psycho-Analysis*, trans. W. J. H. Sprott (New York: W. W. Norton, 1933), p. 184. The same essay is called "Femininity" in *The Standard Edition of the Complete Psychological Works of Sigmund Freud*, vol. 22, trans. James Strachey (London: Hogarth Press and The Institute of Psychoanalysis, 1964).

19 Freud, "The Psychology of Women," p. 158.

20 Gayle Rubin, "The Traffic in Women," p. 185.

21 Sherry B. Ortner, "Oedipal Father, Mother's Brother, and The Penis: A Review of Juliet Mitchell's *Psychoanalysis and Feminism*," *Feminist Studies* 2,

no. 2/3 (1975): 179. As Michele Barrett has remarked, "no substantial work has yet been produced that historicizes the [gendering] processes outlined in psychoanalytic theory." *Women's Oppression Today: Problems in Marxist Feminist Analysis* (London: Verso and New Left Books, 1980), p. 197.

22 Freud, "The Psychology of Women," p. 179. By female masculinity is meant the preoedipal object choice of a female; by femininity is meant the oedipal object choice of a male.

23 Nancy Chodorow, *The Reproduction of Mothering: Psychoanalysis and the Sociology of Gender* (Berkeley: University of California Press, 1978), p. 122.

24 Chodorow summarizes the female's "emotional, if not erotic bisexual oscillation between mother and father—between preoccupation with 'mother-child' issues and 'male-female' issues." *The Reproduction of Mothering*, p. 168. I am indebted to Chodorow for the concept of oscillation.

25 "The asymmetrical structure of parenting generates a female oedipus complex . . . characterized by the continuation of preoedipal attachments and preoccupations, sexual oscillation in an oedipal triangle, and the lack of either absolute change of love object or absolute oedipal resolution." Chodorow, *The Reproduction of Mothering*, pp. 133–34.

26 In an analysis related to my point here, Elizabeth Abel sees the theme and presence of same-sex friendship in literary works by women as an expression of female identity and the particularities of female oedipalization. As well, Abel offers striking remarks on the theory of literary influence that can be derived from Chodorow. "(E)Merging Identities: The Dynamics of Female Friendship in Contemporary Fiction by Women," *Signs* 6, no. 3 (Spring 1981): 413–35.

27 For example, H.D. was psychoanalyzed by Freud, and engaged, according to Susan Friedman, in a constant interior debate with Freud on several issues, including gender. *Psyche Reborn: The Emergence of H.D.* (Bloomington: Indiana University Press, 1981). Virginia Woolf noted her "very amateurish knowledge of Freud and the psychoanalysts" and admitted that "my knowledge is merely from superficial talk." In her circle, however, the talkers might have included James Strachey, the translator of Freud's *Complete Psychological Works*, cited in note 18. *The Letters of Virginia Woolf, Volume Five: 1932–1935*, ed. Nigel Nicolson and Joanne Trautmann (New York: Harcourt Brace Jovanovich, 1979), pp. 36 and 91.

28 Freud, "The Psychology of Women," p. 177.

29 Freud, "The Passing of the Oedipus-Complex," in *Collected Papers, Volume 2* (London: Hogarth Press, 1957), p. 275. The paper dates from 1924.

30 Virginia Woolf, *Moments of Being*, ed. Jeanne Schulkind (New York: Harcourt Brace Jovanovich, 1978), pp. 132, 129, 132.

31 Simone de Beauvoir, *The Second Sex*, trans. H. M. Parshley (New York: Bantam Books, 1972), p. 47.

32 John Berger, *Ways of Seeing* (New York: Viking Press, 1972), p. 46.

33 Gerda Lerner, *The Majority Finds its Past: Placing Women in History* (Oxford: Oxford University Press, 1979), pp. xxi, 52.

34 Nancy Cott, "Introduction," in *Root of Bitterness: Documents of the Social History of American Women* (New York: E. P. Dutton, 1972), p. 3.

35 Sheila Rowbotham, *Women's Consciousness, Man's World* (London: Penguin, 1973), pp. 30–31.

36 Alice Walker, "In Search of Our Mothers' Gardens," in *In Search of Our Mothers' Gardens* (San Diego: Harcourt Brace Jovanovich, 1983), p. 235.

37 Virginia Woolf, *Three Guineas* (New York: Harcourt, Brace and World, Inc., 1938), p. 5. Abbreviated in the text as *TG*.

38 Virginia Woolf, "The Leaning Tower," in *The Moment and Other Essays* (New York: Harcourt Brace Jovanovich, 1948), p. 154.

39 Raymond Williams, "Base and Superstructure in Marxist Cultural Theory," *New Left Review* 82 (November–December 1973): 7.

40 Raymond Williams, *Marxism and Literature* (Oxford: Oxford University Press, 1977), p. 112.

41 Edwin Ardener, "The 'Problem' Revisited," a coda to "Belief and the Problem of Women," in *Perceiving Women*, ed. Shirley Ardener (New York: John Wiley and Sons, 1975), p. 22. Elaine Showalter made Ardener's analysis available to feminist criticism in "Feminist Criticism in the Wilderness," *Critical Inquiry* 8, no. 2 (Winter 1981), especially pp. 199–201.

42 "Double-consciousness" is, in fact, the influential formulation of black identity made in 1903 by W. E. B DeBois in *The Souls of Black Folk* (in *Three Negro Classics*, ed. John Hope Franklin [New York: Avon Books, 1965], p. 215). "It is a peculiar sensation, the double-consciousness, this sense of always looking at one's self through the eyes of others, of measuring one's soul by the tape of a world that looks on in amused contempt and pity. One ever feels his twoness—an American, a Negro; two souls, two thoughts, two unreconciled strivings; two warring ideals in one dark body, whose dogged strength alone keeps it from being torn asunder." Richard Wright made a similar point in 1956: "First of all, my position is a split one, I'm black. I'm a man of the West. These hard facts condition, to some degree, my outlook." (*Presence Africaine* [November 1956], cited in *The Black Writer in Africa and the Americas*, ed. Lloyd W. Brown [Los Angeles: Hennessey and Ingalls, 1973], p. 27).

43 Ellen Moers, *Literary Women: The Great Writers* (Garden City, N.Y.: Doubleday, 1976).

44 Elaine Showalter, *A Literature of Their Own: British Women Novelists from Brontë to Lessing* (Princeton, N.J.: Princeton University Press, 1977), p. 11. The postulation of "unity" is also generally assumed in this study. However, other perspectives on women's writing might make other assumptions, now that "women's writing" is an accepted critical category.

45 Sandra M. Gilbert and Susan Gubar, *The Madwoman in the Attic: The Woman Writer and the Nineteenth-Century Literary Imagination* (New Haven: Yale University Press, 1979), p. 49.

46 Mary Jacobus, "The Difference of View," in *Women Writing and Writing about Women*, ed. Mary Jacobus (London: Croom Helm, 1979), pp. 19–20.

47 Myra Jehlen's summary of the relationship of women to culture is exemplary.

> Women (and perhaps some men not of the universal kind) must deal with their situation as a *pre*condition for writing about it. They have to confront the assumptions that render them a kind of fiction in themselves in that they are defined by others, as components of the language and thought of others. It hardly matters at this prior stage what a woman wants to write; its political nature is implicit in the fact that it is she (a "she") who will do it. All women's writing would thus be congenitally defiant and universally characterized by the blasphemous argument it makes in coming into being. And this would mean that the autonomous individuality of a woman's story or poem is framed by engagement, the engagement of its denial of dependence. We might think of the form this necessary denial takes (however it is individually interpreted, whether conciliatory or assertive) as analogous to genre, in being an issue, not of content, but of the structural formulation of the work's relationship to the inherently formally patriarchal language which is the only language we have. ("Archimedes," p. 582)

The proposal this book makes for the "structural formulation" analogous to genre is the act of critique, drawing on the oscillations of female identity.

48 The sex-gender system involves a linked chain of institutions such as the sexual division of labor in production and in the socialization of children, valorized heterosexuality and the constraint on female sexuality, marriage and kinship, sexual choice and desire, gender asymmetry and polarization.

49 We have omitted a closing "survey of several contemporary works," which shows "how the critique of story is not only a thematic fact but an indication of the moral, ideological, and political desire to rescript the novel" (DuPlessis)—eds.

INDEX

Addison, Joseph, 140, 178; *The Spectator*, 178
Agamemnon, The, 27
Aesop, 470; fables, 361; "The Town Mouse and the Country Mouse," 459, 470
Alcott, Louisa May, 389
All the King's Men (Robert Penn Warren), 451
Althusser, Louis, 387
Alter, Robert, 423–27
Amazon Utopias, 396
Antonioni, Michelangelo, 421
Ardener, Edwin, 485
Ardener, Shirley: *Perceiving Women*, 388
Aristotle, 2, 3, 5, 51, 54, 72, 139n6, 172, 178, 227, 240, 267, 269, 358, 411; *Poetics*, 2, 139n6, 153, 172, 240, 358
Atwood, Margaret, 476; *Lady Oracle*, 473; *Surfacing*, 393
Auerbach, Erich, 265, 338; *Mimesis*, 266n11, 340
Auerbach, Nina, 382; *Communities of Women: An Idea in Fiction*, 389
Austen, Jane, 33, 40, 44, 45, 46, 47, 171, 176, 181, 187, 199, 221, 270, 395; *Emma*, 181–82; *Mansfield Park*, 45; *Persuasion*, 46, 303; *Pride and Prejudice*, 32, 33, 181–82, 254, 264
Authority of Experience, The (ed. Lee Edwards and Arlyn Diamond), 399, 402n28

Bader, A. L., 458
Bakhtin, Mikhail M., 7, 70, 313
Bal, Mieke, 12
Balzac, Honoré de, 5, 123, 144, 148–49, 194, 203, 206, 207, 210, 211–14, 216, 217, 270, 279, 285, 325–26; *César Birotteau*, 279; *Le Chef d'Oeuvre Inconnu*, 207; *Duchesse de Langeais*, 279; *Eugénie Grandet*, 234; *Les Illusions perdues*, 325; *Le Père Goriot*, 313, 316, 317, 321, 322, 323, 324–25, 328, 332
Barnes, Djuna, 85–86, 95, 118; *Nightwood*, 85, 88, 95–99, 192, 197; *Ryder*, 95
Barth, John, 71, 338, 422, 423, 430, 431, 432; "The Literature of Exhaustion," 419, 432, 433
Barthelme, Donald, 419, 421, 422, 426
Barthes, Roland, 71, 319, 387, 419, 426; *S/Z*, 319; *Writing Degree Zero*, 144, 426
Bate, Walter Jackson, 433; *The Burden of the Past and the English Poet*, 433
Baudelaire, Charles, 421
Beardsley, Monroe, 368
Beattie, James, 132

Beauvoir, Simone de, 228, 326, 483; *L'invitée*, 228

Beckett, Samuel, 270, 421; *Comment C'est*, 232; *Texts for Nothing*, 430

Beckson, Karl, and Arthur Ganz, 253; *A Reader's Guide to Literary Terms*, 266n1, 301, 312n3, 424

Belinsky, Vissarion G., 5, 78

Bell, Currer, Ellis, and Acton (pseud-onyms of the Brontë sisters), 395

Belle Journée, Une, 319

Bellow, Saul, 421, 422, 426; *Henderson the Rain King*, 183; *The Victim*, 179

Bennett, Arnold, 24, 26, 31, 32, 33, 34, 36

Benveniste, Emile, 314

Berger, John, 483

Besant, Walter, 14, 16, 17, 18, 21, 22

Binding, Rudolf, 200

Blake, Nicholas, 315

Blanchot, Maurice, 149, 199, 226; *L'Arrêt de mort*, 196

Blankenburg, Friedrich von, 56, 68n6; *Versuch über den Roman*, 55

Bloom, Harold, 382

Bloomsbury group, 25, 196, 198

Boccaccio, Giovanni, 3, 187, 431; *Decameron*, 3, 333

Boileau-Despreaux, Nicholas, 51

Booth, Wayne C., 5, 253, 261, 314, 358, 366, 369–70; *The Rhetoric of Fiction*, 5, 8, 9, 170, 253, 266n6

Borges, Jorge Luis, 338, 421, 424, 429, 432

Bowen, Elizabeth, 351

Boyers, Robert, 382–83; "A Case Against Feminist Criticism," 382

Brecht, Bertolt, 428

Brontë, Charlotte, 47; *Jane Eyre*, 345; *Villette*, 32. See also Bell, Currer

Brontë, Emily, 106, 196; *Wuthering Heights*, 103, 105–7, 448–49. See also Bell, Ellis

Brooks, Cleanth, 96

Brooks, Gwendolyn, 476

Brooks, Peter, 237

Brooks, Van Wyck, 80; *The Ordeal of Mark Twain*, 80

Brower, Reuben, 300

Browning, Elizabeth Barrett, 380, 389–90; *Aurora Leigh*, 390

Browning, Robert, 75, 186, 390; *Men and Women*, 390

Burke, Kenneth, 301, 308, 359; *The Philosophy of Literary Form*, 359

Butler, Samuel, 26; *The Way of All Flesh*, 26

Butor, Michel, 236–37, 421; *L'Emploi du temps*, 237, 315; *La Modification*, 315

Byatt, A. S., 222

Byron, Lord George Gordon, 52, 60; *Childe Harold*, 52; *Don Juan*, 52

Calvino, Italo, 421, 422, 431; *The Castle of Crossed Destinies*, 422; *Cosmicomics*, 422, 431; *Invisible Cities*, 422; *The Path to the Nest of Spiders*, 422

Camus, Albert, 199, 315; *La Chute*, 199, 316, 317, 333, as *The Fall*, 183; *L'Étranger*, 199, 226, 229, 326, 329, as *The Stranger*, 179; *La Peste*, 199

Cantatrice chauve, La, 324

Carlyle, Thomas, and Jane Carlyle, 27

Cary, Joyce, 200; *The Captive and the Free*, 174; *The Horse's Mouth*, 183

Castle of Otranto (Horace Walpole), 193

Cayrol, Jean, 149–50

Céline, Louis-Ferdinand, 370; *Journey to the End of the Night*, 370

Cervantes, Miguel de, 3, 13, 63, 118–19, 220, 431, 432; *Don Quixote*, 3, 119, 127, 194, 325, 421, 431, 432

Cézanne, Paul, 96

Chanson de Roland, La, 328

Chateaubriand, Vicomte François René, 196

Chatman, Seymour, 143, 251, 371; *Story and Discourse: Narrative Structure in Fiction and Film*, 366

Chaucer, Geoffrey, 7; *Troilus and Criseyde*, 7, 178

Cheever, John, 422

Chekhov, Anton, 78, 467–68; "On The Road," 462

Chernyshevsky, Nikolai G., 78

Chesterton, G. K., 209
Chodorow, Nancy, 480
Christian Socialism, 390
Christie, Agatha, 147
Cixous, Hélène, 399
Cloches de Bâle, Les, 329
Clough, Arthur Hugh, 390
Coleridge, Samuel Taylor, 132, 194, 309
Colet, Louise, 426
Confessions of Zeno, 171
Conrad, Joseph, 32, 102, 108, 191, 196, 258, 346, 370, 439–40, 445, 451, 454; Chance, 442–43; Heart of Darkness, 162, 168, 258, 320, 327, 328, 333, 351, 371, 439, 441–43, 452; Lord Jim, 374, 434, 438–44, 445–46, 448–50, 451, 453, 454; Nostromo, 449, 450, 451; "An Outpost of Progress," 162; The Secret Agent, 272, 370, 375, 449, 452; The Secret Sharer, 260; Under Western Eyes, 370, 452; "Youth," 439
Constant, Benjamin, 408; Adolphe, 405–14
Contemporary Approaches to English Studies (ed. Hilda Schiff), 381, 401n1
Conversation, The (film), 408
Cooper, James Fenimore, 122
Coover, Robert, 419, 421
Cortazar, Julio, 421
Cott, Nancy, 483; The Bonds of Womanhood: Woman's Sphere in New England 1780–1835, 389
Crane, R. S., 9, 190, 238, 239, 240, 350, 358–59; "The Concept of Plot and the Plot of Tom Jones," 131, 169n1, 239, 250n1, 364n22
Crane, Stephen, 468; Maggie: A Girl of the Streets, 362
Cross, Wilbur L., 134

Daly, Mary, 384
Dante Alighieri, 206, 333, 370; Divine Comedy, 370; The Inferno, 371
Decline and Fall (Evelyn Waugh), 182
Defoe, Daniel, 4, 44, 104, 105, 346; Robinson Crusoe, 4; A Journal of the Plague Year, 4; Moll Flanders, 4, 103, 104, 105, 260

Demian (Herman Hesse), 192
Dickens, Charles, 12, 43, 44, 46, 125, 171, 176, 272, 274, 428, 429, 431; Bleak House, 345; Dombey and Son, 382; Great Expectations, 13, 121, 155, 160, 180, 181, 377, 431; The Old Curiosity Shop, 327
Dit d'aventures, 52
Döblin, Alfred, 200
Doolittle, Hilda (pseud. H. D.), 476, 481; Helen in Egypt, 481; Tribute to Freud, 481
Dos Passos, John, 123
Dostoevsky, Fyodor, 12, 47, 81, 121, 200, 428, 436; The Brothers Karamazov, 135, 201, 315; Crime and Punishment, 241, 245, 436, 444; Notes from Underground, 352; White Nights, 60
Douglas, Norman, 42–43
Dreiser, Theodore, 123–24, 302; Sister Carrie, 302–3, 306
Dryden, John, 5, 72, 173–74; "An Essay on Dramatic Poesy," 173
DuBois, W. E. B., 486
Duerrenmatt, Friedrich, 201; Die Panne, 201
Dujardin, Edouard, 194, 196
Durrell, Lawrence, 200; Alexandria Quartets, 200, 244, 445; Justine, 320

Écriture feminine, 381
Edel, Leon, 381
Eliot, George, 196, 232, 338, 340–41, 383, 390, 391, 395, 396; Adam Bede, 328, 388; Middlemarch, 174, 391; The Mill on the Floss, 391
Eliot, T. S., 6, 12, 26, 37, 71, 81, 88, 93, 95, 98, 104, 197, 421, 424, 425, 429; The Waste Land, 96, 98
Elkin, Stanley, 421, 426
Elliott, George P., 423; The Modernist Deviation, 423
Ellison, Ralph, 10; Invisible Man, 10
Elton, Oliver, 134
Engels, Friedrich, 75–77, 211, 214
E. T., 112; D. H. Lawrence: A Personal Record, 112
Euclid, 83, 429; Elements, 83

496 Index

Evan Harrington, 42
Existentialism, 143

Fascism, 215, 217; Fascist ideology, 205
Faulkner, William, 8, 12, 115, 123, 180,
    272, 349, 421, 423, 451, 454, 467;
    Absalom, Absalom!, 11, 243, 249,
    444, 450, 451, 465, 466; *As I Lay
    Dying*, 184; "Barn Burning," 154;
    Intruder in the Dust, 183; *Light in
    August*, 173; "A Rose for Emily,"
    462, 466; *Sanctuary*, 270, 326; *The
    Sound and The Fury*, 13, 183, 249,
    303, 305, 306, 444, 446–48, 466
Fellini, Federico, 421
"Female World of Love and Ritual,
    The" (Carroll Smith-Rosenberg), 389
Feminist, 476–77; feminist critique,
    385–87; feminist criticism, 382–83,
    385–401, 473, 474, 486
The Feminization of American Culture
    (Ann Douglas), 389
Ferguson, Suzanne, 349; "Defining the
    Short Story," 152
Fern, Fanny, 393, 396
Fernandez, Ramon, 98, 263
Fielding, Henry, 4, 5, 47, 52, 55, 126,
    131–41, 176, 180, 184, 187, 196, 221,
    241, 310, 340, 371; *Amelia*, 369;
    Jonathan Wild, 180, 369; *Joseph
    Andrews*, 4, 310, 369; *Shamela*, 4;
    Tom Jones, 5, 55, 131–41, 168, 173,
    175, 178, 179, 184, 186, 240, 244, 315,
    327, 330, 371, 378
Fitzgerald, F. Scott, 123, 125, 161, 299;
    "Babylon Revisited," 154, 160; *The
    Great Gatsby*, 101, 161, 170, 178, 182,
    301, 449, 465; *Tender is the Night*,
    301, 305, 450; "Winter Dreams," 161
Flaubert, Gustave, 6, 20, 85, 86–90, 123,
    149, 176, 192, 194, 206, 221, 256, 297,
    325, 421, 426, 459, 467, 468; "Un
    coeur simple," 23n2, 320, 326–27,
    329; *L'Education Sentimentale*, 326;
    Herodias, 328; *La Légende de Saint
    Julien l'Hospitalier*, 319; *Madame
    Bovary*, 32, 86–88, 121, 142n11, 241,
    256, 314, 325
Foley, Martha, 351, 353

Ford (Hueffer), Ford Madox, 108, 232,
    243, 451; *The Good Soldier*, 243, 246,
    248, 444, 445–46, 448, 450, 451, 462,
    465, 470; *Joseph Conrad: A Personal
    Remembrance*, 445
Forester, Fanny, 396
Formalism, Russian, 436
Forster, E. M., 10, 24, 26, 171, 234, 356;
    Aspects of the Novel, 10, 40, 141n10,
    356; *The Longest Journey*, 127–28
Fourier, François, 390
Fowles, John, 421
Frank, Joseph, 12, 101, 278, 434, 435,
    438, 453, 457, 465
French symbolism, 72, 194–96
Freud, Sigmund, 79, 81, 128, 478–81;
    Freudian analysis, 80; Freudianism,
    473; Freudian theory, 478–81
Friedman, Norman, 258, 265, 314, 349,
    457, 458
Frye, Northrop, 343, 345, 348n11, 398;
    Anatomy of Criticism, 398

Galsworthy, John, 24, 26, 32, 33, 34,
    354
Gardner, John, 422, 423, 430; *On Moral
    Fiction*, 423
Gaskell, Elizabeth, 338, 389, 396
Gass, William H., 419, 420, 430
Genette, Gérard, 9, 12, 85, 375
German romanticism, 194–95
Gide, André, 148, 196, 199, 234, 421;
    Les Faux Monnayeurs, 198, 322, 327,
    328; *L'Immoraliste*, 320, 327–28, 333
Gilbert, Sandra, 486
Gilbert, Stuart, 88
Gillespie, Gerald, 351, 357
Gilman, Charlotte Perkins, 396–97
Godard, Jean-Luc, 421
Goethe, Johann Wolfgang von, 58,
    68n8, 77, 206, 214, 216; *The Sorrows
    of Young Werther*, 193, 330; *Wilhelm
    Meister*, 55, 195
Gogol, Nikolai, 64, 272
Gold Pot, The, 323, 327
Golden Ass, The (Lucius Apuleius), 3
Golding, William, 199–200; *Pincher
    Martin*, 199
Goldsmith, Oliver, 367

Gombrich, E. H., 346; *Art and Illusion*, 340

Goncourts, Edmond and Jules de, 194

Gordimer, Nadine, 458

Gorky, Maxim, 79, 214, 216

Gothic literature, 193, 466, 486

Gourmont, Rémy de, 194

Graff, Gerald, 423–27; "Babbitt at the Abyss," 423; "The Myth of the Post-modernist Breakthrough," 423

Greene, Graham, 200; *Brighton Rock*, 180; *The Power and the Glory*, 183; *The Quiet American*, 180

Greenwood, Grace, 396

Grimm's fairy tales, 470

Gubar, Susan, 486

Guerard, Albert J., 449

Gullason, Thomas, 458

Gynocritics, 385, 388–89, 397

Hardy, Thomas, 32, 196, 346, 386–87; *The Mayor of Casterbridge*, 32, 254, 380, 386–87; *The Return of the Native*, 241

Hartman, Geoffrey, 384

Hassan, Ihab, 422, 423, 426–27, 428; *The Dismemberment of Orpheus: Towards a Postmodern Literature*, 423

Hauptmann, Gerhardt, 52

Hawkes, John, 419, 420, 422

Hawthorne, Nathaniel, 7, 13, 122, 468; *The Scarlet Letter*, 327, 388; *Twice-Told Tales*, 7

H. D. *See* Doolittle, Hilda

Hegel, G. W. F., 56, 74; Hegelian dialectics, 205

Heilbrun, Carolyn, 385–86

Heine, Heinrich, 52

Heinrich von Ofterdingen, 194

Hemingway, Ernest, 8, 123, 125, 262, 467; "Cat in the Rain," 462; *A Farewell to Arms*, 331; *For Whom the Bell Tolls*, 162; "The Gambler, the Nun, and the Radio," 464, 470; "Hills Like White Elephants," 157, 167, 462; "Indian Camp," 459; "The Killers," 176, 178, 325, 371; "The Short Happy Life of Francis Ma-

comber," 154, 160; "Soldier's Home," 262, 470; *The Sun Also Rises*, 321; "Ten Indians," 158

L'Heptameron, 333

Herder, Johann Gottfried von, 74; *Ideas on the Philosophy of History*, 74

Hoffmann, E. T. A., 194, 421

Homer, 7, 73, 74, 76, 125, 132; *Iliad*, 7, 59, 173, 140n6; *Odyssey*, 73–74

Horace, 51

Houston, J. P., 282, 295, 297; "Temporal Patterns in *A la recherche du temps perdu*," 282

"How Beautiful with Shoes" (Wilbur Steele), 154, 160

Howe, Irving, 386, 423–24; *The Decline of the New*, 423

Howells, William Dean, 122, 357

Hugo, Victor, 428

Hurston, Zora Neale, 476, 483

Hutton, Richard, 393

Huxley, Aldous, 180; *Brave New World*, 175; *Eyeless in Gaza*, 450, 451; "Nuns at Luncheon," 175

Huysmans, Joris Karl, 194

Hyperion, 194

Ibsen, Henrik, 42, 314

Ingarden, Roman, 438; *Vom Erkennen des literarischen Kunstwerks*, 438

Jacobus, Mary, 487

Jakobson, Roman, 315

James, Henry, 5, 6, 8, 24, 102, 108, 252–53, 260, 263, 270, 273, 274, 299–300, 206, 314, 325, 349, 350, 354–55, 356, 357, 358, 381, 436, 468; *The Ambassadors*, 142n11, 174–75, 241, 245, 263, 376, 378; "The Art of Fiction," 6; *The Art of the Novel*, 252; *The Awkward Age*, 178, 187; *Daisy Miller*, 352; "The Death of the Lion," 361; *The Golden Bowl*, 301, 304, 306; "The Jolly Corner," 470; "The Lesson of the Master," 356; *The Portrait of a Lady*, 135, 361; *The Princess Casamassima*, 126, 128; *The*

James, Henry (*Cont.*)
  Sacred Fount, 259–60, 261; *The Spoils of Poynton*, 183; *The Turn of the Screw*, 261; "What Maisie Knew," 376; *The Wings of the Dove*, 107, 301
Jameson, Fredric, 235
Jarry, Alfred, 421
Johnson, Samuel, 5, 72, 74; *Lives of the Poets*, 80
Jonson, Ben, 72; *The Alchemist*, 132
Journal de Salavin, 329
Joyce, James, 8, 12, 24, 26, 37, 88–90, 94, 96, 108, 113–14, 167, 171, 186, 196, 197, 220, 254, 264, 270, 349, 421, 423, 424, 426, 428, 429, 430, 444, 467, 468; "Araby," 459, 466; "Clay," 462–63; "The Dead," 352, 461; *Dubliners*, 467; "An Encounter," 461; "Eveline," 378n9, 463; *Finnegans Wake*, 197, 232, 243, 425, 428, 429; "Ivy Day in the Committee Room," 464, 470; *A Portrait of the Artist as a Young Man*, 8, 89, 104, 112–14, 186–87, 264, 331, 374; "The Sisters," 461; *Stephen Hero*, 113; *Ulysses*, 11, 13, 37, 85, 88–90, 96, 99, 112–14, 166–67, 173, 242, 243, 246–47, 249, 254, 301, 326, 374, 425, 459, 461, 465
Julie de Carneilhan (Colette), 360

Kafka, Franz, 149, 200, 421, 424, 426; "The Metamorphosis," 180, 352
Kaplan, Cora, 390
Keats, John, 301; "On First Looking Into Chapman's Homer," 155
Keller, Gottfried, 210
Kellogg, Robert, 452, 453
Kenner, Hugh, 423, 433; *A Homemade World*, 423
Kinflicks (Lisa Alther), 393
Kingsley, Charles, 390
Kipling, Rudyard, 467; "Love O' Women," 462; "Mrs. Bathurst," 462
Klabund, 200
Klinkowitz, Jerome, 421
Kolodny, Annette, 392
Kott, Jan, 230

Lacan, Jacques, 387
Laocoön (Gotthold Lessing), 435
Larbaud, Valéry, 196
Lardner, Ring, 180; "Haircut," 179
Lawrence, D. H., 26, 42, 110–12, 122, 196, 244, 467; *Collected Poems*, 110; *Sons and Lovers*, 103, 110–12, 178, 262
Leavis, F. R., 96
Lee, Holme (pseud. of Harriet Parr), 396
Lenin, V. I., 78, 214
Lerner, Gerda, 483
Lessing, Doris, 476; *The Four-Gated City*, 481; *The Golden Notebook*, 383, 481
Levin, Harry, 88
Levine, George, 11
Lévi-Strauss, Claude, 2; *The Savage Mind* (*La Pensée Sauvage*), 2
Lewes, George Henry, 390, 393
Lewis, Sinclair, 123
Liaisons dangereuses, Les, 371
Llosa, Mario Vargas, 445, 454; *The Green House*, 445
Locke, Richard, 422
Lodge, David, 337
Loraine, Philip, 316
"The Lottery" (Shirley Jackson), 154
Lubbock, Percy, 171, 178, 253, 263, 353; *The Craft of Fiction*, 253, 266n7
Lucian, 65
Lucinde, 55
Lukács, Georg, 7, 221, 268
Lunacharsky, Anatoly, 78
Lyly, John, 3

Macaulay, Lord Thomas Babington, 37
Macherey, Pierre, 387, 399
MacLeish, Archibald, 79
McLuhan, Marshall, 432
Maeterlinck, Maurice, 194
Magny, Claude-Edmonde, 234
Mailer, Norman, 421; *The Naked and the Dead*, 422
Mallarmé, Stéphane, 232, 421
Malraux, André, 199; *La Condition humaine*, 198, 329
Maltese Falcon, The, 325

Mann, Heinrich, 200
Mann, Thomas, 200, 214, 243, 421, 426, 430; *Death in Venice*, 352, 356, 361; "Disorder and Early Sorrow," 168; *Dr. Faustus*, 177, 179, 182, 200; *Tonio Kröger*, 360, 426
Mansfield, Katherine, 467
Marienbad (film), 236
Márquez, Gabriel García, 12, 421, 425, 431–32; *One Hundred Years of Solitude*, 425, 431
Marvell, Andrew: "To His Coy Mistress," 155
Marx, Karl, 75, 76, 77
Marxism, 70, 77, 143, 203, 204–6, 381, 397–99
Master of Ballantrae, The, 182
Matthews, Brander, 458
Matthiessen, F. O., 96
Maupassant, Guy de, 180, 468; "The Necklace," 180
Mauriac, Claude, 421
Mauriac, François, 229, 232; *Le Noued de vipères*, 329, as *Knot of Vipers*, 180
Maurice, Frederick Denison, 39
Mayakovsky, Vladimir, 79
Mehring, Franz, 77
Mellen, Joan, 383; *Women and Their Sexuality in the New Film*, 382
Melville, Herman, 10, 122, 272, 340; "Bartleby the Scrivener," 352; "Benito Cereno," 352; "Billy Budd," 352; *Moby-Dick*, 170, 174, 184, 270; *Redburn*, 180
Meredith, George, 98, 176, 196; *The Egoist*, 173, 178
Michelet, Jules, 74, 76, 144
Michener, James, 430
Mill, John Stuart, 397
Milton, John, 75, 340; *Paradise Lost*, 140n6, 371
Mirsky, D. S., 72
Modernism, 143, 150, 220, 337, 419, 422, 423, 424, 426, 427, 428, 432, 433, 454; modernist/modernists, 11, 13, 48, 85, 86, 205, 420–30 passim, 454
Moers, Ellen, 486
Molière, 177

Montherlant, Henri Millon de, 370; *Les Jeunes Filles*, 370
Moore, George, 468
Moravia, Alberto, 458
Moréas, Jean, 191
Morrison, Toni, 476
Murdoch, Iris, 199, 221–22, 226, 231; *Under the Net*, 228
Musäus, Johann Karl August, 68n3; *The Second Grandson*, 52
Musil, Robert, 200, 218, 219–20, 421; *The Man Without Qualities*, 219–20

Nabokov, Vladimir, 244, 338, 353, 421, 423, 429, 430; *Pale Fire*, 244, 430
Nashe, Thomas, 3
Naturalism, 206–8
Nemerov, Howard, 350, 363n3
Nerval, Gérard de, 196
New Criticism, 70, 300, 311
Nietzsche, Friedrich, 97
Nightingale, Florence, 391; "Cassandra," 391
Nochlin, Linda, 341, 346, 347n6, 347n8
Nouveau roman, 10, 22, 229, 445
Novalis, 194; *Heinrich von Ofterdingen*, 194

Oates, Joyce Carol, 422
O'Brien, Edward, 352, 353
O'Connor, Flannery, 362, 467; *The Violent Bear It Away*, 362; *Wise Blood*, 362
O'Connor, Frank, 458, 460, 467
O'Faoláin, Sean, 467; "Sinners," 159
Olsen, Tillie, 476
Olson, Elder, 155, 168n2, 358
Origin of Species, The, 346
Ortega y Gassett, José, 220, 222
Ortner, Sherry, 479
Orwell, George, 10; *Animal Farm*, 10
Owen, Robert, 390

Parr, Harriet, 396
Partlow, Robert, 382
Pater, Walter: *Marius the Epicurean*, 136
Petronius, Gaius, 3; *Satyricon*, 3
Piaget, Jean, 416

Picasso, Pablo, 271
Piercy, Marge, 476
Pinget, Robert, 421
Plath, Sylvia, 389; *The Bell Jar*, 392
Plato, 73, 83, 367
Plutarch, 61
Poe, Edgar Allan, 7, 122, 154, 458, 467, 468; "Cask of Amontillado," 175; "The Fall of the House of Usher," 459
Pope, Alexander, 5
Porter, Katherine Anne, 184, 356, 467; "Noon Wine," 360; "Old Mortality," 360; *Ship of Fools*, 356
Portnoy's Complaint, 320, 327
Postmodernism, 419, 420–22, 423, 424, 427, 431, 432, 433; postmodern/ postmodernist, 9, 419–33 passim, 454
Pound, Ezra, 6, 88, 421, 429; *Cantos*, 428; *Pisan Cantos*, 429
Powers, J. F., 274–75; "The Prince of Darkness," 275
Prévost, Abbé Marcel, 76; *Manon Lescaut*, 76
Proudhon, Pierre Joseph, 97
Proust, Marcel, 9, 41, 47, 90–95, 96, 125, 148, 150, 196, 220, 278–98 passim, 315, 421, 444, 452, 453; *Un amour de Swann*, 330; *A la recherche du temps perdu*, 9, 85, 90–95, 96, 277–98, 315, 322, as *Remembrance of Things Past*, 9, 177, 179; *Le Temps retrouvé*, 232, 325
Pushkin, Aleksandr, 77; *Bronze Horsemen*, 78; *Eugene Onegin*, 327
Pynchon, Thomas, 419, 421, 422, 423, 430

Queneau, Raymond, 421

Rabelais, François, 3, 63
Realism, 11, 12, 178, 203–4, 206–7, 211, 212, 214, 335–46, 419; feminist socialist realism, 397; moral realism, 128–30; Russian realism, 204, 315
Resnais, Alain, 421
Rhys, Jean, 476
Rich, Adrienne, 384, 392, 476; *Of Woman Born: Motherhood as Experience and Institution*, 384; "Song," 392
Richardson, Dorothy, 197, 397, 475, 476, 481
Richardson, Samuel, 4, 13, 44, 56, 180, 191, 193, 241, 242; *Clarissa*, 4, 241, 242, 244; *Pamela*, 4
Rivière, Jacques, 196; "Roman d'aventure," 196
Robbe-Grillet, Alain, 10, 171, 199, 223, 229, 232, 236, 286, 338, 421, 426; *La Jalousie*, 286, 325; *Le Voyeur*, 199
Robins, Elizabeth, 394
Rohde, Erwin, 50, 67n1
Romanticism, German, 194–95
Rosaldo, Michelle, 388; *Woman, Culture, and Society*, 388
Rousseau, Jean-Jacques, 55; *La Nouvelle Héloïse*, 55
Rowbotham, Sheila, 483
Russ, Joanna, 476

Sacks, Sheldon, 358–59; *Fiction and the Shape of Belief*, 359
Sade, Marquis de, 181; *Les Infortunes de la vertue*, 327–29; *Justine*, 320
Sainte-Beuve, Charles, 5, 74, 80
Saintsbury, George, 72, 81
Salinger, J. D., 172; *The Catcher in the Rye*, 179; *Nine Stories*, 172
Sand, George, 390
Sarraute, Nathalie, 10, 199, 221, 244, 421
Sartre, Jean Paul, 178, 199, 223–37, 244, 270, 326, 329; *Les Chemins de la liberté*, 228; *L'Etre et le néant*, 225, 236; *Les Mots*, 225; *La Nausée*, 198, 218, 223–37, 315, 328; *Le Sursis*, 199
Savage, D. S., 110
Sayers, Dorothy, 389
Scholes, Robert, 452, 453
Schopenhauer, Arthur, 194, 270
Schorer, Mark, 116, 144, 300, 353–54
Schreiner, Olive, 476; *Story of An African Farm*, 391
Scott, Sir Walter, 45, 133, 214, 216, 218, 220, 241; *The Bride of Lammer-*

moor, 41; "Wandering Willie's Tale," 470

Seduction and Betrayal (Elizabeth Hardwick), 388

Shakespeare, William, 74, 75, 77, 78, 97, 98, 120–21, 206, 270, 301, 311; Antony and Cleopatra, 98; As You Like It, 77; Hamlet, 176; King Lear, 181, 309; Macbeth, 181; A Midsummer Night's Dream, 121; Twelfth Night, 77

Shaw, Bernard, 27, 77

Sherlock Holmes, 31

Shklovsky, Victor, 436

Short Story Theories (Charles May), 458

Showalter, Elaine, 486; A Literature of Their Own, 395

Simon, Claude, 421, 454; Flanders Road, 445

Simpson, Richard, 393

Sinclair, Upton, 209

Smith, Norman Kemp, 81

Smitten, Jeffrey R., 449, 452

Smollett, Tobias, 241; Humphry Clinker, 241

Snow, C. P., 200, 237

Sophocles, 72, 83, 134, 270; Oedipus Rex, 118, 135–36, 181; Oedipus Tyrannus, 132

Sorel, Charles, 52, 68n2; Le Berger extravagant, 52

Spark, Muriel, 222–23, 380, 389, 392; The Driver's Seat, 391; The Prime of Miss Jean Brodie, 391

Spinoza, Baruch, 309

Staël, Madame de, 390

Stegner, Wallace, 422

Stein, Gertrude, 86, 421

Steinbeck, John, 84, 126, 164, 165; "Flight," 163–65; The Grapes of Wrath, 302, 303; The Wayward Bus, 126

Stendhal, 5, 12, 192, 270, 325, 414; Armance, 410, 414–16; La Chartreuse de Parme, 323; Le Rouge et le noir, 201, as The Red and The Black, 241, 271

Sterne, Laurence, 180, 191, 194, 197,

315; A Sentimental Journey, 193, 303, 305; Tristram Shandy, 32, 33, 175, 177, 179, 181, 193, 303, 305, 325, 371, 421, 459

Stevens, Wallace, 223

Stimpson, Catherine, 385

"Stopping by Woods" (Robert Frost), 157

Strachey, Lytton, 26, 37; Eminent Victorians, 37; Queen Victoria, 37

Strong, L. A. G., 458

Stroud, Theodore, 458

Structuralism/structuralist, 366, 381, 397–99, 431, 458

Styron, William, 422

Swift, Jonathan, 4; Gulliver's Travels, 4, 175

Swinburne, Charles, 77

Symbolism, French, 72, 194–96

Symons, Arthur, 439

Taine, Hippolyte, 74, 75, 76; History of English Literature, 74–75

"Telephone Call, A" (Dorothy Parker), 157

Tel Quel group, 421

Thackeray, William, 47, 196, 200, 338; Henry Esmond, 175; Vanity Fair, 32, 175, 254, 317

Thibaudet, Albert, 87

Thody, Philip, 231

Thousand and One Nights, A, 316, 328, 332

Tillich, Paul, 223

Tillotson, Kathleen, 369; The Tale and the Teller (lecture), 172

Tocqueville, Alexis de, 120

Todorov, Tzvetan, 314, 434, 454n3; Poétique, 406

Tolstoy, Leo, 10, 78, 167–68, 206, 210, 213, 214, 215, 216, 272, 349, 424, 428, 429, 436; Anna Karenina, 255, 425; The Death of Ivan Ilyich, 160–61, 167–68, 349, 351; War and Peace, 13, 32, 47, 168; What Is Art?, 78

Trilling, Lionel, 3, 11, 71, 131, 203, 268

Trollope, Anthony, 184, 196, 200, 272; Barchester Towers, 179

Trollope, Frances, 396

Trotsky, Leon, 78, 79; *Literature and Revolution*, 79
Turgenev, Ivan, 6, 20, 467, 468
Twain, Mark, 80, 180, 428; *Huckleberry Finn*, 170, 179, 183, 431

Unamuno, Miguel de, 270, 421
Under the Volcano (Malcolm Lowry), 272, 451
Updike, John, 422, 431, 467

Valéry, Paul, 275, 427
Vathek (William Beckford), 193
Vico, Giambattista, 73, 74, 76; *La Scienza Nuova*, 73
Victoria Press, 394
Vidal, Gore, 431
Vidan, Ivo, 12, 86
Vigneron, Marcel, 296
Vinci, Leonardo da, 80–81
Vonnegut, Kurt, Jr., 419, 421, 422; *Cat's Cradle*, 361

Walker, Alice, 476, 483; "In Search of Our Mothers' Gardens," 483
Wallace, Irving, 430
Walser, Robert, 200
Warnock, Mary, 225
Watt, Ian, 310
We Happy Few (Helen Howe), 126
Weil, Simone, 231
Weldon, Fay, 391; *Down Among the Women*, 391; *Female Friends*, 391
Wells, H. G., 24, 26, 32, 33, 34, 44, 101, 107–9, 261, 468; *Tono Bungay*, 44, 103, 109, 112
Welty, Eudora, 467
West, Rebecca, 261, 391
Wezel, Johann Carl, 55, 68n5; *Tobias Knouts*, 55

Wharton, Edith, 154; *The House of Mirth*, 391; "The Other Two," 154
Wheatley, Phyllis, 483
White, E. B., 157; "The Door," 157
Wieland, Christopher Martin, 55, 68n4; *Agathon*, 55
Wilde, Oscar, 344–45; "The Artist as Critic," 344; "The Decay of Lying," 344
Williams, Raymond, 485
Williams, William Carlos, 219; *Paterson*, 221, 227
Willingham, Calder, 183; *Natural Child*, 183
Wilson, Edmund, 92, 101–2, 115–16, 131, 144
Wimsatt, W. K., 360
"With Rue My Heart Is Laden" (A. E. Housman), 157
Women's studies, 384
Women Writers Suffrage League, 394–95
Woolf, Leonard, 390
Woolf, Virginia, 8, 12, 40, 48, 70, 102, 116, 131, 190, 196, 197, 199–200, 218, 244, 265, 268, 338, 340, 346, 384, 389, 390, 395, 397, 421, 435, 452, 465, 472, 474–77, 481–84; *Mrs. Dalloway*, 159, 249, 265; *Orlando*, 481; "A Room of One's Own," 395, 473, 474–77, 481–83; *Three Guineas*, 484; *To the Lighthouse*, 265, 383, 470, 481; *The Waves*, 197, 198; "Women and Fiction," 389, 476

Yeats, William Butler, 185–86, 301

Zamyatin, Evgeny, 429; "On Literature, Revolution, and Entropy," 429
Zola, Émile, 20, 194, 203, 206, 207, 208, 211, 213, 217, 326, 341
Zweig, Stefan, 200

Library of Congress Cataloging-in-Publication Data
Essentials of the theory of fiction.
Bibliography: p.
Includes index.
1. Fiction—History and criticism—Theory, etc.
I. Hoffman, Michael J., 1939–   . II. Murphy,
Patrick, 1951–   .
PN3331.E87   1988   801'.953   87–36606
ISBN 0–8223–0826–6

About the Editors

Michael J. Hoffman is Professor and Chair of
English at the University of California, Davis. He
is also Director of the University of California at
Davis Humanities Institute and Executive Director
of the statewide California Humanities Project.
Professor Hoffman's previous books include three
on Gertrude Stein, a novel entitled *The Buddy
System,* and *The Subversive Vision: American
Romanticism in Literature.* He is working on a
book on literary modernism and is a regular contributor to *American Literary Scholarship.*

   Patrick D. Murphy is Assistant Professor of
English and a member of the Graduate Faculty at
Indiana University of Pennsylvania. He has coedited *The Poetic Fantastic: Studies in an Evolv--
ing Genre,* "Feminism Faces the Fantastic," a
special issue of *Women's Studies,* and edited
"Feminism, Ecology, and the Future of the Humanities," a special issue of *Studies in the
Humanities.* He is currently editing *Staging the
Impossible* and *"For the Waking That Comes":
Essays on Gary Snyder.* He has published a number of essays on modern American poetry, fantasy,
and science fiction and is particularly interested
in dialogics, feminism, and environmentalism in
relation to the production and reception of contemporary literature.